More Shipwrecks of Florida

More Shipwrecks of Florida

A Comprehensive Listing

Steven Danforth Singer

PINEAPPLE PRESS

Palm Beach, Florida

Pineapple Press
Published by Rowman & Littlefield
An imprint of The Rowman & Littlefield Publishing Group, Inc.
4501 Forbes Boulevard, Suite 200, Lanham, Maryland 20706
www.rowman.com

Distributed by NATIONAL BOOK NETWORK
Copyright © 2020 by Steven Danforth Singer

British Library Cataloguing in Publication Information Available

Library of Congress Cataloging-in-Publication Data
978-1-68334-026-3 (cloth)
978-1-68334-037-9 (electronic)

♾™ The paper used in this publication meets the minimum requirements of
American National Standard for Information Sciences—Permanence of Paper for
Printed Library Materials, ANSI/NISO Z39.48-1992.

In memory of my Aunt Roma and Uncle Elmer (El), my other parents.

Contents

Acknowledgments

In addition to all those previously mentioned in the first two editions of *Shipwrecks of Florida*, I'd like to thank my wife Debby; the crew at Pineapple Press; John de Bry; Karuna Eberl; Cathy Sheehan; Robert Westrick; State Archives of Florida, Jacklyn Attaway, and Adam Watson; Law Library of Congress, Shameema Rahman; Stavanger Museum, Norway, Anna Helgoe; Aust-Agder Museum, Norway, Hannele Fors; Mandarin Museum, Florida, Sandy Arpen; Larvik Museum, Norway, Gro Stalsberg; Maritime Museum of Denmark, Thobjørn Thaarup; University of Florida Archives, Terrence Phillips; University of South Florida, Tampa Library, LeEtta Schmidt; Land and Sea Surveying, Merritt Island, Florida; NOAA, David Hall, Keeley Belva; Monroe County Library, Key West, Tom Hambright; Naval History and Heritage Command, Lisa Crunk; Armed-Guard.com; Elliot Museum, Florida; Palm Beach Historical Society; National Archives; National Park Service; The Marine Historical Society of Detroit, Roger LeLievre; and fellow divers Bill Winkler and Capt. Hadley Alley.

Foreword

This new book is meant to be an accompaniment to my second edition of *Shipwrecks of Florida*. It includes over 1,500 new shipwrecks not previously listed, plus additional information on many of the shipwrecks that were previously listed in the first two editions of *Shipwrecks of Florida*. I've also included more information on Florida's maritime history including the wreckers of Florida, a chapter on piracy and privateers, in which Florida saw

Illustration of a shipwreck circa 1868, by Jules Noel. *Great Shipwrecks*, 1880.

much of this activity over the years, and some tales and truths on buried and sunken treasure around Florida.

Since I finished the second edition in 1998, technology and the Internet have made research so much easier. I can contact a museum on the other side of the globe with a simple e-mail now, and so many records previously only available at the source, are now readily available over the Internet.

I've added more stories which hopefully will give the reader a better insight into Florida's interesting, colorful, and sometimes tragic maritime history.

Introduction

Shipwrecks continue to be found off our shores, and the stories some could tell! Did vanity cause many ships of the 1641 Spanish plate fleet to become lost? Find an ancient Egyptian artifact diving in the Keys? Did the movie

Recent shipwreck on Pompano Beach due to a storm.

1

Jaws come to life for some on board a vessel off Florida? Abandoned aboard ship and almost eaten alive? Saved by being locked in a water cask? These are just a few tales I relate in this new book.

I'd love to include all the unidentified wreck sites myself and others have found over the years, but that would take up a whole new book. *Shipwrecks of Broward County*, self-published with James Dean in 1985, mentioned all the unidentified sites known at that time off Broward County. *Diving to a Flash of Gold*, by Martin Meylach, lists many locations for unidentified wrecks in the Keys. Many older divers I've talked to from Florida know of an unidentified wreck site near where they live and dive. Back in the 1950s and 1960s off Miami and Biscayne Bay, many of these unknown wrecks were given names like the *Ring Wreck*, which lies off Ajax Reef and where Swedish cannon dated 1778–1779 were recovered, the *Bed Springs Wreck*, the *Brick Wreck*, the *Schooner Wreck*, and the like. Off Broward and Palm Beach we dove on the *Windlass Wreck*, the *Lumber Wreck*, the *Chillingsworth Wreck*, the *Cannon Wreck*, the *Slate Wreck*, and others. I always sought out the older divers who knew where all these wreck sites were. Hopefully this new book will help in the identification of the hundreds of wreck sites divers, fishermen, and snorkelers have found over the years that are still unidentified. Some like the *Ivory Wreck* off Delta Shoal, which I mention further on,

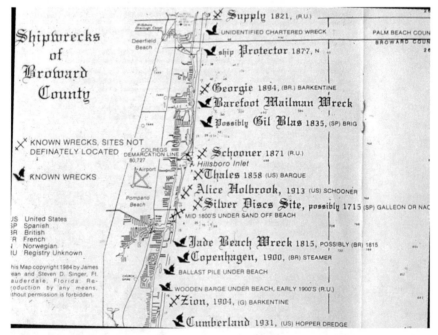

Section from a map of shipwrecks along the coast of Broward County, Florida, including unidentified ones. *Shipwrecks of Broward County*, by James Dean and Steven Singer.

This small Spanish cannon found by lifeguard Paul Hurt in the 1960s just north of the Pompano Beach Pier.

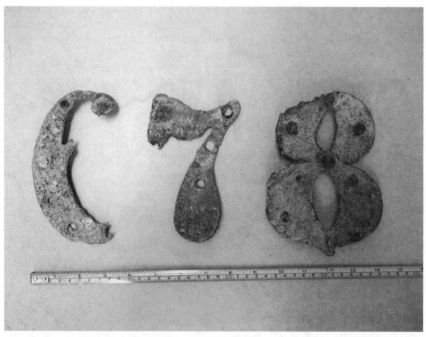

Lead draft markers numbers 6, 7, and 8 that were nailed to the hull of a wreck believed to be the *Georgie*, lost in 1894.

A block of "Crown Patent Fuel," manufactured by the Crown Preserved Coal Co., Lt., Cardiff, Wales. These were made by crushing good quality steam coal and mixing it with hot pitch and tar and molding into blocks. Found by a diver years ago in the upper Keys. Information provided by Robert Protheroe Jones, The Maritime Waterfront Museum, Swansea.

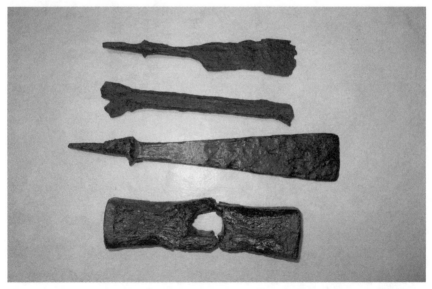

Some tools recovered years ago from a wreck believed to be the *Tifton* (1926.) A couple of scrapers, a nail puller, and a small sledge. Author.

were salvaged back in the 1950s and are known about. Others like a 1750s wreck two miles off Elliot Key in 18 feet of water are not as well known. I'd never heard of it until I found an article recently in the 1954 *Sarasota Herald Tribune* that also had a photo of some artifacts from the wreck. Some amateur archaeologists discovered it in 1954. John and Charles Fales, Sam Corbett, and A. T. Tommedlin of Sarasota and Homestead found it while looking for old wrecks. A few timbers remained, but it was loaded with Spanish tile. They also recovered some dishes and a large piece of olive jars that dated it around the 1750 period. They hired a local Miami crew to salvage the Spanish tile which was stacked 6–8 feet deep, for a third of the recovery. Just another shipwreck whose identity remains a mystery. Are those 250-year-old tiles now decorating some local buildings or homes? Several newspapers in 1889 reported the death of two men during an accident while blowing up a wreck said to be the old Dutch brig *Nevada*, which was obstructing a channel off Mayport. I have found no reference for the brig *Nevada* though.

A ship's bell found by a beachcomber after a storm in Palm Beach County.

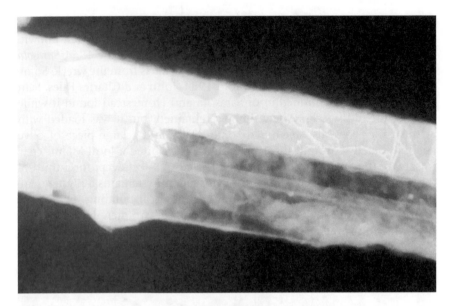

X-ray of a 19th century pistol found by a diver off Boca Raton years ago.

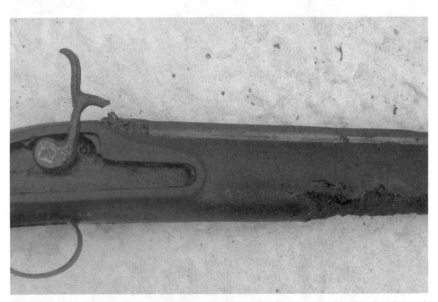

The 19th century pistol after conservation. It is believed to be associated with a British wreck found in the 1960s nearby.

The Keys were the resting place of many a shipwreck. An article from an 1871 *Harper's* magazine called "Along the Florida Reef," and later reprinted in *Tales of Old Florida,* published in 1987, and edited by Oppel and Meisel, relates a scene of those aboard a schooner in the Keys:

We were anchored off Old Rhodes Key, and now stood off toward Plantation Key, and took to our boats as soon as the water became too shoal to admit the schooner farther in. Everywhere along the beach were fragments of wrecks. Old hulks are seen on the shoals, and at high-water mark winrows of wood lined the shore. Here was a Turkish maiden, the figure-head of some unlucky ship, lying half buried with splinters and fragments of gilded panels, the remains of a wrecked steamship. Farther on a handsome sign-board bearing the Yankee name of *Joseph A. Davis* in gilt letters. Figure-heads in scroll-work, handsomely carved. On another key, great numbers of new hogsheads and bundles of staves for barrels; part of a cargo, no doubt, destined for the "ever-faithful isle." I can only imagine finding a scene like this today. The *Joseph A. Davis* mentioned, was a bark that wrecked on Grecian Shoals in 1866.

Hurricanes and storms have uncovered many wrecks these last few years on the beaches of Florida. Tropical storm Gabriel uncovered a wreck over 125-feet long on Ponte Vedra Beach in 2001. Another hurricane uncovered a wreck in 2004 on New Smyrna Beach. I first saw a photo of this wreck on eBay, when someone wanted to sell spikes and such from it. The state

ASHORE ON A FLORIDA REEF.

A 19th century illustration of a wreck on the Florida Reef. Baldwin Library of Children's Historical Literature, Special and Area Studies Collection, George A. Smathers Libraries, University of Florida, Gainesville.

archaeologists heard about it, had the eBay auction shut down, and visited the wreck and deemed it a historical site. The city though hadn't heard about that, and they scooped it all up and hauled it to the dump!

A shipwreck uncovered by a storm in 2001 on Ponte Vedra Beach. John J. Paskoski.

A section of a shipwreck washed up onto Ponte Vedra Beach, March 2018. Marc Anthony/Spanish Main Antiques, St. Augustine, Florida.

As I'm finishing up this book, regional news reported that a large section of a 19th-century sailing ship washed up on Ponte Vedra Beach, March 28, 2018. It appeared to be from a fairly large ship with frames and inner and outer planks fastened with wood trunnels. I would need to investigate, but looks to be around the mid-1800s. It obviously had been buried under sand all these years since it looked to have no growth on it and likely just been recently uncovered from nearby and washed up onto the beach.

Hurricane Michael in 2018 just uncovered some large vessels on Dog Island believed to have wrecked there during the 1899 hurricane.

Many other wrecks still lie under the beaches around Florida. I investigated a couple of construction sites being developed along the beach over the years and did find remnants of a shipwreck just as they started excavation for the foundation at one site. No time to investigate further as there was soon a very large building on top of it. My friend and one of the original keys wreck divers, the late ex-Miami detective Carl Ward, told me about a few cannons and other shipwreck material that was found when they were building on Miami Beach in the 1960s near Lincoln Road and the beach. All the cannons appeared to be English, and there were quite a few of them. He believes most of the ship now lies under the street there. In 2007, construction workers stumbled upon a large cannon off Biscayne

One of the shipwrecks uncovered after Hurricane Michael on Dog Island, 2018. This may be the *Jahfner* or *Vale*, which wrecked in 1899. Kai Nelson.

This cannon was found just off Biscayne Bay during construction on a hotel. City of Miami Beach.

Bay while working on the Lido Hotel. As no conservation lab was available, it was reburied where it was found. Remains of an early wreck along with a large cannon were found in 1961 during the construction of the beachfront Casa Blanca Motel in Panama City, believed to be from the 17th or 18th century. I'm sure there are numerous other stories construction workers could tell about what they found while building along Florida's shoreline.

Storms and hurricanes continue to uncover treasure along the beaches where the 1715 Fleet wrecked, and those that know where to look are still being rewarded. The beaches here from south of Ft. Pierce to north of Sebastian have given up much treasure over the years. We went up the coast after a good Nor'easter, but seeing that the beach wasn't cut away, we never even took out our metal detectors. That day though, a lady found an 8 escudo "Royal" (a rare gold coin) in the washed-out dune line right in the same area we decided it wasn't worth detecting! I did find a wood plank from an old ship that day that washed up on the beach with numerous sheathing nails. I made it into a nice table which now proudly sits in my living room.

Years ago, before all the beach renourishment projects began, the sand along the beaches of southeast Florida would move naturally offshore in the winter months and then back inshore during the summer, exposing many shallow water wrecks during the winter. North of Boynton Inlet we could snorkel or dive four to five wrecks dating from the 16th to the 19th century all in one morning or afternoon (one had many musket balls, the

Plank from a shipwreck with sheathing nails that author found on Wabasso Beach after a storm. Was later made into a table.

state having now named it the *Military Wreck* after we showed a later lease-holder the location), and on another wreck a diver friend of mine found some eight-real coins dated 1793. The *Protector* (1877), off Deerfield Beach, and the "Lumber Wreck," off Boca (possibly the *Tifton*), were regular dive sites we would explore in the winter. Except maybe after a hurricane, I've not seen these exposed for probably 20 years or more now. Some say these wrecks are now protected due to the sand cover (some are now permanently under the new beaches), but unfortunately, many of the shallow water reefs that were always exposed are now buried under sand from these projects which is washed offshore, especially when the northeast storms arrive in the fall. The 20-foot reef off Deerfield Beach, which was a favorite area to fish for Spanish mackerel and also to dive for lobster, has been completely buried for miles in the last couple of years, killing all the corals and sponges, and no longer a habitat for sea life.

As a member of the Marine Archaeological Council (MAC) for many years, I had the pleasure to work under and later study under the father of marine archaeology, Peter Throckmorton. While living in Greece and Turkey in the 1950s, he got to know the local sponge divers, who would take him to dive on some of the wrecks they had found. Peter's work on these ancient shipwrecks was the beginning of underwater archaeology as we know it today. He taught me a lot, and unlike most mainstream archaeologists, he was willing to share his knowledge with anyone, even those in the private salvage business. Though archaeology was his passion, he ironically found the main pile of coins on a wreck that noted author Arthur C. Clarke's group found off Sri Lanka back in the early 1960s. In fact, it was Clarke's book, *The Treasure of the Great Reef*, that really got me interested in shipwrecks. I believe it was the first book I had ever bought, a paperback

Famous underwater archaeologist, Peter Throckmorton, teaching a class while anchored over a shipwreck.

I saw at my grade school book fair, and which I still have! Peter started a marine archaeological program here in south Florida at Nova University in which I became one of the first students to sign up, but my friend and mentor Peter was taken away from us way too early, as was the program.

I later became the president of MAC and was the one who submitted a proposal, along with a video of the wreck site of the *Lofthus*, to the state of Florida to be considered as an underwater preserve. The wreck had been buried for many years but was now completely uncovered and has remained uncovered ever since. The state was very interested, and we took their archaeologists out to the site on Don Kree's boat. Soon after, it became one of the state's Underwater Preserves. Years earlier, I had positively identified the *Copenhagen* (also a State Underwater Preserve) a wreck site that was incorrectly being called the *Cumberland*, which wrecked a few miles to the south, found and submitted the photo of the wreck used in all the state brochures at the St. Augustine Historical Society, and even got a copy of the original plans of the ship from England, along with helping map the site. While president of MAC, I came up with the idea of establishing a "Shipwreck Trail," and with help from the group's members, it became a reality and is now a popular snorkel and dive site off Lauderdale-By-The-Sea, with concrete cannons, a real anchor, and a ballast pile. I also obtained a research permit from the state of Florida, and a dredge and fill permit from the Army Corps of Engineers, through both MAC and the Graves Museum of Archaeology, which permitted us to excavate the 1835 wreck site of the *Gil Blas*, which had a direct impact on the development of Broward County. We were able to excavate the site and completed a nice site map of the wreck. It lies only 180 feet south of another 19th century unidentified wreck site that MAC worked on with Peter Throckmorton back in the 1980s.

Though treasure diving and archaeology often seem to be at odds, I dove for many years with noted treasure hunter, Navy UDT diver/officer, and author, Bob "Frogfoot" Weller. Bob was one of the most knowledgeable people on the planet regarding shipwrecks, and he was as interested in preserving their history as any archaeologist. He was another good friend who's passed over the bar but not forgotten. I later worked as a subcontractor for the famous treasure hunter Mel Fisher on the 1715 wreck sites with my own salvage boat. I've had the pleasure to know the late Sir Robert Marx, who lived in Florida and was a noted explorer, diver, and author of more books about shipwrecks and their history than probably anyone. I've been lucky to have met and worked with so many interesting people in this field

First mapping of the *Copenhagen* wreck site (running a tape alongside the pillow block), mid-1980s.

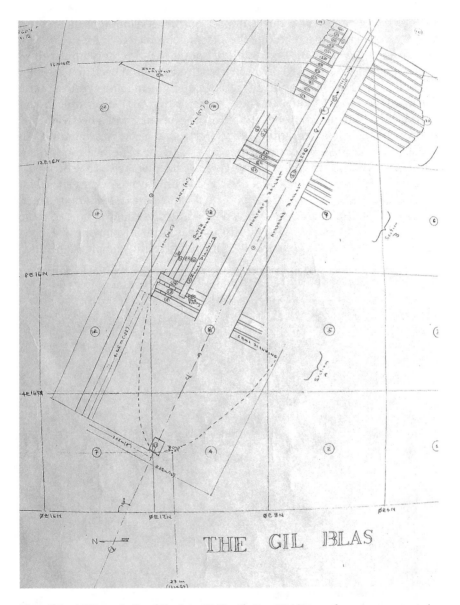

Map of the 1835 wreck site of the brig *Gil Blas*. By Rene Haldimann, from measurements by author and the Marine Archaeological Council.

Part of the hull and keel of the *Gil Blas* after uncovering site using author's salvage boat.

Author and Bob "Frogfoot" Weller, with some gold coins we found on the 1715 "Douglas Beach" site that day.

Author alongside famous treasure hunter Mel Fisher.

such as my late friend Phil Masters, who's company found Blackbeard's ship, the *Queen Ann's Revenge*.

The Internet now provides so many sites to explore regarding shipwrecks. Websites like Cathy Sheehan's florida-keys-vacation.com offer a wealth of information on shipwrecks in the Keys, some which I shared in this new edition. GPS coordinates of many shipwrecks are available here and on many other websites. Some good sites are listed in the bibliography.

I have not included wrecks sunk as artificial reefs as they are not actual shipwrecks having been sunk on purpose, but many do have a colorful past. While studying marine archaeology under Peter Throckmorton, he would often take us on field trips. One was to a floating restaurant called the *Ancient Mariner* to see one of the few riveted built steel ships still afloat. After customers got sick from something caused by a kitchen worker, the restaurant soon closed, but later became an artificial reef off Broward County. Local fishermen called a spot off Pompano in 500 feet of water the "sub" for years, which on sonar did appear to look like a submarine and which the old timers all said was a lost German U-boat. MAC got the Navy interested, and we went out on the Navy research vessel *RSB1* to search for it. It turned out to be a reef though. What also turned out to become an artificial reef a few years later was the *RSB1*! For anyone interested in the

Author with famous explorer Sir Robert Marx on the "Jupiter Wreck" site.

Author on the vessel *RSB1*, which is now an artificial reef.

Painting of the *Maple Leaf*, by Donald J. Ingram. Mandarin Museum, Jacksonville, Florida.

history and photos of these artificial reef wrecks, Michael Barnett's book, *Encyclopedia of Florida Shipwrecks*, goes into detail on many of these. Interesting finds continue to be made off Florida's coast. Recently, a 16th-century French ship was found off Cape Canaveral with bronze cannon and may be one of Jean Ribaut's lost ships. Though as so often with shipwrecks, it is now in a legal dispute with France, the state, and the finders.

The Civil War wreck of the *Maple Leaf*, found off Mandarin Point on the St. John's River, has probably given up some of the best-preserved Civil War artifacts to date, many which are on display in several museums now. Most of the cargo of armament and supplies still remain on the wreck! It is now a protected site.

Though they have been worked on since the 1950s, the 1715 Fleet wreck sites have given up millions in gold and silver these last few years. In 2015, the 300th anniversary of the loss of the fleet, millions in gold coins were found by two groups working the wrecks, one on the "Douglas Beach" wreck, and the other on "Corrigan's Wreck," just a stone's throw off the beach. The weather that year was the best I've ever seen. In 2010, a bronze cannon with gold and silver coins inside was found on the Corrigan's site. A gold statue was also recovered around this period.

For anyone who finds anything in Florida waters, be aware of the laws. Anything over 50 years old found in Florida waters is now deemed historic and can't be removed—so don't pick up that 1965 penny! I love to dive for fossils, and a $5.00/year permit is obtainable from the state so you can legally remove these. Sharks teeth though do not require a permit to take. I found a very nice mastodon tooth while working on the 1715 "Cabin" site years ago, and still dive for fossils with my daughter Monica off the west coast of Florida.

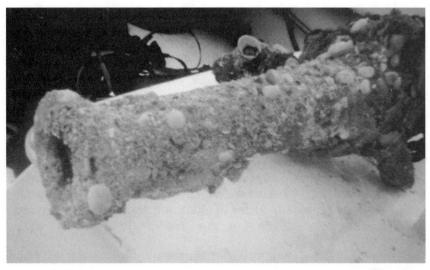

Encrusted bronze cannon found in 2010 on the 1715 "Corrigans" site. It was filled with gold and silver coins. Mark Silicato.

It's not unusual to find fossils from the "Ice Age" mixed in with artifacts from the 1715 wrecks. This is a mastodon tooth the author found on the 1715 "Cabin" site.

Author with a fossil shark tooth found while diving off Venice, Florida. Monica Singer.

1

Florida Life-Saving Stations

Before any life-saving stations were built along our coasts, there were attempts to provide mariners some assistance in case of being shipwrecked. An article in the November 1, 1820, British *Monthly Magazine* reported that, due to the many shipwrecks along the Florida coast, the French consul at New Orleans announced an establishment at Cape Florida, similar to the later Houses of Refuge/Life-Saving Stations. It goes on to say where shipwrecked sailors may find help along this stretch of Florida,

> captains, &c. in any danger, passing by the north of Guya-Biscane, will find the entrance of the Boca-Eastonces, which may be passed in entire security, and that they will perceive houses before them on the continent. In case of shipwreck to the north of Boca-Eastonces, they will find, at the distance of two miles, certain places fixed upon, whence houses may be seen, and where, by making signals with fires or otherwise, due aid will be afforded them. If lost in the south part of the New River, they must proceed in a southerly direction, along the shore, and they will find, at the distance of every four miles, posts with inscriptions in English, French and Spanish, pointing out the spots where pits of fresh water have been dug.

Boca-Eastonces is mentioned as "Boca Ratones" (see Biscayne Bay Station), and refers to the entrance into the bay at present-day Miami, not present-day Boca Raton. This was one of the earliest published maritime safety guidelines for Florida that I've ever seen. The information soon changed as the Seminole Wars made much of this area now unsafe for any nonnative settlers or shipwrecked sailors. Lighthouses and lightships built or stationed along Florida before 1876 also served to help anyone shipwrecked along this coast.

The first five Life-Saving Stations on the east coast of Florida were built in 1876. They were the *Bethel Creek* (also called the *Indian River Station* until the new *Indian River Inlet Station* to the south was built in 1885), *Gilberts*

20

Hillsboro Inlet Lighthouse.

Bar, Orange Grove, Fort Lauderdale, and *Biscayne Bay* stations. Five more were built on the east coast, and one on the Panhandle in 1885 and 1886, for a total of 11 stations in Florida. The east coast stations were in District 7, and the *Santa Rosa* station was in District 8, though as more stations were built along the coasts of the United States, that soon changed to Districts 8 and 9. The distinction between a House of Refuge and a Life-Saving Station was that the Houses of Refuge were just that, places where shipwrecked sailors could stay and recuperate, offering rooms, for example, for the sailors. Except for the *Jupiter* and *Santa Rosa* station, all the others in Florida were considered a House of Refuge. All were considered a Life-Saving Station as they were all equipped with lifesaving equipment. The U.S. Life Saving Service lasted for 44 years until it was incorporated into the U.S. Coast Guard in 1915.

Many shipwrecks are listed as having wrecked near a particular station. Some vessels are listed as wrecked a distance from, or nearby a particular station number, without giving the station's name. An example would be something like "four miles north of Station #2." There were only the five stations in Florida from 1876 until 1885 when more were built, so depending on the year of the wreck, station numbers did change. Here is the list of stations starting from the northernmost to the southernmost. The only station I know of on the west coast/Panhandle side is the *Santa Rosa Station.* Information is from the Life-Saving Service records, which published annual reports (Lat/Long coordinates are from the 1891 annual report).

Also, lighthouses and lightships also kept records of shipwrecks, and some of these records are available in the National Archives. I have some wreck reports from the *Light Station at Alligator Reef* from 1876 onward from the National Archives.

The Gilberts Bar Station as it looks today with author's wife Debby in foreground.

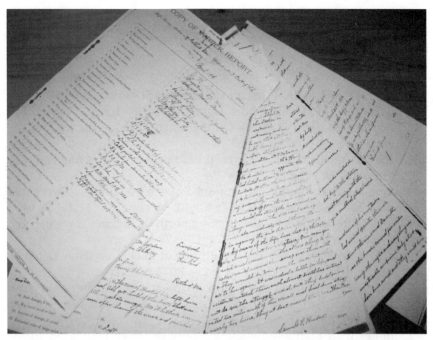

Copies of a handwritten wreck report of the brig *J.H. Lane*, from the Gilberts Bar Station.

Painting of the *J.H. Lane*, by G.C. Whiticar. Laura Kay Whiticar Darvill.

The *Gilbert's Bar Station* is the only one still in existence on the East Coast and is now a museum.

East Coast

1. **Smith's Creek Station** (renamed the **Bulow Station** in 1903)—Twenty miles south of Matanzas Inlet. Lat. 29°26'10" N, Long. 81°06'15" W.
2. **Mosquito Lagoon Station**—On the beach opposite the lagoon. Lat. 28°51'30" N, Long. 80°46'20" W.
3. **Chester Shoal Station**—Eleven miles north of Cape Canaveral. Lat. 26°36'40" N, Long. 80°35'50" W.
4. **Cape Malabar Station** (discontinued March 30, 1891)—Thirty miles south of Cape Canaveral. Lat. 28°03'10" N, Long. 80°32'45" W.
5. **Bethel Creek Station**—Eleven miles north of Indian River Inlet. Lat. 27°40'00" N, Long. 80°21'20" W.
6. **Indian River Inlet Station**—South side of inlet (*Note:* Now called Ft. Pierce Inlet). Lat. 27°29'45" N, Long. 80°17'50" W.
7. **Gilbert's Bar Station** (now a museum, open to the public)—On north side of St. Lucie Inlet by the St. Lucie Rocks (also called Gilbert's Bar). Lat. 27°12'00" N, Long. 80°09'50" W.
8. **Jupiter Inlet Station**—On south side of the Inlet. Lat. 26°55'40" N, Long. 80°04'00" W.
9. **Orange Grove Station**—South end of Lake Worth, 32 miles south of Jupiter Inlet. Lat. 26°27'30" N, Long. 80°03'20" W.
10. **Fort Lauderdale Station** (or **New River Station**)—Seven miles north of the New River Inlet. Lat. 26°08'00" N, Long. 80°06'00" W.
11. **Biscayne Bay Station**—Ten miles north of Boca Ratones, Narrows Cut. Lat. 25°54'10" N, Long. 80°08'00" W. *Note:* "Boca de Ratones" or "Boca Ratones" meant a Rocky Inlet, and on maps well into the 1800s, was a passage in Biscayne Bay (also called Bear Cut). Obviously, the Life Saving Service in 1891 (where this information was found) still considered Boca Ratones as in the Miami area and not at present day Boca Raton.

West Coast/Panhandle

1. **Santa Rosa Station**—On Santa Rosa Island, three miles east of Ft. Pickens. Lat. 30°19'00" N., Long. 87°14'30" W.

2

More Florida Maritime History

Florida's maritime history encompasses hundreds of years, some which I spoke of in *Shipwrecks of Florida*. Here I'll try and explain the difficulty researching shipwrecks around Florida due to its unique history and ever-changing geography. The Spanish, French, and British controlled parts of it at one time or another. At one time, Florida was really two regions with East Florida and West Florida, each controlled by different countries. Florida's

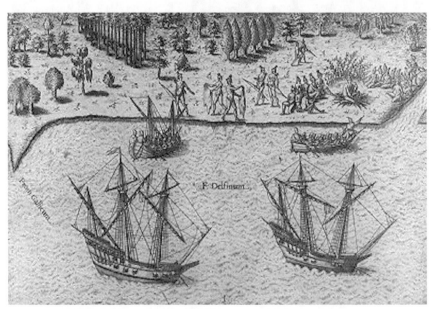

A 1591 engraving by Theodore de Bry, depicting the French landing in Florida. Library of Congress Prints and Photographic Division.

boundaries also changed through time. Early shipwreck reports can be very misleading when mentioning where a ship wrecked. Three treasure-laden Spanish vessels that wrecked off Padre Island, Texas, in 1554, were said to have wrecked off Florida in one early report that I had read. Looking at an early map of that time, much of the Gulf Coast, including present day Texas, is all called "Florida." Early maps of Florida could also be misleading as some showed areas differently than later maps did, or place names were different or incorrect. Major inlets went by different names over the years. When researching Florida's Life-Saving Stations, the Biscayne Bay Station was listed as 10 miles north of Boca Ratones, Narrows Cut, and this was a report from the later 1800s. Thinking that can't be right, as Boca Raton is much further north, I checked a few old maps, and Boca Ratones was indeed a passage in Biscayne Bay and also known as "Narrows Cut," (the cut just north of Bear Cut). The name meant something like "Rocky Inlet." Looking up the history of Boca Raton, it says the name Boca Ratones was mistakenly moved on maps in the early 19th century to where Lake Boca Raton is. An 1823 map shows Boca Ratones and Bear Cut both as the same place in Biscayne Bay, and further north shows Boca Ratone Sound (Lake Boca) on the map and calls the area "Boca Ratone Rio Seca" (Dry River) and

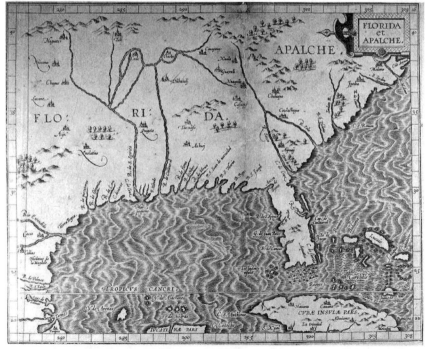

A 1597 map of Florida and the Gulf Coast. Note: Most all of Gulf Coast is called Florida. Florida et Apalche, Digital Collections, Tampa Library, University of South Florida.

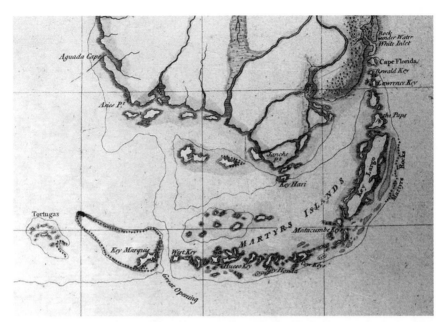

Part of a 1769 map showing the Florida Keys. Note: Keys are called "Martyrs Islands." East Florida, Digital Collections, Tampa Library, University of South Florida.

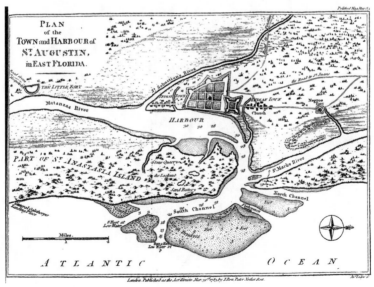

A 1783 map of St. Augustine. Note Fort Mantanzas is called "Little Fort." Also note Fort Mose, the first free black settlement in The Americas. *Political Magazine*, London, March 1, 1783.

Author photographing one of the bronze cannon at fort Castillo de San Marcos, St. Augustine. Monica Singer.

shows an inlet there called "Dry River Inlet." This inlet was usually closed off through most of the 18th and 19th centuries. But then again, looking at a 1760 English map of Florida, "Boca de Ratones" is marked about where Boca Raton is today. If this isn't confusing enough, read on!

From the 17th century and into the 19th century, many ships were simply said to have wrecked in the "Gulph of Florida." This was a very general area and could also include parts of Cuba, the Cay Sal Banks, and other areas of the Bahamas or elsewhere, so a vessel reported as wrecked in the Gulph or "Gulf" of Florida may have wrecked nowhere near Florida. Toward the end of the 18th century and the beginning of the 19th century, it was more likely that a vessel listed as wrecked in the Gulf of Florida, did actually wreck in Florida waters. Toward the end of the 18th century, reports were starting to be somewhat more specific as to where a vessel actually wrecked and would specify as wrecked at or near places such as Cape Florida, St. Augustine, Cape Canaveral, the Martiers (spelled a few different ways and generally meant the Florida Keys), the Tortugas, and Pensacola.

Many ships wrecked in the Florida Keys. The many reefs and Keys they wrecked near went by different names over the years. The Florida reefs of the Keys in the 18th century were simply referred to as the Martiers, Martieres, Martyr's, or Martyr Reefs, depending on who made the report and how they spelled it. A 1769 map shows the reefs off Key Largo as the "Martyrs Rocks." Into the 19th century, the reefs were simply referred to as the "Florida Reef." Cape Florida was also used as a common place name which could encompass any part of the Keys and further up the coast and over to the Cape Sable area. Long Key was previously called Viper Key or Cayo Vivora on Spanish maps. After the Civil War, it was changed to Long Island and then Long Key, probably because of confusion with Long Island, Bahamas. Marathon and the surrounding keys were originally called Cayo de Bacas (or Vacas) by the Spanish, vacas meaning cow. Maybe named after manatees or sea cows? Eventually it was called Key Vacas or Vaccas (spelled both ways) in the 19th century. An 1856 map shows both Key Vaca and Cow Key near each other. Ajax Reef was also called Hay Jack Reef in the mid-1800s. Crocker's Reef was also called Crow's Reef, as one wreck was listed on both, and it said Crow's Reef was six miles below Conch Reef. Grecian Shoals also went by Triangle Reef, and the list goes on.

Into the later 18th and early 19th centuries, more and more of the reefs and shoals of the Florida Keys and elsewhere were given specific names, many of these names originating from a vessel which wrecked or stranded upon them. Carysfort Reef was one of the first reefs to get named due to a ship. The *HMS Carysfort* stranded there in 1770, but was gotten off after spending nine days on the reef. She continued to serve and later captured several American vessels off Florida during the Revolutionary War, but this

An 1861 sketch of Ft. Jefferson, Tortugas. Courtesy of the Monroe County Library, Key West, from *Harper's Weekly*, February 23, 1861.

reef was now associated with her stranding and given her name. Surprisingly, most of the early reports mentioning this reef called it "Carysford Reef," and not until later into the mid-1800s was it then correctly called "Carysfort." Also confusing is the fact that Carysfort Reef was used to describe most all the reefs off the Key Largo area and north until more of the area reefs got their own individual names such as Molasses Reef, Pickle's Reef, and French Reef. I'm sure the wreckers sometimes referred to different reefs as "where we salvaged so and so ship," or where "we salvaged all that molasses," and the name would then stick to that particular reef. Turtle and Conch Reefs most likely had a great abundance of turtles and conch. Though no longer legal, catching turtles was big business in the 1800s. Conch, sponges, and shrimp eventually got fished out in the Keys. I used to go shrimping during the full moon off Broward and Palm Beach, but haven't done so in a few years as I just don't see them anymore. Hopefully they will come back.

Other reefs and shoals attributed to a shipwreck are: Ajax Reef, also called Hay Jack Reef (Ship *Ajax* wrecked there in 1836); Ledbury Reef (snow *Ledbury* wrecked there in 1769); Pulaski Shoal (ship *Pulaski* wrecked there in 1832); Tennessee Reef (attributed to the ship *Tennessee*, which went aground there, but got off in 1832); Triumph Reef (ship *Triumph* wrecked there in 1838); Alligator Reef (*USS Alligator* wrecked there in 1822); Fowey Rocks (*HMS Fowey* struck here in 1748—drifted off and sank in Biscayne Bay though); Looe Key (*HMS Looe* wrecked there in 1741); Brewster's Reef (ship *Brewster* wrecked there in 1848); Hetzel Shoal (lies east of Cape Canaveral, was named after the U.S. Survey Steamer *Hetzel*, which wrecked on the beach a couple of miles south of Cape Canaveral, but through the perseverance of

Capt. Rogers, she was eventually gotten off which was a truly remarkable feat considering her state). The ship *Pacific* and the bark *Grecian* were both said to have wrecked on Carysfort Reef in 1836, but since most of the reefs in that area were all referred to as Carysfort Reef at that time, and if I was to make a guess, I'd say "Pacific Reef" and "Grecian Shoals" were named after those vessels and are probably where they actually wrecked. I don't know how "Molasses Reef" got its name, but molasses was a very common cargo of the time, and several ships full of molasses wrecked in the Keys, though I don't see the name "Molasses Reef" used in the Florida Keys until around 1880. The reef named "Molasses Reef" in the Caico's Bank (also referred to as part of the Inagua's, Bahamas, in the 19th century) goes back much earlier. Some areas were also named after Florida's pirates (see chapter 6).

I thought I solved the mystery of how "Pickle's Reef" got its name, but looks like the mystery remains! Some thought a ship carrying a partial cargo of pickles may have wrecked there. Others thought that the remnants of a lost cargo of concrete in the area, which some say look like pickle barrels, could be how it got its name. But the name Pickle's (or Pickel's or Pickell's or Pickle) Reef goes back to at least 1829, long before concrete was being manufactured in the United States (it's possible the concrete is from the wreck of the *Linda* in 1871, which wrecked in that area with a cargo containing barrels of concrete, brimstone, etc.). So how did Pickle's Reef supposedly get its name? Here's an excerpt from an article about the reef in the *American Republican and Baltimore Daily Clipper*, July 18, 1845, and it's spelled "Pickell's Reef" in the article, not "Pickle's Reef":

> The name was given to it by a crew of wreckers, about six or seven years ago, who touched upon it while on their way to Key West, from Key Biscayne, and in compliment to an officer of the army whom they became acquainted with while at the Capes, and whom had distinguished himself in the Florida war.

So, it turns out the reef has nothing to do with pickles, but was named in honor of an Army officer whose name was Lt. John Pickell! The first reports should have used the name "Pickell's Reef," though most early reports I've seen only said "Pickel's Reef," leaving out the extra "L." I did find one report regarding the wreck of the *Dorothy Foster* in 1836 in a London paper which correctly spelled it "Pickell's Reef." Looks like soon after this, newspapers mistakenly used the name "Pickle's Reef," and the name stuck. I briefly looked up Lt. Pickell, who was under General Jessup's command. He wrote a journal on his experience in Florida during 1836 and 1837. He was somewhat of a naturalist, in that he describes Florida's flora and fauna in some detail. He did seem sincere in trying to end the hostilities between the Native Americans and the Army. So, what was originally named "Pickell's Reef," in honor of an Army officer, has over time become known as "Pickle's Reef." Now my only concern about this explanation is that the earliest mention of the reef I've found was regarding the schooner *President*, reported wrecked on "Pickle's Reef" in 1829. I know Lt. Pickell was here in 1836, but was he here in 1829, and why is the first mention in 1829 spelled "Pickle"? The Second Seminole War didn't start until 1835, and the first war ended back in 1819. I believe Lt. Pickell was an 1822 graduate of West Point, so he wasn't here during the First Seminole War. One wreck was reported on "Little Pickle Reef" in 1834. I guess there's still a bit of a mystery about Pickle's Reef yet to be solved. In the wreck section, I spelled the reef's name as it was reported at that time.

Coffins Patch (or Patches) Reef was originally called "Collins Patch" or "Collins Patches" (no idea who or what Collin was), and I don't know when the name got changed from Collins to Coffins but appears to be after the Civil War. Up until the war, even the light there was called Collins Patch Light. I saw mention of a "Rieuzi Reef" in an old report, also called "Big Conch Reef" which is present-day "Conch Reef," which was most likely named after the ship *Rienzi*, which wrecked in that area in 1845 (said to have wrecked on both Carysfort and Pickle's Reefs, though probably wrecked on what is now "Conch Reef"). Was "Davis Reef" named after the brig *Davis*, which went aground in the Keys, and was gotten off by the wreckers in 1828? Who knows! Would be interesting to see where "Washerwoman Shoal," the "Samboes," "Rebecca Shoal," "Crocker's Reef," and many of the other reefs and shoals got their names from. I'm sure there is a great story behind each one.

Key West was previously called Thompson's Island for a brief time and before that was called Cayo Hueso. A 1769 map called it West Key. Looking at different maps of Florida through the years, and depending on the

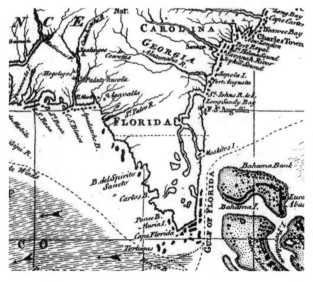

A 1740 English map of the Caribbean detailing the routes of the Spanish treasure fleets. Enlarged the portion showing Florida. Note where the place names "Gulf of Florida," "Cape Florida," "Moskitos Island," etc. lay. *Gentleman's Magazine and Historical Chronicle*, 1740.

nationality of who made the map, the names of areas around Florida went by many different names. Cuba, for instance, was called "Fernandina" by the Spanish in the early 16th century.

Key West at the end of Duval St, circa 1870. Courtesy of the Monroe County Library, Key West.

A 1900 photo of Key West Bight, end of Elizabeth St. Courtesy of the Monroe County Library, Key West.

Many shipwrecks were reported by other vessels who witnessed these wrecks during their voyages and would then share this information when they reached their destination which could be months or even a year or more later. Local newspapers would then report this information and not always be correct. The names of wrecked ships were often incorrectly spelled or completely wrong. Just one example is that of the 1874 wreck of the *Barao de Teffe*. Other reports spelled it the *Baras de Tiffe, Barrao De Teffe, Baris de Tiffe*, and *Barrao de Taffe*. Where some ships were reported as wrecked was also sometimes incorrect. I looked into one wreck reported as lost off Cape Sable, Florida, but turned out it was wrecked off Cape Sable, Nova Scotia. Looked into another as wrecked off St. Augustine, but after further review it turned out as having wrecked off St. Augustine, Brazil, not St. Augustine, Florida. There's Molasses Reef in the Keys, and Molasses Reef in the Caico's Bank; Elbow Cay in the Bahamas, and Elbow Reef, Abaco (reports of wrecks on Elbow Reef up until the Civil War referred to the reef off Abaco), and Elbow Reef in the Keys; Great Isaac in the Bahamas and Isaac Shoal near the Tortugas; Sound Pt, Key Largo, and Sound Point, Eleuthera; Indian River, Florida, and Indian River, Delaware; Bird Key Shoal, Tortugas, and Bird Cay, Bahamas; Matanzas, Cuba, and Matanzas Inlet/Bay, Florida; Fowey Rock, England, and Fowey Rocks, Florida. One wreck which confused me was listed as wrecked on Alligator Reef, but was incorrect and should have said Alligator Pond Reef, which is off Jamaica. So, as you can see, where a vessel was listed as wrecked, can sometimes be incorrect or misleading due to a simple misunderstanding of a place name. The Indigenous people had lived on Amelia Island well before any Europeans, and they had their own names for it. I had no idea, but once the Europeans started to arrive, eight different flags flew over Amelia Island at one time or another. French, Spanish, British, Floridian/Patriot, Green Cross, Mexican, Confederate, and the U.S. flags all flew over the island. During the later 18th century it was called Egmont Island, and later during the Revolutionary War, Hillsborough Town. There could have been some confusion with Egmont Key and Hillsborough (or Hillsboro) Inlet, or Hillsborough Bay (also spelled Hillsboro) over the years.

Here's a short excerpt from a manuscript captured from one of Jean Lafitte's French privateers around 1810 that describes the east coast area of Florida from a mariner's point of view. It was reprinted in the *Savannah Republican* in 1825:

> When you see the Coast of Florida or the islands that lie near it bearing North and South, you may steer north and north by east, keeping always in sight of land; for if you are in Channel, that is to say, when you have made the land which bears N. and S. at WNW, you may approach the coast within two leagues, as far as Cape Canaveral: large vessels, however by no means approach nearer than three leagues; and when the wind is favorable, you may steer your

course within from 5 to 6 leagues from the coast. . . . The land of the Florida shore is very low and almost inundated. You can hardly see anything but the trees that grow on it.

I've tried not to list any vessels that were salvaged. Some vessels originally reported as wrecked, were later floated off a reef, raised, or towed back to a port and repaired or condemned. The schooner *Emma Knowlton,* which was abandoned off Jacksonville in March 1911, and presumed sunk soon after, was found drifting off Bermuda four months later and towed into port. I was listing the schooner *Mary Ann* as lost off Florida in 1837, but later found it was towed off the beach and towed into Key West. Same as the French brig *Glameuse,* first reported as wrecked, but then brought to Key West and condemned in 1834. I started to list the Danish tanker *Scandia* as wrecked, as all the newspapers listed her as a total wreck (one even said she broke in three pieces), on a reef 40 miles south of Miami in 1929. Being over 8,000 tons and carrying over three million gallons of fuel, I then thought why haven't I heard of this wreck. Being in an area that divers frequent, it should have been found by now. I did some further research, and with some help from the Danish Maritime Museum, found it was salvaged, towed to New York, and was repaired. I started to list the steamer *Alicia A. Washburn* as it was reported abandoned off the Panhandle in 1886, leaking and engulfed in flames, but checking the *Annual List of Merchant Vessels,* she was still listed in service for the next two years, so must have been salvaged. A few vessels I reported as wrecked or possibly wrecked in the first two editions, I've since found were salvaged, and that information is updated in this book.

Pensacola was an important port going back to the 18th century. As mentioned in the first two editions of *Shipwrecks of Florida,* the lumber industry boomed here in Florida in the later 19th century and early 20th century, and ports like Pensacola, Apalachicola, Fernandina, Jacksonville, Tampa, and St. Augustine flourished. Quite a few lumber ships were wrecked during this period. The Cedar Keys area and the reefs around Key West supported a thriving sponge business, and Tarpon Springs is still a popular tourist destination where one can still see the sponge boats and sponge divers still operating. Agriculture, which is still Florida's major industry next to tourism, helped with the expansion of shipping from Florida ports. The age of sail soon came to an end by the late 1920s, and steam, gas and diesel-powered vessels took over. Agriculture and tourism are now Florida's main industries, and the building boom continues to this day, with construction supplies being shipped into Florida ports on a daily basis, and tourists from all over the world can be seen coming and going from one of the many large cruise ships based here in Florida. Warships and submarines, fuel tankers, cruise ships, freighters, yachts, and smaller pleasure craft can be seen everywhere off Florida's coast, in her many inland waterways and lakes, or

Sketch of Pensacola Harbor circa 1760-1770s. Courtesy of the State Archives of Florida.

An 1886 photo of the Pensacola waterfront. Courtesy of the State Archives of Florida.

A 1902 photo of the Fernandina Lumber Wharf. Courtesy of the State Archives of Florida.

A 1926 photo of abandoned lumber schooners at Miami (toward the end of the age of sail.) Courtesy of the State Archives of Florida.

The new port at St. Petersburg, early 1900s. Library of Congress Prints and Photographic Division/ Keystone View Co.

The lumber wharf on the St Johns River, Jacksonville. Library of Congress Prints and Photographic Division/Detroit Photographic Co.

docked in her many ports or Naval and Coast Guard bases, making Florida a busy state, if not the busiest state, for all types of ships and watercraft in the United States. Unfortunately, as you will find in this book, all types of vessels continue to be wrecked or lost both here and all around the globe.

A 1794 map of East and West Florida. Euriskodata, Inc.

3

Mystery Wreck

I'm giving this wreck its own chapter, as the previous chapter describes the difficulties in trying to identify a shipwreck or pin down a wreck's location from old records. What first appeared to be a no-brainer as to the identity of this wreck, turns out to be far from it.

My previous editions listed the wreck of the *Spring of Whitby*. A ship's bell with her name inscribed on it was found off the coast of Florida, so there could be no doubt as to her identity, or could there? The following details some research I did on this wreck site.

In 1965, a shipwreck was discovered a few hundred feet off the beach of Wabasso, Florida. A bronze bell was recovered from the site and inscribed on the bell was the name *Spring of Whitby* and the date 1801. Now one would think that with this information, the history of this wreck, and the date she wrecked, would be easy to research. Having dove the area of the wreck in the 1990s, I was interested in finding out more, so I recently did some research on this vessel as nobody as yet has determined for sure her true identity or any details of this wreck's demise. The best source for my research was the book *The Ancient Port of Whitby and Its Shipping*, by Richard Weatherill, published in 1908, which lists all the vessels built or owned at that port. I also checked *Lloyd's Register of Shipping* and *Lloyd's List* (one is simply a register of all vessels, and the other lists vessels' movements and any disasters), along with newspaper records of the time. First thing I found was that there never was a vessel called the *Spring of Whitby* ever built or owned at Whitby, nor could I find any vessel with that name anywhere else! I did find three vessels with the name *Spring*, two which were built at the Whitby shipyards, and one that was owned at Whitby but built elsewhere that fit this time frame. I immediately eliminated one as it was built in 1807 and was lost near Dunkirk. That left two vessels, the "ship" *Spring*, built 1800 (probably launched 1801), 397 tons, 110 feet x 29.2 feet, built at Whitby by Fishburn and Brodrick, and the "brig" *Spring*, built elsewhere in 1801, but owned at Whitby.

The "ship" *Spring* was sold to the government and used as a transport out of London. She later became a merchant ship sailing between London and Quebec and other eastern Canadian ports. She was listed in Lloyd's Register until 1825, when she was no longer listed. In the 1824 register, the captain was listed as James Skelton. Lloyd's List of 1824 has no mention of either the ship *Spring* or Captain Skelton. This was the vessel that others had previously attributed as the vessel wrecked off Wabasso.

The other vessel was the 138 ton "brig" *Spring* (after 1807 was listed at 145 tons), built 1801 at Portrack near Stockton, but owned at Whitby. She disappeared from Lloyd's Register after 1815. In 1815, she was listed as single decked with beams and copper bolted. Her last captain was J. C. Smith. She returned to Liverpool from Rio in May 1815, and soon after made her last and final voyage to Wilmington, North Carolina. Lloyd's List of October 1815 says she became a total wreck in late August 1815, on the "Cape Roman Shoals" (now called Cape Romain, South Carolina), and all the crew were saved. So that vessel was eliminated, or was it?

I then checked newspapers for the year 1824, as that was when the "ship" *Spring* appears to have been lost. Searching English papers, I found a September 1824 paper that mentions the British ship *Spring* not being heard from for over three months and thought this could be the one lost off Florida. The captain was named Quelch, and she was on a voyage from Southampton to Mexico (which put it in the area of Florida). On board was the ex-emperor of Mexico, General Iturbide, who most attribute to Mexico's independence from Spain. The voyage was for the sole purpose of landing the general at a predetermined area along the Mexican coast in hopes of his gaining control of Mexico again. He had previously been exiled not long after he was named emperor. Unfortunately for the general, he was soon captured and executed by a firing squad, and the *Spring* returned to

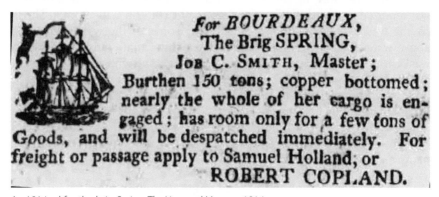

For *BOURDEAUX*,
The Brig SPRING,
Job C. Smith, Master;
Burthen 150 tons; copper bottomed; nearly the whole of her cargo is engaged; has room only for a few tons of Goods, and will be despatched immediately. For freight or passage apply to Samuel Holland, or ROBERT COPLAND.

An 1814 ad for the brig *Spring*. *The Liverpool Mercury*, 1814.

England later that year. I also determined that this *Spring* was an entirely different English ship, and not built or owned at Whitby. I now eliminated this English ship called the *Spring*, though the very interesting story of the ex-Emperor sidetracked me for a couple of hours!

So back to the ship under command of Captain Skelton. This ship is no longer mentioned in Lloyd's Register after 1824. Looking through Lloyd's List, which mentions shipwrecks and vessel's ports of call, I could find nothing on the *Spring* after 1823. No mention of her or Captain Skelton anywhere. Lloyd's list of 1823 mentions her arrival in Quebec in July 1823. Then in December 1823, in both Lloyd's List and some British newspapers, it was reported that the ship *Spring*, of London, with a cargo of lumber, wrecked in a terrible storm on the shore near Bovenbergen, December 9, 1823, on the west coast of Jutland, and immediately went to pieces with the loss of all on board. The captain's name is not mentioned in the reports, though I'll bet it was Skelton. This was a pretty violent storm, and a number of other vessels also wrecked nearby, so there wasn't much detail given on the *Spring*. She usually carried lumber from Canada, and it's been reported that this was the cargo, so I'm fairly sure that this is the wreck of the "ship" *Spring*, of Whitby, built in 1800, and maybe launched in 1801. Not the wreck off Florida! And as others have questioned, what would she be doing off Florida when on a voyage from Canada back to Europe? Piracy was now just declining from one of its bloodiest and busiest engagements throughout the Caribbean and up the eastern coast of America, and it's not entirely improbable that a ship could be captured by pirates off Canada and taken south, but in this case, I don't think that is a possibility, as another ship would most likely have reported seeing her along such a voyage, and all evidence indicates that this is the ship that wrecked off Jutland!

So back to the mystery of the bell. The inscription was probably meant to say: "*Spring*, of Whitby." Looking at all the evidence, I'm led to believe the bell is from the "brig" *Spring*, built in 1801, and owned at Whitby, though not built there. How did the bell end up off Florida, you ask? Well, the brig was reported as wrecked off South Carolina in 1815 on Cape Roman Shoal, so she was likely accessible and probably some of the wreck remained above water. Like all accessible wrecks, anything that could be salvaged, was! Though only conjecture, I'm thinking that along with the sails, rigging, and whatever else, the ship's bell was also salvaged, and most likely placed onto another vessel which later wrecked off Florida's coast. Just my guess, but if I'm right, the identity of this vessel, and the nature of her demise, still remains a mystery yet to be solved!

Many of the shipwrecks in this book have a unique story to tell, and many more still have secrets yet to reveal!

4

The Wreckers

With so many vessels being wrecked along the Florida coast, more and more individuals made a living from the salvage of these vessels. Some of the early Keys residents like Jacob Houseman made a name for themselves in the wrecking business. These "wreckers" were a hardy bunch of seafarers. Before Key West was established, they would come from the Bahamas or ports along the U.S. coast to search for wrecks along Florida to salvage. Spaniards from Cuba would also engage in the wrecking business before the Bahamians and Americans took it over in this area, and the local indigenous tribes would also engage in the salvage business whenever the opportunity arose. If a hurricane or storm was reported, these hardy individuals would set sail for Florida to go "wrecking," hoping to find abandoned vessels or cargo. After Key West was established, wrecking became the main

Wreck on the Florida Keys.

A 19th century illustration "Wreck on the Florida Keys," by E. Moran. Note the wrecking vessels nearby. *Intermediate Geography* (1800s).

A 19th century illustration of an early salvage diver. Courtesy of Baldwin Library of Children's Historical Literature, Special Area and Studies Collection, George A. Smathers Libraries, University of Florida, Gainesville (from *St. Nicholas Magazine*).

business there, and as mentioned in *Shipwrecks of Florida*, Key West was the wealthiest city per capita in the United States for a time due to the wrecking business. Were there unscrupulous individuals in this business? I'm sure there were, just as there are in many businesses today. The schooner *Hiram* claimed she wrecked in 1837 due to false light on the beach at Key West. In 1851, the brig *John French* reported a "False Light" off Key West. Most wreckers though put their lives on the line to save vessels, cargoes, and other lives. The wrecking vessel *Mount Vernon* was lost along with 12 men during the October 1844 hurricane, while trying to save the ship *Atlantic*. The pilot boat/wrecker *Florida* was lost helping salvage cargo from the ship *Crown* in 1857, though no lives were lost. Seventeen wrecking vessels and 200 men spent three weeks saving most of the *Crown*'s cargo and materials.

The work was backbreaking. The *New York Herald*, January 16, 1849, relayed a report from the *Courier* about the salvage of the steamboat *Anglo Saxon* in 1848.

The A S ran ashore on Ledbury Reef (about 5 miles from Caesar's Creek, and 15 miles from Cape Florida) on the 23d Dec, at 7 40 PM, and was boarded by the wreckers on the following day at 11 A.M. the wind at the time blowing a strong gale from the ENE. She is said to be very much injured, and was so badly ashore that the coral, sand, &c, had to be dug from under her guards, as also every thing of weight removed previous to her getting off. She was towed down by the sloops *Texas* and *Parallel*, which, with the sloop *R.H. Green*, and 50 men, got her off, at top high water, morning of the 27th. The captain had given up all hopes of getting her off, and the passengers had removed their baggage to the wrecking vessels. Owing to the boisterous weather, greater than ordinary exertion had to be used, or she never could have come off: this, combined with the superior abilities of the captains of the wrecking vessels alone saved her.

Usually, a stranded vessel would have to agree with some sort of percentage the wreckers would receive before they would attempt to save a vessel or its cargo. Captain Thompson of the ship *Erin go Bragh* went aground on Sand Key in 1850 and described the wreckers as "hovering around his ship like a swarm of bees." He refused their help, and to the wrecker's disappointment, he and his crew got her off after five days on the key. Many times, a dispute would ensue after the vessel or cargo was salvaged, and just as it is today, lawyers would end up in court and try and settle these disputes, or the dispute would be settled by a judge in a salvage court.

I remember a story about a Key West pastor, who was also a wrecker, which may or may not be true. While giving his sermon on a Sunday morning, he saw a vessel go aground out in the harbor. All the wreckers in town were in the church, and he being the only one looking in that direction, continued on with his sermon while slowly making his way toward the door, and also giving his crew a signal. He quickly ended the sermon as he and his crew bolted out the door to their wrecking vessel so as to be the first on the scene!

Though wrecking was a very profitable business in Key West, many wreckers were also shipwrights, or worked with the many shipwrights in Key West, who also made a very good living repairing the many vessels towed into Key West. An example of how good they were at their job was the repair of the bark *John Parker*, of Boston, which wrecked in April 1846 and was towed into Key West that month. This was not a small vessel as I'm guessing over 100 feet long, and in less than two months, she's loaded again and sets sail. Could you find a shipyard today that could do this work in less than two months? The *Boston Post* of May 2, 1846, had a report from Key West dated April 18:

> The bark *John Parker* must land everything moveable of weight, together with all her spars but lower masts. In heaving down yesterday she fell on the shears, and it requires the services of 20 men to raise her up; 40 feet of main keel abaft is good; fore foot split, bilge planks very much chafed, fastenings and copper started all along the bilge; several plank must come out—400 boxes sugar damaged, all the ground tier being wet. Materials can be had here to make repairs, and 10 or 12 men as carpenters and caulkers are employed.

They had to replace part of the keel, replace some planking, install new lower rudder pintles (pins), and so on, and it was all repaired by the end of May, and she set sail after reloading the beginning of June.

Old S.H. Kress & Co. postcard showing wreckers around the steamship *Alicia*, wrecked in 1905 on Ajax Reef. From author's collection.

A fleet of wreckers clustered about the steamer "Alicia," of Bilbao, which went ashore on Ajax Reef. The steamer was bound for Havana, with a full general cargo

The *Alicia* on the reef, with the wreckers around her. *Yachting Magazine* "Wreck Ashore," April 1942.

The *Louisiane* on the reef next to Sombrero Light. Was saved by the wreckers. Courtesy of the Monroe County Library, Key West.

An 1868 ad for divers for the sale of two wrecks near Pensacola. *New York Herald,* 1868.

For more information, I highly recommend the book, *The Florida Keys, Volume 3, The Wreckers,* by John Viele (see suggested reading in the Bibliography).

THE "OTHER WRECKERS"

Once the Seminole Wars ended in 1858, more settlers made Florida their home. The east coast area from St. Augustine to Cape Florida was largely uninhabited by Europeans up until that time. By 1873, there were cattle ranches on the mainland, orange groves along the coast, and settlers along the Indian River regions who became part-time wreckers whenever a vessel or its cargo came ashore along this coast. These part-time "wreckers" aren't to be associated with the "wreckers" of the Florida Keys who saved and salvaged vessels and cargoes legally as a full-time occupation, with a government license to do so. Those wreckers worked with the owners of both the vessels and cargoes that they salvaged. The part-time wreckers further up the coast when salvaging any vessels, did so with absolutely no legal authority.

The following is from an article I found reprinted in the *Savannah Morning News*, May 10, 1873, titled "The Florida Wreckers—The Winged Wagons of the Indian River and the Gulf Stream." Far from salvaging anything legally, this article gives a whole new insight in how many of the wrecks along the mid-eastern coast of Florida were salvaged, along with living conditions of the time along this coast. It was a pretty desolate coast from Cape Canaveral to Cape Florida, and the sudden storms that frequented this coast wrecked many a vessel. The article also went on about insurance fraud which I go into later in this chapter.

WINGED WAGONS—The beach varies from fifty yards to five miles in width. It separates Mosquito Lagoon and Indian River from the ocean. The lagoon and river are connected by a short cut or canal, hewn through a bed of soft coquina rock during the Seminole War. This canal, or "haulover," as the natives call it, is about a mile from Dummitt's celebrated orange grove, and is nearly four hundred yards long. The mainland, with its vast growth of pines, stretches beyond the lagoons.

The Indian River is a sort of public highway. Not more than fifteen families live upon its banks. Each family owns a winged wagon, or cat-rigged sailboat. There are but few land roads, and all the travel and business are done in those centre-board buggies. Some of the inhabitants are compelled to sail two hundred miles to reach a store or a church. Others go as far for a doctor. The dead are buried in the garden in homemade coffins. There are no schoolhouses within a week's journey. In some cases it takes four days to go to a post office and return. Everything depends upon the wind. People look for the course of the wind the first thing in the morning. "When do you think the wind will shift?" is a common question. Instead of "How's the weather," you hear. "How's the wind?" I found a Swede living upon an island in Lake Worth who was in the habit of sailing two hundred miles to borrow a book or a newspaper. He usually returned it within a month. As this necessitated two trips, he actually traveled eight hundred miles for the sake of a little reading.

NEWS OF A WRECK—Such are the people who look upon a wreck as a godsend. It furnishes them with shoes, muslin, calico, buttons, hooks and eyes, and a thousand little necessaries of life which they can get in no other way. A storm arises, and a vessel is driven ashore. The sailors wander across the beach to Indian River. They hail some straggler and are forwarded north in the little cat-rigged wagons. The news of the wreck spreads like wildfire. As the country is flat, the spars of a stranded vessel can be seen at a great distance. "A wrack, a wrack," is the cry, and within twenty-four hours, Indian River is dotted with winged phaetons, all striving for the nearest point to the ship. The wreckers fight their way through the almost impenetrable palmetto scrub to the beach, and pick up whatever they can find. When the dead bodies become bloated and offensive, they are buried in the sand. Each wrecker piles his plunder in a heap. Some hunt in couples. One man watches the pile, while the other adds to it. Occasionally whole parties club together. A part of them operate upon the wreck, one of them guards the stores, and the others tote the booty through the sand and scrub to the boats, which may be miles away from the wreck. Thus a pathway is opened, which is used by all. At times the water is so shallow that the fleet of cat-rigged sailboats are compelled to anchor a quarter of a mile from shore, and the wreckers have to wade out to them with their plunder on their backs. As fast as the boats are loaded they put for home, and return for a second cargo as soon as possible. Some men are weeks in securing all their booty. Occasionally parties build a shanty upon the sand from the driftwood of the ship. They occupy it until the last vestige of the cargo has disappeared. Then they strip the vessel of all the brass and copper they can reach, and leave her for good.

WHERE THE BULL DRIVERS COME IN—Those living on the Indian or Banana Rivers generally get the first chance at the wreck, but after three or four days the news spreads among the bull drivers of the vast cattle ranges on the main land, and they flock to the beach like hungry crows. Knowing that the tidbits of the cargo will be picked up long before their arrival, they bring with them all their ringboned and spavined nags, and barter them for wrecked goods. They are sharp at a trade and make curious bargains. When the *Ladona* was wrecked, a bull driver swapped a mare to a man named Summelin for 125 pairs of brogans, a peck of buttons, a half bushel of spool thread, and a pint of fish hooks. Summelin thought he had made a good bargain, but the mare died within a week for want of something to eat. The bull drivers generally bring with them a lot of provisions, which they trade with the wreckers, who are nearly famished, for articles that strike their fancy.

Water is usually very scarce in the vicinity of the wreck. An old cove named Harris turns this scarcity into money. On the announcement of a wreck he arms himself with a two-gallon jug filled with water, jumps into his boat, hoists his sail, and puts for the ship. On his way over the beach he meets a dozen men in the hot sun bending under the weight of plunder which they are toting to the boats. Some of them have not tasted water for twenty-four hours. As Harris meets them he kindly offers them a drink. They drop their loads and gladly seize the jug and turn its bottom to the sky. Meanwhile Harris steals the most valuable part of their booty, receives the thanks of the thirsty victims for his kindness, and travels on. If he is caught stealing, he coolly says, "Well, Tom, you've got more of this than you want, an' I reckon you won't miss this here roll of flannel, so I'll just confiscate it." In nine cases out of ten the victim, in gratitude of the water, will say, "All right, Harris; take it along." Should Harris meet a man bearing a load not worth stealing, he will turn away his head as if intensely interested in something beyond him, and not see the thirsty wrecker. Harris and his jug turn up at every wreck. The old man's peculiarities, however, have become well known, and his business is falling off.

FLORIDA PHILOSOPHY—Most of the inhabitants here wear wrecked goods. Even their hats and shoes come from stranded ships. Their wives and daughters have dresses and aprons made of wrecked calico, their tables are covered with wrecked linen, and their beds are spread with wrecked muslin. A good wreck will supply an economical family for years. The ship ashore is regarded as legitimate prey. The people are honest and passably industrious, but they will go for a week like gulls after a dead fish. They reason like philosophers. A vessel freighted with merchandise runs ashore. The goods drift upon the beach in a sandy wilderness, miles away from any residence. Before the authorities can take any action, everything will be ruined. The people declare that they might better secure what comes ashore than leave it upon the beach to rot. So they take what they can find. They look upon it as a gift of Providence. The difficulties in transportation are such that it will not pay the underwriters to secure a ship's cargo unless it is unusually valuable and imperishable. In nine cases out of 10 a Government official will help himself to the booty, and consequently the wreckers seem to think it a duty they owe themselves and the country to get ahead of him. They are kind-hearted and generous to shipwrecked passengers and sailors, and unhesitatingly peril their lives to save them. They will go miles out of their way to forward them on their way north, feeding and clothing them without asking for a cent in return. They throw out no false lights, but calmly await whatever the wind and the Lord may send them. They bury the dead in the sand, and regard the cargo as common property. Ministers, deacons, Freemasons, Christians, and sinners all run a race for the plunder. They do not call it stealing, but simply saving an immense amount of property from being wasted. A man would be safe among them with a million of dollars in his pocket—much safer than he would be in New York City, but they would plunder a wrecked bum—boat without a qualm of conscience.

The article goes further to state how the Seminoles, under young Tiger Tail, salvaged most of the wrecks to the south of Jupiter Inlet. It went on to say how his band salvaged linens and silks from a British ship wrecked north of Biscayne Bay in 1872 and traded the linens with settlers on the east coast, but brought the more valuable silks to the west coast to trade with those in Tampa and Cedar Keys. It also mentioned that all the dogs and cats around Cape Canaveral came from all the wrecked ships in the area. The writer says that while he was at the Cape Canaveral Lighthouse, a crew from a Prussian ship from Cardenas, loaded with iron, which they had to abandon at sea in the boats, came ashore there and left a cat they saved from the ship.

EARLY SALVAGE TECHNIQUE

Many salvage divers including myself have used a 55-gallon drum to raise an object from the sea bed. Starting back in the 1840s, instead of a 55-gallon

The salvage vessel *Ella Warley III*. Note the prop wash deflectors (blowers) that lower over the propellers, working on the "Jupiter Wreck." These could move over 20 feet of sand in order to reach the bottom.

Jack Pennel's outboard "blower." We used this one year on a 1715 wreck site to move sand in the shallow reef area.

Author's old White's PI 1000 underwater metal detector, which still works after 25 years, though had some help.

The latest White's Surfmaster PI Dual Feed underwater metal detector. White's Electronics.

Then MAC president Bill Raymond, on our floating commercial dredge, on a later 1800s wreck-site during an archaeological investigation.

This and the next four photos show the progression of salvaging an anchor we found about ten feet from some 1715 cannons we discovered on the north end of the "Cabin" site. The anchor belonged to a later wreck though. One of the arms was quite bent from trying to hold the vessel it belonged to in place, and judging from how it lay, the vessel must have wrecked right up onto the beach. What a story it could tell! This photo shows the lift bags I used to tie to and lift the anchor. We then slowly towed it about ½ mile to Mel Fisher's salvage vessel, which had a crane. Author.

drum, the early wreckers used a "hogshead," which was a large cask, usually of 63 gallons but came as large as 140 gallons in size. Mentioned throughout the book is the word "bilged," which meant the ship's lower hull was damaged to allow the water to pour into it. According to Albion's book,

> The favorite method of salvaging a stranded hull which had "bilged" was to fill the hold with empty hogsheads at low tide while the water was out of the hull. The breaches in the planking would be plugged up; steam pumps set to work; and, when the tide came in again, the buoyancy of the hogsheads was sometimes enough to enable a steamer to tow her clear.

Search and salvage equipment continues to improve. Where we used to use a sextant to pinpoint our location using beach markers, we now use a GPS. Chirp or side-scan sonar is now available on many common fishfinders and just installed one myself.

A discussed in *Shipwrecks of Florida*, most older objects recovered from the sea will need some sort of conservation, which can be very time-consuming.

Mel Fisher's salvage vessel lifting the anchor with its crane.

The anchor was kept wet until conservation could start. That's conservator Noel Vassallo in the Marine Archaeological Council's conservation tank along with another anchor, preparing them for electrolysis.

The anchor after conservation.

The anchor had the letters "MLD" stamped in the middle of where the arms meet the shank and have yet to identify them.

Photo of the *Global Hope* in a sinking condition off Key West in 1978. Coast Guard and salvage companies (modern wreckers) saved her and towed her to Texas to be scrapped. Courtesy of the Monroe County Library, Key West.

INSURANCE FRAUD

Insurance fraud also reared its ugly head. Some ships were being intentionally wrecked or sunk in order to collect insurance money. Some of these incidents were investigated. The ship *William Hitchcock* was reported as wrecked on the Tortugas in February 1848 by the captain and crew who made it to Key West. The wreck was investigated by Captain John Hoyt, agent for the underwriters, and found five auger holes on each side opposite the fore hatch in order to sink her. He had these plugged and she was then pumped out and gotten off with the assistance of the wreckers. Also in 1848, the brig *Benjamin Litchfield* grounded near Sand Key and her captain refused any help from the wreckers. Her cargo of lime soon caught fire and most everything was lost. The wreck was later investigated, and the hull was found to have had auger holes drilled through it. Most likely another case of insurance fraud.

The Captain of the *Brother's Pride* had loaded her with a worthless fake cargo and purposely wrecked her off Florida in 1879 in order to collect on the insurance. Just a few months later that same year, the brig *George Harris* was beached near Cape Canaveral, having reported she was in a sinking condition due to a storm. An agent for the underwriter, Mr. Ellis, investigated and found an auger hole, falsified log, very little water in her hold, and the fact that there was no storm!

In 1896 at Pensacola, the captain of the ship *Mabel Taylor* refused to obey the pilot's order to anchor up, and all through the night, while in site of the life-saving station, never issued a distress signal. She was found aground the next morning a total wreck. She was totally insured though! The captain had no answer as to why she wrecked.

The earlier 1873 quoted article, "The Florida Wreckers," also mentioned a schooner which wrecked below Cape Canaveral with $50 worth of shingles on board. Government officials saved the cargo, though it cost the taxpayers $4,000 to do so. It goes on about insurance fraud at that time: "There is little doubt that the Florida coast is turned to good account by dishonest shippers and captains. When a vessel gets old and unseaworthy, it is an easy matter to load her with a nominal cargo, and insure both vessel and cargo double their value. She can be scuttled or run ashore on the Florida coast miles away from any habitation, and the insurance companies are none the wiser. It is said that one-third of the wrecks are caused by rascally captains. Col. Titus gave me the name of a steamer which went ashore near Lake Worth in January last, which he places in this category. I have forgotten her name, but she came from New York, and Titus declared that he would prove what he said."

Implying that one-third of the wrecks around this time were wrecked on purpose may be stretching it a bit, though who knows. Would be interesting to follow up on many of these insurance investigations and see if anyone got prosecuted, and if so, what the outcome was. Sometimes a wreck was reported that never even existed such as with the supposed wreck of the *America* in 1846. It appears the whole story was made up.

Wrecks also brought opportunity to some wheeler and dealer types. Take for instance the wreck of the ship *Bombay*, which went aground in the Tortugas, February 1838. She was gotten off and her cargo saved by the wreckers. They then towed the ship into Tortugas Harbor where they left her after removing much of the materials. The captain sold her at auction for $1,450. Half the profit from the sale of the cargo went to the wreckers. The buyer, finding the hull not that badly damaged, had her repaired in the harbor and he immediately resold her to a merchant in New Orleans for a $7,000 profit via a quick claim deed. The ship then went to New Orleans where she was refitted and fully repaired. By May 22, 1838, with a full cargo of cotton, she sailed for England and by late September 1838, she was back in New York. She was insured for $30,000. It was reported on May 10 that the underwriter for the insurance company came to Key West from Boston in order to seize her, and when he learned she was now in New Orleans, he proceeded there. No idea what transpired after that as she may have already sailed for England by the time the underwriter arrived in New Orleans.

Reality shows like *Storage Wars* on television have been a big success. Salvaged material from shipwrecks were auctioned in a similar manner. A number of papers reported how a bidder bought 12 crates at $12 each off the wreck of the *Lima* in 1825 at Key West. All were filled with crockery (some broken), along with lace and silks, and the bidder made a profit of over $500, which was a very large amount in those days (would be equal to over $11,000 in profit today).

Ships and small craft continue to be lost or rescued annually, even with the most sophisticated equipment on board. Salvage companies like Titan, which used to be based in Florida, now work all over the globe salvaging wrecked ships. But it's the crews of the Coast Guard who are usually first on the scene off our coast and who continue to place themselves in danger in order to save lives. Even the Navy steps in when needed. During Hurricane Hugo in 1999, the 150-foot tug *Gulf Majesty* was towing a 750-foot barge. Hit by the storm about 300 miles off Jacksonville, with 40-foot waves and 60-mph winds, they needed to cut the barge loose, but the tug was filling with water before they were able and had to be abandoned. An SOS was sent before they abandoned her. The Coast Guard got the coordinates but had no vessels in the area and contacted the Navy. The Navy's *John F. Kennedy* had left Mayport to ride out the storm and was the closest vessel to the wreck. They launched two SH-60 Seahawk's which took an hour to reach the scene in 35–45 knot winds. One found three of the eight crew in the water and rescued them. Low on fuel, they returned to the ship. They returned later and found the rest in a life raft and all were rescued.

5

Some Noteworthy and Interesting Items

Additional information related to a wreck can be found in chapter 8.

Sharks

Sunk by a shark!—The crew of the shrimper *Christine Nicole* must have been playing scenes from the movie *Jaws* in their minds when a massive bull shark rammed their vessel in 2007, which caused it to sink.

The original "Shark Hunter"—Capt. Quint from the movie *Jaws* had a burning hatred toward sharks due to his experience from having survived the sinking of the *USS Indianapolis*. That same hatred was shared by a Mr. Wainwright. Back in 1887, the wife of Mr. Wainwright fell overboard in Jupiter Inlet and was devoured by a shark. The *Detroit Free Press* had an article in 1891 called "He Loved Her," and noted that after three years, Mr. Wainwright had killed over 800 sharks from Jupiter Inlet, and had no intention of stopping!

Jupiter Inlet must have had a reputation as a shark haven as a number of papers published a story about shark attacks in 1873, which related an incident during the Civil War about a boat which was upset about 20 feet from shore by Jupiter Inlet with 14 sailors on board. "There was a foaming of the waters, and in half a minute twelve of the fourteen men disappeared." Two did make shore, but were so badly bitten that they soon died from their wounds.

Shark by another name—In 1875 it was reported from Pensacola that a sailor had stolen a boat there and it soon capsized in the bay where he was "immediately gobbled up by a Sunday School Trout, known elsewhere as a shark." First time I've heard of that reference.

Crew lost—See chapter 8 to read about the fate of the *Carrie Strong* in 1916.

ABANDONED AND LOCKED BELOW DECK
ONLY TO BE EATEN ALIVE!

Makes a great headline, but this was the fate of one on board the schooner *Jessie P* in 1896!

TERRIBLE EXPERIENCE OF A
SAILOR.

ALONE ON ABANDONED SCHOONER.

ATTACKED BY RATS.

FEARFUL STRUGGLE FOR LIFE.

An 1896 article headline about the *Jessie P.* The Shields Daily Gazette & Shipping Telegraph, July 1896.

Unusual cargoes—Imagine finding an ancient Egyptian artifact on a wreck site in the Florida Keys. That would be history making, or maybe not! An Egyptian mummy was salvaged from the wreck of the ship *Spermo* in 1827 on Alligator Reef. Were there more Egyptian artifacts that went down with her? Maybe so! If you do find one there, don't call *National Geographic* just yet—it's most likely from the wreck of the *Spermo*!

Find an intact safe on Ledbury reef? Don't get too excited. The ship *Quebec* had gone ashore on Ledbury Reef, January 21, 1848, and though she was gotten off, she threw much of her cargo overboard, which consisted of Salamander safes (Salamander was a popular safe manufacturer), ploughs, dry goods, castings, and so on. The wreckers dove and recovered much of the cargo. So if you find a "Salamander" safe while diving on Ledbury Reef, it will likely have nothing inside, but if it's not a "Salamander," well, then you just might want to get excited.

What if you came across a pile of 69 cannon in Tortugas Bay. You may think you found a Spanish Galleon or a great warship, but those were just part of the cargo of the schooner *E. Richardson*, which wrecked there in 1870.

Just about everything was transported by ship back in the day, including a complete dinosaur skeleton destined for a museum in 1845, and salvaged by the wreckers.

The strange tale of the *Helen Mar*—She was reported wrecked in 1835, though eventually found abandoned and floating. Her tale is told in the chapter 8, and it's definitely a strange one.

James Bond's DB5—It's not a shipwreck, but one of the most famous movie cars, the original Aston Martin DB5 that Sean Connery drove in the movie *Goldfinger*, may lie off the coast of Florida. It disappeared from a Boca Raton aircraft hangar in June 1997 and has never been seen since. The story was covered on Brad Meltzer's TV show *Lost History*, where one theory was a freight plane had flown in that evening, picked it up, and dumped it in the ocean off Florida for the insurance money. There was some evidence that a freight plane did fly in that night. There may be a reward for the finder!

Saved after being locked in a barrel—You could not make up a story like this! As punishment for not obeying the captain, a rambunctious 14-year-old boy was confined to an empty water cask overnight on the ship *Alexander* in 1870, but was washed overboard during a terrible storm that evening. The boy survives after 30 hours at sea; the ship does not!

The slave trade—The slave trade flourished in the 17th, 18th, and 19th centuries, and many a pirate took part in this trade. One was found off the Marquesas in 1984 and identified is the *Henrietta Marie*, which wrecked in 1700, though she had already dropped off her cargo of slaves in Cuba. It was investigated and many artifacts relating to this nefarious trade are now in a traveling exhibit bringing the story of slavery to thousands of people all over the world. Though Congress banned bringing slaves into the United States in 1807 (to begin January 1, 1808), that didn't stop many from continuing the trade. Florida though didn't become a state until 1845, and though it was known as a sanctuary for runaway slaves, the trade also continued here.

In 1817, a small Spanish schooner from Africa arrived at Amelia Island with a cargo of slaves, not realizing the island was now under control of

Recently found anchor (found in the area the *Nimble* went aground chasing the *Guerrero* in 1827) that may help locate the pirate/slave ship *Guerrero*. Note how much sand nature moved, as only the encrusted portion was previously visible. Though barely visible in photo, much of the wood stock was still there having been buried for many years. Boy Scout Nautical Group 32, Ft. Lauderdale, and Mr. Frank Brinson, P.E.

the Florida/Patriots. It was immediately captured by an 18-gun privateer stationed there.

A number of groups have searched for the wreck of the pirate/slave ship *Guerrero* that had captured most if not all the slaves from other slave traders off Africa, and wrecked in 1827 in the upper Keys, but it is yet to be found. Some new evidence has come to light and may help reveal the site of the wreck. See *Guerrero* in chapter 6 for resources and information.

One of the first still to be identified wrecks found in the Keys was called the "Ivory Wreck," due to the elephant tusks recovered from the site. It was located back in the early 1950s on Delta Shoal, and many artifacts including a cannon were recovered. Though believed to be a 17th-century wreck from the artifacts recovered, the cannon had some markings near the breech. The story of this wreck and how it was found is told in the book *Treasure Diving Holidays* by Jane and Barney Crile. It describes the cannon markings as: "near the breech was the letter P. Below that, engraved in a flowing script, was a provocative JN and the number 170 1/11 24." They tried to have it identified but could not. They heard back from the Hague Museum which said they doubted it was Dutch. Archaeologist Mendel Peterson believed it was made in Amsterdam, so it may be a Dutch vessel. What everyone does believe is that it was most likely a slave ship.

The slaver *Bell* sank with 150 souls on board in the Keys in 1788, though the fate of the captain and his mate could be attributed to karma, and they may have wished they drowned too. The slaver *Dove* wrecked on Florida's coast in 1773, and 80 poor souls were lost.

Many of these slave vessels brought their human cargo to Cuba or other Caribbean islands, though it appears Florida was also active in this trade in the 18th and 19th century with slave ships operating from Florida ports. The sloop *Active*, from Jamaica for Florida, with slaves and rum, was captured by an American privateer in 1779 and taken to the Carolinas. Florida though offered the first free black settlement in the Americas by the Spanish at Fort Mose in St. Augustine.

The *St. Augustine News* reported on August 17, 1844, that the U.S. Revenue schooner *Vigilant* had arrived there with a demand from the governor of Louisiana through the Florida governor for eight Africans who had escaped from Belize in the pilot boat *Lafayette* and got stranded on the Tortugas Reef. It seems a few days earlier, six of them were sold as slaves to a Mr. V. Sanchez, by the U.S. Marshal at a public sale. Sanchez was refusing to deliver the six, and the case was causing much interest. Why Louisiana was involved I have no idea.

> *From the Royal Gazette of Sierra Leone.*
>
> Freetown, July 17, 1819.
>
> From recent and authentic information, we have to lay before our readers a distressing memoranda of the traffic in slaves at Gallienas and the river Sheabar, close to our happy and free colony.
>
> Brig 180 tons, name unknown, Perry master—fitted out from the Havanna; 306 slaves; crew English and Americans; sailed in July.
>
> Schooner 49 tons, Cook master, from St. Augustine, East Florida, 56 slaves, crew Americans, sailed in July inst.
>
> Schooner 180 tons, Breton master, fitted out from St. Thomas, West Indies, cargo English goods, 317 slaves, crew French, sailed June last.
>
> Schooner, name unknown, Muinard master, from Guadaloupe, cargo English goods; 340 slaves, crew French, now trading.
>
> Brig, name unknown, Blackwood master, Havana; American cargo, 420 slaves, now trading.
>
> Schooner, name unknown, Marteau master, from St. Thomas, West Indies, cargo English, 300 slaves, to be sold in the British West India Islands; now trading.
>
> Schooner, name unknown, Jones master, (an Englishman,) cargo American, 260 slaves, now trading.
>
> Schooner, name unknown, has made trade at Sheabar for 180 slaves, and still remains there. Slaves at an average of 100 bars per head.

An 1819 newspaper article reprinted from a Sierra Leone newspaper listing slave ships, one from St. Augustine. *Annapolis Maryland Gazette & Political Intelligencer*, March 1820.

The slave trade continued up until the Civil War. One report has the schooner/slaver *Experiment* dropping off her cargo near Jupiter in 1859 and then wrecking the vessel to get rid of any evidence. The story of the *Horatio*, found abandoned off Key West in 1855, is another strange tale of trying to hide evidence of the slave trade and may have hidden a tale of a horrible atrocity. The schooner *Florida* wrecked off the southeast coast of Florida in 1825, and had 20 Africans in her hold who all drowned, though reports make no mention of them as being slaves.

Though slavery still goes on today, even in this country, these wrecks would be a stark reminder of man's inhumanity to man.

Immigration and Florida—The Mariel boatlift, Cuban rafters, Haitian and South and Central American immigrants, these are stories we read about daily, and Florida has always been one of the epicenters for migrants entering this country, whether legally or illegally. Back in the early 1900s, Chinese immigrants were being smuggled into Florida as the wreck of the *Viola* in 1921 can attest to. I saw firsthand the aftermath of the wreck of the Haitian vessel *La Nativite* in 1981, as they pulled numerous dead bodies from the ocean and off the beach in front of the homes of millionaires. Some of the poorest people in the world struggling for a better life only to die where some of the wealthiest people in the world lived. It happened again in 2008 off Fisher Island, which was the most expensive postal zone at that time and may still be, where the average home there in 2008 was $3.8 million. An old freighter of about 45 feet grounded in a heavy surf with about 40 persons on board. Most on board were from the Dominican Republic and some from Brazil. Three were drowned and others were missing and feared lost. The one summer when hundreds of Cuban rafters set forth for Florida, we made a trip on Don Kree's Whaler to the Bahamas. I remember all the rafts (though all now empty and drifting in the Gulf Stream) we came across both going over and coming back. Some of these were constructed out of the craziest things you could imagine, and none were anything I'd like to be sailing on in the open ocean. An overloaded boat capsized off Miami in 2009 carrying Haitian immigrants from Bimini, and a number of people died. Reports of immigrants landing on the beach continues to this day, and as I'm wrapping up this book, I just read in a January 5, 2019, newspaper, that eight of 10 people were rescued off Florida from an overturned 18-foot boat smuggling them to Florida, though two of the 10 were lost including a nine-year-old child. If a small boat returning from a fishing trip to the Bahamas had not seen them, all 10 would likely have been lost. Immigration seems to be the hot topic in Washington these days.

Mutiny and murder—This was not an uncommon occurrence as the story of the *Enterprise* in the previous editions can attest to. What was the difference between a mutineer and a pirate? As some stories in chapter 6 can attest to, there really isn't a difference. Some sailors who signed on as crewmen had already planned to take over the vessel once at sea. The captain of the *Port Factor* made a big mistake when taking on three Spaniards as crewmen in 1742. The sloop *Ajax* was found near Cape San Blas in 1832, and all the crew were missing and presumed dead. Two men had previously shown up in Apalachicola with gold and fine clothes in the vessel's boat. Suspecting foul play, they were arrested, but had been released before the

Saw this abandoned raft about 20 miles off the Palm Beach coast during the Cuban rating exodus in the 1980s. Imagine making the crossing on this!

vessel was found and was later determined the two were part of the crew. The brig *Neva* wrecked in 1866 on the St. John's Bar. Some of the surviving crewmen were later arrested after local officials found some bodies washed ashore a couple of days later, including the captain and a woman, which after examination, were determined to have been murdered.

Cannibalism—Having to resort to cannibalism to survive was nothing new to sailors. *Moby Dick* was a story loosely based on the wreck of the whaleship *Essex* in 1820. I recommend watching the movie, *In the Heart of the Sea*, as it tells the story of this ship. Cannibalism was not unknown to these shores either. The ship *Tiger* wrecked near Cape St. George in 1766, and the story of the survivors was written about in a couple of books which included cannibalism in order to survive. A Captain Hestley picked up four survivors of a wreck off Florida in 1774 who had been in a boat for 19 days. The remains of one dead man was still on the boat which the rest had devoured to survive. The ship *Mersey* sunk off Florida in 1865, and some survived by drinking the blood from a wounded man's arm, and fortunately, they were rescued and the wounded man survived. One tale of cannibalism that really is disturbing is that of the Norwegian bark *Drot*, which wrecked off Florida in 1899. The story was reported in almost every newspaper here and abroad and briefly described in this new edition.

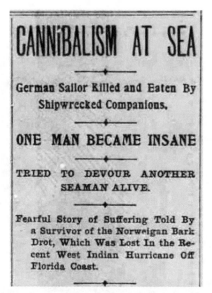

An 1899 newspaper headline about the
Drot. The Salt Lake Tribune, September 1899.

Disease—Disease crippled many a ship as sickness could debilitate an
entire crew. As with the wreck of the *Athenaise* in 1804, the crew were so
sick, that there was literally nobody left to man the vessel (second edition,
page 266). The same happened with the *HMS Winchester* in 1695, with
most of the crew dead or sick from scurvy, there was nobody left to man
her. The bark *Robert Morris* wrecked in 1853, as her crew were also too sick
to man the vessel. The same happened to the bark *Gloria* in 1891.

Ships entering a port suspected of having anyone on board who were
sick were told to anchor in a quarantine area or "quarantine station" as
they became known. The *Olivette*, a 224-foot hospital ship, which cared for
the sick and injured during the Spanish-American War, foundered in Fernandina Harbor at the Quarantine Station, where she would anchor due to
her having sick on board, though was later raised and put back in service.

The brig *Ajax* anchored off Key West in 1833. She was 15 days out from
New Orleans with almost 150 immigrants bound for Liberia. Most had
been slaves from Tennessee, Kentucky, and Ohio, in which the Richmond
Palladium newspaper stated had been had been "manumitted" (released
from slavery) with the condition that they be deported to Liberia. The mate
and two immigrants became sick and died two days after leaving New Orleans, and between 30 and 40 died from the cholera while anchored off Key
West. After the sickness subsided, the *Ajax* then set sail again for Liberia on
May 19. Of the 200 or so residents at Key West, about 10–15 became sick
and nine died with no new cases since May 27. Though it appeared nobody

left the ship, there was correspondence with and maybe supplies brought out to the brig. Nevertheless, some in town did catch the disease. The survivors of the *Ajax* may have met up with the survivors of the pirate/slaver ship *Guerrero* once reaching Liberia.

In September 1858, a steamer found the British brig *Esperanza* drifting in the Gulf off Bay Port, Florida. The captain and all the crew were found dead from the "fever," except two men and a boy. They towed the brig to Apalachicola and placed her in quarantine.

When the California steamship *Philadelphia*, carrying 250 passengers and California gold, arrived at Key West from Aspinwall on June 28, 1852, a cholera epidemic had struck those on board, and 22 had already died. Capt. McGowan asked if some could come ashore, but was refused for fear of spreading the disease. Sand Key and the light there were presently abandoned as it was under construction, and it was agreed to let the *Philadelphia* use the island. It was soon anchored nearby and the passengers not sick were placed on the island and a sail placed over the construction area for shelter. A dismantled brig was then set up as a hospital, and anchored near Sank Key. The *Philadelphia* had enough food, though those at Key West did supply them with anything they needed such as lumber and ice. Eventually the epidemic passed, the *Philadelphia* was cleansed and fumigated, coal was shipped in as it was almost out of fuel, and she sailed for New York, July 14. A total of 55 had died by the time she sailed, though others had also

Photo of an FEC R/R barge ashore after a hurricane. Courtesy of the Monroe County Library, Key West.

suffered from Chagres fever, which also plagued the ship. Many survivors ended up recuperating at Key West, but only after it was deemed safe.

The Florida Railway—The Florida East Coast Railway (FEC), which still exists today, eventually brought those from the mainland all the way to Key West by rail, and Key West soon became a popular vacation spot. Remnants of the old railway can still be seen in the Keys today. What most don't know is that hundreds of workers lost their lives during hurricanes while building the railway. Many lived on railway Houseboats or Quaterboats, some which were destroyed in these storms, especially during the 1906 hurricane.

Hurricanes and Storms—Much has been written about the Spanish treasure fleets of 1622, 1715, and 1733, which were devastated by hurricanes, but hurricanes also account for so many other wrecks off Florida, some with great loss of life, such as the steamers *City of Vera Cruz, Evening Star,* and the *Valbanera.* Over 240 men were lost when the *USS Warrington* sank during a hurricane off Florida during World War II. Even today, with all the modern navigational equipment, excellent hurricane weather forecasts, and safety equipment, ships are still lost due to hurricanes as was the 790-foot *El Faro* in 2015 off the Bahamas after she left Jacksonville. As you will find by reading this book, hurricanes are not uncommon here in Florida. The 1840s were a particularly bad time for hurricanes as they slammed the coast of Florida in 1842, 1844, 1846, and 1848. The 1846 hurricane almost completely destroyed Key West. In 1896, a strong hurricane hit the Cedar

A schooner sunk in Key West Harbor after the September 1919 hurricane. Courtesy of the Monroe County Library, Key West/Art and Historical Collection.

A 19th century illustration of launching a lifeboat during a storm. Not an easy task. *Shipwrecks and Tales of the Sea*, 1887.

Illustration from an 1831 account of shipwreck survivors on a piece of wreckage. *Shipwrecks & Disasters at Sea*, 1836.

An illustration depicting survivors clinging to the ship's boat from a 1784 account. *Shipwrecks & Disasters at Sea,* 1836.

Keys area. At that time, there were around 100 sponge vessels working the sponge banks near Cedar Keys. Each of these vessels had a crew of 4–10 men on board. Almost every one of these vessels were lost in the storm, resulting in one of the greatest losses of life off Florida's shores, though hardly ever mentioned. How exactly the *Valbanera* wrecked still remains a mystery, though resulted in the greatest loss of life off Florida's coast in the 20th century (three freighters and a tanker were also sunk during this same storm with well over 100 lives lost).

In the previous editions, the narrative of the *City of Vera Cruz* gave a glimpse of the horrors one would encounter in a hurricane. Many from that ship were killed due to all the wreckage or "flotsam" drifting along with the survivors. Imagine surviving the sinking of your ship, clinging to some piece of wreckage, when a large wave sends a piece of that wreck slamming into your head or body! I've again added a number survivor's accounts from vessels such as the *Varuna, Mississippi, Lodona,* and many others, which describe their experiences being wrecked during a hurricane, which from their accounts, can give you a better insight of what it must have felt like to be in such a terrible situation.

Florida is also known for the sudden squalls that can sweep in so quickly, that one only has a brief amount of time, if any, to get ready before it

One of the familiar squalls that can appear quite suddenly.

View from the salvage boat *Pandion*, during a squall with gusts over 100 mph on the 1715 "Nieves" site. Only had time to throw off our three anchors and head east.

arrives. Anyone who has been caught in one of these knows the damage they can cause. I've been caught in ones with gusts over 100 mph, and are quite scary to say the least. Those working the 1715 fleet are all too familiar, as these squalls are quite common some years (some years we hardly ever saw one, and other years were quite frequent). We'd see one coming, and if close to the inlet, would try and beat the storm to get inside for protection, or if coming up too fast, or too far from any inlet, would either get out to deeper water and anchor up, then swinging in a 360-degree circle from the bow anchor until the storm passed or would just head east, keeping an eye on the compass as the bow was about as far as you could see. The worst one I remember was off Pompano Beach, the storm came up so quick, we just made it in the inlet as we were luckily nearby. With hail the size of golf balls, I had to hold a swim fin over my head to deflect them from hitting me as my bimini top was torn off. I also had to don my dive mask to be able to see anything, just making it inside the inlet when visibility went to zero. My buddy jumped into the cabin, but not before he got pelted by some hail, which left a bruise on his leg the size of a softball. My friend's much larger 60-foot boat, which was out near us out at the same time, got hit by lightning which fried all his electronics. Just how devastating these squalls can be was related by the survivors of the *Speedwell* in 1898, a truly sorrowful tale!

As I'm finishing up this book, we've just gone through Hurricane Irma in 2017 and Hurricane Michael in 2018. At first it looked like my home was in the direct path of Irma, but it slowly kept going west and we rode it out at home here on Florida's east coast. We were without power for a few days, but had a generator I luckily found the day after Hurricane Wilma a few years before and it kept the refrigerator cold and we had no damage to speak of. Irma was a monster storm, as was Michael, and we are still hearing about the devastation in the lower Keys and elsewhere. It could have been much worse. And then another hurricane comes and hits Puerto Rico a week later! Looked like everything settled for another year in Florida, but Hurricane Michael comes out of nowhere, and slams the Panhandle.

The ocean is definitely getting warmer as I find every year I go diving here. I believe global warming is an issue we better start dealing with. As for shipwrecks, hundreds of vessels were lost, damaged, or destroyed during these last hurricanes. One washed up on Melbourne Beach a couple weeks after Irma and made the local and Internet news. The 45-foot two-masted sailboat *Cuci* was found relatively intact, both masts still there, and with two manakins on board up on the beach. Appeared only the manakins were on board as the owner was listed as in jail, and last registration sticker was from 2014, so probably just a liveaboard which must have broken loose from its mooring in Key West during the hurricane and drifted the 360 miles north to Melbourne. I was watching the *Miami Early Evening News* the night before

Hurricane Irma even struck our area, when they showed one boat already sunk at its dock, and two others that broke free from their moorings out in Biscayne Bay and were now up on the beach, and the winds were not even that bad yet! Some of the Keys got the worst of the storm, and days later, photos of many sunken boats or others alongside roadways and wrecked up on land were on social media. Fuel leaks were also becoming a problem from all the sunken boats in the Keys after the storm. Last I had heard, almost 1,700 sunken boats had been removed from the waters of the Keys due to Hurricane Irma. Most everyone watched on TV as Hurricane Michael slammed our coast. Days later, a number of vessels wrecked over 100 years ago were found uncovered on Dog Island.

A 92-foot yacht sunk inside Hillsboro Inlet after Hurricane Irma in 2017.

Bermuda Triangle—No doubt there are some strange stories regarding losses at sea in the triangle. I have no doubt that many vessels listed as missing were simply victims of piracy, even in this day and age. As mentioned previously, storms have sunk many more. The steamer *Cotopaxi*, which went missing off our coast in 1925, was recently part of a YouTube hoax showing her sudden reappearance off the coast of Cuba as a modern-day *Flying Dutchman*. There are pilots and sailors who have told of navigational equipment going awry, or actually losing time in the triangle. Aliens, Atlantis, I've heard it all. I've seen some strange weather patterns off the coast, heard of rogue waves, mention a commercial fishing boat sunk by a shark, so who knows. What I can say for sure is that one must fully respect the power of Mother Nature, especially when sailing upon our great oceans and lakes.

Wildlife—Wild animals were also a problem for anyone wrecked along the Florida coast. Besides having to worry about sharks and alligators, wolves, bears and panthers were also a threat as the crew of the *Admiral Saultzemann* can attest to when they wrecked here in 1858.

Mosquitoes were another hazard if one was wrecked off our shore. I've read a number of reports of survivors burying themselves in the sand to prevent being eaten alive by these pests. I've always wondered what those who lived here used to ward off these pests. I've heard bear grease, but never verified this. I've been on a remote beach in the Bahamas when the mosquitoes and the no-see-ums attacked at dusk, and swear they could drive one mad.

The Teredo Worm and Indian River—Fighting the ravages of the teredo worm, which burrows into and destroys wood, was a constant maintenance issue for vessels in the West Indies and Florida. Maybe it was the mix of fresh and salt water of that area, but the worms of Indian River were known to be unusually devastating to a ship's hull. The government chartered steamer *James Boatwright*, which sank in 1838 in the Indian River due to the teredo worms, had her owner's case heard in a government hearing in 1846 to hopefully be compensated for her loss. Witnesses stated that another ship had gone aground in the river during the same period with one half of her hull out of the water and in very good shape. After six weeks in that position, the vessel was needed by the Army, so they did some minor repairs to the exposed hull and then had her heaved over only to find the other half completely destroyed by the worms, and it was abandoned there as it was too far gone to repair. Another witness mentioned that the brand-new schooner *Venus*, which had been in the Indian River, had her hull "completely honey-combed by worms, in four months." A Naval Lt. told how one of their launches (largest boat on a warship) was destroyed and sunk in Pensacola Harbor due to the worms in just three weeks, saying the hull was "completely perforated." He went on to say he'd also seen the solid oak stock of a frigate's anchor destroyed by worms in only six weeks.

It was stated in the hearing regarding the *James Boatwright* that, "Owing to the prevalence of worms in said river, whose ravages are generally so rapid and destructive, it is not regarded safe for any boat not coppered to remain in the waters of that river for more than six or eight weeks without being examined and repaired" (Source 14).

Frostbite in Florida?—It does occasionally get below freezing in Florida, but one doesn't necessarily attribute frostbite as ever occurring in the State of Florida, but many of the survivors of the steamer *Lamplighter*, which wrecked near Dog Island in February 1841, suffered just that before being rescued.

When rescuing a crew from a schooner wrecked on the rocks at Cedar Key in January 1886, it was reported that it was so cold, that the salt water froze on the reefs in the area, and dead fish could be seen floating for miles.

Florida's Indigenous Tribes—Many shipwreck survivors tell the tale of being attacked by the indigenous tribes along our coast. As many of the indigenous people in the New World (though not new to them), had been enslaved, killed, or wiped out from European diseases, it should have been no surprise then that they would become hostile, and that's probably the only thing that kept many of them alive. There's no doubt that the indigenous peoples of Florida were treated badly by the Europeans. One of the earliest stories of a shipwreck survivor told how a tribal chief called Difcaptici was tortured and killed by the Spanish. In 1753, a Captain Bell told a story how he met a native chief who told him of the Englishman's treachery. They had helped some Englishmen save a wrecked sloop which was then refloated. A boy from their village who also helped was the only one of them who could speak English. While on the vessel helping to get it ready to sail, he overheard the English say how they were going to kidnap all those still on board (most likely to be sold into slavery). The boy quickly let the others know, who then all jumped overboard and swam to shore. Unfortunately, the English got hold of the boy and took him away. Where did the taking of scalps originate from? From what I've heard, it was the European settlers who began this practice in this hemisphere. A report in 1856 tells of some volunteers who skirmished with the Seminoles in Florida and took 17 Seminole scalps, though lost five of their own men. The Seminoles were one of many tribes forced from their homelands further north in the 19th century, and many made their way to Florida, resulting in the Seminole Wars. The indigenous people previously here in Florida were basically wiped out from European disease. Though a few Seminole chiefs did surrender, there never was a formal surrender by the Seminole Nation from what I can gather, and the very few that did remain in Florida at the end of the Seminole Wars eventually created the tribal lands now in place here in Florida.

Aircraft—Though most everyone has read or seen on television the mystery surrounding the loss in 1945 of Flight 19 (the five TBM Avenger bombers whose loss has been attributed to the Bermuda Triangle), somewhere off or over Florida, finding any of these would solve a great mystery and certainly make headlines.

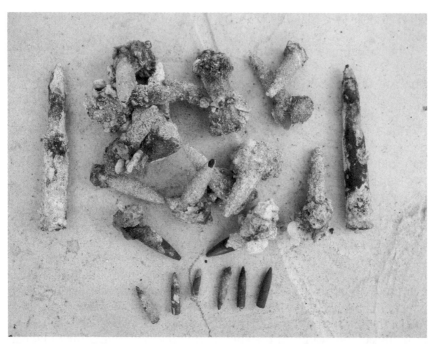

Some encrusted 50 and 30 caliber bullets from World War II found off Lauderdale by the Sea.

I only list in the wreck section a couple of aircraft that wrecked off Florida, though quite few have over the years including a WU2 spy plane reported a year after the Cuban missile crisis in November 1963, as being lost 40 miles northwest of Key West. One I did list would definitely be worth finding. One of the most famous of all aviators, James "Jimmy" Doolittle (a true American hero), wrecked a plane while attempting a cross country record in 1922 off Jacksonville. Though most of the plane was likely salvaged, I'm sure some pieces still remain just off the beach.

On December 31, 1920, some residents of Melbourne saw a giant wrecked seaplane floating off the beach. Turned out it was one of two abandoned from a Naval flotilla from Washington bound for Key West. One had been forced to land in rough seas off Stuart, which ripped her bottom out. A second seaplane attempted to land in order to save the crew and met the same fate. A third seaplane managed to rescue both crews though.

A number of planes were lost off Florida in World War II. Many a Navy pilot trained at Ft. Lauderdale including former President Bush, and I encourage anyone interested to visit the Naval Air Station Museum at the Ft. Lauderdale Airport. A number of people onshore witnessed a Navy Martin Mariner bomber from the Banana River Station crash about five miles off Melbourne. Nine lives were lost, though three of the crew inflated their life vests and floated to shore after 12 hours in the ocean. Divers still find live

Instead of tourists on the beach at Lauderdale by the Sea during World War II, these 50 caliber gun turrets were set up for practice! Courtesy of the Naval Air Station Fort Lauderdale Museum.

ammunition off Florida's coast from World War II. Years ago, I found many 50 and 30 caliber bullets and shells while diving off Lauderdale by the Sea, where aircraft gun turrets were set up along the beach so gunners in training could practice their skills.

World War I—World War II came right up to Florida's doorstep, but did World War I? German subs were operating in the Atlantic off the United States and Canada, one even fired on the town of Orleans on Cape Cod in 1918. A number of very strange stories appeared in a number of newspapers in September 1914, and though the United States had not entered the war yet, Britain and Germany were now heavily engaged in battles on the high seas.

The first strange reports were about a German cruiser sunk by a British warship off St. Andrews Bay. On September 6 and 7, some newspapers reported that a German warship with large guns was seen by a few named vessels about 10 miles off the Pensacola Bar. At this time the Hamburg-American Line freighter *Navarra* was loading up with 6,000 tons of coal and other supplies at Pensacola. The next day it was reported that the *Navarra* was seen unloading cargo onto the warship under blackout that evening. Later reports said a British warship from Cuba was now nearby and had sent a plane to look for the German cruiser. Shortly after, it was reported from St. Andrews that a gun battle could be heard offshore between there and Port St. Joe for about 40 minutes. The next day it was reported that some small craft from St. Andrews went out to investigate and saw the British ship about 18 miles from St. Andrews Bay but did not approach it. Also seen was wreckage from the supposed German warship that was scattered for miles including crushed boats and life preservers. I can find no records of any German warship sunk during this time off Florida or any information about any naval engagement by the British in this area. Was this all an elaborate hoax or misinformation given to the local news organizations? Most likely, but there was reliable information a German warship was in the area.

The next strange reports were reported in other newspapers a few weeks later. Those reported that a carrier pigeon had flown in from the ocean at St. Augustine in late September 1914. It had a cylinder attached to it which read: September 29, 1914, off Florida Coast: "Just sunk two British Warships (signed) German B.S.L 12-12." Cylinder was inscribed "Germany 12-12." Another hoax or misinformation? Probably. I know of no British warships sunk off Florida during that time, though there's no reason to believe German subs couldn't have operated off the Florida coast in World War I.

Carrier Pigeon to the Rescue—Speaking of carrier pigeons, one was known to have saved Capt. Tom Moore's fishing vessel *Miss Florida*. The *Galveston Daily News* reported in 1935 how the *Miss Florida* went aground in the upper Keys on October 19, 1935. Mr. Dealy and his wife had chartered her for a day of fishing. He was the vice president of the *Dallas News* and *Dallas Journal*. Unable to get the vessel off, Mr. Dealy sent a carrier pigeon with a note attached explaining their predicament. The pigeon went straight for the Florida Fishing Docks at Miami, where I presume the *Miss Florida* sailed from. The note was then given to the commander of the Coast Guard cutter there, who in turn radioed the Coast Guard station at Port Everglades who dispatched a patrol boat to the scene which managed to pull the *Miss Florida* off safely.

Was it a common practice to have carrier pigeons on board in case one got in trouble? Early version of our VHS emergency radio? I'm thinking maybe it was. After the steamer *City of Boston* was lost in 1870, I saw one newspaper call for ships to start keeping carrier pigeons in case of emergencies. A Navy balloon that left Pensacola Air Station in March 1921 was found in the water half submerged about 20 miles off St. Andrews on April 9 after those onshore received a number of messages sent from her by carrier pigeons. The last message said they were within 100 feet of the ocean and falling fast. Chief Quartermaster C. K. Wilkenson and the four crewmen were believed lost.

April Fool's Joke Gone Bad—With all the talk of fake news today and stories going viral, here's a fake story that did go viral way back in 1895. As an April Fool's joke, and obviously not thinking rationally, an unknown individual reported a vessel as lost in Biscayne Bay. The vessel reported was the chartered sloop *Robinson Crusoe*, which had been hired by wealthy and well-known businessmen William Ziegler and John Wells of New York. Also reported to have been on board was Mr. Henry Flagler, the wealthy Florida businessman, along with others. The story was picked up by almost every newspaper across the country and reported! The sloop was never in any trouble and continued on her cruise. Those on board may not have even been aware of the report until afterward. Relatives and friends of those on board who read the articles could only imagine the worst!

Oiling the Water—Some of the wrecks listed mention oiling the seas to calm the waves. Many vessels in trouble used this method to flatten out a rough sea to either lower the lifeboats and get close to a sinking ship using lamp or fuel oil. This process did work and probably saved a number of lives. They even came out with a projectile full of oil that could be fired from a gun in 1883.

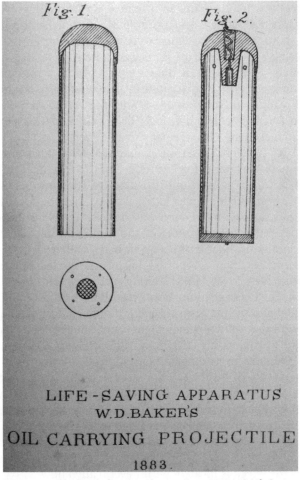

Illustration of projectile for oiling the sea. From 1883 U.S. Life Saving Service annual report.

Is the Money Worth It?—You may find some coins belonging to the captain of the *Henrietta*, which wrecked in 1832. Tied around his waist was $500 in specie, and that was enough to weigh him down, ending his life as he tried to swim to shore. I'm sure this isn't the first time this has happened. Did some of the 1715 fleet sailors find themselves in the same predicament?

Message in a Bottle—As you will find in this book, a number of losses were only known due to someone finding a "message in a bottle." Some described being captured and burned by pirates such as the schooner *Euphrates* in 1823, and others being shipwrecked, such as with the *Ladras* in 1897. The Navy also used bottles with a message to track currents, hoping the finder would report where they found the bottle. Most times the finder did report where, and this information was sometimes posted in the newspapers. The following is just a couple of unverified accounts regarding shipwrecks that may relate to Florida. As indicated further, I'm sure many of these messages found over the years were a hoax.

A few papers reported that a "message in a bottle" was found near the St. Johns Bar in 1854. It was written in pencil using part of the bottle's label and it read: "September 6, 1854, Ship *Marion* is lost; all hands dead but me; and I on a float. John Dooly, Richmond VA." This next one may have been a cruel hoax. The steamer *City of Boston*, Capt. J. J. Halcrow, of the Inman Line, had left New York, January 25, 1870, for Halifax, and left there on January 28 bound for Liverpool with 191 people on board. She was never heard from again. Built in 1864 near Glasgow, 2,278 tons, 332' x 39' x 27'6", iron hulled. It was later surmised that she must have struck an iceberg and sank with no survivors, though it was also said the two-bladed propeller that recently replaced the damaged three-bladed one, was not strong enough to handle the ship in bad weather. Four years later in 1874, numerous newspapers reported that a "message in a bottle" had been found near the New River, Florida, along with a piece of the wreck of the *City of Boston*. The message in the bottle read: "Steamship *City of Boston*—To all whom this message may come. That I, the undersigned, a passenger on this ship, write the following statement: On Sunday night a heavy storm arose; 12:30 P.M., increasing; 1:20 A.M., all hopes lost; 2 A.M., going do— JOHN CASWELL, London, England." A short distance away a board was found headed "City of Boston." Some penciling on it read, "We have now taken to the boats as our last resort." Some papers said it's likely a hoax as other bottles had been found off Canada since it disappeared, and thought to be genuine. Also, no J. Caswell was listed as a passenger, though he may have boarded late. And did a board and a bottle drift together that far south to the Florida coast? Is any of the steamer lost off Florida? Though likely a hoax, unless the wreck is located, we'll never really know.

Piracy and Intemperance—The temperance movement started in the early 19th century and culminated in Prohibition 100 years later. The pirate Fernandez, who sailed the Caribbean and Florida coasts, blamed his unspeakable crimes on his abuse of alcohol, and the book on his trial, confessions and execution, had a warning on its cover about the use of alcohol along with a whole chapter on intemperance and its harmful influence. (See chapter 6 on pirate Nicholas Fernandez.)

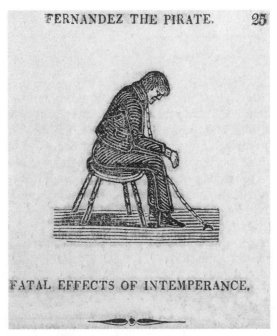

Illustration of the pirate Fernandez awaiting execution from the 1830 *Dying Declaration of Fernandez.* Law Library of Congress.

6

Florida Pirates and Privateers

Florida saw many a pirate and privateer sail along its vast coastline over the last few centuries. There's no doubt, pirates such as Jennings, Teach (Blackbeard), Lafitte, and many others sailed along the coasts of Florida. Romanticized in many a movie, the thought of being free to sail wherever you wanted and do whatever you wanted, answering to nobody, is just the thing to let one romanticize this type of life, though it was far from that for most. For a few, the pirate life was one of adventure and sometimes great wealth, but for many others, only death and destruction. Pirates, gunslingers, and outlaws. We all grew up hearing the stories of these legendary bandits. With the likes of Blackbeard, Billy the Kid, or Bonnie amd Clyde, what is it that attracts us so to these outlaws, so much so that hundreds of books, television shows, and movies continue to be made about their lives? Piracy still exists today, and for many of those who lived to tell the tale, romance and adventure were not usually part of the story, but more often than not, misery and death were.

Many pirates started off as privateers, who with a letter of marque from whatever country they were loyal to or had some

Portrait of a Gentleman---of Fortune

An 1921 Illustration of a "Gentleman of Fortune," by Will Crawford. *New York Tribune*, April 1921.

A "Letter of Marque," issued by the Continental Congress and signed by its President, John Hancock, October 24, 1776, issued to James Powell of the 30-ton schooner *Northampton*, of Virginia, with a crew of 30 men and armed with some carriage guns. Courtesy of the State Archives of North Carolina.

sort of agreement with, could then legally go and take any ship that was an enemy of that country, and a share of whatever was taken was divided among the crews, the rest going to the country who offered the marque. The ships themselves were often worth more than their cargoes, so sinking a vessel was not something a privateer wished to do. After a ship was captured, the ship and its cargo were brought back to a safe port either under control of the country whose letter of marque the privateer sailed under, or to a port controlled by an ally of that country. During the Revolutionary War, Congress required that one-third of a privateer's crew be lands-men, so as not to lose seamen who may otherwise enlist in the fledgling Navy. Britain, which already had a large Navy, also encouraged privateers during the war, and those amounted to almost as large a fleet as their Navy. Florida was

Notice in a 1745 newspaper for where the privateer crew of her majesty's ship *Tyger* could collect their prize money for the capture of a Spanish sloop off Florida. *London Daily Advertiser*, May 1745.

mostly under British control during the Revolutionary War, and Governor Touyn of East Florida fitted out a large number of privateers there to disrupt shipping off the coasts of Georgia and the Carolinas.

I love some of the names given to some privateer vessels such as the *True Blooded Yankee*, *Saucy Jack*, *Fame*, *Dragon*, *Revenge*, *Tyger*.

Wars came and went, and once a peace treaty was signed, the privateer could no longer go and plunder. The 18th century was not without its abundance of wars and as such the opportunity to become a privateer, as there was the *War of the Spanish Succession*—also known as *Queen Anne's War*—(1701–1713); *War of the Quadruple Alliance* (1718–1720), *Anglo-Spanish-French War* (1727–1729), *War of Jenkins' Ear* (1739–1748); *The Seven Years War*, or *French and Indian War* (1756–1763); the *American Revolution* (1775–1783); and the first *Napoleonic War* (1796–1802). And let's not forget the undeclared *Quasi-War* (1798–1800), between the United States and France fought almost entirely on the high seas. When a war was over, many then turned to piracy.

Sir Francis Drake and John Paul Jones were privateers. Drake attacked St. Augustine in 1586 and captured and burned it to the ground. The Spanish called him a pirate. St. Augustine was attacked again in 1668 by the Jamaican privateer Robert Searles (alias John Davis). Searles was unaware that his letter of marque had been canceled and was later arrested in Jamaica for piracy, though soon pardoned and became part of Henry Morgan's army that sacked Panama. During the *Seven Years War*, there were about 230 privateer vessels operating from the ports of Boston and New York, consisting of around 5,000 sailors. Privateering became so lucrative that it caused a recruitment problem for the British Navy. In 1757, so many sailors deserted Her Majesty's ships to go privateering, they didn't have enough men to sail the ships from New York Harbor. Desertion continued to be a problem, even for the Continental Navy during the *American Revolution*, our second most successful captain, just behind John Paul Jones, was Gustavus Conyngham. Not as well known, he had just as a

Two advertisements from a 1746 London paper for the sale of an American built privateer, the *Sandwich*, and a 350-ton Spanish prize *Nuestra Senora del Carmen*, taken by a privateer. *General Advertiser* (London), October 1746.

distinguished career as Jones, and even briefly sailed with Jones after having escaped a prison, though through many different circumstances, was both an officer of the Continental Navy, a privateer, and even sentenced to a British prison as a pirate during the war.

The distinction between a privateer and a pirate became hazy during both the Revolutionary War and the Civil War as neither the United States or the Confederacy were recognized as a sovereign state by the other side as yet. Some in Britain did not recognize any of the rebels as privateers, but only as pirates during the Revolution, but fortunately the more moderate voices did. The *Declaration of Paris* in 1856 was signed by most European nations, but not the United States. This declaration made privateering illegal to an extent. (See suggested reading in Bibliography, letter by Charles P. Daly, which addressed the difference between piracy and privateering and describes the case of the Confederate privateers from the *Jefferson Davis*, on trial for piracy.)

When the Civil War began, the South offered a letter-of-marque to anyone who wished to become a privateer for their cause. How many became privateers for the Southern cause and how many did for the possibility of getting rich would be an interesting statistic. Many a privateer operated off Florida during the war, and supplies for the southern cause were smuggled into many of Florida's bays and inlets. Some of the privateer crew of the Confederate brig *Jefferson Davis*, which wrecked off Florida in 1861, were later tried and convicted as pirates in Philadelphia, even though they had letters of marque from the Confederacy. Confederate President Davis was outraged by this and had some captured Union officers placed in a criminal prison. He then sent a warning to President Lincoln that if any of the convicted privateers were executed, so would these Union prisoners. The North relented, and all privateers were then treated as POWs. Unfortunately for the South, their court system was now in shambles, and the Southern privateers soon found that getting any share of any prize was almost impossible. Not worth the risk any longer, privateering for the Confederacy was coming to an abrupt end, though many Southern privateers then joined the Confederate Navy.

Honest seafarers who found themselves captured by pirates often had to make a choice. Pirates were always looking for talented men such as sailors, carpenters, navigators, doctors, and cooks. Once captured, it was not uncommon to be given a choice, join the pirates, or be cast away in a small boat with maybe a chance of survival, or worse, be put to death. Many chose the pirate's life. Those that chose that life under duress were often referred to as "forced men," and on more than one occasion, many of these "forced men," when given the chance, would side with a captured crew and would turn on their fellow pirates and kill or take them prisoners, preferring to go back to an honest life and see their families again. That was the case of some on the *Birch Galley* in 1730. Many a slave from Africa joined the pirates as it seemed a much better life than that of a slave. The more I read about the slave trade though, the more it seems that pirates were also deeply involved with the trade and slave ships were a favorite target of many pirates. A Portuguese slaver was reported sunk by pirates off Angola in 1770 after they plundered all on board and killed all the crew, it's likely the slaves were brought to the West Indies or the Americas, similar to the pirate/slaver *Guerrero* in 1827.

Now there was a very fine line between privateering and piracy. Some used a letter of marque to commit piracy as detailed further on. The pirate Jean Lafitte (believed correct), or Laffitte, depending on who you ask or who was writing about him, was a mystery. Privateer, pirate, war hero, slaver, governor of Galveston (he was then issuing his own letter-of-marques to his crews after a brief appointment in 1819), take your pick. Even his death remains a mystery. The following is a letter from Lafitte himself to the editor of the *Aurora*, dated 1815, shortly after being pardoned after the Battle of New Orleans, though reprinted in another paper. A little hard to read, so here is what it says:

Letter to the editor of the *Aurora* in 1815 by the pirate Laffitte (as spelled in letter), explaining how he was not involved in piracy. *The Republican* and *Savannah Evening Ledger*, October 1815.

To the Editor of the Aurora,

Sir-Several columns having appeared against me for two years past in various gazettes of the United States, I take this method to give them formal and public contradiction. It has been asserted that privateer vessels belonging to me, committed acts of piracy, in making prizes without being duly commissioned, and in capturing American vessels. In answer to such assertions, I offer the inspection of the letter-of-marque, under which my privateers sailed, to all who may wish to examine them; and if any one knows of any piracy, or injustice perpetrated by me or by my orders it will of course be his duty to give information of it to the officers authorized to prosecute such offenses; who will find me always ready to appear when duly called upon. I remain, very respectfully, sir, your obedient servant

Joseph Laffitte
Baltimore, South Gay-Street, No.4
September 25, 1815

Here he Americanized his name to Joseph. He was in the Washington, D.C., area at this time and was said to be quite the figure in the social circles while there and spent a small fortune entertaining. While a pirate, it's said he did have a strict code as to the treatment of those on board any captured vessels, that they should all be treated well, and any of his men who did otherwise were severely punished or killed. After he left Galveston, his story is mostly speculation, but he may have still sailed off Florida as he supposedly had a base in Cuba toward the end of his career. A New Orleans paper had reported in January 1823 that Lafitte was shipwrecked off Cuba, was captured, and placed in the Port Pricipe Prison, but soon escaped. In April through June, a number of papers reported the destruction of the infamous pirate vessel *La Gata* (also spelled *La Cata* and *La Guita*) off southern Cuba near the mouth of the River St. John's, March 20, 1823, by the British cutter *Grecian*. Most papers reported its captain was a Joseph Sabina, though some papers said the captain was Lafitte. Being that this vessel had burned and murdered the crews of over 40 vessels in the last few months, and that Lafitte was known to treat captured crews quite well, the captain was most surely Sabina. A survivor who was a "forced man," also never mentioned Lafitte as the captain. During this same time though, a number of papers also reported that the pirate Lafitte was killed in an engagement at sea with a British sloop-of war, and that the pirates shouted "No quarters," before all being killed. This is all speculation as I found no proof of this. Lafitte's death still remains a mystery!

Long before Commodore Porter headed the fleet in Key West, he headed the New Orleans Station in 1809–1810. He had captured a number of French privateers in that area, others said pirate vessels, supposedly controlled by Jean Lafitte. Was later said that this engagement had halted the privateer's plans to make a settlement at "St. Esprit or Spiritu Santa" (the Tampa Bay area, also spelled Espiritu Santo, Bay del Spirito Samento, etc., depending on who's map you had). One of Porter's officers recovered a manuscript in French from one of the captured vessels. After it was translated to English, it contained a wealth of information regarding much of Florida that any mariner would appreciate, demonstrating these privateers or pirates were quite familiar with the coast and inland waterways of Florida (see chapter 2 for an excerpt from this manuscript).

The French minister complained, and Porter was transferred to another station. An excerpt from Porter's response is such: "The vessels I captured were tried and defended in the district court at Orleans, and if I have not shown probable cause for seizure, I consider myself bound to make good in a pecuniary way, and no other." Seems most likely these vessels were engaged in nefarious activities.

Between 1680 and 1730, piracy flourished throughout the Caribbean and the Eastern seaboard of the Americas and has been called the "Golden Age of Piracy." Many pirates did have a "code" that they lived by, and the pirate ports like Port Royal and Nassau had strict rules which all pirates abided by or suffered the consequences. A pirate vessel would reach an agreement before they left for any adventure on what the percentage of any spoils everyone on board would receive. There were even extra rewards in some cases for those who went above and beyond, such as who first caught sight of a potential prize, who struck down the enemy's captain. They even had a sort of pension plan for anyone injured, though it varied from captain to captain. Henry Morgan gave 500 crowns, or 15 slaves, to anyone losing both their legs; 500 piastres, or six slaves to anyone losing one arm or leg, and the list goes on. The War of Jenkins' Ear, which lasted from 1739 to 1748, was between Britain and Spain and soon after France, and saw so many privateers operating off the Florida coast, the Caribbean, and Europe, that British and other newspapers were constantly reporting what ships from what country were captured, recaptured, or wrecked. Though piracy continued in this hemisphere through the 18th century to a lesser degree, it wasn't until the end of the Napoleonic Wars and the War of 1812, that piracy flourished again. Privateering on the other hand would flourish whenever a war ensued. Compared to a seaman in the King's or other country's navy, a privateer could possibly make a fortune, which was a big incentive. Both in this and the shipwreck chapter, you will find many accounts of privateering off the Florida coast.

Soon after the War of 1812, piracy was again flourishing around the Florida Peninsula and the Caribbean, though many a ship was plundered by privateers before this. *The Northampton Mercury* of October 26, 1816, had this to say:

> By letters from Nassau, New Providence, it appears that 14 sail of pirates, well-armed and manned, are cruising in the Gulf of Florida, and capture, destroy, or plunder every merchantman coming through the Gulf either from Jamaica or the Spanish colonies. The commerce in the Bahamas is in consequence totally destroyed. Many vessels belonging to Nassau, bound to the Havannah with English manufacturers, have been captured, and stripped of every article of value: and many merchants of Nassau have been ruined by their losses. The pirates rendezvous at the small islands of the keys, called the Dry Tortugas, which overlook the passage through the Gulf, at the southern extremity of the Peninsula of East Florida.

A 19th century illustration of pirates boarding a vessel. *Naval Battles of the World*, 1894.

Florida offered many bays, islands, and inlets to hide, though the native tribes kept most from making any permanent settlements along much of Florida until after the Seminole Wars ended. The natives had seen enough death brought by the Europeans, that they were usually not too kind to any who set foot on their shore. Africans who wrecked along our shore were usually spared.

Some of the names appearing on Florida maps could be traced to pirates. Supposedly a slave turned pirate named Black Caesar used an area off Florida as a base of operations, and "Caesar's Creek" off Biscayne Bay was supposedly named after him. An 1834 map of Florida has it called "Black Cesar's Creek," but another map from the same year has it as "Black Sarah's Creek." Jose Gaspar (second edition, page 49) is a well-known pirate name here in Florida, but as described in my first and second editions, he never existed and may have been confused with a pirate named Richard Coeur de Lion. Ross Island in Tampa Bay has been attributed to a pirate named Henry Ross, but it appears he is a fictitious pirate and Ross Island was actually named after an inhabitant of the island, Lorenzo Ross. John's Pass in Tampa Bay was named after John Levique who some say was a pirate (see chapter 7). How Gasparilla Island got its name I do not know, though it was on Spanish maps well before the fictitious Jose Gaspar was reported to have lived. The Gilbert's Bar House of refuge was named after the rocky shoreline where it was built called "Gilbert's Bar." That name originated from the

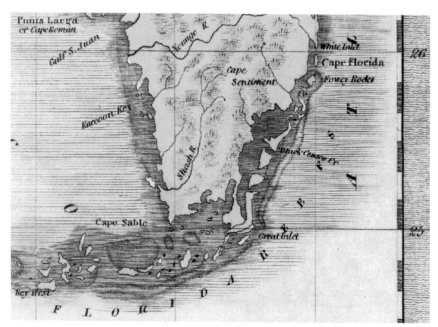

An 1834 map depicting "Black Cesare Cr." Note the spelling and also that other place names that have changed. Euriskodata, Inc.

PEDRO GIBERT, *Captain.*
(CONVICTED.)
Born in Catalonia.—Married.—Age, 38.

An illustration of the pirate Pedro Gilbert drawn during his trial. Law Library of Congress.

Spanish pirate Don Pedro Gilbert, who sailed these waters in the 1820s and 1830s. He was later captured off Africa and was one of the last pirates to be hung in Boston, March 11, 1836. The name "Gilbert's Bar" soon appeared on maps of this area after his trial.

A BRIEF TIMELINE OF PIRATE AND PRIVATEER ACTIVITY

In 1683, a group of pirates including Thomas Jingle and Andrew Ranson, who with a fleet of six ships, were operating off the Florida coast and had recently captured a Spanish vessel. They then planned an attack on St. Augustine, but a storm delayed their assault. A small group including the pirate Ranson, landed in a small boat north of St. Augustine to collect some food and water, but were captured by the Spanish. Ranson was sentenced to death by garrote, but the rope broke before he was strangled and the Franciscan monks gained his freedom. Ranson later helped to finish the fort there and also helped defend St. Augustine against a British attack.

The pirate Henry Jennings left Jamaica with around 100 men when he heard about the wrecked Spanish treasure fleet of 1715 on the Florida coast, hoping to retrieve some of the treasure for himself and his crews. They found the Spanish salvage camp at present-day Sebastian, and managed to drive off the Spaniards guarding the treasure, making off with a small fortune. After returning to Jamaica though, Spain demanded his arrest, and he escaped leaving his estate behind to become a full-time pirate. He earned the respect of most all the pirates of the Caribbean and became their spokesman so to speak. When pardons were offered by King George to all pirates in 1717, he presided over the meeting of many of the "Pirates of the Caribbean," and was one of the first to accept the pardon, and soon retired in style. At that meeting were the likes of Hornigold, Teach, Martel, Fife, Winter, Brown, Williams, Bellamy, La Bouche, Penner, England, Burgess, Cocklyn, Sample, Vane, and others. When Governor Rogers entered the harbor at New Providence (Nassau) in June 1718, many of those mentioned were there, and all accepted the pardon

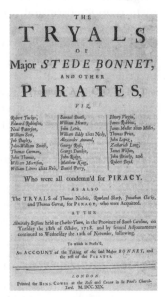

Cover of a book about the trial of the pirate Major Stede Bonnet, along with others who sailed the southeast coat of America. Law Library of Congress.

except Vane, who made a daring and successful escape from the harbor. Following Jenning's example, about 150 other pirates accepted the pardon from the governors of Bermuda and New Providence, but many returned to piracy "like the dog to the vomit," as quoted in newspapers of the time. The fate of those mentioned at the meeting was as follows: Hornigold, Burgess, and La Bouche were later lost when their ships wrecked; Teach and Penner were killed; Fife was killed by his own crew; most of Martel's crew were killed and he and a few were left on a deserted island where they escaped, though he later made it back to the Bahamas; Cocklyn, Sample, and Vane were hanged; Winter and Brown surrendered to the Spanish at Cuba; and England went to Madagascar. I'm sure all these pirates sailed along the Florida coast at one time or another.

In 1716, the *Berkley Galley*, from Jamaica, was boarded by pirates off Florida who shot Captain Saunder's arm off, took all the gold and silver along with most of the crew, and then let the rest go.

The *Stamford Mercury* in late 1717, printed a letter reporting: "That the pyrates in the West-Indies having landed upon the island of Cuba 1500 men, plundered several Spanish towns, but 5 Men of War lying ready at the Havana in the same island, gave chase to the pyrates and forced one of them ashore on the Coast of Florida, where she was burnt." But not before the crew got the provisions and guns ashore, and raised a battery and a fort in a night's time.

In 1718, Major Stede Bonnet (had been a Major in the Army), and a number of other pirates, were all condemned at Charleston. Bonnet was a respected man with a wife and much land in Barbados, but some say may have lost his mind and became a pirate. He left the island in his vessel the *Revenge* and sailed all along the southeastern coast of the colonies and Florida. Early on, he encountered Blackbeard, who took over his vessel and Bonnet's crew, which he did not like at all, but Bonnet soon regained the *Revenge*. He had no love for Teach and wanted to engage his ship but never found it or Teach again. For someone with no seafaring experience, Bonnet was quite successful, and even accepted a pardon, and was granted a letter of marque to be a

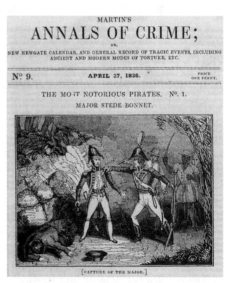

MARTIN'S

ANNALS OF CRIME;

OR,

NEW NEWGATE CALENDAR, AND GENERAL RECORD OF TRAGIC EVENTS, INCLUDING ANCIENT AND MODERN MODES OF TORTURE, ETC.

Nº 9.   APRIL 27, 1836.   PRICE ONE PENNY.

THE MOƧT NOTORIOUS PIRATES. Nº. 1.

MAJOR STEDE BONNET.

[CAPTURE OF THE MAJOR.]

An 1836 illustration of the capture of Bonnet. Law Library of Congress.

Illustration of a smaller pirate vessel attacking the merchant ship *Seabird* between Florida and Cuba. The pirates lost this battle. *Shipwrecks & Tales of the Sea*, 1887.

privateer for England, but soon the urge to go pirating took over again and he ended up in the hangman's noose at Charleston.

The pirate "Calico Jack" Rackham was another well-known pirate we've all read about or have seen recently on television shows. In 1719, he supposedly made camp on the west coast of Florida (see chapter 7).

If you were to be captured by a pirate, Calico Jack would be one you'd probably feel better about as he usually only plundered what he could and would let everyone go on their way once he was done. The pirate Edward (Ned) Lowe (or Low), on the other hand, was one you would not want to be captured by. Many that had crewed with him left when the first opportunity presented itself, as his brutality went far above what most men, and even most pirates could take. In 1723, he took a Portuguese ship. The captain hung a bag of 11,000 moidores in gold out the cabin window to try and negotiate. Lowe went for it and the captain dropped it in the sea. Enraged, Lowe cut his lips off and broiled them in front of his face, then killed him and all 32 of the ship's crew. He terrorized up and down the East Coast of America, the Caribbean, to the Azores and elsewhere, but whatever the final fate of this bloody madman was has remained a mystery. Those that unfortunately had the misfortune of meeting Lowe who flew the black flag with the red skeleton surely never forgot. A seaman by the name of Philip Ashton wrote a memoir of his life after being captured by Lowe in 1722 off Cape Sable on the northeast coast of America, along with his band of pirates including Farrington Spriggs. Lowe's vessel had two great guns, four swivels, and about 42 men. Ashton became a "forced man," who reluctantly joined the pirates, and said that Lowe would not take any married men on as crewmen fearing they would not be loyal to him, though doesn't mention any of the barbarity he was known for, but likely killed them all. After sailing to the West Indies, Ashton finally escaped to an uninhabited island in the Bay of Honduras where he survived for 16 months in solitude.

The pirate Shipton, who was a consort of the pirate Spriggs who had sailed with Lowe, had lost his sloop of 12 guns on the coast of Florida in 1725. On board was a crew of 70 men. The natives took all the crew except Shipton and 12 others who managed to escape in a canoe. The natives kept 16 of the crew (probably as slaves) and took the rest to Havana. The British Man of War *Diamond* later captured the canoe with four Africans and one white man and $3,000 in money, but Shipton and the rest had escaped again. The *Diamond* was well known in these parts; in 1719 she took a 24-gun prize off Florida with 30,000 pieces-of-eight on board.

Tales of mutiny, where some of a ship's crew would take over a vessel for the purpose of pirating, were not uncommon. It's likely that many of these pirates had planned all along to crew on a vessel and take it over once out to sea. In April 1726, the snow *Elizabeth*, Capt. John Green, sailed with a fleet from Jamaica, bound for Guinea. It left the fleet while off Florida, and the next night, the crew of 11, except the mate, carpenter, and gunner, mutinied and killed the captain and chief mate and threw them overboard on May 27. They then turned pirate and began to take vessels all the way up the coast to New England. After taking a schooner from Marblehead, seven of the pirates transferred to that vessel, leaving the snow to Capt. Fly, who had been the boatswain under Capt. Green before he was murdered. Now there were only three others with Fly who were all in as pirates, the others all being "forced men." One of these was William Atkinson, a passenger on one of the vessels they had taken, and was forced to be their navigator. He persuaded three of the forced men to help him overtake the ship, which they did, and secured the four pirates. They brought the snow to Boston, where the four pirates were tried, and most likely saw the hangman's noose.

Here's an example of how busy and lucrative privateering could be. On June 13, 1728, a Spanish privateer from Havana took six English vessels off Cape Florida, four from Boston, one from Rhode Island, and one from South Carolina. With the brisk business of shipping goods back and forth from Jamaica, the British merchant ships soon sailed in fleets from Jamaica back to England or the colonies similar to the Spanish treasure fleets, usually with a British warship or two alongside to prevent being captured by pirates or privateers.

A British ship, the *Birch Galley*, Capt. Joseph Turner, was captured by a Spanish privateer in May 1730, or as the Spanish called them, the Guarde Costa (their Coast Guard). They took the ship to one of the Florida Keys and kept them prisoner there for four days, plundered the ship of all her stores and part of the cargo, and took all their clothes and bedding. They put the thumbs of all her company "under the cock of a gun," to force them to say they had money or logwood, which they did not.

The British privateer vessel *Diamond*, Capt. Knowles, brought into Jamaica two prizes in October 1739. One was a Spanish ship they captured (most likely off Florida) on September 26, and had on board 74,000 pieces of eight and clothing for the soldiers at St. Augustine.

A privateer sloop under Capt. Bennet, wrecked on Loggerhead Key, August 20, 1740, during a hurricane. It was in company with another privateer, the schooner *Ranger*, of Jamaica, Capt. Thrasher, who saved the crew and took them to Charles-Town. They had captured a number of merchant vessels along with two Spanish privateers while cruising the Caribbean, and ransomed one of the privateer captains for 2,000 pieces of eight.

The vessel *Fame*, under Capt. Griffith, was a famous privateer who sailed the waters off Florida. He captured a Spanish sloop off this coast in 1742, one of a number of vessels from St. Augustine for Havana to get supplies. Its captain and crew abandoned her and made the Florida coast in the sloop's boat, leaving 25 Spanish soldiers, a lieutenant, two Frenchmen, and two gentlemen on board who were all sent to a Georgia prison. The *Fame* took the prize sloop into Amelia Sound. A number of British privateers operated off Florida and surrounding areas during this time.

In December 1744, her Majesty's ship *Rose*, Capt. Frankland, was operating between Cape Florida and Matanzas, Cuba. Early on the morning of the 31st, she came upon a large Spanish ship called the *Concepcion of St. Malo*, Captain Adrian Mercan, from Cartagena bound for Havana and Cadiz. Soon, a fierce battle ensued between the two which lasted between 7 a.m. and 12:30 p.m., all the time a fresh gale was blowing and the seas were rough. They came alongside each other a few times during the battle. The Spanish finally struck their colors after one side's guns were completely disabled, but not after almost 100 men were killed. The *Rose* lost only five men, though 10 or 12 were severely wounded including the Captain. The *Rose* brought her prize into South Carolina. On board were hides and cocoa, 70 chests of gold and silver, containing about 310,000 pieces of eight, and from the passengers on board, they also collected another 5,000 ounces in gold, consisting of doubloons, pistoles, and bars. The *Rose* had 177 men and boys on board; the *Concepcion* well over 200, though outgunned.

In 1745, a Capt. Gardner operated a small privateer out of New Providence and brought back an advice boat from the King of Spain loaded with arms that he captured off the Florida Keys. A few days before that he had captured a small convoy of 10 sloops and schooners off Cuba escorted by a French sloop of about 20 tons, and after a few hours engagement, he took the whole lot. Their cargo consisted of powder, sugar, tallow, and candles, of which I'm sure he helped himself to. That little convoy had 70 men, he had seven!

The English privateer vessel *Dragon*, Capt. William Waynman, of and from New York, captured a Spanish privateering vessel under Capt. Barnoes, that operated out of St. Augustine and menaced the coast up to South Carolina, either late 1747 or early 1748. The Spanish vessel had 14 carriage guns, 60 men, and 1,000 pieces of eight along with several prisoners. That was the third prize the *Dragon* took on that voyage. The Spanish privateers also had success at this time taking the English ship *Elizabeth* in 1748, Capt. Boyd, from London for South Carolina, and brought her into St. Augustine, and the *Dolphin*, listed in the shipwreck chapter. Another English man-of-war, under Capt. Forrest, captured a French ship said to be worth $100,000 in the Gulf of Florida in 1748, and took it to South Carolina.

Imagine capturing a treasure fleet only to have to give it all up. When the War of Jenkins' Ear ended, not everyone was happy about it. Not knowing that the war had ended, a British fleet (and believe some were privateers) had been waiting off the Tortugas in Florida for the Spanish Fleet from Vera Cruz. A fleet of British merchants from Jamaica under convoy of the *Lenox*, Capt. Holmes, was bound for England via the Windward Passage, but the currents not being favorable, they made for the Gulf of Florida instead. On September 29, 1748, they saw seven large ships which they soon realized were Spanish men-of-war bearing down on them. The *Lenox* had almost 200,000 pounds in specie on board and had no intention of letting the Spaniards get any of it, though they were duty bound to protect the merchant vessels. Capt. Holmes instructed the merchant vessels to be on their way as best they could, and they made for the Spanish to hopefully give the merchants some time to flee. It soon became dark, and knowing that Admiral Knowles and his fleet were not that far away off the Tortugas, they were able to meet up with him by the next morning. Informing Knowles of the Spanish fleet, they all made haste to catch them. On October 5, they caught up with the Spanish. A major naval battle soon ensued between the two fleets. The Spanish had seven ships, the *Invincible, Conquestadore, Africa, Dragon, New Spain, Royal Family,* and the *Galgo*, with a total of 400 guns and 4,150 men. The British also had seven ships, the *Tilbury, Stafford, Cornwall, Lenox, Warwick, Canterbury,* and the *Oxford*, with a total of 426 guns and 2,995 men. The Spaniards were soon on the losing end of the battle and had been making their way toward Havana in order to save themselves. By the time the coast was in sight, it became too dark to continue the fight and the British decided to wait until morning. The Spanish Admiral's ship *Africa* was so badly damaged he ran her ashore. The *Conquestadore* had been taken as a prize, but the others managed to get into port at Havana. The next day the British made toward the admiral's ship, and seeing this, the Spanish set her on fire, and within an hour she blew up. The fleet then sailed for Havana where they met an advice boat from Old Spain which gave them the most unwelcome news that the war had ended. They estimated the Spanish Fleet had close to $50 million on board, and if they only had two more hours of daylight the day before, they would have captured or destroyed the whole fleet. Now with the war having ended, the treasure that was so close at hand was now lost. I can't say for sure, but they probably had to give up the one prize and all the treasure she had on board too. It was estimated the Spanish lost close to 2,000 men, and the English around 60, though many were injured. There's probably a good amount of treasure still buried off the Cuban coast where the *Africa* blew up.

The Spanish sloop *Santa Maria*, Capt. Don Martin d'Hamassa, was a successful privateer operating out of St. Augustine. It had captured or sunk a number of vessels after taking all their cargo and valuables in late 1762 and early 1763, including the schooner *General Wolfe*, which was wrecked at Matanzas, January 1763, though three Spaniards drowned. She arrived in St. Augustine soon after with her prizes after waiting offshore for the winds to subside (see chapter 8). Another small privateer schooner with six three-pounders also operated out of St. Augustine and had captured a number of vessels around the same time.

Some pirate vessels were well armed for their size. A pirate vessel called *The Free Thinker*, which had 16 guns and 12 swivels, boarded the vessel *Enterprise*, Capt. Fearne, off Florida in 1771. The vessel *Leveret* was boarded off Florida by the pirate ship *Fancy* of 18 guns which took some provisions and then bade them farewell in 1772.

In 1776, the British privateer *Minerva*, of 18 guns, was sunk in the Gulf of Florida by two American privateers (see chapter 8).

The *Newport Mercury* printed a report from Charleston, dated May 2, 1794, that said they received a letter from an officer of the French privateer *L'Aime Point Petre*, Capt. Talbot, that had sailed from Charleston not long ago. It

The pirate Wansley, from a book about his trial. Law Library of Congress.

said they had captured the ship *Grenada Packet*, of London, which they captured after it left Pensacola and then took the prize into Savannah. Its cargo consisted of furs and skins and a small amount of specie. What was also mentioned was that there was supposedly five hogsheads of gold and silver hidden aboard. What gave credence to the report was that the British Consul was offering "any price for the ship and cargo as she stands." Don't know what the outcome was.

In 1798, the vessel *Nancy*, Capt. McAllister, from Charleston for Pensacola, was taken by a privateer vessel and brought into New Providence. May have been a French privateer as the undeclared *Quasi-War* was going on at this time.

In 1802, one of William Augustus Bowle's privateers took a Spanish brig from Havana bound for St. Augustine worth 40,000 pounds sterling, and also took a Spanish schooner loaded with flour.

In 1807, two days after leaving Laguna, a brig under Captain Hubbell was boarded by the British frigate *Orpheus*, Captain Brigs, who detained him six hours and then took off all his crew except the mate and ordered him for Jamaica. Brigs put on board one officer and six men. Off Cape Florida, Capt. Hubbard, along with his mate, managed to retake the brig.

In 1810, the British vessel *Nelson* was captured by a French privateer in the Gulf of Florida after a seven-hour battle, in which Capt. Valpy and one other were killed. The French lost one man. The *Nelson* was then plundered and the guns thrown overboard before she was released.

Though the rewards could be lucrative, being a privateer could also be deadly. The British sloop-of-war *Observer*, captured a 14-gun French privateer in the Gulf of Florida in 1812, but not before killing 30 of the 90 on board the French vessel.

Another tale of mutiny, the vessel *Florida*, Capt. Stubbs, was taken over by her crew at Amelia Island in 1812, which sailed away with her, likely to go pirating.

Treasure was still being shipped back to Spain in 1812. The American privateer *Revenge* plundered the vessel *Iris*, Capt. Castanos, from Havana for Cadiz, of $24,000 and a large amount of gold and silver, on November 24, 1812.

The pirate Louis-Michel Aury had taken over Amelia Island and claimed it under the new Mexican flag. He used it as his base of operations until he surrendered it to U.S. forces in 1817.

In 1817, a privateer/brig operating under the Carthaginian flag, wrecked near Cape Florida in June 1817. It was reported to be the Portuguese ship *Marquis de Pombal*, which was captured in March by the privateer *Patriota de Buenos Ayres* (the crew of the *Pombal* were let go and another vessel landed them at Fayal), under Capt. Joseph Stafford of Baltimore, operating under the Buenos Ayres flag. It and other captured vessels were taken to Cartagena and it was outfitted under the new name *Europe*, Capt. Doane Rich. On board was $140,000 in specie, which was saved by the Providence wreckers and taken to Nassau. A boy from the brig turned King's evidence against the crew saying it had plundered several English vessels and threw her armament overboard when wrecked. The order was then given to arrest the crew as pirates. Some of the rescued crew stole a wrecking vessel, the *Venus*, and escaped, including the first lieutenant, who was from Nassau. The 18 to 20 left in Nassau were jailed and would probably be hung after a trial. Captain Webb of the schooner *Hope* had said he was also boarded by a Carthaginian privateer brig around the same time and plundered of provisions. He said it looked New York built and was possibly the well-known privateer brig *True Blooded Yankee*. He also stated that most of the crew were Spanish and was told the captain was French. While plundering his ship, the pirates told him that they had also captured five Spanish ships.

On December 19, 1818, the Hamburg ship *Emma-Sophia*, bound for Havana, was boarded by pirates between the Bahama Banks and Key Sal (now Cay Sal). They were about 30 in number and their vessel was about 30 tons. They put 12 pirates on board the *Emma* and the two vessels then sailed to the pirate's base of operations in the lower Florida Keys, where she was then anchored in a small and snug harbor. The pirate captain was Spanish but the crew were from all nations including Americans, German, and French. Three more piratical vessels soon arrived, and over the next two days, the *Emma* was plundered of over $50,000 in cargo and personal belongings under the penalty of death if the crew did not offer up all valuables. All the pirates carried foot-long knives, which they constantly brandished to threaten the *Emmas*'s crew and passengers. Thankfully, they left without killing anyone and the *Emma* left the Keys on Christmas day and arrived at Havana the day after.

In 1819, the sloop *Lawrence*, in command of Captain Attwick, out of Charleston, had sailed from Havana to the east coast of Florida to cut lumber. It fell in with a pirate sloop off Florida who boarded her and after hanging the Captain up in the shrouds in order for him to tell where all the money was, the pirate was then convinced he had given him all the money on board, which wasn't much. He then convinced Attwick and the crew to join him as pirates. One of the crew named Reed reluctantly agreed as a forced man, as he probably would have been killed otherwise. Reed later turned State's evidence against the pirates who were later captured. The two sloops then sailed along the Florida coast and fell in with the British brig *Ann*, of Scarborough, Captain Thomas Sunley, which had sailed from Matanzas bound for Falmouth, England, loaded with coffee and some sugar (see chapter 8 for more on the *Ann*). She was in distress and had a crew of 10. She was easily boarded and soon six of her crew joined the pirates. The captain, First Mate David May, Wm Quince, the cook, and one sick seaman,

John Hall, were brutally murdered and then thrown overboard. The pirates then ran the brig ashore near Mosquito Inlet, where they loaded up the coffee onto the sloops. The schooner *Francisco* was also seized by one of the pirate sloops and forced alongside the brig and loaded up with coffee and sugar which was to be taken to Mobile. It stopped in St. Augustine where it was seized. The *Lawrence* sailed back to Charleston where they falsely reported they found a brig abandoned on the Florida coast and salvaged the coffee. Knowing otherwise, and with testimony from Reed, most were arrested. Captain Attwick had escaped, the six crewmen of the *Ann* were later captured, and a manhunt for the rest was underway. Some, if not all those responsible, got to meet the hangman's noose. The cabin boy of the *Ann* described Captain Attwick (dark whiskers and a face pockmarked by smallpox) and also said that he was no forced man, but was complicit in the murder of the *Ann*'s captain and crew. The cabin boy survived by hiding out on the *Ann*.

The July 20, 1820, *Annapolis Maryland Gazette* related a story regarding privateers and slavery. In early 1820, Spanish East Florida was governed by José Coppinger. A small American privateer had captured the Spanish Guineaman *General Ramez*, a brig from Africa, with 250 slaves on board. The privateer wrecked soon after near St. Augustine and the crew transferred to the brig. On board the brig was the governor's son. The captain of the privateer anchored off St. Augustine and sent word to the governor that he would release his son if they provided him food and water. The governor refused, but two friends of the son who were American citizens were given permission to go and negotiate but would get no help or boat from the garrison. The two soon borrowed a boat from an American vessel in the harbor and gained the release of young Coppinger. The *Ramez* soon left and entered the St. John's River to sell the slaves on board.

Piracy was flourishing everywhere, including the East Indies. The cruelty inflicted by some pirates in that hemisphere was reported in a British magazine in 1820. A report from Bombay, India, in January of that year mentions a pirate vessel capturing a merchant vessel with no cargo except 80 Byragee pilgrims (both men and women). They beheaded 40 pilgrims and threw them overboard, pierced the rest with lances, took four women with them, and tried to sink the vessel before they left. A few survivors managed to get the vessel into port.

In 1821, the 23-ton schooner *Fancy*, from Savannah, on a cruise to the Florida Reef to catch turtles, was taken over by most of the crew, who tied up Captain Hayes and set him adrift in a small boat with no provisions. He got loose and made his way to two other crewmen abandoned on an island a few miles away, and all were later picked up by the smack *Boxer*. A description of the *Fancy* and that of the three crewmen who mutinied and turned pirate was posted in local newspapers to aid in their capture. The names of the three who turned pirate, and from their descriptions, would make perfect characters for the next pirate movie: Mate, Hezekiah Lee, of Connecticut, was in the late war and was first lieutenant of the privateer *Macdonough*, his face scarred from smallpox and very red. George King, a seaman and Englishman, about 26 years old, with the tattoo G.K. on one arm and formerly served on the U.S. frigate *Guerriere*. James McCloud, about 35 years old, stout build, with a large scar across his nose, and said he was formerly on the Patriot brig *Irresistable*. Don't know if they were ever captured, but Lee was reportedly seen in Savannah afterward.

The Columbian armed privateer schooner *Centella*, Capt. Hopner, was known to purposely wreck many of his prizes in the Florida Keys in the 1820s. Believed he had some sort of an arrangement with the local wreckers.

By 1823, piracy was again out of control, this "Message in a Bottle" tells a terrible tale of piracy. The bottle was found by the pilot boat *Favorite* in Boston Bay which read:

Off Cape Florida, March 17, 1823. This is to inform all those whom it may concern, and particularly my friends in the City of New York, that having left Bordeaux on the 27th of December, 1822, on board the *Euphrates*, Captain Henshaw, bound for Cuba and Charleston, South Carolina, we left the island of Cuba on the 5th of March and fell in with, and were captured by a piratical schooner, Captain H was treated with every indignity-the mate (Mr. Harris of Baltimore) was cruelly put to death by the inhumane wretches-for refusing to give up the papers without the Captain's orders-after setting fire to the ship, they confined us on their schooner, where I have stolen the opportunity to inform my friends of my situation—I never expect to see them again—any one who may find this will oblige a sufferer by inserting the above in public prints. Charles McFadden, native of Ireland M.H.B.

What ever happened to Mr. McFadden?

The brig *Mechanic* of Savannah, Capt. Ray, had been captured off Cuba in 1823 by the pirate schooner *Despacho*. After plundering the brig, and taking any money the Captain had, they hung and shot all the crew and passengers on board. A few days later, the schooner was captured by an English cruiser who found some papers from the *Mechanic*. Some soon confessed of the murders and also of murdering all on board another brig and ship they recently captured. The pirate captain was put on board a schooner with 20 soldiers in order to hunt down the remaining pirates. As an incentive for the pirate captain, if the others were not found, the governor ordered that the pirate captain be executed, and his head brought back to port.

One of the worst atrocities reported in 1823 was the torture of Capt. Perkins, whose Kennebunk brig was captured off Campeche by a pirate schooner of about 50 tons with 40–50 men on board. They stabbed him numerous times, cut off both his arms and one of his legs above the knee, and then dipped a quantity of oakum in oil, and after filling his mouth with it, placed him on the oakum and set fire to it. Around the same time, the schooner *Junior*, of Baltimore, was also taken and the captain, crew, and two passengers were killed.

With shipping so disrupted by the ever-increasing attacks by pirates, and also the increasing brutality, Commodore David Porter was given command of a fleet of vessels in 1823 outfitted at the Norfolk Navy Yard to head down to the waters off Florida and the Caribbean, especially around Cuba, to hopefully put an end to this piracy. They made a temporary base at Thompson's Island (later renamed Key West). With 16 vessels at his command, from a Sloop of War, schooners, and steamers named the following: *Shark, Decoy, Grey Hound, Fox, Jackall, Peacock, Sea Gull, Wild Cat, Ferret, Terrier, Weazel,* the three cutters *Midge, Musquito,* and *Sand Fly,* and two galleys *Nipper* and *Gnat,* he meant business. A local poet penned this as the fleet was ready to depart:

> Then go forth, Porter, in thy might,
> Let sudden vengeance on them light-
> Pursue them with a fiery hail,
> From which no refuge may avail-
> Alike from ocean and from land
> Sweep off the vile marauding band-
> Let every monster of them fail,
> Not one be spared-destroy them all.

Porter's fleet began the pursuit of these pirates with names like Diableto or "Little Devil," who's vessel the *Catalina* used the coast of Cuba and probably Florida to hide. Many were caught or killed as was Diableto, though piracy still continued, as did the brutality, but to much less of an extant.

In December 1824, the brig *Edward*, under Captain Ferguson, left Havana bound for Boston. On February 17, it was captured off Florida by a pirate schooner commanded by an American by the name of William Paul (formerly of Baltimore), that had a crew of 40–50 men. They immediately started assaulting the crew with swords and such and killed the captain by cutting off his head. Some of the crew were stranded on a small island but eventually were seen and rescued by a wrecker and brought to Cape Florida.

Another awful act of piracy occurred off Florida in June 1827. The brig *Crawford*, Capt. Henry Brightman, had left Matanzas, Cuba, bound for New York, but had taken on board in Cuba, three Spaniards, and Mr. Alexander Tardy, who said he was a doctor. The crew had become violently sick (due to all being poisoned by Tardy) and when about midway up the Florida coast, the captain and crew were attacked by the Spaniards, and being weak from the poison, some were stabbed, throats slit, or bludgeoned to death. Some took to the rigging though all were injured, others were thrown overboard or jumped to escape immediate death. Only a couple of the crew survived as they were needed to help man the ship. After entering Norfolk, one survivor notified authorities, and the three Spaniards were arrested. Tardy remained on board, and knowing he could not escape, slit his own throat.

The *Guerrero* was a Spanish pirate/slave ship under command of the pirate Capt. Gomez. She wrecked December 17, 1827, around 10 miles from the Carysfort Light Boat while being chased by the *HMS Nimble*. There's much to the story, and the book *Slave Ship Guerrero* by Gail Swanson and the documentary *The Guerrero Project* on DVD by Karuna Eberl tells the story in detail. A brief description of the aftermath had some of the Spanish crew of the wrecked *Guerrero* stealing two of the wrecking vessels along with many of the Africans (including all the women prisoners) and sailing to Cuba. The *Nimble* had also wrecked while chasing her, but was later got off a couple of miles from where the *Guerrero* wrecked. With help from the wreckers, they took the rudder from the *Guerrero* to replace the damaged one on the *Nimble* so she could sail again. The remainder of the Africans numbering 121 (41 had drowned) were taken to Key West on the *Nimble*. They were eventually transported to St. Augustine under the custody of U.S. Marshal Waters Smith, who personally helped many of them. In 1829, about 100 of the Africans were returned to Liberia, Africa, as free men. The search for this wreck continues today.

The famous Keys wrecker, Jacob Houseman, had a run-in with pirates in March 1829. He saw a distressed schooner inside a reef off Cape Tavernier. He brought his wrecking sloop the *Sarah Isabella* by her and then boarded her to offer assistance. He soon regretted that decision as the pirates ordered him to pilot their vessel into the gulf, threatening to shoot him if they touched bottom. It was a Baltimore built schooner, with a long-gun amidships, and had no name on the stern. There were about 50 men on board, all Spaniards, and he learned that they had left Cuba to fish off the Cay Sal Banks and was chased inside the reef here by a U.S Cutter from Key West.

Having safely gotten them outside the reef, the pirate captain realized Houseman's vessel was better than his, and also needing more men, decided to take him and his vessel back to Cuba. Soon though, the wrecking schooner *Thistle* was in pursuit. Houseman told the pirates she was an armed vessel, and not wanting a fight, released Houseman, his vessel and crew, and even "payed him fifty dollars for his pilotage."

In 1829, the *Washington National Intelligencer* had this to report. The brig *Dromo*, Capt. Morgan, arrived in New York from Havana. It reported that while at Havana, the Catholic Majesty's schooner *Habanera*, Capt. Juan Olavola, brought in a prize pirate schooner captured off the Colorado's, Cuba. Most of the pirates had escaped, but they captured a few, one who was a forced man that said he was from the French brig *Amedee* and was only spared after agreeing to join the pirates, as all the other crew had been murdered. He said the pirates had murdered over 115 souls while he was a member. They had captured or destroyed a number of vessels, and probably some off Florida. The *Habanera* found on board 14 signal flags of various vessels which had been captured or destroyed. On the cabin table of the pirate schooner, written in Spanish, were these words:

> This is a Corsair brave,
> Which cru'zes hereabouts,
> The eternal enemy
> Of English rascals.
> Though thwarted everywhere,
> They still are vigilant,
> Pursuing every sail,
> The Slaver without mercy,
> And yet with greater wrath
> The poor corsair.

Another pirate who used Cuba as his base during this time, but attacked vessels off Florida, the Bahamas and along the east coast, was an American by the name of Charles Gibbs (real name was James D. Jeffers). Not as well known, he captured many a vessel (he burned and destroyed most after plundering them) and he kept a low profile as the phrase "dead men tell no tales," fit him to a tee. When he and his crew captured a vessel, they usually killed all on board, including women and children. He was reported to spare some crews whom were from his birthplace in Rhode Island, and he had even dropped off a Capt. Bell and some officers from the privateer *Maria* at Pensacola, after taking their vessel, I believe, as a mutineer in 1816. He started his career of piracy in 1816 on the vessel *Sans Sousee* from Margaretta, and semi-retired in the United States and Europe after 1819. Missing the action of warfare, he then supposedly joined the U.S. Navy as a lieutenant in 1826, and later tuned a privateer/pirate again. He was finally captured and hanged in New York on Ellis Island in 1831, along with one of the other mutineers, not as a captain of a pirate vessel, but as a simple seaman who had squandered all his money after retiring from piracy. After signing on the vessel *Vineyard* in New Orleans, he joined a mutinous crew who were alerted to a rich cargo of $50,000 in Mexican silver specie previously loaded on board by one of the first of the crew to sign on, some who only heard about it after a week at sea and told of it while off the Tortugas. While off Florida, they planned their mutiny. Did Gibbs sign on after being told of the treasure, or just happen to find out once on board? After a time planning to steal the treasure, they killed the captain and mate in November 1830, and later wrecked and burned the vessel, and barely made it to land on Pelican Beach on Barren Island, which lies inside Jamaica Bay, between Brooklyn and Rockaway, New York. The mutineers left the

TRIAL
AND
SENTENCE,
OF
Thomas J. Wansley and Charles Gibbs,
FOR
Murder and Piracy,
On board the Brig Vineyard.

NEW YORK:

Printed and Sold by Christian Brown, 211 Water-st.

1831.

The cover of a book on the trial of the pirates Wansley & Gibbs. Law Library of Congress.

burning vessel in a longboat and a jolly boat but a storm soon approached and the seas became rough. The jolly boat was capsized drowning all those on board along with some of the treasure, and the longboat barely made shore, but only after having to throw most of the heavy specie overboard. The jolly boat was later recovered along with a small amount of specie. The mutineers who landed ashore buried what had been saved which was estimated to be around $5,000 to $6,000, though it was reported it was recovered later but never verified. The rest of the treasure still lies off the coast New York. Gibbs confessed to all of his atrocities just before he died and a couple of books were published with his confessions and details of the trial and execution including *The Confession of Chas. Gibbs alias James Jeffreys* (misspelled his true name), in 1831. The other pirate who was tried and convicted along with Gibbs was Thomas J. Wansley, who also confessed. A book of his confession and his tale of piracy on the *Vineyard* was also published the same year.

Gibbs was asked why he killed so many (reported as many as 400 people), and he replied: "because a man has to suffer death for piracy; and the punish for murder is no more. Then you know, all witnesses are out of the way, and I'm sure if punishment was different, there would not be so many murders."

Another confession translated into English in 1830 similar to that of the pirate Gibbs was one by the pirate Nicholas Fernandez, given just before he was hanged and quartered in Cadiz on December 29, 1829. He and his pirate crew operated out of Cuba and sailed off Florida and throughout the Caribbean. They murdered and tortured hundreds of innocent people including women and children, many who were on American vessels. He blames his many sins on his abuse of alcohol.

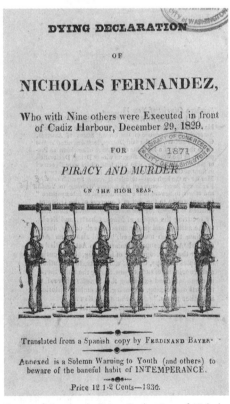

Cover of the book *Dying Declaration of Nicholas Fernandez*. Note the "warning" at the bottom. Law Library of Congress.

The wreck of the sloop *Ajax* was found in 1832, but not before two suspicious men (who were later found to be part of the crew of the *Ajax*) landed in a row boat at Apalachicola. They were held on suspicion of theft (had allot of valuables with them that they could not explain and fine clothing with initials not their own), but were let go before they could be arrested. Was feared they killed the captain and rest of the crew. Warrants were later issued for their arrest.

In 1835, the brig *Olive Branch*, which had left Apalachicola bound for New York, reported that on May 13, they saw a suspicious vessel off the Tortugas. It was a hermaphrodite brig with a main topsail, and it fired into a Dutch bark from New Orleans several times, though the bark got away. The next day, the *Olive Branch* met up with the bark and was told it was carrying a large sum of specie on board. Her captain believed the pirate brig must have heard about her cargo and followed her from New Orleans. Though Jean Lafitte was now dead, it could have been one of his ex-comrades, as Louisiana was their old haunt.

Captain Benners, of the wrecking schooner *United States*, reported from Indian Key March 31, 1837, that he found the wrecked hull of what he believed was a relatively new Spanish schooner, upset, dismasted, and full of water near the Cape Florida Light House. They found about 30 boxes of cochineal and a bunch of hides which he and some other wreckers salvaged and took to Key West. When Capt. Benners investigated further, he found in the hold the body of a man with a large gash across his forehead. Even more gruesome was what else they found. Body parts strewn about, four feet, two hands, and one upper and one lower jaw of a man. He could not find the name of the vessel, but estimated it was around 100 tons and copper fastened. He also found a trunk which contained children's clothing, and a shirt with the initials E.P. Another report said that along with the body, four hands and three feet were found, a box with a globe, atlas and Courier newspapers, and a brass plate engraved Luciano Fornasari. That report says the vessel was likely foreign built as much of the schooner was constructed of mahogany. The hull may have been towed to Key West. One can only imagine the horrors that took place on board this vessel, and the thought that children were on board only makes it worse. Piracy or mutiny was likely involved.

The Belgian brig *Maria Antoinette* left Antwerp on May 12, 1849, bound the West Indies. Her Captain was Leopold Laurvere, first mate was named De George, and second mate Christian Kessen. Nothing unusual happed until July 4 when the captain took his usual nap around 2 p.m. A crewman named Lov, entered the captain's cabin and cut his throat as he slept. At the same time, the first mate was sitting on the upper part of the cabin sewing and old sail when a crewman named Vandevagen grabbed him by the throat and cut his throat too. The knife didn't kill him though, and the mate ran forward into the hatchway, but very weak now, Vandervagen easily caught up with him and then beat his head in with an old musket barrel. The two mutineers now turned pirates, forced the rest of the crew to throw the two bodies overboard. They then had a meeting and decided to run the ship onto the Florida Reef and take the boats (and I'm sure any money and valuables on board) and make their escape. They might have succeeded if they hadn't ran it aground where they did. Before they could escape, the lighthouse keeper and wrecker Reson Duke saw the wreck, and with five of his men, approached the vessel as they saw it could be saved and offered their assistance. The two pirates told Duke that the captain and first mate were killed by lightning, and so as not to raise any suspicion, made a deal with the wreckers to get the brig off the reef for $600. They got her off with not much trouble, and left Reson's son and a Henry Cole on board to pilot her to Key West. That night though, the second mate and another crewman told Cole about the murders and that the two pirates were planning to kill them the next evening. Cole got to one of the boats and made for the lighthouse where Reson was told the story. Reson and his men were soon back on board, and being well armed, took the two pirates into custody and brought them to Key West where they were put in chains until they could be delivered to their Vice Consul in Havana. They probably saw the hangman's noose once they were returned to their country, if they even made it that far.

In 1858, the British brig *E.A. Loud* was found abandoned in Dead Man's Bay. At first it appeared she wrecked due to the crew having the "fever," but soon the local authorities believed mutiny and murder may have taken place, as the three survivors may have faked their sickness and were found to have an abundance of money (see chapter 8).

So, is piracy a thing of the past? Not even close. It's never stopped and continues to this day. Somalia, the South China Sea, Brazil, and probably just about anywhere off the beaten path, piracy still continues. Since I've lived in Florida, I've read about more than one local vessel taken over by pirates. We used to go to the Bahamas quite often on small boats and usually carried a gun or two on board, especially when going off the beaten path, and were glad we did on one occasion. Of all those vessels listed as lost in the "Bermuda Triangle," I'm sure piracy had a hand in some of those disappearances.

I saw a story by Keys historian Brad Bertelli about Angus Boatwright, who was the second permanent resident of Lower Matecumbe Key, and was well known as a charter captain and fishing guide. He operated his boat, the *Muriel III*, out of Holiday Isle. In April 1960 or 1961, he had a fishing charter, and they sailed for the Cay Sal Banks. Meanwhile, two men in their 20s, and the young wife of one who just recently met him, had stolen a boat in Key West, which they wrecked at N. Elbow Cay. Boatwright saw a signal from the three stranded thieves on the island and cautiously approached.

One swam out and an argument ensued. Boatwright pulled out his rifle but it jammed, and the thief pulled out his pistol and shot the captain twice. The mate and four passengers were left on the island along with the dying Boatwright, and the three headed to Cuba where they wrecked again and were arrested. Extradited to the Bahamas, they were tried, and the two men hanged at Fox Hill Prison for piracy and murder in May 1961.

I previously listed a shrimp boat called the *Gunsmoke*, which was scuttled by drug smugglers in January 1977 off Florida. What I didn't know at the time was the crew was complicit in the murder of four innocent bystanders, two who were teenage girls, who had stumbled upon their operation up the East Bay at the mouth of Sandy Creek. It became known as the "Sandy Creek Murders." While offloading their cargo of marijuana, worth about $21 million, four Springfield residents had driven down a dirt road to Sandy Creek to go fishing, only to find themselves at the wrong place at the wrong time. One was shot right then by a lookout, and the other three were shot hours later and then dumped into a sinkhole about 100 miles away. It's said the murder spooked the crew of the Gunsmoke and they soon left, and another report says a passing tug had shone a spotlight on the operation, and the crew of the *Gunsmoke*, believing the tug may have seen the drug operation and would report it, decided to quickly end the operation. They decided to scuttle the boat a few hours later near Tampa, and the crew got away. The tug never did report anything, and an overturned johnboat hiding 3,000 pounds of marijuana was left behind at the scene. It was said there were five crewmen on the *Gunsmoke* and about 20 onshore to offload the drugs. When law enforcement found the johnboat and drugs that were left, that evidence helped in the arrest of some of the people who were ashore, though no one on the *Gunsmoke* were ever caught.

What does this have to do with piracy? Well, docked at Apalachicola at the same time was a 75-foot yacht aptly called the *Pirate's Lady*. On board were the captain and a college student to help sail her to Clearwater. The fisherman in this area are a close-knit group, and rumors among them soon spread that some of the crew of the *Gunsmoke* hijacked her, killed the two on board, and sailed her to either Mexico, or South America. Two informants, who would not go on record fearing reprisals, said that the *Gunsmoke* first went to Apalachicola, where two crewmen took a skiff and boarded the *Pirate's Lady* that night, killed the two on board in the engine room, and followed the *Gunsmoke* south which was scuttled that day near Tampa. Realizing the yacht was too high profile, they later scuttled her too. There were some sightings of the vessel down south to believe this may have been the outcome, but in 1992, the sunken wreck of the *Pirate's Lady* was found by commercial divers off Carrabelle in 92 feet of water, about 50 nautical miles southeast of Apalachicola. Though it is possible they did take her south and brought her back on a drug run and scuttled her at a later date, it

seems most probable she was scuttled not long after the *Gunsmoke*, probably heading back near Apalachicola, and sunk her near home as I presume
the pirates were from that area (it's about 120 miles between where the two
were scuttled), taking the skiff back to shore. The *Panama City News Herald*
of August 6 and December 18, 1983, had two articles on the disappearance
of this and other vessels in that area, supposedly linked to piracy and drug
smuggling. Only a few months before the *Pirate's Lady* disappeared, the
47-foot sport fisherman, *Flying Dutchman*, also disappeared after leaving
Apalachicola, October 26, 1976. It is believed to be hijacked by pirates and
the four on board murdered. It goes on to say that the Bay County Sheriff's
found a 30-foot boat floating bottom up with 14 bullet holes in her hull
and all the electronic gear stolen. Also mentions other vessels missing since
1969 such as the *Mirage*, *Kacky Jean*, *Quick & Easy*, and the *Wee Too*.

Will the crew of the *Gunsmoke* ever be tried? I'm sure some are still alive,
and hopefully someone's conscious will help them to come forward and
testify. The wreck of the *Gunsmoke* lies 24 miles off Johns Pass, St. Petersburg.

I remember hearing about the local charter boat *Rapscallion*, which operated out of the Pier 66 Marina in Ft. Lauderdale. Two men chartered it for
$4,000 in 1995 to take them to the Bahamas. Just before reaching Bimini,
one of the men pulled out a MAC-11 submachine gun and ordered then to
go to Cuba. The captain got into shallow water, jumped overboard, and the
boat ran aground. The two then took a raft after handcuffing the mate to the
boat railing. They were later captured off Cat Cay, posted bail of $185,000,
and were never seen again.

A similar story happened again in 2007. Two men chartered the boat *Joe
Cool*, out of Star Island, Miami, for $4,000 (something about $4,000 here)
to take them to the Bahamas. Besides the two passengers, there was the
captain, his wife, his cousin, and a friend. When they did not return the
next day, the Coast Guard was notified, and they found the *Joe Cool* adrift
and out of fuel about 30 miles off Cuba. There was blood on the deck and
foul play was immediately suspected. The two pirates were soon found in
the boat's life raft, with a story of Cuban pirates killing the other four. The
two, one a Cuban, and the other a thief and child molester wanted in the
United States were arrested. The younger Cuban soon confessed that the
other killed the four and threw them overboard, planning to go to Cuba the
whole time. Both now serving life terms.

Three Republic of Georgia men had rented some personal watercraft in
Boynton Beach in 2016, took them to Freeport, Bahamas, and were abandoned there. They then chartered a 26-foot boat. The three now had two
Brazilians, which they had been paid over $20,000 to smuggle into the
United States. Soon after leaving Freeport, they threw the captain overboard. He tried getting back on board, but they stabbed him. He fortunately
made it back to shore and recovered. The five then headed back to Florida

where they docked at the Sailfish Marina in Palm Beach, and abandoned the boat there. The three were later arrested in Broward County.

Movies like *Captain Phillips*, which told the story of a 2009 hijacking off Somalia, East Africa, or the release of the American captain and chief engineer of the commercial vessel *Edison Chouest Offshore*, kidnapped off West Africa in 2013 by Nigerian pirates and ransomed for a supposed $2 million, attest to the fact that piracy lives on. In 1992, there were 106 cases of piracy reported worldwide, 370 in 2002, 445 in 2010, 191 in 2016, and 156 in the first nine months of 2018. These are just what were reported and believe mostly commercial craft. There were 70 acts of piracy reported in 2017 for just the Latin America and Caribbean region, which was a 163 percent increase over 2016 for the same area. A number of these cases resulted in murder. So even today, it's still a good idea to keep a watchful eye when out on the ocean. If something looks suspicious, be very careful—there still be pirates!

7

Buried and Sunken Treasures

Stately Spanish galleons coming from the Isthmus,
Dipping through the Tropics by the palm-green shores,
With a cargo of diamonds,
Emeralds, amethysts,
Topazes, and cinnamon, and gold moidores.

—Excerpt from the poem "Cargoes," by John Masefield

The previous tales of pirates off Florida would lead many to believe that some must have buried their booty along the coasts or waterways of Florida. Shipwrecked sailors from any treasure laden vessel obviously would be more concerned about their survival than treasure, but it does seem plausible that many would have buried any treasure or money washed up or saved from a shipwreck in a safe place they could later retrieve by using some type of landmark or markings. Buried pirate treasure? Well, pirates usually spent their money as fast as they got it, though some circumstances may have required some to hide it for a time. Now if they wrecked, or were being hunted, or had to go into a port where they may be searched, it's quite probable they may have buried or hid their loot to retrieve at a later date. There's no doubt that the native tribes salvaged much treasure over the years from the many shipwrecks along this coast and may have buried or hid some of it for safekeeping. Any of the local beach hunters along the Treasure Coast will tell you there's still much treasure to be found buried under the beaches there, washed ashore from wrecked Spanish treasure galleons. Beaches along the Florida Keys have also offered up Spanish coins and treasure through the years from wrecked ships. Can't tell you how many stories I've heard of people finding coins or lost treasure along Florida's vast coastline and beaches, from the Panhandle to Amelia Island, as almost every area of Florida I've been to has a tale or two.

BURIED TREASURE

Since coming to Florida years ago, I've heard many tales of buried treasure. Most are just that, tales. People have invested tons of money over the years looking for treasure both on land and under the sea. Many were scams from the start. Treasure scams have gone on for years. One of the first I found was reported in a newspaper article in 1837. A known pirate named Mitchell, who had recently been pardoned, scammed a Mr. Roberts of Philadelphia out of some money telling him he had buried over $1 million near Key West. He acquired the money in the last war and needed another investor to outfit a vessel to go and retrieve it. Of course, Mr. Roberts never saw Mitchell again. The popular movie actor of the 1930s and 40s, John Carroll, was actually discovered by the studios while working on a treasure hunt in Florida (he would take tourists treasure hunting for a fee) and soon signed on with RKO studios.

I've heard many tales of the famous pirate Jean Lafitte's treasure being buried along Florida's coast. There's no doubt that the pirate Jean Lafitte, and many of his consorts, sailed and stopped along the Florida coast, and in 1810, even planned to make a settlement in the Tampa Bay area. After he left Galveston, it's said he had a number of bases for operations including Cuba.

In 1950, Florida's Assistant State Attorney General, Ralph E. Odom, along with a State Road Department draftsman named Warner Sanford, drew up a colorful Florida treasure map for tourists that Mr. Odom had done some considerable research on. You can still find copies of this map being sold today.

There's no doubt there's treasure yet to be found in the waters in and around Florida, and definitely still under the beaches where the 1715 Fleet wrecked, and I believe some will also be uncovered elsewhere on land. Most all the following stories were reported in local and national newspapers, and I believe some are true and the treasures likely came from a wrecked ship, others have some basis in fact, and some are simply a bit far-fetched, but I'll let the reader decide, and besides, who doesn't love a good treasure story!

Marco Island Marriot/Calico Jack Treasure

One story has it that in the year 1719, Calico Jack Racham supposedly found a safe haven to repair his vessel on the west coast of Florida around Estero Island, along with his pirate lover Anne Bonny. It's said that they saw a Spanish galleon in distress off the Florida coast, but a severe storm swept the area just as they were about to investigate. After the storm, they found the ship wrecked on the beach near Cape Romano, buried in the sand, the crew having already left in their boats, probably for Havana. They found some gold coins and other treasure but the rest was buried in the hold of the ship deep under the sand. They left intending to return and get the rest of the treasure at a later date, but were later captured off Jamaica. Calico Jack was found guilty of piracy and hung. It was said the treasure wreck lay in an area with a crescent shaped beach. When the Marriot Hotel was being built on Marco Island back in 1970, a treasure hunter approached the construction supervisor, and with an old map in hand, told the story of the treasure galleon and how the beach in front of the hotel was a perfect match for the "crescent beach." The supervisor was swayed by the tale and soon they were excavating and drilling in the beach in front of the hotel. They soon found pieces of wood, just like those from a ship, but the tide was coming in and before they could shore up the area to continue digging, an executive from the project immediately shut down this activity and got the crew back to the work of building the hotel and no more work looking for the ship was allowed. Is this a far-fetched tale, or is there a treasure ship buried under the sand in front of the Marco Island Marriot?

John's Pass Treasure

Between Treasure Island and Madeira Beach lies John's Pass. Supposedly a pirate named John Levique had buried a chest of treasure there. In 1848, he had gone to New Orleans to sell some turtles he had caught, and on his way back encountered a hurricane. They found a safe place to anchor during the storm, but when he got back, he found a channel had been cut through the exact area where he had buried his treasure, now called "John's Pass" in his honor. Now from what I've found, he did exist, though found no evidence he was ever a pirate. In 1842, the Armed Occupation Act offered homesteaders 160 acres in areas of Florida if they would farm it and fight the Seminoles if needed. John Levique was one of those who took advantage. He and another homesteader named Joseph Silva did go to New Orleans to sell turtles, and they faced a hurricane on their way back. They were the first to go through a new pass which was later called "John's Pass," after Levique. Was Levique ever a pirate and did he ever bury treasure there? Highly unlikely. If he did bury anything, it would probably be on his 160 acres!

Jupiter Treasure Chest

Well, there's one story of buried treasure I believe to be true. In 1915, while having a pool constructed on his Jupiter Island Estate, Major E. C. Lewis, of Nashville, who was a chairman of the board of the Louisville and Nash-ville Railroad, uncovered a chest of gold and jewels valued at over $50,000 (that's about $1,195,000 in 2019). There's a good chance this was from the "Jupiter Wreck," which most believe is the *San Miguel el Archangel,* wrecked in 1660, and lies just off Jupiter Inlet.

Red Reef Treasure

This is one story I've never seen reported in any newspaper, but have heard too many locals from back in the day tell me about it. A similar story to the Jupiter chest tells of buried treasure being uncovered when the Red Reef Golf Course in Boca Raton was being built. A backhoe operator supposedly uncovered two sacks or chests full of treasure. The golf course is right on the ocean, and from what I've researched, there may be some truth to it! A number of wrecks lie offshore and Spanish cannons have been found close by.

Bayou Chica Treasure

A paper reported in 1913 that a contractor from Pensacola named Charles H. Villar had found an iron chest buried in the shallow waters of Bayou Chica while doing some work there. Inside, he found Spanish doubloons and silver lires worth around $70,000 (that's about $1,723,000 today). It was believed to be buried by pirates, as this was a known rendezvous for them in years past.

Pirate Bell's Treasure

In February 1876, the steamer "Bill Keysen" arrived at Cedar Keys which had on board a company of treasure hunters. A large crowd gathered to see what they had and witnessed a large chest being brought ashore to the local hotel, which was well guarded by other men of the party with both rifles and pistols. Nobody in the party or the crew of the steamer were talking, but some information was gained. They had been searching for two treasures, one of silver and one of gold and jewels. Believed the chest brought ashore contained the silver, amounting to a half million dollars. Others of the party were now searching for the gold on an island, having chartered the schooner *Charry M.* Another later report from Savannah gained some additional information as this party of treasure hunters had passed through that city on their way back to Washington County, Georgia. The news of the treasure had followed them, and some in Savannah were obviously curious to know more. Accompanying them was a reporter from the *New York Herald* and some more information about the treasure was reported in the local papers. It seems the leader of this treasure hunt had been given a treasure map and location of the treasure by a person who knew the pirate named

Bell. The story goes that Bell and his crew had captured a Spanish ship and took the treasure on board and buried it on one of the islands in Sarasota Bay. They then sailed to Wilmington under government protection where Bell went ashore. While he was ashore, the crew mutinied and set sail back to Sarasota Bay. Before reaching their destination though, they wrecked on the Florida coast and all of them perished. Bell was now the only one who knew the location of the treasure. He made a trip back and retrieved one box of treasure. On a second trip he found he was being watched and did not retrieve any of the treasure. He had brought along a friend on these trips, and after Bell died at St. Marks where he lived, the friend became the only one who knew the location of the treasure. Upon the friend's death bed, he gave the maps and information given to him by Bell to the leader of the treasure hunting party. That person then sold shares of this enterprise to finance this expedition. The reporter from the *Herald* would only say that he was sworn to secrecy, but the expedition was not without some success.

Cedar Keys Treasure

A report in 1875 told of an old Spaniard by the name of Rios de Ralfo, who said that he was a pirate in his younger days and came to Cedar Keys to retrieve some treasure he helped bury many years before. The locals all wondered if he really knew about any treasure. That year though, he took passage on the steamer *Wilmington* bound for Havana, and as some corroborated, he had recovered an iron box containing precious stones and Spanish coins valued at $10,000.

The Sea Horse Island Treasure

A story published in 1876 tells about the Spanish pirate Moreno, who along with his pilot named Gardin, scuttled their brig off Bay Point, Florida, killing the rest of the crew. They then took off $127,000 in gold and silver from the wreck and buried it on Sea Horse Key after taking $15,000 each. With the brigs boat, Moreno took Gardin to Cedar Key and dropped him off and returned to Sea Horse. He then marked a palmetto tree near the buried treasure with a crow's foot, but before he could leave, he was approached by a Captain Sam Johnson who was a well-known pilot along this coast and who lived at Alsena Otie. Asking what he was doing there, Moreno said he was fishing. Having no fishing equipment though, Johnson didn't believe a word, but Moreno was already in his boat and headed to New Orleans. Asked about the strange encounter in 1874, Captain Johnson remembered it vividly. In 1863 Moreno was in Texas and had approached a Captain Crooker for passage in his schooner back to Sea Horse Key with a promise to split the loot 50/50, which he said was in one tin box and an iron chest. Crooker abstained, and Moreno was killed soon after by a Mexican. Is any of this true? Would a pirate drop off the pilot knowing he could go back and retrieve the treasure? Did he not drop off the pilot but kill him instead? Why would he not have marked the tree while they were there in the first place? Who knew about the crow's foot mark, Captain Crooker? That's the problem with most treasure stories, so many just don't make much sense. Captain Sam Johnson does give the story some basis in fact though.

Capt. Kidd's Treasure?

Is there no place on earth that Capt. Kidd didn't bury some treasure? Reported in the *New York Times* in 1893 was a story about Oceola Smith, who with $5,000 from investors, started a company to find Capt. Kidd's buried treasure. They sunk a shaft 23 feet deep on the Ft. Brooke Reservation just outside of Tampa when they hit water. They then used a steam pump and had gotten to 33 feet but nothing except fossils and shark's teeth had been found. Money soon ran out but Mr. Smith soon got some new investors and work was continuing.

The *Times* noted that Mr. Smith was using different types of divining rods to locate the treasure. They asked him to prove they worked, and after a few tests, they all failed to do so.

Carl Creek Treasure

In 1897, a group seeking treasure searched the Carl Creek area which is a few miles west of Punta Gorda, supposedly used by the pirate "Old Gasper." They found some pirate markings and began to dig. They had been digging almost two days when that night, they were scared off by people screaming and by gunshots, though they did leave one person to guard the area. The next morning, they went back to where they had been digging and found their friend bound and gagged and the hole much bigger. They could see where a chest had been dragged out of the hole and found some Spanish doubloons scattered about, along with pieces of copper and fragments of silver. The person they left to guard the site said about 10 or 12 black bearded men arrived by boat and after binding him, dug out the original hole and found a chest about five feet by three feet and carried it onto the boat and left.

Now this one is hard to believe. If "Old Gasper" is referring to Jose Gaspar, we know he didn't exist. And if you were out in the woods at night, heard a bunch of people making noise, and bullets were flying by your heads, would you leave an unarmed person there? And who would volunteer to do that?

Amelia Island Treasure

In 1897, it was reported that two groups had found buried treasure on Amelia Island. The first was a group of strangers claiming to be scientists. They had brought along some charts supposedly showing where some treasure was buried. A local named Chris Pinckney saw them recover a box of gold coins. That night, he snuck into their camp and stole the charts from them. Without the charts, the group soon left and that's when Pinckney approached his employer George Gause, a local lumberman, and the two soon uncovered a chest of Spanish doubloons with a value of around $35,000 (would be close to one million in today's dollars). The story gets a bit weird after this as Pickney soon disappears to New York. Gause got local lawyer W. A. Hall involved, but then Gause disappears. Hall did see some of the coins, and also the hole under an old oak tree where the treasure was recovered. He said he could see the outline of where the chest had been when he was shown the hole they retrieved it from. Also, some local merchants still had some of the gold doubloons which Gause paid them with before taking off. Whatever the case, the story got out, and Amelia Island soon had a bunch of holes being dug near big oak trees!

Lone Oak Treasure

In 1904, a Mrs. Julia Crawford was found dead in her boarding house in San Francisco due to a gas leak. She was the sister of the late Lt. Jenkins, who was lost on the battleship Maine. When the landlady was going through her things, she found numerous letters, maps, and so on—supposedly with clues to a buried pirate treasure at a place called Lone Oak, near St. Petersburg on Tampa Bay. The treasure was supposedly buried by the crew of a pirate ship which had wrecked on the north side of the bay many years ago. So, whatever happened to all those clues?

Fort George/Fanning Island Treasure

Reported from Jacksonville in December 1911, and picked up by papers both here and in England, was the story of two boys, who after finding an ancient chart in the ruins of a coquina (or shell) house on Fort George Island, unearthed a treasure on Fanning Island worth about $150,000 dollars (that would be over 3.5 million in today's dollars!). They say the gold, silver, and copper coins were "buried in an iron chest of about one cubic foot in size, some five or six feet under the sand." The boy's names were, Loring Hewen and John King, one being 17 and the other 18 years old, the sons of local and respected families. Those that saw the coins said they were dated over a century ago and were Spanish. Now there is at least one ruin of an old coquina house still standing on Fort George Island today. I'm inclined to believe this story.

Miami Beach Treasure

Another story reported in 1913 was of buried treasure found on an island off Miami. The first report I read was that a Mr. E. C. Cole, a wealthy Chicago businessman, had found a 2.5-pound chunk of melted gold while looking for corals on an old wreck site. A couple of weeks later a different report was made. Mr. Cole said that while he was looking for a suitable site to build a vacation home on one of the islands near Miami, he stumbled upon an old rusty "boarding pike." He said it had "strange charts and figures traced in the iron which had almost been obliterated by the rust." A few days later, he examined it closely with a magnifying glass, and saw what appeared to be a chart etched in it. He also realized that the island was of a similar shape as the boarding pike.

> The broad line running from the head of the pike to a small dent in the center, he decided, was the line to a buried treasure, and the pike represented the island. It was easy to decipher the figures which he concluded to indicate how far a line was to be drawn from the water's edge.

Running a line, he marked a spot, and along with some friends began to dig. When they got about 6 feet deep, they hit something solid. They retrieved some objects and washed them off. What they found were lumps of gold and silver and later some jewelry.

They melted down the gold and silver into squares. They sent one of the gold lumps to an assayer, who reported it was pure gold. Mr. Cole said he planned to do a systematic survey of the area. Not long after, Mr. Cole had a new yacht built, aptly named the *Treasure Trove*!

More Miami Treasure

A more modern treasure story began when two burglars were jailed in Mobile on robbery charges in 1957. They gave the police some information about some stolen merchandise buried along Miami Beach. Detectives arrived at the property of television star Arthur Godfrey, who owned the Kenilworth Hotel on the beach. Following the thief's directions, they walked 200 yards north of the hotel and dug in the sand. What they found were three strong boxes with over $100,000 in stolen bonds and jewelry!

Green Cove Spring's Treasure

Reported in 1948 was a story about how a treasure hunter named G. B. Mobley, using a type of divining rod, actually had part of Walnut Street in

Green Cove Springs dug up to look for treasure. Supposedly some gold was found but saw nothing more on this story.

I never believed in divining rods, but while at a shipwreck symposium, there was a man who said he used a divining rod and it works. He happened to have it with him at the time. Well-known author and diver Robert Marx was there also, and both of us being skeptical, asked this man to prove it, which he agreed to do. I witnessed Mr. Marx take a Spanish gold escudo and hide it outside the hotel to actually see if this guy could find it using the divining rod. Using his metal divining rod, it pointed right toward it, and he found it within a few minutes!

Florida Treasure Maps

Reported in the paper in 1948 was a story about some treasure maps. A man named Faust, who was a planter on Santa Rosa Island, received a cane stick with 12 maps inside from a Capt. Andrea who had been shipwrecked on the beach by Faust's farm, but died not long after Faust rescued him. Faust never pursued investigating these maps, but his grandson, Capt. Walter N. Brown, did do so after he inherited them. He examined the maps, and using the two easiest maps to follow, he went on a treasure hunt and supposedly found $350,000 in French coins using the first map, but which were soon stolen, as he talked a little too freely about what he found and word got around. Following the second map, he found a much smaller treasure consisting of a small pot of gold coins.

The article goes on to say how a Mrs. Beulah E. Crocker (also known as the Cherokee Indian Princess) was now involved as an investor in a treasure hunt using two more of the maps. Ms. Crocker was the widow of New York City Tammany boss Richard Crocker, who was quite wealthy and had a mansion in Palm Beach before his death. No idea how their treasure hunt ever turned out, but a 1952 Sarasota newspaper article mentions Ms. Beulah Crocker. It said she was presently leaving on a search again after 12 previous attempts to look for the treasure in two Florida bayous, one in Bay County and another along the Gulf Coast. It goes on to say she owned the property where the largest treasure, worth $75 million, was supposedly buried, and leased the property from the state where the other treasure, worth $4 million, supposedly was. She had already spent $25,000 of her own money in the search, but now had a partner, Mr. Hugh Ridenour, of Pahokee. She's mentioned again in a Ft. Walton paper in 1973, but she died in 1957, and was likely referring to her expeditions back in 1952. It said the property she bought was in the Panhandle along a river there. The treasure was said to contain millions in plate, coin, jeweled church ornaments, and silver, and was in four wooden and iron chests. It also said she was in possession of the 12 maps then. I wonder if anything was ever recovered and if there was any truth to the finds, and where are those maps today?

Marco Island Treasure

Besides the story of buried treasure on Marco Island regarding the pirate Jack Rackham in chapter 8, a paper in 1897 had run a story on recent searches for buried and sunken treasures, including Capt. Kidd's, the *De Braak* wreck, Lafitte, and so on. It mentioned that an ex-miner named Nicholson, who was basically broke, was seen in his cabin on Marco Island with a pile of 10 and 20-dollar gold pieces, along with some gold "slugs" (octagonal shaped pieces used for currency in California for a brief time). Nicholson died soon after, and having no relatives, a search was on for his treasure but never found. Most believed he buried it near his home. Sounds like California gold-rush coins. A number of ships from California with gold, which was shipped regularly to the East Coast, wrecked.

Key West Treasure

In 1979, the brothers Kent and Jim Pepper were renovating their home in Key West. While working on an old water well in their backyard, they discovered a gold nugget. Digging deeper, other objects were found and they got help from some of the workers from Key West contractor Sackett Construction Company, who were offered one-third of anything found. They soon found more gold nuggets, a ships spike, an old hinge which appeared to be from a chest, and an 1800s half dime. They believed a treasure chest may be deeper down. The gold recovered weighed over two pounds.

The Hidden Treasure

I'll leave this section with a story written by S. G. W. (Samuel Greene Wheeler) Benjamin, published in the 1874 edition of the magazine *St. Nicholas* (story and illustration reprinted with permission from: Baldwin Library of Children's Historical Literature, Special and Area Studies Collections, George A. Smathers Libraries, University of Florida, Gainesville, Florida). Mr. Benjamin was a historian, art expert, and statesman (was the first minister to Persia). All his books and works seem to be nonfiction, including a short story on William Phips salvage of the treasure wreck *Concepción* back in 1687. *The Hidden Treasure* was again published in 1887 in Benjamin's book *Sea-Spray; or Facts and Fancies of a Yachtsman*, and under the title *The Hidden Treasure*, is this caption: "**Founded on Fact!**" Enjoy.

At a fort in Florida, during the Seminole War, a man named Richard Blount lay wounded and dying. A keen observer might have discerned in the emancipated features, well covered by an iron-gray untrimmed beard, traces of refinement-almost effaced, it is true, by the unmistakable marks of a turbulent, and perhaps criminal career.

The surgeon in charge of the stockade seemed a man of warm heart and tender sympathies, which had not been blunted by familiarity with suffering. He carefully tended the dying soldier, doing all in his power, by words and actions, to soothe his last hours. This kindness was not without results. Impressed by the attentions to which he had long been unaccustomed, Richard Blount—taciturn and reserved by habit, if not by nature—grew more communicative, and, at last, made certain revelations concerning transactions of which no other living man had any knowledge.

One afternoon, as the sun was setting red and broad in the burning haze behind the motionless palmettoes, and the mocking-bird was pouring forth his wealth of music by the still bayous where the alligator basked unmolested, Richard, who was feeling stronger than usual, after a period of silence and mental struggle with himself, said:

"Doctor, you've been mighty good to me. You are the first person who has spoken a kind word to me for many years. I've led a hard life of it, and very likely don't deserve any better than I've received, yet I can't forget that I was once a better man and used to kind words from these who loved me. And now, although I am both poor and forsaken, yet believe me when I say that it is in my power to make you as wealthy as your wildest fancies could desire."

"I was born in England; I have not a single relation now living, and to you it can be of no consequence what were the early circumstances of my life. It is enough to say that I was the younger son of a good family, and was destined for the church, for which I was totally unfitted. I was sent to Oxford, but an insatiable thirst for adventure caused me to run away. After various fortunes in many parts of the world, in which the cards were generally against me, it was at last my luck to find myself shipped with a crew of a pirate schooner, and a motley set we were—Spaniards, Englishmen, Frenchmen, Italians, Yankees, Greeks—men of all races. Two or three years I sailed in her, boarding and burning vessels in the Spanish Main. At length a rumor reached the nest of pirates which I belonged that the English government was about to take vigorous measures to capture our vessels and destroy our rendezvous. As we had for a long time been very successful, without any serious molestation, there was all the more reason to believe the report. A council of war was called, in which words ran high. But it was decided that, as our rendezvous was well known and would most likely be attacked first, and we should be unable to defend ourselves successfully against such forces as could be sent against us, we ought at once to remove our possessions and conceal them for awhile in some unknown hiding place. With us to decide was to act, and without further delay the treasure, which was enormous, being the accumulated spoil of many hard fights and scuttled ships, was stowed in the holds of our vessels. (A little water, surgeon, if you'll be so good.)

IN THE BAYOU

Illustration from the story "A Hidden Treasure," *St. Nicholas Magazine*, 1874. Baldwin Library of Children's Historical Literature, Special and Area Studies Collections, George A. Smathers Libraries, University of Florida, Gainesville.

"So Immense," continued Richard, after a moment, "was the stock of dollars and doubloons and jewelry that no other ballast was needed for the schooners. When everything was on board, we set fire to the cabins on shore, and by the glare of the burning houses dropped down the lagoon and made an offing. We headed for the coast of Florida, and the moon being at the full shoved the schooners into an inlet whose whereabouts was known to one of our captains, a native of Florida, borne at Key West, son of a wrecker, I think. It was a very quiet part of the country, without so many people as there are about it now; and they aren't over thick even now. We had sent some men ashore in a boat in the morning to find the exact entrance, and after dark they lit a fire on the beach; so we knew just where to put the schooners. At daylight we sailed a long way up the bayou, winding about from bent to bend, with sweeps, or tacking along the shore, and blazing the trees as we went along, until we came to a clearing in the woods, where the trees seem to have been felled by a hurricane. It was gloomy and silent enough—a solitude which we disturbed perhaps for the first time. Here we made the vessels fast to the trees, and all hands went ashore. We made tents of old sails and in a few hours, to see the smoke streaming up from among the trees, and see the boys capering after squirrels and climbing after birds' nests, or flinging sticks at the alligators, you would have thought it was an old settlement."

After a brief interval of rest, Richard went on: "When the provisions and everything else had been taken out of the schooners we hove out the ballast (you remember it was dollars), and carried it into the middle of the clearing. Each man put his share into an earthen pot; his name, written on a piece of parchment, was placed inside, and his initials were scratched on the outside, and it was then sealed up carefully. The pots of gold and silver were then buried in a circle in holes dug tolerably deep in the ground, and every man planted a small tree over his treasure. Our common stock of treasures were next sealed up in a large jar, and we buried this in the center of the circle and planted a good sized tree over this also."

"After we had secured our valuables, as considerable time had been spent in doing all this, it was decided that the schooners should go off on another expedition at once, and they put to sea, leaving a few men under my charge to look after the camp and the treasure. Several weeks went by, and no news came from the absent schooners. Our stock of provisions began to run low, and it was impossible to get anything in that desolate maze of a morass, overgrown with tangled forests and cut up by muddy streams and bayous, especially as we had planted nothing in the clearing, and had not cleared any more of the land, as we expected that, of course, the schooners would soon return with a fresh stock. We had always been so lucky that not a soul of us dreamed any trouble. Anyhow, the schooners never came back, nor did I ever afterwards get any clue to their fate. They were probably captured and burned, or more likely foundered in a hurricane.

"The rainy season was coming on, and before long several of our number had fallen off with starvation and disease. My comrades and I talked over the situation, and finally concluded to look out for number one, and leave the treasure to take care of itself.

"Well, we had a ship's boat with us and one day, after putting a few moldy biscuits in our pockets, we took to our boat and followed the bayou until we came to the sea. Then we skirted the coast until we reached a settlement, and after that separated in different directions, for there was no tie of friendship to bind us, and we each had a sort of dread that the other might some way betray him. For years after I wandered about the country—sometimes on the frontier—until I enlisted in the Army, not caring much what became of me, but half hoping that perhaps I should be sent to Florida, as turned out to be the case, to fight these Seminoles, and so perhaps get a chance to look up the treasure we had buried in the forest. I never had the ready money, nor, I'm not ashamed to say, the courage, to go back alone to that spot; but I got this shot in the leg, and here I am, and much good that treasure has done me! But it don't seem quite the thing, you see, that all that treasure and money should be buried there and be of no use to anybody, and as you are the first and the last person to be kind to me these many years, I'll trust you to see that I have a decent burial, and will tell you just how to go find the treasure. It's all truth I've been telling you, and you needn't be afraid I'm spinning you a forecastle yarn, but just do as I direct you to do, and it'll make you the richest man in the country; and I don't know who deserves it better."

Richard Blount, after this, gave the surgeon very minute directions as to how to go in quest of the treasure. On the next day the pirate died. As soon after this as the surgeon could get leave of absence, he made arrangements with a friend to go after the supposed mine of wealth concealed in the forests of Southern Florida. He could not quite believe the story, but the circumstances under which it had been disclosed, and the fact that money had often concealed by the freebooters of the sea, made it sufficiently probable to warrant his chartering a small, light draught schooner and engaging a crew of blacks able to work the vessel and willing to dig in the mud after gold.

It was only by a very close and tedious observation of the coast that the mouth of the bayou was found. On entering it from the sea, the line of trees that had been blazed was also discovered with some difficulty and traced from bend to bend in the dusky light of the primeval forest.

Guided by this clue, often but faintly distinguishable, the treasure-seekers, after slowly sailing along the devious mazes of the silent waters of the wilderness until they almost despaired of reaching the end in view, at last burst suddenly upon a sort of clearing in the dense mass of vegetation, overgrown with trees of young growth, arising from which a circle of large trees could be distinctly traced, with a central shaft lifting its feathery tuft of foliage far up into the blue sky. Tent stakes and other relics of extinct life were also visible amid the rank grass which overgrew the soil.

Everything, thus far proved exactly as described by Richard Blount, and it was reasonable to suppose that, as the story had been found to tally in the minutest details with the facts, it would continue consistent throughout. It was therefore with renewed zest and with the burning impatience which tortures the soul when one is confident of the results and sees the desired object almost in his grasp, that the doctor seized a pick-axe and ordering his men to follow suit, broke ground in the last stage of the quest after a treasure which his fevered fancy pictured as more and more colossal as the rapturous moment approached when it would be opened to view. Such was his impatience that he was the first to make a discovery. The point of the pick, after turning up the soft soil almost noiselessly for some anxious minutes, at last struck something hard with a most decided click. The next stroke the sound was repeated, and at the same time a bit of red pottery was thrown up. The doctor perspiring with excitement, flung aside the pick-axe and, falling on his knees, began to draw out the earth with his hands, while everyone stopped his work and looked on with breathless expectation. It took but a minute to bring to light an earthen jar, but on trying to raise it they found it was cracked in several pieces, and that the bottom had fallen out. What was more important was that the jar was empty! Here was a disappointment, to be sure; but they would not give up heart; there were still many jars and perhaps this one was only a "blind." But jar after jar was turned up and all were found more or less broken, and not a dollar did one of then contain. Last of all the searchers cut down the central tree and unearthed the last jar over which it stood. This also, crowning disappointment of all, was in the same condition and contained only earth-worms. Baffled, but not quite disheartened, the treasure seekers, as a last resort, dug several feet below where the central jar had been. They did not find the treasure they sought, but they ascertained where it had gone.

They came to water, and thus discovered the solution to the mystery, and what had robbed them of the gold. They stood on a mere alluvial crust of oozy soil, under which the water percolated at some depth below. The moisture of the earth had softened the jars, and the weight of the treasure had carried away the bottom and caused it to sink lower and lower, as in a quicksand, until it had dropped into the water, and of course out of site.

There was nothing more to be done but abandon further operations for the time, as such a result had not been foreseen and the means for raising the money were not at hand. But the following year the doctor returned to the bayou with a pumping machine and ample apparatus for his purpose, and after much labor was partially rewarded for his trouble.

Doubloons and guineas, vases and caskets of precious metals elaborately chased, the handiwork of skilled artisans of various races and ages, gems of price, which had long lain concealed in the slime of the forest again flashed in the sunbeams. But all the lost treasure was not regained; some of it eluded the closest scrutiny of avarice and enterprise, and still lies buried forever under the waters and the sod of Florida.

SUNKEN TREASURE

The Spanish fleets carried untold treasures back to Spain, many which wrecked off Florida's shores and described in chapter 8. Many of these shipwrecks such as most from the 1622 fleet, the "Jupiter Wreck," 1715 fleet (four yet to be found), and 1733 fleet wrecks, have been found. The Spanish recovered much of the treasure from some of these shallow water wrecks

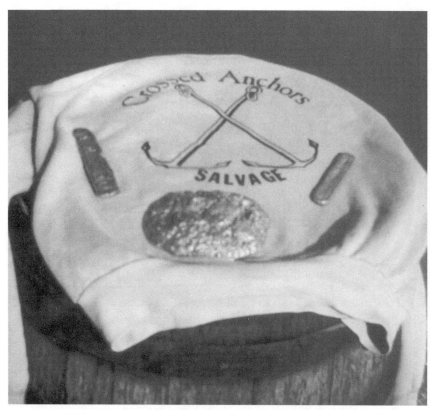

Gold disk and bars recovered from the 1715 Fleet off Florida. Bob Weller.

soon after they wrecked, and most were then forgotten. Some of the treasure wrecks off Florida had been found going back to the late 1920s, though weren't really pursued until divers and treasure hunters like Art McKee and Kip Wagner started making incredible finds. After that, the treasure hunt was on, and continues to this day.

A recent television reality show linked a NASA astronaut and treasure hunting. Actually, back in 1961, some of the NASA astronauts and the helicopter pilots that caught the nose cones were working with an old-time resident of Cocoa Beach who knew of some shipwreck locations. They were recovering coins off that coast, and it was reported in 1961 that they already sold about $50,000 worth of coins and had started a company to recover more. I've heard this story more than once, and I believe coins and treasure were definitely recovered off the Space Coast.

Most merchant vessels carried some money on board, so it's not uncommon to find some coins on a wreck site. The *Supply* in 1822 had $4,000 in specie on board. The *Helen Mar*, in 1835, had $109,000 in specie on board,

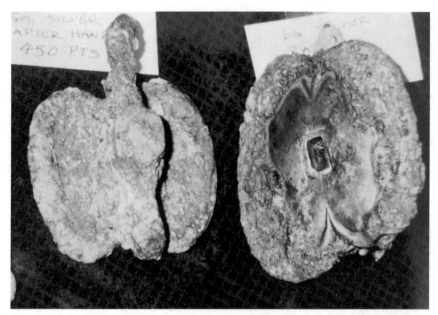

Semi-encrusted silver rapier handles recovered from the 1715 "Douglas Beach" site.

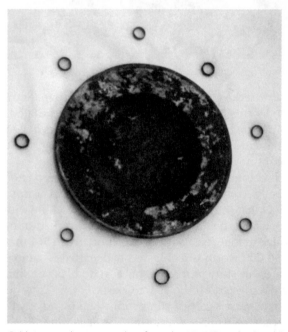

Gold rings and a pewter plate from the 1715 "Douglas Beach" site. Bob Weller.

Diver using a metal detector on the "Jupiter Wreck."

Diver with a "piece of eight" on the "Jupiter Wreck."

Prop wash deflectors used to move more than 20 feet of sand on the "Jupiter Wreck."

though $21,000 was salvaged leaving $88,000 (that's over 2 million in today's dollars). The brig *Stanley* was carrying silver ore when she wrecked in 1845, and the list goes on. The *Victorioso* lost in 1771, supposedly carrying a rich treasure back to Spain. The *North America* wrecked on Delta Shoal in 1842 and had $10,000 in gold on board, though neither the crew, passengers, or the wreckers seemed to have any idea where it went—was it stolen, still there? The *Hector* in 1800, sank with $200,000 in specie. These are just some examples. Researching pirates and privateers off Florida, it was not uncommon for many a merchant ship that had been looted to report $25,000, $50,000, or more in specie having been robbed from them. It seems before bank deposits were the norm for payment of goods, payment for cargoes delivered, and payment for cargoes bought were paid in cash much of the time, so large amounts of money were sometimes carried on these voyages.

I've heard many stories of treasure found, but usually with no proof to back them up. Almost anywhere off the coast of Florida, someone has heard a story of someone finding a sunken wreck with treasure on board. Most though are just that, stories. In April 1965, newspapers across the country reported that a treasure galleon had been found 90 miles south of St. Petersburg by a Mr. John Sykes in water so shallow, you could wade in it and pick up coins. It went on to say that two gold Aztec statues, a silver

Author's old salvage boat *Chelsea*, on one of the 1715 wreck sites.

hilted sword, coins, and other treasures were recovered and had been catalogued by the state and were now in a bank safe. The state did get involved and had catalogued and photographed the finds. This all turned out to be a fraud as all the objects were fake.

If by chance you do find something, as I've stated before, it is illegal to remove anything in state waters older than 50 years. Make sure you know the laws, and if finding anything of value, you may be able to apply for a state salvage lease. Some waters off Florida are under Federal control, so be aware of any rules and regulations.

Author with gold and silver coins from the 1715 "Douglas Beach" site.

Keys Treasure

A paper reported a treasure found in the Keys in 1898. It was reported that a Key West sponge fisherman had found treasure. While looking underwater off one of the many islands in the Keys, he saw what looked like a chest near an entrance in the side of the island. Diving down to investigate, he entered the entrance and soon was inside a cave. He found that it had been inhabited. Inside was deteriorated clothing, a chain mail suit, swords and muskets, and old box with around 100 Spanish copper coins, and in one corner a skeleton chained to a rock. He grabbed some of the coins along with a pair of compasses and went back to his boat. He then dove back down and tied a rope to the chest by the entrance and hauled it aboard. Inside he found it filled with very ornate silverware.

Sounds like the makings for a great book or movie. Any truth to it? I'll let the reader decide.

The Silver Ballast Bars

In 1903, a Captain Jennings and the crew of the wrecking schooner *Osceo* supposedly found a wreck in five feet of water off Miami that had silver ore. He filed a claim on the wreck. The story made a number of newspapers and goes like this:

Supposedly a ship wrecked near Miami in 1835 loaded with silver bars. The one survivor kept the secret, but being a drinker, befriended a local seaman named Ned Pent, also known as "Uncle Ned Pent," who also being a drinker, soon got the story from the survivor after they got drunk one evening. The survivor ended up leaving Florida to go to New York, but Uncle Ned kept looking for the wreck when he wasn't at sea. In 1859, he finally found the wreck uncovered by the sand, and carried away a number of bars thinking them to only be lead. He used them for ballast in his small boat. When he got to Key West, he sold the boat to go drinking, and soon after signed onto a vessel and sailed away. The new owner thought the bars looked strange and had them checked out. Word soon got around that they were pure silver and the owner quickly sold them all. He looked for Uncle Ned, but never found him. The Civil War then broke out and all thoughts of treasure hunting ended. "Uncle Ned" was back, but was busy working as a seaman on a blockade runner, though he had heard through the rumor mill that his lead bars turned out to be silver. As soon as the war was over, old Ned was back looking, but the sands had long covered the wreck up again. The survivor who moved to New York had never forgot about it either and had gotten an investor to help look for the wreck. Soon there were a number of people looking for it until Captain Joseph Jennings said he found it and filed a claim through local lawyer C. C. Chilingsworth. The papers reported it was found 30 to 40 miles above Miami, was about 100 feet long and ran onto the beach bow first. Also reported that using an auger, they had already recovered silver shavings. A cofferdam was to be placed around it to further excavate. After filing the claim, Jennings was appointed wrecking master by the courts.

Another story called it "Brown's Wreck," after old man Brown, who lived near the New River. He supposedly found the bars after a storm, and thinking they were lead, he then sold them at Key West, only to find out later that they were silver. Jennings found a couple of wrecks in this area and recovered a number of iron cannon from one and a few coins on another; the cannons which ended up as decorations on the Clarke property in Palm Beach.

These were reported in a number of papers all over the country. That seemed to be the end of the story as I found nothing more ever printed about it. I've heard the story before about the lead ballast bars years before I ever read the newspaper articles. So, whatever happened to his wreck? Another treasure story to unravel!

Treasure in a Crab Claw!

In 1908, Mr. J. R. Chard, of Greenwich, Connecticut, landed a large crab off New Smyrna while fishing, and sticking out among one of the claws was an encrusted piece of metal. The fisherman scraped it off, and to his amazement it was a Spanish doubloon dated 1608! Mr. Chard said he was going to extend his vacation hoping to find some more.

Ocklawaha River Chest

One tale that was reported in the *Pensacola Journal* in 1908 was of a copper chest that was seen on a ledge of rocks on the bottom of the Ocklawaha River. It was reported from Candler, Florida, that Mr. W. R. Caldwell had found it but was too heavy for him to retrieve. He would not tell its exact location and was even offered $1,000 for half of what was recovered. I seriously doubt anyone would reveal this information before they retrieved the chest, if there ever was one!

Suwannee River Treasure

A newspaper in 1953 reported that Lakeland hotel owner, William F. Sneed Jr., had recovered a treasure chest in 16 1/2 feet of water near the mouth of the Suwannee River while using a metal detector. Inside were 4,500 Spanish gold doubloons, and 3,500 silver pieces of eight. Also, inside the chest was a silver cup he thought was of English origin. He valued the gold coins between $100 and $150 each, and the silver between $50 and $90. The low value of all was put at $650,000 (almost six million in today's dollars). The story was soon reported in papers all over the country, and one mentioned that the tax man was interested, as taxes would have to be paid on anything found. Soon after, newspapers reported that Mr. Sneed said there was a misunderstanding, and that only about 15 gold and 15 silver coins had been found, and the silver cup and the ornate silver scissors he's seen holding in one newspaper's photo, were loaned to him by others. The earliest dated coin was reportedly dated 1757 and another he showed a reporter was dated 1792.

Destin Florida Treasure

A dredge operator named Bill McFarland had been dredging sand for fill to develop the Holiday Isle subdivision in the mid-1960s. This development was where the original entrance to the Choctawhatchee Bay was years before. Around 1965, his dredge was becoming fouled with old ship's timbers and ballast stones that had been buried under 20 feet of sand. Bronze spikes and metal sheathing were also found. But most interesting were the gold coins he was finding. It wasn't until 1968 that he began to tell the story and it soon made the local paper. He had dredged three canals and all the fill was now placed where homes and condominiums were to be built. He was sure gold and other artifacts must be buried in the fill. How much Mr. McFarland ever recovered will probably never be known. The developer of the property was CBS Corp. and was owned by a Congressman, a former State Senator, and a local Public Works Director. McFarland said the major part of the wreck was in the middle of one canal opposite lots 21 and 32 in Block E. The local paper even had a map and photo of where the shipwreck artifacts were being found. McFarland also said some ships timbers were charred and a piece of silver appeared to have been burned. It never gives a date of any of the coins, but the local paper does have a photo of McFarland holding one, and only says it was very similar to the ones being found from the 1715 Fleet wrecks. The coin photo does appear to look like those from 1715. Another photo shows him holding a large brass spike and has some metal sheathing (say brass) with nail holes. Now whether brass or bronze or some composite type sheathing, I couldn't tell, but if the coins are from the 18th century, the ship's material seems to date the wreck much later. The Holiday Isle development lies between the Gulf and the Old Pass Lagoon, where many a ship over the centuries have passed. Was there more than one wreck he found? The state was soon notified about the finds and sent their archaeologist to investigate. I could only find a few articles regarding the find, the last two were very brief, one about the legality of it all, and the final one showed a photo of McFarland, Robert Williams, who was the State Director of Archives and History, and State Archaeologist Carl Clausen, at the Holiday Isle site, with Clausen holding a piece of the ship's timber. I'm sure some sort of state report must exist about what was observed. This I'd like to see.

A Haunted Reef

I'll leave this chapter with a story I uncovered in an 1891 issue of the *Salt Lake Tribune* titled "A Haunted Reef," by Rene Bache. As I once had a part-time business cleaning boat bottoms, changing zincs, and recovering lost items, I can certainly relate. While reading it, I drifted back in time and could visualize how Florida looked over 100 years ago. Like many treasure stories, most are purely fiction, though a few are based upon some facts. The name of the Florida Key mentioned in the story does exist! Any basis in fact? You be the judge. Enjoy!

> My business is diving. The trade isn't romantic as most people think it. There isn't anything worth telling about going down in the water to scrape barnacles off the bottom of vessels, or mend holes in them. That's what I do mostly, though now and then there's a wreck, and I'm employed to fetch up property, or more likely to get corpses. Those are unpleasant, but then the pay is extra. Sorrowing relatives are the most liberal folks I have to deal with,

Commercial divers in the Keys, circa 1910. Courtesy of the Monroe County Library, Key West.

"THE VONSTER SNAPPED ME UP AS A BIG FISH DOES A MINNOW."

Illustration from the story "A Haunted Reef," by Rene Bache. *The Salt Lake Tribune*, 1891.

and they'll often come up $10 an hour without haggling a bit. It's worth it too.

All the same, the work is sort of precarious. It's by the job, ordinarily, and there's times when for a long while I earn little or nothing. A wreck may be a godsend then, especially if lives are lost; but I'm not hankering after another such as the one I was hired to dive for three years ago. That is what I was going to tell you about, because I'm very sure that no other man ever had an experience like it. Of course, you're at liberty to say that it was a delusion and all that, but I'm an honest man and a Christian, and you're welcome to my oath that what I say is a solemn fact. If it wasn't true, I wouldn't own this little house today, and my wife, God bless her, mightn't be putting a baby of mine to sleep in that bedroom yonder.

Work was pretty slack in Charleston Harbor in December 1888. I remember the date well, because about that time I was in awful trouble, not only was I out of money, having had nothing to do for weeks, but things threatened to go smash about a matrimonial project I had on hand. To put it in these words—I was in love with the sweetest little bit of womanhood that ever drew breath, and thanks to the reckless way in which I'd spent every cent I earned while having no thought beyond bachelorhood, I didn't have a dollar of my own to show the old gentleman I wanted for a father-in-law.

I could understand the way he looked at it well enough. My business was uncertain, and even dangerous sometimes. He liked me, but he didn't want to take chances for his daughter's happiness. What he said was: "Show me that you are a bit ahead in the world and can support her. Put a couple thousand dollars in her name, just to stand between her and want if something should happen, and my girl is yours."

Now, you can imagine how I felt. Only two thousand dollars between myself and heaven. Yet how was I to get it? You might almost as well said two million, the possibility of procuring it seemed so remote. Even if I saved every penny, it would take me years. What might happen meanwhile? No man who hasn't known what it is to be in such a position can imagine the agony of it.

The blackest hour of my life I spent one evening in that month of December, in my little lodging near the waterfront, eating my heart out with the thought of what might be so easily attained if only I had two thousand dollars. Two thousand dollars! Why, it seemed so small a matter to stand between two lovers and bliss. Yet what a hopeless sum of money from our point of view.

It was a bare little room I had in the lodging-house, almost unfurnished, with not much in it besides a cot-bed, a chair or two, and a queer, three-cornered table with a smoky lamp on it. Poor as it was, I owed two weeks' rent for it. The lamp threw shadows of myself in all sorts of shapes upon the wall and ceiling, as I walked about and thought and thought until it seemed I should go crazy. What made me most miserable of all was that I had suggested to my girl this very afternoon, in a moment of desperation, that she should marry me anyhow, against the old man's wish. She refused in such a way—not angry, but only shocked, and as if I had lost something in her eyes—that I could almost have cut my throat for having done it.

The sound of footsteps coming up the stair broke in on my thoughts. There were two persons, I judged from the noise, and one man was lame. His crutch went "clump, clump" up the steps. When they got to the top one of them laughed. I shall never forget that laugh, because I heard it many times afterward. It always made a sort of chill down my backbone.

There came a knock at the door, and a tall man in a black cape-coat entered. It occurred to me off-hand that I had never seen a living person look so like a corpse as he did. Not only was his clean-shaved face deathly white, or rather, gray, and his lips colorless, but the frame of his body had so little flesh on it that he was hardly more than a literal skeleton. He was followed by quite a different individual—the one with the crutch.

The lame man was not more than five feet high, but very muscular. I remember being struck by that at once, because in place of an overcoat he wore a slight jacket of worsted. The most remarkable thing about him, however, was an extraordinary scar down one side of his face, which I afterwards learned had been made by the slash of a "curvo"—the deadly curved knife that the Chileans use. One of his eyes had been destroyed by the cut, which extended nearly to the chin and had healed in such a way that, when he smiled his mouth was drawn up on one side in a distorted fashion, so as to produce a most ghastly effect.

It was the tall one who began the talking. He sat down in the chair I offered him and went right to business.

"You are a diver?" he said.

"That is my trade." I replied.

"I am told," he added, "that you understand your business and are to be trusted."

"I hope so," I admitted.

"The latter point is very necessary," he said. "If we employ your services, one condition will be absolute secrecy. You will be required to take an oath."

That made me feel a little nervous. I didn't much like the looks of my visitors any way. Between the corpse in the cape-coat and the one-eyed man with the scar there wasn't much to choose for agreeableness. The notion of sharing a secret with them wasn't pleasant.

"You are accustomed to fetch valuables from sunken wrecks, I believe?" said the tall man.

"Yes, sir."

"At how many fathoms' depth can you work effectively?"

"Fifteen fathoms certainly," I answered. "I have worked as deep as twenty fathoms, but not for long, on account of the pressure."

"Very well so far. You do not object, I suppose, to going a long distance for a job, if the pay corresponds?"

"It depends on what the pay is to be."

"We will satisfy you on that point. Secrecy being guaranteed, we are willing to pay $1,000 for one month of your time. You will have to travel several hundred miles, however, expenses being allowed."

"That is big money!" I said, quite astonished. "Where is the place?"

"You will know in due time. In fact, you will not be informed on that subject until we arrive there. Furthermore, before any steps are taken we shall require you to swear that you will never under any circumstances reveal anything respecting the transaction. So long as you keep faith all will be well, but, we give you clearly to understand that if you break it you will not escape us. It is as well to have these matters thoroughly settled beforehand."

"You mean that you-you fear the law?" I asked.

"Perhaps. However, that is not your affair. Do the work as we direct, keep your mouth shut and you will receive the money. There the bargain ends."

"I won't do it." I said, drawing back. "A thousand dollars means a good deal to me, but even for that money I won't go into such a blind scheme with strangers like you. How do I know that it mightn't get me into prison?"

"We will make it $2,000," replied the tall man, quietly."

Two thousand dollars! Why, that sum meant all the world to me. A month's work, and I could come back and marry the girl I love. I shivered and hesitated.

"Well, what do you say?" asked the corpse in the cape-coat. "Will you undertake the job for that price, or shall we find another diver? We are liberal, but we mean business."

"Will you give me any guarantee that I shall not be obliged to take part in anything criminal?" I said.

"We promise you that," answered the tall man. "In fact, you will be at liberty to withdraw in such a case. All we demand is secrecy on your part, because otherwise we might be placed in peril. But there is no danger for you whatsoever. You see, I speak frankly. I cannot perceive why you should hesitate."

"I don't any longer." I said. "Two thousand dollars, you say? It's a bargain. But I must be sure of getting my pay."

"We will give you $500 when we start, and the balance when the job is finished."

"Then it is agreed," I said. "When do we start?"

"Within forty-eight hours. You will be notified as to the time of departure, and I will hand you the $500 at the railway station."

"You say that my expenses will be paid?"

"Yes. You will be required to bring with you all the necessary apparatus for diving. We must not lack anything. You have the equipment I presume?"

"I do not own an air-pump."

"Then I will buy one. You have everything else?"

"Everything."

"All right. Be in readiness, and pack your equipment in as small compass as possible. We wish you good night."

When the door closed behind them I dropped into a chair in a cold perspiration. The whole thing was like a dream. Two thousand dollars! Why, it seemed like Providence. Yet I felt afraid. What could this extraordinary job be that was worth such a sum? There was something wrong about it somewhere, certainly, for the corpse in the cape-coat had implied as much. At the same time he had said that there was no danger for me and that I should not be obliged to do anything criminal. All right so far; but the men themselves were so strange and even horrible. I didn't like the notion of having to take an oath of secrecy either. However, that wouldn't prevent me from backing out if I found I daren't go ahead. Anyway, I was in for it, and, if all turned out well, what happiness it would be!

The next morning I went to Caroline and told her the whole business. She wanted me to break the contract. She didn't approve of my going away to an unknown place with two such men. Finally she cried, and begged me to give it up.

But I had made up my mind already. I couldn't help thinking that it was a risky venture somehow, but I proposed to gamble for that $2,000. So I wiped away her tears, and cheered her up a little by telling her that I would take the best possible care of myself and be on the watch for mischief. We arranged it that she should know when I was to leave, and see me off.

That afternoon I got a note by messenger. It had no signature, and read simply: "Eleven-thirty train tomorrow morning for Jacksonville, Florida. Be at station promptly with all traps."

By the time I received this communication I had made all my arrangements and was ready to go. That evening I spent with Caroline, and the next morning we went to the railway station together. I found my two employers there. They were conversing together earnestly in a corner of the waiting room. The lame one with the scarred face shook hands with me and offered to do so with

Caroline, but she shrunk away. At that he laughed. It was the same mirthless and unnatural giggle that I had heard on the night before the last when my strange visitors were coming up the stairs. On the rare occasions when the man uttered it his face became queerly distorted, the corner of his mouth on one side being drawn up in a hideous fashion. I always felt like shivering when I heard it. However, he only said: "I know I ain't a beauty, but never mind."

At that moment, the corpse in the cape-coat drew me aside and handed me a roll of money, asking me to count it over. I did so, and found that it amounted to just $500, all in good twenty-dollar banknotes. That made the thing seem real for the first time.

"That binds the contract," he said. "We have decided that our final consultation and understanding shall be deferred until we get to Jacksonville tomorrow afternoon. You have all the traps with you?"

"Yes; I've had them taken around to the baggage room. A trunk and a box are all; they have my name printed on them."

"I will see to them with our own luggage," said the tall man. "The train leaves in just fifteen minutes."

I spent those fifteen minutes saying good-by to Caroline. She begged me again to give up the whole affair, declaring that my two acquaintances were the most dreadful looking men she had ever seen in her life and that she believed that they would surely play me foul in some way. But I told her that it was too late to go back now, since I had taken the money and made the agreement, and I did the best I could to console her, finally handling her $400 of the amount I had received before I stepped upon the train. The last I saw of her, she was sitting on a baggage truck and weeping into a handkerchief. So I didn't start out on that journey in any very cheerful frame of mind, notwithstanding the little fortune I hoped to earn.

There wasn't anything very remarkable that occurred on the way to Jacksonville. I felt so depressed, not being able somehow to shake off my melancholy, that I sat by myself sulkily, while my two employers played euchre in a solemn sort of fashion in the smoking compartment. It was a relief to me when we arrived and were driven to the St. James Hotel.

After dinner the tall man, whose name was Crawley, told me that I should join him and his partner in the room which they had engaged for themselves. We sat down around a table and the talk went straight to business. I was then informed for the first time that I was engaged for the purpose of getting certain treasures of large value from a sunken vessel. That much had been hinted at before, but I was now told that the craft in question had been wrecked on the Florida reefs, among the coral islands called "Keys" at the south end of the peninsula. They did not mention the locality exactly, but said that the spot was perfectly known to themselves, so that we should have no difficulty in reaching it. We were to leave Jacksonville the next morning and would be obliged to make part of our journey by sail-boat.

Before going any further, I was required to enter into a solemn agreement respecting my part in the transaction, guaranteeing that I would never under any circumstances reveal any facts concerning it. How it was that subsequent occurrences released me from this bond of secrecy will appear before my story is ended.

Considerably more at ease in mind now that I understood more definitely what was expected of me, I left Jacksonville with my employers the following morning. We took the steamer "Volusia" for more than 150 miles southward by the St. John's River, and after some delay caused by getting aground on a shoal, arrived forty-eight hours later at a flourishing little town called Titusville. Titusville was founded twenty years ago by an interesting old gentleman named Titus, who had been a desperado of some note in his time and had been compelled to seek the seclusion of what was then a wilderness by reason of having cut to pieces with a bowie knife an inoffensive person whose only weapon of defense was a blue cotton umbrella. The town is near the head of the great lagoon called Indian River, whereon are situated numerous plantations which produce the finest oranges in the world.

After some bargaining, Mr. Crawley succeeded in purchasing quite a large sail-boat, with a half-cabin which afforded a narrow shelter as well as sufficient room for storing a quantity of provisions. We loaded those aboard, together with our boxes, and set sail with a fair wind.

Indian River is fully four miles broad some distance below Titusville, but its lower part is comparatively narrow. I had never seen so beautiful a country, the landscape in December being green with all the loveliness of summer and the air as balmy as a June day. The shores were dotted with groves of ripening oranges, with long stretches of cypress woods bearing streamers of Florida moss and here and there groves of palmetto trees. We sailed about a hundred miles down the lagoon to Jupiter Inlet, where there is an opening through to the Atlantic and a lighthouse also. Passing out into the ocean at that point, our voyage was outside until we reached Cape Florida, from which point it was plain sailing in calm water behind a long string of big islands.

During the journey, the weather being remarkably clear and the breeze constantly fair, I had an opportunity to become somewhat better acquainted with my employers. Crawley was a silent man and not at all communicative, but the other, whose name was Grimshaw, found plenty to talk about. He was full of the scheme for recovering the treasure, and, now that we were fairly embarked in pursuit of it, he showed no hesitation in telling me pretty nearly everything about it. So he beguiled the tedious passage for both of us with the details of what struck me as a very remarkable story.

It seems that the recent war between Chile and Peru had wound up with the sacking of Lima, the capital of the latter country. While buildings were blown up and public works of art recklessly destroyed by the victorious soldiers, eager for blood and plunder, the churches were generally respected. There was one such sacred edifice, however, which did not escape the seekers after booty, it having become known that a large sum of money and other valuables had been hidden there for safe-keeping. The building was broken into at night by armed men and a great quantity of gold was taken away together with rich ornaments belonging to the church.

The party of plunderers that looted the church was not composed of Chileans, but of a crew of desperate characters, which, for the sake of pillage, had sought the scene of strife in a vessel commanded by a citizen of the United States. Having transferred the booty to the ship, they sailed away as promptly as possible. It was next a question whither to carry it. The first mate of the brig was none other than my friend Grimshaw, who told the tale with a horrible relish that showed how much he had enjoyed the tragic occurrences which led up to the robbery of the treasure. I could understand already why it was that secrecy on my part had been demanded as a condition of my employment. However, it was none of my business how they got it, and I felt rather relieved in mind than otherwise at learning the facts.

The captain of the piratical craft, who was picturesquely named Suaggs, seems to have been very much feared by the cut-throats he commanded. For reasons best known to himself, and not at all understood by the rest of the ship's company, he refused to sail for San Francisco, where the plunder could readily have been disposed of, and deliberately started southward toward the Horn, not declaring for what port he was bound. By the time they had rounded the Horn, and turned the vessels nose toward the north Atlantic, the crew was in a mood for mutiny. One night, Captain Suaggs got very drunk, struck one of the men, and was promptly murdered with a knife. First Mate Grimshaw, whom I suspect of having had some hand in the tragedy, took command.

"All went well after that little event until we reached the West Indies," said Grimshaw in telling the story. "I had made up my mind to steer for Havana, divide the treasure, and see what could be done toward disposing of it there. Unfortunately, the weather turned very foul, and after four days of the worst storm I ever encountered, the brig was driven at night upon the Florida reefs. Both masts went by the board when we struck, and the vessel would have gone to pieces within a few moments, only that a great wave took her and hurled her bodily over the reef between two keys shaped like a horseshoe and into deep water beyond, where she sank immediately. I grabbed a stick of timber and got ashore on one of the keys, more dead than alive. Not another soul on board was saved; and small loss it was for a more precious set of rascals never swabbed a deck, and I had all along feared that there would be trouble when it came to sharing the booty.

"At the same time, my own prospects weren't bright just then; I spent a night of exposure on the coral key, with no shelter but a few mangrove bushes and the storm howling above the thunder of the breakers. Luckily, the next morning it broke, and the weather turned beautifully fair, though the waves still rolled in tremendously high and washed half over the little islet where I had found a landing. As I said, there was a sort of horseshoe formed by two long keys, with the ends of the horseshoe toward the mainland and a stretch of reef that was just awash in the middle. That is as I found it when I had a chance to survey the situation by daylight. The mainland was not over ten miles away, but to reach it seemed hopeless, partly because of sharks.

"Presumably I would have had to take my choice between starving and being gobbled by the sharks, if it hadn't been that a wrecking schooner hove in sight about noon. I was meditating how I could catch or kill a lonely pelican that had lighted on the islet, and wondering how long it would take me to perish of thirst, when I saw the sail and jumped up and shouted with all my might. Within half-an-hour I was safe on board the little vessel, which was out hunting for wrecks after the storm. This is quite a profitable business among the Florida reefs, those engaged in it usually plundering whatever craft they find stranded, or at all events grabbing everything they can lay hands on and claiming a share as salvage. In this case the captain of the schooner was much disappointed at finding no booty. I knew better than to tell him of the treasure that was sunk behind the reef, and all he got was my thanks for conveying me to Key West, whence I worked my passage to Charleston on board of a lugger.

"The captain asked me rather mysteriously if I had noticed anything queer while I was on the key. I said no, except for a remarkably big shark.

"'Was it a real shark?' asked the captain.

"'Why, certainly,' I answered. 'Don't you suppose I know a shark when I see one?'

"'Mebbe so,' said he taking a long whiff at his pipe.

"'What on earth are you driving at?' I asked.

"'Oh, nothing,' he said. 'I was only just askin.' You never heard, I s'pose, that Horseshoe Key is haunted.

"'Is the ghost male or female?' I inquired, jokingly.

"'It ain't human' he replied. And that's the last word I could ever get him to say on the subject."

If Grimshaw's story is to be believed, he had in view from the first idea of recovering the treasure from the wreck, but he perceived that the thing could not be done without a considerable investment of money. Therefore, happening to meet in Charleston a former partner of his who had means, namely, Mr. Crawley, he confided the whole business to him and an agreement was made between them to dive for the valuables and divide the proceeds. Learning that I was an expert diver and accustomed to searching wrecks, they employed my services, stipulating secrecy for two reasons—first, because the matter was not one to be blabbed, and secondly, because the treasure had not been come by honestly to begin with. I thought it at the time rather a mistake on their part to confide so much to me as they did, but the knowledge I subsequently gained of their plans led me to conclude that they knew what they were about.

Before leaving the horseshoe shaped key, Grimshaw had made sure of their location, so that he could find them again, and it is thus that we were able to steer straight to them. It was still the loveliest weather imaginable, and sailing among the keys was like a summer dream. The water in that region is clear as crystal, so that one can see the bottom at a depth of twenty fathoms with a perfect distinctness. Bright-colored fishes—blue, scarlet and every other tint of the rainbow—are plainly visible to the eye, as they swim about over the white coral sand far below, the boat almost seeming to float in the air. Here and there the sea is dotted with islands of coral, some merely shoals washed over by the waves, while others are fringed with mangrove bushes, and the bigger ones bear trees and a varied vegetation. These are the "Keys."

Waterfowl of many kinds frequent them, and pelicans and long-legged cranes walk about solemnly upon their margins.

Our destination, when we reached it, I found to be one of the most beautiful spots in the world. The horseshoe formed by the two keys was completed in shape by the strip of reef connecting them together, which in calm weather slightly out of water. We arrived there, I well remember, on the afternoon of December 23—two days before Christmas. It was none too soon, for within an hour a big squall came up from the southwest, and it soon blew great guns. We were safe enough in the little harbor, but my companions were angry at the delay. They were anxious to set to work at diving for the treasure immediately. However, before we had time to do so much as locate the sunken wreck, the storm was upon us, and we were compelled to seek shelter in the crowded little cabin.

In some way my experience thus far had been rather pleasant than otherwise, but I can't express to you the distress I suffered from the necessity of associating on terms of such close intimacy and companionship with the two extraordinary men I have described. I know one of them to be a cut-throat by his own confession and I did not doubt that the other was quite as bad. But it was not on that account chiefly that they were disagreeable to me. There was something about both of them that was horrible and well-nigh inhuman, it seemed to me. I can't tell which I loathed most, the one-eyed man with the crutch or his corpse-like partner. Once in a while I would catch Crawley's fishy eye fixed upon me with a look that have me a strangely uncomfortable feeling, though I didn't know exactly why. He rarely had a word to say, but remained apparently wrapped in his thoughts, never taking any part in the handling of the boat, which he left entirely to Grimshaw and me.

The storm lasted until about midnight on the December 24—Christmas Eve. Then the weather cleared, and Christmas Day was a beautiful one, a gentle breeze from the south scarcely making a ripple on the embayed water behind the bend of the horseshoe. Our first move was to get our traps and provisions out of the boat, drying in the bright sun whatever had become moist from the soaking of the rain. We set up on the key a tent which we had brought with us, and also put together a little stove for cooking purposes. I shot half a dozen chocolate-colored curlew, Grimshaw caught a small loggerhead turtle, and soon we had a good breakfast in course of preparation. We ate with good appetites, notwithstanding our anxiety to find the exact location of the wreck, and to make sure that the treasure was still there in the sunken bulk. I myself could not help sharing the excitement which my employers felt concerning the issue of the adventure.

Accordingly, as soon as we had done breakfast, we shoved off the boat, and paddled in the direction of the reef on which the vessel had been wrecked. Behind it was deep water, as much as a dozen fathoms, I should say, and there, sure enough, lay the broken hulk on the bottom of white coral sand, every part of her as clearly visible in the crystal water as if she had been on dry land. The story Grimshaw had told was real enough to me now, after we had found the ship just as he had said we should find it, and his account of the treasure inside of her no longer seemed to me a fairy tale. I was as anxious to begin operations for recovering it as my companions were, but at that point Crawley asserted the authority which he had all along assumed-over the expedition and declared that the diving must not be done in the day-time. He pointed to three sails that were in sight, and said:

"Those are probably wreckers. I've heard it said that they can scent plunder 100 miles. Do you think that we would be wise to risk being caught at this work by daylight, after all our trouble and expense, only to divide the trea-sure with others? Oh, no. At it is, I have feared lest the object of our presence here might be inquired about, and I suggest that, in such a case we shall pre-tend to be on a fishing expedition. I propose that our diving shall be done a night, and I have brought along for that express purpose an electric lamp of the newest pattern for diving purposes. There ought to be no difficulty about fishing up the valuables inside of a few hours work in this calm water, and my plan is that we shall start in to-night, when it will be starlight and no moon."

Grimshaw and I saw the force of what Crawley said, sad so, we made all necessary arrangements for diving that night. We unstepped the mast and took it out of the boat, together with everything that wasn't necessary for our purpose. Then we set up amidships the equipment which is used to supply the diver with air while he is under water, and I unpacked my gear. It was about 9 o'clock in the evening and as dark as we could wish when we pad-dled out to the wreck and began operations.

Somehow, although I had been long accustomed to such work, when it came to finally undertaking the job, I felt a strange sense of dread that I could not account for. My companions helped me to adjust my helmet, to which we attached the electric light, and, thus prepared, I was lowered into the depths below.

There was no difficulty in climbing aboard the wreck, which lay like a dead thing on the coral bottom. She was fairly broken in two in the middle, having been "hogged" by the reef, as the term is, when she was carried over it by the breakers. Both masts were gone close to the deck, but all the loose spars had drifted away and nothing was left but the bare hulk, into which I might have crawled through a big hole in her side.

The deck was inclined at an angle of about 45 degrees. I clambered up to the companion-way which led to the cabin, because it was in that direction that I had been instructed to make my search. You must understand that the vessel was built with a poop deck, so that the upper part of the cabin was above the level of the deck. Three or four steps descended from the deck into the cabin. I crawled through the doorway and found a scene such as is not unfamiliar to a diver but which would seem appalling enough to anyone else. All the furniture in the cabin was in a confused mass overhead, toward the side of the room which was uppermost, and mingled with this floating debris were three corpses of human beings, the flesh half eaten by eels and fishes.

My business on this occasion, however, was not to resurrect dead bodies. Merely glancing around upon the scene of death and destruction, gloomily lighted as it was by the electric lamp on my helmet. I made my way through the cabin to a door on the side opposite from the companionway. All the time, you must remember, I was compelled to crawl along a floor that slanted up-hill. Finally, I reached the door and paused to get from my little diver's knapsack and chisel that I had brought for the very purpose which I had now to accomplish. The wood had swollen so much that it took me nearly half an hour to break the door open.

The broken door gave admittance to a compartment about ten feet long and shaped like a half oval. It occupied the entire space inside the hollow of the vessel back of the cabin. Such spaces are commonly utilized on board small ships for stowing valuables or liquors, access to it being only to be had through the cabin itself. I found the compartment fairly crowded with a medley of objects in such indescribable confusion that I could not for the life of me make any selection. There seemed to be a mass of junk of all sorts and I at once perceived that to clear it out and get at whatever was of most value would require considerable time. Now, one can't stay down at such a depth for very long without difficulty and so I concluded to get to the surface again and report progress. I managed to disengage from the rest of the stuff what looked like a small iron-bound trunk, and this I fastened to my belt with a piece of rope that I found handy, because in that way I could get it to the top of the water more easily. I could hardly have lifted the little trunk on dry land, but the density of the water made it easy to carry comparatively. Half lifting and half dragging it I succeeded in making my way out through the companionway to the deck.

It is now that I come to the dreadful and horrifying incident without which this story would hardly have been worth the telling. I had not fairly set foot upon the deck, dragging the little trunk with me, when there rose from behind the black hulk of the vessel a gigantic object. To describe it is difficult, because it did not look like anything real that was ever seen in this world. It was an enormous fish—yet not a fish, inasmuch as it looked to have no solid form and body. A shape it seemed, and nothing more—the phantom of a vast shark. Not less than one-half as long as the ship itself it was, and it floated slowly toward me with jaws distended, turning slightly on its side. I saw two rows of great saw-like teeth. Most wonderful and contributing above all else to the spectral aspect of the monster was a sort of phosphorescent radiance that seemed part of it.

In my terror of the ghastly creature, I could have shrieked aloud, only that my cry was stifled in my helmet. My blood froze in my veins. I was unable even to make an attempt to escape, fascinated as I was by the glare of the Thing's hideous eye, as it swam slowly toward me. With a frantic effort, I jerked the signal rope which connected me with the boat, but it was too late. An instant more and the monster had snapped me up as a big fish does a minnow, closing its awful jaws upon me.

Imagine how feelings of horror and amazement swept over me when I found myself actually passing through the body of the phantom—for such it was—and presently I was dragged into the boat by my companions, almost unconscious from fright. I must have fainted away immediately, for I remember nothing until I came to myself in the tent on the key, whither I had been conveyed.

The view that me my gaze when consciousness returned was so dreadful that for some time I could not believe it real. I thought it must be some horrible nightmare. My two companions were lying on the ground, weltering in blood, and apparently dead. I got to my feet with difficulty and swallowed a gulp of whisky from a bottle that stood on a rude improvised table of our own construction. Alongside the bottle stood an empty flask with a single lighted candle in the neck of it which threw a flickering illumination upon the dismal scene.

I took the candle in my hand, and stooping down, examined the body of Grimshaw, which across the doorway of the tent. He was quite dead, the blood still flowing from a knife wound in the temple. Perceiving that my attentions could be of no benefit to him, I turned to the other. To my surprise, Crawley was still alive. As I propped him up in my arms, he met my gaze with his fishy eye and made a motion toward his mouth. I poured some liquor down his throat, and he spoke in a husky voice and with evident effort.

"We fought over the treasure," he said. "Grimshaw—shot me—here,—I cut him. See—it was a good stroke. He is dead. No—I can't live. I am hurt here—internally. Now you will have all the gold. You are a lucky man. If this—hadn't happened, we meant to kill you and bury you here—on the key—so that no one should—ever know—the secret."

There came a rattle in his throat, and with a gasp, he died.

I buried them both in the sand of the coral key at daybreak, so that they met the very same fate which they had intended for myself. The little iron trunk I found had been open. It was filled with gold pieces, and it was doubtless over this they began quarreling. I lost no time in putting the tent and other property aboard the sail-boat, clearing away every trace of our visiting the place, and that afternoon set sail for Key West. There I sold the small craft, and, shipping the diving apparatus to Charleston as freight, I took passage in a coasting vessel for home, carrying with me the box of gold. It contained just $4,200 in Peruvian coin, and the sum made a very nice little portion for Caroline and myself to begin married life upon.

As for the bulk of the treasure, it still lies in deep water behind Horseshoe Key, 80 miles northeast by east from Key West. Anyone who wishes may go in search of it. For myself, I have had enough of the mysterious treasure and the phantom shark that guards it.

8

Shipwrecks

As in the previous editions, the ships tonnage is listed as gross tons unless otherwise noted. In this book, I've listed the shipwrecks by years. The first two editions listed wrecks by sections and date (section 1, Panhandle; 2, Florida's west coast; 3, Lower Keys/Tortugas; 4, Upper Keys; 5, Lower East coast; 6, Upper East coast; 7, Inland waterways; 8, Unknown Florida locations). At the very end of all new wrecks listed or at the end of any previously listed wrecks where correct "section" location is now known or changed is the "section number" in parentheses. New shipwrecks not previously listed in the first two editions of *Shipwrecks of Florida* are listed first after each year, and the ship's name is in All CAPS. Any previously listed shipwrecks in the first and second edition of *Shipwrecks of Florida* are listed after the "new" wrecks, and the ship's name is not all caps and include new/additional or corrected information (all are preceded by the page number they are located on the second edition of *Shipwrecks of Florida*). As mentioned in the foreword of this book, this new book is meant as an accompaniment to the second edition of *Shipwrecks of Florida*. The locations of many of the wrecks may be spelled differently as I used the spelling as given from many wreck reports, so you may see Gulph, or Gulf of Florida, Carysford, or Carysfort Reef, Martiers, or Martyrs Reefs. Many 19th-century reports of wrecks do not give the date it wrecked, so I can only assume it's close to the report date, which may be months or more. If I list a wreck in the year 1730, and the report date is March 1730, it's very possible the vessel wrecked in 1729, so bear that in mind.

Supposed verified GPS coordinates for some of the wrecks in this book and previous editions are at the end of this chapter, along with the GPS coordinates for the shipwrecks included in Florida's Underwater Preserves. It includes unknown wrecks that hopefully this book or previous editions will help to identify. I've started with wrecks from the west end of the Panhandle going east and down and around the coast of Florida up to the Florida/Georgia

"The Storm." *Shipwrecks & Tales of the Sea*, 1887.

Timbers of an 1860s era shipwreck off Hillsboro Beach. Many would not recognize this as a shipwreck, so be aware of what to look for as discussed in "Shipwrecks of Florida."

border. Coordinates for the 1715 and 1733 fleet wrecks are also listed in this chapter after those dates. Coordinates not verified or just approximate are listed after any wreck associated with those coordinates. For more information on GPS coordinates or for websites offering information, see the bibliography.

After 1900 I've used the following abbreviations for many gas and diesel vessels: Here are the abbreviations: G/V (gas vessel); G/P (gas passenger vessel); G/C (gas cargo vessel); G/F (gas fishing vessel); G/T (gas tow vessel); G/Y (gas yacht); O/V (oil vessel); O/P (oil passenger vessel); O/T (oil tow vessel); O/C (oil cargo vessel); O/F (oil fishing vessel); O/Y (oil yacht); F/V (fishing vessel).

1500–1600S?

1) *ELIZABETH*—The one survivor of the ship *Elizabeth* told the story how he was wrecked on the Florida coast and saved by the Spanish, he being a Christian was treated very well by them, though his tale tells how cruelly the Spanish treated the native Americans as he witnessed some of their torture and executions. He goes on to say how brave the native Americans were and mentions one in particular, a war captain by the name of Difcaptici. *Source:* British Magazine, 6/1/1747, taken from story *The Moralist No X.* (8)

1553

1) Page 22. **Spanish Fleet**—Looks like this fleet was scattered as some wrecked off Mexico and elsewhere. *Source:* 13.

1554

1) Page 206. *Santa Catalina*—Chaunu says the gold and silver was not taken by the French and that she was lost later in the Gulf. *Source:* 13. (8)

1555

1) *SAN ESTEBAN* and the *SANTA MARIA la BLANCA*—Capt. Damyan Martin, and Capt. Francisco de Sanctana. Both 220-ton naos. Both lost on the coast of Florida and some of the gold and silver was saved. *Source:* 13. (8)

1563

1) Page 49. *Capitana* and the *El Angel Bueno* (Capt. Sebastian de Quesada)—The 1563 Spanish treasure fleet ran into a hurricane after leaving

Havana in the Florida Straits and the ships were soon separated. These two were lost. Only 30 survived from the *El Angel Bueno,* having drifted in the ship's boat for 6 days until rescued off South Carolina. Three ships made it back to Santo Domingo and the others to the Azores. Both those lost carried a large quantity of treasure. As to their whereabouts, that remains a mystery. Fontaneda, a Spanish shipwreck survivor who had been captured in 1549 and living with the Florida Calusa tribe, mentions in his memoir having come across one of these wrecks in Florida. I originally listed it as wrecked near Charlotte Harbor, but new evidence points to the Keys and that it is the *El Angel Bueno.* The Calusa did salvage some treasure. One group believes they are now on the trail of the wreck in the area of American Shoals. The other is said to have wrecked anywhere from Bermuda to a cay off Cuba. *Source:* 9; 13; Research by Robert Westrick & the Bronze Cannon Corp. (8)

One of the five bronze cannon found in the 1980s near American Shoals. Possibly from the 1563 *El Angel Bueno.* Bill Robinson, Bronze Cannon Corp.

1586

1) Page 208. **Ships of the New Spain Fleet**—Chaunu says five vessels were lost at the entrance to the Florida Straits, though the crews and most, if not all the treasure, was saved. Possible Florida wrecks. The five he lists are:

a) *Nuestra Señora de la Concepción*—600-ton nao, Capt. Martin de Vittoria.

b) *Nuestra Señora de los Remedios*—120-ton nao, Capt. Francisco Ximenez.

c) *San Juan*—120-ton nao, Capt, Martin de Irigoyen.

d) *Santa Maria de Jesus*—400-ton nao, Capt. Antonio Jorge.

e) *San Vincente*—50-ton nao, Capt. Blas Gonzales. *Source:* 13.

1589

1) Page 133. **Two ships** of the 1589 New Spain Fleet—Chaunu lists two vessels as lost in the Bahama Channel (Straits of Florida), the **Santa Catalina**, 350-ton nao, Capt. Domingo Ianez Ome, and the **Jesus Maria**, 400-ton nao,

Capt. Francisco Salvago. C. Bonifacio only list the *Jesus Maria* and says lost between Florida and Bermuda. Correct spelling for the commander of the New Spain fleet is: Mártin Perez de Olazabal. If one of these wrecked near Cape Canaveral, the other may also be near. *Source:* 9; 13.

1593

1) *LA NUESTRA SEÑORA de las OLAS*—Spanish merchantman, was lost on the bar coming into St. Augustine for repairs in 1593. *Source:* 38. (6)

1600

1) Page 208. **Spanish nao**—Believe a 50-ton nao, of the Neueva España fleet, Capt. Diego Rodriguez, from Mexico. May have been a "situado" and carried some money for the troops in Florida. Believe it wrecked on the west coast of Florida. *Source:* 13; Misc. research. (8)

1622

1) Pages 65–66. **1622 Spanish Fleet**—The search for treasure from these wrecks has never stopped since I last wrote about them. They are still actively being worked, and though nothing like the 1985 mother lode find on the *Atocha* has been located, treasure is still being found!

Markings on a gold bar recovered from the 1622 wrecks. One can see the royal stamps, the assayer's marks, and the stamp "En Rada." The few with this stamp became known as the EN RADA bars, and the mystery was later solved, as the stamp was associated with the Peña-Randa family of Columbia, who were in the gold smelting business there, and produced gold bars. Information provided by Ernie Richards.

One of the more unique finds from the wreck of the *Atocha*: A pair of ornate silver stirrups. Kane Fisher found one, and Edward Stevens found the other the next year. Captain Edward Stevens.

1624

1) *ENDRACHT*—Dutch ship, wrecked at the mouth of Caloosahatchee River, June or July 1624. Some cannon were salvaged later on. May have had some treasure and cargo of a prize Spanish ship it had captured, and which the crew took back to the Netherlands. *Source:* 16. (2)

1634

1) Page 67. *El Buen Jesus*—Capt. Juan Cuello, 80-ton fragata. This vessel was listed as lost. The fleet ran into a storm at Lat. 27°30' N. Possible Florida wreck. *Source:* 13.

1641

1) Pages 167–68. **The 1641 fleet wrecks**—None of the five ships supposedly lost on the Florida coast have been found that I've heard. The facts about the whole fleet, and how many ships were actually in the fleet is also

a bit sketchy, so could have been more wrecked off Florida than thought. Supposedly 31 ships left Havana. *The Treasure of the Concepcion*, by Peter Earle, says the Nueva España (New Spain) fleet left first without waiting for the Tierra Firme fleet to arrive at Havana. *The Nuestra Señora de la Concepción* was the Almiranta of the fleet, a 600-ton galleon, and her captain was Don Juan de Villavicencio (Chaunu has her tonnage and captain's name different). This ship and probably some others were not in good condition when they left Havana. Capt. Villavicencio wanted to fully repair his ship, as he knew it had problems, and wait for the other fleet to arrive before leaving, plus they were now at the height of hurricane season and were leaving at a time Villavicencio knew could put the whole fleet at risk. His wishes were not heeded though, as the Captain-General, Juan de Campos, had no intention of waiting. It appears vanity was the real reason. Campos did not want to wait for the Tierra Firme fleet to arrive under command of Admiral Francisco Diaz Pimienta. Pimienta was a hero in Spain, and Campos did not want to share any of the glory in returning to Spain with the much-anticipated treasure (Pimienta didn't leave for Spain until 1642). When the hurricane hit, they were all in the Florida Straits/Bahama Channel (most say off St. Augustine), and they were all scattered by the storm though three sank that first day. Most believe any lost off Florida would have been north of St. Augustine, though others think further south. One ship, the *Rosario*, survived and made it into St. Augustine. Another, name unknown, was located by the Spanish after the storm and some treasure salvaged. Two wrecked off Cuba. As for the Capitana and Juan de Campos, they did make it back to Spain, only to wreck at the mouth of the Guadalquivir River, though most of the treasure was salvaged along with much unregistered treasure which Campos had to explain to his superiors. Chaunu lists all 31 ships that left Havana for Spain, though there are some discrepancies as with the *Concepción* mentioned previously:

1) *San Antonio de Padua*—Capt. Juan Idiaquez, 200-ton nao.

2) *El hijo prodigo*—Capt. B. Estebes, 30-ton nao.

3) *San Marcos*—Capt. Juan de Castros, 860-ton galleon.

4) *San Juan Bautista*—Capt. M. de Chavarria, 600-ton galleon.

5) *San Genaro*—Capt. A. de Yruren, 620-ton galleon.

6) *Santa Teresa*—Capt. D. de Ypeñarrieta, 680-ton galleon.

7) *San Geronimo*—Capt. S. de Casabarite, 580-ton galleon.

8) *Santiago de Napoles*—Capt. J. de Cassaos, 500-ton galleon.

9) *Santiago de Galizia*—Capt. P. de Olabarria, 600-ton galleon.

10) *La Concepcion*—Capt. Don Juan de Yzarraga, 406-ton galleon. (per Earle, *Nuestra Señora de la Concepción*—Capt. Villavicencio, 600-ton galleon, Almirante of the fleet under Campos).

11) *San Nicolas*—Capt. D. J. de Chavarri, 400-ton galleon.

12) *Jesus Maria Josefe*—Capt. D. J de Leyba, 600-ton galleon.

13) *San Francisco de Sol*—Capt. D. R. de Contreras, 300-ton galleon.

14) *Nuestra Señora de la Vittoria*—Capt. D. D. Ponce de Leon, 400-ton galleon.

15) *San Francisco Javier* (aka *la Gata*)—Capt. D. A. de Tacio, 60-ton patache.

16) *San Elifonso* (aka *El pajaro*)—Capt. M. de Torre y Ulloa, 60-ton patache.

17) *San Josefe y San Antonio*—Capt. L. de Baroa, 60-ton patache.

18) *Nuestra Señora de la Candelaria y San Francisco*—Capt. J. de Arriola, 330-ton nao.

19) *Santa Cruz y San Josefe*—Capt. M. de Arbide, 270-ton nao.

20) *San Antonio*—Capt. M. de Chavarria, 170-ton nao.

21) *Nuestra Señora de Rosario*—Capt. J. de Narganes, 200-ton nao.

22) *San Diego*—Capt. L. de Trompes, 300-ton nao.

23) *Nuestra Señora de la Esperanza*—Capt. P. de Trujillo, 250-ton nao.

24) *Nuestra Señora de la Candelaria y el Rosario*—Capt. F. Gamarra, 250-ton nao.

25) *Jesus Maria Josefe*—Capt. D. Batista de Chaves, 300-ton nao.

26) *La Esperanza de Dios*—Capt. M. de Lili, 230-ton navio.

27) *San Juan evangelista*—Capt. J. Ruiz (Guillen), 240-ton urca.

28) *Nuestra Señora de Valvaneda*—Capt. A. de Serra, 50-ton ship.

29) *San Pedro y San Pablo*—Capt. Don Juan de Campos, 550-ton nao, Capitana of the fleet.

30) *Nuestra Señora de la Candelaria* (believe changed name to *Nuestra Señora de Atochá y San Josef*)—Capt. G. Belano, 400-ton nao.

31) *Nuestra Señora del Rosario*—Capt. Benlusi Benerio, 80-ton fragata.

Source: 13; 15. (8)

1660

1) Page 134, 232. *San Miguel el Archangel*—Though not positively identified, it's most likely the wreck commonly referred to as the "Jupiter Wreck,"
which was initially known about for years, but found again by lifeguard
Peter Leo just off the beach in 1987. I had the pleasure to dive the wreck
on Allan Gardner's salvage boat when the weather was too rough to work
the 1715 wrecks with my own salvage boat. After moving more than 20 feet
of sand over the site, the bottom would be uncovered. Some of the nicest
looking coins I've ever seen recovered from a wreck were from this site. You
could actually read the dates on some while on the bottom. The site is still
being worked by Dominic Addario and others, and I believe the remaining
wreckage lies to the north of Jupiter Inlet. I found a silver spoon I believe is
from this wreck on the beach just north of the inlet after a good northeaster
washed much of the beach sand away down to the bedrock.

Diver recovering a coin on the "Jupiter Wreck."

Two eight real coins dated 1658 from the Potosi mint, along with a silver spoon, recovered from the "Jupiter Wreck" site.

1695

1) Page 104. *HMS Winchester*—Remnants of the wreck are still visible today. She actually wrecked because she did not have enough men to man her. Most all the crew had died or were sick from scurvy, and she eventually ran aground and sank near Carysfort Reef. Found in 1938 and much salvaged in 1939, she was again salvaged in the 1950s. Probably the most interesting artifact recovered from the wreck was a lime juicer! If only they had used it! See GPS coordinates at the end of the chapter. *Source:* 8.

1705

1) *NUESTRA SEÑORA de ROSARIO y SANTIAGO APOSTAL*—Part of the Spanish Windward Fleet out of Vera Cruz, she wrecked during a storm in Pensacola Bay in 1705. Built in Mexico, 450 tons, originally had 44 guns. The wreck was found by a diver in the 1980s, and the University of West Florida has excavated it and identified it as the *Apostol*. *Source:* Research available from University of West Florida. (1)

1715

1) Pages 135–36. **1715 Spanish Plate Fleet**—I didn't go into that much detail in the previous editions, as others have devoted whole books to this fleet. I worked many years on these wrecks. In 1988, Bob Weller and I recovered three gold coins one day on the Douglas Beach site. At this time, the site was divided in two lease areas, with Richard McAllister holding the lease on the south side of the site, and Mel Fisher with the lease to the north side. I was working for Bob who sublet from McAllister. Word soon got out about our gold find which was just on the south side of the dividing line between the two lease areas. Treasure salvor Mo Moliar was working Mel's lease area, and as soon as heard about our find, his boat, the *Virgalona*, was anchored over the north side of the dividing line from where we found our coins. He immediately found millions in gold escudos! We were so close, but yet, so far! A few years later, we located some 1715 cannon previously unknown on the north end of the "Cabin Wreck." We briefly worked around them, but found nothing else except an anchor from another wreck only a few feet away. I tied an airbag to it, towed it to one of Mel's salvage boat, who with their crane lifted it up, and it now resides in my backyard. I ran into Mel that night, and he said to keep working around those cannon. I didn't heed his advice, as we went back to another area where we were finding silver coins. We were only working the wrecks about four days a week as we still had to make money, and soon left for our regular jobs. Again, Mo, who was also working the "Cabin" site at this time, heard about our cannon finds, was anchored over them as soon as we left, and found some beautiful gold jewelry nearby. If only I had listened to Mel!

Much is still being recovered. As mentioned in the introduction, millions in gold and silver have recently been found. Of the 12 ships in the fleet, four still haven't been found! The *La Galeria* and a small frigatilla (both said to be lost in deep water with no survivors), *Nuestra Señora de la Concepción* (most believe off Cape Canaveral), and the *San Miguel*, which some say sank close to shore off north Florida (coins from this period are said to be found on Fernandina Beach). One other, the ex-Dutch sloop *Señora de la Popa*, went high up on the beach and was used as headquarters for a time during the Spanish salvage operations. Though I've never seen them, a site off Pompano Beach supposedly produced silver disks dated 1714, salvaged under state permit E#-19, and has been dubbed the "Silver Discs Site."

Remember, it is illegal to take anything from the water from these wrecks unless properly permitted. Anything found between the high and low water mark along the beaches is legal, though metal detectors can't be used in some parks. Be aware of the laws. Here are the GPS locations of some of these wrecks:

1715 Spanish Plate Fleet GPS Coordinates—Coordinates from *Sunken Treasure of Florida Reefs*, By Bob Weller; State of Florida. *Note:* Coordinates near ballast area, as most of these wrecks are scattered over a great distance.

1) *Neustra Señora de la Regla*—"Cabin Wreck"—Lat. 27°49.48'N, 80°25.48'W.

2) *Santo Cristo de San Roman*—"Corrigan's Wreck"—27°43.7'N, 80°22.65'W.

Author's wife Debby, with some silver coins recovered on the 1715 "Douglas Beach" site.

3) *Nuestra Señora del Carmen*—"Rio Mar Wreck"—27°38.25'N, 80°20.50'W.

4) *Nuestra Señora del Rosario*—"Sandy Point Wreck"—27°35.8'N, 80°20.45'W.

5) *Urca De Lima*—"Wedge Wreck"—27°29.4'N, 80°17.4'W. State mooring buoys at 27°30.317'N, 80°17.950'W.

6) *Nuestra Señora de las Nieves*—"Douglas Beach Wreck"—27°25.3'N, 80°16.3'W.

For those interested in learning more about this fleet, there are a few new books I highly recommend. *The Rainbow Chasers Tricentennial*, by T. L. Armstrong and Tommy Gore; *Finding the Fleet*, by Robert F. Westrick; and *The Quest for the Queen's Jewels*, by Robert F. Marx. My old standby, *Sunken Treasure on Florida Reefs*, by Robert "Frogfoot" Weller, is one I've always recommended. For those who want to search the beaches by these wrecks, I recommend the website by Lee Wiese: www.mdhtalk.or/articles/beaches/1715-fleet/1715-article.pdf. It shows just how to get to the beaches where many coins have been found over the years, especially after a good Nor'easter or hurricane.

I worked on these wrecks for many years with Bob Weller and then on my own along with my dive partners. We found many coins and artifacts, and though it takes a lot of hard work, these were some of the best times of my

Some gold coins or "escudos" found by the author and Bob Weller on the 1715 "Douglas Beach" site. Ernie Richards.

Rochelle, Nov. 10. We have hear the following Relation of the Loſs of the Spaniſh Flotilla, commanded by Don Juan de Ubilla, and the ſix Ships from Cheves. On the 24th of July, the eight Ships of the Flota, the ſix Galleons from Cheves, and the Griffin, ſet Sail from the Havana, and were by four in the Afternoon out at Sea, ſteering their Courſe to the Mouth of the Canal of Bahama ;. but the Wind not ſerving right, they had more Work to get thither than uſual. But having reach'd the Channel, they found themſelves 40 Leagues too far from the Coaſt of Florida, and were ſurpriz'd by a terrible Hurricane from the North-Eaſt, without being able to make any Way, or get out to Sea. The Waves run ſo high, breaking upon one another, and the Storm was ſo furious, that the Sails were torn to Pieces. The bad Weather continuing, all the Ships were oblig'd to cut down their Maſts ; and on the 31ſt they endeavour'd to ſet into the Land, but were caſt upon the Shoals, where they were ſoon torn to Pieces ; and all the Ships but one, nam'd the Flying-Stag, periſh'd, with all the Men and Paſſengers, computed to be 500 in Number. The News of this Misfortune being brought to the Havana the 17th of Auguſt, divers Ships went out immediately to fiſh up the Gold and Silver. They have already recover'd a great Part of what was on Board the Urca de Lima, and they hope to ſave a good deal of the reſt.

Actual article from a 1715 English newspaper, relating the loss of the 1715 Spanish treasure fleet. *The British Weekly Mercury*, 1715. Note: Report is not entirely accurate.

Large encrusted iron cannon on the 1715 "Corrigans" site.

One of the many grenades the author and crew recovered on the 1715 "Cabin" site. Note the wood plug that the fuse went through. The bottle next to it has some of the gunpowder from the grenade, and when dried, still lit. Also note the original encrustation that fully encapsulated the grenade. Would never recognize it underwater without using a metal detector.

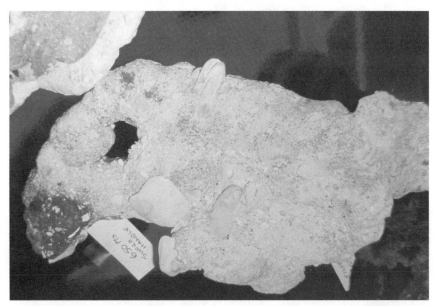

A heavily encrusted object from the 1715 "Douglas Beach" site. An x-ray confirmed it was an intricate sword handle.

Lead sounding weights. The one on the right was recovered by the author from the 1715 "Cabin" wreck, and the other is from a later 1700s wreck.

Author with encrusted musket recovered from the 1715 "Cabin" site.

Don Kree on the stern of the *Chelsea*, with a pottery shard and artifact from the 1715 fleet.

The name "Vitoria" inscribed on a silver plate was recovered by the author from the 1715 "Cabin" site. Who was Vitoria?

The same plate had the makers mark and partial assayer "GO" and and "L" on the obverse, but that was all. This photo is of the complete markings on some silverware recovered on the 1715 "Corrigans" site. These were made in Mexico, and the assayer was Nicholas Gonzales de la Cueva, assayer from 1701 to 1713. Mel Fisher's Treasure Museum, Sebastian, Florida.

life. There's still much to be found, and having done more research, I may be back looking for one of the lost ships soon.

1720

1) **Eight French SHIPS**, and several **English** and **Spanish SHIPS**—Reported from Cadiz in 1720 that these were cast away on the Florida Coast. *Source:* Weekly Journal or British Gazeteer, 10/1/1720. (8)

1722

1) **Reynolds**—Ship, from the Jamaica fleet, was lost on a rock in the Gulph of Florida. All on board saved. *Source:* Newcastle Courant, 8/11/1722. (8)

1725

1) **Pirate SLOOP**—Of 12 guns, Capt. Shipton (see chapter 6). *Source:* London Journal, 5/15/1725; London Parker Penny Post, 5/10/1725. (8)

2) *JANE AND MARY*—Ship, sailed from Honduras with the ship *Mermaid* when they were taken by pirates in the Gulph of Florida, and the *Jane and Mary* was sunk. *Source:* Ipswich Journal, 6/12/1725. (8)

3) *JOHN AND MARY*—From Jamaica for Virginia, was also lost in the Gulph of Florida around the same time as *Jane and Mary*, and all on board saved. *Source:* Ibid. (8)

4) *WESTMORLAND*—Capt. Straiton or Stretton, from Jamaica for Bristol, was lost in the Gulf of Florida. Crew took to the longboat and made South Carolina after much hardship. *Source:* Ipswich Journal, 9/11/1725; Caledonian Mercury, 9/23/1725.

5) *ROBERT AND SAMUEL*—Captain Austin, from Jamaica for London, was lost near Cape Florida. *Source:* Stamford Mercury, 12/16/1725. (5)

1727

1) *NEPTUNE*—Capt. James Lock. Stranded and lost on the Florida Keys, November 6, 1727. Some if not all the crew were saved. *Source:* Stamford Mercury, 2/22/1728. (8)

1728

1) *WESTMORELAND*—Ship, Capt. Joseph Warren, left Jamaica July 7, 1728, bound for London, but was lost soon after on coast of Florida. Captain and crew took to the boat and got to Havana seven days later. *Source:* Historical Register, 1/1/1729. (8)

1733

1) *BELVEDERE*—Capt. Oliver, from Jamaica for Carolina, was "lately lost in Gulph of Florida," crew saved. *Source:* Daily Journal London Middlesex, 3/20/1733. (8)

2) **Two Spanish MEN OF WAR**—A report dated July 21, 1733, which reported the 1733 plate fleet wrecks in the Keys, also mentions two Spanish Men of War that wrecked at St. Augustine which were from La Vera Cruz bound for Cadiz. *Source:* Weekly Miscellany (London), 10/6/1733. (6)

3) **Unk. SLOOP**—Of Rhode Island, entirely lost on the Martiers, Gulf of Florida, December 18, 1733. Nine white and five black men were on board. Capt. Thomas Wells, of New York., Capt. Richard Cupit, two white and three black men took to a canoe they had saved and made shore. The Native Americans immediately killed all the whites. A mate named Charles Morino and the rest took to the boat and were picked up by Spanish sloop and taken to Havana. *Source:* LDA, 7/2/1734. (8)

1) Pages 104–105. **1733 Spanish Plate Fleet**—As with the 1715 fleet wrecks, I didn't go into that much detail as there are books that go into greater detail on this fleet. My favorite is *Galleon Alley*, by Bob "Frogfoot" Weller (Florida, Crossed Anchors Salvage, 2001). The state of Florida put out a great booklet called the *1733 Spanish Galleon Trail* a few years ago, which has all GPS coordinates (see the end of this entry) and photos of each site. Some of the wrecks are no longer visible, while others still have timbers showing, and ballast piles intact. Besides the Spanish recovering most of the treasure soon after they wrecked, modern salvors have recovered most of the remaining treasure, though there is still some to be found. Ever since fisherman Reggie Roberts showed diver Art McKee the site of the *El Rubi* in 1938, the hunt for treasure in the Keys has never stopped.

1733 Spanish Plate Fleet—Ships went by different names, so using the most common ones. Coordinates are from *1733 Spanish Galleon Trail*, published by the state of Florida, and the website, *florida-keys-vacation.com*. All north latitude, west longitude.

1) *Nuestra Señora del Populo*—25°21.85'N, 80°09.69'W. Protected by the Biscayne National Park.

2) *El Infante*—24°56.556', 80°28.531'. In 20 feet of water, a ballast pile and timbers still visible.

3) *San José*—24°56.919', 80°29.334'. In 30 feet of water, mostly buried now.

4) *El Rubi*, Capitana—24°55.491', 80°30.891'. In 19 feet of water, not much visible. This was the first of the 1733 wrecks to be salvaged in modern times by Art McKee.

5) *Chaves*—24°56.179', 80°34.985'. In only 8 feet of water, some remains visible.

6) *Tres Puentes*—24°53.612 ', 80°35.012'. In 15 feet of water, most under sand last I saw.

7) *Herrera*—24°54.326', 80°35.538'. In 20 feet of water with scattered ballast.

8) *San Pedro*—24°51.802', 80°40.780'. State Underwater Preserve, with concrete cannons and a later anchor placed there. Has mooring buoys. In 18 feet of water. Nice ballast pile.

9) *El Terri*—24°50.761', 80°42.850'. Relatively intact ballast pile in about 15 feet of water.

10) *San Francisco*—24°49.185', 80°45.425'. One of my favorite 1733 sites as the ballast pile is relatively intact and some ships timbers can still be seen. Shallow water, so it's a great wreck to snorkel and visibility was usually good.

11) *Almiranta*—24°48.633'. 80°45.932'. In 14 feet of water, ballast visible.

12) *Nuestra Señora de las Augustias*—24°47.455', 80°51.738'. Lies in the Long Key Channel and currents and visibility can be a problem. Lots of ballast about.

13) *Sueco de Arizón*—Has two areas of ballast. 24°46.625', 80°53.372'; and 24°46.728', 80°53.480'.

14) *San Ignacio*—24°41.70', 80°56.44'. Near Coffin's Patch and in the Marine Sanctuary; so look but do not touch.

Extract of a Letter from the Havanna, Aug. 19, N. S.

'THIS goes by an Auviso bound to Cadiz, with
the melancholy News of the Loss of all
'the Flota in the Night of the 15th ult. on the
'Keys, or broken Islands, near Cape Florida, except
'the Africa Man of War; the San Ignacio and the
'Florida Ship were beat to Pieces, so that only 12
'out of about 300 Men were saved; the San Joseph
'y las Animas sunk; the rest of the finest Fleet
'that ever went from hence, are whole, but with-
'out Masts, having cut most of them down, and in
'such a Condition that they say it's not possible, so
'won't endeavour to get any others off than those
'commanded by Don Juan de Espeleta, Don Anto-
'nio Chaves, and the Auviso; they have lost but

'12 Men, and those by having over-loaded them
'selves with Plunder. It's certain much more Mo-
'ney is saved than was register'd, for our Gover-
'nor has near Ten Million of Pieces of Eight in
'his Custody, and there is full Three Millions
'more known to be saved, expected here in a few
'Days, with the Commander in Chief, Don Ro-
'drigo; but as to the rest of the Effects but little
'is saved, and of that, little without Damage.
'The following is a compleat List of the Flota,
'which sailed from this Port of the Havanna, un-
'der the Command of the Rear-Admiral Don Ro-
'drigo de Torres y Morales, the 13th of July this
'present Year 1733, and the 16th following in the
'Morning, appeared lost on the Keys of Baca, Vi-
'vora, and Matacumbe, viz.

Ships Names.	Captains Names.	Length of the Keels in Spanish Codes, or Cubits.	Men.	Guns.
	KING's SHIPS.			
Admiral. The Ruby,	Don Juan de Arnaud,	64	500	64
Vice-Admiral. The Cock,	Don Fr. Thomas Aguirre,	60	450	56
Infante,	Don Pablo Aguirre,	51	450	60
New Ship, St. Joseph, alias Africa,	Don Daniel Huony,	66	500	66
The Pink. The Populo,	Don Juan de Egues,	58	350	20
	MERCHANTS SHIPS.			
N. S. del Rosario, y S. Vincente Ferrer,	Don Juan de Arizon,	57	125	26
St. Philip,	Don Joseph del Villar,	64	130	34
N. S. del Rosario,	Don Juan de Espeleta,	60	135	30
N. S. de los Dolores, y S. Yzabel,	Don Antonio de Loaiza,	60	130	30
San Fernando,	Don Juan de Reyna,	61	150	34
N. S. de las Augustias, San Raphael,	Don Francisco Sanchez de Madrid	60	130	30
San Ignacio,	Don Christoval Urquixo,	60	150	30
San Francisco,	Don Vincente de Ycurribarria,	57	120	26
San Joseph y las Animas,	Don Xaval Fr. Franco,	60	130	30
St. Peter,	Don Gaspar Lopez,	56	125	24
El gran Poder de Dios,	Don Joseph Sanchez de Madrid,	52	75	20
N. S. de Belen y San Antonio,	Don Luis de Herrera,	53	70	20
N. S. del Carmen, S. Ant. y las Animas,	Don Antonio de Chaves,	45	50	18
El Auviso,	Don Joseph de Aramvido,	35	20	8

Also a Frigate bound for Florida,
which sailed in Company with
the Flota.

The following is an exact Account of what Treasure and Effects were shipp'd in the Flota, and re-
gistur'd, at La Vera Cruz.

GOLD and SILVER.
358 Castiliana's of wrought Gold.
6400 Pieces of 8 Value, in coin'd Gold.
284 Marks, 4 Ounces, of Silver in Ingots.
145953 Marks of wrought Silver.
10748747 Pieces of 8 in coin'd Silver.

Cochineal	2323 Serons
Ditto Silvester	158 Serons
Vanillas	391275000
Chocolate	101 Chests
Guatamilla Indigo	1361 Serons
Sugar	2766 Arroves
Snuff	1062 lb.
Tanned Hides	13955
Presents	100 Cases
Earthen Jarrs	185
Tortoise-Shell	1 Case

DRUGS.

Jallap	6594 Arroves
Sarsaparilla	252 ditto and 7 lb.
Liquid Amber	49 ditto
Cortex Contra Yerba	49 ditto
Balsam	271 ditto 13 lb.
Zevadilla	487 ditto
Achiote	188 ditto
Axiete de Baria	34 lb.

The Directors of the South-Sea Company have
received Advice, by way of the Havanna and Cadiz,
of Mr. James Holland, one of the Supercargoes of
their Ship the Royal Caroline, being dead at La
Vera Cruz.

By the Dutch Mail which arrived Yesterday, we
hear the Normanton, Capt. Charles Rigby, from London and Madeira, bound for the East Indies, was
well the 17th of May last between the Capes of
Good Hope and La Aguaillas. This News comes by
a Dutch Ship which met her.

Yesterday in the Afternoon one William Johnson,
who served his Apprenticeship to a Cooper in London, against whom a Warrant had been granted three
Weeks ago for Deer-stealing, had the Assurance to
ride through the City, about four o'Clock, with a
Sack full of Venison, and being known by some Persons in the Street, as he was passing through Budge
Row two Men laid hold of him, and pulling from
his Horse and seizing him, another Man, his Com-
rade, attempted to rescue him; and after a great
Struggle the said Johnson getting loose, left his Horse
and betook himself to his Heels, and was pursued
with an Outcry of his being a Deer-stealer; and
having a long Knife in one Hand and a Pistol in the
other, ran as far as Hind Court in Thames-street
without any one daring to lay hold of him, at last a
Carman seizing him by the Collar, he threatened,
if he did not quit his Hold, to shoot him, who refused

Actual report from a 1733 London paper relating the loss of the 1733 Spanish treasure fleet. *The Daily Journal*, October 1733.

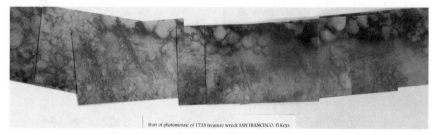

Start of photomosaic of 1733 treasure wreck SAN FRANCISCO, Fl Keys.

Photomosaic of the edge of the ballast pile with ships timber underneath on the 1733 wreck of the *San Francisco*.

Bob "Frogfoot" Weller next to the ballast pile of the 1733 wreck of the *San Pedro*.

Photomosaic of the 1733 wreck *San Jose*, by Dimitri Rebikoff. One can clearly see two mast "steps" along the keel, plus the ship's timber frames and ballast. Courtesy of Mrs. Dimitri Rebikoff.

1734

Note: Both captains of the following two vessels were either very unlucky or very lucky depending on how you look at it. After both lost their ships off Florida, they took passage on the *Friendship* from Carolina bound for London under Capt. Davis. It then wrecked off the coast of New Jersey where Capt. Davis and two others drowned. Capt. Barkley and Capt. Marshal survived though. *Source:* LEP, 12/31/1734.

1) *MILK-RIVER*—Capt. Berkely or Barkley, for London, was abandoned in the Gulf of Florida after she sprung a leak was and unable to reach any port. Crew took to the boat and made Carolina after 20 days at sea. *Source:* LDA, 10/10/1734. (8)

2) *WESTMORELAND*—Capt. Marshal, was also lost in Gulph of Florida about the same time as the *Milk-River*. Crew were saved and got to Carolina. *Source:* LEP, 1/31/1734. (8)

1736

1) *ASHELY* or *ASHLEY*—Capt. Jenkins, from Jamaica for London, was lost off Cape Florida. Captain and crew took to the longboat and were later picked up by a ship and taken to Carolina. A total loss. *Source:* Dublin News Letter, 2/8/1736; London Reed Weekly, 2/5/1737. (5)

2) *KING GEORGE*—Capt. Tristman, from Jamaica for Liverpool, was lost in the Gulph of Florida, August, 1736. *Source:* Daily Journal London Middlesex, 10/5/1736. (8)

1737

1) *BETTY'S HOPE*—Capt. Souers or Sewers, from Jamaica for London, was lost 12/12/1737, near Cape Florida. Captain and crew made it to South Carolina. *Source:* LEP, 7/22/1738; Stamford Mercury, 7/27/1738. (8)

2) *ENDEAVOUR*—Sloop, Capt. Elderton, from the Bay of Honduras for New England, was lost in the Gulf of Florida, August 26, 1737. *Source:* Newcastle Courant, 1/21/1738. (8)

1738

1) *MARY*—Capt. Thomas Gladman, of and for London from Jamaica, went ashore on one of the seven islands 30 leagues from Cape Florida, June 18, 1738, a total loss. Capt. Crow said he investigated the wreck in August

1739 on the Tortugas, and the name of the ship, date lost, and name of the captain, mate (John Saunders) and carpenter (Samuel Hogsflesh) were neatly written on a molding and nailed to a mast. *Source:* LEP, 8/1/1738; Williamsburg Virginia Gazette, 10/5/1739. (3)

2) *CROWN*—Ship, Capt. Jeffery, left Jamaica August 11, 1738, for London, and on September 5 at Lat. 25°N, they saw land, thinking they were near Cape Florida. They anchored that night and in the morning found themselves in the middle of some reefs and unable to get out. Saw a Spanish sloop and schooner about five miles distant and the captain took the boat over and asked for a pilot to help them but was denied. They wanted some rum before they would talk. The captain returned in the boat and now kept a lookout fearing an attack by either the Spaniards or the Natives on the shore. Still unable to get the ship out and believing they would soon be attacked, they all took to the longboat and made for Carolina and eventually fell in with a sloop that took them there. *Source:* Daily Post, 1/23/1739; LEP, 11/21/1738. (4)

1739

1) *EARL GALLEY*—Capt. Robert Codd, of Bristol, from the Bay of Honduras bound for Isle of Wight, stranded 4/27/1739, about 20 leagues north of Cape Florida. The captain and 14 crew took to the longboat and made Charles-Town, May 19. *Source:* LDA, 7/17/1739. (5)

2) *LOVELY BETTY*—Capt. Spence, left Jamaica May 12, 1739, but soon went ashore in the Gulph of Florida. *Source:* Daily Post, 1/23/1739. (8)

1740

1) **Privateer SLOOP**—Was one of two English privateers that just took a Dutch prize, Capt. Marshal, who lost his sloop on the Florida shore, April or early June 1740. He and his crew were all saved by the other privateer. *Source:* Williamsburg Virginia Gazette, 5/9/1740.

2) **Spanish SLOOP**—Was sunk by a British ship under Capt. Peter Warren near St. Augustine. They also captured another sloop with the Spanish Commodore aboard, who was on his way to Havana to buy provisions for the garrison, and which had 8,000 pieces of eight on board. The other sloop probably carried some specie too. *Source:* Derby Mercury, 7/17/1740. (6)

3) **Privateer SNOW**—A Jamaican privateer, Capt. Mackey, was lost on the Florida coast after his vessel was badly damaged by a French warship and which he lost some men. A Rhode Island privateer picked up the survivors and brought them there. *Source:* Williamsburg Virginia Gazette, 7/11/1740.

4) **Privateer SLOOP**—Capt. Bennet, was lost on Loggerhead Key during a hurricane, 8/20/1740. See Chapter 6. *Source:* Dublin News Letter, 12/20/1740.

1741

1) *PORT FACTOR*—Ship, Capt. Bennet, from Carolina for Lisbon, had taken three Spaniards on as part of crew. Story is they murdered the captain and some of the crew and took the ship to St. Augustine, where it wrecked going over the bar. As Spain and England were at war, one paper put the blame on the captain for bringing the Spaniards (the enemy) on board in the first place. *Source:* Daily Post 1/16/1742. (6)

2) **Spanish PACKET BOAT**—From Vera Cruz for St. Augustine with a large sum of money for the fort there. Was lost on the St. Augustine Bar. All the money was lost. *Source:* Caledonian Mercury, 10/12/1741. (6)

3) *NASSAU*—Capt. Bradshaw, was lost on the Martiers, crew saved by a Virginia brig. *Source:* Daily Post, 10/16/1741. (8)

1) Pages 209 and 317. *H.M.S. Wolf*—Commander was Charles Turner, Esq. Previously to being wrecked, she delivered at Jamaica a prize French sloop from Campeche, which had 100,000 pieces-of-eight on board. May have had some on board the *Wolf* when she wrecked. Crew were saved. Believe this may be the wreck which lies off Hallandale Beach Boulevard, and whose cannon are pictured on page 316 of the second edition. While a member of the MAC, I helped conserve those cannons and they are now on display in front of the City of Hallandale's administration building. *Source:* Derby Mercury, 5/7/1741.

1742

1) *CHARMING NIGHTINGALE*—Capt. Pallister (died during voyage), from Jamaica for England, was lost in the Gulph of Florida. *Source:* Daily Post, 3/30/1742. (8)

1) Page 67. *HMS Tyger* (also spelled *Tiger*)—General dimensions/armament for a 50-gun ship at this time was 130' x 35' x 14', and had 22-18 pounders, 22-9 pounders, and 6-6 pounders. Went aground on a reef near Garden Key, Dry Tortugas (where Fort Jefferson now sits). A Spanish map made after the British left shows the wreck about 1.5 miles, 190° off the west end of Garden Key. The crew built a fortified camp on the island, bringing the 6 and 9 pounder cannon ashore. Thinking they wrecked in the

Bahamas, a boat was sent to find New Providence, but soon realized they were in Florida and returned to camp. A Spanish sloop was seen removing some of the *Tyger's* rigging and masts but soon left. Another sloop returned a couple days later and the *Tyger* was set afire by Lt. Dennis. Ten days later a Spanish sloop with 100 men anchored offshore. The British soon attacked hoping to capture it, but failed. That sloop was later captured by a vessel under Capt. Charles Davidson, whose captain told him only he and 19 men returned to Havana after the battle. The entire crew of the *Tyger* finally left March 19, eventually making their way to Jamaica on some smaller craft they had captured or found abandoned. *Source:* 11; 28 (for full story); Ipswich Journal, 8/21/1742; Wikipedia.

1744

1) Page 68. *HMS Looe*—*Note:* All the papers including Lloyd's List of the time called the vessel the *"Loo* man of war." The correct name though is the *Looe.* The website FloridaKeysTreasures.com, had an article on Florida Keys names, and how they got them. It said the vessel that the Looe had captured and that was in tow, was the ex-English merchant ship **Billander Betty**, which had been captured by the Spanish, and which also wrecked along with the *Looe.* I could find no mention of this name in Lloyd's though. In my second edition, I had the name of the vessel as the *Snow* (page 358), though a snow was also a type of vessel (a large two-masted type vessel rigged as a brig).

1745

1) *HMS CHESTERFIELD*—Possible Florida wreck. She was bringing troops from North America to Havana, when she was lost on the rocks in the Gulf of Florida. Colledge says she foundered 10/31/1745 "near" the Bahamas. A court-martial a few years later cleared the Captain and officers of any wrongdoing. *Source:* 11. (8)

2) **British PRIVATEER**—Was reported that a privateer under command of Capt. Marshall was lost in the Gulf of Florida, and the crew were saved by the 350-ton Dutch prize vessel it and three other privateers had recently taken and now in command of Capt. Dennis. They arrived in Newport. *Source:* LDA, 8/28/1745. (8)

1746

1) **Unk. SNOW**—Believe a privateer, was driven ashore at Cape Florida and beaten to pieces along with the *Cruizer*. *Source:* Penny London Post 2/11/1747; Ipswich Journal, 1/14/1747. (5)

2) *CRUIZER*—Privateer, of Philadelphia, reported from Charlestown, December 15, 1876, that she was lately taken by a Spanish Xebeques (Xebec-type of ship a bit smaller than a frigate), and was fitted out at Havana and drove ashore at Cape Florida and beat to pieces. *Note:* The above snow and *Cruiser* appeared to have wrecked at the same place and time. *Source:* LEP, 2/10/1747. (5)

3) **FIVE SPANISH XEBEQUES** (Xebecs) along with **two captured British ships**—Were all lost near Cape Florida, some cargo saved. *Source:* Penny London Post, 6/26/1847. (8)

1747

1) *NEW BALION* or the *NEW*, Capt. Balion—From Plymouth bound for North Carolina, was captured by a Spanish Privateer after two days sail, and lost near Cape Florida while being taken to Havana. *Source:* General Advertiser, 8/26/1747; The Scots Magazine, 10/2/1747. (5)

2) **Unk. SPANISH VESSEL**—From Havana bound for South Carolina under a flag of truce. On board was Captain James of the ship *Harrington*, recently captured after a 14-hour battle with a Spanish 70-gun Man of War off Havana. The vessel foundered a few leagues off the Florida coast and all made shore safely in the ship's boat. *Source:* LDA, 8/8/1747. (8)

3) Reported by different newspapers that between 25 and 30 vessels were lost off the coast of Florida around October 1747 within 60 leagues of St. Augustine. A few of those named were:

a) *DOLPHIN*—Capt. Stephens, from Carolina for Antigua, was lost on the coast of Florida, October 5, 1747.

b) *ELIZABETH* and the *SEAFLOWER*—Both of and from Carolina for Cape Fracois, sailing under a flag of truce, captain of the *Elizabeth* was named Hutchins.

c) **Unk. VESSEL**—Capt. Seymour, was returning to England with prisoners.

d) **Unk. VESSEL**—Capt. Jewer, from Carolina for St. Augustine sailing under a flag of truce.

e) Also reported from London, August 11, 1748, with no dates given, were that four **Spanish XEBECS**, and some **British SHIPS** were lost near Cape Florida. Was there a hurricane in October 1747, and were these also part of the ships mentioned earlier, or maybe wrecked later in 1748? Probably all lost during the 1747 storm but can't say for sure. Could also be a late report and be the same vessels listed in 1746.

Source for a–e: Whitehall Evening Post, 1/14/1748; Derby Mercury, 6/10/1748, 8/12/1748. (8)

1748

1) *JOSEPH AND JANE*—Capt. Lane, from South Carolina bound for Antigua, was lost near Cape Florida. *Source:* General Evening Post, 5/21/1748. (8)

2) *DOWNTOWN* or *DOWNTON*—Capt. Grundy, bound for North Carolina, was taken by a Spanish Privateer, and wrecked near Cape Florida while being taken to Havana. *Source:* Whitehall Evening Post, 6/2/1748; Derby Mercury, 6/3/1748. (8)

3) *JUDA*—Spanish ship with cocoa and 57,000 dollars. This was the prize that also wrecked along with the *HMS Fowey* (page 105). All the money and cargo were saved. *Source:* General Advertiser, 9/19/1748; LL, 1747–1748. *Note:* Though the *HMS Fowey* drifted off the rocks and sank a distance away, I believe the *Juda* remained wrecked at or near Fowey Rocks. (4)

1) Page 106. *Dolphin*—Capt. Bagott, for North Carolina, had been captured by a Spanish privateer, and was being taken to Havana when she wrecked by accident near Cape Florida. *Source:* General Evening Post, 10/15/1748; The Scots Magazine, 12/3/1748.

2) Page 106. *Howlet*—The ship was fitted out in Boston for a trading voyage to the Gulf of Mexico by a Mr. Winslow. The cook on the *Howlet* was the servant of Winslow's brother, General Winslow, a provincial governor, and the *Howlet* wrecked in 1748. The general was in England in 1760 on business and was on board a West Indiaman when he ran into his old servant who relayed the story. After being wrecked on the coast of Florida near Cape Florida, he was the only one spared by the natives because he was black, though they sold him to a Spanish merchant of Havana, where he was kept a slave until the year before as he was always watched and unable to escape. When he saw a New England ship in the harbor about two miles off, he stripped off his clothes and swam to it, and to his joy they took him on as the cook and the ship then returned to London. The cook who had

been treated well by the general, returned with him back to Boston. *Source: Public Ledger,* 5/24/1760.

1749

1) *SWAN*—Capt. Finch, from Carolina bound for Antigua, was lost on the Florida coast. *Source:* Whitehall Evening Post, 5/25/1749. (8)

2) **Unk. SHIP**—Capt. Garnon or Garnock, from Jamaica bound for Rhode Island, was beat to pieces in a storm in the Gulph of Florida. Crew were taken up by a vessel bound for New York. *Source:* Penny London Post, 11/3/1749; Aberdeen Press and Journal, 11/14/1749. (8)

1750

1) *CADOGAN*—Capt. Phillip Corwall, from Jamaica for Rhode Island, was lost in the Gulf of Florida, the crew saved by another vessel. *Source:* Whitehall Evening Post, 4/5/1750. (8)

1) Page 210. *Betsey*—Crew took to the boat and taken up by a sloop to Providence. Four other ships were also lost, but nationalities unknown. *Source:* LDA, 5/14/1750.

1751

1) *SEA FLOWER*—Brigantine, Capt. John Bristow, of RI, from Bay of Honduras for Rhode Island, wrecked at Cape Florida, July 10, 1751. Crew took to the boats and spent 21 days in them before reaching Charleston, South Carolina. *Source:* Aberdeen Press and Journal, 12/3/1751. (5)

2) *ISABELLA*—Capt. Powers, from Bay of Honduras bound for New York, was lost to leeward of Cape Florida along with her cargo. All the crew arrived safely at St. Augustine. *Source:* LDA, 8/28/1751. (5)

3) *SUCCESS*—Sloop, Capt. Shourt, of New York, left the Bay of Honduras in April 1751. After encountering bad weather along their way, and having to man one pump due to a leak, they eventually were in site of Matanzas, Cuba, mid-September, when they were overtaken by another gale. She lost her sails, and with the seas pounding over them and with both pumps working, they wrecked on a small key near Cape Florida. The crew took to their boat and made their way through the keys for about two weeks arriving at the Martiers. They were surrounded by the natives there and captured. Would have been killed except for a Spanish sloop who took some of them

to St. Augustine, as the natives had some sort of treaty with the Spanish at the time. The others were left with the natives to help salvage another wrecked ship nearby which was from Jamaica for London, loaded with rum and sugar. *Source:* Aberdeen Press and Journal, 5/26/1752. (5)

4) *HARRIOT*—Brigantine, Capt. Powell, from the Bay of Honduras, was lost to the leeward of Cape Florida. Captain and some crew and cargo saved by a ship bound for St. Augustine.*Source:* LDA, 11/18/1751. (5)

5) *HOPEWELL*—Capt. Isaac Hudson, of New York, was lost a few leagues off Cape Florida. Captain, crew, and some cargo saved. *Source:* Salisbury and Winchester Journal, 11/18/1751. (5)

6) *HANNAH*—Brigantine, Capt. George Matthews, from Carolina for Philadelphia, was lost in Gulf of Florida, some crew saved. *Source:* LDA, 12/5/1751. (8)

1) Page 210. **Great Britain**—Wrecked September 15. Crew saved by the *Charming Peggy*, Capt. Conry, and taken to Falmouth. *Source:* General Advertiser, 12/3/1751; LL, 12/3/1751.

1752

1) **BRIDGET**—Brigantine, Capt. Simpson, from South Carolina bound for Philadelphia, was lost in the Gulf of Florida Some on board saved. *Source:* London Read Weekly, 6/20/1752. (8)

2) **DELIGHT**—Brigantine, Capt. Waller Newton, from Philadelphia for South Carolina, was lost in the Gulf of Florida. Crew saved by a vessel bound for Jamaica. *Source:* LEP, 7/9/1852. (8)

3) The following were lost during the October 22, 23, 1752, hurricane. Source for all the hurricane losses: PA, 2/8/1753; LEP, 1/13/1753, 1/30/1753, 2/6/1753; LDA, 3/10/1753; LL, 1/16/1753, 3/9/1753, 4/20/1753.

a) **French SNOW**—Came ashore on the Florida coast, November 4, 1752, due to a hurricane. All 37 on board were killed by the natives. (8)

b) *RUBY*—Was one of many vessels lost, part of a fleet sailing from Jamaica, Capt. Edwards, drove onto the Florida coast, November 2, 1852, due to a hurricane, and bilged. Next day was boarded by the natives that arrived in two canoes. They took their clothes and while rummaging through the ship, the crew escaped in the longboat and sailed for the Savannah Inlet. Fourteen other American vessels also wrecked along the coast. (8)

Reported missing which sailed with and the same time as the *Ruby* from Jamaica (all possible Florida wrecks):

c) *THREE FRIENDS*—Capt. Gotterney, from Jamaica for Bristol. (8)

d) *BOSTON*—Light brig, Capt. Dane, from Jamaica for Virginia or Boston. (8)

e) **Unk. SHIP**—Capt. Hill, from Honduras for NY. (8)

f) **Unk. SCHOONER**—Capt. Boyd, bound for Virginia. (8)

Other vessels reported missing due to the hurricane:

g) **Spanish MAN OF WAR** and **SCHOONER**—Listed by Lloyds as missing in the hurricane. Possible Florida wrecks. (8)

h) *SPEEDWEL*—Capt. Smith, from Jamaica for Philadelphia. (8)

Additional information on October hurricane wrecks previously listed:

1) Page 210.

a) *Alexander*—Capt. Mudie.

b) *Fanny* (correct)—had this listed as the *Lancaster*, page 210. Capt. Lowery, for Lancaster, was lost in the Gulph of Florida.

e) *May* should be *Mary* (correct)—She left with 26 other vessels. First encountered the storm on October 18, which got worse, and on October 21, they lost their bowsprit and foremast. On October 23, went ashore in the Florida Keys near three other wrecks. She carried cargo of rum. The Spanish found them soon after, and having no weapons, they boarded the ship and took their clothes and other things and then set the ship on fire. They were rescued by a Spanish schooner November 13, which took them to Havana.

g) *Statia* (correct), not the *Statea*.

h) *Phillis*—Captain, second mate, and five sailors drowned.

i) *Kingston*—Lloyd's says Capt. McDugal.

j) *Pompey*—Bound for London, also lost in the October hurricane.

End of October hurricane losses.

1753

1) *MARTHA*—Brigantine, Capt. Joseph Powers, from Bay of Honduras, was lost to the leeward of Cape Florida. Captain and some crew saved. *Source:* LEP, 7/19/1753. (5)

2) *NICHOLAS AND SARAH*—Capt. Lutton, from Honduras, was lost near Cape Florida. Captain and some of the crew saved by a ship bound for St. Augustine. *Source:* LDA, 8/31/1753. (8)

3) *TWO BROTHERS*—American vessel, Capt. Clavering, bound for Jamaica, was lost in the Gulf of Florida. Captain and crew saved. *Source:* LDA, 11/16/1753; PA, 11/16/1753. *Note:* Not to be confused with the British ship *Two Brothers*, lost earlier this year. (8)

1) Pages 210–211. *Two Brothers*—Of London, Capt. Coates, from Jamaica for London, was lost in the Gulph of Florida, March 17, 1753 (Lloyds says 4/26/1753), all the crew saved by two other vessels, one was the *Earl of Effingham*, commanded by Capt. Bellamy. *Source:* London Evening News, 7/5/1753; LEP, 6/9/1753; LL, 6/12/1753. (8)

1754

1) *SEAHORSE*—Brigantine, of Boston, Capt. Adams, from the Bay of Honduras along with 13 other vessels all bound to London, New York, and Boston, wrecked on the Dry Tortugas Banks, May 23, 1754. The mate and seven crew arrived in Philadelphia in a sloop under Capt. Hardy. Some cargo of logwood and some sails were salvaged by Hardy. *Source:* Annapolis Maryland Gazette, 8/8/1754; LEP, 10/10/1754. (3)

1755

1) *JAMES AND SARAH*—Capt. Cook, of and from Jamaica, was lost in Gulf of Florida. *Source:* London Read Weekly, 6/5/1756; Gazetteer and London Daily Advertiser, 6/9/1756. (8)

2) **MYSTERY SHIP**—Capt. Morris of the *Enterprise* reports he found an abandoned ship on the Florida coast July 5, 1756, at Lat. 25°30'N. The ship looked fairly new, English built, and loaded with logwood and pimento, and had a double horse-head, was lute stern'd, and had a woman painted blue on it. Some letters were found, dated 1750 or 1751, directed to Andrew Young, Esq., at Kirkwell. No boats on board. *Source:* Gazetteer and London Daily Advertiser, 8/11/1756. (5)

1757

1) Page 211. *Myrtilla* (believe correct), or *Myrtle*—Capt. Marsh or March. *Source:* LEP, 10/29/1757; PA, 11/2/1757.

1758

1) *DRAGON*—Ship, Capt. Dixon, from Jamaica bound for London, was lost in the Gulf of Florida. Crew was saved and taken to Philadelphia. She was the last of the missing Jamaica Fleet. *Source:* LEP, 2/22/1759. (8)

1759

1) **Unk. SLOOP**—Reported from Charleston, December 29, 1759, that a Spanish vessel brought into that port the crew of a sloop that wrecked on the Martiers early November. They made shore on pieces of plank where they spent 20 days before being rescued, subsisting on prickly pears. *Source:* Whitehall Evening Post or London Intelligencer, 3/6/1760. (8)

1760/1761

1) *HARWICH*—English man-of-war, Capt. Marsh, was lost in the Gulf of Florida in 1760. Crew made it to Havana in their boats. Also listed as lost "near the island of Cuba." Possible Florida wreck. *Source:* Ipswich Journal, 2/7/1761; Caledonian Mercury, 5/16/1761. (8)

2) *PROVIDENCE*—Capt. Marshal, of Liverpool, from Jamaica for London, was lost in Gulf of Florida, crew saved. *Source:* Whitehall Evening Post, 2/3/1761. (8)

1) Page 211. *Jamaica Packet*—Capt. Flynn. Crews of all three vessels were taken up by the vessel *Hawke*, Capt. Ritchie, who also saved 90 puncheons of rum and 4 hogsheads of sugar from the *Mary*. *Source:* PA, 7/4/1761.

1762

1) *PEGGY*—Brig, of New England, foundered in the Gulph of Florida. From Jamaica bound for London. *Source:* LL, 9/27/1762. (8)

1763

1) *GENERAL WOLFE*—Schooner, Capt. Higgins, with a cargo of indigo, sugar, etc., was captured by Spanish privateer and wrecked at Matanzas near St. Augustine, January 1763. *Source:* Annapolis Maryland Gazette, 3/17, 1763. See chapter 6. (6)

1) Page 107. *Alexander*—Lost on the Martiers (keys). *Source:* LEP, 10/10/1763. (8)

2) Page 168. *Charming Sally* or *Charming Nelly*—This source says *Charming Nelly*, from St. Augustine and of and for Charles-Town, Capt. James Brown, wrecked near Matanzas around late October 1763. The two **French sloops** in the Spanish Transport Service, from Havana bound for St. Augustine, were lost near Matanzas and the other near St. Augustine around the same time. *Source:* LSJC, 1/12/1764.

3) Page 211. *Albinia*—Ship, Capt. Gilbert, made shore and the crew saved by a sloop under Capt. Folger. Ship and cargo of indigo lost. *Source:* Leeds Intelligencer, 6/14/1763; LEP, 6/4/1763.

1764

1) Page 168. *Industry*—Supposedly found in 1997 with eight cannons. One cannon is now on display at the St. Augustine Lighthouse. *Source:* 38.

1765

1) *VIGILANTE*—French Frigate, 28 guns, wrecked at the Dry Tortugas. Since not listed as a French naval vessel, it's most likely a privateer. *Source:* LEP, 1/21/1766. (3)

1766

1) **New England SNOW**—From the Cayenne Settlement (French Guiana) bound for Pensacola, with 85 French passengers on board, which "drove ashore to the westward of Cape Florida and bilged." Crew and passengers made it to St. Augustine. *Source:* Dublin Courier, 4/4/1766. *Note:* This was when the settlement was ceded to the Dutch, though went back to France years later. (5)

2) *HAPPY RETURN*—Capt. Denwiddie, from Virginia for Pensacola, wrecked on the Florida shore. *Source:* Gazetteer and New Daily Advertiser, 10/18/1766. (8)

3) **French SHIP**—A report from Pensacola said a French ship from St. Domingo bound for the Mississippi, with muskets, gunpowder and Indian stores, was run ashore on the Florida coast to the westward of the Cape and lost with most of her cargo. *Source:* Williamsburg Virginia Gazette, 5/23/1766; General Evening Post, 4/8/1773. *Note:* Some British newspapers

repeatedly posted this exact same report giving no dates year after year up until 1881! (8)

4) *SANTA BARBARA* or *ST. BARBE*—Spanish ship, from Honduras. Lloyd's says "2000 serons of indigo" on board. A report from Cadiz only mentions money on board and that she wrecked in the "Canal of Bahama," July 16 or 17, 1766. The man-of-war *Brilliant* saved a considerable amount of money from the wreck, but "the remainder of her cargo, to the amount of a million of piastres, was all lost; and the whole crew, which was very numerous, perished, except nine or ten persons." Possible Florida wreck. *Source:* LL, 10/14/1766; Derby Mercury, 10/31/1766. (8)

5) October 23, 1766, hurricane at Pensacola. There were 12 vessels in the bay when the storm hit. Many were driven ashore.

a) *WETHERILL*—Brig, Capt. Freeman, from Honduras, went ashore on other side of the bay and all the crew drowned except three. *Source:* LL, 2/24/1767. (1)

b) *REBECCA*—Capt. Craig, from Carolina, went ashore on Rose Island about three leagues from town and was not known if she could be saved. *Source:* Ibid (1)

c) **Unk. SCHOONERS**—One went ashore on the other side of the bay and another schooner foundered at anchor. *Source:* Ibid. (1)

End of October hurricane losses.

6) *MARY*—Sloop, Capt. James Sheffield, from Savannah for St. Augustine, was reported from South Carolina on December 5, 1766, that the sloop *Mary* wrecked on the Florida coast south of Matanzas. On board was the Hon. William Grover, Esq., Chief Justice of East Florida, along with other passengers. All made it to shore except two of Mr. Grover's servants who drowned. The survivors were eventually rescued by a Bahamian sloop and taken to St. Augustine, but not before Mr. Grover died on board the sloop. *Source:* 25; The Ipswich Journal, 1/31/1767. *Note:* In Bernard Roman's book, it's mentioned he was wrecked on the Florida coast in 1766. Possibly the same vessel. (8)

1767

1) *JEMIMA*—Capt. Hastings, from Rhode Island bound for Pensacola, wrecked at Cape Florida (maybe late 1766). Vessel and cargo lost. *Source:* PA, 3/17/1767. (5)

2) *ACHILLES*—Capt. Jackson, from Antigua for Rhode Island, with rum and sugar, wrecked in the Gulf of Florida. *Source:* LEP, 12/12/1767. (8)

1768

Note: The Georgia Gazette reported that the *Polly,* the 18-gun Spanish ship, and the *Anna Maria Theresa,* were all wrecked on the "Martiers," and the Bahamian wreckers were salvaging them.

1) *POLLY*—Brigantine, Capt. John Bartlett, from Jamaica of and for New England, with molasses, wrecked on the Martiers. Crew saved by the sloop *Rainbow. Source:* London Lloyd Evening Post, 9/26/1768; PA, 10/11/1768. (8)

2) **Spanish SHIP**—Of 18 guns, from Havana for Spain, with sugar and tobacco, etc. (one source says richly laden), ran on shore of the Martiers, July 17, 1768. Crew saved. *Source:* London Lloyd Evening Post, 9/26/1768; PA, 10/11/1768. (8)

3) **Unk. SNOW**—Of New York, Capt. Roach, from Pensacola with 160 officers and soldiers, wrecked on the bar of St. Augustine. All on board saved but the vessel and all baggage was lost. *Source:* St. James Chronicle, 1/28/1769. (6)

1) Page 211. *Anna-Theresa* (or *Anna Maria Theresa*)—Captain Valentine Dyer, from Pensacola for Charles-Town, was lost on July 27. Mails, sails, and rigging saved by a Providence wrecker. *Source:* London Lloyd Evening Post, 9/26/1768; PA, 10/11/1768.

1769

1) *SEAFLOWER*—Sloop, Capt. Whitpain, from Honduras for Philadelphia, wrecked off Cape Florida, May 8, 1769. Vessel lost. Crew, passengers, and some cargo saved. *Source:* The Pennsylvania Gazette, 6/23/1769 (from North Carolina's Office of Archives and History "Colonial Records Project"). (5)

2) **Unk. Spanish SHIP**—Richly laden, from Caracas, wrecked on the Matiers on a reef near Cape Florida. *Source:* Middlesex Journal 2/27/1770. (4)

1) Page 107. *Ledbury*—Capt. Lorrain, from Jamaica for Bristol, England, "after being out nine weeks was drove on shore 15 leagues to northward of Cape Florida, in a violent gale of wind, 29th September" Crew and some cargo saved. *Source:* LL 12/19/1769. Lloyd's possibly has it wrong and it likely wrecked on what is now called Ledbury Reef.

1770

1) *HAPPY DELIVERY*—Capt. Carter, from Halifax bound for Pensacola, was lost in a gale on coast of Florida, and only three of her crew were saved. *Source:* Middlesex Journal, 7/17/1770.

2) **Spanish SHIP**—A report from Charles-Town, South Carolina, July 18, 1870, says about six weeks earlier, a Spanish ship of 74 guns, having on board General O'Reilly and other officers, and a large quantity of money, from Havana for Spain, was cast away on the Martiers near Cape Florida. The general and all on board got to Cuba by assistance of some Bahamians and the ship's boat. The ship and all cargo except the money were reported as lost. *Source:* LEP, 9/13/1770. (8)

1) Page 212. *St. Mary*—Was lost on Cape Florida. *Source:* PA, 9/15/1770. (5)

1771

1) *HECTOR*—Captain Norris, from Jamaica bound for Bristol. After being 11 weeks out, she was driven ashore during a violent gale 12 leagues to the northward of Cape Florida. Crew and some cargo saved. *Source:* LSJC, 5/25/1771. (5)

2) *KING FARMER*—Capt. Pitts, from Jamaica, was lost in the Gulf of Florida. *Source:* Kentish Gazette, 6/22/1771. (8)

3) **Spanish SHIP** and **SNOW**—Wrecked on Cape Florida, 1771. They were part of a treasure fleet of 13 ships from Vera Cruz and Havana bound for Cadiz. A snow from the fleet fell in with a British ship off Carolina and told them that a Spanish ship and a snow wrecked ashore at Cape Florida, and were lost, whereas they took off everyone numbering about 80, most who were troops being relieved from the Mexican station, some passengers, and some English prisoners, along "with as much specie, &c. as possible." It was said they recovered over half a million in specie, and probably much remains on the wrecks. *Source:* Pennsylvania Gazette, 9/5/1771; Virginia Gazette, 9/26, 1771; Leeds Intelligencer, 11/19/1771. (5)

4) *VICTORIA*—A few British papers only said it was from Vera Cruz for Cadiz, and lost off Cape Florida. Most likely one of the two listed previously. *Source:* Ipswich Journal, 10/26/1771. (5)

1) Page 107. **HMS** *Carysfort*—Though she got off the reef, I'll mention her grounding here as Carysfort Reef was named after her, though for many years some referred to it as Carysford Reef. Though I've read different dates, I believe she grounded on October 22, 1770. She had sailed from Jamaica

under Captain William Hay for the Gulf of Florida with a pilot from Jamaica supposedly familiar with those waters. According the report, they ran aground due to "perverseness, obstinacy, and ignorance of the pilot," and ran ashore at night on the Martyr Reef (other reports spell it Martiers). The captain and crew worked nine sleepless days and night to get her off (another report says they got off by October 25). By cutting away the masts, throwing the cannon overboard (reports say 17 or 18 nine pounders), and carrying an anchor out astern, they finally got her off and through an intricate passage through the reefs, which Robert Hunter (who later became Governor of New South Wales) had placed markers, and suffered a number of injuries during the whole ordeal. They set sail under jury mast and made Charleston where they repaired. *Source:* The Naval Chronicle; Caledonian Mercury, 1/3/1771.

2) Page 107. *El Nauva Victoriosa*—British papers called it the *Victoria* or just *Victorioso* and as wrecked near Cape Florida. In my previous editions, I mentioned this may be the wreck referred to locally as the "Pillar Dollar Wreck," discovered in the 60s. Different sources give different dates on the coins found. One said 1770, other says 1760–1764 (maybe two different wrecks?). Site has recently been investigated by archaeologists. *Source:* LL, 10/22/1871; PA, 10/22/1771. (5)

1772

Note: A ship reported that on July 27, 1772, they saw a ship high up on the beach, 10 to 12 leagues north of Cape Florida, with only her two lower masts standing. This could be one of the following vessels. *Source:* Annapolis Maryland Gazette: 9/27/1772.

1) *MERCURY*—Capt. Aprey, from Jamaica bound for Liverpool, supposedly lost in Gulf of Florida. *Source:* PA, 7/20/1772. (8)

2) *HIBBERT*—From Jamaica bound for London, went ashore on Cape Florida, and most if not all the cargo was saved. *Source:* Middlesex Journal, 9/8/1772. (5)

3) Sixteen Spanish SHIPS (two were frigates)—Were reported lost in the Gulf of Florida, August 1772. *Source:* LEP, 11/26/1772. (8)

4) Large Spanish SHIP—A vessel arrived in St. Augustine and reported a Spanish ship with a rich cargo from Curacao, wrecked on the Martyrs, a reef of rocks to the west of Cape Florida, September last. *Source:* Caledonian Mercury, 12/12/1772. (4)

1) Page 107. *Marie Beckford*—Some cargo was saved. *Source:* LL, 1772.

2) Page 212. *Fortune*—Lost on the coast of Florida, a man and a boy drowned. *Source:* St. James Chronicle, 2/18/1773; LL, 2/19/1773.

1773

1) **French WARSHIPS**—Possible Florida wrecks though most likely false information. A number of newspapers reported four French men of war as lost in the Gulf of Florida. Two ships names (of 74 guns) were mentioned but I looked those up and both remained in service after 1773 including the *Palmier* which sailed until lost off Bermuda in 1782 and the *Defenseur*. *Source:* General Evening Post, 2/23/1773, 3/2/1773, 1/13/1774; London Craftsman, 10/23/1773.

2) *LOVELY NANCY*—Ship, Capt. White, foundered in the Gulf of Florida, March 10, 1773, and the crew saved by the vessel *Black Prince*, and taken to England. *Source:* St. James Chronicle, 4/13/1773. (8)

3) *APPLE*—Capt. Waketon, of and for Dublin, from the W. Indies, sprung a leak and foundered in the Gulf of Florida. All hands lost. *Source:* Caledonian Mercury, 9/27/1773. (8)

4) *SAVANNAH* or *SUSANNAH*—Brig, Capt. Gore, from Jamaica bound for Georgia, was lost in Gulf of Florida. *Source:* LL, 12/24/1773; General Evening Post, 12/23/1773. (8)

5) *LIBERTY*—Schooner, from Mississippi, Capt. John Hunt, was capsized near Cape Florida in 1773. On board was Bernard Romans, who mentions this wreck in his book. *Source:* 25. (5)

1) Page 212. *Dove*—Slave ship, from Africa bound for St. Augustine, when she wrecked on the St. Augustine Bar. Barnette says she wrecked one league south of Smyrna. *Source:* 7; 38. (6)

1774

1) *RYE GALLEY* (believe correct) *or REY OALSEY*—Ship, Capt. Robert Hunter, from Honduras bound for Glasgow, with mahogany and logwood, wrecked near Cape Florida, May 20, 1774. Vessel and cargo were a total loss; crew and sails were saved. *Source:* LEP, 8/9/1774; St. James Chronicle or British Evening Post, 8/18/1774. (5)

2) **Two Spanish MEN-OF-WAR** (one of 64 guns, other of 50 guns) and a **New England SHIP**—Reported from Jamaica that these were all lost during a gale in the Gulf of Florida, and all on board drowned. *Source:* London Craftsman, 7/16/1774. (8)

3) *ST. PETER*—French man-of-war. A letter from Cape Fear, reported the *St. Peter* had wrecked on the Dry Tortugas (believe in 1774). *Source: Stamford Mercury*, 1/26/1775. (3)

1775

1) *TRINIDADE*—More than one English paper reported that a French man-of-war *Trinidade*, of 74 guns foundered in a gale in the Gulf of Florida, and all on board perished. This may be a false report, as I've found no French ship by that name. *Source:* LEP, 4/18/1775. (8)

REVOLUTIONARY WAR PERIOD

1775

1) **Unk. SHIP**—Capt. Robinson, from Jamaica bound for Bristol, was cast away on the Martiers, September 24, 1775. *Source:* Morning Post and Daily Advertiser, 1/4/1776. (8)

2) **Spanish GALLEON**—Also mentioned in the report of Capt. Robinson's loss was that five Spanish galleons from Campeche were caught in a storm and four were dismasted. Two made it to Georgia and two to South Carolina, the other feared lost. Possible Florida wreck. *Source:* Ibid. (8)

1776

1) *MERIDETH*—Brig, 200 tons, two 6 pounders and eight 4 pounders, of Liverpool, Capt. W. Woodville, left St. Augustine for Liverpool in mid-January 1776, and never heard from again. Possible Florida wreck. *Source:* LL, 5/14/1776; LR 1776. (8)

2) *AMHURST* or *AMHERST* (Lloyds)—British ship, Captain B. Francis, 300 tons, built 1755, was lost at Pensacola. *Source:* LL, 11/22/1776; LR, 1776. (1)

1) Page 212. **Minerva**—A letter from Jamaica said, "His majesty's armed brig the *Minerva*, of 18 guns, commanded by a Lieutenant of the navy belonging to this station, is sunk in the Gulf of Florida by two American privateers, (who were cruizing for the homeward bound West-Indiamen) and the crew perished." Capt. Callahan. *Source:* General Evening Post, 8/3/1776; Public Advertiser, 4/19/1777. The *Minerva* is not listed as a royal naval ship, so I'm assuming she was acting as a privateer. Lloyd's Register of 1776 lists her at 180 tons and built in Boston, Capt, J. Callahan.

1777

1) *JAMAICA*—Capt. Mackey, from Jamaica bound for Liverpool, was burned due to lightning in the Gulf of Florida. *Source:* PA, 10/7/1777. (8)

2) *KEEPER*—British armed brig (privateer) was sunk in the Gulf of Florida by two American privateers in 1777. The crew were saved by the Americans. *Source:* Oxford Journal, 10/25/1777.

3) *BUTE*—English armed ship escorting the Jamaica Fleet. She sprung a leak and it was decided to scuttle her in the Gulf of Florida. The *HMS Pallas* took off all on board. *Source:* Kentish Gazette, 1/21/1778; Northampton Mercury, 1/19/1778. (8)

1) Page 213. *Glaudina* (correct name)—Left London, April 1877 for Pensacola. *Source:* Morning Post and Daily Advertiser, 4/18/1777; LL 12/23/1777.

1778

1) *GENERAL HOWE*—Ship, Capt. Thomas Salkeld, of Glasgow, was lost on the bar of the St. John's River. Captain and crew got ashore in the long boat, and some of the cargo was saved. Vessel went to pieces. *Source:* LEP, 4/4/1778. (6)

2) *ST. JOHN*—Report from Pensacola says the French ship *St. John*, from St. Domingo bound for the Mississippi, with gunpowder and Indian stores, was driven on the Florida coast to westward of the Cape, and lost with the crew and cargo. *Source:* LSJC, 4/28/1778. (*Note:* May be false as it sounds like the same French ship mentioned as lost in 1773 and continually reported for almost 10 more years.) (8)

3) Three British naval vessels the *Carysfort* (same *Carysfort* that the reef is named after), Capt. Fanshaw, the *Perseus*, Capt. Elphinstone, and the *Lizard*, Capt. McKenzie, either captured or destroyed 35 vessels off the Florida and Carolina coasts. Several which were armed vessels (these they took as prizes). Most were from France or the West Indies, loaded with clothing, ammunition, and salt. Ships destroyed are (can't say if lost off Florida or Carolina):

a) *WETHERAL*—Ship, was driven on shore. *Source:* LSJC, 6/2/1778, General Advertiser and Morning Intelligencer, 6/4/1778.

b) *BUCKSKIN*—Schooner, with tobacco and flour, was scuttled. *Source:* Ibid.

c) *THOMAS*—From Providence, was burned. *Source:* Ibid.

d) *NISBITT*—Burned. *Source:* Ibid.

e) *RACHAEL*—Burned. *Source:* Ibid.

f) *WOODCOCK*—Driven ashore. *Source:* Ibid.

g) *HOPE*—From Charles-Town, with rice and Indigo, and another *Ship*, also from Charles-Town, both foundered at sea, but the crews were saved by the British. *Source:* Ibid. Also of note, the British ship *Galtea* sent eight prizes into St. Augustine, and the privateers *Greyhound* and *Georgie*, along with the *Active* sent in 12 prizes. *Source:* Ibid.

4) *COMET*—British vessel, from Pensacola bound for Jamaica, was lost in a storm (October 1778 hurricane?) off Florida. Crew and mail saved. *Source:* LL, 3/9/1779. (8)

5) *WILLIAM*—Capt. Thomas, from Jamaica bound for Bristol, was lost on the coast of Florida. *Source:* LSJC, 12/8/1778. (8)

1) Page 108. *Mary*—Capt. Horncastle, 300 tons, built 1861 at and of Scarborough. *Source:* LR, 1778.

2) Page 136. *HMS Otter* (correct). *Source:* 10.

1779

1) *SALLY*—Capt. Hatten, from Jamaica bound for England, was lost on the east coast of Florida. *Source:* LSJC, 7/8/1779. (8)

2) *DOROTHY & MARY* and a **three-decked Vessel**—British vessel, 200 tons, Capt. P. Seward, had four 4-pounder and four 6-pounder cannons, from Jamaica bound for London. It was lost in the Gulf of Florida. An unknown three-decked vessel, of the Jamaica Fleet, also went on shore in the Gulf of Florida and was lost. *Source:* LL, 9/28/1779; EA, 10/1/1779; LR, 1779. (8)

3) **Spanish FRIGATE**—Was sunk by the *HMS Ferdinand* in the Gulf of Florida. They kept company for three days before engaging due to severe weather. The crew of the frigate was lost. *Source:* EA, 10/19/1779. (8)

1780

1) A large **Spanish fleet** sailed from Havana October 16, 1780, to take Pensacola which consisted of 11 warships and 51 transport ships. Two days later, the fleet was hit by a hurricane and some ships were lost and damaged, and what could, limped back to Havana. Most probable some of these wrecked off Florida.

Not to be deterred, another Spanish Fleet left Havana February 2, 1781, and by May 1781, Pensacola fell to the Spanish after a brutal battle there.

A British newspaper dated June 23, 1780, relayed a report from May 1780, which speaks of a Spanish fleet meant to invade West Florida. It says 105 vessels left Havana, but only 34 returned; the rest lost by storm or taken by the British. *Source:* EA. 6/23/1780. Another report said this fleet sailed for New Orleans with 3,000 men, when it encountered the storm, and two Spanish frigates and several transports were lost along with 700 men. Many did reach New Orleans and marched to Mobile, only to be defeated there by General Campbell and his West Florida troops. *Source:* Derby Mercury, 6/16/1780.

1781

1) *Le Defensuer*—Reported from Barbados, that the 74-gun French man of war *Le Defensuer*, with several land forces on board, foundered in the Gulf of Florida in a gale and all the crew perished. *Source:* London Chronicle, 10/18/1781. *Note:* The *Defenseur* was still listed in service in 1784, so this is likely incorrect.

1782

1) **Spanish SHIP**—Reported from Barbados that a Spanish ship with $60,000 on board, foundered in the Gulf of Florida and only seven of the crew survived. *Source:* Bristol Journal, 8/17/1782. (8)

1783

1) *FORTUNE*—Capt. Roach, from Barbados for London, was "lately lost on coast of Florida and all the crew perished." *Source:* LSJC, 3/6/1783. (8)

2) *NANCY*—Brig, Capt. Bayn, from St. Augustine for St. John's, Florida, was lost on the bar of St. Mary's, being drove to leeward by contrary winds. *Source:* London Chronicle, 9/27/1783. (6) *Note:* It was reported from Charleston on September 6 that a hurricane had hit St. Augustine and several vessels went ashore, including a London ship with a great number of Carolina refugees (loyalists), all who perished. *Source:* Annapolis Maryland Gazette, 10/2/1783.

1) Page 169. *Tonyn* (correct)—British ship, 200 tons, French built, 20 6-pounder cannons, from Charles Town, South Carolina, for St. Augustine and then London, Capt. P. Welsh, was lost on the St. Augustine Bar during

a violent gale (most likely one of the vessels mentioned earlier). Most of the crew were saved by lashing themselves to rafts. A Mrs. Abbot and her child drowned, not allowing themselves to be lashed to a raft. *Source:* LL, 11/4/1783; LR 1783; Leeds Intelligencer, 11/11/1783. (6)

END OF REVOLUTIONARY WAR PERIOD

1784

1) **SAILING FLEET**—Reported from New York, March 1784, "that 12 sail of small vessels, belonging to the fleet which left Charles-Town last December, were wrecked on St. Augustine-Bar; and a sloop near the Bar of St. John's." *Source:* Manchester Mercury, 4/29/1783.

2) *FORTITUDE*—Ship, Capt. Jones, from Jamaica bound for Bristol, was "lately lost on coast of Florida" and most of the crew perished. *Source:* London Chronicle, 4/15/1784. (8)

3) *REBECCA*—Schooner, Capt. Stewart, left Jamaica for Philadelphia, October 1784, was lost on the coast of Florida, crew saved. *Source:* Whitehall Evening Post, 4/7/1785. (8)

1785

1) *CYRUS*—His Majesty's ship, Capt. Brown. A letter from Nassau dated November 14, 1875, states that the *Cyrus*, on leaving St. Mary's, struck on the bar. To prevent her from grounding further, one anchor was let out, but the wind then changed driving her over the anchor which then went through her bottom. She was off and into the harbor on the bank just before she sank. On board were his Excellency Governor Tonyn and suite, embarked for England. Colledge lists a *Cyrus* as a transport ship, 461 bm (an early tonnage measurement), 111' x 30.5', purchased in 1771, lost off Barbados April 22, 1786. She was possibly salvaged or even a different vessel. Only other *Cyrus* I found was a store ship, filled with valuable naval stores, which sank off Antigua, April 18, 1876, which is likely the same vessel Colledge mentions. *Source:* London Chronicle, 1/21/1786; 10. (6)

1786

1) Page 213. *Caroline*—Brig, Capt. C. Grant, 180 tons, built at Boston, was actually lost in the Bahamas on some rocks called the Southern Rokuses some 20 leagues from land, and landed on Andrew's Island (likely Andros)

in their boat. *Source:* London Chronicle, 5/27/1786; LR, 1786; Annapolis Maryland Gazette, 8/10/1786; Kentish Gazette, 6/2/1786 (full story).

1787

1) Page 108. ***Nobel Bounty***—Built 1771, of Ipswich, 300 tons, single deck with beams, from Jamaica for London. Crew saved by the vessel *Friendship*, who also saw two ships ashore on coming around Cape Florida. Some of the cargo was saved. *Source:* London World Fashionable Advertiser, 9/16/1787; LR, 1787.

2) Pages 213–14. ***Alfred***—Ship, 300 tons, built 1749, Capt. Stuart or G. Stupart, of Jamaica, wrecked along with the *Albion* on the Florida shore, the middle of August 1787, during a gale north off Cape Florida. Crews and some cargo saved. *Source:* PA, 1/9/1788; London Chronicle, 10/11/1787; LR, 1787. (5)

2a) ***Albion***—Ship, 300 tons, built 1774, Capt. T. Whitehead, wrecked along with the *Alfred*. *Source:* Ibid. (5)

1788

1) ***BELL***—Slave ship, of Glasgow, from Jamaica bound for Georgia, was struck by lightning, April 1, 1788, instantly killing 11 of the crew. The captain and two crewmen survived but were injured. A few hours later the vessel with 150 slaves went down. Captain and the two others lashed some spars together for a raft and reached a key near Cape Florida where they remained for five weeks in dire condition. Only two survived, being picked up by a New Providence wrecker. The captain lost both legs and an arm, and the other, a Robert Boyd, could not use his legs. The loss of all the poor souls left on board makes this one of the worst maritime disasters off the coast of Florida. Were they left shackled or locked below decks so there was no chance to escape? One can only imagine the nightmare they must have endured. *Source:* Historical Magazine, 1/1/1789. (4)

1) Page 169. ***Betsey***—Sloop, lost October 25, 1787. Twelve of the 16 on board drowned, including two children. *Source:* PA, 4/5/1788.

2) Page 214. ***Everly*** (correct)—She was got off and continued to London. *Source:* London Chronicle, 11/15–18/1788.

3) Page 214. ***Mary & Jane*** or ***Mary & James*** (papers say *Mary & James*, Lloyd's says *Mary & Jane*)—Brig, of Whitehaven, 190 tons, built 1785 at Whitehaven, Capt. James Perriment or Penniment. From Old Harbour, Jamaica

bound for London, with 280 hogsheads of sugar, 50 puncheons of rum, 70 bags cotton, and some dyewood and ginger, stranded on the Martyr's Reef, August 28, 1788. Some cargo saved and taken to Nassau. Vessel lost. *Source:* Ibid, LR, 1787.

1789

1) **Unk. Large SHIP**—Ship *Ark* reported on July 29, 1789, that she saw a wreck of a large ship off Cape Florida which was a home-bound West Indiaman. Was burned to the water's edge. A number of hogsheads with sugar were in her hold with letter "PC" and a diamond in between. *Source:* LSJC, 11/17/1789.

1) Page 108. *Hazard*—Capt. T. New, of Stockton, 300 tons. *Source:* LR, 1789.

1790

1) *NUESTRA SEÑORA de la CONCEPTION*—Spanish ship, abandoned at Lat. 24°30'N, 84°00'W, October 14, 1790. From Truxillo for Trinidad. *Source:* The Times London, 1/19/1791. (2)

1) Page 108. *Apollo*—Ship, 300 tons, built 1781, Capt. Cragg, wrecked on the Florida shore near the *Edward & George. Source:* LR, 1790.

2) Page 108. *Edward & George* (correct)—Capt. T. Rainey, 343 tons. Wrecked near the *Apollo*, three leagues west of Cape Florida. *Source:* PA, 10/13/1790; LR, 1790.

3) Page 214. *Thetis*—Ship, 250 tons, Capt. C. Moore, of Bristol, built 1781, lost near Cape Florida. *Source:* LSJC, 10/12/1790; LR & LL, 1790. (5)

4) Page 214. *Abby*—Brig, 168 tons, Capt. Braithwaite, built in 1786, of White-haven, bound for Dublin, was lost near Cape Florida with a cargo of rum and sugar. *Source:* LSJC, 10/12/1790; Dublin Journal, 10/19/1790; LR & LL, 1790. *Note:* Was also reported as the brig *Albion*, 168 tons, also built in 1886 but must be the *Abby* as the *Albion* is still listed in service later on. (5) 1791

1) *GALGO*—Spanish brig (royal packet), Capt. Joseph Rodriga Cabsers, with a cargo of some Lumber, and passengers, left New Orleans June 21, 1791, bound for Havana. At 5 a.m. on June 23, she was capsized in a storm about 40 leagues from Pensacola. Eight persons were immediately lost including a Mrs. Palao and her daughter, most being trapped in the cabin though a few escaped swimming underwater and grabbing onto some

rigging. The survivors then clung to the side of the wreck. The *Annapolis Maryland Gazette* of 9/15/1791, reported the disaster:

> When the party, for about the space of four hours, conceiving every moment the last, had sustained the violence of the waves, in a boisterous storm, rain, and thunder, amidst the dreadful scene of floating deceased friends; (for the portion between the cabin and the main deck was at this time destroyed by the irresistible force of the sea, and consequently everything washed out,) the masts at once gave way at the deck, and cleared the wreck by the agitation of the sea, which gave liberty to the hull, to right itself so as to admit the crew to enter the highest side of the quarterdeck, in which situation, filled with water, and loaded with green lumber, she at best floated very deep, and in consequence of her pitching but seldom above water.
>
> In about fifty-five hours after this disastrous event, the wind and waves fortunately abated, which afforded an opportunity to kindle a fire, which a flint and steel, which a peculiar circumstance had preserved:—Night now coming on, the people fatigued and exhausted by the want of fresh water, &c. found means to tie themselves on the highest places on the hull, to indulge in some degree a requisite repose, secured from the dangerous washing of the ocean; first establishing a watch by turns to keep up the light, in hopes to draw attention, if any vessel should, by the will of Providence, be directed that way; which had the wished for effect.

One vessel passed them by and offered no help, but the next day, Capt. Dolhonde of the vessel *Amiable Maria*, rescued the 19 remaining survivors and landed them in Cuba on July 19.

1) Page 214. *Hope*—Ship, of New Brunswick, Capt. George Chappell, from Jamaica for Charleston, in ballast, was driven ashore in a gale, December 10, 1790, about 40 leagues south of St. Augustine. Crew, sails, and rigging saved by the sloop *Tamar*. *Source:* Lloyds Evening Post, 2/11/1791. (6)

2) Page 214. *Lively*—Capt. W. Morse, of Bristol. *Source:* LR, 1791.

3) Page 214. *Prince of Austurias*—French ship, about 200 tons, continued to be listed in *Lloyd's Register* after 1792, so believe saved. *Source:* LR, 1794.

1793

1) Page 215. *Brothers*—Ship, copper bottomed, 325 tons, Capt. J. Withers. *Source:* LR 1793.

2) Page 215. *General Clary* (this is the other name reported besides the *General Clark*)—*Source:* Edinburgh Advertiser, 7/2/1793.

1794

1) *NANCY*—Brig, of Norfolk, Capt. Beesom, from Jamaica for Norfolk, "was cast away on the coast of Florida. The captain, crew, and part of the cargo saved, and the brig lost." The crew were picked up by the schooner *Hopewell. Source:* GUS, 6/14/1795. (8)

2) *COLUMBUS*—Went ashore on the Martiers and was a total lost. *Source:* LSJC, 10/14/1794. (8)

3) *LUCY and MOLLY*—Brigantine, of Boston, built 1789 at Plantation Four, Maine, 87 tons, 62' x 21'2" x 7'11", one deck, two masts, square stern, Capt. Joseph Doalbeare. Was lost off St. Augustine in 1794. *Source:* 27. (6)

1) Page 215. *Catherine Green*—Ship, copper sheathed, 316 tons, had 10 12-pounder cannons. Part of large fleet that left Jamaica, Capt. William Rose. Lost on the Florida Reef near Matecumbe Bay, with rum, sugar, coffee, pimento and cotton, August 8, 1794, in a hurricane. Most cargo saved. *Source:* LL, 1794; LSJC, 9/25/1794. (3)

2) Page 215. *Vigilant*—Capt. Richardson, was lost off Cape Florida, August 28, 1794, during a hurricane (another says driven ashore on the Martyr's Reef, August 25 after losing masts in the storm (believe they went through bottom). Some cargo of mahogany saved. *Source:* LL, 10/16/94; LSJC, 12/2/1784; LR, 1794. (8)

1795

1) *OLIVE*—Sloop, of Portsmouth, New Hampshire, Capt. Chaberlayne, from Jamaica for New York, with coffee, was driven ashore, February 22, 1795, on Martyr's Reef. Next morning the wreckers saved the crew, cargo, and part of the ship's materials. *Source:* GUS, 3/20/1795. (8)

2) *CA-IRA*—Privateer schooner, Capt. Harvier, "was cast away in a severe gale of wind on the coast of Florida about 45 miles from Augustine." Crew saved, vessel a total loss. Captain and part of the crew confined to the castle, and the sick sent to the hospital. *Source:* GUS, 6/25/1795. (6)

3) *ALLIGATOR*—Of Norfolk, bound for the Turks Islands for salt, foundered in the Gulf of Florida. Some crew saved by the brig *General Green* of Philadelphia. *Source:* Morning Post and Fashionable World, 11/10/1795. (8)

1) Page 215. *Noah's Ark*—Brig, Captain Jacock, wrecked on the Martyrs around May 1, 1795. Had a number of French passengers bound for Philadelphia. The captain went down to his cabin to get some papers before

abandoning ship, but before when he came back on deck, "a Mr. Robins, with three of four others, jumped in the brig's boat and went off to sea." The 30 or so left now had no means of escape and the captain prepared: "Thus circumstanced he was under the necessity of preparing a raft, on which he, the crew, and the remainder of the passengers entered, and committed themselves to the mercy of the waves: In that situation, they remained for about thirty hours, at which time they were providentially picked up by Captain Churnside of the brig *Swallow*." *Source:* GUS, 5/13/1795.

Illustration of shipwreck survivors on a raft, by Hildibrand. *Great Shipwrecks*, 1880.

1796

1) *SPIRITO SANTO*—Spanish ship, wrecked at St. Augustine with the loss of four crewmen. *Source:* Times London 3/9/1796. (6)

2) Some of the following may be part of the fleet of merchantmen that sailed from Jamaica under the protection of the *HMS Sampson* of 64 guns. The *Sampson* arrived at Plymouth January 4, 1797, and reported she lost track of all 14 vessels in a severe gale in the Gulf of Florida and feared the worst. *Source:* Evening Mail, 1/6/1797.

   a) *MARIA*—Transport, Capt. Gilchrist, from Jamaica, was lost on Ledbury Reef. *Source:* BWM, 10/16/1796. (4)

b) *VIGILANT*—Transport ship, Capt. McPherson, from Jamaica, cast away on the Florida Keys in a heavy gale and entirely lost, September 1796. Captain and crew saved by the schooner *Two Brothers* and taken to Savannah. *Source:* London Star, 11/10/1796; GUS, 10/10/1796. (4)

c) *WILLIAM and MARY*—Capt. Courton, of the *Two Brothers*, saw another ship on shore believed to be the *William & Mary*, which soon after went to pieces and was feared all on board were lost. *Source:* GUS, 10/10/1796. (4)

d) *CLARISSA*—Sloop, Capt. Jef. Cougdon, of New York, was also lost on the same Key as the *Vigilant*. Crew and some cargo also saved by *Two Brothers*. *Source:* GUS, 10/10/1796. (4)

e) *FELICITY*—Schooner, of Philadelphia, was abandoned after being upset in a storm, at Lat. 27°30'N, off Florida. After three days in the boat, were picked up by the schooner *Active*. The next day the *Active* saw two wrecks on the reef within Key Largo with wreckers nearby. *Source:* GUS, 10/4–10/1796. (4)

1) Page 108. *HMS Bermuda* (correct)—Loss of all 121 on board. *Source:* 11.

2) Page 109. *Hope*—Brig, of Philadelphia, was seen ashore on Hais Reef (sic), June 15, 1796 (Lloyd's List states wrecked near Cape Florida). From Havana. Ship *Louisa* took off her captain and his trunks and believed the cargo would be saved. *Source:* GUS, 7/9/1796; BWM, 8/21/1796.

3) Page 215. *Ranger*—Bark, Capt. N. Dobson, 231 tons, of Stockton. *Source:* LR, 1796.

4) Page 215. *Jolly Tar*—Capt. Brayman, was lost during a gale on the Florida coast, August 25, 1796, cargo, rigging, sails and crew saved. *Source:* GUS, 10/10/1796.; London Star, 11/25/1796.

1797

1) *BETSY*—Brigantine, of Philadelphia, built 1783 at Osborne, Virginia, 122 tons, 79' x 20' x 18', two decks, believed wrecked on the Florida coast around January 1797. *Source:* 27. (8)

2) Hurricane of October 15–16, 1797. A number of vessels were lost on the Florida coast. Some are:

a) *COMMERCE*—Brig, of Baltimore, Capt. Gardiner, was totally lost on Key Largo. After three days with no food or water, the crew were rescued from the Key by an English privateer and treated well. *Source:* GUS, 11/20/1797; Newport Mercury, 11/28/1797. (4)

b) **Unk. BRIG**—Of Bristol, RI, from Havana, Capt. Trownston, totally lost off the Florida coast, some cargo saved. *Source:* Ibid. (8)

c) *EXPERIMENT*—Ship, Capt. Brownlow, from Charleston bound for Havana, foundered in the Gulf. Captain arrived in New Providence after 10 days in boat. Possible Florida wreck. *Source:* Ibid. (8)

1798

1) *DURCAS* or *DORCUS*—Brig, of Washington, North Carolina, Capt. J. Britte, 140 tons, from Kingston for Washington, wrecked on the Dry Tortugas. Crew took to the boat and made for Cuba. A privateer came across them and took all except the captain, one crewman, and a boy who all had the fever. The captain and crewman died, but the boy made landfall alive on the shore of Cuba about 15 miles from Havana. Another report has a different story. It said the *Dorcas* wrecked on the Dry Tortugas, January 11, 1798, under Captain Nathaniel Mitchel, and was a total wreck. The privateer brig *Lark* came to their assistance the next day and took off the mate and four crew, the captain and four others staying by the wreck. The mate and two of the men were then transferred to the brig *Polly* later on. Likely the *Lark* did find the whole crew, but fearing the fever, only rescued those who were not sick. *Source:* The Pennsylvania Gazette, 5/2/1798; LR 1798; LR, 1798; GUS, 2/7/1798. (3)

1799

1) Pages 23–24. *HMS Fox*—Bilged in 7 feet of water. Crew made it to a coral reef and stayed for 33 days. The privateer *Providence* rescued them. *Source:* Observer London Middlesex, 3/2/1800.

2) Page 136. *HMS Amaranthe* (correct)—The captain and others were supposedly captured by the Spanish, and exchanged for their prisoners and sent to Jamaica. *Source:* EA, 4/1/1800.

1800

1) *MARY AND NANCY*—Brig, Capt. Crimpton, of Philadelphia, was lost on the Florida Reef around June 1800. A sailor from the brig was placed on the brig *Fame* by a New Providence privateer. *Source:* GUS, 7/18/1800. (8)

2) *MOLLY AND FANNY*—Brig, Capt. Benjamin Kempton, from Havana for Philadelphia, left Havana May 24, 1800, and when off Florida in a heavy sea, she let go her bower anchor and spun round into the wind striking a

reef or bar and lost her rudder. She soon had six feet of water in her hold. The crew tried to save her, but when water reached above the cabin floor, she was abandoned, and the captain and crew took to the boat. They were picked up by three New Providence privateers. *Source:* GUS, 7/25/1800. (8)

3) *TANNER*—Ship, of New York, Capt. J. O'Brien, 215 tons, copper sheathed with iron bolts, five years old, from Vera Cruz for Spain, with the Vice King on board as a passenger. She was captured by a British frigate who let her proceed to Havana to drop off the Vice King. She was then taken to Kingston where a lieutenant was placed on board as prize-master along with some seamen. She wrecked on the Martyr's Reef soon after. She was a large ship, copper bottomed, mounting 16 guns. *Source:* GUS, 7/25/1800; LR, 1799–1800. (8)

4) *BELLONA*—American privateer ship, reported by a British vessel on December 27, 1800, that the 16-gun rebel privateer *Bellona*, wrecked on the bar at St. Augustine Harbor. The crew of 68 were taken prisoner there and most of the cannon and stores were saved. *Source:* London Chronicle, 2/17/1801. (6)

1) Page 215. *Hector*—This is an unusual story. This was a Spanish ship previously owned by an Englishman named Reid, and who was also on board as an agent. She sailed from Havana in August 1800, bound for Nassau. Though England and Spain were at war, the Bahamian governor had signed a license giving the ship protection from any English ships. The cargo was reported to consist of raw hides, logwood, and 270 boxes of sugar of which 200 of these contained 1,000 Spanish dollars each, "made up in rolls, called cartridges, and amounting, in the whole, to two hundred thousand." The cargo was insured in England, and would be worth much more today. The captain and owner was Don Juan De Villers. On her fourth day out, though the weather was calm, she struck a reef, got off, but struck another soon after near Cape Florida called the Martyr's Reefs, the pilot blaming the strong currents. They had to abandon ship and took to the boats, landing on a deserted island for shelter from the weather. They lit a fire, and some Bahamian wreckers took them aboard the next day. The wreckers tried everything to float the ship and save any cargo using a diving bell and other equipment, but as only her gunnel was above water, there was no saving the ship. Only a few hides, some logwood, and some wet sugar were saved. The bottom of all the sugar boxes had fallen out, and all the specie sank to the bottom and none was recovered.

A few years later, Mr. Reid sued the underwriters for the loss of the cargo. There were many legal problems considering Spain was considered an enemy, the money was illegally being transported as per Spanish law, and there were other legal problems, as there was no proof the money was even on board, that the cargo and ship were Spanish property (supposedly previously owned by Reid), and so on. It appears Mr. Reid did at least partially win his case. *Source:* Globe (London) 12/24/1805; London St. James Chronicle or London Evening Post, 11/26/1806.

1801

1) *ELIZA*—American ship, from Jamaica for New York, foundered off Florida, at Lat. 29°N, Long. 82°W (incorrect as would be in the middle of Florida) in 1801. *Source:* LL, 1/29/1802. (8)

1) Page 216. *Eagle*—Capt. Dennett, from Havana for Philadelphia, wrecked December 15, 1801, on the Florida side of Maranzie's Reef (probably meant Martiers—another report just says Florida Reef). Crew and cargo saved. *Source:* London Star, 2/6/1802; LL, 6/1/1802. (8)

1802

1) *NANCY*—American schooner, Capt. Chace, from Tobago for Charleston; was "cast away on the Martyr's Reef," February 13, 1802. Crew arrived in Nassau on the schooner *Venus*. *Source:* Georgia Gazette, 3/4/1802.

2) *OAKS*—Schooner, Capt. Nipkins, from Charleston for Havana, was lost on the Martyr's reef, February 17, 1802. Crew andd some cargo saved by the schooner *Adventure*, and taken to Nassau. *Source:* Ibid.

3) *UNION*—Brig, Capt. Long, from Mariel, Cuba, for New York, was lost on the Martyr's Reef, May 1, 1802. All on board saved. *Source:* Georgia Gazette, 6/17/1802.

1) Page 216. *John*—Capt. Dawson, wrecked on Martiers Reef (Keys), June 17, 1802. Crew saved and arrived at Charleston. *Source:* London Star, 10/21/1802; Edinburgh Weekly Journal, 6/30/1802.

2) Page 216. *Neptune*—Capt. Cashbury, from New Orleans bound for Greenock. *Source:* BWM, 8/29/1802.

1803

1) **Spanish SHIP** and a **SNOW**—Both of Cadiz, were lost on Mocus (sic) Reef, Florida shore, January 1803. *Source:* LL, 3/25/1803. (8)

1804

1) *CHARLOTTE*—Sloop, Capt. Dickenson, of New London, from Charleston, wrecked on the Florida Reef and robbed of most all her cargo by the Spanish wreckers. Capt. Haley of the schooner *Sally*, fell in with her on June 15, 1804, and took off the captain, crew, and the remaining cargo of rum (seven puncheons) on board. *Source:* Morning Chronicle, 10/13/1804. (8)

2) *BEAVER*—On July 9, Capt. Haley of the *Sally* fell in with another wrecked ship, the brig *Beaver*, of Savannah, stranded on a reef off the Tortugas which had been abandoned by her crew. Capt. Haley took off 82 puncheons of Jamaican rum and some sails, rigging, and the like. *Source:* Morning Chronicle, 10/13/1804. (3)

3) *SUSAN*—Ship, of Providence, Rhode Island, Capt. John Gladding, built 1794 at Warren, 238 tons, 89'3" x 24'8" x 12'4", two decks, three masts, had a woman figurehead. Lost on the Florida Reef around October 5, 1804. *Source:* 27. (8)

4) *SALLY*—Sloop, Capt. Burlbutt, wrecked November 10, 1804, "on the Florida shore, to the southward of New River." Reported as wrecked about two miles from the *Athenaise* (page 266; this is the sloop mentioned in that story). If not for the provisions on the *Sally*, the crew and prisoners on the *Athenaise* would have been in much worse shape and many may have starved. *Source:* Courier (London), 2/28/1805; Evening Mail (London), 3/1/1805. (5)

1805

1) *CONCORD*—American ship, was detained by *HMS Fly* and *Rattler* and wrecked along with those two ships on Carysfort Reef in 1805. *Source:* LL, 5/3/1805. (4)

2) *BROMDEN*—Capt. Gibson or Gibsen, from New Orleans for Bordeaux, lost on the Florida Reef. *Source:* British Press, 11/22/1805; London Star, 11/21/1805. *Note:* This may be the same ship as the *Providence* (page 216), as both are listed with the same captain's name. Lloyd's lists a *Providence*, Capt. Gibson, as wrecked on the Florida Reef, though it also lists another *Providence* in the same report as wrecked at Orfordness. Lloyd's may have gotten the names mixed up as a number of papers say the *Bromden*, which I believe is correct. (8)

1) Page 109. *HMS Fly* (correct)—*Source:* 11.

2) Page 109. *Rattler*—Ship, 287 tons, sheathed with copper, iron bolts. *Source:* LR, 1805.

1806/1807

1) *SEAFLOWER*—Capt. Fitch from Jamaica and Havana for New York, was lost off the Florida shore. *Source:* LL, 3/20/1807. (8)

2) *TRUSTY*—Capt. Smith, wrecked on the Florida Reef (Lloyd's just says in Gulf). The *Trusty* and the *Minerva* both left Jamaica in a fleet escorted by *HMS Hunter* which also struck and lost her rudder. Crews of both, and most cargo and materials were saved. *Source:* LL, 5/20/1806; Royal Cornwall Gazette, 7/5/1806. (8)

3) *MINERVA*—Brig, from Kingston for Quebec, went ashore near the wreck of the *Trusty*, March 19, 1806. *Source:* Ibid. (8)

1) Page 217. *Flora*—The Hibernian Journal, June 3, 1807, reported that the *Flora* arrived at New Providence having been aground on the Florida Reef.

1808

1) *MERCHANT*—Schooner, from Havana for Charleston, wrecked off Key Largo, January 1808. Most of the crew and some cargo saved by some Bahamians. Survivor Vincent Nolte wrote about it in his memoirs. *Source:* 37. (4)

1) Page 109. *Ohio*—Ship, Capt. A. Hall, of New York, 175 tons. *Source:* LR, 1808.

1809

1) *DRAGON*—British ship, Capt. Ayres, from Haiti and Barbados for London, was totally lost on the coast of Florida. *Source:* LL, 3/24/1809. (8)

2) *GENERAL BERESFORD*—British ship, Capt. Appleby, from British Honduras for Bristol, was lost in the Gulf of Florida. *Source:* LL, 12/8/1809. (8)

3) *TWO FRIENDS*—Brig, Capt. Hand, from Savannah for Amelia Island, parted cables and bilged in a gale on Amelia Island. Cargo of cotton saved. *Source:* RSEL, 12/19/1809. (6)

1810

1) *GENERAL PINKNEY*—Ship, of and from Charleston for Amelia, bilged on the north breakers of Amelia Island. Cargo saved. *Source:* RSEL, 3/20/1810. (6)

2) *INDUSTRY*—Sloop, Capt. Moorhouse, wrecked at Cape Canaveral in 1810. Cargo of cotton saved. *Source:* RSEL, 5/19/10.

3) October 1810 hurricane:

a) *ANNA*—Capt. Hooper, of Baltimore, from Havana for Baltimore, was totally lost October 25 or 26, 1810, on the Florida shore, at Lat. 26°30'N. Crew saved. *Source:* BWM, 1/20/1811; RSEL, 12/6/1810. (5)

b) *MARIA-GERTRUDE*—Spanish brig, Capt. Don Pedro Munis, wrecked same time and place as the *Anna*. *Source:* RSEL, 12/6/1810. (5)

c) *ARGUS*—Brig, Capt. Bronham, from New Haven for Barbados, was driven ashore near the *Maria-Gertrude*, October 28, 1810. A total loss, crew saved. *Source:* BWM, 1/20/1811; RSEL, 12/6/1810. (5)

d) *JOSEPH*—Schooner, Capt. Frothingham, of Boston, from Nassau for Philadelphia, was lost October 26, 1810, on the Florida coast. Crew took to the boat and landed on shore. Took the boat overland to a lake and left it there November 13. *Source:* BWM 1/20/1811; RSEL, 12/6/1810. (6)

e) *OLYMPUS*—Brig, of Boston, from New Orleans for Ronningen, Norway, was lost October 28, 1810, on the Florida coast. Crew took to the boat and went through a lake with it. They found a tent with a man named John Williams of New York, barely alive and left by his comrades (likely from the *Joseph*), who was in bad shape from his injuries and later died. *Source:* RSEL, 12/6/1810. (6)

f) *U.S. GUNBOAT #159*—Left Savannah for St. Mary's and never heard from again—believed lost in the same gale. Possible Florida wreck. *Source:* RSEL, 11/15/10. (8)

g) *AMELIA*—Sloop, Capt. Morrison, driven ashore October 1810, on Amelia Beach. From Charleston for Amelia. Crew and cargo saved, vessel lost. *Source:* RSEL, 11/10/1810. (6)

h) *KITTY-ANN*—Schooner, Capt. Rudolph, from Charleston for St. Mary's, was driven ashore on Amelia Beach during a gale, October 18, 1810. Expected to be a total loss. *Source:* RSEL, 11/6/1810. (6)

i) *HURON*—Ship, Capt. Toby, of New Bedford, from New Orleans for New York, with tobacco, cotton & logwood. Wrecked at the same place as the *Cabinet* (Key Biscayne), October 26, 1810. Most cargo saved from both vessels along with passengers and crew by wrecking schooner *Rake's Delight*, and arrived in Nassau. *Source:* RSEL, 11/27/1810.

j) *NUESTRA SEÑORA DE CARMEN* alias *la Arancarra*—Schooner packet, from Havana for Cadiz, with the royal dispatches from Havana, Cartagena, and Vera Cruz. Wrecked on Aliot Key (believe Elliot Key), October 27, 1810. Passengers and crew got safely on the island, and were rescued by wrecking vessel *James & Charlotte*, and taken to Nassau. *Source:* Ibid.

1) Pages 136 and 140. *Triton*—Of Philadelphia, with sugar, coffee and logwood, wrecked October 19 in same area as the *Fame*. Vessel, cargo, and one man lost. *Source:* RSEL, 11/15/1810.

2) Page 140. *Caroline*—Of New Orleans, built at New Market, New Hampshire, in 1800, 189 tons, 77' x 24' x 12', two decks, three masts, square stern. Wrecked about six miles south of Indian River. Capt. Daniel Curtis, with cotton, wrecked October 25, at Lat. 27-23. One crew lost. Ship and cargo a total loss. *Source:* 27; RSEL, 11/5/1810.

3) Page 140. *Union*—Capt. Domingo Antonio Lordua, from Havana for London, with logwood, wrecked same time and near the *Caroline* (page 140). Captain and four crew lost, 15 others saved. *Source:* RSEL, 11/15/1810.

4) Page 140. *African*—Spanish brig, Capt. Don Francisco Garcia, from Havana for New York, went ashore same time and place as the *Union*. Vessel, cargo and one man lost. *Source:* RSEL, 11/15/1810.

5) Page 170. *Hanover*—Ship, of New York, Capt. Baxter, from Liverpool for Amelia Island, wrecked October 26, 1810, four miles south of Mosquito Inlet. *Source:* RSEL, 12/6/1810. *Note:* One report has the name of the ship as the *Andrew*.

5a) Page 170. *George*—Brig, of New York, Capt. Decone, from Liverpool, was lost in same gale near St. Augustine, ship and one man lost. *Source:* RSEL, 11/15/1810. Another report says she was a ship, of New York, from Liverpool for Amelia Island. One crewman was lost. *Source:* London Pilot, 1/18/1811.

6) Page 170. *Intrepid*—Sloop or schooner, with passengers, Capt. Fowler, from St. Mary's for Savannah, with salt and cotton, wrecked at St. Augustine, November 1810. A number of lives were lost including the captain's wife and children. *Source:* London Pilot, 1/7/1811; RSEL, 11/10/1810.

7) Page 217. *Fame*—Ship, Capt. Bennett, from New Orleans for Liverpool, with 500 bales cotton, was cast away on Martyr's Reef around October 14,

1810, near Key Tavernier. All crew saved and taken to Charleston. About 390 bales of cotton saved. *Source:* RSEL, 11/27/1810.

8) Page 217. *Cabinet*—Ship, of New Orleans, with cotton and a few tons of logwood, wrecked near Key Biscayne, October 25, 1810. *Source:* Ibid.

1811

1) *AMBROSIA*—British ship, Capt. H. Moon, 217 tons, 11 years old, copper sheathed. Left Jamaica July 7, 1811, for London. Wrecked on the Florida Reef, July 21, 1811, crew saved. *Source:* Liverpool Mercury, 11/15/1811; London St. James Chronicle and Evening Post, 11/12/1811; LR, 1811. (8)

2) *TRIDENT*—Brig, of Portland, Maine, Capt. Robinson, from Havana for New York, with sugar and coffee, wrecked on the west coast of Florida, October 16, 1811. Crew and cargo saved and taken to Nassau. *Source:* RSEL, 11/23/1811. (2)

3) *ELIZA*—Brig, Capt. Collins, from Havana for Boston, with rum and sugar, was lost off the west coast of Florida, October 10, 1811. Crew and cargo saved and taken to New Providence. *Source:* Ibid, 11/23/1811. (2)

4) *MOUNT ROYAL*—British ship, 170 tons, 20 years old, had six guns, Capt. Hall, from Pensacola bound for England. Wrecked during a gale, at Pensacola, October 11, 1811. *Source:* LL, 12/27/1811; LR, 1811. (1)

5) *MARY*—Capt. Forbes, was a total loss on Amelia Island, October 1811. Probably the same vessel listed on page 170 as the *Maria*. *Source:* LL, 12/27/1811. (6)

6) **PILOT BOAT**—A pilot boat was on its way to the steamer *William Gaston*, which lay outside the bar at Ft. Pierce, October 25, 1811, when she capsized in the rough surf. Mr. Ashlock, a boy, two crewmen, and seven U.S. soldiers all drowned. The captain of the *Gaston* immediately sent one of his yawl boats to look for survivors, but it also capsized, drowning three of the four on board. *Source:* Gettysburg Adams Sentinel, 11/22/1811. (5)

1) Page 170. **North Star**—In November 1810, the brig *Musquito* reported she saw the *North Star* abandoned and drifting at Lat. 29°18', dismasted and with 6 feet of water in her hold. She also reported her as a brig, of Hartford, and believed from the West Indies as still had some fruit on board. *Source:* RSEL, 11/20/1810. Probably drifted till she wrecked on Amelia Isle.

1812

1) **Unk. BRIG**—Of Boston, from New Orleans, with cotton, reported from Charleston, July 22, 1812, as wrecked on the Florida shore. Crew and cargo saved by the Bahamian wreckers and taken to Nassau. *Source:* RSEL, 7/25/1812. (8)

2) *ONTARIO*—Capt. Mix, from Liverpool, struck the bar at Amelia Island, April 29, 1812, during a gale. She was severely damaged and was believed she would be condemned. *Source:* LL, 6/30/1812. (6)

1) Page 109. *Highlander*—Brig, copper sheathed and fastened, 209 tons, built in Denmark. *Source:* LR, 1812.

1813

1) The August/September 1813 hurricane slammed Florida's northeast coast and further up the eastern seaboard, destroying many houses on Amelia Island, Fernandina, St. Mary's, Georgia, and all along the St. Mary's River. The storm had previously swept the Caribbean causing much damage. It hit the island of Dominica on July 23 and eventually made its way to Nassau, Bahamas, where it destroyed 130 sailing vessels and much of the town. The packet-boat *Eclipse*, which arrived at Charleston on September 23, and who rode out the storm in the St. Mary's River, reported the following. The privateer *SAUCY JACK*, of Charleston, was driven into the marsh, but probably could be saved. One **Gun-boat** was sunk with the loss of 23 of the 29 crew on board. Two other **Gun-boats** were driven on shore. The **Custom-house barge** was sunk and two crew drowned. The Commodore's gig was destroyed. The large British ship *EMPEROR* was drove on shore high up the river, and the Florida Patriots were threatening to burn her. Lloyd's list her as captured, was four years old, 575 tons, and copper fastened. Other reports said every vessel in the harbor at Fernandina was blown ashore except a Swedish brig. Other reports say **three Gun-boats** were sunk at St. Mary's, and some were high and dry on the Florida side. All the smaller vessels at St. Mary's are all ashore on both sides of the river. Also reported that the schooner *GOOD INTENT*, Capt. Williams, bound to Amelia Island with a load of cotton, "wrecked at the Musquito in the gale-the cargo saved." *Source:* The London St. James Chronicle and Evening Post, 11/18/1813; Gettysburg Adams Centinel, 10/13/1813; Annapolis Maryland Republican, 9/18/1813; LR, 1813. (6–7)

2) **Unk. BRIG**—Had been captured off Jamaica in 1813 by the American privateer *Lovely Cordelia* and was wrecked on the Florida coast on her way to St. Mary's. *Source:* RSEL, 11/2/1813. (8)

1) Page 170. **Flor de Guadiana** or **Flor Guardiana** (formerly the *Alexander Hamilton* and likely correct name)—Portuguese ship (not Spanish). Wrecked on the south end of Cumberland Island during the September hurricane, and much of the cargo of sea island cotton and materials from the ship were saved and sold at auction. *Source:* RSEL, 9/23–25/1813; Gettysburg Adams Centinel, 10/13//1813.

1814

1) *AMERICANO*—Capt. Abren, from Havana for Lisbon, wrecked July 26, 1814, on one of the Florida Reefs. *Source:* BWM, 9/4/1814. (8)

1815

1) Page 217. **Watt** or **Watts**—British brig, Capt. McGee, from Montego Bay for New York, wrecked on the Florida Reef, early Sept 1815. *Source:* Morning Post, 10/28/1815; BWM, 10/29/1815. (8)

1816

Note: Appears two hurricanes hit the Florida coasts in 1816, one in June (5th–8th) and another in September.

1) *WILLIAM*—British Brig, Capt. Kennedy, from Charleston for St Mary's, wrecked near the *Due Bill & Water Witch* at the same time. *Source:* LL 8/13/1816. (6)

2) *ORPHEUS*—British ship, 306 tons, copper sheathed, three years old (built in America). From New Orleans for Liverpool, Capt. Bathgate. Foundered in the Gulf of Florida, at Lat. 31°N, Long.81°W, June 10, 1816. Crew rescued. *Source:* LL, 7/23/1816; LR, 1816. (6)

3) *DUKE OF WELLINGTON*—British ship, Capt. Pearce, from Jamaica for Savannah, wrecked on the Amelia Island Bar, October 20, 1816, crew rescued. *Source:* The Morning Post, 12/10/1816; Public Ledger & Daily Advertiser, 12/10/1816. (6)

4) *HAZARD*—Brig, Capt. Rogers, from Boston for Havana, lost during the September gale on the Florida Reef. *Source:* SR, 9/28/1816. (8)

5) **Unk. English SHIP**—From Honduras for London, was lost on Florida coast during the September hurricane. *Source:* SR, 9/28/1816, 10/26/1816. (8)

6) **Unk. SHIP**—Capt. Armstrong, of Philadelphia, became a total loss on the Florida coast during the September hurricane. *Source:* SR, 9/28/1816, 10/26/1816. (8)

7) **Unk. English SHIP**—From Havana or Jamaica for Savannah, with specie to buy cotton for Liverpool, wrecked inside the Florida Reef and supposedly would be lost. *Source:* SR, 9/28/1816, 10/26/1816. (8)

1) Page 68. *Sir John Sherbrooke* (correct)—American ship, built in Nova Scotia, 141 tons, Capt. D. Cowan, wrecked on a reef off the Eastern Key of the Dry Tortugas, October 12 or 19, and bilged. After all the passengers and their trunks were put ashore, the captain, mate, some crew, and two steerage passengers went back aboard and removed all the specie, which were stowed in boxes and barrels in the hold, and brought these ashore. It was said the captain offered the two steerage passengers £500 each, if they would go along with him in the longboat, taking all the money to the United States. *Source:* LL, 12/13–19/1816; LR, 1816; EA, 12/13/1816.

2) Page 109. *Martha Brae*—British brig, of Whitehaven, Capt. Wm. Farish, 240 tons, copper bottomed, wrecked near the mouth of the Indian River, June 6, with the loss of two lives. Brig went to pieces within a few hours. *Source:* The Times London, 8/13 and 8/23/1816; Courier, 8/13/1816; LR, 1816.

3) Page 109. *Three Sisters*—Ship, of and from New York for New Orleans, wrecked on Carysfort Reef, and was burned by the captain, Aug, 1816. Some crew saved by a New Providence wrecker. *Source:* SR, 9/28/1816.

4) Page 171. *Due Bill*—Schooner, wrecked and was a total loss a few miles south of St. Augustine Bar, during the June 5–8, 1816, hurricane. *Source:* SR, 6/27/1816.

4a) Page 171. *Water Witch*—Schooner, also drove ashore at the same place as the *Due Bill*, but believed would be gotten off. *Source:* SR, 6/27/1816.

4b) Page 171. *Huron*—Was driven ashore south of St. Augustine during the June 5–8 storm. *Source:* SR, 6/25/1816.

5) Page 218. *Catherine* or *Catharine*—Brig, Capt. Cox, of Salem, was lost on the Florida Reef during the September hurricane. *Note:* Was also reported as *the Catherine Osmond*, Capt. Vicary, from Havana & believe for Salem. Lloyds does have a *Catharine & Edward*, Capt. Vickary, registered this year, but it did not wreck. *Source:* LL, 12/10/1816; SR, 10/26/1816; LR, 1816.

6) Page 218. *Zanga*—Schooner; was saved and continued to sail. *Source:* SR, 10/12/1816.

7) Page 218. *General Pike*—Schooner; was saved and continued to sail. *Source:* SR, 10/31/1816.

8) Page 218. *Atlas*—British ship of the Clyde Line, was lost near Cape Florida on a reef June 5, during a severe gale, crew and some cargo saved. A Savannah paper says wrecked in the Bahamas. *Source:* EA, 8/9/1816; SR, 7/30/1825. (4)

9) Page 218. *Cossack*—Brig, of Salem, Capt. H. Flint, wrecked June 5 on Martyr's Reef, crew and some cargo saved. *Source:* EA, 8/16/1816; Courier, 8/13/1816.

10) Page 218. *Narragansett*—Of Bristol, Rhode Island, Capt. Levi Dewolf or D'Wolf, from Havana bound for St. Petersburgh, Russia. Arrived at Savannah in their longboat late June 1816. They had encountered a gale/hurricane, June 6, 1816, at Lat. 26°05'N, which eventually drove them into white water and over two reefs and onto the beach. Vessel and cargo lost, all the crew saved. *Source:* SR, 6/27/1816.

11) Page 218. *Rebecca*—Ship, of Savannah, Capt. Ewing, with a cargo of wines, drove ashore on the Florida Reef, September 19, and soon went to pieces. Crew took to the longboat and landed about 15 miles from the wreck on Key Tavernier. A small amount of cargo was saved. Crew and salvaged cargo were taken to Nassau. *Source:* SR, 10/26/1816. (4)

12) Page 218. *Magdalen*—Brig, 183 tons, four years old, Capt. J. Sawyer, American owned. Wrecked on the Florida Reef, 12/31/1816. *Source:* LR, 1817; EA, 11/14/1817.

1817

1) *HAMBRO*—Ship, of Hamburg, Capt. Patterson, from St. Ube's for Savannah, wrecked on the Florida coast, March 12, 1817, 12 miles south of St. Augustine. Crew saved, but most of the cargo lost. *Source:* London News, 6/8/1817; Public Ledger & Daily Advertiser, 6/5/1817. (6)

1) Page 110. *Dispatch* (correct name). *Source:* LL, 8/22/1817.

2) Page 110. *Unity*—Had rescued the crew of the *Sisters*, Capt. Swiney, which had wrecked on Grand Cayman, when she later wrecked on Carysfort Reef. Crews of both vessels were then rescued by the vessel *John*, Capt. Vaux. *Source:* BWM, 10/5/1817.

3) Page 218. *Marquis de Pombal*—Capt. Hernandez; see chapter 6. *Source:* LL, 8/26/1817; Perthshire Courier, 8/7/1817; Public Ledger and Daily Advertiser, 8/13/1817; SR, 7/22/1817; BWM, 8/31/1817. (5)

1818

1) *ANCHOVY*—Schooner, Capt. Maraton, from Charleston for St. John's, for timber, wrecked on the bar off the St. Johns River, March 1818. *Source:* DSR, 4/16/1818. (6)

2) *AMELIA*—British ship, 379 tons, of Whitby, eight years old, copper sheathed, Capt. P. Williams, wrecked off Cape Florida, May 7, 1818. Some cargo and rigging saved. *Source:* DSR, 6/20/1818; LR, 1818. (5)

3) *QUEEN*—British ship, Capt. Fiott, or Fivot (Lloyd's), or Flint, 380 tons, 14 years old, from Jamaica for London, was lost on the Florida Reef, 8/7/1818. All the crew saved, though one died later. *Source:* DSR, 9/15/18; London News, 10/12/1818; LR, 1818. (8)

1) Page 68. *Acasta*—Brig, 225 tons, copper bottomed, of Whitehaven, Capt. H. Parkin, from Jamaica for Liverpool, wrecked on the Tortugas prior to December 5, 1818. Most cargo to be saved. Two crew were lost to sickness. *Source:* Carlisle Patriot, 1/30/1819; LL 1/27/1819; EA, 10/29/1819; LR, 1818.

2) Page 110. *Eliza*—(Brig?), wrecked on Carysfort Reef during the September hurricane, in ballast. Three boxes of Spanish dollars were saved along with the crew by a passing schooner (another report says six boxes of dollars saved). *Source:* SDR, 10/22/1818; EA, 11/13/1818.

3) Page 219. *Betsey*—American schooner, wrecked on the Florida Reef, as reported from Nassau, May 13, 1818. Some of the cargo of molasses saved and brought to Nassau. *Source:* DSR, 6/11/1818. (8)

4) Page 219. *Solway*—Capt. W. Bennett, 273 tons, six years old, copper sheathed. *Source:* LR, 1818.

1819

1) *GOLDEN FLEECE*—From Jamaica for Liverpool, wrecked on Long Key, prior to February 6, 1819. Crew and cargo saved. *Source:* Public Ledger & Daily Advertiser, 4/23/1819; LL, 4/26/1819. (4)

2) *SARAH-ANN*—Brig, Capt. Banks, of Portsmouth, New Hampshire, from New Orleans, wrecked in a Hurricane, August 26, 1819, on the Florida Reef and immediately bilged. The longboat was wrecked and they hastily made a raft and were saved as the brig sunk just after they abandoned her. Brig was a total loss. *Source:* SDR, 9/4/19. (8)

3) *KINGSTON*—British ship, Capt. Horncastle, sprung a leak and was abandoned in the Gulf of Florida. From British Honduras bound for London. *Source:* LL, 12/3/1819. (8)

1) Page 110. *General Jackson*—Brig, Capt. Taylor, from New Orleans for Rotterdam, with tobacco, stranded on a reef of rocks, five leagues southeast of Cape Florida. Most cargo saved. *Source:* SDR, 5/31/1819.

On Thursday, the 8d inst.

Will be sold on Jones' upper wharf, for account of all concerned,

3¼ hogsheads TOBACCO,

saved from the American brig General Jackson, captain Taylor, stranded on the coast of Florida, on her passage from New-Orleans to Rotterdam. Terms, cash.

Sale to commence at 11 *o'clock,*

M. Herbert, auct'r.

june 1———29

An 1819 auction add for cargo salvaged from the *General Jackson*. *Savannah Daily Republican*, June 1819.

2) Page 219. *Bonne Adele* (believe correct)—*Source:* Public Ledger and Daily Advertiser, 4/23/1819.

3) Page 219. *Ann* (correct)—British snow, Captain Thomas Sunley or Sundly, of Scarborough, England, 218 tons, four years old, copper sheathed. From Matanzas bound for Falmouth England, with coffee and sugar. She was purposely driven ashore by pirates who had captured her, in 2-1/2 fathoms of water on the Florida Reef near the New River, June 29, 1819. Vessel and cargo were a total loss. While in distress, the *Ann* was boarded by two pirate sloops, who later killed the captain, mate, carpenter, cook, and one sick seamen. Unsure of the fate of the captain's little boy, though the cabin boy survived by hiding and may be one and the same. The rest of the crew joined the pirates. One pirate sloop was the *Lawrence*, Capt Attwick. He was persuaded to join the pirates when confronted by the other pirate sloop off Florida, though the cabin boy said otherwise. Many were arrested

when arriving back in Savannah with a hold full of coffee for piracy and murder. One of the pirates was arrested when found on another vessel and went by the name James Carley, alias Carroll, alias Caslin. The owners sued a salvager later in court. The *Ann* was later found abandoned by the sloop *Sailor's Rights* with topmasts and running rigging carried away and 4 feet of water in her hold. They salvaged much of the cargo that was left by the pirates, and then burned her, June 29, 1819. (See Chapter 6 for additional information.) *Source:* LL, 9/3/1819; EA, 9/7/1819; SDR, 8/14–28/1819; SR, 7/17/1819, 8/3/1819; LR, 1819.

4) Page 219. **Barrila**—Brig, 151 tons, 68' x 21' x 12'9", Capt. Thomas Jones, of and from New Orleans for Philadelphia, was driven over a reef to the inside during a storm, the same time as the *Lively*. Cargo, rigging and anchors saved. *Source:* 26; LL, 11/26/1819; SDR 9/4/19.

5) Page 220. **Lively**—Schooner, of Baltimore, went over reef and anchored inside and lost both masts the same time as the *Barilla*. Cargo and crew saved. *Source:* LL, 11/26/1819; SDR, 9/4/19.

1820

1) **USS LYNX**—Baltimore clipper rigged schooner, six guns, 150 tons, 80 feet long. It had 50 men on board under Lt. J. R. Madison, and had been employed in the suppression of piracy. She left St. Mary's, Georgia, January 11, 1820, for Jamaica, and last seen on the 22nd. Never heard from again. Possible Florida wreck. *Source:* 14; The Pensacola Journal, 6/2/1918. (8)

2) **Small American PRIVATEER**—Wrecked near St. Augustine early 1820 (see chapter 6). *Source:* Annapolis Maryland Gazette, 7/20/1820.

3) **HIPPOLITE**—French brig, Capt. Francis Couguand, from Havana for Havre, with sugar, liquor, and cigars, stranded October 6, 1820, on the east coast of Florida. Cargo salvaged by a number of wreckers and brought to Savannah. Crew saved. The owners disputed salvage costs in court. *Source:* SDR, 10/24/1820, 12/2/1820. (8)

By J. B. Herbert & Co.
On Tuesday next, 7th Nov,
At 11 o'clock.
Will be sold on Hunter's wharf.
For account of the underwriters and all concerned,
50 boxes white Havana Sugar
33   do   Brown   do   do
12 boxes Segars
saved from the wreck of the French brig Hippo-
lite, capt. Cougnaud, wrecked on her passage from
Havana to Havre, and sold by consent of the
French Consel and all concerned.
Terms cash   oct 31   195

An 1820 add for the salvaged goods from the wreck of the *Hippolite*. *Savannah Daily Republican,*
November 1820.

1821

1) *SANCHEZ*—Brig, lost on Nassau Bar, January 27 or 28, 1821. *Source:* DG,
2/15/1821. (6)

2) *HOPE FOR PEACE*—Schooner, Capt. Baker, from Belize for Charleston,
with sugar and molasses, made Great Isaac on January 25, 1821, and hove
to due to the bad weather. That evening the storm became a hurricane. All
the crew were below except one man who was at the helm when a huge sea
turned the vessel bottom up. The seaman topside was washed overboard but
regained the ship when she righted herself. The captain was able to make
it on deck and found the "foremast, mainboom and tiller had been carried
away, the boat badly stove, and the vessel nearly a wreck, with three foot
of water in her hold." Many below had been badly injured including the
mate, who was the captain's brother. The next day they found themselves
drifting into the breakers off Florida about 26 miles north of Cape Florida,
and dropped the anchors in 7 or 8 fathoms of water and remained there
until the 30th when she parted cables and drove onto the beach and bilged,
filling with water. The crew repaired the ship's boat and made St. Augustine
along with the crew of the brig *Supply* which had also wrecked about half
mile from them. Some rigging was saved. *Source:* DG, 2/19/1821. (6)

3) *ELIZABETH*—Schooner, Capt. Vail, of Middleton, from Matanzas for
Savannah, was upset in a squall, February 26, 1821. They cut the masts and

Illustration of a brig after righting itself from an 1821 account, by Hidibrand. *Great Shipwrecks,* 1880.

she righted. She was found at Lat. 30°15'N, Long. 79°10'W, by the brig *Statirs,* which took off the remaining crew (had lost three), after 11 days adrift. *Source:* DG, 3/12/1821; SDR 3/30/1821. (6)

4) *RICHMOND PACKET*—Schooner, from Havana bound for Baltimore, was wrecked on purpose for insurance money in the Florida Keys in 1821. Captain stayed in Florida and the crew took passage on the sloop *Hiram,* which they believed to be a wrecker, but turned out to be a pirate sloop. All made it to Savannah. *Source:* Courier, 12/6/1821. (8)

5) **Unk. SCHOONER**—A schooner about 80–100 tons, which appeared to be new, with masts gone and which had an Indian figurehead, was found abandoned and full of water by the ship *Prudence,* at Lat. 28°30'N, long. 79°30'W, on March 16, 1821. *Source:* SDR, 4/5/1821; Georgian and Evening Advertiser, 4/4/1821. (6)

6) **Swedish SHIP**—From Havana for Cadiz, wrecked on Carysfort Reef, 3/9/1821. Crew saved. *Source:* SDR, 4/5/1821. (4)

7) *LE ROYAL DESIRE*—French ship, 240 tons, Capt. Feuar-Went, from Havana for Havre, with sugar and coffee, was lost near the Florida coast early June 1821 after she sprung a leak and filled with water. Crew took to the longboat and were later picked up by the brig *Siren*. *Source:* SDR, 6/16/1821. (8)

8) *MARYLAND*—Was reported that the *Maryland* and five other vessels were driven ashore during the September 16–17 gale, and that it was believed the *Maryland* would be lost. These vessels are mentioned on page 24, 2nd edition. *Source:* Courier, London, 11/23/1821.

9) *MARQUERITE or MARQUERITTE*—Dutch brig, Capt. Teddens or Teddins, from Havana for Antwerp, with coffee, wrecked on the east coast of Florida during the September 14, 1821, hurricane. Some cargo could be saved. Some of her cargo was taken by pirates (another source says "by a schooner under the Independent flag") the second day after she left Havana (they took 80 bags of coffee). *Source:* LL, 11/27/1821; New Times London Middlesex, 11/29/1821. (8)

10) *THREE DAUGHTERS*—British brig, Capt. Mc Masters, from Kingston, Jamaica for St. Andrews, wrecked December 9, 1821, approx. 50 miles south of Cape Canaveral. The vessel was a total loss, crew saved. *Source:* SDR, 1/23/1822. (5)

11) *CAROLINE*—Schooner, of Edenton, North Carolina, was driven ashore on Santa Rosa Island (Pensacola) during a gale, December 21, 1821. From St. Thomas for Mobile, had anchored off the island after being robbed by pirates off Cape Cruz on the 4th, to get provisions. One passenger, one crewman, and owner Mr. Meyer Pollack, were left on board, as Capt. Taber, a passenger, two crew and a boy went on shore in the boat. Two of those on board survived though the owner drowned. *Source:* SDR, 1/29/1822. (1)

1) Page 110. *Parley, Pearl, or Du Pearl*—Danish ship, Capt. J. Johnson, with 1,100 boxes of sugar and 300 bags of coffee, was driven ashore at Cape Florida, March 2, 1821, vessel and cargo lost. Crew took to the boat and a launch, the boat with the captain was blown south 70 miles and picked up by a wrecker, and the launch is believed to have made a British sloop of war they saw nearby the wreck. *Source:* Georgia and Evening Advertiser, 4/20/1821. Another source says her name is *Du Pearl*, and wrecked on a reef off Soldiers Key. *Source:* SDR, 3/29/21. Probably the *Pearl* on page 110, same Capt. Johnson, as wrecked off Soldier Key 3/8/1821. The *London Statesman*, 5/9/1821, says the Danish ship *Pearl*, with 1075 boxes sugar and 360 bags coffee. Captain and four men made Charleston; nine others took the longboat and have not been heard from since.

2) Page 140. *Supply*—Wrecked half mile from the *Hope for Peace*. It was a total loss, including the cargo of rum, tobacco, dry goods, and $4,000 in specie. All on board got ashore and made St. Augustine or were picked up, some in their boat and others in Capt. Baker's boat from the *Hope for Peace* which also wrecked nearby. *Source:* SDR, 1/23/1822; The Georgian and Evening Advisor, 4/20/1821; DG, 2/19/1821.

Illustration depicting taking to the boats from a sinking frigate from an 1816 account. *Shipwrecks and Tales of the Sea*, 1887.

1822

1) *NELSON*—English brig, wrecked on the Florida shore, January 31, 1822. Crew saved by the vessel *Beaver* from Jamaica, and taken to Eastport. *Source:* LL, 4/9/1822. (8)

2) *LADY WASHINGTON*—Sloop, of and from St. Augustine for Pensacola. Encountered a gale off Pensacola, July 7, 1822, and couldn't get into port. On board the ship were members of the Florida Legislative Council. On the 9th she swamped but righted herself and was run onto beach at Ship Island. All crew and passengers were saved. *Source:* SDR, 8/6/1822. (1)

3) *MARGARET*—Pilot boat, was believed lost in the same storm as the *Lady Washington*. *Source:* SDR, 8/6/1822. (1)

4) *OROZIMBO*—Brigantine, of Bristol, Rhode Island, 197 tons, built 1807 at Dighton, Massachusetts, 77'2" x 24'5" x 12'3", 2 decks, had an alligator figurehead, wrecked on the Florida Reef around September 27, 1822. *Source:* 27. (8)

5) *FRANCES & LUCY*—Capt. Barnaby, from Jamaica bound for Halifax, was lost on the Florida Reef, January 14, 1822. *Source:* 27. (8)

1) Page 111. *USS Alligator*—Some experts who have been to the wreck site now believe it may not be the *Alligator*, but another vessel entirely. They say the *Alligator* would have had iron ballast, but only stone ballast is found at the site. Also, remnants of the hull do not seem to correspond to the *Alligator*'s construction. I guess more investigation is needed. *Note:* Ten guns from the *Alligator* were salvaged by the wrecker Capt. Houseman of the schooner *William Henry*. See GPS coordinates at end of chapter. *Source:* 34; SDR, 2/19/1823.

2) Page 220. *Ann* (correct)—British brig, of London, Capt. Campbell, from Havana for River Plate, with sugar, indigo and spices, was lost late April 1822 on the Florida Reef near Cape Florida during a squall. One source says she had a cargo of sugar, coffee, mahogany, and the like, bound for Buenos Ayres, and wrecked on East Florida Key. Some cargo saved. *Source:* LL, 6/28/1822; DR, 5/25/1822; Morning Advertiser, 6/25/1822. (4)

3) Page 220. *Dunkirk*—French brig, with indigo, logwood and mahogany, wrecked on East Florida Key, late April 1822, near the wreck of the *Ann*. Another source says on Elbow Reef, 4/18/1822. Last reported, brig was burnt after most of the cargo and materials were saved, though another report says she was floated off. *Source:* Morning Chronicle, 7/3/1822; LL 5/14/22; SDR, 4/20/22; 5/25/1822; BWM, 5/19/1822. (4)

4) Page 220. *Neptune*—Believe to be saved though can't confirm, as a ship *Neptune*, Captain Duncan, continued to sail in 1823. *Source:* LL, 1824.

1823

1) *FLY*—Schooner, wrecked 10 miles north of the St. Augustine Bar, January 6, 1823. It was also reported that a brig with lumber, and a sloop, were ashore near the same place. *Source:* SDR, 1/25/1823. (6)

2) *CONSTANT SPANIARD*—Armed Spanish ship, from Havana for Spain, with sugar and coffee, was wrecked at Cape Florida, January 27, 1823, some sails and rigging saved. *Source:* LL, 3/14/1823; SDR, 2/19-20/1823. (5)

3) *FARMER*—Brig, Capt. R. Lancaster, from Honduras for Liverpool, was lost the night of March 10, 1823, on the Florida Reef. Crew and some sails and rigging saved and taken to Charleston by the schooner *Florida*. *Source:* LL, 5/2/1823; SG, 3/27/1823. (8)

4) *EUPHRATES*—Ship, was burned off Cape Florida, March 1823, by pirates. See the story in the chapter 6. *Source:* SDR, 4/30/1823. (5)

5) *BELLA DELORES* or *Bella de Lores*—The Columbian armed schooner *Centella*, Capt. Hopner, had taken a prize Spanish palacre-brig, the *Bella Delores*, which then wrecked on a reef near Long Key, June 7, 1823 (another report says June 9 on Key Vacas). Most cargo saved. Believed captain Hopner wrecked these on purpose (believe he was working with the wreckers), as this was not the first prize that Hopner had that wrecked in this area. Hopner had captured a number of vessels off Cuba in the past. An article in 1824 again has the *Centella* wrecking a prize at Key West or northwest of Key Vacas, on the lee side of this key. *Source:* SG, 8/5/1823, 11/3/1823; SR 7/24/1824; Public Ledger and Daily Advertiser, 9/9/1823. (4)

6) *ORBIT*—British brig, of Liverpool, Capt. Baxter, from New Orleans for Liverpool, with 1,207 bales of cotton, wrecked on Ledbury Reef, June 30, 1823. She got off after lightening the vessel and came to anchor. A northeast gale then blew in and carried away the windlass and she went ashore again and bilged. Her hull full of water and masts gone, she was abandoned. All the crew were saved by the schooner *Florida*, which also salvaged 100 bales of cotton. *Source:* SDR, 6/11/1823. (4)

7) *TELEGRAPH*—Brig, Captain Swain, from Mobile, of and bound for New York, wrecked July 16, 1823, on the Tortugas bank. Crew saved. *Source:* SG, 8/26/1823. (3)

8) *REAPER*—Schooner, Capt. Morse, from Cuba for New York, went ashore at Cape Canaveral during a gale, October 2, 1823. Crew and some cargo saved. *Source:* SR, 10/16/1823. (6)

9) *WASP*—American sloop, from Havana for Savannah, wrecked on the Florida Reef. Nassau wreckers saved the crew and cargo. *Source:* SG, 10/26/1823; LL, 12/9/1823. (8)

10) *ENDEAVOR*—Sloop, of and built at Newport, Rhode Island, in 1816, 35 tons, 47'6-1/4' x 16'10.5" x 5'4-3/4", one mast, was reported lost in June 1823, believe at or near Pensacola, either on or between January 5, 1822 and June 1823. *Source:* 27. (1)

1) Page 221. **Parker & Sons**—From New Orleans for Greenock, with 411 bales cotton, wrecked, August 15, 1823, near Bahia Honda (lower Keys). Cargo saved and taken to Havana. *Source: LL,* 10/17/1823; SG, 9/23/1823. (3)

1824

1) **GOVERNOR SHELBY**—Sloop, Captain Collio, from Fernandina bound for the St. John's River, went ashore in a gale on the middle ground within the bar by St. John's. *Source:* SDR 2/12/1824. (6)

2) **COMET**—Schooner, of New York, Captain Johnson, wrecked on Key Vacas, February 26, 1824. Sails, rigging, and anchor saved by the schooner *Florida. Source:* SDR, 3/15/1824. (3)

3) **GEORGE III** (brig) and **SPANISH BRIG**—Both reported lost near the Basin Bank—coast of Florida (possibly Basin Hills Shoals near Key Largo). The *George* on February 25, 1824, and the Spanish brig on March 2, 1824. The Spanish vessel had a cargo of sugar, and the sails and rigging were saved. The *George*, was from Honduras, with mahogany. *Source:* SDR, 3/15/1824. (8)

4) **MARY**—British brig, Capt. Woofendale, of St. Johns, New Brunswick, with rum and sugar, from Montego Bay bound for New Brunswick, was abandoned about 50 miles off Florida's coast after the gale of September 14, 1824. The crew drifted for four days in their boat until landing on Amelia Island. The wreck was later seen off St. Augustine. *Note:* A fleet consisting of nine British and one American vessel (from Honduras and Jamaica) were all caught in a hurricane September 14 at Lat. 29°N, Long. 80°W, the *Mary* and the *Ceres* being two of them. One of the fleet came ashore on St. Catherine Island, Georgia, and at least one made Charleston in bad shape. *Source:* SR, 10/5/1824. (6)

5) **USS WILD CAT**—Schooner, three guns, 48 tons, had 31 men on board under Lt. J. E. Legare. One of Commodore Porter's fleet to rid the Caribbean of piracy (see chapter 6). She left Cuba for Key West and was lost during an October storm. Supposedly an armchest and some other wreckage from her was found on Carysfort Reef. *Source:* 14; The Pensacola Journal, 6/2/1918. (4)

6) **Three small VESSELS**—Reported destroyed by pirates near Cape Florida, crews escaped to shore. One was the Bahamian sloop *Whim*, and another a Spanish sloop. *Source:* 28; SR, 11/8/1824.

1) Page 68. **Swift**—Wrecked July 30, 1824, on Long Island Reef (probably meant Long Reef). All the cochineal and indigo were saved along with

906 boxes of sugar and taken to Key West. *Source:* London Morning Post, 9/16/1824.

2) Page 68. *Ceres*—British brig (one of the Honduran Fleet along with the *Mary* also mentioned), Captain William Bird, from Honduras bound for London with logwood and mahogany, was swamped in a gale, September 14, 1824, off the Florida coast. Only two seamen of the 14 on board survived; the others having been swept overboard and drowned. They were rescued by the schooner *Mars*, September 23, 1824, at Lat. 30° 10'N, Long. 81° 15'W, after eight days clinging to the wreck with nothing to eat or drink except raw salt pork and whatever rainwater they could capture. *Source:* SR, 10/20/1824.

3) Page 171. *Sarah*—British brig, about 250 tons, was found ashore near the mouth of the St. Johns River with mast gone and was copper bottomed. The wreck washed ashore September 23, 1824, and two people were found dead on board. *Source:* SR, 10/7/1824; LL, 11/16/1824. (6)

1825

1) *CALULIAN*—Swedish brig, Capt. Prom, from Havana for Genoa, with 1,200 boxes sugar and coffee, went ashore on the Florida Reef, February 17, 1825. Only 40 boxes of sugar saved. *Source:* SG, 4/27/1825. (8)

2) *FLORIDA*—Schooner, of New Haven, Connecticut, Aaron C. White, Master, left St. Augustine for Havana, February 26, 1825, with flour, naval stores, and the like, and 30 passengers. On March 3, at Lat. 26°45'N, near the Florida coast, she was upset in a squall and instantly filled with water. Twenty-one passengers and one crew drowned, the remaining 16 clung to the side of the vessel. After two hours they managed to get the boat free and cut away both masts allowing the vessel to right itself. They then let go an anchor in 40 fathoms, but soon parted her cable and went adrift in Gulf Stream. For two more days, they weathered the storm with waves breaching over the wreck. The boat could only hold 10 persons, and they took turns in 12 hour shifts in the boat and on the wreck and remained this way for two more days. They just changed shifts when the wreck was upset again and the remains of the mast were nearly in the water. Those left on the wreck believed she would soon sink and jumped into the water and made for the boat. Those on the boat cut the lines and drifted away from the wreck as there was no more room for any others, and they left their comrades to die. It had no sail and only one oar. They made a sail from a lady's shawl and a piece of linen, and soon the seas calmed down. After three days and nights, they landed on Amelia Island and were taken in by plantation owners Mr. Bond and Harrison. Next day some took the

boat to St. Mary's and then took passage to Savannah. Unknown is the fate of the six left aboard the wreck. *Source:* SG, 3/24/1825. An earlier report not mentioned in the "story" a number of days later, was that the *Florida* also had 20 Africans in her hold (likely slaves). By this account, she capsized the night of the 3rd, and was driven onto the Florida Reef. Captain, three passengers, and the crew of six got into the boat and soon after cut from the wreck leaving six on board and believed all those below had drowned including the 20 Africans. One survivor, a Mr. Travers, said he lost his mother, wife, and two daughters. It would be interesting to see if there was an inquiry, as it sounds like the *Florida* was illegally smuggling slaves. *Source:* SG, 3/16–24/1825. It was also reported the Florida was seen three days after it was abandoned with nobody on board. *Source:* Belfast Commercial Chronical, 6/1/1825. (8)

3) *US Barge DIABLETA*—Lt. Pearson, after a cruise looking for pirates off Cuba, she could not make Thompsons Island (Key West) due to a storm, and made for Pensacola, where she wrecked ashore on Santa Rosa Island, 3/19/1825. *Source:* SR, 3/26/1825. (1)

4) *FOX*—Schooner, from Savannah for St. Johns, assorted cargo and merchandise, wrecked on the Florida coast, April 15, 1825. Vessel and cargo were a total loss. *Source:* SR, 4/28/1825. (8)

5) *HENRY*—American ship, Capt. Ingersoll, of New York, from New Orleans for Liverpool, wrecked on the Dry Tortugas, April 18, 1825. Crew and some cargo saved. *Source:* SR, 5/13/1825; SG, 5/23/1825. (3)

6) **Unk. Spanish SCHOONER**—A prize of a Columbian privateer, she went to pieces on the Tortugas, believe early July. Some cargo saved and taken to Key West. *Source:* SG, 7/19/1825. (3)

7) **LIGHT VESSEL**—Intended for mooring on Carysfort Reef, Capt. Jas. Hart, from New York for Carysfort, went ashore on July 9, 1825, during a gale, at Lat. 26°30'. Captain and crew stayed on the beach for eight days until a schooner from Cape Florida took them off. It was originally reported she was a total loss, but was got off and saved. *Source:* SG, 9/9/1825.

8) *BRUTUS*—Two-masted brig, of Newport, Rhode Island, built 1815 at Freetown, Massachusetts, 197 tons, 77'2" x 24'5" x 12'3", two decks, Capt. Collins, from Havana for London, was lost July 27, 1825, on the Florida Reef. Crew and only 14 boxes of sugar saved. *Source:* 27; LL, 8/2/1825. (8)

9) *LIMA*—Brig, from Havana for Philadelphia, Capt. Stoneman, with a misc. cargo (silks, crockery, etc.), wrecked on Elbow Reef, some cargo saved. *Source:* SR, 8/6/1825; SG, 8/9/1825. (4)

10) *REVENGE*—French brig, from Campeche for Marseilles, was cast away early September 1825, on the Florida Reef. The captain filed a complaint against wrecker Jacob Houseman, who took off some logwood and cochineal. The St. Augustine court awarded Houseman 95 percent of this. *Source:* SG, 11/1–15/1825. (8)

11) *ANN*—Brig, from the West Indies for London, with coffee and sugar, was lost near Key Tavernier during a gale, November 1, 1825. Crew saved, ship and cargo a total loss. *Source:* SR, 11/23/1825. (4)

11a) **Unk. SCHOONER**—From Charleston for Mobile, wrecked near Key West in the same gale as the *Ann.* Cargo and passengers taken to Key West. *Source:* SR, 11/23/1825. (3)

12) *INDEPENDENCE*—Schooner, Capt. Hazelton, from New York for St. Augustine, drove ashore about 40 miles from St. Augustine. All the crew and passengers were lost, along with the vessel, some cargo saved. *Source:* SR, 11/7/1825. (6)

13) *HOBBY*—Schooner, from New York for Cape Florida, while on a wrecking voyage, was lost near New Smyrna, December 2, 1825. Capt. Bedell and crew saved. *Source:* SR, 12/15/1825. (6)

14) *BARACOA*—Schooner, Capt. Reed, of New York, from Norfolk for Mobile, went ashore on one of the Florida Keys, and was abandoned. Wreckers were removing cargo and doubted vessel could be saved. *Source:* SR, 10/20/1825. (8)

15) *MARY BUNTIN*—Schooner, from Charleston for New Orleans, became a total loss on Sambo Keys in 1825. Some or all crew and passengers saved. *Source:* SG, 12/12/1825. (3)

16) *BLISS*—Brig, 217 tons, of New York, 15 years old and sheathed, Capt. Auld, from Jamaica for Baltimore, wrecked on the Florida coast, December 15, 1825. *Source: Source:* LL, 2/24/1826; LR, 1825. (8)

1) Page 221. *Hercules*—Brig, was saved and taken to Key West and repaired. *Source:* SR, 4/23/25, 12/12/1825.

2) Page 221. **John Carl** or **Johan Carl** or **Carl Johan** (believe correct)—Swedish or Finnish ship, from Havana for the Mediterranean, with 1,000 boxes of sugar, was lost on Carysfort Reef, February 1825, around same time as *Point a Petre.* About half the sugar saved along with some sails and rigging. Believe the correct name is *Carl Johan.* There's a Finnish ship of same name of 201 tons, 20 years old, Captain S. Alm, registered with Lloyd's in 1825 but no longer in 1826, but a Swedish ship of the same name was also reported in British papers as wrecked off England in 1825. I'm led to think

the Finnish ship is what wrecked here. *Source:* British Press, 4/30/1825; LL, 4/29/1825; LR, 1825. (4)

1826

1) *ADELE*—Capt. Tabout, from New Orleans for Havre, was lost February 28, 1826, on the Florida Reef. Crew and most of the cargo saved and taken to Key West. *Source:* Courier, 4/24/1826; LL,4/21/1826. (8)

2) *CHART*—Capt. Holland, of Kingston, Jamaica, was reported from Norfolk, February 23, 1826, as lost on the Florida Reef. *Source:* LL, 4/11/1826. *Note:* This may be the British ship or schooner reported lost on Florida Reef, March 1, 1826. *Source:* New Times London, 5/22/1826. (8)

3) *GREYHOUND*—Of Philadelphia, Capt. Watkins, from Mobile for Bordeaux, reported from New York on November 11, 1826, as lost on the Dry Tortugas. Crew saved and arrived at Havana. *Source:* LL, 12/28/1826. (3)

1) Page 112. *Ellen*—Capt. Coit, of Philadelphia, crew and some cargo saved. *Source:* American Watchman & Delaware Advertiser, 3/3/1826.

1827

1) *SPERMO*—Ship, Captain M'Pherson, from New York bound for New Orleans, wrecked on Alligator Reef, January 1827, and the vessel became a total wreck. Some cargo was saved including an Egyptian mummy and taken to Key West. They removed a multitude of folds of linen from the mummy and only found a skeleton with its neck dislocated. The source goes on to say that it smelled so bad that the collector of customs ordered it to be burned. *Source:* SG & SR, 2/5/1827. (4)

2) *GLOBE*—Schooner, from Boston for Pensacola and Mobile, wrecked on the westernmost Sambo Key, February 1, 1827. Most cargo saved. *Source:* SG, 2/28/1827. (3)

3) **Unk. BRIG**—Prize to Commodore Porter's squadron, was lost on one of the Tortugas, February 6, 1827, and the cargo of wine was saved. *Source:* SG, 2/28/1827. (3)

4) *MARGARET*—Ship, Capt. Lancope, of and from Philadelphia for New Orleans, wrecked on Dog Keys (southwest coast of Florida by Estero), March 20, 1827, in a gale. The vessel was lost, some cargo saved. *Source:* SR, 5/1/1827. (2)

5) *GENERAL PIKE*—Schooner, of Fairfield, Connecticut, Capt. Pike, from New York for Tampico, wrecked March 18, 1827, on the beach 18 miles north of the Key West Lighthouse, vessel lost, some cargo and all the passengers and crew were saved. *Source:* SR, 4/7/1827. (3)

6) *ANN MARIA*—Schooner, of Newburyport, Capt. Wm. Brown, from New Orleans, with rum, sugar and molasses, wrecked off Suwannee, May 15, 1827, in a gale. Only two of the crew survived and made it to Tallahassee. Their account was suspicious though. *Source:* SR, 5/25/1827. (2)

7) *FLORIDA*—Schooner, of New London, Connecticut, Capt. Keilogg, capsized in a squall WSW, 20 miles south of Indian River, vessel and cargo total loss. Crew and passengers took to the boat and landed at Indian River 14 hours later. They made it to St. Augustine seven days later. *Source:* SG, 5/19/1827. Almost the same fate as the New London *Florida* wrecked in 1825. (5)

8) *JAMES MITCHELL*—British ship, from Liverpool for Havana, had run aground off Cuba. Next day was boarded by USS *John Adams* and USS *Hornet*, and was gotten off and taken to Key West, where she beached and became a total wreck, July 1827. *Source:* LL, 7/27/1827. (3)

9) **Unk. French BRIG**—From Trinidad for Nantes, was lost on the Florida Reef. Reported from New York, November 27, 1827. *Source:* Trade Free Press, 12/23/1827. (8)

1) Page 112. **Guerrero**—See chapter 6. *Source:* SR, 1/22/1828; *The Guerrero Project* (DVD); *Slave Ship Guerrero*, by G. Swanson.

1828

1) *FAVORITE*—Brig, of Portland, Capt. Sweetzer, from Havana for Portland, Maine, wrecked March 22, 1828, on Carysfort Reef. Crew, sails, rigging and some cargo saved. *Source:* SG, 4/16/1828; SR, 4/15/1828. (4)

2) *SUPERIOR*—Sloop, Capt. Carey, of and from St. Augustine for Philadelphia, with live oak, wrecked September 2, 1828, on St. Augustine Bar. Crew, passengers, and some cargo saved, vessel lost. *Source:* SG, 9/11/1828. (6)

3) *ORLEANS*—Of Boston, from Havana for Europe, wrecked on Carysfort Reef, late September 1828. Some cargo saved. *Source:* LL, 11/21/1828. (4)

4) *MERCURE*—French ship, Capt. J. J. Aubray, from Campeche for Havre, with logwood, wrecked on the Florida Reef, November 1828. The crew abandoned her in their longboat along with $6,000 in specie, her arms, and provisions, though later got passage from some wreckers (the wrecker in

court was awarded 5 percent of the specie). Key West wreckers saved some of the cargo. *Source:* LL, 12/23/1828; G, 2/9/1829. (8)

1829

1) *WILLIAM*—Sloop, Capt. Mitchell, from Savannah for and of St. Augustine, went ashore on Anastasia Island and bilged after crossing the bar, January 17, 1829. She broached in a swell, and anchors let go, but the cable parted and she drifted ashore three to four miles inside the bar. Cargo saved. *Source:* SDR, 1/22/1829. (6)

2) *ALLIANCE*—Capt. Latterman, from Guayra for Marseilles, reported from Boston, May 1, 1829, as wrecked on the Florida Reef. *Source:* LL, 6/2/1829. There was an *ALLIANCE* from Campeche for London that wrecked on the Florida Reef, November 17, 1828, and was taken to Key West and condemned. Possibly the same vessel, but ports of call completely were different. *Source:* London Times, 8/7/1829. (8)

3) *PRESIDENT*—Schooner, one mast, built 1820 at Pawcatuck, Connecticut, 118 tons, 71'2.5^2 x 22' 1.5^2 x 8'9^2. Capt. Ebener Baker, of Providence, Rhode Island, from Matanzas with molasses, wrecked on Pickle's Reef and bilged, July 14, 1829. Sails and rigging saved and she was then burned to the water's edge. *Source:* 27; SR, 8/13/1829. (4)

4) *FRANKLIN*—Schooner, Capt. Sheppard, from Charleston for St. Augustine, was lost on the bar off St. Augustine, November 1829. Passengers, crew, and small portion of cargo saved before she went to pieces. *Source:* G, 12/16/1829. (6)

1) Page 112. *Corrico, No.1* (correct)—Lost April 3, 1829. *Source:* Morning Journal, 6/15/1829.

1830

1) *CHARLOTTE CORDRIA*—Brig, Capt. Mix, was a total loss on the Florida coast, January 1, 1830, 14 miles south of the St. John's Inlet and 18 miles north of St. Augustine. Crew saved. *Source:* DSR, 1/8/1830. (6)

2) *WILLIAM & HENRY*—Of London, Capt. Wright, wrecked January 10, 1830, at "Key West, Bahamas" (misprint?). Only the mate Christopher Gwynn was saved. Possible Florida wreck. *Source:* LL 5/21/1830. (8)

3) *MARY ADAMS*—Schooner, Capt. Riberon, from Savannah for St. Augustine, with U.S. Stores for Ft. Marion, went ashore on the St. Augustine Bar, May 11, 1830. Vessel lost, though cargo saved. *Source:* DSR, 5/17/1830. (6)

4) *ANN JANE*—Schooner, of Bristol, Maine, Capt. Floman, from Charleston for St John's, with a full cargo, wrecked on the St. John's Bar, May 23, 1830, while attempting to cross the bar at low tide. A total loss. Captain and crew saved. Some cargo came ashore on North Beach, eight miles from St. Augustine a few weeks later. *Source:* SDR, 6/14/1831. (6)

5) *WILLIAM*—Brig, from New Orleans for Havana, with 180 hogs that came down the Mississippi from Indiana, foundered off Key West in 1830. All on board, and most if not all the hogs, were saved by the wreckers, who were awarded one-fourth of the saved hogs. *Source:* Lawrenceburg Indiana Palladium, 5/22/1830, 6/19/1830. (3)

6) *ROME or ROMEO*—Schooner, Capt. Hughes, from New York for St. John's and Palatka, with merchandise, wrecked, September 22, 1830, 10 miles south of St John's Lighthouse. Captain and crew saved. Most cargo saved though damaged. *Source:* G, 10/2–7/1830. (6)

7) **Unk. British SHIP**—The U.S. survey sloop *Florida*, Lt. Gedney, reported a wreck, this from her logbook:

> September 3rd, Lat. 28°33'N, Long. 80°27'W, fell in with the mainmast, topmast & topgallant mast, of a large ship; the lower mast painted white above and green below; carried away about the spar-deck partners, fidded royal mast, black yards and chain top-sail sheet. At 2 PM picked up a puncheon of Jamaican rum, branded I.B near the bung. Sept 4th, about 4 miles north of Cape Canaveral, at 7 PM boarded the wreck of a large ship (about 600 tons) sunk in five fathoms of water, to which the mainmast we fell in with yesterday belonged and from appearances, supposed to be a British ship.

Source: SR, 10/14/1830. *Note:* Possibly the *Lady Canning? Amity?* (6)

8) *SARAH, AMITY, ISABELLA*, and *LADY CANNING*—Reported from New York, October 21, 1830, that between Cape Canaveral and St. Augustine, wreckage and cargo were strewn along the shore. Wreckage with the names *SARAH, AMITY, ISABELLA*, and *LADY CANNING* were all found here. The *Sarah*, Capt. Boyd, for London and the British bark, *Lady Canning*, Capt. R. Allen, for Liverpool, both left from Jamaica around August 1, 1830. The British ship *Amity*, Capt. Wilcox, left Laguna for Cork July 23. None had been heard from since. Some London papers say the *Amity* wrecked, August 15, 1830, on the Florida coast and the *Lady Canning* on August 16, 1830, with the loss of all hands. The *Lady Canning* was 305 tons, copper sheathed, and two years old. *Source:* LL, 11/26/1830; LR, 1830. (6)

9) *KATHERINE* or *KATHARINE*—American ship, from New Orleans for Marseille, wrecked on Dog Island, October 31, 1830. *Source:* The Times London, 1/5/1831; LL, 1/4/1831. (1)

1) Page 68. **Vineyard**—Was actually purposely wrecked and burned off Long Island, New York, by the mutinous crew who murdered the captain and mate and buried some of the specie they stole on the beach. One of the mutineers on board was one of the most notorious pirates of the time, Charles Gibbs (see chapter 6).

1831

1) *TOISON*—Schooner, Capt. Cobb, had wrecked in the Keys, believe on Pickle's Reef. Wreckers were awarded 30 percent of the cargo salvaged and 15 percent of the $2,800 found on board. The hull was to be sold (probably as she lay on the reef, though possibly towed to Key West). *Source:* Washington National Intelligencer, 3/25/1831. (4)

2) *USS SYLPH*—Schooner, one gun, 41 tons, Lt. H. E. V. Robinson in command, built 1831. It left Pensacola in July 1831, and never heard from again and believed lost during the August storm. Possible Florida wreck. *Source:* 14. (8)

3) *SYLVIA*—British ship, 322 tons, copper sheathed, five years old, of Bristol, Capt. Purnell, from Jamaica for Boston, was lost July 7, 1831, on the Florida Reef. Crew and passengers saved. One source says it was later found burned. *Source:* Courier, 8/22/31; LL, 8/23–26/1831; The Standard, 8/22/1831; LR, 1831. (8)

4) *DASHER*—Brig, 160 tons, built 1829 at Hull, England, copper sheathed, single deck with beams, Capt. Brend, from Laguna for London. Went ashore and bilged on Little Conch Reef, 8/11/1831. Some cargo saved and brought to Key West. *Source:* LL, 10/4/1831; LR, 1831. (4)

5) *MARIA* (likely same as *Maria*, page 221)—Was a new ship, Capt. M'Mullin, was 15 days from Philadelphia bound for New Orleans, loaded with dry goods, provisions, and so on, and 230 laborers for the canal (presume a canal being built in New Orleans). She wrecked on Carysfort Reef, November 25, 1831, and was lost. Crew, passengers, and most all the cargo (though damaged), were saved by the wreckers and taken to Key West. *Source:* BMP, 12/24/1831. (4)

1) Page 69. **Exertion**—Brig or bark, of Eden, from New Orleans for Providence, Rhode Island, with 428 bales of cotton, wrecked on some rocks near

the Dry Tortugas, April 27, 1831, and bilged. Cargo (damaged), sails and rigging, and the crew saved. *Source:* G, 5/23/1831, 6/15/1831

2) Page 69. *Concord*—Capt. McGown (believe correct), most cargo saved. *Source:* Washington National Intelligencer, 11/1/1831.

3) Page 112. *Marcelly* (correct)—Capt. D. Munro, 299 tons, copper bottomed, built in New Brunswick, reported from Key West that she wrecked near the Florida Lighthouse and all her cargo of cotton drifted to the beach. *Source:* LL, 4/29/1831.

4) Page 112. *Amulet*—Of Plymouth, Massachusetts, built 1826 at Duxbury, 252 tons, 98'1² x 23'11.5² x 11'11-3/4', two decks, three masts, square stern. Cargo was mostly stores for Sutler's Department at Cantonment Jesup, of which mostly all was saved, though damaged. Her hull was sold at auction where she lay for $35.00. *Source:* 26; Washington National Intelligencer, 3/25/1831.

1832

1) *AJAX*—Sloop, from Matamoros for Mobile, Capt. Tishow, was found wrecked near Cape San Blas (another report says off Port of Mobile), and barrels of flour were picked up and taken to Apalachicola. Previously, two men named Davis and Stephens, had arrived at Apalachicola in April in the ship's rowboat with a large sum of money in gold and wearing fine clothing (with initials that did not match their name), along with jewelry, silverware, two gold and one silver watch, and a valuable spyglass. They were held for suspicion of theft but then let go. The two left town before they could be arrested and were now wanted men. After they left it was found they were listed as part of the crew of the *Ajax*. It's believed they murdered the captain and crew of this vessel. *Source:* G, 6/8–15/1832. (1)

2) *STERLING*—Schooner, was found by the brig *Albeona*, from Providence bound for Matanzas, on her beam ends and on fire at Lat. 27°22'N, on June 8, 1832. They rescued all on board who had been in that situation for 31 hours, and the *Sterling* sank soon after. Possible Florida wreck. *Source:* BMP, 6/25/1832.

3) *SHEPARD*—Ship, built 1825 at Bath, Maine, by George Shepard, 349 tons, 108'2" x 26'10.5" x 13'5.25", copper bottomed, of New York, Capt. Blaland, from Havana for Hamburg, with 2,450 boxes of sugar, wrecked at Key Tavernier (one report says Carysfort Reef) and bilged, August 3, 1832. Crew saved. Wreckers saved about half of the sugar and the sails and

rigging. *Source:* 6; G, 8/16/1832, 9/27/1832; LL, 1832; Cork Constitution, 10/9/1832; LR 1832. (4)

4) *JOSEPHINE, JOSEPHALO or JOSEFA* (believe correct)—Spanish ship, from Havana bound for Barcelona, with sugar and cotton, wrecked October 24, 1832, near the same place as the *Kentucky* (50–70 miles north of Cape Florida). Crew, passengers, and part of cargo were saved and taken to Key West. Vessel a total loss. *Source:* G, 11/28/1832; LL, 2/8/1833. (5)

5) *SARAH*—British brig (Lloyd's says a ship), from Matanzas for St. Johns, New Brunswick, with 10 boxes of sugar, believe wrecked in same area as the *Kentucky*, October 29. Crew & seven boxes of sugar saved and taken to Key West, vessel a total loss. *Source:* G, 11/28/1832; London Bell, 1/6/1833; LL, 12/14/1833. (5)

6) *MONTPELIER*—Brig (another source says British ship), Capt. Winchell, from Savannah for Kingston, with lumber, went ashore about 10 or 16 (believe this is correct) miles north of Cape Canaveral during a gale, October 29, 1832. Vessel and cargo a total loss, crew saved, some swimming to shore. The captain and all but three who wished to remain by the wreck took to the longboat and made St. Augustine, losing the boat in the breakers a bit south of the light. They said they saw wreckage all along the coast from the storm. "Flour, beef, tar, oil, and half barrels of butter, were strewn all along the coast." *Source:* G, 11/15/1832; DSR, 11/14/1832; LL 12/14/1832. (6)

7) *HENRIETTA*—Schooner, Capt. Douglas, of and for Newbern, North Carolina, from St. Domingo and Exuma, with coffee and salt, went ashore about 50 miles south of Cape Canaveral during the late gale. Captain and crew took to the longboat which was soon swamped. The captain drowned as he had $500 in specie tied about his waist, which must have weighed him down. The others all made the shore and were saved. *Source:* G, 11/22/1832. (6)

8) *THOMAS*—British ship, Capt. Walker, of St. John's, New Brunswick, was wrecked near the mouth of the "Indian River (Key West)," during the October 29, 1832, gale. Crew and cargo saved. Either Key West is a mistake as Indian River is much further north, or it possibly meant near Indian Key, or simply meant Key West. *Source:* London Guardian and Public Ledger, 2/2/1833; LL, 2/1/1833. (8)

9) *TEMPLE*—Schooner, Capt. Moore, from Charleston bound for Key West, went ashore between Mosquito Inlet and Cape Canaveral, October 16, 1832. Crew took to the longboat and arrived at Mosquito on the 29th. *Source:* DSR, 11/14/1832; BMP, 11/26/1832. (6)

10) *ALEZANDERO*, or *ALEXANDER*—Spanish brig, Capt. Magroldi, from Havana for Malagra, with mahogany, logwood, and sugar wrecked about October 10, 1832, near Cape Florida during a gale and bilged. Some sugar, coffee, and rigging saved. Several other wrecks were reported near Cape Florida and Cape Canaveral. *Source:* DSR, 11/20/1832; Morning Advertiser, 12/21/1832. (5)

1) Page 70. *Splendid*—Was got off and continued on her voyage to Havre after throwing off 500 or 600 bales of cotton. *Source:* BMP, 3/6/1832.

2) Page 70. *Pulaski*—Packet ship, Capt. E. D. Post, from New York for Mobile, with 40 cabin passengers and 28 in steerage, struck on NE key of Tortugas and bilged, October 20, 1832. Twenty-five of the cabin passengers went onto the key where the lighthouse stands (Garden Key) after all hope of saving the vessel was lost. The steerage passengers landed on an adjacent key. Thirteen days later a fishing smack picked up the captain and two passengers from the wreck and took to them Key West where the captain chartered a schooner and went back to get rest of passengers. It had a valuable cargo, but ship filled with water in 10 days. About half of the cargo was saved and brought to the beach by the Lighthouse's boat. *Note:* Originally reported by mistake as the ship *Alabama*. *Source:* G, 11/20 & 22/1832; DSR, 11/20/1832; BMP, 11/26/1832.

3) Page 70. *Othello*—Was got off with the assistance of some wrecking vessels; continued on her voyage to England. *Source:* LL, 4/27/1832.

4) Page 70. *Eliza Plummer*—British ship, 359 tons, copper bottomed, Captain Griffiths, from Montego Bay for Liverpool, wrecked August 14, 1832, on the Samboes. Vessel a total loss, some cargo of rum, sugar and pimento saved. She was later set fire to by unknown persons who illegally salvaged materials off her. The captain had complained how the first wreckers on the scene acted badly. *Source:* G, 8/14-16-30/1832, 9/27/1832; LR, 1832.

5) Page 70. *Tennessee*—Ship was got off the reef and taken to Key West for repair. Believe Tennessee Reef was named after her. *Source:* G, 9/27/1832.

6) Page 113. *Kentucky*—Ship, a coastal packet which held a speed record for several years, Capt. E. S. Dennis (correct), 415 tons, 118'8" x 27'10" x 13'11", built 1827 at New York by S.&F. Fickett, from New Orleans bound for New York, with, cotton, sugar, corn, lead, and sarsaparilla, wrecked 50 miles north of Cape Florida (another report says 70 miles north of Cape Florida). "The vessel struck in about five fathoms, and when only three hundred yards from the beach." She remained in this situation for the next 36 hours with the seas breaking over her. Finally, four made shore in the

boat and the remainder were "hauled ashore by lines, except the cook and one seaman, who were drowned." Another report says three men were lost. The ship and most of the cargo were a total loss. Some of the cargo (200 bales of cotton) were saved and taken to Key West along with the rest of the crew and passengers. *Source:* 2; DSR, 11/28/1832; G, 11/28/1832; Washington National Intelligencer, 12/8/1832. (5)

7) Page 365. *Henry Bennett*—From Mobile for Havana, was thrown on her beam ends during a severe gale, August 16, 1832, and abandoned the next day. Crew and passengers rescued by the schooner *Grecian* and taken to New York. The brig *Regulator* fell in with the *Bennett* within sight of Tortugas light, "stripped and abandoned," August 31. *Source:* BMP, 9/3–20/1832.

8) Page 366. *Glasgow*—Captain Higginson, from New Orleans for Liverpool. All the crew and most of the cargo was saved and taken to Key West. *Source:* G, 7/18/1832.

1833

1) *HELEN GRAY*—British bark, 286 tons, eight years old, Capt. William Mabee, from Jamaica for London, with pimento, rum, sugar, coffee, and logwood. It was lost of Conch Reef (Lloyd's says Little Conch Reef, March 10, 1833. Wreckers saved about 600 bags of pimento, 10 hhds of rum, and some materials, and brought them to Key West. LR, 1833, G, 4/12/1833.

2) *MARSHAL NEY*—Ship, 296 tons, of New York or Boston, built 1831 in Maine, Capt. Curtis, from New Orleans for Havre, with 1,100 bales of cotton, stranded on the Quicksands and bilged, about 40 miles west of Sand Key Light, March 9, 1833. She was abandoned and all the crew made Key West in their longboat. *Source:* G, 4/2/1833; LR, 1833. (3)

3) *BONNETS OF BLUE*—Sidewheel steamboat, Capt. Davis, 71 tons, built 1833 at Charleston, from Savannah for Mobile, encountered a gale June 24, 1833, when about 40 miles SE by S of St. Augustine. She soon broached and lost steering.

> Soon after, the boat was found to be leaking badly, and the pumps became choked-the leak gaining fast, the squaresail was then taken in, and both anchors let go in 15 fathoms of water, and all hands employed in hailing— Finding it impossible to keep her free, slipt the chains, cut the hawser, and set the square sail, for the purpose of driving the boat on shore—at the same time commenced lightening her by throwing the wood overboard.

When it was obvious she was about to sink, they made the longboat ready and the captain, a lady and two children, two passengers, and all the crew except two Africans got in the boat. Report says boat was too small for everyone, and all in the boat made shore at Burysville, Florida. The steamer sank soon after the boat left her. One of the Africans made shore on a piece of the wreck and was saved, the other unfortunately drowned in the surf. The wreck of the steamboat drove on shore minus the engine which fell out of her when she rolled over and sank. *Source:* 21; SR, 7/15/1833. (6)

4) *BROTHERS*—British brig, of and for Guernsey from Havana, Capt. Lemassure, wrecked on Carysfort Reef, July 20, 1833, near the lightship, and immediately bilged. Only a small portion of cargo saved. About 260 boxes of sugar and 20 bags of coffee were saved along with the sails and rigging. It was mentioned in the report that many of the old charts placed the lightship outside the reef, when in fact it was anchored in an inner basin, which may or may not cause a ship to wreck, though the light can easily be seen from 10 to 12 miles away. Captain insinuated this may have been the cause of the wreck. *Source:* G, 8/3–6/1833. (4)

5) *HICKERU*—Schooner, Capt. Hardy, from Baltimore for St. Marks, went ashore on Pelican Reef, November 20, 1833, and bilged. Crew and cargo saved, vessel a total loss. *Source:* DSR, 12/11/1833. (3)

6) *PONTIFF*—Ship, of New York, Capt. Hathaway, from New Orleans for Havre, wrecked on the Florida Reef, December 20, 1833. (One paper says wrecked on Cat Key, Bahamas.) Crew and some of the 1,800 boxes of sugar saved, vessel a total loss. *Source:* London Guardian Public Ledger, 2/12/1834; DSR, 1/28/1834; G, 1/20/1834. (8)

7) *MARY JANE*—Brig, Capt. Card, from Baltimore for New Orleans, with an assorted cargo of dry goods, went ashore and bilged on Collin's (now Coffin's) Patch, off Duck Key, about December 29, 1833. Vessel a total loss, some cargo and all crew and passengers saved. *Source:* G, 3/26/1834. (3)

8) *BRAGANZA*—From Jamaica, wrecked on the Florida Reef (1832 or 1833). Cargo saved and taken to Key West. Unknown if salvaged. *Source:* London Times, 2/8/1833. (8)

1834

1) *ANNA MARIA*—Believe an Austrian ship, Capt. Janson or Jansens, from Trieste bound for La Guayra (La Guaira?), wrecked on the Dry Tortugas, April 16, 1834. Crew and most of the cargo saved. *Source:* True Sun, 6/5/1834. (3)

2) **Spanish BRIG**—Loaded with rice, wrecked on Carysfort Reef around May 16, 1834, a total wreck. *Source:* London Morning News and Public Ledger, 6/23/1834. (4)

3) *POMONA*—From London for Xagua, Capt. Malzard, struck on Indian Key, August 1, 1834. It was doubtful she could be got off. Captain and some crew made Cuba and later came back to save her cargo. Unknown if vessel was saved. *Source:* LL, 8/26/1834. (4)

4) *RESOLUTION*—First reported she came into Key West July 16, after being on a reef for six days. Then reported she struck a rock on the "Marques Cay," July 22, 1834, and on the 28th had to be abandoned in a leaky state, at Lat. 25°N, Long. 80°W. *Source:* LL, 9/2–12/1834. (3)

5) *ROBERT BRUCE*—American ship, wrecked on the Dry Tortugas. *Source:* Times London 7/29/1834. (3)

6) *WILLIAM*—Brig, Capt. Martin, of and from Philadelphia for Havana, with an assorted cargo, wrecked on Carysfort Reef and bilged. Vessel was a total loss. Most cargo saved though damaged and brought to Key West. *Source:* Washington National Intelligencer, 10/4/1834. (4)

1) Page 368. **Amiable Gertrude**—Wrecked at or near Key West, November 12, 1834. *Source:* Caledonian Mercury, 1/24/1835.

1835

1) *OLIVE BRANCH*—Schooner (possible slaver), Capt. Lightburn, from Savannah for New Orleans, capsized off the Tortugas, February 9, 1835, during a squall and filled with water. Two slaves drowned. The survivors took to the boat and were later picked up. *Source:* G, 3/7/1835. (3)

2) *DREAD*—Smack, of Groton, was lost in Tampa Bay, May 9, 1835. Sails and rigging saved. *Source:* G, 5/27/1835. (2)

3) *PEDEE*—Schooner, Capt. George Tolson, from New Orleans for Charleston, capsized during a gale off the Tortugas, August 15, 1835. There were 11 on board (four were passengers). Only one crew survived and was picked up by ship *Marengo* after five days without sustenance. *Source:* BMP, 9/9/1835. (3)

4) SEPTEMBER 15, 1835, HURRICANE IN KEYS: Source for a-j: G, 10/7/1835, 11/3/1835; Caledonian Mercury, 11/23/1835; LL, 11/20/1835.

a) *BRILLIANT*—Sloop, wrecked at Bahia. (3)

b) *CAROLINE* and the *AMELIA*—Schooners, both high and dry at same place. (3)

c) *OLIVE BRANCH*—Wrecked at Bahia. (3)

d) *THISTLE*—Wrecked at Key Largo. (4)

e) *FLORIDA*—Schooner, ashore with mast and rudder gone.

f) **Spanish BRIG**—With sugar AND cigars, went ashore 50 miles north of Cape Florida (probably the *Gil Blas*). (5)

g) *HERO*—Sloop, ashore near the same place as above, from New York for Key West, with dry goods. Passengers, crew, and some materials saved. Vessel lost. (5)

h) *GALLANT*—Fishing smack, ashore 70 miles south of cape Canaveral. Crew saved, vessel lost. (5)

i) *EMPRESS*—Fishing smack, from New Bedford for New Orleans, went ashore 15 miles south of Cape Canaveral. Captain and three crew drowned, only one saved, vessel lost. (5)

j) *THOMAS*—British ship, from Laguna for Liverpool, with logwood, was driven ashore on or near Indian Key, September 15, 1835. Cargo and some rigging saved. (4)

End of hurricane wrecks.

5) *EDWIN*—Brig, from New York for Apalachicola, was lost on the Apalachicola Bar, 1835. *Source:* G, 10/7/1835. (1)

6) *FELICITY*—Schooner, Capt. Stratton, from New York for St. Johns, with U.S. stores for Fort King, wrecked on the St. John's Bar, November 1, 1835. Crew and some cargo saved, vessel a total loss. Hull, sails, spars, and rigging to be sold on beach as she lies. *Source:* DSR 11/9–18/1835. (6)

7) *CONDE*—Spanish/Cuban brig, Capt. Villanova, from Charleston for Havana, with rice and lard, went ashore 20 miles south of St. Augustine, September 18, 1835, during a hurricane. Two crew drowned, some cargo saved, vessel a total loss. *Source:* G, 10/5/1835. (6)

8) *HELEN MAR*—Brig, of Philadelphia, Capt. E. D. Stewart, from Tampico for New York or Bermuda, with jalap, fustic and $109,000 in specie. This is an unlikely Florida wreck even though many reports say so. Some said she was totally lost on Washerwoman Shoal (others say Washerwoman's Shoal, Key Sal Bank), April 22, 1835, and the brig sank immediately though the crew were saved with only the clothes on their back. The captain took passage on the brig *Speed* from Havana, and three of the crew, named Henry Hillman, Francis Dillon, and William Jacobson, were left on the key. Soon there were ads posted offering a $20,000 reward by the Philadelphia/New York underwriters, say she stranded on Washerwoman's Shoal, Key Sal (Cay Sal Banks?), though Washerwoman Shoal is in the Florida Keys. A later

paper including those with the $20,000 reward offer stated that a Bahamian wrecker got at least $21,035 from the wreck and deposited it in Admiralty court in Nassau. More was also reported as recovered, and reports say it was buried on nearby keys. These were all reported in May and June 1835. What becomes even stranger is what was reported in several British papers in September 1835. Those said the *Helen Mar* was found abandoned off Cuba with nobody on board, but she still had $20,000 (they say piastres or Spanish dollar newly dated 1835) left on board! Papers found on board indicated she had taken on $109,000 at Tampico.

So, a brig with $109,000 on board (that would be close to three million today after inflation) either wrecks and sinks or gets stranded on Washerwoman Shoal in the Keys or Cay Sal. The captain leaves on another vessel, three crew are left on the key, some of the money is salvaged by a Bahamian wrecker and legally deposited in Nassau, and some money is buried by others, but $20,000 is left on board. Then the brig gets afloat all by itself (so she had to have only been stranded), and six months later is found floating off Cuba with the $20,000 still on board! It would be hard to make up this stuff. There had to be some sort of board of inquiry regarding this brig, and that would definitely be an interesting read. *Source:* G, 5/8/1835; Washington National Intelligencer, 6/29/1835; London Courier and Evening Gazette, 9/7/1835; BMP, 5/2/1835.

1) Page 70. **United States**—Schooner, from Charleston for Key West with the U.S. mail After 35 days out, was totally lost, 12 miles north of Cape Florida Light, August 12, 1835. Crew and mail, though damaged, were saved along with some cargo. *Source:* BMP, 9/2/1835. (5)

2) Page 140. *Gil Blas*—See carronade photo.

3) Page 366. *Collector*—Of Newport, Rhode Island, built 1826 at Stueben, Maine, 104 tons, 72'10^2 x 21'9^2 x 7'1/2^2, one deck, two masts. *Source:* 26.

4) Page 366. *Mary*—Was lost September 6, 1835, eastward of Sombrero Key. Some cargo saved and taken to Key West, vessel a total loss. *Source:* Madison Republican & Banner, 10/22/1835.

5) Page 366. *Majestic*—The *Georgian*, October 7, 1835 reports:

A bronze carronade found by diver Henry Taylor off Indian Key years ago. Believe this was originally salvaged from the 1835 wreck of the *Gil Blas* and then brought to Indian Key, when it was lost again after falling off a barge.

"ashore at Caesar's Creek & bilged, some cargo saved." Lloyd's List also says she wrecked near Caesar's Creek.

6) Page 367. *Blakely*—Captain J. F. Safford. *The Georgian*, October 7, 1835, as with the *Majestic*, listed it as wrecked further north and ashore on Carysfort Reef, some crew saved, all else a total loss.

7) Page 368. *Lion* (correct)—Most all the cargo saved and brought to Key West, 330 hhds, 9 tcs, and 2 bbls sold there for 12 to 16 cents per gallon, half decreed by the court as salvage. *Source:* G, 5/27-30/1835.

8) Page 368. *Isabella*—Capt. Fenner. Crew, spars, sails, and rigging saved and sold at Key West. *Source:* Ibid.

9) Page 369. *Noble* and the *LaFayette*—Of Brunswick, went ashore 100 miles south of Cape Canaveral, crew saved, vessel lost. Schooner *LaFayette*, went ashore 56 miles south of Cape Canaveral. *Source:* G, 10/7/1835.

1836

1) **UNITED STATES**—Steamboat, wrecked at the mouth of the river at St. Augustine. *Source:* G, 11/10/1836. (6)

2) *PACIFIC*—Ship, Capt. Fisk, from New York for Mobile, with dry goods, went ashore on Carysfort Reef and bilged, mid-December 1836. Vessel a total loss, but the crew and most of the cargo saved. *Source:* G, 1/14/1837; DSR, 1/16/1837; London Shipping Gazette, 2/7/1837. (4)

3) **Unk. TRANSPORT**—A story about a Mr. Robert Akbab Abeauef Wright told how he was a crew member on a troop transport that took troops under a Capt. Pratt from New Orleans to Tampa in 1836 and was later wrecked on the beach near Hillsboro. He was taken prisoner by the Native Americans, taken to St. Augustine, and turned over to a Col. Taylor. *Source:* The Morning Call, 8/25/1890. (5)

4) **Unk. SCHOONER**—From Thomaston for St. Joseph, with lime, burned near the Tortugas, early December 1836. Passengers and crew saved by a brig from St. Joseph bound for New York. *Source:* G, 12/27/1836. (3)

5) *SUPPLY*—Sloop, built 1839 at and of New Bedford, 12 tons, 33' x 10'3" x 4'5", lost at Pensacola, 1836. *Source:* 27. (1)

1) Page 70. *Stranger*—Brig, from New York for Apalachicola, Capt. Soule, wrecked on the Western Dry Rocks, February 28, 1836. It had an assortment of new type and paper for the *Herald Newspaper*. Some cargo salvaged.

Source: G, 3/30/1836. The *Boston Morning Post,* March 24, 1836, says she was got off by wreckers and taken to Key West with all the cargo.

2) Page 70. *Eleanor*—Vessel was saved.

3) Page 70. *America*—The *Vesper* rescued her crew. Believe wrecked near the Dry Tortugas Lighthouse, on Garden/Bush Key. Unknown if hull salvaged as reported that some of the damaged ship was sold (may be as she lay on the reef?). *Source:* Washington National Intelligencer, 12/9/1836; BMP, 12/6/1836; G, 12/27/1836; USCG records.

4) Page 113. *Grecian*—Of Portland, Maine, some or all cargo saved. Vessel condemned so may have been brought to Key West. *Source:* BMP, 4/16/1836.

5) Page 114. *Dorothy Foster*—Of London, 328 tons, Capt. Tilley, wrecked on Pickell's Reef (only newspaper report that had the name of the reef spelled as intended—of course it's now Pickle's Reef). *Source:* True Sun, London, 9/27/1836; LR, 1836.

6) Page 114. *Lowell*—Had wrecked on Loo Key Reef, but was got off and taken to Key West. The schooner *Vesper* rescued those on board and also the passengers from the ship *America*. *Source:* BMP, 12/6/1836.

7) Pages 140–41. *James*—Another source says from Mobile for New York, Capt. John S. Place, and ran ashore 40 miles north of Cape Florida. *Source:* DSR, 4/23/1836.

1837

1) *HARRISON*—Schooner, Capt. Powers, from Tabasco for New York, was lost on the Tortugas, January 15, 1837. Cargo saved and taken to Key West, vessel lost. *Source:* G, 2/16/1837. (3)

2) *HIRAM*—Schooner, Capt. Perry, for Mobile with a cargo of lime. It went ashore at Key West, March 1, 1837, "due to a false light exhibited from beach." When the water came in contact with the lime, she caught fire and burned to the water's edge. Captain and crew saved. *Source:* G, 3/20/1837. (3)

3) **Unk. Spanish SCHOONER**—A gruesome tale (see chapter 6). A vessel's hull was found near the Cape Florida Lighthouse in March 1837, of a schooner about 100 tons, no name found. The hull was towed to Key West by the wrecking schooner *United States. Source:* DSR 4/10/1837; Washington Globe, 4/19/1837. (4)

4) *MARY MARIE*—Capt. Parrington, from New York for New Orleans, went ashore on Pickel's Reef. Cargo saved. She was condemned and sold, though

unknown if brought to Key West or sold as she lay on the reef. Source; NYH, 5/4/1837.

5) *OCTAVIO*—Brig, from New Orleans for Charleston, wrecked near St. Johns, April 1837. Articles and cargo sold on the beach near Nassau Inlet, including bacon, lard, whiskey, and rigging. *Source:* North Carolina Standard, 5/17/1837.

6) Hurricane of 8/1/1837 (NE Florida)

a) *GEORGE & MARY*—Schooner, Capt. Willey, from Charleston for Black Creek, wrecked on the beach during a hurricane, August 1, 1837, 12 miles north of St. Augustine, another report says just south of the St. Augustine Lighthouse, and went to pieces. Crew and passengers were saved, along with some cargo. *Source:* G, 8/12/1837; DSR, 8/11-16-17/1837. **[AQ: are these date ranges or three separate dates?]** (6)

b) *FAVORITE*—Brig, drifted over the St. John's Bar and sunk at Jacksonville Wharf. Her cargo of U.S. stores was lost. Believe vessel saved. *Source:* G, 8/12/1837. (6)

c) Unk. **SLOOP**—Sunk near Fernandina and "her masts were barely visible." *Source:* Ibid.

End of August 1, 1837, storm wrecks.

Note: The St. Augustine packet *S.S. Mills*, of 90 tons, was lost off Jekyll Island, Georgia, during the storm.

7) **Unk.** *fore & aft SCHOONER*—A ship reported seeing the sunken wreck about 15 miles north of St. Augustine. Ends of the spars were painted green. *Source:* G, 8/29/1837. (6)

8) Hurricane at Apalachicola (also at Pensacola), August 31, 1837.

a) *HENRY CROWELL*—Steamer, went to pieces and the hull sunk at Columbus Wharf.

b) *EDWIN FORREST*—Steamer, went to pieces and the hull sunk at Columbus Wharf.

c) *MINERVA*—Steamer, decks all off, sunk along Bate's Wharf.

d) *ORLEANS* or *NEW ORLEANS*—Schooner, was high and dry in the Florida Promenade.

e) *SELECT*—Sloop, ashore on Commerce Street near a Grog Shop.

f) *PLOUGH BOY* and the *THREE POLLIES*—Sloops, were a total loss.

Source for a–f: G, 9/16/1837. (1)

1) Page 25. I mention a couple of vessels wrecked at Pensacola during the hurricane. Another report says the date of the storm was August 7, 1837, and that most all the vessels except the warships anchored in Pensacola Harbor, dragged their anchors and went ashore, and the cutter *Jefferson* was driven aground in the Navy Yard. *Source:* Annapolis Maryland Gazette, 8/31/1837.

End of August hurricane wrecks.

10) *HUNTER*—Schooner, of and from Philadelphia for St. John's/Black Creek, Capt. Somers, with govt. stores, went ashore in the breakers at mouth of St. John's (St. John's Bar, October 1837). Vessel and cargo a total loss, crew saved. *Source:* DSR, 10/19/1837; G, 11/16/1837. (6)

11) *PRESIDENT JACKSON*—Of New York, with government stores and a deck load of lumber, left Tybee Light and struck Nassau Shoal and lost her rudder 10 hours later. To save the crew, the captain ran her ashore onto the beach about 10 miles south of St. John's Lighthouse. Vessel lost, some cargo saved. *Source:* DSR, 10/19/1837; G, 10/20/1837. (6)

12) *MARIA J. ESTILL*—Ashore near St. John's Bar and bilged, a total loss. *Source:* DSR, 10/19/1837. (6)

13) *HEBREW*—Ship, Captain John B. Carr, 399 tons, of the Merchants Line, from New Orleans for Tampa Bay, with 118 bales hay, 434 sacks of corn, 85 mules, and 15 horses. It was lost on Anclote Key, 35 miles north of Egmont Island, October 30, 1837. Crew saved, and of all the cargo, only the mules were saved. *Source:* 12; G, 11/14/1837. (2)

14) *LOVELY KEZIA*—Schooner, Capt. McWilliam, of Charleston for Havana, with rice, wrecked about 100 miles north of Cape Florida, about quarter mile offshore, on December 1, 1837. Another report has a brig sighting a wreck which they believed to be the *Lovely Kezia*, with a number of native Americans around her, at Lat. 26°54', Long. 79°50', on December 7, (which seems more likely since the *Industry* would be closer to that). Fearing the natives, they went south and came across the wreck of the *Industry* (page 141) of Montreal, which was reported as 45 miles north of Cape Florida. *Source:* DG, 1/9/1838, DSR, 1/4/1838.

15) *WILLIAM HENRY*—Schooner, Capt. Gomez, from Charleston for Mosquito Inlet, Florida, wrecked on Mosquito Bar, December 18, 1837. It wrecked on the south bar and bilged while trying to get to the pilot boat. Crew and passengers saved. Vessel and cargo a total loss. *Source:* DG, 1/18/1838.

1) Page 71. *Sarah Ann*—Capt. N. Patch or Hatch, of and from Key West (or Charleston) for Mobile, was lost on Sombrero Reef, August 29, 1837. She immediately bilged and filled with water. Crew and passengers saved from the wreck (had tried to make a raft from some spars but failed). Vessel and cargo a total loss. Another source says some did get on a raft which was rescued by the schooner *James Webb*, who then proceeded to the wreck taking off the women and children and rest of the crew on the 31st. *Source:* G, 9/14/1837; North Carolina Standard, 9/27/1837; Oxford Chronicle and Reading Gazette, 10/21/1837.

2) Page 114. *Rosalind* (believe correct), and also reported as *Rosland*, *Rosalin*, *Rosaland*, or *Rosalina*—British bark (believe 289 tons), Capt. A. Alexander, with rum, sugar, logwood, mahogany, Spanish cedar, and ginger. Two-thirds of the cargo saved. One source says wrecked 6/26/1837. *Source:* London Shipping Gazette, 9/6/1837; G, 7/11/1837; NYH, 7/13/1837; LL, 8/25/1837.

3) Page 114. *Pee Dee*—Capt. Cole, from Indian Key for New York, with copper, iron, and cotton, wrecked on the bar approximately a half mile off Key Biscayne and bilged. She had been dismasted previously and sprung a leak and then was run ashore. Cargo would be saved, vessel a total loss. *Source:* G, 11/15/1837.

4) Page 141. *Cyrus Butler*—Bark, Capt. Suchet Mauran, wrecked at Lat. 27°05'N, August 1, 1837. About 200 bales of cotton saved as well as all crew and passengers. *Source:* 12; G, 10/13/1837; North Carolina Standard, 9/27/1837.

5) Page 141. *Industry*—British three-masted schooner, of Montreal, Capt. Dickson, from Montego Bay for Quebec, with rum, sugar, pimento, and other supplies, was found ashore about four miles north of Cape Florida, September 13, 1837, at Lat. 25°13'. Vessel a total loss. Most of the rum was saved. Crew and passengers made it to Key West. They first walked south to Cape Florida Lighthouse which was deserted at that time. *Source:* DSR, 10/24/1837; SG, 1/9/1838; Public Ledger and Daily Advertiser, 11/21/1837. (5)

1838

1) *CHARLES WHARTON*—Ship, 396 tons, built 1828 at Philadelphia, 114.7' x 27.7' x 13.85', two decks, three masts, square stern, and had a man's figurehead, Capt. Wm. C. Rogers, of and from Philadelphia for Tampa with volunteers and troops, stranded on the bar off Tampa and bilged, late December 1837. It was reported from Key West January

11, 1838, that the rigging and materials were saved and the wreckers were awarded 60 percent. All on board were also saved. She sailed regularly from Philadelphia to Liverpool, and many immigrants came across on her. *Source: 27*; Gore's Liverpool General Advertiser, 8/24/1837; Richmond Indiana Palladium, 1/20/1838; Washington National Intelligencer, 1/31/1838. (2)

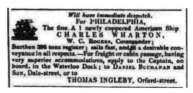

An 1837 ad for the ship *Charles Wharton*. *Gore's Liverpool General Advertiser*, August 1837.

Illustration of a vessel that was driven onto a sandbank, by W. Dickes. *Perils and Adventures of the Deep*, 1844.

2) *CUSHIER*—Brig, reported ashore on St. John's Bar, a total loss. *Source:* DSR, 1/30/1838. (6)

3) *NEW JERSEY*—Schooner, Capt. West, from Philadelphia, went ashore on the St. John's Bar and was stripped of all valuables. Vessel a total wreck. *Source:* DSR, 1/30/1838. (6)

4) *JAMES BOATWRIGHT*—Steamer, 185 tons, about 10 years old, Capt. Donnell, of Charleston. The vessel had been chartered by the U.S. Army to be used on the Indian River to tow vessels up river with provisions and government stores for the Army at Ft. Pierce, which lay six miles above the mouth of the river. She sprung a leak April 23, 1838, after about four months service there. She lay at anchor alongside the sandbar at the mouth of the river where she usually lay when not towing vessels over the bar when the leak occurred. She was taken to shallow water and the pumps manned. Soldiers from the fort also came to help but to no avail. They did salvage the engine, but that's about it. The loss was brought to court due to damage done by the worms to the hull. The captain had repeatedly asked to go to Charleston for repairs but requests were denied as this was the only tow vessel available. She was not copper bottomed, so was in danger of worm damage to her hull. The Indian River was known to be very destructive to wood hulls due to the Teredo worm. In court, it was stated a non-coppered vessel should not stay in the Indian River more than six to eight weeks without being examined and repaired. *Source:* 10 (Congressional hearing records from 1846). See chapter 5 regarding Teredo worms. (5)

5) *JULIA*—Ship, of Philadelphia, Capt. James B. Ames, from Mobile for Liverpool, with 1,100 bales of cotton, was hit by lightning during a storm off Sand Key Light, June 23, 1838, and caught fire. Crew had to abandon her and took to the boats. They were soon picked up by another vessel and taken to Key West. A wrecking schooner found her on a reef later on and scuttled her to put out the fire. She saved some 65 bales of cotton which were floated off after she was scuttled. *Source:* SR, 7/13/1838. (3)

6) *GRAND TURK*—Ship, of Boston, Capt. Thompson, from St. Ubes for New Orleans, with salt, ran aground on Fowey Rocks, July 5, 1838. The U.S. steamer *Poinsett* got her afloat and anchored inside the reef. By the next day, even with the pumps constantly manned, it was apparent she could not stay afloat and she was run ashore to keep her from sinking. Wreckers came on site and stripped her clean and brought the crew and all they salvaged to Key West. The hull as she lay was sold at auction for $165. It was stated the ship wrecked due to no light at Cape Florida. *Source:* BMP, 8/28/1839; Morning Herald, 8/31/1839. (4)

7) *SUCCESS*—Schooner, Capt. Stackpole, of Nantucket, from New Orleans for New York, with lead, castor oil, and furniture. Wrecked on the Florida coast about 35–40 miles south of St. Augustine, September 9, 1838. On the 5th she had collided with a brig during a gale who tore off her bowsprit and then lost both masts. When close to shore she dropped her anchors, but they soon parted and she went ashore and went to pieces. One passenger drowned. Others walked to Matanzas Inlet. *Source:* SR, 10/3/1838; DG, 10/6/1838. (6)

8) SEPTEMBER 1838 HURRICANE

a) *PALESTINE*—Schooner, of Bangor, Maine, Capt. Philbrook or Pillsbrook, from Matanzas for Boston, with molasses. After losing all sails and spars, they cut away her masts, but with no means to navigate, decided to abandon her off Florida. All the crew were rescued from their boats near Cape Florida. The hull was sound when they left her, so no idea how far she may have drifted. Possible Florida wreck. *Source:* Washington Globe, 10/16/1838; SMG, 10/29/1838. (8)

b) *FOUR BROTHERS*—Schooner, Capt. James Madison, wrecked on the Florida Reef and all on board were lost. *Source:* London Standard, 10/29/1838. (8)

Wrecks previously listed and lost in the September Hurricane.

a) Page 114. *Export*—Brig, of Kennebunk, Capt. C. M. Morrill, wrecked on Ledbury Reef and bilged in 15 minutes. It had 1,569 boxes of sugar and one bag of coffee. The brig bilged in 15 minutes and was partly broken in two. The crew took to the longboat and safely made land. They were later picked up by the wrecking sloop *Globe*. A ship had struck near them an hour earlier believed to be the *Triumph*. *Source:* Vermont Phoenix, 10/12/1838; Washington Globe, 10/16/1838; SMG, 10/29/1838.

b) Page 115. *Caroline*—Wrecking schooner; was raised and brought to Key West. *Source:* Washington Globe, 10/16/1838.

c) Page 115. *Triumph* (Correct name; not the *Thracian*)—Ship, of Boston, from Philadelphia with a locomotive and other cargo, went ashore on some rocks about 15 miles south of Cape Florida Light. Another vessel saw the longboat and two jolly boats being lowered but all were soon swamped not far from the ship. After a few hours, she went entirely to pieces. After the storm subsided, the wrecking schooner *United States* pulled up some white lead, domestics, bar and sheet metal, and part of a locomotive steam engine. All hands were lost. Believe "Triumph Reef" is named after this wreck. I wonder if any of the locomotive is still there.

Source: London Standard, 10/29/1838; BMP, 10/15/1838; Bloomington Post, 11/9/1838.

d) Page 115. *Caledonia*—Wrecked off Cuba. Colorado's Reef is off Cuba, not Florida.

e) Page 141. Mystic *fishing smacks*—Of the two Mystic fishing smacks, one wrecked 5.5 miles from Ratones (Biscayne Bay's Bear or Narrows Cut) and the other near the New River. *Source:* Washington Globe, 10/16/1838.

f) Pages 278–81. *Alna*—Wrecked six miles north of the Ratones. *Source:* Washington Globe, 10/16/1838.

g) Page 141. *Courier de Tampico* or *Courier de Vera Cruz* (believe this is correct)—Seven of the 16 crew were saved (Native Americans spared the French). One source says wrecked near the Ratones (Bear Cut). Brig and cargo a total loss. *Source:* Vermont Phoenix, 10/12/1838; Washington Globe, 10/16/1838.

End of September 1838 Hurricane wrecks.

9) *COMET*—Schooner, wrecked near New Smyrna around November 1838, and all crew were killed by native inhabitants, except the cook who was a black man. *Source:* Farmers Gazette, 7/22/1840. (6)

10) *TRIUMFANTE or Triumphante*—Spanish brig, Capt. Gonzales, from Havana for Cadiz, wrecked December 11, 1838, and found ashore 60 miles north of Cape Florida, or soon after, by the U.S. Schooner *Wave*, who salvaged 60 muskets, 1,500 pounds of lead, 280 bales of cotton, and other supplies, and took them to Key West after setting her on fire. Crew and passengers already saved. *Note:* May have wrecked further south as a Spanish brig was reported by one of the vessels in the *Wave's* fleet as having wrecked south of the steamer *Wilmington*, which they reported about 50 miles north of Cape Florida. *Source:* 4; Washington Globe, 5/7/1839; Morning Chronicle, 1/5/1839. (5)

11) *SHOCCO*—U.S. barge (these were oar driven with a 15-man crew and carried two light swivel guns), and was one of three vessels under Lt. Shubrick, which had just saved the crew of the steamer *Wilmington*. On the way back south, they spotted a wrecked Spanish brig. Shubrick sent the *Shocco* and a schooner (borrowed wrecking schooner), under Lt. Howard to the wreck and they saved the crew, along with 30 slaves and much of the cargo. The *Shocco* was lost though, as a strong wind blew her offshore before she could be made fast to the schooner, and she capsized, though no lives were lost. *Note:* The Spanish brig mentioned is most likely the *Triumfante*. The *Shocco* was part of a group under the *USS Wave*. *Source:* 4. (5)

12) **ESTELL & SON**—Schooner, from New York for Jacksonville, with hay and bricks, was lost on the St. John's Bar, December 11, 1838. Some cargo saved, vessel lost. *Source:* DSR, 12/27/1838. (6)

1) Page 71. **Ella Hand**—Wrecked on Stirrup Key, Bahamas, not off Florida.

2) Page 114. **Hebrus**—Capt. Chegwin; "177 boxes of sugar saved; 94 which are damaged." *Source:* LL, 5/4/1838.

3) Page 115. **Wilmington**—Sprung a leak and was run ashore and sank in two fathoms about 50 miles (correct and reported by naval vessels) miles north of Cape Florida. It went to pieces the next day. Crew and passengers totaling 30 were saved by the U.S. Schooner *Wave* and sloop *Panther*, and taken to Key West after eight days ashore. *Source:* Washington Globe, 5/7/1839. DSR, 12/12/1838. (5)

4) Page 141. **Muscogee**—Capt. H. W. Van Vechten, of Columbus, Georgia, from Indian River for Apalachicola. She anchored in calm weather to repair the boiler when a storm hit. Of the 22 on board, three were washed overboard and lost. The remaining crew took to the boats just before she sank and were picked up four days later by the steamboat *Giraffe* and taken to Key West. *Source:* DSR, 6/14/1838; The Columbia Democrat, 7/14/1838.

1839

1) **FALCON**—Brig, of and from Savannah (Georgia Line) for Tampa Bay, 165 tons, Capt. A. Jones, with grain for the Government troops, wrecked on Carysfort Reef, January 20, 1839. Crew and some cargo saved, vessel a total loss. *Source:* 12; DSR, 2/21/1839. (4)

2) **HOPE**—Schooner, Capt. S. Haley, from Apalachicola for New Orleans, capsized in a squall, December 20, 1839. Only the captain survived, and seven crew and three passengers lost. Vessel and cargo were a total loss including $3,000 in specie belonging to the captain. It was formerly a mail boat that ran between Charleston and Key West. Another report says a U.S. mail Schooner wrecked on Washerwoman's Key, September 7, 1839. Crew saved. *Source:* DR, 1/6/1840; Morning Post, 10/16/1839. (3)

3) **SUSAN & ELIZA**—Capt. Crowel. The story of this wreck was posted in a number of newspapers, though it was more about paper currency versus bank drafts. The vessel met with a storm south of St. Augustine. By the next morning the sails were lost, and the cook's house, along with the cook, were swept overboard. Soon they had to abandon ship, and all took to the longboat with some provisions. Overloaded, one passenger had to throw his

bags of paper money overboard, but the one passenger who had about the same amount in bank drafts in his wallet was able to keep his as it added no weight. After a day and a half, they made it to St. Augustine. *Source:* Liberty Advocate, 11/14/1839.

4) *NEW CASTLE*—Sidewheel steamboat, 253 tons, built 1926 at Philadelphia, of Mobile, with 200 Mexican soldiers for Tampico, was a total loss near Tampa, December 12, 1839. All the crew and soldiers were saved. *Source:* 21; Weekly Georgian, 2/1/1840. (2)

5) *INDEX*—Sloop, of Brookhaven, from Key West for St. Joseph and Pensacola, wrecked December 27 or 29, 1839, about 30 miles from Point St. Joseph. It's believed that all the crew were lost. One body was found lashed to a spar. *Source:* Weekly Georgian, 1/18/1840. (1)

6) *ELIZABETH CAROLINE*—Capt. Downey, of Harwich, Massachusetts, capsized during a gale, December 27, 1839, off Cedar Keys. Schooner *Elizabeth Ann* fell in with the wreck the middle of January and towed her into the harbor under Cedar Keys. Possibly hands were lost. *Source:* DR, 2/14/1840. (2)

1) Page 71. *Mary Howland*—Crew and passengers saved, along with all the cargo, and most of the rigging. Hull was sold at auction for $310.00. *Source:* BMP, 11/8/1839.

1840

1) *BOY*—Brig, of Newport, 139 tons, Capt. Charles Williams, from Havana for New Orleans, with coffee, sugar, and 12 passengers, went ashore on the sea side of the peninsula opposite St. Joseph, Florida, January 1, 1840, in 5 feet of water and listed over. Cargo saved as were all persons on board. *Source:* DR, 1/17/1840. (2)

2) *STAR*—Ship, of the Star Line, 596 tons, Capt. John Mallett, from New York for New Orleans, wrecked on Carysfort Reef (another says near Indian Key), January 24, 1840. Crew and all 40 passengers were saved along with some cargo. Vessel was a total loss. *Source:* 12; DR, 2/29/1840. (4)

3) *EMBLEM*—Schooner, of New Bedford, Capt. Leonard Russell, from Apalachicola for Havana, was thrown on her beam ends during a gale, March 25, 1840, when about 50 miles west of the Tortugas. After eight hours, her masts went by the board and she righted herself full of water. She drifted for four days with sharks circling like this until the survivors were saved by the brig *Charles Miller*, who fell in with her off the Florida Reefs about 15 miles north of Viper Key (now called Long Key), about 180 miles from where she was

thrown over. Some died during this time including passengers. One survivor said he saw 23 vessels pass by, one so close they could see it getting the boat ready, but they changed their mind and left them to die. Only four out of 11 on board survived. One survivor was a Mrs. Judah, who all said was very courageous. Her husband had died in her arms, as did one of their children, and she also lost her other son who died where he was lashed in the ropes. She stated that her feet hung in the water from where she was lashed, and had to keep constant vigilance and pull them up frequently, as the sharks would try and grab them if she hadn't. Imagine seeing your whole family die, and then having to keep the sharks at bay for four days lashed to a wrecked ship. For the four days before they were rescued, they only had one lemon, one apple, and a little water to survive. *Source:* Vermont Telegraph, 4/20/1840. Weekly Georgian, 4/25/1840; BMP, 8/8/1840. (4)

4) *EMERY*—Brig, of Bath (believe 285 tons, built 1827 at Topsham, Maine, 99' 5" x 25'4.5" x 12' 8.25"), Capt. Merryman, from Matanzas for Boston, with sugar, coffee, and molasses, was reported from Key West, July 25, 1840, that she went ashore on Carysford Reef and bilged. All the coffee and sugar was saved, but none of the molasses, of which 500 hhds was still in the lower hold. *Source:* 7; BMP, 8/8/1840. (4)

5) *MORRIS*—British brig, Capt. Russell, from Montego Bay for London, with rum, logwood, and pimento, sprung a leak and was run ashore about 20 miles north of Mosquito Inlet, October 8, 1840. Vessel a total loss, crew and cargo saved. *Source:* Weekly Georgian, 10/31/1840. (6)

6) *Wm. E. JESTER*—Schooner, with government stores, wrecked on the St. John's Bar. Crew and cargo saved. *Source:* Weekly Georgian, 10/10/1840. (6)

7) *HENRY BARGER*—Schooner, Capt. Chase, of New York, believe 147 tons, from Baltimore for Palatka, with government stores, wrecked on St. John's Bar, October 19, 1840. Some cargo, sails and rigging saved. Vessel was a total loss. *Source:* SDR, 10/26/1840; 19. (6)

8) *GLOBE*—Schooner, from Baltimore for Palatka, with supplies for the U.S. Army, became a total loss on the St. John's Bar, December 9, 1840. Crew saved. *Source:* SDR, 12/16/1840. (6)

9) *JOHN McCLANE*—Schooner, Capt. W. H. Freeman, of Philadelphia for St. Thomas, with a small cargo, sprung a leak and was abandoned at Lat. 30°N, Long. 79°W. The crew took to the boats and ended up off Mosquito Bar three days later, but the boat swamped about a quarter mile off shore and four of the six drowned in late December 1840. *Source:* Daily Georgian, 1/1/1841. (6)

1) Page 221. *Cora Nelly*—French ship, Capt. Claro, from Havana for Marseilles, with sugar and coffee, ran aground on Carysford Reef and became a complete

wreck. The crew, most if not all cargo, and materials were saved and brought to Key West. *Source:* Weekly Georgian, 7/4/1840; SMG, 7/16/1840. (4)

1841

1) *AFFLECK*—British brig, of Whitehaven, 237 tons, built 1825 at White-haven, sheathed with felt and copper, from Savanilla for Liverpool, Capt. John Banks, of the SR Mallory Line, with sea island cotton, fustic, dye woods and dividivi, bilged on the Tortugas, May 5, 1841. Most of the cotton and some dividivi were saved along with some sails and rigging. *Source:* SDR, 5/26/1841; BMP, 5/26/1841, 6/11/1841; LR, 1841. (3)

1) Page 25. *Lamplighter*—Capt. Woods, from Mobile for Cedar Keys and Tampa Bay. She broke her shaft off Dog Island, February 13, 1841, and dropped anchor to wait for assistance. The next day, the steamer *Caroline* came by and a boat was sent to her with three men for assistance. The *Caroline*'s Captain refused as he thought it more important to get his passengers (some were of the Hurt Theatrical Co.) to Apalachicola and he left them.

The three in the boat rowed to the St. Marks Lighthouse where they procured a schooner to go back but weren't able until Monday when no trace of the *Lamplighter* was found.

On Saturday morning, a gale blew in from the north and continued throughout the day, and by midnight it was ascertained the ship would not last. Two boats were lowered but the seas being so rough the crew could not get the boats near the steamer, and eight of those on board had to jump into the water to get to them. At this moment the steamer suddenly sank, drowning all those left on board including women and children.

The men in the boats had no provisions. It was below freezing with the temperature being 28 degrees F. Three men died on the boats as they both drifted apart, but found each other three days later when the two left in the smaller boat climbed into the larger one. They finally made land Wednesday morning, though didn't find any water till the next day.

The Steamer *James Adams*, Capt. Chase, had left St. Marks for Cedar Keys on the 16th and had run aground on a sandbar later that evening. The next day they spotted a man walking in the water toward their vessel. Fearing the native tribes, they looked through the glass and saw it was not and sent a boat to see who it was. When they reached the poor soul, he told them he was a survivor of the *Lamplighter* and that there were five more about two miles south. They went and got them too, all exhausted and suffering from frostbite on their hands and feet, some very badly. They were all brought back to the *James Adams*, which got off the sandbar and later made port. *Source:* Daily Georgian, 3/7/1841.

2) Page 115. *Manchester*—She was sold on the reef for $1,250. It was gotten off Carysfort Reef and taken to Key West where she was repaired and was to be sold. *Source:* SDR, 4/25/1841; BMP, 5/27/1841.

3) Page 221. *St. George*—A report from the survivors says she wrecked on Cat Keep, off the Florida shore (probably Cat Cay, Bahamas). She ran into a violent gale on April 29 and rode it out for 14 days until wrecked on the rocks at "Cat Keep, off the Florida shore," "Capt. Allen, the Chief mate, and 15 of the crew were immediately swept overboard by the heavy sea." Only three survived who took to the rigging and were later saved by the schooner *Comet. Source:* London St. James Chronicle and Evening Post, 8/3/1841.

1842

1) *GARLAND*—British brig, Capt. Dobie, from Liverpool for Apalachicola, with 2,200 bags of salt, "struck upon the western of a number of flats, off the reef of Cape St. Blas," (Cape San Blas), February 10, 1842. One report says in a fog, and another during a storm. The captain, three men and a boy took to the jollyboat to make shore and get help, but capsized in the breakers about 200 yards from the brig. Two of the men drowned and one made shore and went for help. The captain and the boy clung to the jollyboat until help arrived about two and a half hours later. The brig soon broke in two, the mainmast falling to the south and the foremast falling to the north, and was a complete loss. *Source:* Lancaster Gazette, 4/2/1842; NYTR, 3/7/1842; BMP, 3/8/1842. (1)

2) *MARIA* (may be a false report)—Schooner, Capt. Thompson, from Boston for Mobile with an assorted cargo, went ashore during a gale, March 9, 1842, near Cape Canaveral. It was a total loss except for the spars and sails. Three of the crew marched north to Fort Mellon (about 200 miles) and were arrested as deserters. I did not find out the outcome of this, but the three may have made up the story as it was hinted they could be deserters from the *Jefferson*, as it was said they were caught and brought to Fort Mellon which they had tried to avoid. *Source:* SDR, 4/5/1842. (6)

3) September 1842 Hurricane

a) *SUPERIOR*—Fishing smack, of Key West, Capt. Haley, was at anchor in the Marquesas and lost will all hands. A portion of her stern was found near Key West. *Source:* SDR, 9/21–28/1842. (3)

b) *VAN BUREN*—Fishing smack, of Key West, Capt. Kemp, from Havana for Key West, was lost in the Gulf with all hands. *Source:* SDR, 9/21–28/1842. (3)

c) *HURON*—Fishing smack, of Key West, Capt. Comstock, supposedly lost on the Quicksands with all hands. *Source:* SDR, 9/21–28/1842. (3)

d) *CAROLINE*—Schooner, was high and dry on Mule Key. Unknown if salvaged. *Source:* SDR, 9/21–28/1842. (3)

e) *CUBA*—Brig, of Mystic, believe the 187-ton brig, built 1839 at Stonington, Connecticut, 92' x 24'3" x 9'6", Capt. Benjamin R. Latham. From Galveston for New York, with cotton, staves and passengers, was lost in the September hurricane. Some wreckers saw part of the stern near Key West and feared all on board were lost. A portion was towed into Key West. Some of her cargo was found floating and a broken trunk with some ladies clothing and a locket with the name Mary E. Haswell inside. Believed she was from Texas. Another report says a waist buckle was found in a trunk with the name Mary E. Hall engraved on it. That report also said a child's coffin was found with the letters CT in brass nailed on top of it. *Source:* 37; NYH, 10/13–21/1842; SDR, 10/13/1842. (3)

f) *BOSTON*—Schooner, of Key West, on a turtling voyage, was found near Cape Florida abandoned and full of water. Believe all hands were lost. *Source:* SDR, 10/13/1842; BP, 10/15/1842. (5)

End of September hurricane wrecks.

4) *VIRGINIA*—Bark, of New York, Capt. Sinclair, from Matanzas for Cowes, with sugar, was abandoned after being hove onto her beam-ends and

Illustration of a bark "on her beam ends," similar to the fate of the *Virginia* in 1842. *Naval Battles of the World*, 1894.

dismasted, October 7, 1842, at Lat. 30°30' N, Long. 78°30' W. All the crew saved by the schooner *Maria. Source:* Colonial Gazette, 11/23/1842. (8)

5) *FRANCIS*—Schooner, of Key West, wrecked at the mouth of the Indian River, and the crew supposedly killed by the native Americans. *Source:* BP, 11/4/1842. (5)

6) *VENUS*—Schooner, of Surry, Maine, Capt. Johnson, from New London, Connecticut, bound for St. Augustine, with granite, went ashore on Pelican Bank between the bar and St. Augustine Lighthouse, November 22 or 25, 1842, during a northeaster where she bilged and filled with water. She had a pilot on board. She was sold as she lay. *Source:* SDR, 12/9/1842; BP, 12/16/1842. (6)

1) Page 71. *Pequot*—Of Warren, Rhode Island, built 1838 at Westerly, 59 tons, 62' x 19'8" x 5.9", two masts. Capt. Elisha P. Phinney, had a cargo of western produce. The cargo and ships materials were saved. There was some speculation she was run aground on purpose. A September report says the purchaser of the hull got it off the rocks. *Source:* 27; SDR 8/1/1842; BP, 9/8/1842.

2) Page 71. *New York*—Capt. B. F. Lane, some cargo saved. *Source:* SDR, 5/26/1842.

3) Page 71-2. *North America*—Built 1833 in Bath, Maine, 499 tons, 130.1' x 29' x 14.6'. Wrecked on Delta Shoal and has been located (see GPS coordinates at end of chapter). She originally went aground and broke her rudder south of Orange Keys. It was there that the passengers were taken off while they fixed the rudder. When one wrecker arrived at that location, she had already left, but soon wrecked again off Key Vaca and bilged. The hull was sold as it lay on the reef for $302. Part of her cargo consisted of $10,000 in gold. It was reported from Key West, December 19, that her case was to be heard in court that day and the gold was missing. The *New York Herald* said this: "The $10,000 in gold by the North America, is missing." Did the gold sink with the ship? Is it still on the reef? Was it taken off when the passengers first left? Did one or more of the crew or the wreckers steal it? Another mystery yet to be solved. *Source:* 6; 34; SDR, 12/19/1842; NYDT, 12/19/1842; NYH, 12/10–17/1842.

3) Page 115. *Herald*—British brig, Capt. Hancock, from Vera Cruz for Swansea, went ashore on Elliot's Key, December 26, 1842, most of the cargo of copper and jalap was saved. Another says wrecked on rock at Collins Patches near Vacas Key. *Source:* London Magnet, 2/9/1843, BP, 10/19/1842; Morning Advertiser, 1/31/1843; London Evening Standard, 1/30/1843.

1843

1) *FRANCES ASHLEY*—Brig, Capt. Randall, from Matanzas for New York, with coffee, honey, tobacco, and palm leaf, sprung a leak in the Gulf, January 19, 1843. They tried to make Key West with the help of a wrecking sloop, but was run ashore inside a reef. Cargo was saved. Something did not seem right and the wreck was investigated and found to have some auger holes bored into the hull. The hull later saved and taken to Key West. This was likely an insurance scam. *Source:* SDR, 2/14/1843. (3)

2) *MARION*—Ship, Capt. Freaks, of Portsmouth, from Boston for Apalachicola, went ashore on American Shoals about 18 miles windward of Key West and bilged March 13, 1843. Most cargo was saved. *Source:* SDR, 3/30/1843. (3)

3) *OPELOUSAS*—Brig, of Baltimore, 10 days out from St. Thomas for New Orleans, went ashore on Little Pickle Reef, five miles northeast of Key Tavernier (other source just says Pickles Reef), March 24, 1843. Vessel was a total loss. Sails, rigging, and so on were taken into Key West. *Source:* BP, 4/14/1843; NY Daily Tribune, 4/13/1843; NYH 4/24/1843. (4)

4) *HOYT*—Sloop, Capt. Coffin, of Charleston, from Havana for Charleston, with molasses and sugar, was lost at Cape Florida, April 6, 1843. Some cargo saved. *Source:* SDR, 4/25/1843. (5)

5) *COUNSELLOR*—Two-masted schooner, of Newport, Rhode Island, built at Prospect, Maine, in 1829, 94 tons, 68'2" x 20'2.5" x 7'11", one deck, lost at Apalachicola, 4/24/1843. *Source:* 27. (1)

1) Page 71. **Rudolph Groning**—It was saved, taken to Key West and repaired and re-coppered. Same brig that wrecked again on the Tortugas in 1847. *Source:* NYH, 12/17/1843.

2) Page 72. **Pilgrim**—Built 1831 at Gouldsboro, Maine, of New Orleans, 199 tons, 83' x 23'5.5" x 11'8-3/4", two decks, two masts, square stern. Capt. William J. Philbrook. Vessel bilged, all cargo was to be saved. *Source:* 27; SDR, 12/8/1843.

1844

1) *FATHER MATTHEW*—English ship, with cargo of sugar box, and shooks, of St. Stephens, New Brunswick, for Matanzas, went ashore off Caesar's Creek and bilged, February 1844. Cargo expected to be saved and taken to Key West. It was a new ship on her second voyage. *Source:* BP, 2/20/1844, LL, 3/5/1844.; North Devon Journal, 3/7/1844. (4)

2) *MARIA*—Schooner, Capt. Atwell, from Baltimore for St. Augustine, with Govt. Stores, struck St. John's Bar, February 1844, which caused a bad leak. Captain ran her ashore near St. Augustine to save her and the crew. Cargo was damaged. *Source:* NYH, 2/9/1844. (6)

3) *LAUREL*—Brig, of New Bedford, built 1821 at Hallowell, Maine, 119 tons, 67'3" x 21'10" x 9'7", one deck, two masts, square stern. From Boston, with provisions for a lumber company cutting live oak at New Smyrna, wrecked on Mosquito Bar, April 4, 1844. *Source:* 27; SDR, 4/19/1844. (6)

4) *ROZANA*—Brig, was lost at the same place as the *LAUREL* a few weeks previously with timber bound for the north. *Source:* Ibid

5) *ECHO*—Schooner, Capt. Hastings, from St. Augustine for the Turks Islands, in ballast, wrecked June 17, 1844, on the Mosquito Bar. Crew saved, vessel a total loss. *Source:* SDR, 6/28/1844. (6)

6) *SOBIESKI*—Ship, of New Orleans, from Apalachicola for Liverpool, was ashore off Santa Rosa Island, August 30, 1844, in 15 feet of water. About 500 bales of cotton, some cedar, and most of the rigging was saved. Expected the vessel would be lost. *Source:* BP, 9/12/1844. (1)

7) *J.D. NOYES*—Brig, wrecked near St. Marks, prior to the gale of October 1844. The brig *Statira* saved a lot of chain, rigging and anchors from the wreck, but she was later wrecked herself off Key West in the October Hurricane. *Source:* Vevay Indiana Palladium, 11/16/1844. (2)

8) OCT 5th 1844 HURRICANE at Key West. Eighty passengers and the crew from the ship *Atlantic*, which wrecked at Carysfort, were saved. The ship was later got off and taken to Key West much damaged, though 12 crew on the wrecking sloop *Mount Vernon* who were trying to save the *Atlantic* were lost. The storm came from the northeast on the evening of the fourth and continued for 18 hours wreaking havoc among the Keys. The following were lost in the storm.

a) *HUDSON*—Schooner, Capt. Millen, of New York, from Washington, D.C., was drove to sea while at anchor at Key West. She dragged her anchors and was presumed to be lost. *Source:* Vevay Indiana Palladium, 11/16/1844. (3)

b) *LOUISA*—Pilot boat (schooner), dragged her anchors and sank. She was later found and raised near Sand Key (a crewman was found from the *Louisa* off Cape Florida two days after the storm and said the vessel capsized). *Source:* Ibid.

c) *ORBIT*—Schooner, Capt. Sully, was run ashore. *Source:* Ibid.

d) *PEQUOT*—Schooner, Capt. Pent, sunk at Wall's Wharf. *Source:* Ibid.

e) *SOPHIA*—Schooner, sunk. *Source:* Ibid.

f) *EMPIRE*—Schooner, Capt. Wood, cut through and sunk by the British ship *Victoria*. Loss of $1000. *Source:* Ibid. The following were all driven ashore:

g) *ROME*—Schooner, Capt. Kemp. *Source:* Ibid.

h) *BRITTANNIA*—British schooner, Capt. Kelly. *Source:* Ibid.

i) *TEXAS*—Sloop (saved). *Source:* Ibid.

j) *REFORM*—Sloop, Capt. Roberts. *Source:* Ibid.

k) *AMERICA*—Sloop, on shore, Capt. Maloney. *Source:* Ibid (not to be confused with the ship *America*, which wrecked on Carysfort, but got off and repaired at Key West).

l) *RANGER*—Schooner, on shore. *Source:* Ibid.

m) *RIVAL*—Sloop, sunk at Tift's Wharf. *Source:* Ibid.

n) *MOUNT VERNON*—Wrecking sloop, lost with all hands except two who were picked up clinging to the quarterdeck. One body of a crewman believed to be Jacob Gomez was found near Indian Key and buried there. She was in the process of trying to salvage the ship *Atlantic*, stranded on Carysfort Reef, when the hurricane struck. The *Atlantic* was first reported as also lost but was later brought into Key West. *Source:* Ibid; SDR, 10/25/1844; NYDT, 11/6/1844.

o) *U.S. Revenue cutter VIGILANT*—Coast Guard records list her at 43 tons, 56' x 18.5' x 4', schooner rigged, commissioned in 1843. Her armament consisting of two brass 4-pdrs, five muskets, 12 pistols, five cutlasses, and five boarding pikes. Capt. W. B. G. Taylor, of New Orleans. She was blown from her anchors out of the harbor at Key West during a severe gale and capsized, October 5, 1844. Only three out of 14 of those on board survived. The *Boston Post*, October 23, 1844, said the three "caught hold of a very small canoe, which got loose from the schooner when bottom up; they there retained their hold for two days and nights, the sea continually breaking over them—when taken off by the ship *Ilzaide*, they were nearly speechless and quite exhausted." One hour later near Cape Florida, they rescued another sailor from the schooner *Louisa*, which also capsized in the same storm at Key West. *Source:* SDR, 10/20/1844. *The Savannah Daily Republican* of February 26, 1845, had a report from Key West dated February 1, 1845, regarding the search for the *Vigilant* by the pilot of said vessel who was fortunately on land when the hurricane struck:

> Mr. Johnston, late pilot on board the Cutter *Vigilant*, has for some weeks past been engaged in searching for the remains of the ill-fated vessel. He returned

to this place on the 29th ult., and has given us the following particulars of his cruise. At the Miami he found one of the cutter's boats in good order, and five miles above New River two other boats which he recognized as belonging to the *Vigilant.* Also, mainsail and mainboom, water casks and breakers, compass, spars and instrument case, but all in such a damaged state to be unfit for use. Between New River and Lake Worth he discovered a great portion of the vessel, which had been burnt-together with gun carriages and other materials, and in his opinion the cutter must have drifted ashore about eight miles north of Boca Ratone River, and was probably there stripped and burnt, as he saw a great number of burnt plank and timber, which he supposed to have belonged to her. About 20 miles North of Boca Ratone he found one dead body, but he could not recognize it. He interred it on the beach. On his return, about 20 miles from Indian Key he met with the skeleton of another person. He will shortly sail in the schr. *Ranger*, Capt. Haley, for New Orleans. (5)

End of October Hurricane wrecks.

8) *ECHO*—Schooner, Capt. Snow, with live oak bound for Norfolk, was lost on the bar at New Smyrna on the South Breakers, December 14, 1844. Vessel and cargo were a total loss. Crew saved. Paper reported: "When within one hundred yards of the bar, going out, one of the blocks on the lee forebrace parted from the strop, and the topsail flew into the wind and became aback, which set her on the South breakers." *Source:* SDR, 12/27/1844. (5)

1) Pages 72 and 358. *Zotoff*—Of Kennebunk, 370 tons. Bilged within a few hours. All the cargo except 450 bales of cotton were saved, but most were damaged. Most all materials from the ship were also salvaged. Cargo consisted of: "688 bales cotton, 40 bbls beef, 1016 do flour, 251 do molasses, 648 hides, and 3016 pigs lead, part of which would be saved in a damaged state." *Source:* BP, 1/9-14-18/1845.

2) Pages 72 and 358. *Conservative*—British brig, 289 tons, bottom sheathed with composite metal, Captain Thomas Carrey or J. Carry, of Belfast, Ireland, with 750 bales of cotton and 80,000 pounds of tallow. Only 263 cotton bales were salvaged in a damaged condition. Vessel had bilged. Hull sold as it lay on the reef for $78., the materials for $772.08, and the damaged cargo (232 bales) for $4,281.04. *Source:* BP, 12/9/1844; SDR, 12/27/1844; Civilian & Galveston Gazette, 12/21/1844; LR, 1844; SMG, 1/15/1845.

3) Page 367. *Wellington*—Of Belfast, wrecked on Tortugas Shoals, April 31, 1844. Some cargo saved. *Source:* LL, 5/16/1844.

4) Page 367. *Alwida*—Of Waldoboro, Maine, Capt. Tallman, from Manzanilla for New York, with mahogany, cedar and palm leaf, wrecked on Alligator Reef around June 29, 1844. Wreckers got her off, but she was leaking

so badly they immediately ran her onto the beach. They saved most all of the cargo. *Source:* BP, 7/19/1844, NYH, 7/24/1844.

5) Page 367. *Louis XIV*—Believe she was got off and then condemned at Key West. In June, she was off Louisiana smuggling cargo to shore and some arrests were made and the ship was supposed to be confiscated. *Source:* The Whig Standard, 6/6/1844; The N.Y. Daily Tribune, 8/30/1844.

6) Page 367. *Select*—Of New Orleans, Capt. Thomas Lewis, with 500 bbls pork and 50 bbls flour, ran ashore on a reef off Key Vacas, July 21, 1844, and bilged. Most cargo and materials saved. *Source:* SDR, 8/7/1844.

7) Page 367. *Statira*—Had a cargo of 282 bales cotton, 85 boxes tobacco, along with the chains, rigging and anchors salvaged from the wreck of the *J.D. Noyes*. According to a report from Key West in the *Vevay Indiana Palladium*, November 16, 1844, she was anchored in the harbor when the October hurricane struck and she:

> dragged her anchors, 4000 pounds weight, and drifted out and struck upon the dry rocks, where she now lies a complete wreck. Her decks are cut up fore and aft, and she is broke in two by parting abaft the mainmast. The captain's trunk, containing $1,000, was washed away at the time the cabin went.

All those on board were saved. The wreckers only saved 164 bales of cotton, and the wreck was sold as she lay for $845. *Source:* Vevay Indiana Palladium, 11/16/1844; SMG, 11/15/1844.

1845

1) *STANLEY*—British brig, from Savanilla (Sabanilla?) for Liverpool, with fustic, tobacco, salted hides, silver ore, etc., wrecked on Sea Horse Island (by Cedar Keys), September 28, 1845. *Source:* SDR, 11/14/1845.

2) *Unk. British BARQUE*—Went ashore on Pickle's Reef around September 9, 1845. From Matanzas for Europe, with sugar and coffee, and was a total loss. *Source:* SDR, 10/1/1845. (2)

1) Pages 115–16. *Rienzi*—With a valuable assorted cargo, wrecked on Pickles Reef and bilged, most cargo saved, though some damaged. *Source:* SDR, 6/9/1845

2) Page 116. *Newark*—Captain Merwin, of New York, 306 tons, 104'10" x 25'6" x 12'9", built in New York by Fickett and Thomas in 1835. It had 640 bales cotton and some merchandise, most of the cargo saved. The most interesting of the cargo was a complete skeleton of a 104' long dinosaur that

had been excavated in Alabama and was destined for New York. The bones were packed inside 20 boxes, all which were saved, even though the ship's hold was full of water. The wreckers went out of their way to save these. *Source:* 3; BP, 6/27/1845; The Spirit of Democracy, 7/19/1845.

1846

1) *MARINER*—British ship, Capt. H. Stansbury, of Philadelphia, was reported lost on the Florida Reef. Captain, crew, and passengers saved. *Source:* BP, 5/16/1846. *Note:* I could find nothing more on this vessel, so unsure of validity.

2) *St. MARK*—Ship, Capt. Cave (believe correct) or Martin, of New York, from Mobile for Liverpool, with 1,757 bales of cotton. wrecked on Carysfort Reef, July 27 or 28, 1846. She went ashore, broke her rudder and bilged. Ship was a total wreck, most cargo saved though some damaged. Crew were taken off by the schooner *Mary Ellen. Source:* SDR, 8/12/1846; DG, 8/20/1846; Nat. Standard and Steam Navigation Gazette, 9/5/1846; LL, 8/29/1846. (4)

3) *AMERICA*—The following was all reported in the papers, but most likely a hoax as you will see. Brig, of Boston, Capt. Childs, 255 tons, about two years old, from Kingston, Jamaica for New York, with an assorted cargo, went ashore about 16 miles north of Cape Canaveral near the mouth of Indian River on September 27, 1846, in a violent gale from the northeast. Went ashore and broke in two, crew and passengers narrowly escaped by swimming to shore including a Mr. Flouroy who was the last U.S. Consul to Martinique. Vessel and cargo were a total loss. *Note:* The story of this wreck was told by a Mr. Sherwood who arrived in Savannah and said he was the first mate of the vessel. The *Boston Daily* responded to this report

> As there is no brig *America* belonging to this port commanded by Captain Childs, nor any that we know of performing a similar voyage, it is probable the man is an imposter (referring to Mr. Sherwood), and framed the story to raise money by exiting the sympathy of the good citizens of Savannah.

Mr. Sherwood also stated the brig was owned by Allibone & Troubot of Boston and Philadelphia, but the *Philadelphia U.S. Gazette* stated that the company owned no such vessel. Seems this was most likely an elaborate ruse perpetrated by Mr. Sherwood, though it was a pretty convincing story. *Source:* SDR, 10/7-20/1846. (6)

4) *GENERAL TAYLOR*—U.S. Steamer, was burned to the water's edge at her wharf at the Pensacola Navy Yard, early October 1846. There was

speculation that foul play was involved. She was rebuilt and continued to serve. *Source:* 14; Daily Georgian, 10/21/1846. (1)

5) *NEW ENGLAND*—Bark, Capt. William Long, of and from Boston for New Orleans (of the Merchant's Line), with assorted cargo including bbls of mackerel, wrecked on American Shoal in December 1846 and bilged. Some cargo and rigging saved as were all the crew. An old ship built in 1827, 359 or 357 tons. *Source:* 12; BP, 1/16/1847, 2/3/1847, Daily Georgian, 1/20/1847. (3)

6) 1846 HURRICANES at Key West and the East Coast in September and October. Key West was in ruins after the October 11 hurricane. The light-houses at Key West and Sand Key were washed away along with 22 lives. No trace of either remained. The fort was much damaged, and the caissons were washed away. Here's a list of just some of the vessels wrecked in the lower Keys near Key West, and at least one further up the coast. Some of these were likely saved and others condemned and sold.

a) *GUNS* off the *U.S. Brig Perry*—Brig was saved but had to throw some of her guns overboard (four guns lost), which may still be there. She was ashore near Sombrero Shoal inside the reef. She had eight 32 pounders on board, two cannons, and six carronades. *Source:* 14; AS, 11/9/1846. (3)

b) *COMMADORE KEARNEY*—Schooner, Capt. Payne, was ashore in 2 feet of water, unknown if salvaged, though was discharging her cargo and thought she would likely be gotten off. *Source:* AS, 11/9/1846; NYH, 11/6/1846; BP, 11/14/1846. (3)

c) *MATAMOROS*—Brig, from New York for St. Marks, Capt. Bunco, dismasted and now high and dry, threw some cargo overboard. Unknown if salvaged (believe she was, as a *Matamoros* is listed in service in 1847). *Source:* AS, 11/9/1846; BP, 12/5/1846. (3)

d) *GENERAL WILSON*—Brig, from New York, Capt. Miner, went ashore in 3 feet of water with the loss of foretopmast near Key West. It may be gotten off but doubtful. Cargo saved. *Source:* AS, 11/9/46; BP, 12/5/1846. (3)

e) *LAFAYETTE*—Pilot boat, sunk in Key West harbor, three crew lost. *Source:* AS, 11/9/46; NYH, 11/6/1846. (3)

f) *FALCONER*—Brig, Capt. Bragin, from Portland for Havana, was wrecked and sold for $500 (vessel and cargo). *Source:* AS, 11/9/1846. (3)

g) *LINCEDERO*—Spanish brig, Capt. Baraton, from Barcelona for Havana, went ashore at Key Vacas. Vessel lost, crew and cargo saved. *Source:* Ibid. (3)

h) *ELIZA CATHERINE*—Was ashore high and dry on Key Vacas in a man's garden, and a *brig* went ashore 100 yards above the high-water line at Key Vacas. *Source:* Ibid. (3)

i) *WILLIAM*—Schooner, was on its way to Tortugas with a new lantern for the Tortugas Light, when she was lost on the 10th in the storm. All on board saved. Remains of the lamp for the lighthouse are probably still out there. *Source:* Ibid. (3)

j) *El VENCADORA*—Spanish polacca (ship rigged type vessel mostly in Mediterranean), Capt. Bunatado, of Barcelona for Havana, went ashore near Long Key, and four men were lost. Cargo (though damaged) was saved. Wreck was to be burned. *Source:* AS, 11/9/1846; BP, 12/5/1846. (3)

k) *FIDELIA*—Schooner, of Bristol, Rhode Island, was high and dry in the Keys, 10 miles from Key West, and probably will be condemned. *Source:* AS, 11/9/1846. (3)

l) *LOUISA*—Pilot boat (schooner), sunk in Key West harbor. She had also sunk in the 1844 hurricane but was raised. Unknown if salvaged this time. Crew saved by jumping on board the schooner *C.H. Bacon. Source:* NYH, 11/1–6/1846; BP, 11/4/1846; SDR, 10/29–31/1846, 11/16/1846; LL 11/16/1846. (3)

m) *STRANGER*—U.S. Mail Schooner, Capt. W. C. Hammer, from Key West for Indian Key, was caught in the October 8–11 hurricane, and hove to on her beam ends and her cargo shifted. She eventually righted herself on the 12th and drove high and dry on the beach about 20 miles north of Indian River and bilged. Crew and passengers saved, vessel and cargo a total loss. *Source:* SDR, 11/4/1846. (5)

n) *H.W. SAFFORD* or *W.W. SAFFORD*—Schooner, Capt. McFarlan, from Philadelphia, was ashore high and dry at Key West. It had a cargo of government stores. Captain was waiting for instruction (unknown if salvaged—one reports just said it was to be sold). *Source:* BP, 12/5/1846; NYH, 11/6/1846. (3)

o) *ROME*—Schooner, capsized and sank in Key West Harbor during the October hurricane. *Source:* BP, 12/5/1846. (3)

p) *GOV. BENNETT*—Schooner, Capt. Warfield, of New York, wrecked in the storm and was condemned and sold. *Source:* BP, 12/5/1846. (3)

q) *F.A. BROWN*—Schooner, left Havana October 5, 1846, for Charleston; was missing and believed lost in the hurricane off the Florida coast. *Source:* SDR, 11/10/1846. (8)

End of hurricane losses.

The Boston Post of November 14, 1846, relayed this information from Key West: Bark *Iris* sold for $168, and cargo left onboard for $320. Ship *Warsaw*, $585, cargo spars, lumber, etc., $800. Brig *Napoleon*, $568. Brig *Exchange* & cargo, $536. Ship *Olive & Eliza*, $47. Spanish brig *El Vindacore*, $76. Brig *Commissary*, $100. French ship *Reunion*, $54. Schooner *Gov. Bennett*, $485. Schooner *St Denys*, (private sale) $2,000. Additional information of vessels previously listed as wrecked in the October 11 hurricane.

a) Page 72. *Exchange*—Brig, Capt. Dyer, wrecked "on the Samboes near Key West—vessel lost, cargo probably saved (fish & lumber)." The first mate was lost in the storm. She was sold as she lay on the reef for $595. *Source:* BP, 12/5/1846; NYH, 11/6/1846.

b) Page 72. *Commissary*—Brig, of Bristol, Rhode Island, built 1929 at Charlestown, 231 tons, 92'10" x 23'8" x 11'10", two decks, two masts, Capt. Fletcher. From Havana for Cardenas, in ballast, went ashore and was lost at Boca Chica, December 27, all hands saved. *Source:* 27; AS, 11/9/1846; NYH, 11/6/1846.

c) Page 72. *Iris*—Bark, Capt. Dillingham, of Bath, built 1841 at Topsham, Maine, 330 tons, 114' x 25.2' x 12.7' (correct), from New Orleans bound for New York or Belfast, Ireland, with 986 bbls of beef, 50 bbls of pork, and 14,000 bushels of corn in sacks, wrecked on a reef at Key Vacas, a total loss. All hands and some cargo saved. *Source:* 5; AS, 11/9/1846; BP, 11/4/1846.

d) Page 72. *Eben Preble*—Ship, Capt. Perkins, of Boston for New Orleans, struck Double Headed Shot Key, August 27, 1846, and tried to make Key West in a leaking condition. Had to abandon her with 8 feet water in hold. She was then rescued by the brig *Harriet*, but later found within eye sight of Key West on her beam ends (another report says found afloat a few miles south of Carysfort Reef and towed to Key Tarano (?) to be bailed out). During the October 11 hurricane, she went ashore high and dry on the Northwest Bank and could not be gotten off. *Source:* SDR 9/22/1846; BP, 9/17/1846.

e) Page 73. *La Reunion*—Ship, Capt. Ardison, of and for Marseilles, ashore on the reef near Matecumbe and bilged, some cargo saved. It was condemned and to be burnt. *Source:* AS, 11/9/1846; BP, 12/5/1846.

f) Page 73. *Villanueva* or *Villa Nueva* (believe correct)—Spanish schooner, for Nuevitas, Cuba. Vessel and 20 lives lost, one man was saved by the *U.S. Brig Perry*. She had gone to pieces and disappeared off Key West. *Source:* LL; BP, 12/5/1846.

g) Page 73. *Navigator*—Schooner, Captain Pointer or Poynter, went ashore during the October hurricane at Lat. 26°08' N. A total loss. *Source:* BP, 11/12/1846.

h) Page 73. *Olive & Eliza*—Captain Weeks, from New Orleans for Bordeaux, wrecked on the Quicksands, October 18, 1846, crew saved. She was burned, and only the anchors and chains were saved. *Source:* LL, 12/2/1846; BP, 12/5/1846.

i) Page 73. *U.S. Revenue Cutter Morris*—Topsail schooner, built at the New York Navy Yard, commissioned in 1831, of the Morris-Taney Class vessels, 112 tons, 73'4" x 20'6" x 9'7", usually carried four 6–9 pndrs, though paper said only 2–6 pndrs, Capt. Walden. It went ashore about three miles northwest of Key West during the October 11th hurricane, in 2.5 feet of water, and cut away both masts. Lost anchors, chains, guns, etc., one mile from the channel. Another source says wrecked within a mile of one of the Bahia Honda Keys much further east of Key West. All the crew was saved. Had served as a dispatch boat during the Mexican War. Collector of Customs was told to sell the vessel. *Source:* USCG records; AS, 11/9/1846; NYH, 11/6/1846.

j) Page 73. *Napoleon*—Brig, Captain Libby, of Portland. Condemned and sold at Key West. *Source:* BP, 11/4/1846.

k) Page 73. *Warsaw*—Another source says a French ship, Capt. Crowell, was lost on Matecumbe Key (another says Indian Key and another says near Key Vacas), all hands saved. Had previously been wrecked before the storm, but the hurricane made sure she wasn't salvaged. She was condemned and sold. *Source:* BP, 12/5/1846.

End of October 11 hurricane vessels previously listed.

1) Page 73. *Platina* or *Platena*—Captain Woodworth, from New Orleans bound for Cadiz, had sprung a leak (had 6 feet of water in her hold) and was run ashore on Carysfort Reef, November 27, 1846. The wrecking sloop *America* took off all crew and all materials. Hull was sold. *Source:* BP, 12/5–16/1846. (4)

2) Page 172. *Mutual Safety*—From New York for Charleston and New Orleans, Captain Pennoyer, grounded on S. Point breakers on Talbot Island. She had previously sprung a leak in a storm and was decided to run her aground on land to save all hands. Sold as she lay. *Source:* SDR, 10/16-19-31/1846.

3) Page 221. *John Parker*—Bark, was repaired and saved. *Source:* Daily Georgian, 5/6/1846; BP, 6/3/1846.

4) Page 222. *Mandarin*—British barque, Capt. John Cleland, struck on the northeast end of Alligator Reef, April 24 or 25, 1846, and became total wreck. All the crew saved along with some cargo and most materials. Had originally sailed from Calcutta where she landed "216 coolies at Jamaica." A coolie was an unskilled laborer either from India or China, and many ended up in forced servitude. *Source:* LL, 5/29–30/1846; Allens Indian Mail, 9/24/1846. (4)

1847

1) *AMOS BIRDSALL*—Schooner (also reported as a brig), wrecked on the Mosquito Bar, January or February 1847. May have been carrying government stores as the U.S. government propeller *Ocean* wrecked trying to get into the inlet to salvage four barges from the *A. Birdsall*. Barnette says she went ashore four miles south of the Inlet, January 28, 1847. *Source:* 6; SDR, 3/2/1847. (6)

2) *ST. CLOUD*—Reported March 20 as being wrecked on the Florida Reef; was from New Orleans bound for Europe. *Source:* Morning Advertiser, London, 4/17/1847. *Note:* Not positive, but looks to be she was salvaged and returned to England. (8)

3) *GENERAL JACKSON*—Ship, believed to be the oldest American ship in service at the time. Was taken as a prize in the last war by a privateer. Of Bristol, Rhode Island, 329 tons, 98'1" x 27'8" x 13'10", two decks, three masts, with a man figurehead. From New York for New Orleans, Capt. McIntire or McIntyre, with a cargo of lime and hay. Went ashore and bilged, about 15 miles from Key West, May 20, 1847. She soon caught fire and the ship and cargo were lost. *Source:* 27; Newport Daily News, 6/9/1847; NYH, 6/5/1847. (3)

4) **Unk. British Cotton SHIP**—About 400 tons, went ashore on Washerwoman Shoal, May 23, 1847, about 12 miles from Key West, and her hold was on fire. Wreckers saved some rigging, sails and anchors. *Source:* Daily Georgian 6/2/1847. (3)

5) *LEADER*—Mail packet sloop, Capt. Brown, from Charleston for Key West, sprung a leak on July 18, 1847, and was run onto the beach a few miles north of the New River. Vessel a total loss, most cargo (mail and lumber) saved. *Source:* SDR, 8/1/1847. (5)

6) *MOBILE*—Brig, from New York for Brazos, with 180 troops of the 5th Regiment, wrecked on the Florida Coast according to two sources, but others say Orange Key (which is in Bahamas and more likely). All crew and soldiers were saved. Possible Florida wreck. *Source:* NY Daily

Tribune, 7/17/1847; The Kalida Venture, 7/9/1847; Jeffersonian Republican, 7/1/1847. (8)

7) **DEL NORTEI**—Schooner, from Key West bound for the St. John's River, went ashore south of St. Augustine Light, early October 1847. All hands saved. *Source:* SG, 10/22/1847. (6)

1) Page 73. *St Mary's*—Cargo of coal, struck on the Sambos in view of the Lighthouse; vessel was saved. *Note:* When she wrecked, the cabin boy, fearing possible death, confessed he was actually a girl. Captain Black was a bit remorseful. If he knew she was a girl, she would have been treated a bit nicer. *Source:* Ibid; Indiana State Sentinel, 10/7/1847.

2) Page 74. **Rudolph Groning**—Had lumber for Ft. Jefferson, wrecked December 16, 1847, on North Key, Tortugas. Most cargo saved. *Source:* SDR, 1/8/1848.

3) Page 116. **Yucatan**—British bark, Capt. Casey, of Belfast, went ashore, April 22, 1847, another report says at or near Carysfort Reef and bilged. It was carrying 1,200 bales of cotton, 300 bbls flour, 300 bbls pork, 300 bbls lard, and 5,000 sacks of corn. *Source:* SDR 7/14/1847; NYH, 5/12/1847.

4) Page 116. **Elizabeth Lloyd** (correct)—British Schooner, from Manzanillo for Quebec, ran ashore on Carysfort Reef, June 12, 1847, vessel a total loss. Cargo saved. *Source:* NYH, 6/30/1847.

5) Page 116. **Minerva**—Of Newport Rhode Island. The deck load of lumber, her rigging, and all of the crew were saved. The lumber was destined for Ft. Jefferson. *Source:* BP, 9/6/1847.

6) Page 172. **Narragansett**—Capt. Wilson, wrecked October 21, 1847, just off the beach near the Mosquito Bar. From Charleston for Key West and New Orleans. All crew and passengers took to the boats and made the beach. The next day they all made it to Mr. Stamp's plantation about three miles from the wreck. About $2,500 of cargo and materials were saved.

The first report in the papers did not portray the captain well regarding this event. He later sent the paper his own version of events to clear his name. The *Savannah Daily Republican* on November 2, 1847, had this report of the wreck:

Loss of the Steamer *Narragansett*.—This steamer on her way to New Orleans was on the 21st ult., at 4 o'clock, P.M., run ashore at Mosquito Inlet, on the coast of Florida, under the following circumstances, which we give as they have been detailed to us by passengers whose names are attached to the statement.

The purpose of this statement is that on the 21st ult., they met the steamer *California*, which was about putting back into St. Augustine, on account of the aspect of the weather. The master of the *Narragansett* thought it would be safer to go into Mosquito Inlet, and said he would do so. The boat was beached at about four o'clock, P.M., the lead not having been thrown. There was no boat ahead to sound, nor was any anchor got ready in case the steamer got into the inlet. When the vessel first struck, she was kept under a full head of steam, and no effort was made to get her off-sails all set.

No discipline was maintained aboard after the steamer struck. The Captain was the first one to go ashore, and did not return to the steamer until after everybody was saved. At the time she was beached, the weather was by no means stormy as the night before, nor would the weather be regarded as threatening had not the *California*, putting back, suggested the idea. The passengers and their baggage were all saved, though the Captain is not thanked for their safety. He was the first one to go ashore, nor did he return on board to the knowledge of these passengers during the night.

The passengers were kindly received and entertained by the inhabitants of New Smyrna and Dunlawion, and furnished with means of transportation to enterprise, from which place they were enabled to reach Savannah, arriving here on Sunday morning.

Now here's the Captain's version reported in the *Savannah Georgian*, November 18, 1847:

To the editors of the Savannah Georgian: An article appeared in your paper on Wednesday morning, November 3rd, concerning the loss of the Steamship *Narragansett* at Mosquito Inlet.

I should not have replied to it at this time, but a duty I owe to my friends, as well as myself, demands some explanation. Hereafter I intend to prove all the accusations set against me are unjustly founded.

The steamer crossed the bar at Charleston at 10 o'clock on Wednesday morning, October 20; fine weather and a smooth sea; the evening came on, brisk breezes, a large swell from E.N.E.; by 8 o'clock the steamer was rolling heavily in the weather sea, which caused several of the arms and braces to give way; by 10 o'clock, P.M., the sea and wind both increasing, found the coupling of the shafts were working loose and could work but little steam during the night. In the morning examined the wheel more closely, found three set of arms and two of the braces were gone, the wheel otherwise working loose. I kept off three points to run in for the shore, the land being some twenty five or thirty miles distant, in hope the sea would get smooth and wind lull to enable me to repair the wheel and secure the couplings of the shaft, but 12 o'clock came, no alteration, land at that time being in sight; I sent for my first engineer and consulted him concerning the wheel and engine; he said the sea was using up out weather wheel very fast, and said we must make a lee in some way to make a repair. I told him I would try for Mosquito Inlet as it would be high water about the time we could reach the bar; he advised me to do so.

I accordingly made up my mind to run for that harbor, as my mate said he had sounded that bar a number of times, and was well acquainted, and could take the steamer in. At 2:30 P.M. spoke the steamer *California*, for St. Augustine; at 3 P.M. made Mosquito Inlet; at 4 P.M. crossed the bar in safety some two hundred yards-when the steamer dragged heavy on a sand hove up in the channel, the steering-rods gave way, so did the tiller, likewise the chains attached to the rudder, I set the head sails in the hope of keeping her straight in the channel. I did not stop her engines as I wished to force her over the sand, as the tide was falling, she soon passed over into deep water. Had not her steering tackle given way, she would have been anchored in the harbor in safety. There was not room to anchor between the sand and breakers. Had I stopped the engines, the tide would have swept her on the outer breakers, where there would have been little chance of saving the vessel or the lives of the passengers and crew, I accordingly forced her as far in shore as I could. I succeeded in getting her on the beach, where there was no danger of losing life of baggage, as there was four feet water along-side when the steamer stopped.

I have in my possession such proof as I think will exonerate me from the loss of the steamship Narragansett. H. Wilsom, Late Master of the Steamship Narragansett.

You can be the judge as to the captain's actions. *The Savannah Georgian,* November 2, 1847, also reported the captain as saying he was the first to leave in one of the boats, but he did also have all the ladies on board, along with a couple crewmen, and landed them on the beach. He did not return, but sent the boat back with the crewmen. With the two boats, and after rigging a line from the steamer to the shore to pull the boats with, they soon had all the baggage and people on shore. They all slept on the beach that night and made Mr. Stamp's plantation the next day. They all then made their way to Enterprise, about 30 miles away on Lake Monroe, and had to camp overnight in the woods after traveling through swamps, though the ladies were in a wagon furnished by Mr. Stamp. The passengers did credit the deckhands and especially Mr. Timothy Boole, who was responsible for saving most of the baggage. *Source:* SG, 11/2/1847; Vejay Indiana Palladium, 11/20/1847.

7) Pages 172–73. **Ocean**—U.S. government propeller/steamer from Philadelphia bound for Tampico with government stores, wrecked February 29, 1847, while trying to enter Mosquito Inlet to retrieve four barges salvaged from the wreck of the *Amos Birdsall* which wrecked a few weeks before. All crew saved but vessel a total loss. *Source:* Baton-Rouge Gazette, 3/13/1947; SDR, 3/2/1847.

1848

1) An **Unk. WRECK** (possibly the **VESTA**)—An unidentified schooner was discovered about eight miles (another source says two miles) south of St. Augustine, on the beach in April 1848. She was about 80 tons. A number of bodies or parts were found. The headless trunk of a woman badly

decomposed was found and buried on the beach by the first people who found the wreck. I could not find the name of the vessel but did see the letters PAT on what was left of her stern. A few days later another group visited the site. More bodies, some almost skeletal were found. Still no identity was ascertained though they hoped somebody may have found something to identify her. It must have had passengers as many fine woman's garments were found strewn about. The anchors and chain were salvaged. The next group saw only the letters P, TT, and A. When they got there, the hull was burning as whoever had salvaged the chains had set her on fire. Some think it may be the schooner *Vesta*, from Darien for Charleston, supposedly capsized around February 1848, as those who found the unknown wreck thought it may be this vessel. *Source:* SG, 5/5/1848; SDR, 5/12/1848. (6)

2) **WILLIAM**—Sloop, Capt. D. B. Geddes, from Savannah for Indian River, capsized on the north breakers on Mosquito Bar. *Source:* SDR, 4/21/1848. (6)

3) **MARY JANE**—Wrecking sloop, of Key West, was entirely lost off Cape Florida, June 1, 1848, materials sold for $320. *Source:* BP, 6/22/1848, NYH, 6/2/1848. (5)

4) Hurricane along Florida's west coast, September 25, 1848:

a) **JULIAN**—Sloop, Capt. Talmadge, from St. Marks for Tampa, was lost on Anclote Keys during a storm, September 25, 1848. Vessel and all crew lost. *Source:* SG, 10/31/1848. (2)

b) **CHARLES & EDWARD**—Schooner, of Key West, was high and dry up in the woods near the same place as the *Julian* during same storm. *Source:* Ibid. (2)

c) **CHARLESTON**—Fishing Smack, of Mystic, on a fishing cruise, sunk off Charlotte Harbor in the storm, and one man was lost. *Source:* Ibid, & SDR 10/17/1848. (2)

d) **JOHN T. SPRAGUE**—Schooner, was blown a mile and a half up into the woods at Tampa in the September Hurricane. *Source:* Ibid. (2)

End of hurricane losses.

1) Page 74. **Mortoun** and the **Flora**—Both were condemned, sold, and then burned. *Source:* The Daily Crescent, 1/19/1849.

2) Page 74. **Benjamin Litchfield**—Capt. Bray. See Chapter 4 (Insurance fraud). The hull sold for $5 and materials for $658. *Source:* NYH, 7/12-16/1848; *The Daily Crescent*, 8/7/1848.

3) Page 74. **Henry**—Whaling bark, was lost on Marquesas Islands, Pacific, not Florida.

4) Page 74. **Canton**—Had 3,000 bbls of flour and 550 bales cotton, went ashore and bilged on Loggerhead Key, Tortugas, November 1, 1848. Cargo saved. *Source:* SG, 11/23/1848.

5) Page 117. **Brutus**—Ship, of Boston, with 1,900 bales cotton, went ashore on a reef near Key West. Ship lost, cargo saved, though damaged. *Source:* SDR, 3/31/1848.

6) Page 117. **Brewster**—Ship, Capt. Thatcher, from New Orleans for Boston, went ashore in a dense fog (actually was smoke caused by the locals who every spring set fire to the woods to burn off the grass and make new feed for the cattle), March 18, 1848, on Fowey Rocks opposite Cape Florida, and bilged. Most of the cargo of cotton, hemp and pork were saved (also had copper, brass, metal and railroad iron of which most was saved). One source says old iron also salvaged along with anchors, chain, and rigging. *Source:* SDR, 3/30/1848; SG, 4/5/1848; BP, 4/8–13/1848, 5/30/1848.

7) Page 117. **Kestrel**—Was got off the reef and brought into Key West and examined. One side was badly damaged and other side not yet examined. May be condemned. *Source:* BP, 9/25/1848.

8) Page 117. **Petrus**—From Havana for Havre, with sugar, wrecked on Conch Reef, April 25 or 27, 1848, and immediately went to pieces. Crew took to the longboat and were later rescued by sloop *America*. Captain did save $4,500 in specie. *Source:* SMG, 5/31/1848.

9) Page 142. **Fomento** (correct)—Capt. Germanro, struck a reef, seven miles north of the New River Bar, capsized and sank. All 26 on board saved in the two boats with nothing more than the clothes on their backs. Some 22 pipes of rum and 15 packages of wax were washed up on beach and these later sold for $157.25. The vessel went to pieces soon after sinking. Before found by the wreckers, it was reported that $7,000 in specie was lost in the iron box, though the wreckers said they only found $3,000 in the box and some scattered coin on the bottom. Insurance fraud? *Source:* BP, 4/3/1848.

1849

1) **PALMETTO**—Steamboat, relatively new, snagged and sunk near Chimney Bluff. Cargo of cotton saved and brought down to Apalachicola. *Source:* SDR, 1/11/1849. *Note:* Though reported a total loss, believe saved and is the same *Palmetto* lost in 1852. (1)

2) **CENTURIAN**—Brig, Capt. Richmond, from Cardenas for Philadelphia (of Philadelphia/Baltimore), with molasses and sugar, went ashore off

Key Vacas, April 6, 1849, and bilged. Only the ship's materials were saved. *Source:* BP, 4/16–17/1849. (3)

3) *JEFFERSON*—Brig, from New York for St. Mary's, wrecked on Amelia Island, and was high and dry on the beach, June 4, 1849. Cargo saved, vessel probably a total loss. *Source:* SDR, 7/9/1849. (6)

4) *AMIDE, AMIDO,* or *AMEDEE*—French bark, Capt. Noquez, from Laguna, Mexico, for Havre, with logwood and fustic, went ashore on Pickle's Reef and bilged, June 3, 1849. Wreckers saved 200 tons of logwood. She was uninsured. *Source:* SDR, 6/12/1849; Morning Post, 6/30/1849; Morning Advertiser, 7/3/1849. (4)

5) *IRON QUEEN*—Bark, 310 tons, iron-built bark, built 1841 at Aberdeen, Capt. Robertson (or Robinson), from Honduras for London, with mahogany, ran ashore on a reef near Jupiter Inlet during a gale, October 25, 1849. Captain, his wife, and crew were stranded on the wreck for 10 days before they were taken off by the brig *William,* which also took off some materials. Left the mate and two crewmen on board to watch over the wreck. Vessel a total loss, cargo saved. *Source:* SDR, 11/12/1849, BP, 11/22/1849; LR, 1849. (5)

6) **Unk. Large SLOOP**—About 100 tons, was seen sunk in Biscayne Bay with decks under water after the October 1849 storm. *Source:* Ibid. (4)

1) Page 74. *Maryland*—Ship, Capt. Rouark, of and from Baltimore for New Orleans, with 6,000 sacks of coffee and dry goods, went ashore on Looe Key, December 12, 1849, and soon bilged. Wreckers saved most of the cargo. *Source:* SDR, 12/27/1849; NYH, 12/29/1849. (3)

1850

1) *GANNYMEDE (or GANYMEAD)*—British brig, Capt. Toy, from Jamaica for Nova Scotia, with coffee and copper, wrecked on Matecumbe Key and bilged, January 23, 1850. Cargo and most of the rigging saved. *Source:* SDR, 2/12/1850.

2) *ISABELLA REED*—Brig, Capt. Rogers, from New Orleans for Savannah, with rope, sugar and molasses, went ashore on Conch Reef, February 14, 1850. The captain at first refused the wreckers' help, thinking he could get her off at high tide, but that was a big mistake, as she eventually bilged and was lost, though most of the cargo was saved. *Source:* SDR, 3/12/1850; NYH, 3/1/1850. (4)

3) *JOSEPHINE*—Wrecked on Mosquito Bar, March 30, 1850. The *Charleston Evening News* had an eyewitness account received April 2, part of which stated:

> The *Josephine* reached Mosquito Bar on Saturday, the 30th March, in the afternoon, at low water. She had sprung her main topmast, and her jib sail was badly torn, and as it was blowing hard, Captain Murray deemed it the safest course to try and get in, although the water was breaking in everywhere. He ran in by his usual marks, and got over the outer and worse breakers without touching, but when within a short distance of the smooth water, the *Josephine* grounded hard and fast, about 4 o'clock, P.M. The pumps kept her free of water till the flood tide and the increase of the wind caused the sea to break over her.

Capt. Murray was washed overboard but made the beach on a hatch-cover. The remaining three, Thomas Hall and two seamen, thought it was safer to remain on board than attempt to reach shore in the boat, and they were feared drowned. The vessel eventually drifted ashore bottom up on the South beach. Most of the cargo was lost. *Source:* SDR, 4/11/1850. (6)

4) *HAVANA PACKET*—Belgian brig, Capt. Filkers or Folkerts, from Havana for Antwerp, ran ashore and bilged on a reef near Caesar's Creek (*Lloyd's* says Pickle's Reef), May 4, 1850. About 130 boxes of sugar and some cigars saved, the rest was lost. *Source:* DMN & SDR, 5/13/1850; LL, 6/5/1850. (4)

5) *SUSAN*—Brig, Capt. Hiram Hall, of Boston, from Mobile for Philadelphia, went ashore on the beach, August 24, 1850, 30 miles to eastward of Santa Rosa Island during a gale. She lay in two feet of water imbedded in sand and filled with water. All but one crewman who was sick, left for Pensacola four days later, and one gave out on the way there. *Source:* DMN, 9/10/1850. (1)

6) *PANAMA*—Brig, stranded on the St. John's Bar, July 2, 1850. Vessel was sold as she lay for $180 on the 9th, and by the 12th, with the seas now rough and the waves breaking over her, it was feared she would soon go to pieces. *Source:* BP, 7/24/1850. (6)

7) *NEW ORLEANS*—Brig, from New Orleans, was struck by the gale of August 22, 1850, and soon went to pieces near Sand Key. All were lost except two crewmen who clung to the stern frame of the brig until washed up at Matecumbe Key the next day, 70 miles from Key West. *Source:* SDR, 9/23/1850; The Daily Crescent, 9/30/1850. (3)

8) *CREED*—Brig, of Boston, Capt. Frisby, from New York for Mobile, with mostly hardware and lime. The cargo of lime had caught fire, August 24, 1850, and after two days she was run aground near Indian River, about three miles below the inlet. Only a small part of cargo was saved and she is now under water. *Source:* SDR, 9/25/1850, 10/10/1850. (5)

9) *MORENO*—Spanish brig or polacca, Capt. Galt or Duval, from Trinidad de Cuba for Barcelona, with sugar, aguadiento (probably what we call "aguardiente" today), and cigars, went ashore on a reef off Woman Key, about four miles to the westward of Sand Key and bilged, August 21, 1850. About 150 boxes of dry sugar were saved and the rest in damaged condition. *Source:* SDR, 8/30/1850, 9/23/1850; The Daily Crescent, 9/4-30/1850. (3)

10) *ADIONA*—British schooner, went ashore in Key West harbor and bilged, August 21, 1850. She was loaded with fruit, most of which most was lost. *Source:* Ibid.

11) *GRAZIATA*—Hungarian or Austrian (believe correct) bark, Capt. Bittinch or Batteach, with 708 bales of cotton, from New Orleans for Trieste, went ashore on Pickle's Reef (another says Caesar's Creek) and bilged, November 10, 1850. Cargo saved though some damaged. *Source:* SDR, 11/26/1850; LL, 12/18/1850; BP, 12/2/1850. (4)

1) Pages 74-75. *Sylphid*—Swedish brig, Capt. Ballin, 371 of the 599 bales of cotton on board were saved. *Source:* SDR, 1/13/1851.

1851

1) *CHARLES*—Brig, of New York, Capt. Seth Hammond, from New Orleans for Sagua La Grande, Cuba, with corn, sprung a leak, May 26, 1851, at Lat. 24°02' N, Long. 80°W, and all the crew abandoned her on the 28th. She sank soon after they left in the boats. All the crew were rescued by the ship *Nathaniel Thompson* and taken to Key West. *Source:* SDR, 6/26/1851; BP, 6/28/1851. (3)

2) *MARY ELLEN*—Bark, Capt. Wade, foundered at sea, August 21, 1851, with 1,900 boxes of sugar and a deck load of molasses. Capt. Wade and crew arrived at Key West. Report was from Key West dated August 23, so it couldn't have sunk that far away. *Source:* SDR, 9/2/1851. (8)

3) *SEBAGO*—Brig, of Portland, Maine, Capt. D. P. Shaw, from Carmento (sic), Cuba, where she loaded molasses, and then for Havana for more cargo, was blown off course during a gale and went ashore and bilged, August 23, 1851, on the Tortugas. A small portion of cargo and materials was saved. Crew had abandoned her in the Gulf and were not yet heard from. *Source:* SDR, 9/16/1851. (3)

4) *FERNANDO SEPTIMO*—Spanish brig, from Puerto Rico for Havana, was caught in a gale about 30 miles from Havana, September 19, 1851, and was carried to Cape San Blas where she wrecked and was a total loss. Of the 57

on board, seven men, one woman, and a child were lost. The survivors went to Pensacola. *Source:* DMN, 9/15/1851; SDR, 9/15/1851. (2)

5) *J.W. HOUSTON*—Schooner, of and from Pensacola for Havana, with lumber, was found dismasted and sinking at Lat. 26°27' N, Long. 84°W. Captain and crew were saved by the bark *Maria. Source:* NYT, 10/22/1851. (2)

6) *FAIRY*—Schooner, Capt. Silva, from New Orleans for Havana, was lost. Some of her cargo of 921 barrels of lard, were picked up near Barataria Bay, Louisiana. Possible Florida wreck. *Source:* NYT, 10/7/1852. (8)

7) *JEROME*—Brig, built 1848 at and of Bristol, Rhode Island, 197 tons, 96' x 26'5" x 8'10". From Cedar Keys for New York, with cotton and lumber, was destroyed by fire, November 8, 1851. Four different papers gave different location in Florida. Some of the names listed where it burnt are: Cheesemitskee River, Cheesowooitske, Florida, Chicotika, off Chattahan's Reef, or simply as near Cedar Keys. I assume it burned near Cedar Keys or likely meant the Chassahowitzka River. Maybe there was a Chattahan's Reef on older maps? There is a Corrigan's Reef on current maps. Captain and crew were taken to Key West by another vessel from Cedar Keys. The saved materials from the wreck netted $194. *Source:* 27; SDR, 11/19/1851; BP, 11/21/1851; NYH, 11/29/1851. (2)

8) *PERSIA*—Brig, of Beverly, Capt. Robbins, from Manzanilla for Boston, ran ashore on Pickle's Reef (another says Carysfort), December 22, 23, or 25, 1851, and bilged on Christmas Day. Some cargo of cedar, dyewood, mahogany, cigars, and honey were saved. *Source:* NYT, 1/5/1852; NODC 1/27/1852; BP, 1/5/1852. (4)

1) Page 75. *Mars*—British brig, Capt. Irvin, wrecked on a reef near Caesar's Creek and bilged (another says Fowey Rocks). About 150 of the 500 hogsheads of molasses were saved, as was most of the ship's materials. *Source:* SDR, 3/12-26/1851. *Note:* Though reported also on Dry Rocks, most papers said near Caesar's Creek. (4)

2) Page 117. *Pileta* (correct)—Spanish brig, Capt. Azcue, from Havana for Spain, wrecked on a reef off Soldier Key and bilged, April 1851. Crew abandoned her and landed in Havana. Some sugar and cigars saved. *Source:* DMN, 5/12/1851; SDR, 5/12/1851.

1852

1) *ALPINE*—Sloop, of and from Savannah for New Smyrna, with government stores for the military post there along with several passengers for a pleasure cruise, encountered a gale, March 18, 1852, and went ashore,

March 19, 1852, about 12 miles south of Mosquito Bar. Passengers and crew were saved, as was much of the cargo, vessel a total loss. *Source:* DMN, 4/1/1852. (6)

2) *ELIZABETH*—Ship. Capt. Carr, of Warren, Maine, from Apalachicola for Providence, Rhode Island, with 1,378 bales of cotton, was lost near the bar at Apalachicola. She was a new vessel on her first voyage. About 500 bales of cotton were saved. *Source:* NYT, 4/30/1852. (1)

3) *HARRASEEKET*—Brig, Capt. Adams, of and from Portland, Maine, for Havana, sprung a leak, May 13, 1852, at Lat. 29°10' N, Long. 79°W, and immediately sank, the crew barely having time to get aboard the brig *Telos*. *Source:* NYT, 5/25/1852. (6)

4) *FAIRMOUNT*—Bark, Capt. Whitney, from Cienfuegos for Philadelphia, with sugar, sank off Loo Key, after colliding with the ship *Tennessee*, May 21, 1852. Captain, eight crew, and a female passenger were lost. Two crewmen were saved by the sloop *Plume* of Key West, near Key Vacas, after floating on part of the wreck for two days. Capt. Cook of the *Tennessee* was later blamed for not trying to rescue any of the people on board. *Source:* NYT, 6/2-7/1852. (3)

4) *SARAH*—British brig, Capt. Boyle, from Havana for Nova Scotia (another says Cienfuegos for Quebec), with sugar, struck on Loo Key during the August 22 hurricane, where she lost her rudder and drifted and then drove ashore on Newfound Harbor Point and bilged. About two-thirds of her cargo was saved along with some rigging. *Source:* NYT, 9/13-22/1852; SDR, 9/10/1852; DMN, 9/10/1852. (3)

5) *U.S. Mail Schooner CHATAM*—Capt. Middleton, with the U.S. mail, from Charleston for Key West and Havana, wrecked either 15 or 21 miles south of St. Augustine during the September 5, 1852, gale. Crew and mail were saved. *Source:* DMN, 9/20/1852; SDR, 9/21/1852. (6)

6) *BORNEO*—Brig, Capt. Hodgden, 190 tons, built in Bristol, Maine, in 1851, from New York for Jacksonville, went ashore on the St. John's Bar. It was first reported that the vessel was lost, and the cargo and rigging saved. Papers in January 1853 reported she was gotten off the bar and towed into the St. John's River. In August, another paper reported a brig *Borneo* had just arrived at New York from Jacksonville. Most likely she was saved. *Source:* SDR, 10/7/1852; BP, 10/8/1852, 1/27/1853; G, 8/18/1853.

7) Hurricane of October 9, 1852. *Note:* I'm finishing this book as Hurricane Michael has just struck this same area of Florida, causing major destruction.

a) *CYGNUS*—Pilot boat, Capt. Howard, sunk at the wharf at Apalachicola, and captain and two crewmen drowned. *Source:* The Daily Union, 10/21/1852. (1)

b) *J. VAIL*—Also ashore high and dry at St. Marks, where she "parted her lines and dragged both anchors until she grounded nearly behind the cotton press." *Source:* DMN, 10/18/1852; NYH, 10/25/1852. (1)

c) *JOHN DENHAM*—Bark, of Sippican, Capt. Gray, from Mobile, was anchored on the outer bar at St. Marks where she "dragged and drove across the marsh, and brought up about a mile and a half from the river." Beard and Denham reported her four miles from St. Marks and one mile to the east of the river. *Source:* DMN, 10/18/1852; NYH, 10/25/1852. (1)

d) *METAMORA*—Brig, went ashore on the beach near Sumner and believed will be total loss. Brig *Glenn* also went ashore near her but was gotten off. *Source:* The Daily Union, 10/21/1852; DMN, 10/20/1852. (1)

e) *W.H. BRODIE*—Bark, was blown 100 yards from the south side of the river after dragging her anchors into the trees at St. Marks, where she "remained in an upright position, imbedded about 4 feet in the earth." A report from the firm of Beard and Denham said the *Brodie* lies: "just opposite the East window of our office." Four other vessels also wrecked in the river. A person sent to investigate why these vessels would wreck eight miles from the sea in a river only 150 feet wide, ascertained that four of them simply had nothing available to make fast to. *Source:* DMN, 10/18/1852; SDR, 12/28/1852; NYH, 10/25/1852. (1)

f) *WACISSU*—Schooner, Capt. Delano, of Sippican, Massachusetts, was high and dry at St. Marks, on her beam ends, about 400 feet from the river, between the warehouse and the sheds "where the railroad used to be" (railroad washed away?) *Source:* DMN, 10/18/1852; NYH, 10/25/1852. (1)

a) Page 25. *Palmetto*, and the *Albany*—The steamers were driven from their wharf at Apalachicola and totally wrecked. *Source:* The Daily Union, 10/21/1852; DMN, 10/20/1852; NYT, 10/20/1852.

End of October 1852 hurricane wrecks.

1) Pages 75 and 222. *Telamon* (correct)—Ship, 1,156 tons, Capt. Burgess, of the Eagle and Hazard's NY and NO Line. from New York for New Orleans, struck on Delta Shoal, 1/12/1852. The wreckers floated her off but she was blown on again and wrecked. Some cargo saved including dry goods, drugs, carriages, oils, etc. She was later burned to water's edge. *Source:* NYT, 1/27/1852; DMN, 7/19/1852; SDR, 2/16/1852. (3)

2) Page 118. *Matthew Von Bree* (or *Van Bree*)—From Matanzas for Cowes, with 2,961 boxes of sugar, became a total wreck on Crocus Reef, July 2, 1852. Some cargo saved. *Source:* DMN, 7/19/1852, LL, 1852.

3) Page 118. *Woodside*—Capt. Hodges, 634 tons, 19 years old, with a general cargo. Reported from Key West that her cargo was being saved and the sloop *Empire* had towed a raft loaded with her spars into port. Unknown if ship was salvaged. Another report says the wreck sold for $1,500. Capt. H was going to try and save the cargo but seemed doubtful, as she lies in 17 feet of water outside the reef. *Source:* DMN, 2/14/1853; NYH, 1/19/1853.

1853

1) **Unk. SAILBOAT**—Reported that on Sunday, the 16th, it capsized on the St. John's, between Rice Creek and Palatka, and the four on board, Mr. Allen, Draggers, King, and a slave hand, all got onto the bottom of the boat and remained there for 40 hours. Too exhausted, Mr. Allen and Draggers fell off and drowned. The other two were finally rescued on Tuesday by a passing vessel. *Source:* DMN, 1/24/1853. (7)

2) *AMERICAN COIN*—Schooner, Capt. Doyle, from Savannah for St. Augustine, sprung a leak January 28, 1853 and soon filled with water. The crew manned the pumps but to no avail. They decided to beach her as the neared St. Augustine, but a large wave threw her on her beam-ends. She soon righted but was unmanageable. With the heavy seas washing over her, the crew all took to the boat and safely made shore that night January 29, 1853. The wreck soon broke up and pieces of her floated into the harbor. A small portion of damaged cargo and some ship's materials were saved. *Source:* DMN, 2/4/1853; NYH, 2/14/1853. (6)

3) *VELASCO*—Schooner, of Bucksport, Capt. Farnham, from Nassau, E. Florida for Rockland, with timber, became a total loss on the Nassau Bar, July 2, 1853. Most materials were saved and brought to Boston. *Source:* NYH, 7/23/1853. (6)

4) *VAN BUREN*—Schooner, from Cardenas bound for Bangor, with 138 hhds and 21 tierces of molasses, sprung a leak off Cape Florida and sunk. Crew were taken off by brig *Sagenon* of Boston. *Source:* The Ohio Star, 5/25/1853. (5)

5) *U.S. Mail Schooner E.A. HENNING*—Capt. R. S. Parker, left Key West with the Havana and Key West mails for Charleston, October 12, 1853, and was lost during a gale. Captain, crew, and mail saved by another vessel. *Source:* SDR, 10/30/1853; Wilmington Journal, 11/4/1853. (8)

6) *J. HINCKLEY*—Brig, of Blue Hill, 193 tons, Capt. E.G. Parker, from Boston for Jacksonville, was last seen near the bar of St. John's River, prior to the October 19, 1853 gale, and has not been seen or heard from since. *Source:* DMN, 2/13/1854. (6)

7) *PETITE LIZZI*—Schooner, of Blue Hill, from Boston for Jacksonville, in ballast, capsized during the October 19, 1853, hurricane. Crew cut away her masts to right her. All on board were taken aboard the bark *W.H. Brodie*, at Lat. 29°N, Long.79°08' W. Source; DMN, 10/31/1853. (6)

8) *MARY ANN*—Brig, of and from Falmouth, from Jamaica for Jacksonville, wrecked October 20, 1853, at Lat. 29°17' N, Long. 79°80' W. Crew saved by bark *Brazilian*. *Source:* NYT, 1/17/1854. (6)

9) Cargo of **Bricks**—Though not a wreck, someone may come across a pile of 7,000 bricks off Florida, and wonder where they came from. After leaving Pensacola with cargo of bricks for Ft. Taylor at Key West, the schooner *Montauk* had to throw 7,000 bricks overboard during a storm to relieve her one day out from port. *Source:* SDG, 11/15/1853. (1)

10) **U.S. Coast Survey Schooner *MORRIS***—Was abandoned at Pensacola in 1853 in a sinking condition and as there was an epidemic sweeping the area. As there was nobody to try and salvage her due to the epidemic, she was left there to die. *Source:* NOAA online records.

1) Page 75. *Colony*—Wrecked on Collins (now Coffins) Patch reef and soon broke up. Some materials were saved, cargo a total loss. *Source:* DMN, 2/14/1853.

2) Page 75. *Cimbrus*—Capt. Lodge. The locomotive and some railroad iron were saved. *Source:* DMN, 3/26/1853, 8/8/1853.

3) Page 118. *Palo Alto*—Capt. Key, from Matanzas for Boston, with molasses, collided with the *Nevstine* while sailing in a fog, at Lat. 25°45' N, 79°50' W. All the crew saved by the French bark. *Source:* DMN, 12/19/1853.

4) Page 142. *Cushnoc*—Capt. Lawry, with sugar and molasses, sprung a leak and was forced to beach, June 2, 1853, near Cape Florida. Most materials saved, cargo lost. *Source:* DMN, 6/11/1853.

5) Page 173. *Robert Morris*—Capt. Downs, ran aground and bilged on Pelican Shoal near Key West, July 22 or 23, 1853, due to all the crew being sick. Most cargo of sugar was saved along with the ship's materials and anchor. The salvaged cargo and materials sold for $7,742, and the hull for $45. *Source:* DMN, 9/8/1853; SDG, 8/7/1853; The Daily Union, 7/27 and 8/11/1853. (3)

1854

1) *SARAH JANE*—Schooner, Captain Gooding, of Bristol, Rhode Island, from Boston for Jacksonville, in ballast, drifted ashore after her anchors let go in six fathoms, and bilged in a heavy sea, April 5, 1854, 10 miles south of St. John's Light. A total loss. *Source:* DMN, 4/11/1854. (6)

2) *FRANCENA*—Schooner, 122 tons, of Maine, Capt. Hooper, from Attakapas, Louisiana, for New York, with sugar and molasses, was lost one day out and luckily found by the schooner *Mohawk*, also from Attakapas, while in a sinking state, and took off all on board. Possible Florida wreck. *Source:* SDG, 4/12/1854. (8)

3) *VIRGINIA*—Schooner, Capt. Reeveland, from Savannah for Boston, was caught in a gale, September 29 or 30, 1854, and the next day was dismasted and waterlogged. All hands were later taken off by the ship *Amelia*. Possible Florida wreck. *Source:* DMN, 9/16/1853. (8)

4) Was reported that a **BRIG** and a **SCHOONER**, names unknown, and both from New York for Apalachicola, had gone ashore, September 21, 1854, near the Sand Key Light-boat. Both were a total loss. All on board saved along with some cargo. *Source:* NYT, 10/5/1854. (3)

5) *ATALANTA*—Schooner, reported from Key West in October 1854, as wrecked on the Florida Reef. Cargo saved. *Source:* NYT, 10/21/1854. (8)

6) *ICONIUM*—Ship, Capt. Turner, 550 tons, built 1848 at Wiscasset, owned by D & A Jackson, from New York for New Orleans, in ballast, went ashore on Loo Key and bilged. Wreckers saved the materials, vessel was lost. *Source:* DMN, 11/3/1854; NYH, 11/2/1854. (3)

7) *MANILLA*—British bark, 500 tons, of London, from Belize for New Orleans, burned on the Quicksands, November 31, 1854. Some cargo salvaged. Possibly the bark *Manilla*, of 353 tons, built 1839 at Liverpool, 97.6' x 23.1' x 17.8', sheathed with yellow (composite metal), and was for sale early 1854 and no longer listed in Lloyds in 1855, though maybe re-named. *Source:* NYH, 1/17/1855; Liverpool Mail, 2/18/1854; LR, 1854. (3)

1) Page 76. *Harriet & Martha*—Capt. J. P. Purefoy, of and from Charleston for New Orleans, with 565 tierces of rice, struck a shoal near Ft. Jefferson and bilged. Wreckers saved some or all cargo along with all the sails and materials. *Source:* DMN, 1/26/1854; SDG, 1/26/1854; NYH, 1/17/1855.

2) Page 76. *Athalia*—Capt. C. O. Welton, 236 tons, of New York. *Source:* NYH, 1/17/1855.

3) Page 76. **L.W. Maxwell**—Capt. H. Burt, 160 tons, of New York, from Santa Cruz for New York. *Source:* NYH, 1/17/1855.

4) Page 118. **Elizabeth Bruce**—Capt. Theodore Brown, 586 tons, of Boston, from Liverpool for Mobile, with 350 tons of salt, 70 crates, 4 hogsheads crockery, 50 tons of iron, and eight packages of merchandise, went ashore on the west end of Elbow Reef, January 9, 1854, and bilged on the 16th. Crew tried to save her by throwing the salt overboard for two days until the wreckers arrived. The crockery, iron, and goods were saved along with most of the materials (sails, anchors, chains, etc.), but none of the salt. *Source:* SDG, 1/26/1854; NYH, 1/17/1855.

5) Page 118. **Meteor**—Capt. James Allen, 236 tons, of St. John, New Brunswick, with molasses. It was a new vessel. Cargo lost, but some materials saved. Crew saved, though one report said otherwise. *Source:* NYH, 1/17/1855; Daily National Era, D.C., 2/11/1854; DMN, 2/11/1854.

6) Page 118. **Pauline**—Capt. Townsend Stiles, 199 tons, of Cape May, New Jersey. *Source:* SDR, 8/26/1854; NYH, 1/17/1855.

7) Page 118. **Sterling**—Capt. J. W. Dickey, 144 tons, of Boston, from Matanzas for Montreal, with sugar and molasses. Only a few casks of molasses and materials saved. *Source:* SDG, 5/26/1854; NYH 1/17/1855; Washington Sentinel, 6/8/1854.

8) Page 142. **Saxony**—Capt. J. G. Chase, of Brunswick, 393 tons, from Boston for Matanzas, with lumber and shooks, went ashore near Hillsboro Inlet (another source says a few miles from Hillsboro) and bilged, in 12 feet of water, 4/8/1854. *Source:* SDG, 4/23/1854; DMN, 4/26/1854; NYH 1/17/1855.

1855

1) **SARAH & LUCY**—Schooner, Capt. Hulah, of Richmond, Maine, from Attakapas for New York, with sugar and molasses, was lost in the Gulf of Mexico, March 29, 1855, and all hands saved by the brig *John Alfred*, which was also damaged during the storm but luckily was nearby. Possible Florida wreck. *Source:* SDR, 4/13/1855. (8)

2) **MADAWASKA**—Schooner, from Baltimore bound for St. Augustine, with corn and provisions, wrecked while trying to enter St. Augustine Harbor, April 28, 1855, and very little of her cargo was saved. *Source:* The Daily Dispatch, 5/7/1855. (6)

3) **BONNIE BIRD** (first reported as the brig *Sea Bird*)—Brig, 225 tons, about six months old, of Blue Hill, Maine, Captain Snowball, from Nassau,

Florida, bound for Boston, with lumber, struck so hard on crossing the bar, that a serious leak occurred, and within three hours she was full of water. Crew tried to make St. Mary's, but abandoned her and took to the boats. Were picked up by the steamer *Mount Pleasant*, which tried to get close the brig, but the seas were too rough. She ended up ashore about 18 miles north of St. Johns in the breakers off Amelia Island, May 31, 1855, the seas making a complete breach over her. *Source:* NYH, 6/12/1855; BP, 6/14/1855. (6)

4) *NACOOCHEE*—Bark, of Augusta, Maine, Capt. Howe, from Pensacola bound for New York, with lumber, was abandoned, June 19, 1855, in a leaky condition at Lat. 24°30'N, Long. 81°W. Captain and crew were picked up by the brig *D. Maloney*, which took off most of the rigging and sails. *Source:* NYH, 6/25/1855. (3)

5) *MONTAGUE*—Brig, Capt. Doyle, from Wareham for St. John's, Florida, went ashore late September or early October 1855, on the St. John's Bar, about 16 miles from Jacksonville, where she bilged and filled with water. Crew all made shore the next day and walked 10 miles until they found habitation. *Source:* BP, 10/9/1855. (6)

6) *A.H. STURGES*—Bark, Capt. Baxter, from Jacksonville, with lumber, wrecked on the S.W. Keys, November 10, 1855. All onboard picked up by the schooner *Mantander*. *Source:* SDG, 12/14/1855. (3)

1) Page 50. *George P. Sloate*—These sources say a schooner, Capt. Mershon, of Philadelphia. Went ashore on the north breaker of Charlotte Harbor, December 26 or 27, 1855, and was abandoned. Only the materials were saved. The bricks were for Ft. Taylor. *Source:* NY Daily Tribune, 1/14/1856; DMN, 1/14/1856.

2) Page 76. *Horatio*—Brig, was found stripped of everything and abandoned, and had also been set on fire. She was towed into Key West and eventually repaired and sailed again. What they found out though, was that she was a slave vessel, and was likely left to sink (unsuccessfully) to get rid of the evidence as was the case with many slavers after dropping off their human cargo as it was now illegal to bring slaves into the United States. The *Burlington Weekly Iowa State Gazette*, May 3, 1855, reported: New York, May 26,

> Randolph C. Lasalle, F. A. Meyers, and A. F. Martin were arrested yesterday, charged with fitting out the brig *Horatio*, recently found abandoned off Key West as a slaver. The first named was bailed in the sum of $20,000, but the others were detained in custody, being unable to find sureties.

The plot thickens as the *Bedford White River Standard*, May 24, 1855, reports this:

Arrest of An Alleged African Slave Trader—officer Dulaney of the United States marshal's office, yesterday afternoon arrested a seaman named Brown, on the charge of being recently engaged in the slave trade. The charge is made by Captain James Maguire, who is now sick at the Fountain Hotel. Captain Maguire states, that on a recent voyage of the brig *Horatio*, of which he was master, from New York to the coast of Africa, the crew mutinied and placing him in irons on board, proceeded to the West coast of Africa, where they took on board a cargo of slaves, and conveyed them to the island of Cuba, where they were landed. Capt. Maguire says he managed to escape from the brig, and Brown, one of the crew, having come to Baltimore, the charge was against him. By the laws of the United States, the act is declared to be piracy, and is punishable with death. The accused was fully committed by John Hanna, Esq., United States Commissioner. Baltimore Patriot, May 9.

Further investigation found that Randolph C. Lasalle is actually Rudolf E. Lasala, who was the owner of the ship, though he sent a letter to the press stating that he was not the owner. I found some of the trial proceedings that were printed in the paper and looked like Lasala may not be innocent.

It appears the *Horatio* was fitted out as a slaver from the beginning and brought back 600 slaves from Africa, supposedly landed at Bahia Honda, Cuba, though there was some speculation she may have been chased and threw all 600 overboard. Most bothersome was what the *Evening Star* (Washington, D.C.) reported on June 7, 1855: they had no verification the slaves were landed, but hoped that was the case.

We hope it may be so, for if none of the cargo were landed, we are left to conjecture the possibility that the horrible means was adopted, (of which the history of the African slave trade it is said affords precedents) *of throwing the slaves into the sea* upon being closely chased by a man-of-war! And we are told the appearance of the 'Horatio' allows this suspicion to be entertained as to her. She had recently been, it is quite certain, closely pressed in some chase before she was abandoned, for her rails and stanchions were freshly sawed asunder in several places, manifestly to render her 'limber' or 'springy', and thus promote her sailing; a devise, we are informed, often practices by skillful seamen to escape a pursuing vessel. Upon this whole case of the 'Horatio' is a most mysterious affair, and should be closely investigated by the British and Spanish Governments, as well as our own.

The possibility of the horrible atrocity of six hundred human beings being purposely thrown into the sea to enable the pirates to escape detection, and elude punishment, should prompt it, and it would be wise for the British authorities if seriously and sincerely desirous of putting an end to the Cuba African slave trade, to investigate as to the causes why their officers are not more successful.

3) Page 76. *Rainbow*—Of Warren, Rhode Island, 341 tons, built 1847 at Baltimore, from Swansea. First reports say she went ashore and bilged,

August 30, 1855 (supposedly broke in two) near Cow Keys (another report just says Key Vacas). Only her rigging, sails, anchors and chains were saved. Another report says she was later burned. And then in November, another report said the hull was raised and brought into Key West, along with the entire cargo. It had previously been sold as she lay on the reef. *Source:* SDG, 9/12/1855; NYH, 9/14/1855; DMN, 9/20/1855; London Evening Standard, 11/28/1855.

4) Page 76. *Concordia* (correct)—Capt. Wm. Cushing, of Boston, from Mobile for Liverpool, with 2,200 bales cotton, 604 tons, built at Medford in 1841, newly rigged and coppered. She caught fire in her hold and was forced to run aground about three miles from shore off Cow Keys, near Key Vacas. Some cotton saved, and the wreckers were to also save the anchors and chain. *Source:* SDG, 12/14/1855. (3)

5) Page 193. *Seminole*—After the *Seminole* was cut adrift from the wharf, she was drifting straight for the Coast Survey Schooner *Benjamin Pierce*. Capt. Hawley's report on how he saved his vessel along with another by towing the steamer with his boat, is quite remarkable. *Source:* USCG records.

1856

1) *SIDDONS*—Ship, Capt. Taylor, from London for New Orleans, went ashore on Elbow Reef (another says Carysfort, and another says Grecian Shoal), January 3, 1856, and bilged. Wreckers could only save those and board and most of the ship's materials before she broke up. *Source:* DMN, 1/14/1856; London Express, 1/29/1856. (4)

2) August 27 Hurricane:

a) *DIADEM*—Ship, 657 tons, built at Bath, Maine, in 1838, by Clark & Sewall, 140' 7.5" x 32' 1" x 16' 1/2", from New Orleans for New York, Capt. Kobleer, with 1,395 bbls flour, 250 bbls lard, and 97,061 sacks of wheat, ran into a gale on August 27, and lost four men who were washed overboard. She foundered on August 28, 1856, at sea (one source says 400 miles off SW Pass). The schooner *Yuba* saw the distress flag on the one remaining mast and managed to save rest of crew the next day as it was too rough that evening. The *Yuba* lost her mate and one crewman from the *Diadem* in the process. An October paper says the headboard and other wreckage from the ship was strewn along the Florida shore. The New Orleans papers reported the loss as related by Capt. Kobleer:

> It was very squally-reduced all accordingly; on Thursday morning the storm having increased, hove to under close reefed maintopsail and main spencer; barometer falling fast; and wind increasing, furled maintopsail at 2 p.m., laying

to under main spencer on the port jack with the wind from the northward and eastward; blowing a tremendous hurricane; every other sail being furled with extra caskets. A heavy sea struck the ship; carrying away the bulwarks, with all the stanchions, and all from the fore rigging to within six or seven feet of the taffrail, slitting the plank spar in many places, and sweeping the decks fore and aft of goods, water casks, etc.; bursting open the after hatch, carried away the house on deck. The cabin was stove to pieces, the captain, mate and steward were all covered by the ruins, but were extricated, being badly bruised.

The man at the wheel was swept overboard, with three others of the crew, who were drowned. One man had his head badly cut, and several others were wounded. After this could do nothing more than lash ourselves to the mast; some were lashed to the pumps from which they were swept away several times during the night. After remaining in this condition for some time, a tremendous gust of wind swept over the ship, taking the fore and main top masts; soon after this a gust still more violent broke away the fore and main masts, breaking them off below the deck, leaking huge holes in the deck. The ship by this time was water logged. On Saturday the bark *Yuba* hove in sight; seeing our signal of distress on the mizzen; the only mast we had standing, the captain made for us and waved his hat in signification that he would lay by us. A boat was lowered, to the imminent danger of those that manned her. She was unable, from the roughness of the sea, to get on board, either the *Diadem* or the *Yuba*, so they had to remain in the boat all night; was taken on board the *Yuba's* boat the next morning, and pulling for the bark, was upset twice. Capt. Webber clung to the bottom of the boat and was rescued, but the mate of the bark *Yuba*, who manned her boat was missing; also one seaman belonging to the *Diadem*.

Source: 6; Savannah Georgian and Journal, 9/15/56; The Daily Dispatcher, 9/16/56; DMN, 10/9/56. *Note:* She was assisted off Loo Key by the wreckers only a few months before in June. (8)

b) *JOHN J. TAYLOR*—Schooner, Capt. Bennett C. Anderson. Left New Orleans for Savannah, August 6, 1856, and never heard from again. Believed lost in the August hurricane. Possible Florida wreck. *Source:* DMN, 1/1/1857. (8)

c) *MARIE*—French bark, Capt. Le Port, from Matanzas for Marseilles, with 1,400 hhds (boxes) sugar, went ashore on Loo Key, August 27, 1856, and immediately bilged and went to pieces. Captain and six crewmen were lost, five crew were saved (first and second mate and three crewmen). Vessel and cargo a total loss. *Source:* NYH, 9/16/56; Savannah Georgian & Journal, 9/15/1856, 10/13/1856. (3)

d) *WILD PIGEON*—Capt. Radovich, from Pensacola for Havana. The stern of a brig believed to be the *Wild Pigeon*, drifted ashore on Long Key after the August 1856 hurricane. Her headboard was later found along the Florida shore along with trunks, goods, etc. Was feared all on board were lost.

Source: BP, 10/15/1856; DMN, 10/9/1856; Savannah Georgian & Journal, 10/13/1856. (4)

End of August hurricane losses.

3) *OCTAVIA*—Bark, Capt. Mitchell, from Matanzas for Boston, with cigars and sugar, ran upon French Reef, November 2, 1856, and bilged soon after. About 150 boxes of sugar saved dry, vessel lost. *Source:* Savannah Georgian and Journal, 11/3/1856; BP, 11/18/1856. (4)

4) *USCS BELL*—US survey schooner, 60' x 16' x 4', lost on an uncharted shoal near the entrance of St. Andrews Bay, early December, 1856. *Source:* NODC, 12/22/1856; NOAA online records. (1)

1) Page 26. *Florida*—Was lost August 31, 1856, in St. Joseph Harbor. After dragging her chain with anchors down and under full head of steam, she was blown ashore. A passenger, Col. Winchester, was credited for saving a woman and her two children. *Source:* DMN, 9/24/1856.

2) Pages 76–77. *Lavinia Adams* (correct)—Was temporarily repaired at Key West after being ashore on Looe Key in November 1855, and sailed for New Orleans for permanent repairs on February 18, 1856, but sank a few days later. Crew saved. *Source:* LL, 3/18/1856. Possible Florida wreck. (8)

3) Page 118. *Mariner*—Fairly new clipper ship, around 1,200 tons. Believe wrecked on Pickle's Reef, March 1, 1856, some cargo and materials saved. *Source:* NY Daily Tribune, 3/31/1856.

4) Page 119. *Emigrant*—Capt. Brown, wreckers got her off Alligator Reef and took her to Key West, where she was caught in the August 27 hurricane. She parted her chains and went ashore and bilged on Crawfish Key Shoal (in Key West Harbor). Cargo saved, though some damaged. *Source:* BP, 9/16/1856; Savannah Georgian & Journal, 9/13/1856. (3)

1857

1) *MARGARET ANNE*—Schooner, Capt. Lee, from Apalachicola for Key West, was lost at Charlotte Harbor. *Source:* NYH, 1/16/1858. (2)

2) *FLORIDA*—Pilot boat/wrecking vessel, Capt. Frow, caught fire and was lost right next to the wreck of the *Crown* due to an accident with the bottom of a lantern falling down, while loading cotton from the wrecked ship *Crown* on Ajax Reef, January 26, 1857. *Source:* NODC, 2/19/1857; Memphis Daily Appeal, 4/4/1857. (4)

3) *VISITER*—Schooner, of New Orleans, built 1847 at Baltimore, 76 tons, 69' x 21'1" x 6'1", one deck, two masts, square stern. Wrecked at St. Andrews Bay and abandoned to the underwriters, around May 1857. *Source:* 27. (1)

4) *CARACK*—Ship, of and built at Thomaston, Maine, 900 tons, seven years old, Capt. Stilplien (or Stilphen), from New Orleans bound for Liverpool, with 2,780 bales of cotton, was struck by lightning four days out on July 16, about 250 miles from the Tortugas. She caught on fire and the crew did everything to extinguish the flames. By the next day, when about 80 miles from the Tortugas, the fire was out of control and the ship had to be abandoned. Captain and crew left in three boats but were soon separated by a squall. Two boats were later rescued by two passing vessels and they had not heard from the third boat yet. Crews from the two were taken to Key West. *Source:* DMN, 7/28/1857; Richmond Enquirer, 8/4/1857. (3)

5) *BELLE*—British brig, from Jamaica for Halifax, wrecked on French Reef, October 15, 1857. Materials saved and later sold. *Source:* London Evening Standard, 11/16/1857. (4)

6) *SAMUEL BOLTON*—Schooner (originally a centerboard), 159 tons, built 1854 at Milton, Delaware, of Georgetown, South Carolina, from New York bound for Jacksonville with an assorted cargo, wrecked near St. Augustine, November 13, 1857. Crew and most of the cargo were saved. *Source:* BP, 11/26/1857. (6)

1) Page 78. *USCS Phoenix*—Acquired by the Navy in 1845, 70' x 17' x 7', Capt. Brown., was run ashore and bilged at Key Vacas in order to save the crew after she had sprung a leak. From New Orleans for Key West and Baltimore. Materials and crew taken to Key West. *Source:* DMN, 11/21/1857; NOAA online records.

2) Page 119 (Possibly same **Unk. Bark** on page 78). *Cynosure*—Brig, Capt. Anderson, from Rockland for New Orleans. The cargo of 4,386 barrels of lime caught on fire, and she was run ashore near Elliot's Key. Crew and some materials saved before she completely burned. *Source:* NYH, 1/16/1858; NODC, 6/19/1857.

3) Page 119. *Crown*—Believe it's the 1,259-ton ship, built 1851 at Quebec, of Liverpool, Capt. T. Carrey, sheathed with zinc. Cargo consisted of 3,491 bales cotton, 3,483 bags corn, 660 bags wheat. Some 2,065 bales cotton saved along with some rigging and materials. (Listed as ashore on both Ajax and Pacific Reef—most say Ajax, though another says on a shoal between the two reefs, which is probably correct.) See pilot/wrecker *Florida* above. *Source:* SDR, 1/28/1858; DMN, 3/30/1857; NYH, 2/2/1857; LR, 1857.

4) Page 119. *Helen E. Booker*—Went ashore on Elbow Reef and bilged. "About 600 tons of railroad iron has been saved out of her; the rest will probably be after awhile." *Source:* NYH, 5/31/1857.

1858

1) *ELLA*—Schooner, of Washington, wrecked on the St. Augustine Bar, January 27, 1858, with corn and merchandise, and was a total loss. *Source:* SDR, 2/3/1858. (6)

2) *SARAH VOSE*—Brig, Capt. John H. Curry, from Havana for France, struck on the Florida Reef about 20 miles to windward of Cool Key (maybe Cow Key), April 12, 1858, and is a total wreck. Captain and crew saved and taken to Key West. *Source:* DMN, 4/16/1858. Believe the 153-ton brig *Sarah Vose*. (8)

3) *WEST*—Brig (possibly the 297-ton *West*), of Boston, Capt. Bordington, from Galveston for Liverpool, wrecked on the coast of Florida, July or August 1858. The Bremen ship *Magdalena* fell in with a boat with one survivor of the *West* named George L. Baker about 60 miles NE by E of Key West, who had been two days in the boat. He said waves were breaking over the brig when she wrecked. Believed all the others drowned. *Source:* NYT, 8/23/1858; The Daily Dispatch, 8/25/1858, 9/16/1858; London Magnet, 8/16/1858. (8)

4) *E.A. LOUD* or *ED A. LOUD*—British brig of Digby, Nova Scotia, Capt. Rice, was found ashore in Dead Man's Bay, September 1858. At first the wreck was reported due to the captain and four seamen dying from the fever, and that the three remaining crewmen were taken to Cedar Keys to recover. A couple of weeks later, the U.S. Marshall reported that it was believed the captain and some crew were murdered, and that the three faked having the fever and had murdered the others. The three had allot of money with them. Unsure if saved but reported the pilots were removing the ballast to try and get her off. *Source:* BP, 9/17-27/1858; NYH, 9/27/1858. (2)

5) **Two large SHIPS** and a **SCHOONER**—The U.S. coast survey schooner *Agazzis*, reported sighting three vessels on the beach off Jupiter Inlet, November 16, 1858: "two appeared to be large ships, and one a schooner sunk or buried in the sand—all abandoned." Wreckers from Key West headed that way when they heard the news. *Source:* DMN, 11/30/1858. (5)

6) *CORTEZ*—Spanish merchantman. The British paper, *The Northern Whig*, June 9, 1858, relayed a story from the Dayton (Ohio) Gazette. A woman who seemed out of place begging on Jefferson street in Dayton was asked

where she was from. She told them she was from Spain, that her father had been a member of the Spanish cabinet, and that she had been a countess. Her husband was involved in the recent Spanish conspiracy, and was lately executed. Her estate was seized, and she and her five children were expelled from Spain. Her misery didn't end there. She took passage on the Spanish vessel *Cortez* (I'll have to guess within last year or two), which wrecked near Key West, where three of her children drowned. She made her way to New Orleans, then Dayton, and was trying to reach Detroit where an uncle was living. Article went on to say "Justly entitled to an estate worth two million dollars, she is today a beggar upon our streets." I could find nothing on a vessel of that name recently wrecked near Key West. May just be a made up story, but the ones who reported it believed her.

7) *SAMUEL OTIS*—Brig, 257 tons, of and built at Belfast, Maine in 1855, Capt. Gilchrist, from Jacksonville for St. Croix, with lumber. In late 1858, she had hit bottom while going over the St. John's Bar in charge of the pilot, and sprung a leak. She was then run aground on Amelia Island and wrecked. *Source:* Newport Daily News, 1/1/1859; NYH, 1/1/1859. (6)

1) Page 58. *Pacific*—Capt. Gardner, went ashore July 22. *Source:* DMN, 7/28/1857.

2) Page 78. *Caraquena*—Wreckers saved much of the cargo including hides, sarsaparilla in bales, manila in bales, and 40 or 50 sticks of mahogany. Sails and rigging also salvaged. Cargo and materials were sold at auction as was the hull as she lay on the reef. *Source:* BP, 11/17/1858; NODC, 11/30/1858.

3) Page 78. *Ann Harley*—Capt. Holmes, of Glasgow, from Pensacola for Hull, with 214 pieces of timber, and 1,586 pieces of deal (about 330,000 feet). She immediately bilged after running aground. *Source:* NODC, 12/14/1858.

4) Pages 119–20. *Nathan Hanau* (believe correct name)—Captain Pierce, 513 tons. *Source:* BP, 3/14–24/1859.

5) Page 142. *Admiral Saultzemann* (newspapers all listed her as the *Admiral Zutman*)—"They were frequently attacked by bears, panthers and wolves. Twelve of the former they succeeded in killing, and also three of the later." They found five other wrecks along the beach (some recent). They walked up and down beach for nine days before being rescued. Also found the bodies of 19 men and one shallow grave which had a slab at the head inscribed with name Capt. Adams, found 40 miles below Stryker's Inlet. *Source:* NYH, 4/5/1858.

1859

1) *EXPERIMENT*—Slaver schooner. On June 30, 1859, the U.S. Cutter *James C. Dobbin* heard of a slaver dropping of Africans near Jupiter and went to investigate. It stopped at Indian River and a resident there said that six weeks earlier four seamen came and told him they were from the schooner *Experiment* which just dropped of Africans near Jupiter and they then beached the vessel which soon broke up. They all went south to Key West after that. The cutter searched for the wreck and the crew but found nothing. She then stopped at Jupiter and the man in charge of the unfinished lighthouse said he knew nothing about it. It was also reported from Miami that it had wrecked there, saying the local indigenous people salvaged most everything off the wreck including an abundance of ammunition. *Source:* NYT, 8/1/1859; The Daily Exchange, 3/25/1859.

1) Page 50. *Heidelberg*—Wrecked two lengths offshore and bilged. Around 1,840 dry bales of cotton were saved. *Source:* BP, 11/18/59; NY Daily Tribune, 11/22/1859. (5)

2) Page 79. *Mulhouse*—Built 1853 at Thomaston, Maine, 1,110 tons, 176' x 37' x 18'6-1/2", two decks, three masts, square stern, and had a figurehead. *Source:* 26.

3) Page 119. *Mimi* (correct name)—Capt. Schwartz. *Source:* LL, 3/16/1859.

4) Page 120. *Indian Hunter*—Another source says on a sand bank opposite Key Vaca, and yet another says "went ashore on Pickle's Reef, Florida, on the 26th of June, and settled down on her broadside with a shoal under her lee." *Source:* BP, 7/25/1859; Dublin Mercantile Advertiser, 7/29/1859.

5) Pages 142–223. *Elizabeth Ellen* or *Elizabeth Allen*—Capt. Staigg, had 1,507 bales of cotton, 65 hhds. tobacco, 34 bales tobacco, and six cases merchandise. Left New Orleans on November 18, and on December 3 went aground between Hillsboro and Jupiter Inlets. "A heavy sea running, the anchor which had been let go came home, and the ship was thrown with great violence on her beam ends and into eight feet of water." She bilged the second day, went aground and filled with water. Wreckers arrived on the 7th and it was hoped that two-thirds of the cargo might be saved. *Source:* NODC, 1/19/1859.

6) Page 143. *Eliza Mallory*—Wrecked about 18 miles south of Jupiter Inlet and bilged. *Source:* BP, 11/18/1859.

7) Page 143. *North*—Wrecked about 15 miles south of Jupiter Inlet and bilged. The deck load washed ashore and the starboard side was stove in. *Source:* Ibid; Galveston Weekly News, 11/29/1859.

8) Page 143. *Mary Coe*—Built 1856 at Groton, Connecticut, of Mystic, 123' x 30'6" x 15'3". Went ashore five miles south of Jupiter Inlet and bilged. Another source says one mile north of Jupiter Inlet. *Source:* 42; London Standard, 12/2/1859; BP, 11/18–23/1859.

9) Page 143. *Charles Crooker* (correct)—Built 1849 at Bath, Maine, Capt. Murray. Most of the cotton will be saved, 1,500 bales dry, rest damaged, and tobacco would be lost. Ship had bilged and most of the materials were saved. *Source:* NODC, 1/19/1859. *Note:* At least one paper, *The Daily Exchange* of Baltimore, reported that 31 barrels of silver were also aboard. This was not reported in most papers, and if true, most likely salvaged.

10) Page 223. *Silas Holmes*—Of the Holmes Line, 645 tons, built 1845 at NYC, 146' x 31' x 19', three decks, three masts, male figurehead., from New York bound for New Orleans. She had grounded on East Key, Tortugas, December, 3, and was gotten off by the wreckers on the 5th and taken into Garden Key Harbor. Capt. Griffith gave them a check for $4,500 for their services. She went to leave on the 9th and again went ashore at the mouth of the harbor where she was thumping badly. A dispatch from the *New Orleans Picayune*, December 27, 1859, told of the bark *Doretto* having arrived there after picking up five women and four men in a boat from the *Silas Holmes* which sank at sea. The second mate said they had got off on the 11th but in a leaky condition.

> By 2 o'clock the morning of the 16th, the water was up to her decks, when there being no longer any hopes of saving her, Capt. Griffith put all the women, five in number, on board the best small boat he had, with three of the gentlemen passengers, and the second mate. The ship was then in a sinking condition. There were however two boats left, and the mate supposes the captain, crew, and the balance of the passengers, upwards of 30 souls in all, took to them and a large raft they had nearly constructed when the ship went down. Nothing, however, has been heard of them since, nor is their fate known.

The other 33 souls were lost as was the ship somewhere off Florida's west coast in the Gulf. Later reports of the incident wanted to know why the captain continued on the voyage in the condition the ship was in. The two groundings had obviously damaged the hull. *Source:* 11; 26; NODC, 12/14/1859; 1/19/1860.

11) Page 282. *Enterprise*—The wrecking sloop *Beckwith*, Capt. Franklin, salvaged 20 water casks and 800 feet of lumber from the wreck. Reported her laying broadside upon the beach and bilged. The native people had cut the sails out of the bolt ropes and zinc off the bottom. Two sailors, a Spaniard and a Frenchman, were convicted of piracy and murder in Key West. Two others escaped to Tampa, and another died at Key West. The two at Key West

were sentenced to be hanged on January 9, 1860, but the sentence for one of the two was commuted by the president to seven years in prison. *Source:* DMN, 9/1/1859; The Evening Star, 12/21/1859; BP, 12/3/1859.

1860

1) *CAIRN*—Schooner, 280 tons, from Minatitlan for London, with mahogany, sprung a leak and foundered off Cape Canaveral, March 15, 1860. Crew took to the boats and landed at St. Augustine. *Source:* DMN, 3/26/1860. (6)

2) *REPUBLICAN*—Schooner, of Huron, Capt. Stephen Coville, with assorted cargo, wrecked on Elbow Reef, April 18, 1860, all hands saved. Vessel and cargo a total loss. Papers say Elbow Reef near Abaco, and also off the Florida coast. Elbow Key is off Abaco (Elbow Reef-Florida Keys), so it's one or the other. Possible Florida wreck. *Source:* Sandusky Daily Commercial Register, 5/16/1860. (8)

1) Page 79. *Tiger*—Built 1853 at Camden, Maine, of New York, 169 tons. *Source:* 42.

2) Page 79. *Wm Jarvis*—Capt. Ballard, built 1848 at Castine, Maine, 675 tons, from Boston for New Orleans, with ice in lower hold, and assorted cargo between decks, wrecked, September 12, 1860, to the westward of Marquesas Keys, in a dangerous location where she soon bilged. A total loss. *Source:* 37; NY World, 9/24/1860.

3) Page 79. *Fernandina*—Bark, of Boston, built 1850 in Eastport, Maine, Capt. Tripp, from Mobile for Gibraltar, with rosin and tobacco, went ashore on Elbow Reef, September 8, 1860, and sunk soon after. Ship and cargo total, sails, rigging and anchors saved. *Source:* Civilian and Gazette Weekly, 10/2/1860; New York World, 9/24/1860. (4)

4) Page 79. *Cordelia* (correct) not *Cordelis*—Built 1856 at Warren, Maine, 372 tons, from Cienfuegos for London, Capt. Cook, wrecked October 28, 1860, on Loo Key and bilged. Believed most of the cargo and some rigging will be saved. *Source:* LR, 1859; Evening Star, 11/13/1860; NODC, 11/19/1860.

5) Page 120. *J.W. Rowland*—Was got off the reef and put into Key West in a leaky condition. *Source:* Evening Herald, 1/31/1860.

6) Page 120. *Horace*—Capt. Rodgers. One source says ashore on French Reef (believe correct), another on Carysfort Reef and bilged, night of November 30, 1860. Vessel lost, most cargo saved. *Source:* BP, 12/24/1860; The Daily Exchange, 12/14/1860.

1861

1) *MARY KINGSLAND*—Yacht, Capt. Scott, wrecked about 15 miles south of the Jupiter Lighthouse early in the morning during a gale, March 5, 1861, and went high and dry on the beach. It had the J. R. Scott Theatrical Troupe on board, which had been entertaining along the coast since leaving New York last October, the last performance being in St. Augustine where they left on March 1. All on board were rescued after several day's exposure by the *Cahawba*, whose boat made it through the surf and took off the passengers and crew after two trips. They had subsisted on palmetto tops and wild cabbage. The captain reported that he and his brother walked about 16 miles to the lighthouse, but were refused any provisions or help, but a wrecker in the area accompanied them back to the wreck. Vessel a total loss. *Source:* NYT, 3/22/1861; Cincinnati Daily Press, 3/28/1861. (5)

2) *PHOENIX*—British bark, with mahogany and logwood, was reported from Key West, March 16, 1861, as wrecked on Alligator Reef and full of water, the wreckers were in the process of stripping her. *Source:* Glasgow Sentinel, 4/13/1861. (4)

3) *POCAHONTAS*—Ship, from New Orleans for Liverpool, was ashore on a shoal, 40 miles from Key West, and bilged. Cargo was being saved. *Source:* Nashville Union and American, 3/21/1861.

Civil War: April 12, 1861, to April 19, 1865

1) August 15–16, 1861, Hurricane:

a) *J. APPLETON*—Union schooner, 1,200 tons. Was driven ashore in a gale, Aug. 15, 1861, at Egmont Key near the lighthouse. Was later stripped and burned. *Source:* 41

b) *EMERALD ISLE*—Bark, Capt. Egan, from Key West for London, encountered the hurricane off Indian Key, August 16, 1861, and drove ashore on Matecumbe Key (another report says Crocus Reef) and bilged. Materials to be saved. *Source:* London Magnet, 9/23/1861; NYH, 9/3/1861. (4)

c) *ELIZA ANN*—Capt. Geyer, of Waldoboro, from Ft. Jefferson for New York, in ballast, was driven ashore the night of August 16, seven miles west of Bahia Honda, in one and a half feet of water. Could not be gotten off. Materials saved and will be sold at Key West. *Source:* NYH, 9/3/1861. (3)

d) *GEORGE LESLIE*—Capt. Harlew, from Cienfuegos for New York, in ballast, wrecked on the upper end of Alligator Reef, the morning of the 16th, and immediately bilged and went to pieces. All on board saved. The materials were saved and sold at Key West for $619. Believe the 289-ton bark *George Leslie*, of and built at Thomaston, Maine, 98' x 28' x 13'. *Source:* 37; NYH, 9/3/1861. (3)

e) *ORNATE*—British brig, of Halifax, Capt. McCullough, from Cienfuegos for Boston, with molasses, wrecked on Crocus Reef, September 16, 1861. A total loss. A passenger (Wm Mann of Kingston), two seamen (John Wilson and Charles Brown), and two children were also lost, the rest made Matecumbe on a raft. The lone inhabitant of the island, Mr. Russell, took them in. *Source:* Morning Chronicle, 9/17/1861; NYH, 9/3/1861. (3)

f) *PRIMA DONNA*—British bark, Capt. David Orr, of Londonderry, from Havana bound for New York, in ballast, went ashore on the beach about 20 miles north of Cape Florida and bilged, August 15, 1861. Crew escaped in their boats and fell in with a boat from the wrecked British bark, *Sir Walter Raleigh*, who took in the four survivors, and made Key West. *Source:* London Magnet, 9/23/1861; Morning Chronicle, 9/17/1861; London Evening Standard, 8/17/1861; NYH, 9/3/1861. (5)

g) *ARGENTINA* (*Lloyd's Register*) other reports say *Argentine*—British bark, 245 tons, built 1834 at and from Liverpool, sheathed with felt and yellow (composite) metal, Capt. Bader or Bubaer (Lloyd's), from Cardenas bound for Greenock, Scotland, with sugar, wrecked on a reef near Carysfort Light, and broke up Thursday evening (August 15). An hour after at eight, the first mate Thomas Jones was washed overboard and drowned. Early next morning, seamen William Hubbard and William Kearney were washed overboard and drowned. Soon after, another named Alexander Guild met the same fate. Captain Henry Bader was climbing to the topmast at the same time and was swept away by a huge wave and lost. The keeper of the light, John Jones, could see the tragedy unfolding but was powerless to do anything due to the rough seas. At noon, the poop of the vessel broke off and drifted towards the reef by the lighthouse with seven officers and seamen on board. The keeper Jones and his assistant, at great peril to themselves, launched their lifeboat and rescued the seven men. *Source:* London Magnet, 9/23/1861; Morning Chronicle, 9/17/1861; LR, 1861/2; NYH, 9/3/1861.

1) Page 241. *Malvina* (correct)—French ship, Capt. Cezard, 291 tons, built 1850 at Nantes, of Roscoff, from Manzanillo for Bordeaux, with logwood, honey, sugar, molasses, palmetto leaf, etc., went ashore the night of the 15th, near Knight's Key, and bilged. Cargo, though damaged, was being saved. *Source:* 37; NYH, 9/3/1861. (3)

2) Page 241. *Sir Walter Raleigh* (other papers mistakenly called her the *Sir Walter Allie*, or just the *Allie*)—British bark, 477 tons, built 1852 at Sunderland, sheathed with yellow (composite) metal, of Liverpool, was lost in the hurricane near Cosco Creek (likely Caesar's Creek), and was a total loss.

From Kingston, with rum and sugar. She struck a reef on September 15 and immediately broke up. The captain and 10 men were lost, four were rescued by a boat from the wrecked bark *Prima Donna*. *Source:* NYH, 9/3/1861; Morning Chronicle, 9/17/1861; Londonderry Standard, 9/26/1861; LR, 1861/2. (4)

End of August 1861 hurricane losses.

2) **Lost HOWITZER**—Though not a shipwreck, this should help locate a lost Civil War howitzer. The Union vessels *Penguin* and *Henry Andrew* were at Mosquito Inlet March 1862 to capture any Confederate vessels and establish a blockade there. An expedition of four or five light boats proceeded into Mosquito Lagoon southward past Smyrna about 15 to 18 miles and then headed back. The front two boats were a bit ahead when within sight of the *Henry Andrew*, they went to investigate some earthworks which looked abandoned. When they landed underneath, they came under fire killing five of them including the boat commander, the remaining two, wounded, were taken prisoner. As the other boats approached, they also came under fire. The rear boat had a howitzer, which could not be made to work and the men had to make cover on shore. That night, the acting master's mate, returned to the boats, took one body, all the arms and ammo, and threw the howitzer into the river, and arrived safely on the *Henry Andrew*. The howitzer should still be there in the river. Since it was picked up by one man, I'll assume it was a 12-pound "Mountain Howitzer," which are bronze, 33 inches long and weigh 220 pounds. *Source:* Report of the Secretary of the Navy, 12/1/1862. (6)

3) *STAG*—Schooner. The Union steamer *Hatteras* had gone to Cedar Keys, January 1862, to destroy any Confederate outposts. They captured or destroyed four schooners, three sloops, one ferry-scow (captured), a sailboat, and a launch. The schooner *Stag* was run on shore and fired. One schooner with turpentine did escape. *Source:* Report of the Secretary of the Navy, 12/1/1862. (2)

4) *VANDERBILT*—Confederate steamer, Capt. Smith, from Havana bound for New Orleans, which ran the blockade, foundered, 3/16/1862. Captain, six crewmen, and eight passengers, including two women, landed safely on the coast of Florida four days later on the 20th. Another boat with 17 others had not been heard from. Possible Florida wreck. *Source:* NYT, 4/19–20/1862.

5) *NEW ISLAN*, *FLOYD*, and *ROSE*—Three schooners. These were captured along with some other vessels by the Union steamer *Mercedita*, early April 1862, at Apalachicola a few miles upriver. Tried to get them over the bar but the three grounded in seven feet of water. Unable to get the three off, they

were set on fire, but not until the cargo of cotton was salvaged from the *Rose*. *Source:* Report of the Secretary of the Navy, 12/1/1862. (1)

6) *BRUNETTE*—British schooner, listed as wrecked at Indian Key, but was got off and taken to Key West where it was condemned. *Source:* NYT, 7/9/1862. (3)

7) *FIREFLY*—From Aspinwall for New York, wrecked on the Florida coast. All the crew except the captain were saved. *Source:* Liverpool Daily Post, 7/28/1862. (8)

8) *ANGELINA*—Spanish topsail schooner, from New York for Matamoros, with assorted cargo, wrecked on a reef and bilged near Carysford Lighthouse. Most cargo saved, though damaged. *Source:* NYT, 4/12/1863. (4)

9) *ALICIA* **Unk. SCHOONERS**—Were lost along with their cargoes near Jupiter Inlet, late 1862. Both were from Nassau trying to run the blockade. Also mentioned two sloops, the *Julia*, and the *Avenger*, from Nassau that were captured by the U.S. gunboat *Sagamore* at Jupiter Inlet. It was the captain of the *Julia*, who was from Florida and a secessionist, who was supposedly responsible for destroying the lens and light at the Cape Florida, Jupiter Inlet, and Cape Canaveral Lighthouses, and would be tried. *Source:* NYH, 1/19/1863, 41 (5) (5)

10) *A.B. NOYES*—Union barge. Was burned by the Confederates on October 16, 1863, in Tampa Bay, near Ft. Brooke. *Source:* 41

11) *GENERAL BURNSIDE*—U.S. transport steamer. Reported in late February 1864 newspapers as grounded on the St. Johns Bar, a total loss. Crew saved. *Source:* Philadelphia Age, 2/27/1864. *Note:* This is not the Union gunboat *General Burnside*.

12) *JOSEPHINE*—The *Boston Post* of April 26, 1864 states: "The small sloop *Josephine*, from Tampa for Havana, was burned by the U.S. schooner *Stonewall*, on the Florida coast." (8)

13) *ALICE*—Steamer, Capt. Hezekiah Wingate, with 1,300 barrels on board (at least 300 filled with whiskey), left Apalachicola November 1864 for Columbus, Georgia, hit a snag and sunk 15 miles south of Bristol, Florida, and sunk "like a stone," in the center of the channel, with the loss of the captain and three deckhands. She was almost raised soon after, but a chain broke and she sunk again. A treasure hunter from Chicago named Frank P. Blair, reported to have found her using a magnetometer in 1938. He valued the whiskey at $300,000. Mr. Blair said the magnetometer outlined an area about 156' x 30', which were the dimensions of the *Alice*. *Source:* Humboldt Republican, 3/18/1938. I could find nothing else on a steamer called the *Alice* fitting this description, so can't verify if true or not.

14) *ATLANTA*—Brig, Capt. Johnathan Dow, built 1864 at Searsport, Maine, 362 tons, 110.2' x 30.2' x 12.3', one deck, two masts, square stern, of and from Philadelphia for New Orleans, had on board the crew from the ship *Conqueror*, which wrecked about eight miles from Great Isaac. She made Ft. Jefferson, Tortugas, on April 4, 1865, at 2 p.m., and wrecked on Flapjack Shoal at 2:45 p.m. and bilged. All on board were saved and taken to Key West. Most sails and rigging were saved. *Source:* 27; NYH, 4/27/65; BP, 6/6/1865. (3)

15) *NORRIS*—Steamer, went ashore on the St. Augustine Bar, and soon filled with five feet of water in her hold. Cargo was saved, though damaged. *Source:* Savannah Daily Herald, 4/9/1865.

1) Page 236. **Finland**—Was found discharging salt in Apalachicola Bay, and was boarded just before midnight by *US RR Cuyler* and *US Montgomery*. *Source:* NYT, 4/19/1861.

2) Page 237. **USS Amanda**—Naval records say she went ashore on Dog Island and destroyed by her crew. *Source:* 14.

3) Page 240. **USS Annie** (correct)—Was called the *Anna* when captured, but changed to the *Annie. Source:* 14.

4) Page 241. **Franklin**—Capt. Chisholm, 176 tons, of and built at Maitland, Nove Scotia in 1855, 83' x 22' x 10'. Had cargo of 159 hhds and 160 boxes sugar. This report says lost the night May 21. Most cargo saved and brought to Key West. *Source:* 37; BP, 6/7/1861.

5) **Director**—Page 242. British bark, Capt. Wm. McNeil, 387 tons, built 1846 at Swansea, of London, sheathed with felt and yellow (composite) metal, with sugar and rum, wrecked about four miles above Carysfort Reef Lighthouse, and bilged in eight feet of water. Some rum and rigging saved. All crew and passengers saved. Capt. McNeal said he mistook the light for the Gun Key Lighthouse. *Source:* NYT, 4/12–19/1862.

6) Page 242. **Menemon Sanford**—Had 800 troops for the Bank's expedition on board. All were saved and taken to Key West. Was sold as she lay on the reef for $620 and much salvaged. *Source:* Dawson's Daily Times and Union, 12/20/1862; BP, 1/5/1863.

7) Page 242. **Sparkling Sea**—Capt. Walsh, 893 tons, built 1854 at Bristol, of Boston, 168' x 34', from New York for New Orleans, with the 25th New York Battery, 500 horses, and stores and materials for Bank's expedition. Wrecked on the north point of Ajax Reef near the lighthouse. Some of the crew were accused of mutiny after being wrecked, and many were arrested and jailed, but later pardoned by the president. The accused said the captain was incompetent. Only 12 horses saved, and all the stores were lost. *Source:* 37; NYT, 6/4/1863; Alexandria Gazette, 2/5/63; Green-Mountain Freeman,

1/27/1863. *Note:* Another transport, the *Lucinda*, was also wrecked nearby at the same time, but she was saved.

8) Page 242. *Adelayda*—Spanish schooner, Capt. Echevarria, some cargo saved. *Source:* LL, 4/23/1863.

9) Page 242. *Joseph Meigs*—Built 1842 at Mattapoisett, of New York, 354 tons, 103' x 27'. Wrecked near "Beacon letter P". *Source:* 37; NYT, 8/21/1863.

10) Page 242. *Margaret Kerr*—British ship. Other sources say ashore on Crow's Reef. *Source:* NYH, 3/15/1865.

11) Page 244. **Confederate Schooner**—Likely the 70-ton *Emma*, captured by a Union boat and then grounded near the mouth of the Ochlockonee River, May 24, 1863. She was burned about 250 yards off shore. A Union boat was also lost. Source: 41.

12) Page 245. *Scottish Chief*—Built 1855 at Wilmington, North Carolina, 110 tons. Burned on the north bank of the river by what is now Lowry Park. *Source:* 21; 29.

13) Page 245. *Nan Nan*—Was named the *Little Lily* when wrecked. Built in 1860 at Brooklyn, New York, 147 tons, 156'4" x 27'2" x 8'4". Source: 14; 41.

14) Page 247. *George C. Collins*—U.S. transport steamer, 236 tons, built of oak in Baltimore in 1862, of Hartford, 150' x 28' x 6', from Savannah for Jacksonville and St. Augustine, with commissary stores, went ashore on the St. Augustine Bar, and threw most of the cargo overboard, though some was later saved. As she filled with water, she was abandoned, and a sand-bar formed around her almost immediately. All passengers and crew were saved. Vessel was a total loss. *Source:* 37; Savannah Daily Herald, 4/2/1865.

15) Page 247. *Glen* and the *Santa Clara*—The Savannah Republican reported that both these vessels had been captured and taken to Carolina, not burned.

16) Page 248. *Anglo Saxon*—Was lost off England, not off Florida. *Source:* LL, 1864.

End of Civil War period wrecks.

1865

Oct 23, 1865 HURRICANE—Florida's coasts. Many vessels also wrecked in the Bahamas and up the East Coast including the *SS Republic* which sank off Georgia with $400,000 in specie. I've probably missed some that were lost, and some listed may have been saved, but tried not to list any that were salvaged.

a) *HARRIET B. TYLER*—Schooner, of Philadelphia, 331 tons, built 1863 at Philadelphia, Capt. James McGee, from Galveston for New York, with 780 bales cotton, 67 bales wool, 3,000 hides, and 16 bales of calf skins. Wrecked about eight miles from Cape Canaveral on a barrier island, October 23, 1865. All crew saved except the captain who drowned "while going ashore in a small boat." *Source:* BP, 11/29/1865, 12/25/1865; NYH, 11/29/1865; SNR, 12/1/1865. (6)

b) *JOEL G. SWEET*—Schooner, Capt. Charles F. Marks, of and from Charleston for Apalachicola, with a cargo of lumber, wrecked about the same place as the *Harriet B. Tyler*. Imagine being wrecked and cast ashore during a hurricane with no food or water, badly injured, and having to survive. That was the fate of Capt. Marks and crew in October 1865. The schooner encountered a storm on October 21, which became a full hurricane, and by the 23rd, they sighted land off Jupiter, and had lost all sails. By the next morning, they had been driven north of Cape Canaveral, where she went ashore. Capt. Whitty, who was the navigator on the vessel, later told the story, and many newspapers reported it, a portion related here:

All through the night the gale continued to increase in force, with the sea running mountains high, and the weather being thick and rainy. Early the next afternoon observed the breakers to leeward, tried to keep off, but could not. At this time, they were a few miles to the north of Cape Canaveral. A heavy sea came rolling over them, and swept Captain Marks and Captain Whitty overboard, and at the same time the mainmast was carried away. Captain Marks clung to the mast and was hauled on board; but the sail that was attached to the mast, when it was carried away, fell over Captain Whitty and kept him beneath the waves. He instinctively felt for his knife to cut a place in the sail, so that he might come to the surface and breathe; but the knife was lost, and all the horrors of a death by drowning were suffered by him during the time that he remained under the water. After he had swallowed a great deal of salt water, and just as he was upon the point of giving up all hope of extricating himself from his perilous position, the mast and sail were lifted from over him by a monstrous wave and he arose to the surface, and was hauled on board the vessel, more dead than alive, by those who had given him up as lost. Captain Whitty had his breast badly bruised and his right hand fearfully cut by the mast. Captain Marks had one of his ribs broken and sustained other injuries.

One man made shore with a rope, and the rest then made it to safety where they found themselves on a long stretch of barrier island separated from the mainland. They were so exhausted, they all fell asleep under a small palm tree, but awoke when the storm surge crept up to where they lay. The schooner had disappeared by the next morning, but they found her where she drifted about two miles down the beach. The wind was still blowing hard and they were unable to get to her. Some dug in the sand for fresh water, and a barrel of biscuit washed ashore on the second day. Lots of other wreckage was found along the beach from other vessels, including the remains of a man and woman, their arms tightly clutched around each other. Eventually they got enough lumber together and built a raft, filled a small jug they found with fresh water, and left. They almost reached the mainland when they were picked up by a small schooner and taken to Smyrna. There they met up with the crew of the wrecked *Harriet B. Tyler*, and unable to get to St. Augustine due too rough seas, made it overland to Enterprise on Lake Monroe and eventually to Jacksonville on the steamer *Cosmopolitan*. *Source:* NYH, 11/29/1865; Savannah National Republican, 12/6/1865; BP, 11/28/1865; Daily Union and American, 12/9/1865; Philadelphia Age, 12/2/1865. (6)

c) **REDWING**—Schooner, of Boston, Capt. Randall, from Boston for Jacksonville, wrecked on the same barrier island as the *Harriet B. Tyler*, October 28, 1865, and the crew lived under a boat for 11 days, living on land crabs, until discovered by the one man living on the island who cared for them the next two months when they eventually made St. Augustine. An **Unk. bark** also wrecked on the same island, October 26, and went to pieces. Believe the *Redwing*, built 1838 at Bucksport, Maine, 112 tons. *Source:* 37; BP, 12/25/1865.

d) **MERSEY**—British ship, of Liverpool, 546 tons, built 1848 at Kennebunk, 142' x 28', Capt. Bales (captain and three men had drowned at Santa Anna trying to take the boat through the breakers to the shore, his brother Wm. Bales took over as captain), from Santa Anna, Mexico, for England with mahogany. Weather started getting rough on October 21, and by 23rd, they had to cut away the masts leaving only the foremast. The lee rigging was tangled up with the cut away masts, causing them to smash against the ship's hull which soon caused her to take on water and by 9 p.m. she was on her beam ends. All hands went aft, and at seven the next morning, she rolled over and took some crew with her and others drowned.

One survivor, Robert Smith, related the story at Key West, which the *New York Herald* published, and a portion of his tale of the sinking was such:

> She labored heavily, losing some of her lighter spars, until the morning of the 23rd, when it was resolved to cut away the masts. The weather main shrouds were accordingly cut, and the mainmast went over to leeward; the mizzenmast, foretopmast and the jibboom went by the board at the same time, leaving only the foremast standing. The lee rigging, however, still held the wreck of the masts near the ship, and, in consequence of these breaking in her sides, became waterlogged, and at nine P.M. she lay on her beam ends. All hands got aft, and remained there till seven A.M. of the 24th, when the vessel rolled over and went down, carrying all on board with her.
>
> She had on board at the time thirteen men, all told. Robert Smith states that he went down for some distance with the wreck, and on coming to the surface

he saw several of the ship's company floating about on logs and parts of the ship. Of these the first mate,—Oswell, who was on a log, appeared to be very weak, and was soon washed off and drowned.

The carpenter, steward, one boy and two men were in site for some time, but finally sank.

Seeing more men on a piece of wreck at some distance Smith swam towards it, and found that it was the stern of the ship, to which were clinging the captain (Wm. Bayles), the second mate (Charles Connor) and three men named Charles Clayton, William Dorian and Juste Dubois, a Frenchman.

Just about the time that Smith reached the raft the second mate, who had apparently been much bruised, lost his hold, was washed off and not seen again. The captain, too, was very weak, his right hand being almost severed from the wrist, and his left arm seriously hurt by being jammed between the timbers.

When Smith got on the raft there were five men depending on it for life, without a particle of food or water and very little clothing. They all clung to it, however, till about half-past seven P.M. of the same day, when the captain died, and was washed off the wreck by the next wave."

They were finally rescued on the 26th by the steamer *Newbern*, at Lat. 29-07'N, 80°27'W, off Cape Canaveral, bearing SW about 40 miles.

The men were in a dreadful condition, having been in the water so long a time (four days). Their clothes were all washed off them, their legs very much swelled from the action of the salt water, and they had attempted to quench their thirst by sucking the blood of one of their number, a large wound in whose arm was a testimony to the fact. *Source:* 37; NYH, 11/9/1865. (8)

e) *JOSEPH HOLMES*—Ship, Capt. Crocker, from Key West for Liverpool, with cotton, foundered off Key West in the October hurricane, with all hands. *Source:* BP, 11/14/1865. (3)

f) **Unk. WRECK**—Was seen underwater eight miles NE of Sombrero Light after the storm. *Source:* NYH, 11/6/1865. (3)

g) *HANOVER*—British schooner, Capt. Kingsley, from Boston, was lost on Pelican (one says Sambo) Shoals, November 1, 1865, with mahogany, in six feet of water. *Source:* NYH, 11/6/1865; BP, 11/11–17/1865. (3)

h) *QUEEN MAB*—British bark, 394 tons, of Liverpool, built 1853 at Sunderland, 132' x 27.5' x 18', sheathed with felt and yellow (composite) metal, Captain James Walker, from Portland, Maine bound for Matanzas, with lumber, was sunk in three fathoms of water near Matecumbe. Most materials were saved, along with the crew. *Source:* NYH, 11/6/1865; 12/29/1865; BP, 11/17/1865; LR, 1865. (3)

i) *ANGEL*—Spanish brig, from Havana for Newfoundland, was lost near Carysfort Light. *Source:* NYH, 11/6/1865. (4)

n) *FRANCISCO*—Italian vessel, was lost off the east coast of Florida. *Source:* NYH, 11/30/1865. (8)

j) *GERRASSIMO*— Greek brig, was lost off the east coast of Florida. *Source:* NYH, 11/30/1865. (8)

p) *J.W. LINDSAY*—Schooner, of Fall River, Capt. Benjamin Clark, from Philadelphia for Mobile, was feared lost in the October Hurricane, as she has not been heard from since. *Source:* BP, 12/2/1865. (8)

q) *BALES*—British ship, from Santa Anna, Mexico, for England, foundered off Florida, October 24, after being disabled during the October 22–23 hurricane. *Source:* The Commercial Daily List, 11/21/1865; LL, 11/20/1865. (8)

r) *ALICE*—Schooner, from Pensacola for Cedar Keys, Capt. Oliver, collided with an unknown three-masted schooner, October 28, 1865, in rough sea about 30 miles SW of Cape San Blas. Tried to get her to the coast but had to abandon her before they were able, and she sank the next day. Crew took to the boat and were picked up by the brig *Olga* after being in the boat for 60 hours. She carried merchandise, a large steam sawmill, and boilers for Cedar Keys, 20 bales cotton, 1,500 bushels peanuts, 30 tons old iron, two tons old copper, and a lot of old sails and rigging. Owned by Capt. Oliver. *Source:* NYH, 11/11/1865. (2)

s) *MINNIE*—Schooner, of Mystic for Key West, was lost in the hurricane, October 23, off Jupiter Inlet. Capt. Appleman and four of her crew were picked up from their boat by the steamer *Fung Shuey. Source:* BP, 11/4/1865. (5)

End of new hurricane losses.

1) Page 27. *Convoy*—Steamer, was one of three wrecks reported in the *Boston Post*, February 28, 1876, as an obstruction at the entrance to Pensacola:

> The wreck of the steamer Convoy, lying to the Northward of the channel, inside the harbor entrance, with the beacon of the Bar Range open a little to the Westward of Pensacola Lighthouse, distant 1/2 mile nearly W, and the flagstaff of Ft. Pickens, bearing SE by E 1/8 E, distant 7/8 mile. The wreck is in 12 feet of water, but the steam drum and connecting-rod show above high water, the former about five feet and having the appearance of a buoy.

1) Pages 79–80. *James W. Lawrence*—Schooner, Capt. Moore, 121 tons, built 1861 at Perth Amboy, of and from New York bound for Galveston, with assorted cargo, including a new power printing press and a large amount of type and paper, went ashore on the East Samboes, eight miles from Key West, October 27 or November 1, 1865. Crew and some cargo saved including the press. *Source:* 37; BP, 11/11/1865, Galveston News Tri Weekly, 11/20/1865; NYH, 12/29/1865.

2) Page 80. *Oswingo*—British ship, Captain Daniel Lard, from Liverpool bound for Havana, with coal, went ashore 3/4 miles from Fort Taylor and bilged, October 22, 1865. Half the cargo and some materials saved. *Source:* Commercial Daily List, 11/30/1865; BP, 11/16/1865; NYH, 12/29/1865.

3) Page 90. *Dwight*—Of and built at Biddeford, Maine, in 1861, 138 tons, 87' x 25'. *Source:* 39.

4) Page 120. *Waltham*—Bark, Capt. Minot, from New Orleans and Belize for Boston, was lost on Matecumbe Bar, near Indian Key, with 1,022 bales cotton, 51 bales wool, 1,500 hides, and other goods. Built in Richmond, Maine, in 1851. Some cargo saved. *Source:* NYH, 11/6/65, BP, 1/25/66; Savannah National Republican, 11/14/1865.

5) Page 120. *Dahlia*—Another report says from Kingston for Liverpool with sugar and rum. Wrecked on a reef off Tavernier Key, May 10, 1865, and most all cargo salvaged and taken to Key West. *Source:* Philadelphia Inquirer, 5/27/1865.

6) Page 120. *Caroline Nesmith*—Capt. Cotter, wrecked 15 miles south of Carysfort Light near or on French Reef. *Source:* BP, 11/11/1865; NYH, 11/6/1865.

7) Pages 143–44. *J.M. Harwood* (or *Howard*)—Capt. Delano, from New Orleans for Havre, with cotton, went ashore six miles south of the *John Wesley*. *Source:* BP, 11/17/1865. (5)

8) Page 144. *John Wesley*—Bark, went ashore on the 23rd, about 30 miles north of Cape Florida. Of Searsport, Maine, Capt. Samuel Patten, from New Orleans for Liverpool, with 1,460 bales cotton and 1,200 staves, struck a reef about two miles offshore and then beached. All hands saved. Built at Searsport in 1852, 571 tons. *Source:* NYH, 11/16/65; Baltimore Daily, 11/17/65; Savannah National Republican, 11/14/1865.

9) Page 223. *Morga* (correct)—Spanish brig, from Bilboa bound for Havana, with sardines and flour, wrecked on Sombrero Key. Only 250 lbs. of flour saved. *Source:* The Commercial Daily List, 11/27/1865; NYH, 12/29/1865; LL, 11/25/1865. (3)

10) Page 223. *Indian River*—Originally the *Neptune*, was captured by the USS *Lakawanna* in 1863 and the name changed to *Clyde*, 294 tons, 200'6" x 18'6" x 8', with two 24-pound howitzers. Sold October 1865. Went ashore and wrecked at the mouth of the Indian River, December 3, 1865, a total loss. Crew saved. *Source:* 14, Naval History and Heritage Command website. (5)

11) Page 242. *Anne Baldwin* (correct)—Bark, built in 1831 at and of Liverpool, 310 tons, 99' x 25'1" x 17'4", sheathed with felt and yellow (composite) metal, Capt. Edward Henry Netherclift, from Pedro Cay for Liverpool, with

guano. Wrecked on Little Conch Reef, April 16, 1885. Some cargo and materials (rigging, anchors) saved and brought to Key West. Had a number of problems on the voyage. Captain was exonerated at the inquiry. *Source:* Globe, 5/26/1865; SMG, 7/12/1865 (had the notes of the inquiry); LR, 1865–86.

12) Page 247. *Harriet DeFord*—Was burned on Indian Creek, Virginia, not Indian River, Florida. *Source:* 21.

1866

Hurricane in October.

1) *JENNIE HIGHT*—Ship, Capt. and owner John Nickerson, built at Machias, Maine, 1,117 tons, from Bangor for New Orleans, was a new ship on her first voyage, wrecked at night during a storm on Carysfort Reef, believe first day or so of January 1866, all hands saved along with most materials and some cargo. *Source:* BP, 1/4-6-15/1866. (4)

2) *NEVA*—Double decked brig (one says one deck), of Machias, Maine (built at E. Machias in 1864), 225 tons, 102'7" x 26'3" x 9'5", two masts, square stern, Capt. E. Jerome Talbot, from New York for Jacksonville. Wrecked, January 8, 1866, on the St. John's Bar, on the S. Breakers. Wreck eventually settled on the beach about 12 miles further south of the bar. The second mate, two crew and the cook had stayed on the wreck, and when rescued, said all the others drowned when the boat capsized, which included the captain, pilot, three crew and a woman and child. A couple of days later the body of the captain, the pilot and the woman were found on the beach 12 miles south. The wounds on the captain and pilot included stab wounds that clearly indicated foul play, and the second mate and others were arrested. *Source:* 7; 27; Savannah Daily Herald, 1/15/1866; BP, 1/16-20-23/1866; Barnette says that some or all of the wreck ended up at Ward's Bank at the mouth of the St. John's, and was later removed by the Army Corps of Engineers in 1890. (6)

3) *CONVOY*—U.S. Steamer, reported as burned and sunk near Pensacola, April 1, 1866, due to the upsetting of a lamp in the engine room. Crew escaped in the boats, nothing saved. *Source:* New Albany Daily Ledger, 4/6/1866. (1)

4) *URANA*—Brig, of Baltimore, 285 tons, built 1860 at Brewer, Maine, 101' x 25' x 9', from Savannah for Cardenas, Capt. J. H. Bruce, with lumber, encountered a hurricane, October 1, 1866, and had to cut away foremast, and her hull was full with water. Crew took to the rigging and by the 3rd had drifted near Memory Rock. On the 4th, a boat was seen drifting, and the captain and one man left the brig on a small raft to attempt to retrieve the boat.

They were last seen near the boat, but unknown what happened to them. They lay at anchor that day but the winds began picking up again, and on October 5 they weighed anchor, "continued to drift at the mercy of the waves for five days without food or water." On the 9th, they buried the first mate, Wm. Waters and a seaman, and around noon, they anchored in five fathoms of water about 25 miles south of Cape Canaveral Light. Each man then made a raft and all made shore safely. The next day they made Mr. Henderson's fish camp, who treated them kindly. After taking passage on a couple different schooners, and hiking 25 miles, the survivors all made it to Jacksonville on the *Darlington*. *Source:* 37; Daily News and Herald, 10/29/1866. (5)

5) *EVENING STAR*—Sidewheel steamer, built 1863 at New York, 2,014 or 1,866 tons, 273' x 39'. From New York bound for New Orleans, with nearly 300 passengers which included 59 members of the French Opera troupe of Paul Anthayra, about 30 members of Dr. Spaulding's Circus Company, almost 100 ladies of the night, which had been recruited by a number of New Orleans madams who were also on board, plus a number of regular passengers. Everything was fine when off Hatteras on October 1, 1866. The wind started picking up the next day, and by the third of October, a hurricane was in full force, with giant waves crashing through the deck, putting the fires out and rendering the engines useless. Numerous newspapers printed the story of this wreck from the few witness accounts, as the loss of life was great (believe 247 lives). Tales of bravery (much was attributed to the ladies of the evening) and panic, and the revelation that the ship was not seaworthy, and that this fact was known before she sailed. There were only four lifeboats on board (other reports say six). The steamer went down quickly, though four boats did get away though all were capsized (some numerous times) and had to be righted. The ones who did get into the boats found that there were no provisions. Many were rescued naked, having lost their clothes due to being capsized in the boats, and some drank their own urine in order to survive. Accounts of the sufferings of these survivors were reported in papers all over the United States and Europe. One boat was picked up by the bark *Fleetwing*, another came ashore at Fernandina with eight on board on the 7th, though two were dead, the others too weak to throw them overboard, another was picked up by the schooner *Morning Star* on the 8th, and of the nine originally on board, only five had survived, and the last one which originally had the second mate and 13 women, came ashore off Mayport Mills, Florida. Eleven of the women had already died and the two women who were left, died while trying to get ashore, one of them being devoured by a shark. Of the 132 women on board, only two survived, both were ladies of the evening. There were only 24 survivors out of the 278 on board. Though some reports say she sunk 100 miles off Tybee, others say off the Florida coast. I think it is more probable that she sank off

the Florida coast due to where the surviving lifeboats washed up. *Source:* 2; 21; 37; London Standard, 10/30/1866; Bellows Falls Times, 10/12/1866; Liverpool Weekly, 11/3/1866. (8)

Here's an excerpt from the survivor's accounts printed in the *Liverpool Mail*, November 13, 1866, after the captain informed all on board that the ship was sinking:

> A rush was made for the second, now the upper, deck, and the six lifeboats were speedily filled by the passengers. At 15 minutes past six, or thereabouts, the ship gave a lurch to the right, which was shortly afterwards followed by an equally violent lurch to the left, the vessel sinking almost immediately thereafter. From four o'clock the wreck had been swept by tremendous seas, and many persons had been carried away. It was found utterly impossible to lower the boats, and extremely difficult to keep them upright, even on the ways, and with the assistance of the various appliances used for the purpose. These boats were all crowded when the ship went down, and all were capsized as she foundered, the passengers being thrown into the water and among the floating pieces of the wreck. Many were killed outright by the collision with the heavy timbers; others were drowned at once; others clung to floating planks, furniture, etc., for a time, and then-chilled and hopeless-dropped off to die. Four boats, after various capsizes, succeeded in getting away from the wreck-the last not until nearly ten hours after the disaster.

As to the heroism of most of the ladies of the night,

> they displayed a heroism and unselfishness worthy of the highest praise—they worked at the pumps and at bailing the boat with a vigor that shamed the stalwart men. They cheered up the despairing, they gave new encouragement to the hopeful.

6) *AMBROSINE*—British bark, Capt. William Olsen (formerly the *Chattanooga*, of New York, possibly was the 208-ton brig *Chattanooga*), of Plymouth, England, left Vera Cruz and then picked up a cargo of pitch pine at Pensacola. She left there on September 29, 1886, for Queenstown. On the 30th, she encountered the beginnings of a gale about 15 miles WSW of Jupiter Inlet, and by noon the next day, it was blowing a full hurricane, and she began to take on water, the pumps being tried every two hours now. On the morning of the 2nd, the deck load was washed away and the forward part of the cabin was stowed in. By noon, the sea waves carried away the water casks, spare spars and part of the forward house into the sea. That afternoon the carpenter was washed overboard and drowned. One pump stopped working and the crew kept the other manned. By 8 p.m.,

> the hurricane suddenly increased in violence, and the vessel fell over on her beam ends. About half-past eight a very large sea struck her and carried away

the mainmast about eight feet from the deck and the main topmast above the cap. She then righted, but was now perfectly unmanageable; and about nine o'clock another tremendous sea struck her, causing her to fall apart, and she began to go to pieces rapidly. The crew were now dispersed among the floating wreck and cargo, clinging to various pieces of timber. At the end of about a half an hour the captain, second mate, steward, and one seaman got together on a small fragment of the deck about six feet square. By this time the rest of the crew had disappeared beneath the waves (many of them having doubtless been crushed among the floating timber), except one man who was picked off the wreck of the foremast about eleven o'clock and taken on board the raft.

They remained on the raft with no food or water for 36 hours before being picked up by the steamer *Newbern*, at Lat. 28°N, Long. 78°20' W. Coincidentally, this was around the same area that the *Newbern* rescued the crew of the *Mersey* the previous year. They were exhausted, being without clothes or water, but luckier than the 10 others who drowned. Capt. Olsen said he saw the wreckage of another vessel in the same area. *Source:* NYH, 12/12/1866; Daily Union and American, 10/14/1866; 10/16/1866; Dublin Evening Mail, 10/30/1866; BWM, 11/5/1866; Liverpool Mercury, 10/29/1866. (8)

1) Page 80. *Angela*—Mexican brig, Capt. Daney, from Carmen for Havre. Also reported as wrecked on Pickle Reef. *Source:* LL, 2/6/1866.

2) Page 120. *Isabel*—From Savannah for La-Mar and London. Capt. Landor and crew saved. Some cargo saved. *Source:* Kingston Gleaner, 4/25/1866.

3) Page 120. *Tonawanda*—Most reports said on Grecian Shoals, bilged, and broke in two. Passengers and crew saved along with some cargo. Capt. Berry. See GPS coordinates at end of chapter. The American *Lloyd's Register* says 844 tons, built 1864 at Philadelphia, 176' x 29' x 18'. *Source:* Baltimore Daily Commercial, 4/10/1866; Weekly Georgia Telegraph, 4/16/1866.

4) Page 144. *Sebastopol*—Built 1855 at Bath, Maine, of New York, 566 tons, 138' x 28' x 19'. *Source:* 37.

5) Page 174. *Luella*—Schooner, Captain James Burgess, 104 tons, built 1845 at Waldoboro, of Belfast, Maine, went ashore on the south side of Mosquito Inlet, April 1866. A steamer in May 1866 reported her high and dry with only about six inches of water around her at spring tide. "The vessel is all complete and everything standing the same as when she went ashore." *Source:* 37; Daily News and Herald, 5/23/1866.

1867

1) *ORACLE*—British schooner, (believe 192 tons, 91' x 20'9" x 11'5", built 1865 at Jersey), from Chiltepec, Mexico, for Liverpool, with mahogany, was lost on French Reef, July 5, 1867, crew saved. Most if not all cargo and materials saved which amounted to $3,004.44. Wreckers awarded 55 percent. Cargo sold for $2,123 at Key West. *Source:* Belfast Weekly News, 8/3/1867; BP, 8/21/1867; LR, 1867–68; SMG, 9/3–28/1867. (4)

1) Page 121. *Scandinavien* (correct)—Norwegian bark (originally a brig-changed to bark 1863 or 4), 412 tons, built 1815–1816 at Gavle, Sweden. Cargo consisted of pitch pine. Some materials were saved. Sold for $1,400 (as she lay), wreckers awarded 45 percent. *Source:* 33; Liverpool Daily Post, 4/22/1867; NYH, 4/2/1867.

2) Page 121. *Let Her Be* (correct)—British brig, Capt. Graham, cargo of shooks, struck on Pacific Reef, October 25, 1867, and a total loss. *Source:* NYT, 10/31/1867.

1868

1) *MUSIC*—Steamer, of the Central Railroad Co., sailed the Chattahoochee and Apalachicola Rivers, sank at Moccasin Slough, 40 miles above Apalachicola, early November 1868. Had a cargo of bacon, flour and sundries. *Source:* SMN, 11/9/1868. (7)

1) Page 27. **William Miles**—Ship, built 1853 at Quebec, 1,227 tons, 199'3" x 35'6" x 21'8", Capt. Pollack, from Pensacola for Queenstown, wrecked in 1868, prior to June at Pensacola (one source says on the Middle Ground in sand), was iron fastened and sheathed with felt and yellow (composite) metal. Cargo was sold. Wreck was also said to be sold, though at a 1870 inquiry, it was said the ship was lost (may have sold the hull and salvaged all materials off her, though may also have been re-floated, though no longer registered in Lloyds after 1868). *Source:* LR, 1867–68; NYH, 6/6/1868; SMG, 8/17/1870.

1869

1) *CRICKET*—Screw steamer, built 1867 at Newburgh, New York, Capt. A. E. Lozier (also the owner), from Key West for New York, in ballast, though had some stores. Was running low on fuel and the seas were getting rough, so she made for the St. Augustine Inlet on June 14th. Blew her whistle for the pilot boat but it did not come. With night coming and seas getting

rougher, she ran between the outer buoy and inner buoy number two and ran aground on a bar and broker her back. Three crew took the boat and made shore and the pilot boat finally arrived and got everyone else off. A total wreck. Captain reported the channel had changed almost a half mile southward, and that the buoys needed to be moved. *Source:* SMN, 6/21/1869. (6)

2) *FRANCES ELLEN*—Fishing smack, went ashore off Ft. Pickens, early May 1869, and later drifted into deep water and sunk. Shifting sandbars were to blame. *Source:* Galveston Evening News, 5/15/1869. (1)

3) *LUCY W. ALEXANDER*—Schooner, 111 tons, built 1854 at Rockland, Maine, of Antigua, 80' x 24' x 8', from Cardenas for Baltimore, wrecked on Carysfort Reef, September 25, 1869, in a heavy sea. She cut her cable and was washed ashore. *Source:* 37; NYH, 10/23/1869. (4)

4) *MUTTER* or *MUTTER SHULTZ*—Bark, Capt. Schultz, 690 tons, built 1851 at Burg, 143' x 33' x 20', of Rostock, from Pensacola for Liverpool or West Hartlepool, went ashore on Sugar Loaf Reef (probably a reef off Sugar Loaf Key), and bilged, December 25, 1869. Stores and materials were sold at Key West for $1,300, and hull (believe as she lay) for $100. *Source:* 37; Liverpool Courier, 1/25/1870; NYH, 12/30/1869. (3)

1) Page 80. *Omaha*—Brig, Capt. J. Toothaker, 209 tons, built 1864 at Machias, Maine, of New York, from Key West for Pensacola. After she had left Key West, she was struck by a tremendous gale or tornado the next day around 9:00 a.m., and was soon thrown on her beam ends and turned keel up. The storm lasted about an hour. About an hour and a half later she turned back on her beam ends. The captain, and four others were the only ones to survive, having lost seven crew including the captain's son. They clung to the wreck, though one crewman saved one of the boats which was badly damaged. After a couple of days on the wreck with no water, they managed to repair the boat, patching it with some canvas. After the storm, they estimated their position at Lat. 26°30'N, Long. 83°40'W, about 75 miles from the Florida coast. They left the wreck in the boat, along with a few cans of meat they had saved, though they still had no water. Only had one good oar and two damaged ones. Using a boat hook for a mast and a sail made from some canvas salvaged from the wreck, they steered northeast as best they could as they had no compass, and landed on the Florida coast on May 6 near Cape Roman. There they got some fresh water and then headed for Key West, but made the lighthouse at Dry Bank first, and were welcomed there.

She was later found drifting in the Gulf opposite the Ship Channel by the pilot boat which towed her on the reef about seven miles from Key West, where her spars, sails, etc., were to be salvaged. Lots of brass and old rigging had been saved from her, which sold for $408.88 at Key West. There she was anchored, but she soon sank between the buoys marking the channel between Triangle Shoals. Her bow was held fast by her anchors, and she "swings with the tide." She now posed a problem for vessels using that channel, but was later reported in November that a recent gale had swept her away from channel, and no longer posed a problem, the channel now clear. *Source:* BP, 5/21–26/1869, 6/7/1869, 11/4/1869; NYH, 5/13/1869.

2) Page 80. *Golconda*—Was got off by the wreckers and taken to Key West. *Source:* BP, 6/2/1869.

1870

1) *MAY QUEEN*—British bark, Capt. Mundt, from Havana for Pensacola, wrecked in a thick fog, January 16, 1870, 15 miles west of the Pensacola Bar. The hull was sold at auction as she lay for $30. The sails, rigging, etc., sold for $1,604. *Source:* BP, 1/27/70, SMN, 2/21/1870. (1)

2) *JOHN DAVIES*—British ship 1,041 tons, built in Sackville, New Brunswick, of Port Glasgow, Capt. Cliney, from Greencock for Pensacola, wrecked in a thick fog on Santa Rosa Island, about 20 miles east of the Pensacola Bar, January 16, 1870. Wreckers saved the sails, rigging, etc. Hull sold for $165, and the sails, rigging and other property for $1,521. *Source:* BP, 1/27/1870; Greencock Telegraph and Clyde Shipping Gazette, 3/4/1870. (1)

3) *NORGE*—Norwegian bark, built 1866 at Risor, Norway, 286 tons, Capt. Ellsen, from Havana for Falmouth, with 3,755 boxes of sugar, burned on Triumph Reef, March 3, 1870, some sugar saved. *Note:* Captain Nelson of the steamer *Cortez* reports seeing a large bark completely on fire on Pacific Reef about 10 miles north of Carysfort Light, March 4, 1870. "She was aground upon the reef with her sails set." "She was enveloped in flames from stem to stern." *Source:* 35; BP, 3/9/1870; Galveston Flakes Daily Bulletin, 3/11/1870. (3)

3) *CLARA BELL*—Schooner, 151.1 tons, of Camden, Maine, from New York for Jacksonville, was totally wrecked on the bar at Jacksonville. *Source:* 10; BP, 9/29/1870. (6)

4) October 1870 HURRICANE. May actually had been two storms that month from some of the dates I've seen. Many ships along the Florida coast and the Bahamas were lost or injured.

a) *TOMAS de RESA*—Spanish bark, from New Orleans for Barcelona, with a cargo of staves, was lost on Florida coast (another source says Bahamas Bank) during the October hurricane, vessel and cargo total loss. Crew were saved by the schooner *Rapid*. *Source:* London Daily News, 10/31/1870; NYH, 11/4/1870; Galveston Flakes Daily Bulletin, 10/30/1870. (8)

b) *F.I. MERRYMAN*—Brig 218 tons, 107.9' x 28.2' x 10.2', built in Bath in 1866 and owned there, Capt. Glover, from Baltimore for Galveston, with 200 tons of coal and assorted cargo, was driven high and dry on the Tea Table Bar, during the October hurricane. Driven so far up, that the wreckers could not save her. All cargo saved. Other report says she lay in four feet of water, on a mud bank, near Tea Table Key, between Indian Key and Umbrella Key, and the general cargo was saved. *Source:* BP, 10/28/1870, 11/7/1870; NYTR, 11/15/1870. (3)

c) *HANSON GREGORY*—Bark, Capt. J. B. Gregory, 348 tons, built 1855 at Rockland, Maine, 119' x 28' x 12', of and from Rockland, Maine, bound for New Orleans, with granite blocks, ran ashore on the Florida Reef, October 19, 1870, and bilged. Before she struck, she lost three men overboard. *Source:* 37; New Orleans Republican, 10/26/1870; Galveston Flakes Semi Weekly Bulletin, 11/2/1870; NYT, 11/3/1870; The Charleston Daily News, 10/31/1870. (8)

d) *IDA FOWLER*—Schooner, Capt. Dyer, wrecked on shore about 10 miles south of the *Jefferson Borden*. Another says four miles south of New River, was in ballast, and was up on the beach. *Source:* Ibid; NYTR, 11/15/1870. (5)

e) *E. RICHARDSON*—Schooner, 230.67 tons, of New York, built 1864 at Jonesboro, Maine, bound for Richmond, Virginia, put into Tortugas Harbor leaking, where she sunk along with the 69 cannon she had on board. Salvaged what they could. *Source:* 10; 37; Ibid. (3)

f) *JOHN CROOKER*—Two-masted schooner, 208 tons, 101' x 28.2' x 9.6', built 1866 at Bath, Maine, by Goss and Sawyer, and owned there, Capt. Hogdon, from Savannah for Sagua, wrecked on Cape Florida sandbar during the October hurricane. Crew saved. *Source:* 7; BP, 10/28/1870. (5)

g) *COMPROMISE*—Schooner, of Monument, reported as wrecked off Florida during the October hurricane. *Source:* BP, 11/4/1870.

h) *THREE SISTERS*—British brig, from St. John, New Brunswick, for Havana, was abandoned at sea, October 12, after damage from the hurricane on the 9th, at Lat. 24°N, Long.79°W. Crew were picked up by the schooner *Brilliant*, and taken to Savannah. Later reported she drifted ashore on Wigims Key (there's a Wiggins Pass in Naples, Florida), full of water, and loaded with timber. Likely salvaged, as a brig of the same name is listed in service a couple more years. *Source:* 37; NYH, 10/22/1870; BP 10/26/1870; NYTR, 11/15/1870. (8)

i) *RIGHT BOWER*—Schooner, from New York for Galveston, wrecked on Loo Key during the October hurricane. Wreckers were taking off cargo, but believed vessel was lost. Unknown if salvaged. *Source:* BP, 11/14–15/1870. (3)

j) *EXPORT*—Brig, Capt. Merritt, from Old Harbor, Jamaica for New York, with logwood, encountered a storm September 20, 1870, and suffered much damage at Lat. 22°06' N, Long. 85°20' W. Either late October or early November, encountered another storm at Lat. 24°N, Long. 84°W, lost all sails and was leaking badly. Crew were taken off by the steamer *George Cromwell* from New Orleans and taken to New York. *Source:* BP, 11/15/1870. (8)

k) *ARGUS EYE*—Schooner, 336.46 tons, built 1856 at Wilmington, 122'6" x 28'2.4" x 9'10.8", one deck, two masts, of and from Philadelphia, with U.S. Navy stores, was reported as ashore at Key West Harbor. Unknown if salvaged. *Source:* 10; 27; The Charleston Daily News, 10/31/1870. (3)

l) *HAIL COLUMBIA*—Schooner, was reported wrecked at Luc Key (Loo Key?). Most cargo was saved but unknown if vessel was. *Source:* NYH, 11/11/1870. (3)

m) *SYLVAN SHORE*—Steamer, 143.55 tons, recently bought to be a mail carrier by Capt. Tucker to sail between Fernandina and Tampa and ports in between, was lost in the October hurricane. Capt. Tucker was well known, but may have been negligent as both the engineer in New York where the vessel was purchased from, and the engineer on board who demanded to be put ashore at Mosquito Inlet, both deemed the vessel unseaworthy. Capt. Tucker, his wife and daughters and another couple were lost. The keeper of the light at Mosquito Inlet said he saw her outside dragging her anchor during the gale that night with the seas breaking over her, and that was the last she was seen. *Source:* 10; NYH, 11/10/1870. (6)

n) *DEXTER WASHBURN*—Schooner, 227.46 tons, Capt. C. Harkness, built 1867 at Rockport, 112' x 26' x 15', of and from Camden, Maine, for New Orleans, with granite, wrecked on Conch Reef during the storm, October 30, 1870, and bilged. A total loss. *Source:* 10; 37; New Orleans Republican, 11/23/1870; NYTR, 11/15/1870. (4)

o) *JAPAN*—Schooner, Capt. Sharenberg, from Belize for Havre, foundered in the Gulf Stream, November 4, 1870, about 80 miles off Cape Canaveral. Captain and crew abandoned her in a sinking condition in the ship's boat and landed at Cape Canaveral after 30 hours at sea. They were taken in by the Lighthouse keeper there. *Source:* SMN, 11/19/1870. (8)

p) *PATRIARCO SAN JOSE* or *PALUCA SAN JOSÉ*—Spanish brig, from Havana for Barcelona, bilged on the outside of Pickle's Reef, October 20, 1870. Had a cargo of sugar, coffee, pimento, and copper. Wreckers were in process of removing the cargo. *Source:* NYTR, 11/15/1870; NYH, 11/12/1870; LL, 11/23/1870. (4)

q) *ALEXANDER*—British ship, with 3,733 boxes of sugar, wrecked during the hurricane, and seven men including the Captain were lost. Mate, steward and two men were saved, one was picked up clinging to a submerged rock. Reported lost on Bahama or Salt Key Bank, and survivors brought back to Key West on the pilot boat *Invincible*, but one passenger was lost and came ashore in Florida (see story below). *Source:* BP, 11/3/1870; Charleston Daily News, 10/31/1870.

I have to relate the story of one survivor of the *Alexander* as it's quite incredible and as he was lost off Florida's west coast, I'm including this wreck here even though the ship was lost in the Bahamas. It appears the ship was from New Orleans bound for New York and this happened before the ship was lost. *The Tarboro Southerner* (North Carolina), October 6, 1870, printed the tale of this remarkable survival called *A Wonderful Story*:

> The following beats all the stories of remarkable escapes which we remember ever to have seen: On the passage of the ship *Alexander* from New Orleans to New York, a lad, about fourteen years of age, from a naturally frolicsome and mischievous disposition became so troublesome in his pranks, that he was threatened by the captain if they continued, that he would confine him in a water cask. Our youngster took no heed, however; and at his next offense, was put in the cask which was headed up, leaving, a large bung hole for the admittance of air. That night the ship encountered a violent storm and, in a sudden lurch, the cask containing the boy rolled over into the sea, fortunately the cask struck bung up, and floated about thirty hours, when it was thrown upon the beach at St. Blas (Cape San Blas). Here the boy made desperate efforts to extricate himself from his prison, without success, and, in despair, gave up to die. Some cows however, strolling on the beach, were attracted to the cask and in walking around it, one of them—it being fly time—switched her tail into the bung hole, which the lad grasped with desperate resolution. The cow bellowed, and set off for life, and after running some two hundred yards with the cask, struck it against a log on the beach and knocked it to smash. The boy was discovered by some fishermen on the point, and taken into Apalachicola, where a small collection being made for him, he was enabled to proceed North by the way of Columbus.

Note: The *Alexander* may have run into the beginning of a hurricane when this happened and as stated before, I think there may have been two different storms in October. Nevertheless, the boy was actually quite lucky since if he had stayed on board, his fate may have been quite different.

Notes on the storm: The British steamship *Sapphire*, Capt. Gill (some papers mistakenly called her the *Sophia*), was reported as a total loss in all the papers after the storm, but was gotten off a few months later and saved. She wrecked on Upper Matecumbe Key (others say near Elliot's Key) with a cargo of heavy machinery and steam boilers, which believe were all saved. Was from Liverpool for Havana. The schooners *Alabama* and *Explorer*, both of Key West and owned by Filor and Sons, were reported as high and dry on Bahia Honda and Saddle Bunches Keys, but are listed in service the next couple of years so they were saved. The Key West schooner *Lavinia* was also listed as high and dry on Bahia Honda, but was also saved as she is listed as in service for the next few years. The schooner *Glengary* was also reported from Key West as wrecked, but it was lost near the *Wm Brown* on Dog Rocks, Bahamas Bank. The captain of the *Jefferson Borden*, which wrecked south of Hillsboro, also mentioned that they found a backboard with an English coat of arms in the center, and above in a blue field was the name *Simoda*, and below that "Greenock." They also found the stern of a boat with "*Hyperion* of Glasgow" printed on it, about six miles from their wrecked vessel. I could not find any additional information on these two vessels. The Scottish papers only reported the exact same article. The *Jefferson Borden* was also reported a total loss, but was later sold for $50, floated and towed to Key West, repaired, and sold again for $4,000 and continued in service. A few years later, it was involved in a mutiny. The British ship *Trinidad* was also saved and brought to Key West.
End of hurricane losses.

1) Page 80 and 121. *Star*—Capt. Cockburn, from Calabria for Falmouth, wrecked on Conch Reef or Little Conch Reef, March 20. She had 602 hhds, and 248 boxes sugar. Cargo saved was 237 hhds and 145 boxes saved dry. *Source:* LL, 5/5/1870.

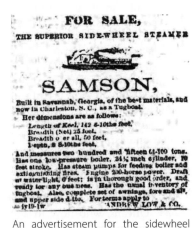

2) Page 144. *Samson* (correct)—Sidewheel steamer (Tug), 215 tons, wrecked at Cape Canaveral, October 7, 1870. Three lives lost. *Source:* SMN, 10/24/1870.

3) Page 144. *Moreno* (correct)—Brigantine, Capt. Phillips, of St. Johns, New Brunswick, from Havana for Sidney, Cape Breton, totally wrecked high ashore by Jupiter Inlet, October 8, 1870. Crew, sails and rigging saved. The hull was too high on shore to be saved. *Source:* SMN, 10/31/1870; BP, 11/3/1870.

An advertisement for the sidewheel steamer *Samson*. *Savannah Morning News*, July 1870.

4) Page 144. **Minerva**—Capt. J (or S). P. Collins, 111.83 tons, built 1847 at Greenport, of Fall River, Massachusetts, from Havana bound for Bristol, Rhode Island, in ballast, sprung a leak October 9, 1870, about 15 miles south of Jupiter Inlet, and was run ashore to prevent her sinking, where she went to pieces within three hours. Another source says 18 miles from Jupiter Light. One man drowned. *Source:* 10; 37; NYH, 10/28/1870; SMN, 10/31/1870; BP, 11/3/1870.

5) Page 145. **William Rathbone** (correct)—Bark, of New York, 1,117.78 tons, built 1849 at Mystic, 158' x 35' x 28', left New York for New Orleans on September 21, 1870, and wrecked October 11, 1870, north of Hillsboro Inlet (most reports say 10–11 miles north, another says 14 miles). She put her anchors out but they soon parted and she broke up within an hour. All the crew saved though Capt. H. H. Doane was badly injured. Capt. was picked up by the steamer *Mississippi* and dropped off at Sand Key. Three men stayed by the wreck on the beach for 19 days and were eventually picked up by the vessel *Morro Castle*. After rounding Hole in the Wall, Bahamas, on October 8, they hove to off the Issacs that evening. The winds began picking up but then subsided (probably the feeder bands we all see before a hurricane in Florida), and proceeded to Bimini and Gun Key the next morning where the full force of the hurricane slammed into the *Rathbone*. *Source:* 37; NYH, 10/22/1870, 11/11/1870; New Orleans Republican, 10/22/1870; The Charleston Daily News, 10/31/1870; 14; NYTR, 11/15/1870.

The following is a partial report furnished by Capt. Doane and reported in the *New Orleans Republican*, 10/22/1870:

October 10, the gale increasing and canting southerly: at 8 A.M. wore to the northeast; during the day gale blowing with unabated violence, accompanied with hail and sleet: 10 P.M., moderating and clearing up; at 4 P.M. on the eleventh, made the land, three miles distant; finding in impossible to work the bark off the lee shore by carrying a press of canvas. Owing to the wind and sea, let go both anchors and veered whole length of cables and held on for fifteen minutes, when the port chain parted and the bark payed off, head to the southward, and struck heavily, the sea making a clean breach over her; found it impossible to ease her of the masts; in less than one hour after the bark struck, she was completely broken up, all hands being saved on a portion of the stern that was run on the beach: on the morning of the thirteenth sent third mate and carpenter down the beach in search of assistance; they returned on the fourteenth, having been as far as Hillsboro, fourteenth miles distant, and could find no aid; saw a steamer, bound south; could render us no assistance, on account of the heavy sea running: October 17, saw a steamer, bound south, which proved to be the *Mississippi*, Captain Henry, bound from New York to New Orleans, who hove to and sent a lifeboat ashore, which, after several attempts, succeeded in bringing me on board, owing to the persevering efforts of the first officer and boat's crew.

6) Page 145. **Varuna**—Additional information on her build from the NYH, 11/4/1870, states: Engine built at Delemater Iron Works of New York City, vertical direct, 26 inches by 30 inches. Two decks, says deck was 120 feet long, beam 28'6", depth 17'6". Square fastened with copper and treenails. Had a cast iron propeller.

While the only people to escape on the boats were Captain Spencer and his crew, though all on one boat drowned, none of the 36 passengers even got onto a boat. Some probably thought the crew only wanted to save themselves. The following is the statement of one of the few survivors, Quartermaster Wallace, which was reported in *The Defiance Democrat*, November 19, 1870, so you be the judge:

We left for New York on Saturday night at seven o'clock, and had fine weather up to the morning of October 20, when the wind sprung up from the south. At noon there was a moderate gale. As the sun went down it was blowing a perfect hurricane. All went well until eight o'clock, when the wind shifted suddenly to the south-west, when the ship became unmanageable, and having a list to port, the sea commenced rushing on board on the lee side of the ship, staving in the bullwarks and the cabin doors. We tried to get her off before the wind, and put on all the steam we could, but it was of no use. I was at the wheel, and we brought her up to the wind again, and tried to fix the cabin door, but the sea was rushing on board to such a degree that the men could not work.

We then twisted her jib to pay her head off, but it was blow to ribbons, although it had been snuggly furled. By this time the sea had stove in the engine house and was running down into the fire and engine room at the rate of many tons per minute, and the ship listing over still more, she was fast filling. I lashed the wheel after I felt the engines stop and went aft to get some water. I was very thirsty, and then managed to get on the hurricane deck, when I found the two ice-boats were gone from the ship and the men were getting the other boats ready. I was still so thirsty that I came back to the Captain's room and got a drink there and opened the weather cabin door to see how the passengers were behaving, but did not see a soul, as they were all in their staterooms unable to come out on account of the ship lying on her beam ends.

I then came on the hurricane deck and got into the after boat, with six others then in. It was lying on the deck waiting for the ship to go down, she then being nearly on her beam ends. The Captain, mate and engineers-ten in all-were in the boat, and in less than five minutes the boats were afloat, but in such a heavy sea that I was afraid we would get foul of the ship's rigging. While the ship was sinking the other boat halted and asked us if we were all right, and after this the steamer got foul of their boat and took her down with the ship.

The boats were Ingersol's metallic life-boats, and I think the captain's boat got clear and came up again, as a boat bottom up was seen two hours after, but no person was in it. After the ship's masthead was out of sight, we thought ourselves all right, as the ship was clear of us, but we counted without a host, for a heavy sea capsized the boat, but all managed after great exertion to right her and get in again. The ship again went down at two p.m., and at midnight the weather moderated and was still. The hardships encountered by the five men was terrible, while braving the fury of the elements for sixty hours in an open boat, without food or water, except a small onion which served to moisten their parched and aching lips.

After being cast on the beach by the breakers, in view of the lighthouse at Jupiter Inlet, only the second mate and a seaman were strong enough to fully drag themselves to the building for assistance. The rest lay exhausted until the keeper sent a boat to take them away. The passengers, thirty-six in number, without doubt, all perished in their state-rooms. When the steamer suddenly lurched over on her beam ends, the water poured into the cabin where they were securely fastened to die a horrible death without even battling for their existence. It would have been madness, the survivors state, to have attempted to rescue them, as the cabin was a trap into which it was certain death to venture. Horrible as the thought is, nothing could be done by the officers and crew but save themselves.

7) Page 145. *Col. I.T. Sprague* (correct)—Of St. Augustine, 37.9 tons. *Source:* 10.

8) Page 225. *Mariposa*—Capt. Willetts, screw steamer, of and from New Orleans, of the Cromwell Line, built 1863 at New York by Webb and Bell, of live oak, and copper and iron fastened, she had a crew of 35 men and no passengers at this time due to a yellow fever outbreak, not wanting to be in quarantine upon arrival at her destination. Cargo consisted of 1,672 bales cotton, 224 bundles hides, 424 hides, 18 bales hides and moss, 29 barrels flour, all valued at $160,000. The stern with her name was found about 15 miles north of Hillsboro Inlet. A lifejacket with her name was also found by the wrecked crew of the *William Rathbone*. They also found a plank near Hillsboro with the words "Mariposa leaking" painted on it. The captain of the wrecked *Jefferson Boardman* (actually the *Jefferson Borden*) also reported finding life- buoys and buckets with her name. *Source:* 37; New Orleans Republican, 10/22/1870; NYH, 10/22/1870; NYTR, 11/15/1870. (5)

1871

1) *CHARRY M*—Sloop, believe 11.62 tons, reported as wrecked on a key leading into Tampa Bay, Capt. D. S. McKay. *Source:* SMN, 1/17/1871. (2)

2) *MARY MATILDA*—Schooner, 34.77 tons, of Apalachicola, Capt. Stokes, ran into a storm which carried away the mainmast, mid-April 1871, and she was beached in order to save her, between East Pass and St. Andrew's Bay. A total loss. *Source:* 10; BP, 5/3/1871. (1)

2) *MARGARETHA*—German brig, Capt. Kroeger, of Stettin, from Laguna for Hamburg, with logwood, wrecked on the St. Johns Bar, August or September 1871. A total wreck, though the anchors, chain, and much of the cargo saved. I found two brigs named *Margaretha* in American *Lloyd's Register* in 1871 from Stettin. One is 259 tons, 100' x 24' x 12', and the other is 152 tons. The Record of American and Foreign Shipping only list the 152-ton brig. Neither two are listed in 1872 in either records. Both had captain's names listed, but neither was Kroeger. *Source:* 7; 37; NYH, 9/6–26/1871; NYT, 9/4/1871; NYTR, 9/4/1871; Barnette says the 152-ton brig. (6)

3) August 17 HURRICANE:

a) *H.G. BERRY*—Brig, 297.91 tons, built 1855 at Boothbay, 106' x 28' x 11', of New York, with sugar and molasses, went ashore 50 yards from the wreck of the *S&W Welsh*. She was dashed to pieces and much of the wreck was on or under the beach. Crew saved, having made shore on pieces of the wreck. A total loss. *Source:* 10; 37; Bloomington Weekly, 8/30/1871; NYH, 9/2/1871. (5)

b) *HILDA*—Norwegian Bark, built 1856 at Boston, 230.5 tons, Capt. F. S. Forjusen, from New Orleans for Cowes or Bremen, with leaf tobacco in hogsheads and staves, went ashore six miles south of St. Augustine during the hurricane, July 15, 1871. A total loss. One man drowned. *Source:* 10; 35; Bloomington Weekly, 8/30/1871; SMN, 8/28/1871. (6)

c) *LINDA*—Bark, 312.07 tons, of and built at Philadelphia in 1859, 113' x 29' x 11', Capt. Smith, from New York for New Orleans, with 1,000 bbls cement, 200 of plaster, 100 of brimstone, 500 cases bitters, 150 do matches and other general cargo, foundered off Carysfort during the August hurricane. Some of the crew reached Cape Florida in the boat. Another report had the steamer *Wilmington* picking up the rest of the crew in the other boat on August 26, at Lat. 26°24' N, Long. 79°51' W, and they said the bark foundered on the 25th at Lat. 25°34' N, 79°32' W. *Source:* 10; 37; BP, 9/2/1871; Greensburg Standard, 9/7/1871; NYT, 8/30/1871; BP, 9/2/1871. (5)

End of August 1871 hurricane losses.

4) *RIVAL*—Steamship, from New York, wrecked after her boiler exploded off the Florida coast, November 6, 1871. Some crew saved. *Source:* New Orleans Republican, 11/30/1871. (8)

1) Page 81. *St. James*—Of Richmond, Maine, built 1867 at Richmond, 1,286.45 tons, 194.6' x 37.5' x 24.6'. *Source:* 6; 10; BP, 11/20/1871.

2) Page 121. *Aquila* (correct)—Italian brig, Capt. V. Fiasconaro, 443 tons, built 1864 at Philadelphia, of Palermo, 132' x 29' x 16', from Havana for Queenstown, with sugar, wrecked and bilged on Pickle's Reef, March 15, 1871, during a storm. Captain and crew saved by the schooner *Ralph*, and taken to Key West. Some cargo saved. *Source:* 37; NYH, 4/5/1871; Gore's Liverpool General Advertiser, 3/23/1871; The Evening Telegraph, 3/20/1871; The Daily Phoenix, 3/21/1871.

3) Page 145. *Mississippi*—Screw steamer of 1,038.44 tons, Capt. W.O. Henry, from New York for New Orleans with a valuable cargo, wrecked August 24, 1871, off Hillsboro Inlet almost in the exact same place where she saved the captain of the *William Rathbone* after a hurricane just a year before. The captain and all on board were initially saved by the steamer *Cortez*. The steamer was later saved and brought to Key West, January 17, 1872, and continued in service for a few more years. *Source:* 10; 37; BP, 9/2/1871; 2/16/1872; *New York Daily Tribune*, September 6, 1871.

Though saved, I've included the interesting story of the wreck told by a passenger originally printed in the *New Orleans Times* and again in *New York Daily Tribune*, September 1871.

THE TEMPEST AT SEA

Thursday morning, the 24th, the wind still being on the increase, the square-sails were furled. At this time the ship was rolling fearfully, the yards frequently touching the sea. Vast bodies of water were constantly being shipped, keeping the decks flooded. At 3 p.m. the storm had increased to a fearful hurricane. The sea was running mountain-high, and the wind whistling through the rigging so as to make it almost impossible to make oneself heard. At about 4 p.m. we shipped a huge sea over the stern, which broke through the rear skylight, flooding the cabin with water. The cabin passengers, although realizing the ferocity of the storm, had tried to preserve their equanimity; but now, seeing one of the sky-light broken open, they commenced to be terrified. The water which had dashed over into the cabin was bailed out by some passengers and stewards, and a wide plank nailed over the opening. The pitching and rolling of the ship was now so constant and severe that, to avoid being dashed from one side to the other, it was necessary to hold on with all one's strength to some part of the state-rooms or cabin. The plank which had been nailed against the broken skylight was quickly torn away by force of the wind, and every stern wave that was shipped would pour down more or less water into the cabin. At 5 o'clock the pilot-house was broken up on the weather side, and the tiller lashed down. The lee boats were torn away by the water, the davits snapping like reeds. Just at this time an awful wave swept over us, breaking through every skylight, dashing one of the boats on the weather side over the main saloon, and sending large quantities of water down the engine-room.

A TERRIBLE SCENE

The cabin passengers, already in a state of terror, were immediately after this startled by successive shrieks, which proved to be the steerage passengers, who had been ordered into the main saloon, as being the safest place, and now who rushed frantically into the cabin, almost mad with fear. Everything now indicated that the ship was about to go down. All knelt down and offered up a fervent prayer to the Almighty to save us from the horrible death. A huge wave washing down the engine-room forced the engineers and firemen from their post, and dashing against Capt. Henry, who was cutting away the drag, which had struck the screw, dislocated his arm. All the lights in the cabin were put out by this sea, and we found ourselves in perfect darkness, struggling to get out of the water, which was getting higher in the saloon every minute. Capt. Henry now dragged himself along the deck, and looking down into the darkness, hailed the passengers, asking whether they were still there. Some one answered, "Aye, aye, Captain, what shall we do?" "Stay where you are," shouted the Captain, "and hold fast." One of the stewards managed to light one of the lamps, and hung it up. In order to keep it from going out again, a passenger held it with one hand, while with the other he grasped the bench for support. The officers were making preparations to cut away the mainmast, when at about eight o'clock, with a shock which can only be compared to that of an earthquake, the ship struck on the Florida rocks. The passengers, unaware of our proximity to the shore, naturally inferred that the *Mississippi* had broken up, and three or four successive waves dashing over us and filling up the cabin, served but confirm the horrible thought. Each one told his neighbor good-bye, and prepared for the end, which we thought had come. At this awful solemn moment, one of the crew procured somewhere a demijohn of whiskey, and commenced drinking himself and handing the liquor to the other men. As soon as Capt. Henry discovered this, he seized the demijohn, and jerking it with his injured arm from the ruffian, poured the contents on the floor. The crew now slunk off in different directions, some going aft, near the end of the saloon, while others went into passenger's state-rooms, pretending to be exhausted from fatigue, while in reality they were ransacking the carpet-bags and packages of the unfortunate passengers.

Enormous waves dashed against the ship almost every half minute, lifting her up as though the immense mass of iron was but a toy, and then dashing her down against the rock, with a horrible grating sound, which seemed to shake every bolt and rivet from its place. And so this long, horrible night dragged slowly along. Occasionally some would make an effort to see the shore, but sky, rain, waves, and spray all seemed one solid, undistinguishable mass, and to see land through the pitchy darkness was impossible.

A ROPE BRIDGE

Pen cannot describe nor imagination picture the horrors of such a night. And when, just at daylight, the captain, going forward and discovering that, by the successive waves, the ship had been beached within a short distance of land, reported the same to the exhausted passengers, and the certainty of being able to save every one, a fervent "Thank God!" was uttered on all sides, and women, children, and strong men wept for joy. The hurricane at daylight, blowing in squalls, indicated that it had passed its height. Two seamen were let down the side of the ship with a strong rope, which they managed to get ashore through the breakers. This rope they made fast to the shore, and on it was then attached what is called a boatswain's chair, which consists of a plank just large enough to sit on, with a rope attached to each side, meeting over the head on a block, which block slides along the large hawser. The first mate, Mr. Cuzzins, then came back to the cabin and announced to the female passengers that they were ready to put them ashore.

Some could hardly realize that they were really saved from the storm. The scene really beggared description: From the depths of despair and the threshold of death they felt themselves saved from the hand of Providence, and were once again to tread God's green earth. Holding on to the wrecked matter and the bulwarks that were not carried away they crawled along the deck, through the spray and rain, to the forecastle, and thence were carried over the breakers, one by one, by means of the boatswain's chair. The male passengers were next landed, and then the crew, the first mate next, and finally the captain. Some sail was sent ashore and pieces of wood and oars, with which a tent was improvised over some low stunted trees on the bank. The passengers, exhausted from constant anxiety and exposure, and wet to the skin, crawled under the tent; some sinking immediately into a deep sleep, while the more robust lent what assistance they could to the crew. Some blankets were next gotten off and distributed, and then some cold provisions, which were greedily devoured, as no one had eaten anything during the long dismal hours of the storm. Nearly the entire day had been consumed in getting off the passengers and crew, and at nightfall the hurricane had swept past us, and the waves were once more calm; still, the scene on the beach was desolate, indeed. Immediately before us stood the ill-fated *Mississippi*, leaning on her side, firmly imbedded in the rock and sand-a noble-looking wreck. Behind, and on both sides of us, nothing was to be seen but sand and briars and stunted trees. A large bonfire was lighted, and then everyone tried to find the driest place possible under the tent to rest their weary limbs. So passed Friday. At daylight on Saturday we were all up. Very few had escaped without some cut or bruise, so that, after sleeping on the wet bedding, still arms and legs were to be seen on all sides. The mates, with some of the men, were again sent on board, and during the day continued to send off provisions and other stuff from the wreck. Two of the small boats were still left unhurt, and these were lowered and hauled ashore. The captain's chart, being brought off, we were found to be at Hillsboro Inlet, about 43 miles south of Jupiter. The inlet, which ran immediately behind our camp, was found to contain fresh water, which relieved us of a great anxiety. Some fish were washed ashore and fried, and crabs seemed to be plentiful in the lagoon, which also swarmed with alligators. All the passengers trunks had been washed overboard from the hatchway, where they were kept, and very few escaped with more than the suit they had on and what few articles they could pick up out of the water in the state rooms.

At 12 o'clock on Saturday we had our dinner served out to us, consisting of flapjack and salt pork. About this time a report was brought that a sail was in sight to the southward. This proved to be unfounded. During the day those of the passengers who had been fortunate enough to save any wearing apparel employed themselves in drying them on the beach., while others strained their eyes in vain along the horizon, like Enoch Arden, "shipwrecked sailors waiting for a sail."

Just about 5 o'clock a sail was discovered to the northward, which in a short time proved to be a steamer. One of the small boats was immediately launched, and the mate was sent off to request the captain of the approaching steamer to land him at Sand Key, that he might return to us with assistance. By the time the mate returned from the steamer it had already grown dark. He reported the steamer to be the *Cortez*, Capt. Whitman, which steamer had left New York on the same evening as the *Mississippi*, and had successfully weathered the hurricane. Capt. Whitman sent some provisions back and sent word to Capt. Henry that he would not leave us on the desolate shore in our wretched condition, but would send his own boats to assist in taking us off, and if necessary would wait all night until every man, woman, and child had been safely transferred to the *Cortez*. The poor passengers, on hearing the manly and generous offer, were wild with delight. There little bundles were soon packed up, and everything prepared to get the females off first. The first boat-load was swamped in the surf, and had to be drawn up on the beach and the boat bailed out before she could be put off again. The second time it succeeded in riding the breakers and got out safely. Boats were kept going from the *Cortez* to the shore until every one of the passengers of the *Mississippi*, and those of the crew who wished to go to New Orleans, were landed on board, which was finally accomplished about midnight. The passengers of the *Mississippi*, who were in a thoroughly wet condition, were furnished with dry clothes, and shown immediately to state-rooms. The *Cortez* then steamed away, and we saw the last of the *Mississippi* as we passed her by. Capt. Henry was landed at Key West early Monday morning, where he has gone to procure the assistance of the wreckers to remove the cargo. During the voyage from Hillsboro to New Orleans, the unfortunate passengers of the *Mississippi* were treated with the greatest kindness and consideration by Capt. Whitman, no difference being made by him in his conduct toward them and his own passengers, the *Cortez* being obliged to take in an extra supply of provisions at Key West to supply the wants of the additional number of passengers and crew.

Note: The 1,215 ton steamer *Juniata*, was also caught in the storm and was beached near the *Mississippi* in order to save the passengers and crew. She was saved by the wreckers and taken to Key West for repairs and all on board survived.

4) Page 145. **Pomona**—Built 1966 at Richmond, Maine, by T.J. Southard, 422 tons, 125.6' x 31' x 15.5', Capt. F. W. Brown, from Galveston, went ashore 25 miles south of Cape Canaveral (reports also say seven miles south of the *S&W Welsh*), August 17, 1871. Cargo of cotton and the ships stores were saved. *Source:* 6; BP, 11/15/1871; Bloomington Weekly, 8/30/1871; NYH, 8/29/1871; New Orleans Republican, 8/29/1871.

5) Page 145. **S&W Welsh**—Brig, Capt. J. Watson, of Philadelphia, 382.39 tons, built 1867 in Wilmington, from Cienfuegos for Philadelphia, with sugar, molasses and railroad iron, went ashore during a hurricane, 15 miles south of Cape Canaveral (wrecked 50 yards from the *H.G. Berry*). Another report says 13 miles southward of the light and 100 yards from the *Berry*. The captain drowned and his body was buried the next day. Vessel a total loss, some sails and rigging saved and maybe some cargo. *Source:* 10; 37; NYH, 8/29/1871, 9/2/1871; Bloomington Weekly, 8/30/1871; New Orleans Republican, 8/29/1871.

6) Page 175. **Lodona**—Capt. Henry R. Hovey (or Hovry), bark rigged iron screw steamer, built in Hull, England, in 1862. Was bought by the Confederacy as a blockade runner but was captured right after and became the *USS Lodona*. Naval records at that time list her at 750 tons, 210' x 27'6" x 11'6". She was later sold by the Navy and in 1871 she was listed at 808.69 gross tons in the annual US Merchant Vessel's list, and papers had her dimensions as 198' x 28.5' x 16' and tonnage at 730 (probably net tons). She had left New York bound for New Orleans on August 12 with a cargo of general merchandise, which one paper said was worth $2,000,000, when she stranded, August 17, 1871, 27 miles south of St. Augustine (another source says six miles north of Cape Canaveral). The beach was strewn for miles with wreckage. On board were 33 souls of which 20 were lost. *Source:* 10; New Orleans Republican, 8/26/1871; Bloomington Weekly, 8/30/1871; The Bolivar Bulletin, 8/31/1871; NYT, 8/26/1871.

Some papers related a couple of the survivor's stories. One was from the mess boy Lewis Wolf. Here's an excerpt from part of his story reported in numerous papers including the *New Orleans Republican*, 9/12/1871:

About 3 o'clock Thursday morning a heavy gale prevailed, and all the firemen were ordered below to keep the fires up. The sea was running into the skylight. About half past 7 we struck a reef and she shifted over on her beam ends.

The captain was in the pilot house at the time she shifted, and he fell out and stumbled while trying to catch hold of the main rigging. The sea broke over the ship and washed him off and carried away the pilot house. Some of the crew got into a boat, and when about thirty yards off the ship the *Lodona* turned over end and capsized. I was amidship on deck holding on to the fore right rigging. It was very hard to hold on with the heavy seas breaking over me. There were fourteen of the crew in the main rigging, the mainmast gave way and the sea broke it right off. All of the fourteen, excepting the captain's son Freddy, fifteen years of age, and the chief cook, Frank, were washed overboard, but they swam ashore as well as they could in the sea which was mountain high.

The Florida coast was nearly ten miles off, and I don't know how they reached the shore. Mr. Stephens, the first mate, got into the only other boat, which was a life-boat, and a heavy sea broke again and washed the boat and himself away. He reached the shore first of all. The crew, the chief engineer, first assistant engineer, five sailors, myself and a fireman, worked our way forward to the gallant forecastle. The wreck was washed ashore gradually, and we remained on her until two hours after the mainmast came down, when we found ourselves on the breakers, three or four hundred yards from the bank. The chief engineer and the fireman swam ashore first, and the second mate followed, and the remaining members of the crew, with the exception of myself, the first assistant engineer and a sailor, remained on the wreck for two days-until Saturday. The sailor made a raft. The first assistant engineer took the raft to go ashore, and he was washed off several times by the breakers. The sailor and myself made it. I broke the bulwarks out of her to make it, and went ashore with the sailor. By this time the chief engineer, captain's son, the second mate and the cook had gone down to the lighthouse, some six miles distant, and the keeper told the party to walk twenty-eight miles up the beach to the first Custom House station.

It goes on to say some tried to make the trek to the Custom House, and came across 14 bodies of their shipmates anywhere from four to 25 miles from where they landed. They could hardly sleep due to the mosquitoes, but eventually came across someone who helped them out. Wolf eventually hailed a small packet boat and made St. Augustine.

The cook, Francis Farrar, also related his story of events as reported in the *New Orleans Republican*, September 12, 1871:

Mr. Farrar was the last person who ever spoke to Captain Hovey, who said to him, "Try and help secure those hatches"—meaning the forward and amidship hatches, which had started. Farrar, noticing that the water was very muddy, asked the captain "if he did not fear going on the lee shore." Captain Hovey replied, "We must try and get her on the other tack." These were the last words the gallant captain ever spoke." He was one of the 14 clinging to the rigging of the mainmast. In this perilous position they remained for two hours, being constantly washed by the waves which were thrown to a great height by the fury of the storm, when, to their horror, the mast was unshipped, and, with its living freight, was cast into the ocean. All on the mast perished with the exception of Mr. Farrar, the cook, and the captain's son.

His story goes on to say that they made camp on the beach from the wreckage, and that he was one that went to the Cape Florida Lighthouse, where they were given food and water, and eventually made Col. Titus' house about 20 miles from Fernandina, where they were given refuge and eventually made it to Fernandina.

The chief engineer, Mr. Scofield, also had his story told. He related how on the 16th they ran into the first of the hurricane, and by that evening it became much worse. The winds had first come from the northeast, and then suddenly veered to the southeast as they most likely were now on the other side of the storm.

The aspect of the sea at this time was awful, ink-black gloom surrounded the vessel on every side, except when the flashing lightning for an instant illuminated the scene and revealed all its horror. Stout hearts quailed as the roaring winds rushed through the creaking cordage with a savage, relentless howl, and the straining ship labored, and creaked, and groaned as if in agony.

"Through hours that seemed ages struggled the gallant ship, and at last the light of morn began to break like a ray of hope through the gloom of that dreadful night. But the light brought with it little relief. Heavy waves were still breaking over the sides, but the violence of the wind had somewhat subsided, and I went on deck to fasten down the skylights, down which the water was pouring. After much trouble, I succeeded and nailed them down, covering them with boards and canvas. As soon as I had done this I passed round on the lee side of the deck-house to seek a little rest, as I felt completely worn out by the fatigue and excitement of the night. Meeting the second officer I remarked to him that the water looked dirty. He said, "Yes, I guess we're in shoal water." At that moment the ship struck heavily, but was carried back by the action of the waves. Again she struck bottom, and again was she lifted back by the waves. Striking the third time, she was thrown on her beam ends with terrible violence. So great was the shock that I was pushed over the ship's side into the water. Fortunately, a mass of the lee main rigging that had been torn away during the night lay in the water, and I was quick enough to catch hold of some floating debris. I then hauled myself on board by the main spencer brails. Just as I reached the deck, almost completely exhausted, the topsail and topgallant yards were carried over the side of the ship. At the same moment, the captain was thrown out of the lee pilot house and cast into the raging sea amid the mass of floating spars and rigging from which I had safely emerged. He must have struck heavily against some of the floating spars for he was drowned in an instant and disappeared from view."

He goes on to say how he and nine others went to the bow to cut away the fore rigging to let the mast go and hopefully right the vessel. At this time, he says he could see land, "which was at no great distance." Was at this time he saw the fourteen crewmen take to the main rigging. He recalls that a large wave later washed the poop deck away along with the mainmast and the 14 men clinging to her rigging. Helpless to do anything, those still on board watched many drown. One man named Miller was able to cling to a floating spar,

> There the poor fellow remained, within sight of his comrades, exposed to the violence of the sea, not more than sixty feet off the ship and almost within speaking distance of his friends, but nothing could be done for him. For twelve awful hours, the man struggled against fate, and fought for life against the terrible odds; but at last human strength gave way, and he dropped exhausted into the furious embrace of the merciless sea, his only dirge a mournful cry of horror from his comrades as they saw him sink under the waves and disappear into the caverns of eternity.

They then made some rafts for those who could not swim, and eventually all those left made it to shore. Seeing the lighthouse that night, the next day he and some other walked about seven miles south and were greeted by the keeper. He gave them some food and water and directions to get to Smyrna to the north. They made it back to camp, and on Saturday the 19th, they headed north. After about twenty miles they could find no good water. "The violence of the storm had driven the waves over the beach into the lagoons and made the water brackish." He and some decided to head back to the camp where there was water, and the others proceeded north. When they got back to their camp about ten that evening, they found their tent occupied by some shipwrecked sailors who had wrecked south of the lighthouse. The next morning, they saw locals or so-called "wreckers," looking to see what they could salvage from all the cargo and wreckage strewn along the beach (see the chapter on Florida's maritime history and the article *The Other Wreckers*, as the *Lodona* is mentioned.)

> The next morning, we made arrangements with some "beachcombers," who came down to the coast in the hope of plunder. I told them they should not plunder while we were present, but offered to go away if they would act as guides and put us somewhere so that we might be able to reach St. John's river. They then took us in their boats and conveyed us to Sand Point, where we landed at ten o'clock P.M. Sunday the 20th. The sandcombers were very anxious to get rid of us, as they wanted to plunder. They treated us kindly, but they were more moved by a desire to get us out of the way than by any motives of humanity, in bringing us to Sand Point. On our arrival at Sand Point, Fla., on the Indian River, we were met by Colonel Titus, the proprietor of a hotel there.

The Colonel took them in, but as soon as he heard about the lucrative cargo strewn along the beach, they were soon forgotten as he was busy getting a boat ready to join the other so-called wreckers. The colonel's wife

Sketch of the *Lodona*, by Commander R. Calhoun. Courtesy of the Naval History and Heritage Command, catalog # NH 51415.

An 1871 advertisement for the *Lodona*. *New Orleans Republican*, August 1871.

though took pity and made sure they were taken care of. The next morning, they made their way three miles inland from Sand Point to a small settlement where they met a Mr. Abbot. A very kind gentleman, he offered to guide them to Enterprise on the St. John's. They proceeded to his house about eight miles from there where he fed them dinner and breakfast the next morning. Mind you, there were 16 of them in their party, from four different wrecks! Enterprise, which is on the St. Johns River, is about 50 miles from Sand Point. The roads, if you can call them that, wound through the swamps, marsh and woods. The journey was far from easy, and many of the men had swollen feat and were still exhausted. At times, they had to wade through mud up to their chests, and at one point had to fell some trees to make a makeshift bridge to cross a deep stream. Luckily Mr. Abbot had brought along his axe. Mr. Abbot left them at Cow Creek, where they thanked him for his help. They then came upon the farmhouse of a Mr. Aiken who let them stay the night. From there, they were taken across Deep Creek by boats, and continued to Enterprise, arriving there on the 28th. Capt. Brock of the hotel there, took care of them for the next three days, and then took them all to Jacksonville on his boat. The Collector of customs at Jacksonville, Mr. Adams, put them all up in a boarding house. The Jacksonville Railroad, and the steamer *Nick King*, then graciously transported them all to their destinations. Could you imagine that today? Capt. Hovey was a very respected captain, and had saved all on board a steamer at great peril to his own ship only a couple of years before.

Story sources: Multiple papers reported the same story, though here are some: New Orleans Republican, 9/10–12/1871; Wilmington Journal, 9/15/1871; NYH, 9/5–8/1871.

7) Page 175. *Nellie F. Burgess*—Capt. McKeen, of and built at Belfast, Maine in 1867, 141 tons, 92' x 25' x 8', grounded on the bar while being towed in rough weather. *Source:* 37; BP, 12/11/1871.

1872

1) *VERONA*—Spanish schooner, wrecked off Boca Grande, Florida, March 8, 1872. One man was picked up, and the fate of the others was unknown. *Source:* LL, 4/16/1872. (2)

2) *AMASIA*, or *AMLIA*, or *AMISIA*—Prussian brig, with mahogany, was wrecked on the Florida Reef, and got off around August 17, 1872, but wrecked again on a reef near Key West and bilged. Most cargo saved. Another source says the Russian brig *Amalia* (believe this may be correct)

and another calls her the *Amisia*. *Source:* NYH, 8/17/1872; Boston Daily Globe, 8/30/1872; LL, 8/23/1872; Glasgow Herald, 8/19/1872. (3)

3) *ST. LOUIS*—Steamer, from New Orleans for New York, Capt. Whitehead, built 1853 in Dumbarton, Scotland, iron propeller, 1,060 tons, 214' x 30', of New York, had struck the sunken steamer *General Grant* shortly after leaving New Orleans, and 24 hours later on December 7, 1872, she sprung a leak when about 170 miles from the SW Bar, New Orleans, and sunk the next morning. All on board took to the boats and made for the Tortugas. All were picked up on the 10th by the British ship *Record*, and brought to Key West. Possible Florida wreck. *Source:* SMN 12/24/1872; New Orleans Republican, 12/29/1872. (8)

1) Page 51. *Evening Star*—Of Cedar Keys, 8.92 tons. *Source:* 10.

2) Page 51. *Eagle*—Of St. Marks, 5.92 tons. *Source:* 10.

3) Page 81. *Amazon*—Wrecked on Carysfort Reef. *Source:* BP, 3/18/1872. (4)

4) Page 81. *S.S. George Cromwell*—Was saved. *Source:* 37.

5) Page 81. *Restless*—Of Boston, 228.24 tons, built 1854 at Madison, Connecticut, 108' x 27' x 9'. *Source:* 10; 37.

5) Page 175. *Elizabeth Fry*—Built 1861 at St. John, New Brunswick, of Liverpool, 1,094 tons, 180' x 35' x 22', wood hull, burned and abandoned 200 miles SE of Tybee (possible Florida wreck). *Source:* 37.

1873

1) *ERNEST MARIA*—Schooner, Capt. Syperick, from Gilbara (sic) for Philadelphia, was abandoned at sea, at Lat. 27°50'N, Long. 79°50'W, in a sinking condition. Captain and crew left in a small boat and landed at Cape Canaveral. Possibly the 114-ton *Ernest & Marie* of Haiti, unknown if saved. *Source:* 37; SMN, 2/13/1873. (8)

2) *H.C. HAND*—Schooner, 187 tons, of and built at Tuckahoe, New Jersey in 1866, from New York for Jacksonville, "parted her hawser while being towed over it (St. John's Bar) on the 1st by the tugboat *Morgan* and went ashore." "She drifted on one of the banks and broke up in 8' of water." Had a cargo of general merchandise of which 25 percent was saved. Vessel a total loss. *Source:* 37; SMN, 11/3/1873; BP, 11/10/1873; Macon Georgia Weekly Telegraph, 11/18/1873. (6)

3) *LUCY*—Steamship, burned 45 miles off Cape Canaveral, August 15, 1873. Fifteen of the crew survived, though two had terrible burns. Believe

the 314-ton *Lucy*, of New York, built at Liverpool in 1863, 212' x 20' x 10'. *Source:* 37; SMN, 9/1/1873. (6)

4) **Unk. WRECK**—This was reported about 18–20 miles south of Cape Canaveral in about 13.5 fathoms of water, bottom up and dragging her anchors. She was now about 40 miles from when first seen a few months ago. Also noted was it lay in the shipping lane of steamers going south. The steamer *Niagara* again reported this as an "old vessel, keel up, south by east of Cape Canaveral, in fifteen fathoms of water, with waves washing over her, and hanging by her anchors." Also reported in 1883 as still in the shipping lane, nine years after the first reports! The same wreck? Maybe the *Western Empire* of 1875? *Source:* SMN, 8/10/1874; The Sun, 1/6/1883. (5)

1) Page 122. *Cornwall*—Built 1863 at Bathurst, England, 136' x 30.7' x 12.0', sheathed with felt and yellow (composite) metal. *Source:* LR, 1873.

2) Page 97. *Nor-Wester*—Capt. Sedgley, 1133 tons, built 1853 at Medford, 183' x 36' x 23', of Boston, from New Orleans for Liverpool, with 2,200 bales cotton, tobacco, and bone dust, found she had caught fire (due to spontaneous combustion) about 30 miles SSW of the Tortugas, and keeping the fire down with great effort, made for Key West where she anchored, February 23, 1873, a few miles from Key West, but due to a gale at the same time, she had to be abandoned, and the residents of Key West watched her burn. She was sold for $975, and the bone dust, which was part of her cargo, sold separately for $3.00. Some of the cotton was saved. *Source:* 37; SMN, 3/18/1873, 4/1–12/1873.

1874

1) *BARAO de TEFFE*—(other papers listed it as: *Baras de Tiffe; Barrao De Teffe; Baris de Tiffe; Barrao de Taffe*, etc.; believe *Barao de Teffe* is correct); Steamer (some said American, but can't find it in records for U.S. vessels), foundered in the Gulf of Florida around January, 1874. Crew were rescued by the ship *Fair Wind* and taken to England. Assume it is American as a couple of British papers later reported that the mayor of Bristol, on behalf of the American President, gave a medal to the captain of the *Fair Wind* for saving the crew of the *Barao de Teffe*. *Source:* SMN, 2/5/1874; NYH, 2/7/1874; BP, 2/7/1874; Galveston Daily News; Sunderland Daily Echo and Shipping Gazette, 7/17/1874. (8)

2) *J. P. CONERGY*—Schooner, of Frederica, Delaware, from Delaware for New Smyrna, to pick up a cargo of live oak for the government, sank inside New Smyrna Harbor, early January, 1874. She was raised by the steam salvage tug *Godfrey Keebler* and was being towed to Jacksonville, February 10,

1874, when a storm forced the *Keebler* to abandon the schooner, but not before saving the crew on board. The schooner eventually sank in eight fathoms of water, approximately 25 miles to the southward of Mosquito Inlet. The wrecking schooner *B & J Baker* salvaged the starboard anchor along with 45 fathoms of chain, one six-inch Andrew's pump, and the engine and boiler with donkey complete. Most of the rigging was already salvaged. *Source:* SMN, 2/12/1874, 5/18/1875. (6)

3) *NATHANIEL*—Norwegian Bark, 642 tons, Capt. J. Berg, from Liverpool for New Orleans and Pensacola, went ashore and bilged during a heavy fog on Santa Rosa Island, in ballast, about 25 miles east of the Pensacola Light, March 16, 1874. A total loss. Crew saved. Her bow was now in five feet of water, and her stern buried in the sand. Hull, stores, rigging, etc., sold for $4,046. *Source:* 35; New Orleans Republican, 3/26/1874; LL, 3/19/1874; SMG 5/6/1874. Likely saved, as still listed in service for a few more years.

4) *HARMONY*—Brigantine, of and built at St. John, N.B in 1865, 307 tons, 115' x 28' x 12', from Matanzas for Philadelphia. Was abandoned due to a storm in 1874, at Lat. 30°57' N, Long. 78°W. Possible Florida wreck. *Source:* 20; 37. (8)

1) Page 82. *Eveline*—Sloop, of Key West, 7.17 tons. *Source:* 10.

2) Page 122. *Gov Troup*—Was saved. *Source:* SMN, 8/8/1874.

3) Page 122. *Mississippi*—Was saved and taken to Key West. *Source:* SMN, 7/30/1874.

4) Page 179. *Nettie Langdon* (correct)—Built at Boston, 303.57 tons, 129' x 30' x 10'. *Source:* 10.

5) Page 194. *Nick King*—Built by Harlan and Hollingsworth of Wilmington in 1865, 165' x 26' x 8', had two inclined engines. After the war, was fitted out as a luxurious steamer with 26 staterooms, a lower dining room, and a 102-foot upper saloon. It did wreck in Georgia in 1873, but may have been salvaged and wrecked again on the St. John's, though I couldn't verify this. What I could verify was that it was still listed in service in *Merchant Vessels of the U.S.* up until 1876. *Source:* SMN, 12/18/1868.

1875

1) *KATE S. COOK*—Schooner, 43 tons, built at Absecon, New Jersey, in 1863, of New York, Capt. Hayne or Haig, from Jacksonville, went ashore November 26, 1875, near Mosquito Inlet after parting her chains. A total wreck, very little cargo saved. *Source:* SMN, 12/11/1875. (6)

2) *ANNA*—Norwegian bark, 560 tons, Capt. Thorstenen (other source says Capt. Reed, who had just purchased her from Spanish owners), from Barrow, England, for Pensacola, wrecked on Santa Rosa Island in rough seas, about three miles east of Ft. Pickens, opposite the city, March 31, 1875, and they cut away the masts to prevent further damage. Crew were taken off by a smack and made camp on the island. She grounded in 12 feet of water but was driven up into shallower water. Hull seemed sound and they hoped to remove the 300 tons of ballast in her hold when the seas subsided to see if

An 1869 add for the *Nick King*. *Savannah Morning News*, July 1870.

she could be saved. The hull and materials were sold, April 7, 1875. *Source:* LL, 4/22/1875; NYH, 4/12/1875; The New Orleans Bulletin. 4/6/1875. (1)

3) **Unk. WRECK**—Was reported in December 1875 that portions of a wreck were found about one degree north of the St. John's Bar. Believed to be a schooner about 100 tons. *Source:* NYH, 12/21/1875. (6)

1) Page 28. *Nettle* or *Nettie*—Was one of three wrecks reported in the *Boston Post*, February 28, 1876, as an obstruction at the entrance to Pensacola: "The wreck of the pilot boat *Nettie*, lying 3/4-mile N by E 1/4 E from the outer bar buoy, in 4-1/2 fathoms water, with her bowsprit awash; the flagstaff of Ft. Pickens bearing, from the wreck, NNW 1/4 W, distant 1-3/4 miles, and the flagstaff of Ft. McRae NW by W, distant 2-3/4 miles." *Annual List of Merchant Vessels* lists a *Nettle*, 31.47 tons, of Pensacola, so that's most likely correct.

2) Page 82. *Mountain Home*—Of New Orleans, 6.43 tons. *Source:* 10.

3) Page 82. *Nordkyn*—Of Tønsberg, 548 tons, built 1849 at Newburyport, 132' x 27' x 19', Norway. From Tabasco, Mexico, for Queenstown. Though reported as wrecked on Coffins Patch, Vacas Key, and near Alligator Reef, believe Coffins Patch is correct. Believe this is the bark *Nordkyn*, built in America in 1849, and refurbished in 1863. Rigging, anchors and chain to be sold by U.S. Marshal. *Source:* 35; 37; LL, 1875; SMN, 9/20/1875; NYH, 10/2/1875.

4) Page 82. *Sparkling Water*—Was saved. *Source:* 10.

5) Page 82. *Athenaise*—Built 1856 at St. John, 171' x 36' x 22'. *Source:* 37.

6) Page 122. *Evandale*—Built 1862 at Quebec, 202' x 37' x 23'. *Source:* 37.

7) Page 122. *Florence Rogers*—Of New York, 406.33 tons, she was saved, as listed in service for many years after. *Source:* 10.

8) Page 146. *J.W. Coffin*—Believe saved as listed in service in 1878. *Source:* 10.

9) Page 146. *Western Empire*—Ship, 1,245 tons, built 1862 at Quebec, 190.8' x 38.1' x 22.9', sheathed with yellow (composite) metal, of London, Capt. Bertie. Had left Pensacola for Grimsby, September 11, 1875, with 1,700 loads of timber. She wrecked about 150 miles south of Pensacola during the late gale. The captain refused to leave her when sighted by the *City of Liverpool*, as he believed they could save the ship. She was dismasted and waterlogged and soon began to break up and had to be abandoned and all took to the boats. One boat was lost with seven men off St. Vincent's Island, the other 17 arrived at Pensacola in a destitute condition. What

happened to the ship after that was described in the *Pensacola Gazette* and reported again in the *Savannah Morning News*, part of which said:

> The abandoned ship has been found, after making a voyage of over five hundred miles without a hand at the helm. Caught in the reflux current, which must have set out southwest from the Bight of Florida after the storm which drove a surcharge of water up into the angle formed by the peninsular coastline, the masterless ship drifted within the influence of the Gulf Stream, was swept through the Strait of Florida and on towards the Atlantic, until she was discovered thirty miles north of Jupiter Inlet, swinging to an anchor. When we reported the disaster, it was stated that in order to enable the hoisting out of the boats both anchors were let go to act as a drag to bring the ship's head to the wind. The length of chain allowed was thirty-five fathoms. Thus the ship has piloted herself remarkably well in navigating round the dangerous coast of Florida, with its keys and reefs, in never less than two hundred and ten feet of water, until her anchor finally reached bottom and brought her to in one of the most frequented of ocean pathways. But for her anchors swinging overboard the ship would probably have gone on with the stream to the coasts of Europe." *Source:* SMN, 9/28/1875, 11/3/1875; LR, 1875; The Andrew County Republican, 10/1/1875.

10) Page 175. *Lizzie Baker*—Built 1864 at Albany, 506 tons, 178' x 29' x 9'. *Source:* 37.

1876

1) *Spanish WRECK*—Unknown date of sinking, but was one of three wrecks reported in the *Boston Post*, February 28, 1876, as an obstruction at the entrance to Pensacola: "A wreck known as the *Spanish Wreck*, on the middle ground, at the harbor entrance, lying in 2-1/4 fathoms water, with one timber awash, nearly in the Bar Range; the flagstaff of Ft. Pickens bearing NE 1/2 N, distant 3/4 mile, and the flagstaff of Ft. McRae NW by W 3/4 W, distant 5/8 mile." *Source:* BP, 2/28/1876. *Note:* The schooner Susan struck this wreck in February and sunk but was saved. (1)

2) *YOLO* or *YOLE*—Both *Lloyd's List* of May 8, 1876, and the *Savannah Morning News* of 6/2/1876, report this wreck, though information is quite different. *Lloyd's* says the Austrian brigantine *Yole*, Capt. Billon, from Pensacola, wrecked on Loo Key. The Savannah paper say the Russian brig *Yolo*, Captain Rodoslovich, from Pensacola, with timber, ran onto Loo Key Reef, Sat. April 29, 1876, about 10 p.m., and at 2 a.m., was discovered on fire and she burned to the water's edge. Wreck was sold at auction for $55. I believe the correct name is *Yole*, as the *New York Herald* paper listed her as arrived and departed from Pensacola in April, though when arrived it said it was a

Russian brig, and when departed said an Austrian brig, though had Capt. Rodoslovich listed both times. (3)

3) *MOHAWK*—Schooner, Capt. Sweeting, from Nassau for Key West, with fruit and 30 passengers. Put into Tavernier the night of October 18 during a storm, but after parting her cables, the captain drove her ashore on Key Largo. Sails and materials saved. *Source:* BP, 11/18/1876; SMN, 11/4/1876. (4)

1) Page 82. *Jalapa* (correct)—Built 1860 at Reiherstieg of oak, of Hamburg, 250 tons, 109' x 26' x 15'. *Source:* 37.

2) Page 83. *Mollie Emma*—Believed saved as a *Mollie Emma* is still listed in service afterwards. *Source:* 10.

3) Page 83. *City of Houston*—Reported to have gotten off and arrived at Key West; was reloading for Galveston. *Source:* BP, 11/1/1876.

4) Page 83. *Galveston*—Of and from Mystic, for Key West, 622 tons, 140' x 36' x 15', built 1866 by C.H. Mallory and Co., of oak, and sheathed with yellow metal. Wrecked at Duck Key, October 22, and attempts to save her were abandoned late January, 1877. *Source:* 37; BP, 2/2/1877.

5) Page 122. *Charles A. Coulomb* (correct)—Of Philadelphia, 361.88 tons, built 1873 at Milton Delaware. *Source:* 10; 37.

6) Page 123. *Godfrey Keebler*—Of and from Fernandina bound for Galveston, 121.88 tons, 108 HP engine, in ballast. Wrecked October 17, 1876. *Source:* 10.

7) Page 123. *David Nichols*—Capt. Wyman, 205.43 tons, built 1845 at Searsport, Maine, 94' x 24' x 9', of Islesboro, Maine, from Philadelphia bound for Mobile, with coal, foundered, October 19, 1876, four miles south of Fowey Rocks. Captain and crew arrived at Key West, October 28. *Source:* 10; 37; BP, 11/1/1876.

8) Page 123. *W.R. Knighton*—Reported to have been gotten off and taken to Key West, October 28. *Source:* BP, 11/1/1876.

9) Page 123. *Catherine Thomas*—built 1848 at New Haven, 71 tons. *Source:* LRA, 1876.

10) Page 175. *Rosa del Turia* (correct)—Of and built at Valencia, 460 tons, 164' x 32' x 19'. *Source:* 37; BP, 5/29/1876.

1877

1) *SPECULATOR*—Ship, of Yarmouth, Nova Scotia, built 1864 at Yarmouth, 747 tons, 172.3' x 33.5' x 19.5', sheathed with felt and copper, Capt. Pittman. Left Hamburg on November 8, 1976, bound for New Orleans, in ballast. She wrecked on Dog Rocks on the night of January 11, 1877. Captain and four crew made Key West in their boat and the rest stayed on board. The schooner *Arietas* picked up the remainder of the crew on January 19, and saved some materials which sold for $800 at Key West. *Source:* 20; LR, 1876; SMN, 1/17/1877; NYH, 2/1/1877. (3)

2) *JOSEPHINE*—Schooner, from New York for St. Augustine, discharged her cargo there and was bound for Jacksonville. She left St. Augustine February 15 and struck going over the St. Augustine Bar with a pilot on board. She only had one anchor, having lost the other in New York Harbor, and let it out but it failed to hold her and she "bounded over the bank and into the slough near the North Beach, upon which she was soon hard on." *Source:* BP, 11/23–27/1877. (6)

3) *CADIZ*—Bark (one paper says Norwegian), from Pensacola for London, wrecked on the North Shoals, Tortugas, March 26, 1877. Vessel a total loss, crew and some cargo and rigging saved. *Source:* BP, 4/9/1877. (3)

4) *LEWIS S. DAVIS*—Schooner, 320 tons, built 1853 at Stony Brook, of Brookhaven, 118' x 29' x 11', from Cardenas for Baltimore, with sugar, was abandoned at sea, April 1877. Crew arrived at Fernandina. Possible Florida wreck. *Source:* 37; SMN, 4/18/1877. (8)

5) *PIONEER*—Steamer, 44 tons, built 1874. One of Captain Lund's boats, caught fire mid-April at 2 a.m. on the Indian River, while anchored close to shore near Sand Point. The watchman was only person on board and awoke to find the ship on fire. He got to shore and notified Captain Lund, who then scuttled her where she burned to the water's edge, a total loss, though the boiler may be saved. *Source:* 7; SMN, 4/21/1877. (7)

1) Page 28. *George Gilchrest*—Built 1865 at St. George, Maine, of Boston, 126' x 30' x 17'. Another report says: Capt. Urann, was disabled night of September 22, 1877, and abandoned when about 50 miles off St. George's Island. All crew saved. *Source:* 37; SMN, 10/20/1877.

2) Page 29. *F.L. Richardson*—Was saved. *Source:* 10.

3) Page 29. *Eliza Jane*—Listed at 46.44 tons, of Mobile. *Source:* 10.

4) Page 83. *Emilie*—Foundered after a collision in six fathoms, at Lat. 26°14' N, Long. 81°52' W. Two survivors were found wading in the water near Harbor Key, one who had become completely insane. Another passenger was

found floating on the skylight. *Source:* Sullivan County Union, 1/10/1877; Columbus Daily enquirer, 1/3/1877.

5) Page 83. *Wm. M. Jones*—Built 1871 at Brookhaven, 126' x 30' x 14'. *Source:* 37.

6) Page 83. *Meggie*—Believe 161 tons, 99' x 21' x 12', built of oak. *Source:* 37.

7) Page 123. *Sverige* (correct)—Built 1857, 142' x 29.6' x 16.6', 424 tons. *Source:* 37.

8) Page 123. *Veto* (correct name)—Schooner was saved. *Source:* 10.

9) Page 123. *Memphis*—Not listed in 1878, 95' x 24' x 11'. *Source:* 37.

10) Page 124. *Merrie England*—Was the last vessel built by Thomas Hobkirk at Whitby in 1862 of oak, 444 tons, 129' x 29' x 18″. Reported as wrecked, December 13, 1877. *Source:* 30; 37.

11) Page 124. *Energia*—Italian bark, 514 tons, of and built at Genoa of oak, 135' x 31' x 19', Capt. G. Cervetto, from New Orleans for Queenstown, wrecked on French Reef, December 31, 1877, and reported would probably be a total loss. *Source:* 37; LL, 1/4-15/1878. (4)

12) Page 146. *Protector*—See photos on next page.

13) Page 176. *Frank E. Stone*—From St. Lucie for New Smyrna, 16.75 tons, wrecked on Mosquito Inlet Bar, a total loss. *Source:* 10; LL, 1877.

14) Page 194. *Lollie Boy*—Capt. E. W. Jones, struck a snag coming down the Ocklawaha in about 18 feet of water, about 15 miles from the St. John's. *Source:* SMN, 11/15/1877.

1878

Another September Hurricane.

1) *OCEAN PEARL*—Schooner, Capt. Henry Fitzgerald, of Baltimore, 124.71 tons, from Porto Bello with coconuts, wrecked on the Florida coast near New Smyrna during the September hurricane. Crew saved. *Source:* 10; BP, 10/4/1878.

2) *BEAUMANOIR*—Brig, 257 tons, built 1867 at Prince Edward Island, 109' x 25.5' x 13.2', Capt. Thomas, of Liverpool. Left Liverpool May 26, 1878, with a cargo of coal for Havana. She left Havana September 3, 1878, with a cargo of sugar bound for New York. On the 5th, the Captain took a bearing at 4 p.m. and were at Lat. 25°24'N, Long. 79°50'W. At 6:15 a.m. on the 5th,

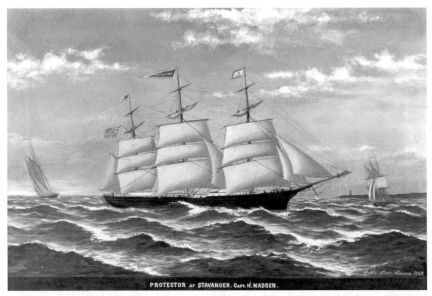

Painting of the Norwegian ship *Protector*, by Anders Ling. Courtesy: © MUST- Stavenger Maritime Museum, Norway.

Some artifacts recovered from the wreck of the *Protector*.

she wrecked on a reef in a heavy gale. On board were the captain and eight crewmen plus the captain's son. They remained on the wreck until the 9th when she began to break up. A piece of the starboard side fell off and they used this as a raft and were carried away by the currents. They had no provisions on the raft and soon one man became delirious, fell or walked off, and drowned. Three others saw land and tried to swim for it and were also drowned. Afterward, the captain's son died in his arms while on the raft. On the 11th, the survivors were picked up by the Swedish bark *Asteroid* and taken to Queenstown. *Source:* London Daily News, 10/12/1878; Liverpool Mercury, 10/30/1878, 11/2/1878; LR, 1878. (8)

1) Page 28. **Besuluida**—Also listed as **Belinda** (believe this is correct). Schooner, 13 tons, from Pensacola bound for Apalachicola, with corn, flour, etc., stranded on the outside beach at Cape San Blas, January 31, 1878. Four lives lost. *Source:* 10.

2) Page 29. **Rhoda B. Taylor**—Believe saved as listed in service a few more years after.

3) Page 29. **Monadnock**—Of New Orleans, 141.525 tons. *Source:* 10.

4) Page 84. **Lewis T. Stocker** (correct)—Was 364.10 tons, may have been saved as listed in service the next year, but not after that. *Source:* 10.

5) Page 124. **Arratoon Apcar**—Built 1861 at Renfrew, Scotland, iron hull, copper fastened, 1,493 tons, 261.7' x 35.1' x 25'. Had 1,243 tons of coal on board. She broke up and very little saved. *Source:* 37; Reading Mercury (England), 3/2/1878.

6) Page 124. **Hope**—Possibly saved as a *Hope* of 371 tons is still listed in service for a few more years. *Source:* LR, 1881.

7) Pages 146–47. **Providencia**—Brig, 129 tons. *Source:* 10.

8) Page 147. **Alexander Nichols**—Built at Cherryfield, Maine, 110' x 26' x 9'. Wrecked September 7, 1878, 1.5 miles south of New River, about 23 miles north of station #5 (Biscayne Bay). Storm was so rough, that the keeper could not search the beaches until the 10th. Beach was cut away in many areas around the station. He found five of the crew that day to the north in bad condition, and half naked. They subsisted on dead fish which had washed ashore. The keeper was barely able to get them to the station. They were given food and clothing and stayed for the next seven days until they could make for Key West. After she stranded, the captain, second mate, and another man reached the shore on top of the forward house which had been torn from the deck by the sea. Another was washed ashore, and the fifth swam to shore. The last man, the first mate, was lost when he got into

Wreck of the Spanish brig *Providencia* in 1878. Courtesy of the State Archives of Florida.

the small boat when they first stranded, and was bailing it out when it was capsized, drowning him. His body was found a few days later 17 1/2 miles from the wreck, by the keeper of the Ft. Lauderdale Station, and was buried by him. They had also lost two men during the storm at sea who had been washed overboard. *Source:* 10; 37.

9) Page 147. *Sevre*—Had a crew of 10, with a general cargo. She ran into a gale on September 6 and weathered it until the 11th when she was driven ashore, 16 miles north of station #1 (Indian River). All swan to shore safely, but one man drowned attempting to swim back to the ship. Eight of the men were found by a man named Peter Wright, who took them to Titusville. The remaining man was found by the keeper of the Indian River House of Refuge in bad shape, and he stayed for 10 days at the station until well enough to leave. *Source:* 10.

10) Page 147. *Virgin de las Nieves*—Spanish bark, of Havana or Barcelona, built 1851 at Grafton, England, 108.9' x 22.3' x 14.1'. The captain and the cook were washed overboard in the storm and lost, the remaining 11 crew members were found by the keeper of the Orange Grove House of Refuge, where they rested for three days. *Source:* 10; 37.

11) Page 147. *Norina*—Capt. Sutora, had sprung a leak off Florida, March 31, 1879, and soon went ashore, 10 miles north of Station #2 (Gilbert's Bar). All 13 of the crew landed in the ship's boat, but lost all provisions when she capsized. Three went for help and reached Gilbert's Bar Station,

April 1. The keeper took them in his boat up the Indian River until they were opposite the wreck. They cut their way through the mangrove swamp and reached the beach and found the rest of the crew. The wreck was about 1/4 mile offshore, with the bow facing the shore, sails set, but the seas were so high, they could not attempt to reach her. The keeper took all the men back to the station to rest and get fed. The next day they returned to the wreck, and seas being much calmer, were able to get the crew's clothes and other items. They stayed at the station for the next five days. The ship and cargo were a total loss. Was built 1868 at Trieste. *Source:* 10.

12) Page 176. *Florida*—Capt. Bagley. From Belfast, Maine, for Jacksonville, with ice. Probably the 286.82 tons, Belfast schooner *Florida*. Was still listed in 1879 so likely saved. *Source:* 10.

13) Pages 176–77. *Elim*—Bark, two-year old vessel, Capt. Hakke, from Santa Anna, Mexico, with mostly mahogany. Crew saved, vessel and cargo a total loss. Believe the 468-ton bark, of Arendal, 117' x 29' x 18'. *Source:* 37; BP, 10/2/1878.

14) Page 177. *Pinta*—Capt. C. W. Townsend (owner), of Philadelphia, from Cartagena for Philadelphia, with coconuts, ran into a hurricane on September 7, and by the 10th had lost all sails and one mast. The schooner was blown upon the shoals and partially capsized near Mosquito Inlet, but was close enough to shore that all on board were able to swim to shore. *Source:* SMN, 9/19/78.

15) Page 177. *Abbie S. Oakes*—From Boston for Jacksonville, of Bangor, 74.23 tons. Lost her anchors and washed far up on the beach. *Source:* 10; BP, 9/18/1878.

16) Page 177. *Sally Brown*—Of Boston, 426.9 tons, built 1862 at Newburyport, 125' x 30' x 15', Capt. Pressey, from Pensacola for Santos. Was abandoned September 8, 1878, and later washed ashore about 12 miles south of Mosquito Inlet. *Source:* 10; 37; BP, 10/8/1878.

17) Page 177. *Hattie Ross*—Capt. Coleman, of Portland, Maine, 182.53 tons, built 1858 at Falmouth, Maine, 95' x 26' x 8', from Old Harbor, Jamaica bound for New York, with sugar and logwood, stranded 15 miles south of Cape Canaveral, September 9, 1878. A total loss. *Source:* 10; 37; BP, 10/4/78.

18) Page 177. *Mary A. Holt*—Of and built at Ellsworth, Maine, in 1867, 193.31 tons, 105' x 28' x 9'. *Source:* 10; 37.

19) Page 177. *Lizzie L. Smith*—Built 1877 at Crisfield, Maryland, 54 tons, 49-5/10' x 17-4/10' x 4-8/10'. *Source:* 37.

20) Page 177. *City of Houston*—Verified it didn't sink off Florida. Captain of the Steamer *United States* saw the wreck the few days later, "15 miles SSE of Frying Pan Lightship in 13 fathoms, her topmasts about 15' out of water." *Source: BP,* 10/29/1878.

21) Page 225. *Lizzie Dakers* (correct)—Built at St. Martins, New Brunswick, 83.7' x 25' x 9'. *Source:* 37.

1879

1) *LA GAULE*—French bark, Capt. Opdebael, from Pensacola for Marseilles, with lumber, wrecked on the Tortugas Reef, February 2, 1879, a total loss. Captain and 14 crewmen took to the boats and were rescued two days later by the Finnish bark *Emeli,* and later transferred to the steamer *Secret* on February 5, which landed them at Jacksonville. *Source: SMN,* 2/11/1879; LL, 2/19/1879. (3)

2) *MINNEHAHA*—Schooner, Capt. Porter, from Pascagoula, wrecked on the Florida coast. *Source: BP* 2/14/1879. (8)

3) *BROTHER'S PRIDE*—Bark, built 1866 at Courtenay Bay, St. John, New Brunswick, of St. John, New Brunswick, 443 tons, 134.6' x 30' x 12.9'. From Cardenas, supposedly with melada (a very thick and valuable molasses), was scuttled off the Florida coast, May 1879. Capt. Tower was later arrested and put on trial for purposely sinking the vessel in an insurance scam. According to witnesses, including a stevedore who testified, the captain took a worthless cargo of casks of dirty water on board at Cardenas. When off the Florida shore in calm water, he bored holes in her hull and it was abandoned to sink. She was insured (have two figures, $38,000 and $70,000). I don't know the outcome of the trial. *Source:* 20; Atlantic Telegraph, 2/18/1880; Bradford Era, 4/18/1880. (8)

4) *IDA SMITH*—Schooner, built 1865 at Esteville, wrecked 12 miles south of St. Augustine, and at low tide was high and dry. She regularly sailed between Jacksonville and Nassau. *Source: Philadelphia Time,* 8/4/1879; NYH, 8/5/1879. (6)

5) *GEORGE HARRIS*—Brig, 221.62 tons, built 1852 at Prospect, Maine, 107' x 26' x 10', from Boston bound for Pensacola to get lumber, supposedly sprung a leak during a storm off Cape Canaveral, September 16, 1879, was reported: "after twelve hours at the pumps, with six feet of water in her hold, she was beached." All the crew were saved. The wreck was investigated by Thomas S. Ellis, agent for the underwriter, who came to a much different conclusion as to how she wrecked: "found a plank bored by an auger, the log falsified, there having been no gale, and only 28 inches of water in her

hold." Another insurance scam? *Source:* 10; 37; SMN, 9/23/1879; The New Orleans Daily Democrat, 10/20/1879. (6)

6) *ANNA BELL HYER*—Schooner, 150.67 tons, of and built at Milford, Delaware, 90' x 28' x 8', for Jacksonville, with terra cotta pipes, struck on the St. John's Bar, October 5, 1879, and was a total loss. *Source:* 10; 37; Alexandria Gazette, 10/7/1879. (6)

7) *BAYARD*—British iron steamer, of Newcastle, 964 tons, was a new ship just launched in June 1878, at Stockton-On-Tees, by Pearse and Co., 240' x 33' x 24', with a compound 130 HP engine, double-bottom, Capt. J. Everett. She left New Orleans, December 4, 1878, for Rouen with 24 men on board. Had a cargo of 60,000 barrels of wheat, when she ran into a storm on December 8 in the Gulf of Florida and the cargo shifted. On the 10th, the waves had crashed through the engine room skylight putting out the fires and she began to sink. Two of the four lifeboats were stove in, and the crew hastily put provisions in both remaining boats (a lifeboat and quarterboat) and cast off, and as soon as they did, the steamer sank and a large wave capsized both boats. The quarterboat sank and only two were able to swim to the lifeboat (the others drowned). They got it righted and the survivors managed to get back on board, though less than an hour later it was capsized again, which they again righted, but full of water. With no provisions and being very cold, one by one they lost their grip and were washed overboard or eaten by the sharks which were following them constantly. Soon only two men were left, the carpenter Edward Simmons and a seaman Thomas Kelly. They managed some drinking water by laying on their backs and letting whatever small amount of rainwater or mist collect there. On the 17th, they were spotted by the Spanish brigantine *Encarnacion* from Fernandina bound for Europe, and were rescued. *Source:* Western Morning News, 1/18/1879; London Week News, 1/25/1879; Belfast Morning News, 1/11–20/1879; LR, 1879. (8)

1) Page 177. *Belle of Texas*—River paddle steamer, 403 tons, of Memphis, from the Mississippi River bound for Jacksonville, wrecked eight miles south of Mosquito Inlet, the night of February 19, 1879. Crew saved. *Source:* 10; Atlanta Daily Constitution, 2/25/1879.

2) Page 177. *Destino A*—Of and built at Fiume in 1871, 120.3' x 27.5' x 17.7'. *Source:* 40.

3) Page 194. *L.T. Knight*—Built at Frankfort, Maine, of Camden, 106' x 27.6' x 9.4'. *Source:* 37.

1880

1) August 1880 HURRICANE.

a) *LONG REACH*—Brig, 226 tons, 113.9' x 28.3' x 9.9', built 1868 at Bath, Maine, from Apalachicola for Philadelphia, with lumber, stranded at Turtle Mound (one source says 12 miles south of Mosquito Inlet), August 30, 1880. Vessel and cargo a total loss, crew saved. *Source:* 6; 10; BP 9/9/1880; SMN, 9/8–11/1880. (6)

b) *ROSA J. EPPINGER*—Three-masted schooner, built at Port Jefferson in 1874, 293.44 tons, of New York, 145' x 32' x 10', Capt. Bayless. Left Cedar Keys, August 18, 1880, bound for New York, with 245,000 feet of yellow pine lumber. One source says she drove ashore 16 miles north of Cape Canaveral, another says 18 miles north of Cape Canaveral abreast of Titusville, August 9, 1880. Captain's son (the second mate), and another man were washed overboard and lost. Reported in the *Daily Gazette*, 9/8/1880, a passenger reported this about the wreck:

We left Cedar Keys heavily loaded. The Captain was powerless to save the ship, the storm was so severe. You never saw anything like it. The schooner was tossed about as though it was an egg shell." Some of the tale reported by the captain in *The Sun* said: "At the time the second mate went overboard the deck load shifted, covering up the pumps. She was leaking badly at the time. The wind was northeast. At 4 A.M. the mainsail was blown clear of the bolt rope. The fore staysail and jib were already gone. The vessel struck at 10 A.M. on Sunday, abreast of Titusville, about eighteen miles to the northward of Cape Canaveral. The cabin was full of water, the partitions and everything washed out, the sea making a clean breach clear through it. The Captain, first mate, cook, three sailors, and four passengers reached the shore. The schooner is a total wreck. Three-fourths of the cargo was washed overboard. The rest lies on the beach.

Source: Ibid; BP, 9/9/80; SMN, 10/19/1880, 9/8–20/80; The Sun, 9/14/1880; LRA, 1880. (6)

c) *Two other VESSELS*—Stranded north of New Smyrna Inlet, and there was a large ship (2,000 tons), newly coppered and dismasted, in the breakers near St. Sebastian with her crew on board. *Source:* Ibid, BP, 9/9/1880. (6)

d) *ALPHONSE et MARIE*—Bark, of Bordeaux, built 1846 at Newcastle, of oak, 112.7' x 27.5' x 17.4'. From New Orleans bound for Rouen, with a cargo of corn. A vessel was reported sunk 12 or 12.5 miles in 54 feet of water off Cape Canaveral, with three masts sticking out of the water, supposedly made of teak. When the wrecking steamer *Resolute* investigated and tore off the deck, she found a cargo of corn, so believed it is the

Alphonse. A dead sailor also washed up on the beach ear Mosquito Inlet with a life preserver that had the name *Alphonse et. Marie* on it. Believed all on board were lost. The floating hull was blown up by Messr. Baker Bros. *Note:* It was also reported to be the *Alphonse & Marie*, also of Bordeaux, but that continued to be listed in service. *Source:* 37; SMN, 10/19/1880; BP, 10/4/1880; LL, 10/5/1880; LR, 1880. (6)

e) *MIRIAM*—Bark, of and built at Camden, Maine, in 1877, 598 tons, 144' x 31' x 17', from Pensacola bound for Rio, with lumber. The forecastle with the name *Miriam* washed ashore 15 miles from Matanzas Inlet. It was believed that the vessel that was bottom up at Matanzas Inlet was the *Miriam*, though were still investigating. Part of the stern of a vessel with "Camden" written on it was also found on the beach near the St. John's Bar which was likely part of this vessel. *Source:* 37; SMN, 10/19/1880; BP, 10/1–4/1880; Daily Dispatch, 9/21/1880. (6)

f) *ADA J. SIMONTON*—Three-masted schooner, of Rockland, Maine, 295.49 tons, built 1872 at Camden, Maine, 125' x 28.8' x 11.5', Capt. Parker, from Pensacola bound for Boston, with lumber, went ashore near Mosquito Inlet near another bark. Crew saved. The *Boston Globe* printed the story from the account of crewman James Thompson:

We left Pensacola, bound for Boston, on the 17th of August. We had bad weather almost from the very start; head winds all along. Every day was worse than the previous one. The wind blew with terrible force and the waves were mountain high. Sea after sea swept over our little craft, and we had no chance to sleep. Everything was soaked with water. Even on the upper bunks there was no such thing as sleeping. The vessel had a cargo of lumber, and almost every-thing on deck was swept away. We were driven in towards the shore steadily, and, at last, on Sunday week last, the vessel went ashore seven miles from Mosquito Inlet, near Port Orange, Fla. It was between 12 o'clock noon and 1 p.m., and the wind was blowing heavily from the northeast. She went right on the breakers about three-quarters of a mile from the shore. The breakers beat with tremendous force and washed right over the deck, and it was with the greatest difficulty the men saved themselves from being swept away. We lashed ourselves to the davits aft and waited there as best we could, and unable to do a thing to save ourselves. There were eight persons aboard in all. Captain Parker, the mate, Lawson, the steward, four seamen and one passenger named Ballard. We lowered the two boats, but both of them sunk almost as soon as they touched the water. Some of the men attempted to get into them and were nearly drowned. The breakers were too strong and no boat could stand them. We remained there till about 10 o'clock, when we Saw the vessel was breaking up. The captain told us our only chance was to get on the deck house and lash ourselves to the framework. It might be swept off by a breaker and floated. Before going up there he said to us that as we were all together for probably the last time, and might never eat another meal, we had better venture below for a few minutes and have a feed. We went down and ate a hasty meal, captain and all together, and fortified ourselves with a good drink. Then we went up on the deck-house, lashed ourselves as securely as we could to the iron framework and lay there expecting death at any moment. The ship was rapidly going to pieces and there seemed no hope for us. The breakers washed over us, and at last a tremendous one came and swept the deck-house right off. We thought it was all over with us, and for a few moments it was awful, but the deck-house remained top up and was floated rapidly toward the shore on the surf. The wind and surf were going in one direction, and we were soon deposited on the shore.

Source: 10; 37; Boston Weekly Globe, 9/15/1880; SMN, 9/6/1880. (6)

g) *FELISA*—Spanish bark, of Barcelona, built 1865 at Sestria Pon'te, 305 tons, 122' x 28' x 18', Capt. J. Anyo. Left S. Pass, New Orleans, August 13, bound for Barcelona, with staves. Ran into the hurricane 30 miles off the Florida coast, and was abandoned in a sinking condition August 30, 34 miles SE of Cape Canaveral, while anchored up in 14 fathoms of water. The crew were picked up by the steamer *New York*, Capt. Quick. She was later found by the wrecking steamer *Resolute*, and towed to St. Augustine, where she was anchored. She later parted her chains and went ashore in the breakers. The cargo of staves was being saved by the wreckers and the vessel stripped. *Source:* 37; SMN, 10/12/1880; The Dallas Daily Herald, 9/5/1880; NYTR, 9/11/1880; LL, 9/23/1880. (6)

f) *NEW REPUBLIC*—Bark, Capt. Dix, of and built at Quebec in 1870 by McKay, 580 tons, 148' x 31.5' x 17.6', sheathed with felt and yellow (composite) metal, from Brunswick, Georgian, bound for Rio de Janeiro, with lumber, wrecked off New Smyrna (Mosquito) Inlet. She left Brunswick, August 27, and by the next day the winds picked up and by the 30th was a full hurricane. She began to take on water and the crew manned the pumps. She lost her sails and by the next day with winds from the east, she had four feet of water in her hold. At 8:40 p.m. she was drove into the breakers and struck bottom which swayed her head toward the shore. All hands took to the rigging as waves swept over her deck. They had to cut away the mainmast at 1:00 a.m. to keep her upright with waves still breaking over her. By 4 a.m., the after house was stove in, and the vessel broke in two. When daylight came, they saw they were only about a half mile from shore. They waited until the waves calmed down and lowered the longboat which they all got into and safely made it to shore, five miles north of New Smyrna Inlet. The anchors, chains, davits, etc., were later salvaged and taken to Jacksonville.

They later related how they saw the *City of Vera Cruz* at 10 p.m. on the 28th laboring heavily, and not long after that the brig *Long Reach. Source:* SMN, 9/13/1880, 11/26/1880; BP, 9/14/1880; LR, 1879. (6)

g) *CAPTAIN MADSEN*—Norwegian bark of Sarpsborg, 510 tons, built 1858 at Lormont, France, 134' x 29' x 18'. From Pensacola for Leith, Scotland, with lumber, was abandoned off Florida and the crew took to the boats and made shore near Jacksonville. She was later found and towed in by three tugs but abandoned again. It was reported she ended up off South Beach, Mayport, and went to pieces on October 1, with much of her lumber strewn along the beach for miles. *Source:* 37; BP, 9/11/1880; LL, 11/5/1880. (6)

h) *SEA BIRD* and a *Mail Boat*—Reported by a Captain Rodgers of the schooner *Dora Ella*, that two wrecks were seen between Point Derassa (sic) and Key West. One was the schooner *Sea Bird* (likely the 27.8-ton schooner *Sea Bird* of Key West), which was torn to pieces and only the crew saved. The other was a *Mail Boat*, which was a total loss with nothing saved. *Source:* BP, 9/17/1880. (8)

i) The wreckage from two vessels washed up on the beach near the St. John's Bar after the storm. Part of a stern with the word "Camden" (likely from the *Miriam*), and a quarterboard with the partial name "Enoch M." Believe the schooner *ENOCH MOORE*, 313.10 tons, of New York, built 1862 at Wilmington, 121' x 31' x 10', as not listed in American *Lloyd's* in 1881. *Source:* 37; LL, 10/5/1880; SMN, 10/14/1880.

1) Page 124. *Excelsior*—Built at Greenpoint, New York, of oak, 150' x 32' x 18.6'. Wrecked May 1880, not 1879. *Source:* 37; SMN, 5/26/1880.

2) Page 178. *Caroline Eddy*—Brig, 337.55 tons, built 1867 at Brewer, Maine, of Bangor, 110.7' x 27.6' x 14.6'. She left Fernandina for New York on the 27th, and capsized during the August 28 hurricane, then righted and drifted until the 31st when she struck bottom about two miles offshore. Crew made a raft and reached shore, two miles north of Matanzas. An excerpt from the *New York Times* article called *Wrecked on the Florida Coast* stated:

> At midnight all hands went aloft to take in sail, and Capt. Warren took the wheel. A tremendous sea struck the vessel forward, and, sweeping aft, washed away the booby-hatch and yawl-boat. The Captain was knocked down at the wheel and stunned, and when he came to himself he saw none of the crew about him, and was about to plunge overboard and drown himself just as one of the sailors called out to him from the rigging, where all the others had taken refuge. The pumps were choked, the brig filled rapidly, and then she capsized. The men clung to the chain-plates, which alone prevented them from being washed away and drowned. The hurricane was now terrific, and the huge seas frequently swept over the waterlogged wreck. Finally the deck load became loose and was washed away. With it went the foremast, and this caused the brig to slowly right itself again. Some of the crew lashed themselves to the lee side of the mainmast, while others took to the rigging for safety. The provisions and

water had all been washed away, and the men suffered the pangs of thirst and hunger in addition to the exposure. The brig was at the mercy of the waves, and tossed about until the morning of Tuesday, the 31st, when she struck bottom about two miles from the beach.

Source: 10; 37; NYT, 9/17/1880.

1881

1) *AMATI*—Italian bark, 813 tons, 174.1' x 35.8' x 22.7', built 1869, of Genoa, Capt. Casanegro, from Pensacola bound for Glasgow, with lumber, was first reported as wrecked on the Florida Reef. Crew all made it to Key West. She was later found abandoned in a sinking condition in Lat. 22°N, Long. 84°W, on January 31, 1881, by the schooner *Xebec*, who salvaged her boat, some sails and a bell. Possible Florida wreck. *Source:* NYT, 1/27/1881; BP, 2/17/1881; LR, 1880. (8)

2) *A.L. FITCH*—Schooner, Capt. Fitch, from Boston, 57.21 tons, of Bristol, Maine, in ballast, went ashore at Mosquito Inlet, February 2, 1881, vessel a total loss, captain and crew saved. *Source:* 9; BP, 2/11/1881. (*Note:* Merchant Vessels has the *A.L Fitch* listed in service in 1882 and 1883 but not in 1884, but American *Lloyd's Register* only list it in 1881, not in 1882, so likely lost.) (6)

3) *HATTIE S. BISHOP*—Brig, 310.89 tons, of Portland, Maine. *Note:* There was a very heavy gale that struck Pensacola on February 6, 1881, and caused much damage to the wharfs and waterfront there. The following vessels were all blown ashore but refloated: Bark *Isabella Ridley;* bark *Governor Langdon;* brig *H.P. Jones;* schooner *A.L Mitchell;* and Norwegian bark *Camschatka* or *Camschaika.* The brig **Hattie S. Bishop** was also floated, but in October 1881, was listed as sold at public auction at Pensacola for a total of $1,244.95. The principal purchaser was a Mr. Levy who bought the hull, spars and standing rigging for $525. "Mr. Levy has not yet determined what disposition he will make of the craft, but the supposition is that she will be towed into shoal water and made a bonfire of." *Source:* 10; BP, 2/10/1881, 11/3/1881. (1)

4) *TOLOMEO*—Listed as both an Italian and Austrian bark, 498 tons, of and built at Lussinpiccolo in 1878 (or Lussini-now Croatia), Capt. Cosulich, from Galveston for Bremen, with 1,655 bales of cotton, became a total wreck on the Tortugas prior to March 7, 1881. Some cargo was salvaged before she caught fire, and some more was later salvaged found drifting (the *State of Texas* picked up 42 bales while on her voyage), and a couple months later from the wreck itself where she was found in six to seven fathoms of

water near the shoal where she had originally wrecked. Cotton sold at auction in Key West for $9,043.25, and the ship's materials for $142.25. *Source:* 37; LL, 5/24–30/1881, 7/12/1881; NYTR, 3/8/1881. (3)

5) *ALPHONSE*—British brig, 294 tons, built in Quebec in 1870, of Montreal, 107.4' x 27.8' x 13', from Cienfuegos bound for New York, Capt. L. P. Thompson, was abandoned (believe far off the East Florida coast) and crew took to the boat and later rescued by the schooner *MC Mosely.* Possible Florida wreck. *Source:* 37; NYT, 10/10/1881; BP, 8/30/1881. (8)

6) *DELTA*—Norwegian bark, built 1867 at Risør, Norway, Capt. Halvorsen, 475 tons, 120.6' x 29.3' x 17', left Pensacola, September 21, 1881, for Dordrecht, and never heard from again. Norwegian source says stranded and wrecked on the Florida coast. *Source:* 35; BP, 5/26/1882. (8)

7) *I. HOWLAND*—Brig, of Boston, 233.42 tons, built 1868 at Waldoboro, 110' x 28' x 10', from Fernandina for Perth Amboy, with 177,886 feet of lumber. She left Fernandina October 3, 1881, at 6 a.m., and when 20 miles out was hit by a northeast gale. By 9 p.m. that night she sprung a leak and the pumps were manned. By midnight they were losing the battle with the leak, and by 1 a.m. the pumps failed. They made for St. Augustine, and at 9 a.m. on the 4th, they ran ashore about one mile south of the St. Augustine Lighthouse, "The sea making a complete breach over her, and she would prove a total loss." The crew all made it safely ashore but by the 7th, the brig had gone to pieces and the cargo was strewn all along the beach. Much of the lumber was salvaged and later sold at auction. *Source:* 10; 37; BP, 10/12–14/1881. (6)

8) *PRIMA DONNA*—British brig, believe 192 tons, 92' x 20.7' x 14.1', built 1848 at Dartmouth, sheathed with felt and yellow (composite) metal, fastened with iron bolts, stranded in Pensacola Harbor, December 25, 1881. Sold at auction and will be broke up. *Source:* BP, 3/7/1882; LR, 1881. (1)

9) *DOVER*—Screw steamer, Capt. Webb, of Mobile, 300.91 tons, from Havana bound for Mobile via Tampa Bay, was sunk during a storm, December 29, 1881, at the mouth of Tampa Bay, in 20 feet of water and will probably be a total loss. Crew saved. *Source:* NYT, 1/8/1882; BP, 1/9/1882. (2)

1) Page 29. *Jessie Rhnas*—Built in Camden, Maine, 116' x 27.8' x 11'. *Source:* 37.

2) Page 178. *City of Austin*—Capt. Edgar O. Stevens, 224' x 36-3/4' x 20', 1,295 registered tons, built of oak, chestnut and yellow pine, launched at Mystic, Connecticut, in August 1871. Schooner rigged steamer/screw propeller, of Austin, of the Mallory Line. From Nassau bound for New

Providence, with cargo of sugar, cotton, sponges, fruit, vegetables, shells, and furniture. All on board saved. *Source:* NYT, 4/27/1881, 5/1/1881.

3) Page 178. *Albina*—Built 1862 at Portland, Maine of oak, 158' x 33' x 21'. *Source:* 37.

1882

1) *RHODA*—British bark, Capt. Billson. Capsized during a storm the night of September 9, 1882, in Pensacola Harbor. The captain and crew clung to the wreck until rescued. *Source:* 4; Knoxville Daily Herald, 9/12/1882. (1) *Note:* Lloyd's lists a ship *Rhoda*, 1,122 tons, of Quebec, condemned in 1882. Only reference I could find. Possibly the same. See GPS coordinates at end of chapter.

2) *GOVERNOR BLOXHAM*—Quarantine dispatch boat, sank during the same storm as the *Rhoda*, en route from the Quarantine Station, and two men drowned. *Source:* Knoxville Daily Herald, 9/12/1882. (1)

3) *IRIS*—Stern wheel steamer, iron built, foundered on the upper St. John's while crossing Big Lake George during a gale, Monday morning at 3 a.m., November 1882. Foundered midway across the lake. The chief pilot, fireman, a deckhand and the cook drowned. Others were rescued by the steamer *Rosa*. The *Iris* was one of the largest freight boats on the St. John's River. Unknown if salvaged. *Source:* Albert Lea Freeborn County Standard, 11/23/1882; Sacramento Daily Record-Union, 11/8/1882.

4) **Unk. MAIL SLOOP**—Some papers simply reported a mail sloop had capsized near Ft. Myers, and three boys drowned. *Source:* Daily Republican, December 11, 1882.

1) Page 52. *Chimborazo*—Built at Thomaston, Maine in 1851 of oak, 171.3' x 34' x 20'. *Lloyd's List* says ashore at Boca Grande, and also on the beach 10 miles north of Charlotte Harbor, with 10 feet of water in her hold. *Source:* 37; LL, 2/24/1882; LR, 1881–1882.

2) Page 84. *R.B. Gove*—Built 1864 at Rockport, Maine, 123' x 30.5' x 18.3'. *Source:* 37.

2) Page 84. *Island Home*—Was gotten off and taken to Key West. *Source:* BP, 3/11/1882.

3) Page 84. *William S. Farwell* (correct)—Of and built at Rockland, Maine, in 1874, 146.14 tons, 103' x 26' x 7'. The mate and three men took a boat to reach shore when on the Tortugas Reef near the lighthouse, but were blown out to sea, though picked up two days later and taken to Cardiff. The *Farwell*

was got off, taken to Key West, repaired, and sailed again. What's strange is that she was found wrecked again (location unknown, may be Florida). Interesting note from the *Boston Post* of July 6, 1883:

> Subsequently she was found a wreck at anchor and was destroyed by the U.S. ship of war *Towhattan*. The fate of the crew is unknown. Her mate and three men who had left her in a boat when she was at Cedar Keys (probably meant Tortugas), were picked up at sea, taken to Cadiz and have since returned home, but it supposed that Capt. Hunt and those who were with him lost their lives.

Source: 10; 37; Lloyd's East, 10/26/1882.

4) Page 225. *Beunaventura* (correct)—The steamer *Beuenaventura*, which went aground on Rebecca Shoals, discharged 150 bales of cotton, and was pulled off by the U.S. transport *Matchless*, and went to Key West. *Source:* BP, 6/6/1882.

1883

1) Page 85. *Lalia*—Built in 1867 at Green Cove, Nova Scotia, 136' x 29.3' x 14.5'. *Source:* 37.

2) Page 225. *Lepanto* (correct)—Bark, 497 tons, built 1868 at Kennebunkport, of oak, 133' x 33.3' x 16.3'. The captain, his wife, and all eight crewmen were saved by the schooner *Olive*, which had to lay by for 14 hours due to rough seas, and landed them all in Roatan. It had left Pensacola, March 21, and encountered a gale and was disabled. Crew were rescued on the 26th. The bark was reported by a number of vessels as abandoned, her deck about level with the sea, and hatches all gone. One reported seeing her at Lat. 22°40'N, Long. 85°40'W, on March 30. Reported that the bark *Vittoria* was next to her with a crew removing materials and bringing them on board. The *Vittoria* later reported that the vessel had broken up near Cuba. That report was false as the steamer *Morgan* reported seeing her abandoned at Lat. 27°08'N, Long. 86°10'W, on April 14, and mentioned it was right in the middle of the shipping lane. The *Vittoria* likely made a false report so as to not deal with any salvage claims. *Source:* 37; NYT, 4/11–26/1883; BDG, 4/4/1883; Galveston Daily News, 4/9/1883; BP, 4/10/1883.

1884

1) **Unk. STEAMER**—Though sunk years before, a reporter mentions that the remains of a steamer (ribs and remains of the boiler) lay right off the front of the Palma Sola Hotel about 200 yards out. Photos and location of the Hotel still exist. *Source:* NYT, 4/6/1884. (2)

2) *HOPE*—Schooner, Capt. Hayes, from Boothbay with a cargo of ice, went ashore on the St. Augustine Bar. Sails, rigging, etc., were saved. *Source:* BP, 2/7/1884.

2) *JOANNA* or *JONNIS*—Greek bark. Was reported wrecked on the Florida coast in December 1884. From Black River, Jamaica bound for Trieste. *Source:* BP, 12/5/1884; Kingston Gleaner; 12/1884.

1) Page 52. **Martha M. Heath**—Built 1970 at St. James, New York, of Providence, 95' x 26.9' x 9'. *Source:* 37.

2) Pages 52–196. **Dictator**—Other source says 202.6' x 29.6' x 9.6'. *Source:* 37.

3) Page 85. **Gutenberg**—Built 1863 at Vegesack, 144.6' x 29.1' x 17.9'. *Source:* 37.

1885

1) *ACORN*—Iron screw steamship, 310 tons, built 1881 at Paisley by Campbell and Co., 165' x 24.6' x 12.9', 75 HP compound engine, Capt. A. Duncan, from New York for Laguna, with grain, lard, oil, etc. Wrecked on Elbow Reef and bilged, February 8, 1885. Crew saved by the schooner *Pocahontas*. She soon broke up and much of the cargo floated away. Wreckers tried saving what they could. *Source:* NYT, 2/12–18/1885; LR, 1885; Richmond Dispatch, 2/12/1884. (4)

2) *CLEAVER*—Swedish ship, from Pensacola for Freensborough, with timber, wrecked on Tortugas Reef, July 1, 1885. Unknown if salvaged. *Source:* Daily Republican (DE), 7/6/1885.

3) *ELWOOD DORAN*—Schooner, Capt. Warrington, of Bristol, Pennsylvania, built 1862 at Milford, Delaware, of oak, 235.66 tons, 117' x 29' x 9', from Philadelphia, grounded on the St. Augustine Bar, December 10, 1885, and was a total loss. She tried to enter the harbor using the short route around Bird Island, but being overloaded, she grounded and could not turn around, was "imbedded in sands of Bird Island and gradually going in pieces." She was loaded with iron pipe from the A. H. McNeal's iron foundry of Burlington, New Jersey, which was bound for the St. Augustine Gas and Electric Light Co. All the cargo and most all materials were saved. *Source:* 10; 37; New York World, 12/21/1885; The Palatka Daily News, 1/25/1885. (6)

4) *CALAIS*—Norwegian brigantine (ex-German *Der Adler*), built 1863 at Barth, Germany, 344 tons, 115.2' x 28.3' x 16.2', stranded and wrecked at Florida in 1885. *Source:* 35. (8)

1) Page 53. *Millie Wales*—Screw steamer, 81 tons, built at Boothbay, Maine. *Source:* 37.

2) Page 85. *Eleanora* (believe correct)—Swedish ship. *Source:* NYT, 7/6/1885.

3) Page 85. *Cetewajo*—Built at Apple River, Nova Scotia, of Parrsboro, 78' x 26' x 9'. *Source:* 37.

4) Page 147. *America*—Wood steamer, built 1863 in Portland, Connecticut, 172' x 32' x 17', Capt. F. C. Miller, sprung a leak during a gale, February 10, and unable to stop the leak, the water rose, put out her fires, and she drifted onto a sandbar, listed and broke in two and sank. All crew made shore safely in the boat, and she broke up soon after. The Life-Saving Station made this report:

> Encountered a heavy gale off the Florida coast on February 11th, during which she sprang a leak, and, the pumps becoming choked, the fires were put out in spite of the efforts of the crew, and they were compelled, for their own safety, to run the vessel ashore. She struck the beach at 11 o'clock at night, about eight and a half miles north of Gilbert's Bar House of Refuge.

She was heavily loaded with a large part of cargo being heavy machinery. *Source:* 10; 37; NYT, 3/3/1885; Wheeling Daily Intelligencer, 2/26/1885; BP, 2/26/1885.

1886

1) **Unk SCHOONER**—Wrecked on some rocks off Cedar Key, January 8, 1886. From Tampa bound for Cedar Keys. Had on board well known civil engineer A. O. Wilson, who had been surveying the area. All hands were saved. It was apparently so cold that the salt water froze on the reefs in that area, and many fish were dead and floating covering the surface for miles. *Source:* NYT, 2/4/1886. (2)

2) *FANNIE W. JOHNSTON*—Schooner, of Bridgeton, 265.84 tons, built 1867 at Cooper's Point or Camden, New Jersey, of oak and pine, 111.5' x 29.5' x 8.7', from Baltimore bound for Mosquito Inlet, with a cargo of bricks, wrecked north of the inlet and was a total loss along with the lives of two crew, 1/15/1886. *Source:* 10; 37. (6)

3) *MAY MONROE* or *MUNROE*—Capt. F. C. Hall, 204 tons, 109.6' x 26.8' x 9.6', of and built at Rockland, Maine, in 1866, of hard woods and oak. Reported from Pensacola early 1886 that the schooner was a total wreck, crew saved. *Source:* 37; NYT, 2/9/1886. (1)

4) *RESOLUTE*—Wrecking steamer, 124.06 tons, 93' x 18' x 5', built 1864 at Wilmington, of the Baker Salvage Co., from Norfolk bound for Haiti, when she sprang a leak off Elbow Key, August 8, 1886. Later had to be abandoned about 200 miles south of St. Augustine off the Florida coast. Crew took to the lifeboat and made it to St. Augustine on August 12. *Source:* 10; The Evening Herald, Syracuse, 8/13/1886; Philadelphia Times, 8/13/1886; Alexandria Gazette, 8/13/1886. (8)

5) *TRES AURORAS*—Spanish bark, of Havana, 371 tons, built 1858 at Nantes, 115.2' x 25.2' x 16'. The captain, mate and four seamen were found floating by the schooner *Annie B. Hutchinson* on part of the cabin-house from the wreck of the *Tres Auroras* (some reports say 15 miles south of the Tortugas, others 50 miles south, and others as just "near the Tortugas") after four days without food or water. She sank during a hurricane, October 10, 1886, and supposedly seven of the crew drowned. She was from Barcelona bound for Havana, loaded with wine. Possible Florida wreck. *Source:* 37; Orleans County Monitor, VT, 11/15/1886; Warren Daily Mirror, 11/4/1886. (8)

1) Page 85. *Rask*—Appears she was salvaged as listed as in service after this. *Source:* 35.

2) Page 85. *Emily J. Watts* (correct)—Built 1883 at Thomaston, Maine, 462.45 tons, 149' x 35' x 12.5'. From Perth Amboy bound for Galveston. Vessel a total loss, but most of the cargo saved. *Source:* 10; 37; BP, 6/9/1886; BDG, 6/7/1886.

3) Page 147. *J.H. Lane*—Built 1869 at Searsport, 134' x 31' x 14.9'. From the records of the Gilbert's Bar Life Saving Station are the following report after she parted her cables and went on the reef about 3/4 miles off shore, 14 1/2 miles north of the Jupiter Light House, SSE 5 1/2 miles from Gilbert's Bar Station, on a reef 3/4 mile from shore: "She lay with her head to the north, and was heavily listed to starboard, or off shore, with the seas breaking on deck and making the situation of her crew extremely dangerous." *Source:* 10; 37.

4) Page 179. *Athlete*—Paddle steamer, 178.85 tons, built 1878 at St. Mary's, GA. *Source:* 10.

1887

1) *OUTING*—Usually don't list anything this small, but was on a record setting cruise. A 24-foot yacht, it was sponsored by the Magazine *Outing*, to go on a "round-the-world tour" with two men on board, Capt. F. A. Cloudman, and mate George Miller (or Muller). They left Boston on November 18, 1886, and had a number of mishaps before being wrecked about one-half mile from the Gilbert's Bar Life Saving Station, January 18, 1886. To keep the waves from swamping them while drifting toward the shore, they threw kerosene oil on the water to calm the waves and it worked, saving their lives. They were going to run her ashore and got about 300 feet from the beach when they saw a 15-foot shark. They waited for it to leave and Muller jumped in the water and swam to the beach and the captain followed and also made shore. The keeper of the Life Saving Station took them in. The keeper of the Gilbert's Bar Station reported seeing the wreck four miles north of the station and about two miles offshore with the two men onboard flying the distress signal on the 18th. He went to find help, and when he came back later that day, he saw that it washed ashore about a half mile north of the station, and followed the footprints of the two on board back to the station where they were taken in and recuperated. *Source:* 10; Weekly Wisconsin, 1/29/1887.

1) Page 31. *Lizzie Ella*—Sloop, built 1876 at Pascagoula, Captain James Dillon, was found wrecked and adrift about seven miles southwest of Cape San Blas by the fishing schooner *J.P. Allen*. Looked to have been at anchor and was run down by a larger vessel. Part of her stern with her name was found, mast was broken in three pieces, and her bottom was gone. Believe all five on board were lost. Besides the captain, there was a George Smith and the others were Norwegian sailors. *Source:* Democratic Northwest, 1/5/1888.

2) Page 53. *Freddie L. Porter*—Built 1865 at Portsmouth, New Hampshire, of oak, 337 tons, 120.4' x 29.5' x 15.7'. *Source:* 37.

3) Page 85. *Joshua H. Marvell*—Capt. Shaw, 104.69 tons, 84.5' x 23.9' x 7', built 1864 at Laurel, Delaware, of Camden, New Jersey, from Cedar Keys bound for New York, with lumber. Crew saved, vessel a total loss. *Source:* 10; NYT, 8/1/1887.

4) Page 85. *Arthur* (correct)—Brig, 210 tons, Capt. Gadsburg or Gardner, built 1878 at Charlottetown, Prince Edward Island, of Mt. Stewart, Prince Edward Island, 105.4' x 24.7' x 12.9', for Galveston, where she recently dropped off a cargo of 1,749 bars of railroad iron. She left Ship Island bound for the Canary Islands and ran into a severe gale where she was dismasted and the deckhouse was carried away, July 26, 1887. She soon filled with water and the crew clung to the wreck for 16 hours with no food

or water. Luckily, a passing steamer, the *Morgan City*, rescued them all and took them to New York. She foundered soon after off the Tortugas. *Source:* 37; Galveston Daily News, 6/10/1887, 1/15/1888; London Evening News, 8/11/1887.

4) Page 86. *Sebulon* (correct)—Built 1884 at Grimstad, 121.5' x 26' x 12.2', from Minatitlan for Queenstown, with mahogany. Crew saved. *Source:* 35; BDG, 12/8/1887.

6) Page 125. *Slobodna* (correct)—Austrian registered wooden ship, of Castelnuovo, built 1884 at Lussinpiccolo by N. Martinolich, Capt. T. Milinovich, 1,199 net tons, 170.6' x 35.4' x 24.4', sheathed with yellow (composite metal), from New Orleans for Raval. Newspaper reports said stranded on Molasses Reef. Most if not all cargo of cotton saved. Hull was condemned and likely sold as she lay on reef. *Source:* LR, 1887/88; BP, 4/23/1887. *Note:* Believed one of the wrecks discovered on Molasses Reef in the last few years. Other record says of Megline? Built 1884 at Lussino, Austria (now Croatia), 173.2' x 35.5' x 25.5'. *Source:* 37.

7) Page 148. *Saragossa*—Correct info is, screw steamer, of Baltimore, 418 tons, 211.2' x 31.5' x 18.2', built 1863 at Philadelphia, of white oak. *Source:* 37.

1888

1) Page 86. *Sabino*—Vessel was gotten off and towed into port. Remained in service until 1891. *Source:* 35; BP, 2/3/1888.

2) Page 86. *Prince Umberto*—Built 1873 at Courtney Bay, New Brunswick, 219.9' x 35' x 23.9'. This source says wrecked on Duck Key, vessel a total loss. Some cargo may be saved. *Source:* 37; BP, 11/3/1888.

3) Page 179. *Virginia Lee Hickman*—Built 1872 at Chester, Pennsylvania, 338.14 tons, 115.6' 30.4' x 9', of Philadelphia. *Source:* 10.

1889

1) *FURMAN F. MULFORD*—Schooner, of Philadelphia, 588.82 tons, built 1877 at Millville, New Jersey, 140' x 35.7' x 12'. From Key West bound for Baltimore, with phosphate rock, Captain J. Thompson. She was abandoned in a sinking condition off Florida at Lat. 30° 10' N, Long. 79°W, November 16 or 17, 1889. All eight of the crew took to the yawl and were picked up the next day by the steamer *Leona*. *Source:* BP, 11/21/1889; The Evening World, 11/20/1889. (6)

1) Page 31. **Urbano**—Italian bark, 698 tons, of Genoa, built 1873 at Varazze, by A. Cerruti, 158' x 30.3' x 20.2', sheathed with felt and yellow (composite) metal, from Buenos Ayres for Pensacola, in ballast, went ashore 30 miles east of Pensacola early January 1889. Crew saved, vessel a total loss. *Source:* Western Daily Mercury, 1/22/1889; LR, 1889; St. Paul Daily Globe, 1/21/1889.

2) Page 32. **Carl D. Lathrop**—Believe saved as listed in service up to 1891. *Source:* 40.

3) Page 86. **True Briton**—Built at Quebec, of oak, elm, hackmatack and yellow pine, 204' x 38' x 24.2'. Capt. Torrance had his certificate suspended for six months, "for not sailing the ship in a seamanlike manner." *Source:* 37; Bristol Mercury, 3/30/1889.

4) Page 86. **Adelaide Baker**—Three-masted British bark (*Lloyd's* says ship, the ex *B.F. Carver*), of Dundee, built 1863 at Brewer, Maine, 810 tons, 152.8' x 34.6' x 20.9'. Left Pensacola, January 19, 1889, for Grangemouth with sawn timber, Capt. Peter McGregor. They thought they had passed Loggerhead and Sand Key Lights and all was well. Then they thought they saw Alligator Reef Light, and around midnight the Captain believing they were off Cape Florida, kept course and at 5 a.m. they wrecked on a reef. They were actually 80 miles south of where they thought they were and had wrecked on Coffins Patch. She had bilged and was full of water and had to be abandoned. At the inquiry, the captain said they were off course due to a faulty chronometer. Now a popular dive site in 23 feet of water (see GPS coordinates at end of chapter). *Source:* 34; NOAA; (Board of Trade Inquiry at Dundee) The Dundee Advertiser, 3/28/1889; LR, 1889.

5) Page 179. **Lady Bannerman**—Built 1855 in Bahamas, 79' x 23' x 9.5'. *Source:* 37.

1890

1) **STARRY BANNER**—Wrecking steamer, 36 tons, 60.6' x 16.2' x 6.7', built 1873 at Bath, from Baltimore bound for Key West. Struck on the bar at Crazy Banks in St. Augustine Harbor in the early morning of November 13, 1890, and sank within 10 minutes in shoal water. Captain and the six crewmen took to the rigging and were saved by the life-saving crew. Steamer was a total loss. *Source:* 10; BP, 11/14/1890; Winnipeg Free Press, 11/14/1890. (6)

1) Page 86. **Bridesmaid**—Built 1875 at Biddeford, Prince Edward Island, 487 tons, 157.9' x 29.7' x 17.2', of Swansea, not listed in 1891. *Source:* 37.

2) Page 125. *Hannibal*—Was saved as listed for a few more years. *Source:* 37.

3) Page 180. *Svanen*—Norwegian bark, built 1878 at Tvedestrand, Norway, 452 tons, 126' x 29.6' x 16.7', wrecked near Fernandina, March 23, 1890. According to the *New York Times*, she "had taken on board a cargo of lumber at St. Augustine and was trying to enter the harbor of Fernandina, when she was caught in a current which carried her some distance to the southward and finally wrecked her on the bar." A pilot boat rescued Capt. Melkesen, his two daughters, and the crew. Captain hoped to save some of the cargo. *Source:* 35; NYT, 4/2/1890.

4) Page 180. *Ethel*—Capt. William D. Garvin. Most papers reported all on board were lost, but they were picked up by the British schooner *Pajaro* and taken to Abaco. Captain of the ship that saw the wreckage believed she went aground on the Hetzel Shoals, as much of the wreckage and cargo washed up on the beach northeast of the shoals, and which the wind at the time would have carried it. Believe it's the *Ethel* built in 1861 at Philadelphia, 34.62 tons, 63.2' x 16.8' x 5.9', of Brunswick. GA. *Source:* 10; NYT, 4/14–19/1890.

1891

1) *MARIE*—Norwegian schooner, built 1876 at Lubeck, Germany, 331 net tons, 121.7' x 26.9' x 13.4', from Laguna with coal, stranded and wrecked off Florida in 1891. *Source:* 35. (8)

1) Page 32. *Dexter Clark*—One source says 142 tons, built at Ellsworth, Maine, of oak and pine, of Providence, 104.4' x 28.5' x 7.3'. *Source:* 37.

2) Page 125. *Edda*—Norwegian bark, Capt. Jensen, from Jamaica for Falmouth, with logwood, sprung a leak May 10, 1891, in the Straight of Florida. The German bark *Oscar Wendt* took all her crew off the sinking bark. *Source:* Kingston Gleaner, 5/28/1891.

3) Page 126. *Erl King*—British iron-screw steamer, of Glasgow, Capt. H. James, built 1865 at Glasgow by A&J Inglis, 2,193 tons, 305.6' x 34.1' x 21.5', 250 hp engine, from Bremen and Swansea for New Orleans. Most of the cargo saved, though damaged. A popular dive site. Used to be called the "Oil King" wreck in the 1960s. *Source:* BDG, 11/17/1891; LR, 1891.

4) Page 148. *Red Wing*—Was lost 2.5 miles south of Indian River Inlet, Delaware (not Florida). *Source:* BP, 10/26/1891.

5) Page 180. *Gloria* (unk. if correct name)—German bark, from Kingston bound for St. Simons, with lumber. She had anchored off Fernandina in

October 1891 asking for a tow from a tug, as three of her crew had died from fever, two more were sick and only five were left for duty. She ended up going ashore between Amelia and Talbot Island and went to pieces before a tug could arrive to help. Crew were brought to the hospital on Talbot Island. She was later burned per the Board of Health. *Source:* The Morning Call, 10/19/1891.

1892

1) Page 88. *London*—Of Dundee, built at Glasgow, 200.5' x 23.5' x 22.5'. *Source:* 37.

2) Page 180. *Minne Louise* (correct)—Vessel and cargo a total loss. Owned in Arichat, Cape Breton Island. *Source:* Boston Weekly Globe, 1/19/1892.

2) Page 198. *Rosalie*—Built at Kissimmee, 41.1' x 12.9' x 6.8'. *Source:* 10.

3) Page 370. *Bessie B*—Likely the schooner *Bessie B*, built 1879 at Port Jefferson, New York, of St. Augustine, 15.46 tons, 55.6' x 13.4' x 3.9'. *Source:* 10.

4) Page 370. *Gladys*—Built 1890 at Peekskill, New York, 58.5' x 11.4' x 4.5'. *Source:* 10.

1893

1) *NETTIE MURPHY*—British ship, 1,373 tons, built 1881 at Tusket, Nova Scotia, of Yarmouth, 205' 38' 23.2', Capt. Cosman. Wrecked during a storm and the whole crew were rescued by the Norwegian ship *Medea* in the Gulf Stream. Left Pensacola for Dunkirk, August 19, 1893. The steamer *Leconfield* saw her drifting August 29, burned to the water's edge with the aft still on fire. Possible Florida wreck. *Source:* The Evening Bulletin, KY, 8/31/1893; Morning Journal and Courier, 8/31/1893. (8)

2) *CARMELITA*—British bark, of Falmouth, built 1865 at Glasgow, 538 tons, 161.7' x 28.6' x 17.7', capsized in Key West Harbor during a storm, October 1893. Condemned and sold. *Source:* 37; BDG, 12/9/1893. (3)

3) *DRISKO*—Three-masted schooner, from Charleston bound for Jamaica, with shingles, Capt. R. D. (or T. A.) Drisko (who had on board his new wife as they just got married). Left Charleston October 8, 1893, and encountered bad weather the next day. Weather soon turned into a hurricane which threw the vessel on her beam-ends. Crew cut the masts and she righted. Captain had lashed his wife to the top of the deckhouse as this was now the only safe place as the waves were breaking over her deck. His wife was washed overboard, but luckily was tied to a long rope and they hauled her

back on board. On October 16 the British steamer *Mexican* took all on board off the wreck. The wreck was later seen off the Florida coast by the *U.S. Cruiser San Francisco*, which then sank her. Likely the 248-ton *Drisko*, built 1888 in Milbridge, Maine, 115' x 31.5' x 9.5', '. *Source:* 10; 37; NYTR, 11/16/1893. (8)

1) Page 33. *J.A. Bishop*—Of Pensacola, 50.4' x 12.4' x 5.6'. *Source:* 10.

2) Page 33. *Kanawha*—Built in Bath, Maine, 172.2' x 29.7' x 16.2'. *Source:* 6.

3) Page 33. *Octavia A. Dow*—Built at Georgetown, Maine, 40.18 tons, 67.7' x 19.9' x 6.2'. *Source:* 6; 10.

4) Page 53. *City of Athens*—Built 1891 at Kissimmee, 36.07 gt, 65' x 16' x 3.7', of Tampa. *Source:* 10.

5) Page 53. *Silver Spray*—Built 1870 at Bay Port, New York, 57' x 16.7' x 4.5'. *Source:* 10.

6) Page 180. *Mascott*—Believe a schooner, of Gloucester, built 1882 at Essex, 80.8' x 22.7' x 8', 77 tons, *Source:* 37.

7) Page 226. *Nellie Parker*—Of St. John, New Brunswick, built 1885 at Tynemouth, New Brunswick, 96.6' x 27.8' x 10'. Capt. C. Barkhouse, in ballast. "The crew were rescued by the life-saving service. The vessel is high aground inside a heavy surf, but is not breaking up." Life Saving service later reported she became a total wreck. *Source:* 10; 37; BP, 4/3/1893.

8) Page 226. *Mary C. Mariner*—Washed up on Lowry Island, MS. *Source:* Pascagoula Democrat Times, 11/3/1893.

1894

1) *MYSTERY*—Sailboat; was on its way to work on a sunken wreck when the boat capsized and sank about one mile from the Santa Rosa Life Saving Station, March 1, 1894. One man climbed into a skiff they were towing and the other three clung to some logs. The life-saving crew immediately went to help and all were rescued. *Source:* 10. (1)

2) *CATHERINE*—Danish ship, of Christiania, Capt. S. Svensen or Stevenson, 1,309 tons, built 1870 at St. John, New Brunswick, 192.9' x 37.7' x 24'. Was driven ashore about two miles west of the Santa Rosa Life Saving Station while trying to enter the harbor, August 7, 1894. Captain Broadbent, who was the keeper of the station, saw the vessel, and as his crew was not on duty at the time, he took his two young daughters, Isabelle and Sarah, ages 16 and 13, to help bring the life-saving equipment to the wreck. They

managed to fire a line to the wreck and saved all the people on board. She was in 12 feet of water and soon went to pieces. *Source:* 37; The Progressive Farmer, 8/14/1894; Alden Times, 2/8/1895. (1)

3) September 1894 HURRICANE—Over 50 bodies washed ashore in the Florida Keys. The storm affected the whole east coast of Florida. Some of the following were likely saved.

a) *BRANDON*—British bark, of Quebec, built 1882 at St. Joseph de Levis, 1,250 tons, 197.5' x 38.5' x 23.4'. Capt. William Redford, from Ship Island bound for Liverpool, with timber, ran ashore on Crocus Reef and capsized after pounding over the reef and going into the channel during a hurricane, September 26, 1894. Four of the 17 on board came ashore on East Matecumbe Key wearing their life preservers. Feared the 14 others, including the captain, were lost. *Source:* 20; Middleton Daily Argus, 10/8/1894; Hamilton Daily Democrat, 10/6/1894.

b) *THIORVA*—Norwegian ship, built 1876 at New Glasgow, Nova Scotia, by J. W. Carmichael, 1,264 tons, 198'6" x 38'5" x 22'7". Cargo of pitchpine, was wrecked during the September 26, 1894, hurricane off Turtle Harbor, all the crew were saved. *Source:* 35. The *Hamilton Daily Democrat*, 10/6/1894 says: "The *Thiorva*, from Pensacola bound for Geestemunde, went ashore in Turtle Harbour. Crew made Key West and taken care of by the English, Swedish and French vice consul there W. J. H. Taylor." See GPS coordinates at end of chapter. (4)

c) *MARIA*—Spanish bark, from Barcelona for Havana, was reported from Key West as totally lost off that port during the hurricane. Some of the crew were saved. Possibly saved. *Source:* Morning Post, London, 10/1/1894. (3)

d) *KATE* and the *NONPOREIL*—Pilot boats, were both driven ashore at Key West. *Source:* Ibid.

e) *CAMBRONNE*—French bark, of Nantes, built 1875 at Nantes by T. Dubigeon and Sons, 109.5' x 23.9' x 13', sheathed in felt and yellow (composite) metal. Capt. Leuthan, from Jamaica, with logwood, was driven ashore on south beach at Key West and condemned. *Source:* NYT, 9/29/1894; LR, 1894. (3)

f) *EDWARD STEWART*—Schooner, was blown across the river at Fernandina, and now lying on the mud flat in five feet of water. Believe salvaged as still listed in service in 1895. *Source:* BP, 9/29/1894. (7)

g) *PRINCESS*—Steamer, sank between Palatka and Picolata during the hurricane. *Source:* Ibid. (7)

h) *DeBARRY*—Steamer, was driven against the drawbridge at Palatka and wrecked. *Source:* Ibid. (7)

i) *MAUDE*—Steam yacht, was sunk near Crescent City during the hurricane. *Source:* Ibid. (7)

j) *MEDIA*—Steamer, of the E. Faber Company, was lost at Cedar Keys in the hurricane. *Source:* Galveston Daily News, 10/13/1894; The Evening Bulletin, 10/12/1894. (2)

k) *EDITH*—Steamer, reported from Palatka as have been driven ashore. *Source:* The Times, Richmond, 9/29/1894. (7)

End of hurricane losses.

4) *AUSTRIANA*—Norwegian ship, 1,544 tons, 215.2' x 39.4' x 24', built 1875 at St. John, New Brunswick, burned while at anchor in Pensacola Bay, December 28, 1894, with one million feet of lumber on board, a total loss. *Source:* 35; Janesville Daily Gazette, 12/29/1894. (1)

1) Page 33. *Alice N*—Most likely the *Alice N*, built 1879 in Miss, of Cedar Keys, 7.4 tons, 34' x 13.7' x 3'. *Source:* 10.

2) Page 33. *George Jurgens*—Schooner, 22.4 tons, 51.8' x 17.4' x 4'. *Source:* 10.

3) Page 33. *David Mitchell*—Schooner, 63.7' x 18.2' x 7'. *Source:* 10.

4) Pages 33–4. *Sea Foam*—Listed at 17.79 tons, 43.9' x 13' x 5.5'. *Source:* 10.

5) Page 53. *Rambler*—Built 1883 at Milwaukee, 60' x 16.7' x 3.4'. *Source:* 10.

6) Page 88. *Nada*—Also listed as Austrian, of and built at Fiume, 430 tons. *Source:* 37.

7) Page 126. *Ida C. Southard*—Page 88. Built 1892 at Waldoboro, Maine, 818.62 tons, 777.69 net tons, 178.7' x 37.2' x 18.3'. *Source:* 10.

8) Page 126. *Oxford*—She was got off the reef and towed to New York for repairs. *Source:* Baltimore Sun, 4/21/1894.

9) Page 126. *Moonstone*—Wreckers got her off Grecian Shoals after dumping part of her cargo overboard and took her into Key West. *Source:* Philadelphia Times, 8/19/1894.

10) Page 148. *Breaconshire*—Screw steamer, schooner rigged, built 1883 at Sunderland, 299.7' x 37.2' x 24.3', iron hull. *Source:* 37.

11) Page 180. *John E. Stevens* (correct)—Steam screw vessel, 38.47 tons, built 1875 at Port Jefferson, New York, of Jacksonville, 57.5' x 16.9' x 6.6'. *Source:* 10.

12) Page 198. *Camusi*—Stern wheel steamer, 130.67 tons, 94' x 22.3' x 5.5', built 1891 at Wilmington, of Savannah. *Source:* 10.

1895

1) *OLLIE*—Two-masted schooner, of East Jacksonville, from Melbourne bound for Jacksonville, wrecked off Ormond Beach and went to pieces, February 3, 1895. Two on board saved. *Source:* Jeffersonville News, 2/4/1895. (6)

2) *CONDOR*—Norwegian bark, 984 tons, 169' x 34.5' x 19.2', built 1876 at Nova Scotia, of Haugesund, abandoned in a fire at Pensacola while in ballast, 7/26/1895. *Source:* 35. (1)

3) *SHAMROCK*—Schooner (sponge fisherman), of Key West, 25.25 tons, built 1887 at Biloxi, MS, 50.5' x 19' x 4.5', foundered off St. Martins Key (near Tarpon Springs), November 1895, in six fathoms of water. Six of the 14 on board were lost (they were below deck when she capsized). *Source:* 10; The San Francisco Call, 11/21/1895; Lorain County Register, 12/7/1895. (2)

1) Pages 88–89. *R. Bowers*—Built 1879 at Camden, Maine, 435.76 tons, 150.5' x 33.5' x 12.2'. *Source:* 10.

2) Page 89. *Walter D. Walett* (correct)—Was gotten off the reef and towed into Key West, where the cargo was sold. She was condemned, and the tug *Underwriter* arrived to tow her to New York. *Source:* BP, 7/30/1895.

3) Page 89. *Harry B. Ritter*—She was saved. In November 1898, she was abandoned far off New Jersey. *Source:* The Wilmington Daily Republican, 1895.

4) Page 89. *Beatrice McLean* (correct)—*Source:* BP, 11/26/1895; Cork Constitution, 11/26/1895.

5) Page 126. *Ingrid*—Built 1877 in Quebec, Canada (originally the *Citadel*), 1,363 tons, 207.3' x 38.3' x 24.4'. *Source:* 35.

6) Page 148. *Nathan Cleaves*—Built at Essex, Massachusetts, 78.7' x 23' x 7.8'. *Source:* 10.

7) Page 198. *Ravenswood*—Built 1866 at New York, 137.2' x 29.8' x 10.7'. *Source:* 10.

Wreck of the Norwegian bark *Ingrid* by Fowey Rock Light in 1895, with wreckers alongside. *Yachting Magazine*, "Wreck Ashore," April 1942.

1896

1) *SEMINOLE*—Trade schooner, believe 37 tons, built 1885 at New Berlin, Florida, of St. Augustine, 65.6' x 18.2' x 4', left Titusville, March 26, 1896, bound for Miami, with lumber. On board was Albert White who just moved to Florida to obtain a divorce and start a new life. He was negotiating the purchase of the *Seminole* and would have bought her if the voyage was successful. Also on board were three other men, and a woman and her two children who was to meet her husband in Miami. On the second day at sea,

a terrible squall hit the vessel and capsized her. The woman and her children were lost, and the four men clung to some wreckage. After a couple of days with no food or water, one drank some sea water and soon perished. Another named Gallagher was later attacked by a shark and bit in two. Only White and a man named Johnson remained. After three days, White became exhausted and lost his grip and drowned. Johnson and the wreckage floated ashore four miles south of Ft. Pierce, where he was rescued barely alive. *Source:* 10; BDG, 4/18/1896. (8)

2) *JESSIE P*—Schooner, 10.87 tons, 34.6' x 13.8' x 4', built 1884 at The Narrows, Florida, of Pensacola, from St. Andrews Bay for Pensacola, with passengers, was caught in the July storm. Believing she was about to sink, all on board took to the boat and abandoned her. Unfortunately, one passenger, Mr. Albert Jackson, was asleep below deck and forgotten during the confusion. When they realized they had left him, it was too late as the seas were too rough to get back to the schooner. When Jackson awoke, he found himself trapped below as all the hatches had been battened down. The *Jessie P* remained afloat and was later found drifting near St. Andrews Bay by a fishing smack. They went aboard and while walking the deck heard a faint tapping. Jackson, in a semi-conscious state, was barely able to tap his boot heels. They immediately opened the hatch and found Jackson in a horrible state. He lay there with enormous Norway rats gnawing at his legs. They got him above and after a few hours he was able to relate his story, which was later reported in many papers both here and in Europe, "on the night of the storm he awoke to find himself alone, with the hatched battened down. When he realized his situation his reason tottered, and he made repeated desperate attempts to burst open the hatch, but was unable to do so. He searched for food, as he found a few biscuits and some water. At last rats appeared around him, grew bolder by degrees, and finally attacked him. He fought them off as long as his strength held out, but in the end, exhausted by fatigue and hunger, became unconscious. He remained in that condition for 48 hours. His legs are terribly mangled."

As to the final stop of the *Jessie P*, I can't say, but she was stricken from the records after this. *Source:* 10; Shields Daily Gazette, 7/20/1896; Fisherman and Farmer, 7/24/1896. (1)

3) September 1896 HURRICANE at Cedar Keys. It destroyed Cedar Key, and hundreds of lives were lost there. A huge storm surge hit this area.

a) Nearly **100 VESSELS** that were engaged in the sponge trade were anchored on the sponge bar just below Cedar Keys when the hurricane struck, and nearly every vessel was sunk. With an average of four to 10 men on each vessel, the loss of life was great. *Source:* NYT, 10/3/1896. (2)

b) *ROSALIE*—Schooner, was lost in the hurricane and only four of the crew of 12 reached Cedar Key in her dinghy. *Source:* Ibid. (2)

c) *GERTRUDE*—Schooner, was dismasted and abandoned 15 miles south of Cedar Key. *Source:* Ibid. (2)

d) *C.D. OWENS*—Steamer, wrecked on the Suwannee River and was fast in the river swamps. *Source:* Ibid. (2)

e) *SATURN*—Norwegian bark, built 1873 at Risør, Norway, 410 tons, 120' x 28.5' x 16.3', Capt. J. Olsen, from Belize for Alloa. Either foundered or capsized off the Florida coast, September 28, 1896. Crew were picked up by the German bark *Hedvig* and taken to Key West. *Source:* 35; Delaware Gazette and State Journal, 10/8/1896; Baltimore Sun, 10/15/1896. (8)

End of September Hurricane wrecks.

4) *TILLY VANDERHERCHEN*—Schooner, 456 tons, 130.9' x 34.3' x 11.7', built 1875 in Mauricetown, New Jersey. Left Jacksonville December 6, 1896, bound for Guadeloupe, with a cargo of lumber. Became waterlogged and was lost off the Florida coast around December 18. Crew saved by the Italian bark *Laboremus*. *Source:* Norfolk Virginian, 2/26/1897; The Morning Times, 1/5/1897. (8)

1) Page 34. *Mary Potter*—Built 1868 at Noank, Connecticut, 53.5' x 18.4' x 8'. *Source:* 10.

2) Page 34. *Mabel Taylor*—Ship, 1,329 gross tons, built 1878 at Tusket, Nova Scotia, by J. A. Hatfield, 205' x 37.7' x 23', Capt. R. Hibbard; had over one million feet of lumber on board. She was towed out of the harbor on the night of the 27th to the outer buoys, and as there was a stiff breeze, was told by the pilot Bassell to anchor up, but the captain refused. A tug went out the next morning and found her aground on Caulkers Shoals at the entrance to Pensacola Bay, a total wreck. Captain Broadbent, of the life-saving station, said he saw lights on the vessel all night and no distress signals from her. Captain Hibbard had no comment as to why she wrecked. Vessel was fully insured though, so that may have been the motive. *Source:* Atlanta Constitution, 2/29/1896; LR, 1896.

3) Page 34. *Florence*—Built at Portland, Florida, 22.77 tons, 42' x 18.6' x 4'. *Source:* 10.

4) Page 34. *Anna Peppina* (correct)—Built 1873 at Savona by F. Sirello, 653 gross tons, 149.2' x 29.7' x 20.1', sheathed with yellow (composite) metal. All the crew were saved. Most all the materials were saved from her, and the wreckers burned her when done. *Source:* 10; LR, 1896.

5) Page 34. **Red Wing**—This vessel was something of a Jonah as a few years before she ran into and sunk a large vessel at Hampton Roads, was then towed up river where she tried to anchor but ended up demolishing several smaller craft. She was later tied up on the Portsmouth side where she then stove a hole in the side of a steamer. She was sold soon after that. *Source:* The Norfolk Virginian, 11/27/1896.

6) Page 179. **Nathan F. Cobb**—Lumber schooner, built 1890 at and from Rockland, Maine, 656.3 toms, 167.2' x 35.1' x 12.7', was discovered in the surf a mile south of the Hotel Cogunua, Ormond-by-the-Sea, with men in the rigging, December 5, 1896 (previous edition incorrectly said 1886). She had originally sprung a leak at sea and filled with water. A gale then threw her on her beam-ends, dismasting her and carrying away the cabin along with two crewmen. She drifted for three days until grounding just offshore Ormond. The Life-Saving Station crew and local citizens all went to help but the high surf prevented them. One of the volunteers drowned when their lifeboat launched from the beach capsized near the wreck. A line was finally made to the wreck by a crewman who swam to the beach with help from those onshore, and the rest of the crew were saved. *Source:* 10; Huntington Weekly News, 12/9/1896.

Wreck of the schooner *Nathan F. Cobb* in 1896. Courtesy of the State Archives of Florida.

An illustration of a rescuer trying to help those on an offshore wreck. As with one who tried to help those on the wreck of the *Nathan F. Cobb*, these brave rescuers sometimes lost their own lives. *The Fisherman's Own Book*, 1882.

7) Page 198. *California*—Measured 47' x 16.3' x 3.7'. *Source:* 10.

1897

1) *BISCAYNE*—Schooner, Capt. Henry Fozzard, from Jacksonville for Biscayne Bay. She was abandoned in a sinking condition, 10 miles off the Bethel Creek Station after colliding with some floating wreckage at 7 p.m., January 30, 1897. According to the captain, three of the crew are believed drowned, as they refused to get in the ship's dinghy. One paper reported there were passengers on board who drowned but the captain said that wasn't true as he refused to take them on board due to bad weather. The captain and mate made shore, and were taken in at the Bethel Creek Station. On February 1, the hull washed ashore bottom up, two miles north of the station, and soon broke up. One paper said a gas motor had exploded causing the wreck. *Source:* 10; BDG, 2/3/1897; Biloxi Herald, 2/13/1897; Iowa Postal Card, 2/11/1897. (5)

2) *LADRAS*—Bark, Capt. Gonzales. A report from St. Augustine was reported in many papers regarding a "Message in a Bottle." A bottle was found on South Beach, seven miles south of St. Augustine. Inside was the log of the bark *Ladras* since it had left Boston. Captain Gonzales said they left Boston January 3 with himself and a crew of 12. On January 12, she sprung a leak and was somewhat repaired by the carpenter: "On January 14th, however, the water began to pour into the hold in great volume. The pumps were manned and the men worked day and night, but at noon on January 15th it was apparent that the vessel was doomed." They took to the boat and watched her sink as soon as they got clear. Ended by saying: "We have little food and water, and must perish unless soon picked up." *Source:* The Cedar Rapids Evening Gazette, 1/21/1897; The Record-Union, 1/22/1897. (8)

3) **Unk. Mystery SCHOONER**—Sank 30 miles due east of the St. John's River Bar, September 23, 1897, and her mast was protruding out of the water in 16 fathoms of water. Believed all on board were lost. It was originally reported as the schooner *Charles S. Davis*, but when the *Davis* arrived safely at Jacksonville, they then reported it as the *Thomas Winsmore*, but that also arrived safely. The identity remains a mystery. I tried searching, but no luck. The *Davis* wrecked off Morehead City in 1899, and the *Winsmore* off the northern Bahamas in 1915. *Source:* The Sun, 9/27/1897; Philadelphia Inquirer, 10/2/1897; Philadelphia Times, 9/27-28/1897. (6)

1) Page 34. *Mary Me*—Built at Freeport, Florida, 17.02 tons, 53.5' x 15.1' x 4'. *Source:* 10.

2) Page 90. *Mathilda*—Built 1872 at Quincy, Massachusetts, 1,795 tons, 219.7' x 43' x 28'. *Source:* 10.

3) Page 126. *Clyde*—Tug, built 1862 at Philadelphia, 56 tons, 70' x 16.1' x 8.6', of Key West. *Source:* 10.

4) Page 181. *Commodore*—Had left Jacksonville New Year's Day, 1897, after loading arms and munitions, and they grounded twice getting out to the open ocean. This must have sprung a leak as the next day she was sinking. Author Stephen Crane wrote of the disaster for the newspapers. *Source:* BDG, 1/7/1897.

1898

1) *OSMOND*—Norwegian bark (ex-Canadian *Osmond O'Brien*), built 1877 at Nova Scotia, 878gt, 173.5' x 35.1' x 20.1'. Wrecked in the Tortugas, January 16, 1898. The steamship *El Rio* saw some of her wreckage floating in

the area on March 15: "Tortugas bearing east-southeast, magnetic, distant, twenty-four miles, passed a large piece of floating wreckage, consisting of after part of a vessel, with stump of mizzenmast, windmill frame and cabin companionways attached, name board on quarter, 'Osmond.'" *Source:* 35; Galveston Daily News, 3/20/1898. (3)

2) *FANNIE KIMMEY*—Schooner, built 1879 at Milton, Delaware, 384.23 tons, 129' x 32.8' x 12', of Philadelphia, Capt. Fisher, from Philadelphia bound for Jacksonville with coal. The vessel grounded in a dense fog and foundered about five miles north of the mouth of the St. John's River, February 2, 1898. Crew saved. Believe will be a total loss. *Source:* 10; BP, 2/7/1898. (6)

3) *THOMAS H. HERNDON*—Dredge, parted her cable during a storm about 15 miles off Cape San Blas along with two scows being towed by the tugs *Nimrod* and *William J. Keyser* (page 35, which also foundered). Twenty-six men on the barge were lost. One report says she washed up on the beach. *Source:* BDG, 8/6/1898; The Times, 8/6/1898. (1)

1) Page 35. *William J. Keyser*—Foundered about 15 miles off Cape San Blas, Captain Allen and three crew lost, the rest of the crew reached shore in an open boat. *Source:* The Times, 8/6/1898.

2) Page 90. *Speedwell*—Capsized March 3, 1898, while from Marco bound for Key West. Truly a tragic tale. As already mentioned, Capt. Collier lost his three sons (ages four, six, and eight) who were part of the nine on board who drowned. Only four survived. Also lost was the entire Nichols family from Bridgeport, Connecticut: Bradley Nichols, his parents, and his wife and his two children. *The Evening Herald*, March 4, 1898, told the story, part of which said:

"About 7 o'clock Captain Collier was at the wheel and the Nichols family and the Collier children were in the cabin asleep. Suddenly a squall came howling up abeam. Gates and Green rushed to take in sail. As the jib flapped loose the squall caught the schooner and blew her clean over on her port side."

Collier, the two deckhands and a passenger were thrown into the sea but all were able to grab onto the rigging and held on for two hours until the storm subsided. They were then able to get the dingy, bailed it out using a hat, broke a thwart (the piece of wood used for a seat in a small boat) in two to use as oars, and rowed towards the Marquesas and were soon picked up by a fishing sloop.

Samuel Gates, one of the deckhands, had this to say,

Captain Collier has been sailing now for 25 years in these waters. He is not to blame for this awful thing. The squall came up like nothing I have ever seen around Key West. Before we knew it we were lifted off our feet and in the water, and as far as those poor people down below, they were penned in like rats. The wife of the younger Nichols, as pretty a woman as ever stepped aboard a ship, rose to the skylight. I was clinging to the rigging. She waved her hand at me, and that's the last I saw of her. When we got off, two hours later, they were all dead.

He also mentioned that he saw the elder Mr. Nichols get out but he immediately went under and drowned. Soon after being brought to port, Capt. Collier and Jesse Green went back out to the wreck with a diver on the vessel *Buccaneer* to recover the bodies.

3) Page 91. *Haroldine*—The correct date she wrecked was January 2, 1898 (not 1906). Built 1884 at North Weymouth, Massachusetts, 1,361.64 tons, 209.8' x 40.5' x 18.7', of Providence, Rhode Island *Source:* 10; The Boston Sunday Globe, 1/16/1898.

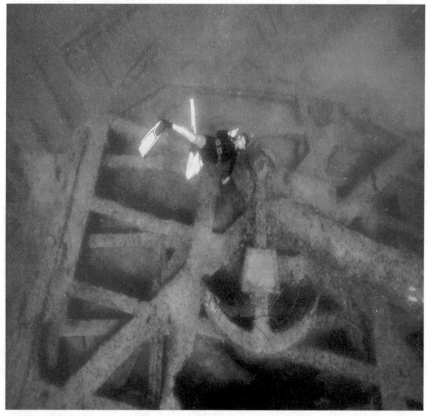

Author snorkeling on the wreck of the Norwegian bark *Lofthus*. First time since the anchor and a plaque were placed on top of the wreck. Monica Singer.

The Norwegian bark *Lofthus* aground on the Reef in 1898. Note the fake gunports to ward off pirates. Courtesy of the Boynton Beach Historical Society.

4) Page 370. *Lofthus*—Built 1868 at Sunderland, England, iron hulled, 1,277 tons, 222.8' x 36.7' x 22.7'. I was the one who submitted this site to be considered as a State Underwater Preserve. See GPS coordinates at end of chapter. *Source: 36.*

1899

A hurricane slammed the Carrabelle and Apalachicola areas on August 1, 1899, causing extensive damage, especially to Carrabelle. A passenger train was even blown off its track (eerily reminiscent of a train derailed in the same area after Hurricane Michael in 2018), and the famous Lenark Inn was blown into the Gulf. Fifteen lumber ships anchored in Dog Island Cove and the upper anchorage were now high and dry on St. George's and Dog Island. Some of these vessels were just uncovered by Hurricane Michael, though other vessels were reported wrecked in this area during the 1852 hurricane (see attached photo). Twelve were loaded with lumber and ready to sail. Most all would be a total loss as they were just a mass of wreckage. Two large schooners that wrecked, the *Mary E. Morse* (she sat upright in the sand with both anchors out front, one sitting under a Russian bark), and the *Emma L. Cottingham*, were refloated though the *Morse* wrecked the next year off the east coast of Florida and the *Cottingham* a few years later on the west coast of Florida. The *Morse* was probably never repaired properly as she came into Key West after leaving Carrabelle leaking badly. I don't know if any of the others listed were saved, but most which were ashore were just auctioned off and probably broken up or got buried in the sand.

1) **LEWIS A. EDWARDS**—Schooner, Capt. and owner C. F. Petersen, built 1851 at New York, 169 tons, 102' x 28.4' x 8.8', of Shieldsboro, Mississippi, from Pascagoula bound for Sagua La Grande, Cuba, with lumber, foundered during the hurricane, August 3, 1899, after leaving Apalachicola. All six on board were lost (one paper reported the rumor that the crew were picked up by a passing schooner but could not verify this). The wreck was sighted about 40 miles southeast by south (or east) of Cape San Blas, the hulk supposedly anchored up and said to be a hazard to navigation. Another report says she was seen dismasted and bottom up with the masts lying beside her near Cedar Keys. *Source:* 10; BDG, 8/19/1899, 9/27/1899; Biloxi Daily Herald, 8/9/1899; The Semi-Weekly Messenger, 9/26/1899.

2) **GRACE ANDREWS**—Schooner, Capt. O. Andrews (also listed as Capt. Brown), built 1874 at Thomaston, Maine, 568 tons, 148.8' x 33.3' x 12.2'. It had 411,000 feet of cypress lumber on board for Boston, when she was dismasted and driven ashore at Carrabelle, and was now full of water. Captain and crew saved, but the captain was badly injured. He later recovered and took command of another ship that had left Carrabelle just before the storm that wrecked the *G. Andrews*. That vessel also got caught in the storm's fury, and though she survived, her captain was washed overboard and drowned. *Source:* 10; Boston Sunday Post, 8/6/1899; BDG, 9/11/1899. (1)

On the west end of Dog Island, the following vessels had wrecked:

a) **CORTESIA**—Italian bark of Trapani, built 1866 at Castellammare, 400 tons, 125.3' x 27.8' x 18.8'. She split in two from stem to stern when she went ashore. From Apalachicola for Bristol with lumber, wrecked at Dog Island Cove. Sold at auction for $55, less sails and rigging.

b) **JAMES A. GARFIELD**—Schooner, was ashore with stern stove in and full of water. She was 510 gross tons, 138.5' x 34.2' x 12.6', built 1881 at Brewer, Maine, out of Bangor.

e) **VIDETTE**—Barkentine, Captain Waldron, was upright but keel was gone. She was 568 gross tons, 141.6' x 33.3' x 16', built 1884 in Milbridge, Maine, of Philadelphia.

f) **RANAVOLA**—Norwegian bark, Capt. Edwartsen, built 1861 at Newcastle, England, 396 tons, 121.2' x 27.7' x 17'. Sold at auction for $270.

g) *ELISABETH*—Norwegian bark, Capt. Pederson. An *Elisabeth* that was listed as missing in the North Atlantic in 1899, but says from Jacksonville for Mersey, with pitchpine. She was built 1893 at Glasgow, 369 tons, 145.5' x 27.1' x 11.8'. Maybe refloated and went to Jacksonville? The wreck was sold privately for $2,000 and resold at auction a few hours later for $3,250.

h) *VALE*—Norwegian bark Capt. Anderson, built 1878 in Kragerø, Norway, 554 tons, 139' x 30' x 17'. Wrecked by Dog Island while loading pitchpine. Sold at auction for $460.

i) *JAFNHAR*—Norwegian bark, Capt. M. Thygesen, built 1877 at Porsgrunn, by Vaugbart and Hoegh, 498 tons, 130' x 29.3' x 16'. Sold at auction for $510.

j) *LATAVA*—Russian bark, Capt. Krantman, of Riga, built 1886, 555 tons, 151.2' x 32' x 15.9', sheathed with felt and zinc. Sold at auction for $615.

Wrecked on St. George's Island were the following:

a) *HINDOO*—Norwegian Bark, Capt. M. Madsen, built 1877 in Apenrade, 622 tons, 147.1' x 31.5' x 17.5'. Sold at auction for $1,185.

b) *BENJAMIN C. CROMWELL*—Schooner, Capt. McClean, built 1883 in Maine, of Portland, Maine, 616 tons, 161.4' x 35.5' x 11.9'. Was reported that a group of alligators had soon made a home underneath her.

The Norwegian barks *Jafnhar* & *Vale* after the 1899 hurricane. Courtesy of the State Archives of Florida.

One of the wrecks uncovered by Hurricane Michael in 2018. Believe it's either the *Jafnhar* or *Vale*, as seen in the 1899 photo (this is the vessel on the left,) as the other was also uncovered about 100 yards away on its side. Kai Nelson.

c) *WARREN ADAMS*—Schooner Capt. Gibbons, lay about 850" from the high-water mark as the high winds carried her 200 feet through the woods where she leveled 57 large trees in doing so. She was 667 gross tons, 163.4' x 35.1' x 13.1', built 1884 at and of Bath, Maine. Snakes were a problem afterward and the mate shot a seven-foot moccasin near the wreck.

Wrecked in same area are:

a) Three **PILOT BOATS** were lost.

b) *OILA* and the *CAPITOLA*—The steamers were lost. The *Capitola* was a stern wheel steamer of 60 tons, 96' x 22.3' x 4.4', built 1898 at Carrabelle, Florida, of Apalachicola.

c) Over **Forty VESSELS** under 20 tons were also lost along with **Six LUMBER LIGHTERS**. Sources for all the others wrecked in the hurricane: 10; 35; 37; Bristol Mercury, 8/9/1899; Albert Lea Freeborn County Standard, 8/9/1899; BDG, 10/10/1899; The Salt Lake Herald, 8/5/1899; The Anderson Intelligencer, 8/9/1899; The Bath Independent, 9/16, 1899; Decatur Wise County Messenger, 8/11/1899; LR, 1899.

Also lost in the hurricane:

2) *CORMORANT*—Norwegian bark, built 1865 at Liverpool, 1,091 tons, 211.4' x 33.6' x 21.6', left Pensacola, September 8, 1899, bound for Buenos Ayres, and never heard from again. Possible Florida wreck. *Source:* 35. (8)

3) *EASTERN LIGHT*—Norwegian bark, built 1869 at St. John, New Brunswick, 1218 tons, 190' x 38.4' x 23.4' left Pensacola with pitchpine, 12/29/1899, bound for Cardiff, and went missing. Possible Florida wreck. *Source:* 35. (8)

1) Page 35. ***Charles A. Swift***—Built in Alabama, 25.72 tons, 54.3' x 19.2' x 4.3'. *Source:* 10.

2) Page 35. ***Albert Haley*** (correct)—*Source:* 10.

3) Page 53. ***Glad Tidings***—Built at St. Andrews Bay, Florida, 38.6' x 15.3' x 3.8'. *Source:* 10.

4) Page 181. ***General Whitney***—Screw steamer, schooner rigged, 225' x 40' x 18', Capt. J. W. Hawthorne, from New Orleans bound for New York. Foundered 50 miles off Cape Canaveral, (others say north of Cape Canaveral.) *Source:* 37; Galveston Daily News, 4/24/1899; Bath Independent, 4/28/1899.

5) Page 369. ***Drot***—The awful tale of this wreck and the cannibalism that ensued was reported in newspapers all over the United States and Europe. She sank after breaking in two during a hurricane in which the captain and seven others drowned. The eight men left clung to some decking. This soon parted and two of the men drifted off on the smaller section. The two were the mate and a seaman, and it was reported the seamen was picked up by the steamer *Titania* and brought to Philadelphia, the mate having committed suicide. The six left, held on for a couple of days with no food or water, though one man caught a few fish. By the third day, the fisherman went crazy and jumped overboard and drowned. Two others died from exhaustion during the next couple of days, the survivors were drinking the victim's blood and eating some of the flesh before dumping them overboard. When only the three remained, and death seemed imminent, they decided to draw straws to see who would be killed in order for the others to live. A German sailor drew the short straw and bravely met his death, the two remaining sailors ate his flesh and drank his blood. Another couple of days went by and both men again were near death. One then went insane attacking the other, biting off pieces of flesh from his face and chest until he was subdued. Soon after this, the two were rescued by a steamer and taken to Charleston. This is truly a nightmare of a tale, and one can only imagine what it was like on that raft. *Source:* The San Francisco Call, 10/1/1899; The Evening Bulletin, 9/4/1899.

1900

1) **ORE**—Norwegian bark (ex-British *John Milton*), built 1865 at Jersey, Channel Islands, 619 tons, 160' x 27.6' x 18', from Cadiz for Carrabelle, in ballast, stranded and wrecked February 6, 1900, about 10 miles westward of East Pass (another report just says ashore on St. George Island), in nine feet of water. A total wreck. *Source:* 35; The Daily News (Pensacola), 2/8/1900; The Philadelphia Inquirer, 2/17/1900. (1)

2) **VENEZUELA**—Norwegian bark (originally a ship), 972 tons, 182.3" x 35.7' x 20.6', built 1879 at St. Mathews, New Brunswick, from Ship Island for Brake, with pitchpine, stranded and wrecked at Turtle Harbor, 9/5/1900. *Source:* 35. (4)

1) Page 54. **John W.Smart**—Built in Newmarket, New Hampshire, 50' x 15.9' x 5'. *Source:* 10.

2) Page 54. **Lula Frances**—Built 1884, 41.6' x 16.2' x 4.6'. *Source:* 10.

3) Page 126. **South American**—Steel barkentine, 382 tons, built 1891 at Carrickfergus, by W. C. Jarvis and Sons, 166.3' x 27.5' x 12.5', of Liverpool, L. E. Schjonemann, Master, from Santiene, Mexico bound for Falmouth, England, with mahogany, ran into a hurricane the night of September 4, 1900, lost all sails, and was driven on French Reef early the next morning. Captain praised the steel hull for saving him and the crew. Vessel was a total loss, but believed most cargo could be saved. It was noted there were other wrecks along the keys due to the storm. *Source:* NYT, 9/9/1900; LR, 1899.

1901

1) **THERMUTIS**—Norwegian bark (ex-German *Dorothea*), built 1872 at Hamburg, 632 tons, 152.5' x 30.5' x 19', from Trinidad for Carrabelle, in ballast, stranded and wrecked on St. George Island, early March 1901. *Source:* 33; Galveston Daily News, 3/4/1901. (1)

2) **NUSTUIN**—Bark, Capt. Tomanowicht, left Carrabelle March 12 with lumber for Cette. Ran into a gale April 1 and lost her sails and rudder. Crew were all rescued by the steamer *Kotendrecht* and taken to Pensacola. Possible Florida wreck. *Source:* The Evening Bulletin, 4/20/1901. (8)

3) **BONIFORM**—Schooner, 147 tons, built 188 at Canning, Nova Scotia, 88' x 27' x 9.7'. From Tampa bound for Honduras, with lumber, was driven ashore near Egmont Light, April 1, 1901, during a storm. Her cargo of lumber was seen floating in Tampa Bay. She was of Tampa and owned by Captain R. C. Jones. *Source:* 37; Portsmouth Herald, 4/23/1901. (2)

4) *TORTUGAS*—Schooner, from Mobile for Apalachicola, with cypress lumber, put into Pensacola Harbor during a hurricane and collided with another vessel and sunk. Four fishing schooners also sunk. Possibly the 72-ton schooner of Charleston. *Source:* 37; Wichita Daily Eagle, 8/24/1901; Sandusky Daily Register, 8/17/1901. (1)

5) *NEPTUNE*—Russian bark, Capt. Zettukoff, left Pensacola on August 10, 1901, for Montevideo and was lost in a storm. Pieces of the wreck including part of her stern with her name on it were found on the outer beach of Santa Rosa Island. *Source:* Santa Fe New Mexican, 9/19/1901. (1)

1) Page 35. *Evelyn*—Another report says she wrecked about eight miles from the Pensacola Bar. She had 1,000 tons of coffee and 150 tons of general merchandise. Some cargo was loaded onto barges and she was refloated and taken to Mobile for repairs. *Source:* Defiance Weekly Express, 8/22/1901; Atlanta Constitution, 9/4/1901.

1902

1) *DORIS*—Four-masted bark, Capt. Masterton, of Baltimore, built 1894 in Belfast, Maine, 944 tons, 189.1' x 36.8' x 17.1', from Tampa bound for Baltimore, with phosphate rock, struck on the beach head on and swung broadside to the beach with waves crashing over her. She was then carried a mile up the beach and the seas ran her on a reef where she broke in two amidships, January 4, 1902. She ended up about one mile from the Boynton Hotel and could be seen from both Lantana and Boynton. Mistook the lights from the hotel for those of a passing vessel. The crew of 12 were saved. Vessel a total loss. *Source:* 10; The Washington Times, 1/6/1902; Indianapolis Sun, 1/7/1902; Alexandria Gazette, 1/11/1902. (5)

2) *NAIAD*—Steamer, 173 tons, built 1884 at Columbus, Georgia, 126.3' x 24' x 3.9', of Apalachicola, of the Chattahoochee River Line. Caught fire and sank, February 26, 1902, at 2 a.m. at Blountstown, Florida. All the passengers got off safely and there was no loss of life. Vessel was a total loss, and most all the cargo, including the U.S. mail, was lost. *Source:* 10; The Indianapolis Journal, 2/27/1902; The Palatka News, 3/6/1902. (7)

1) Page 54. *Caroline Kage*—Went aground on Anna Marie Key, a total loss. Crew and some rigging saved. *Source:* Atlanta Constitution, 1/18/1902.

2) Page 150. *Plunger*—Believe the Maryland-built schooner, 43.4' x 13.8' x 2.6'. From Jacksonville for Miami, with 21,000' of flooring and ceiling lumber. Became beached and everything was stripped off her. *Source:* 10; The Florida Star, 7/25/1902.

3) Page 198. *Lewis*—Built at Fogartyville, Florida, 63.2' x 18' x 5'. *Source:* 10.

1903

1) *AMELIA LYONS*—Schooner (fishing smack), Capt. Sullivan, of Mobile, a new vessel built in 1903 at Milton, Florida, 37 tons, 64.6' x 19.5' x 4.2'. From Mobile, with recently caught fish, capsized and sank during a sudden squall off East Pass, six miles offshore (another report just says 18 miles off Pensacola, July 13, 1903). Three drowned including wealthy Mobile merchant William Ward, who was on a pleasure-cruise. The survivors (four or five), some being naked, were picked up from their open boat which had no oars, after about four hours by a passing steamer, though another report says the survivors clung to a small dory and washed ashore on Santa Rosa Island. *Source:* 10; The Daily Journal (Salem, OR), 7/13/1903; Ottuma Semi-Weekly Courier, 7/14/1903; Atlanta Constitution, 7/14/1903. (1)

2) *MEXICANO*—British tank steamer, built 1893 at Sunderland, 270' x 28' x 22.5', 1,254 net tons, Captain R. S. King, of King Lines Ltd, Middlesex, England. Left Marcus Hook, Pennsylvania, bound for Vera Cruz, with petroleum, September 13, and encountered a hurricane on the 15th. Waves crashed over her until one broke her deck and flooded the fire room causing her to sink soon after. The crew had pumped hundreds of gallons of oil into the sea to try and calm the waves which worked only for short time. The boats were crushed before she sank. One survivor, a Domingo Reyarbaray, had clung to a piece of wreckage and was picked up the next day by the brig *Roxy*. Domingo had gone under with the ship but got tangled in some rigging attached to a spar which floated to the surface taking him with it. Six others were picked up by the steamer *Vidar* barely alive. Capt. Sorrenson of the *Vidar* said he was in his cabin around 9 a.m. when he heard a shout. He went to the bridge to investigate and heard the cry again coming from the ocean and noticed an object in the water. Using his glass, he saw a man stretched out on a hatch and immediately went to rescue him and eventually found the five others clinging to wreckage. There were 22 crew along with the captain, and Sorrenson stated he saw another steamer lower a lifeboat so more were probably saved. One survivor, August Osterlind, of Norway, told how some refused to leave the ship. The boatswain would not leave his bunk saying, "if he had to die he would rather die in his bunk than in the sea," and two firemen refused to leave the stoke room. Just before Osterlind jumped overboard while the ship was in the process of sinking, he heard two gunshots, believing some officers shot themselves rather than face drowning. There were seven men in the water by him and after a while, the second mate gave up his life-jacket to another seaman and

then went under. *Source:* NYT, 9/18/1903; The Kalispell Bee, 9/18/1903; The Semi-Weekly Messenger, 9/22/1903; Lowell Sun, 9/18/1903. *Note:* Most newspaper reports say she sank off the Florida coast, though others say off Virginia, the Carolinas, and Hatteras. I'll list it as a possible Florida wreck for now. (8)

3) *ARABY MAID*—Steel hulled Norwegian bark, 873 tons, built 1868 in Scotland, 194.4' x 32.5' x 19.5', from Mobile bound for Rosario, Argentina, with lumber, was rammed by the Mallory line steamer *Denver*, off the Tortugas, the evening of November 21, 1903, and sank within minutes of the collision. Of the 13 on board, the first mate and a sailor drowned and were buried at sea, and the others were taken on board the *Denver*. Now a popular dive site for tech divers, and sits in 180–205 feet of water (see GPS coordinates at end of chapter). *Source:* 33; 34; Biloxi Daily Herald, 11/27/1903. (3)

Crew on the deck of the Norwegian steel hulled bark *Araby Maid*. Courtesy of Vestfoldmuseene IKS avd. Larvik Museum, Larvik Maritime Collection.

4) *BUNKER*—Pleasure yacht, was reported from St. Augustine, December 15, 1903, as having wrecked on North Beach, one mile from town last night during a high wind. From Jacksonville for Daytona with four people on board (all saved). Owned by F. D. Casey. *Source:* The Atlanta Constitution, 12/16/1903.

1) Page 54. *Nineveh*—Steamer *Maverick* found her abandoned off the Carolinas and after boarding her they later saw her sink at Lat. 32.5°N, Long. 78.29°W. Crew had landed safely in their boat after 52 hours at the Cape Fear Lighthouse. Cargo of coal and buckwheat on board. Someone got Cape Romano and Cape Romain mixed up as *List of US Merchant Vessels* says Cape Romano, Florida. *Source:* 10; Bryan Morning Eagle, 2/1/1903; BP, 1/27/1903.

2) Page 150. *La Barbara*—Auxiliary centerboard yacht, 68' x 15' x 2'5", Capt. J. Lund, of New York, owned by Dr. E. M. Culver (his wife was the daughter of Senator W. A. Clark of Montana) who planned to meet the yacht in Miami, wrecked on shore 20 miles south of Jupiter Inlet, the last Thursday of January 1903. Only the captain and crew were on board and all were OK. They managed to save some of the yacht's costliest fittings. *Source:* NYT, 1/1/1903.

3) Page 151. *Martha T. Thomas*—Capt. Watts. Newspapers says she wrecked nine miles south of Jupiter Inlet and split in two. All the crew saved. *Source:* The Daily Pioneer, 9/16/1903.

3) Page 199. *Trojan*—Built at Palatka, of Jacksonville, 70' x 18' x 6'. *Source:* 9.

4) Page 226. *Celeste*—Not a Florida wreck. Ran ashore with a cargo of guano by the Green Cove Station, Virginia, a total loss. *Source:* 10.

1904

1) *RIMFAXE*—Norwegian bark, built 1876 at Grimstad, Norway, 526 tons, 128' x 29.3' x 17', from Campeche bound for Hamburg, with logwood, stranded on the Marquesas Reef in a storm, October 19, 1904. Crew saved by the schooner *Welcome*. May have been refloated as reported condemned from Key West. *Source:* 35; The Bennington Evening Banner, 10/20/1904. (3)

2) *MELROSE*—Schooner, foundered off the Florida coast, October 15, 1904, with a loss of seven lives (had a crew of eight and four passengers). *Source:* Evening Star, 10/20/1904. (8)

3) *LIZZIE BABCOCK*—Schooner, 589 tons, 145' x3 5' x 17.2', built 1883 at Dennisville, New Jersey, of Somers Point, New Jersey, Capt. Somers. Left Baltimore November 3 or 4, 1904, bound for Cardenas, with coal, and was never heard from again. Most papers thought she was lost off Florida during the hurricane. Possible Florida wreck. *Source:* 10; NYH, 12/30/1904. (8)

1) Page 90. *Sylph*—Yacht, owned by John A. Berkey, from Matanzas. Wreckers saved most materials and all those on board. *Source:* Little Falls Herald, 2/19/1904.

2) Pages 90 and 126. *Sweetheart*—Built at and from Mississippi, 51.8' x 17.9' x 4.4'. *Source:* 10. It was mistakenly placed twice in the second edition, though Long Key is in the middle of the Keys, so could be in either section 3 or 4.

3) Page 151. *Georges Valentine*—Italian iron bark, 882 gross tons, 767 net tons, built 1869 at Liverpool, by Bowdler, Chaffer and Co., 189.7' x 31.2' x 20.5', of Genoa. *Source:* LR, 1904.

4) Pages 151–52. *Cosme Colzada* (correct)—Was 1,405 gross tons, built 1869 at Boston, by Cutis, Smith and Co., 200' x 38.6' x 24', sheathed with yellow (composite) metal, of Barcelona. *Source:* LR, 1904.

5) Page 182. *Mary F. Godfrey*—Lumber schooner. *Source:* 10.

6) Page 226. *E.H. Weaver*—Lumber schooner. *Source:* 10.

7) Page 370. **Four-masted schooner**—This would most likely be the *James Judge* wreck (pages 151–52).

1905

1) *A. HAYFORD*—Schooner, 153 tons, 102' x 27.5' x 7.5', built 1872 at Belfast, Maine. The Assoc. Press reported from Key West, January 12, that she wrecked on the Southwest Reef near the Tortugas and was a complete wreck. From Mobile for Havana, with lumber. All the crew were saved with great difficulty, and Capt. McClennan was taken to a hospital due to his injuries from the wreck. *Source:* 10; Atlanta Constitution, 1/13/1905.

2) *H.B. HOMAN*—British three-masted schooner, 319 tons, 131.6' x 31.2' x 10.6', sheathed with yellow (composite) metal, built 1888 at Portland, New Brunswick, by E. McGuiggan, of St. Johns, New Brunswick. She was 18 days out from Kingston, Jamaica, for Jacksonville, when she went ashore six miles south of Pablo Beach after encountering three days of severe weather, Captain Atkinson and seven crewmen were all found safe on the beach, though suffering from cold and exhaustion. Vessel was a total loss. *Source:* Washington Post, 2/6/1905; Shields Daily News, 2/6/1905; LR, 1905. (6)

3) *LEIF ERIKSON*—Norwegian steamer, Captain Savard, 1,341 tons, from Matanzas bound for Philadelphia, with sugar, collided with the Standard Oil Vessel *City of Everett*, February 4, 1905, off Cape Romano in a dense

fog. The *Everett* cut into her hull to the number four hold well below the waterline. The *Leif's* crew saw no hope in saving her and took to the boats and 20 were picked up by the *Everett*, though two crew drowned trying to escape as one boat capsized. They did not see her sink as she drifted away into the fog. *Source:* Boston Daily Globe, 2/9–10/1905; NYT, 2/10/1905. (2)

4) *HELEN*—British three-masted schooner, Captain J. C. Saunders, built 1903 at Liverpool by J. S. Gardner, of Yarmouth, Nova Scotia, 319 tons, 113' x 31.2' x 11', sheathed with yellow (composite) metal. She was from St. Andrews bound for Philadelphia with coconuts, when she ran ashore on Molasses Reef, March 18, 1905, and the schooner was a total loss. Crew saved. Wreckers saved 100,000 coconuts. *Source:* Daily Press, 3/28/1905; Arizona Republican, 4/3/1905; LR, 1905. (4)

5) *PECONIC*—Steamer, Capt. Jones, built 1881 at Liverpool, 1,855 tons, 270' x 34.5' x 27'8", owned by J. W. Elwell and Co., New York, from Philadelphia for New Orleans. She was caught in a storm off the northeast Florida coast August 27, 1905, when they found themselves in about 10 to 15 fathoms of water around midnight and were ordered to head back out to sea. When they made the turn a large wave caught the steamer and knocked her on her starboard beam-end. The cargo of coal then shifted and she could not recover. She sank soon after. Only two of the 22 on board survived. One was at the wheel and the other nearby and they were able to get into one of the boats which luckily had air tanks to prevent it from sinking. The two landed at Amelia Island the next day. *Source:* 7; 10; NYTR, 8/29/1905; NYT, 8/29/1905; The Bemidji Daily Pioneer, 9/29/1905; *Note:* Barnette states the wreck was locally known as the "Razor Wreck," and is off Georgia, but close to the Florida border. Diving the site, he positively identified it as the *Peconic*. About 40 miles offshore in 70 feet of water.

6) *NOKOMIS*—Schooner, had left Gulfport with lumber, December 1905 for Cuba, but not long after sprung a leak during a gale and rapidly filled with water. Captain Borden decided to abandon her and as they were getting supplies, a large wave capsized her. Luckily one of the lifeboats got free and a jug of water and some cans of meat were saved. All on board spent six days and nights in the open boat until finally washing up on the beach at St. Andrews near death. They were all taken to Pensacola. *Source:* The River Press, 1/10/1906. Possible Florida wreck. (8)

7) *SAKATA*—Three-masted schooner, of Parrsboro, Nova Scotia, 395 tons, built 1905 at Port Greville, Nova Scotia, 149' x 35' x 12.2', Capt. John Conlon (also the owner). Bound for Havana, she capsized off Florida at Lat. 28°'56 N, Long. 86° 10' W, December 19, 1905. She was sighted by the

schooner *Helen Thomas*, December 23, who sent a boat over to her. Only one survivor, mate John F. Williams, was found clinging to the wreck who had been without food or water for four days. He survived by eating part of his oil coat. The captain, his son, and five others were lost. *Source:* 20; BP, 12/27/1905. (1)

1) Page 127. *Pargo*—Built at Jacksonville, 17 tons, 59' x 14.8' x 3.3', of Key West. *Source:* 10.

2) Page 151. *Zion*—Stranded on a reef, four miles north of the New River Station. *Source:* 10.

3) Page 199. *Marguedora* (correct)—Gas yacht, of Chicago, 80.6' x 16' x 7.8'. *Source:* 10.

4) Page 371. *Massa e Gnecco*—Built 1878 at Cornwallis, Nova Scotia, by P. R. Chichton, 1,139 tons, 196.8' x 36.1' x 23', sheathed with felt and yellow (composite) metal, Capt. Pietro Masante. She broke amidships. *Source:* The Ocala Evening Star, 1/18/1905; LL, 1904.

1906

1) *ZETA #2*—Gas yacht, 17 tons, built 1904 in Parkersburg, West Virginia, of New York, 62.5' x 15' x 2', stranded at St. Augustine Inlet, 1/20/1906. *Source:* 10.

1) September 1906 HURRICANE at Pensacola

Pensacola was hit hard by the September hurricane. The lighthouse at Horn Island was swept away, along with the keeper Johnson and his wife and daughter. The Navy yard was also hit hard, "Gunboats *Vixen Isla de Luzon, Gloucester* (former 204-foot yacht of J.P. Morgan called the *Corsair*), *Machias* and *Wasp* as well as Naval tugs *Waban* and *Accomac*, and a number of smaller tugs and launches are complete wrecks." *Postville Review*, October 5, 1906. I checked further, and most of these vessels were salvaged and returned to service as the Navy ordered salvage tugs to Pensacola immediately after the storm. Listed in service in 1908 are the *Gloucester*, *Wasp*, *Vixen*, and tugs *Waban* & *Accomac*.

Note: I'm listing most of the vessel listed as wrecked at Pensacola just to show how devastating the hurricane was, though many I'm sure, just as with the Naval vessels, were salvaged and returned to service. If I found they were saved or definitely wrecked, then I did note that.

Nineteen foreign vessels were on the beach, 25 tugs were either wrecked or on the beach, 25 fishing vessels were lost, and 100 smaller vessels were lost.

Here are a few vessels reported wrecked at Pensacola. Also noted that the Life-Saving Station on Santa Rosa Island was washed away. Appears all the iron hulled or framed vessels survived and continued to sail. Two wrecked a few months later, one off Florida.

a) Five large ships were docked at Muscogee Wharf (the wharf was destroyed and the 38 coal cars on the wharf went overboard) and all are now ashore at the head of the wharf.

1) **SUPERB**—Norwegian bark 1,515 tons, Capt. Ulrich, from Antwerp. This 246' iron bark was saved.

2) **OLIVARI**—Italian bark, 1,055 tons, Capt. F. Costa, built 1876 at Sestri, 192.9' x 35.1' x 23.4', sheathed with yellow (composite) metal, of Genoa. Not listed in 1907, so likely not saved.

3) **ALFHILD**—Swedish ship, 1,445 tons (one report says she foundered), Capt. Svenson, from Port Natal. Appears this 229-foot iron bark was also saved as still listed in 1907, though no longer in 1908.

4) **FERREIRA**—Portuguese ship Capt. deBarros, from Lisbon. This 212-foot iron framed bark was also saved. She was built in Glasgow and her original name was the *Cutty Sark* (though not the famous one).

5) Another vessel, name unknown, also ashore here. Also reported ashore or sunk in the harbor and surrounding area:

b) **CARRIE N. CHASE**—Fishing smack/schooner, 48 tons, 69.5 feet, was one of three vessels blown ashore and into the home of Laz Jacoby, whose home was destroyed, but the crew of the *Chase* were rescued from the front porch! The *Chase* was a total loss. She was built in 1899 in Maine.

c) **CELESTINE**—Steam tug, sunk west of Wright's Mill. Was 23 tons, 50.4' x 14.4' x 6.3', built 1883 at Newburg, New York, of Pensacola.

d) A large *sailing vessel* lay half submerged on the rocks off the timber boom at the foot of Alcanzis St.

e) **OKALOOSA**—Steamer, went ashore; was saved.

f) **FLORENCE WITHERBEE**—Sunk at Palafox Wharf. Passenger screw steamer, 84 tons, built 1873 at New York, of Pensacola, 95' x 17' x 6.5'. No longer listed in 1907.

g) **SIMPSON**—Tug, is on rocks at Sullivan's Ballast Crib. Unknown if salvaged.

h) **MONARCH** and **MARY LEE** are high and dry with noses onto Pine St., though should be saved. Believe the *Monarch* was saved (steamer *Monarch* of Pensacola listed in 1907), though unsure of the *Mary Lee*. A *Mary Lee* is listed in 1906 (screw steam tug, built 1905, 48 tons, 63' x 19.3' x 8.2', of Virginia) and no longer listed in 1907.

i) *A.J. CHAPMAN*—Schooner, 48 tons, built 1860 at New London, of Pensacola, 65.2' x 19.8' x 8.4', stranded at Wright's Mill Beach, Florida (Wright's Mill was in or near Pensacola, was destroyed in the 1906 hurricane).

j) *ISABELLA GILL*—Schooner, 585 tons, built 1891 in Baltimore, of Philadelphia, 153.1' x 35.5' x 14.6', left Mayport August 17, 1906, and never heard from again. Eight lives lost. Possible Florida wreck.

k) *HEREFORD*—Norwegian bark, 241' x 37' x 23', built 1869 at Glasgow, Capt. Jensen, from Luderite Bay, 1,524 tons, was ashore. One report says she couldn't be salvaged and was abandoned, but she obviously was saved and repaired. She left Pensacola for Buenos Ayres, with lumber, and encountered a severe storm on March 29, 1907, which dismasted her and tore away her boats, causing her to be helpless. Three crewmen were lost overboard. Captain Jensen and the first mate were seriously injured. Luckily, the remaining 15 were rescued off Cape Hatteras by a steamer, none too soon, as she was then in a sinking condition.

l) *ANDREA*—Norwegian bark, Capt. Quale, from Port natal, 1,324 tons, was ashore. She was saved and continued in service.

m) *CAMPBELL*—Norwegian bark, 1,155 tons, built 1879 at Weymouth, Nova Scotia, by C. Campbell, 191' x 37.9' x 22', of Haugesund, Norway. She was sunk while loading pitchpine was condemned and sold for $50.00.

n) *AVANTI*—Norwegian ship, Capt. Anderson, to sail for Montevideo, was saved and wrecked the next year in the Tortugas (see 1907 wrecks).

o) *INGRID*—Norwegian iron ship, Capt. Donnell, from Antwerp. Saved and continued in service.

p) *LILLA*—German iron bark, 1125 tons, was ashore. Saved and continued in service.

q) *CHACMA*—British (*Lloyd's* says Norwegian) iron bark, 608 tons, was ashore. Saved and continued in service.

r) *NOACH VI*—Swedish bark, Capt. Bergfeldt, from Nort Nollot, 1,413 tons. Was saved and continued in service.

s) *HEIMDAL*—Norwegian ship, Capt. Hansen, from Hull, 1,467 tons, was ashore. Was saved and continued in service.

t) *AVON*—Italian ship, Capt. Avegno, from Genoa. Saved and continued in service.

u) *MARIE*—German iron bark, 1,057 tons, Capt. Frenk, from Lynn. Was sunk, refloated, and continued in service.

v) *DONNA CHRISTINA*—Schooner, 174 tons, was saved and remained in service.

Sources for the Pensacola wrecks: 10; 35; London Standard, 10/5/1906; The Pensacola Journal, 9/27/1906; NYT, 9/30/1906; 10/1/1906; Washington Post, 9/30/1906; The Atlanta Constitution, 10/1/1906.

OCTOBER 1906 HURRICANE (KEYS)

There was a great number of lives lost during this hurricane, mostly those working on the new railroad. The steamer *Peerless* was damaged, but lost a number of people (she wrecked in another hurricane in 1909). A **PILE DRIVER** with two men was lost. The houseboat *GAMMA* was capsized but no lives lost. Quarterboat *(HOUSEBOAT #3)* was blown ashore near Long Key and all on board were safe. *Four large barges* and a *steam pile driver* were blown out to sea off Long Key and lost. A **COAL BARGE** was lost in the same area. Another **BARGE** with the blacksmith's shop, machine shop, and stove rooms was lost near the Viaduct, but may be raised. Another **BARGE** with decorative work (seven) for the Viaduct arches was lost. Gas launch *ENTERPRISE* was blown ashore and destroyed. Gas launch *EDEN* was ashore, and launches *PALM* and *COLUMBIA* are missing. Launch *ELMORA* was capsized.

At Key West, the schooner *BONITA* sank at Sweeney Dock, the schooner *LEONARD* slammed against the marine railway and was beat to pieces and her cargo of sponge lost. Most of the coal boats were wrecked at Lowe's Dock. *Source:* The Pensacola Journal, 10/21–26/1906.

1) *HOUSEBOAT # 4*—The men on board were working on a concrete viaduct for the FEC Railroad at Long Key, and she was blown to sea at 1:00 a.m., October 18, 1906, and wrecked during the hurricane. One hundred and four men drowned. Only a few survived by clinging to some wreckage and were picked up 90 miles off Key West and taken to Mobile by the steamer *Colorado*. Another report says it wrecked off Long Key and that of the 125 on board (another report says 145 were on board), 75 drowned (though may be more), the others saved and taken to Jacksonville. The crew of the *Colorado* said the four they picked up were waist deep in water when found. Five others were found on another raft of wreckage by the British steamer *Heatherpool* and taken to Norfolk. Those survivors said that just

before they were rescued the sixth man went crazy and jumped into the sea and drowned. *Source:* 22; NYT, 10/23/1906; The Ocala Banner, 10/26/1906; Tulsa Daily World, 10/26/1906; Cameron County Press, 11/1/1906.

2) *HALPY*—Houseboat, the men were also working on the FEC railroad. It was moored off Lower Matecumbe Key about a mile from the mainland to work on the railroad bridge there. On October 18, the hurricane struck her. There were 32 men on board and all were asleep when the storm hit about 11 p.m. At 1 a.m. they were all on deck, the storm caught her and she dragged her three anchors and went aground about 100 yards from the beach and the 22 men who were on the port side were washed overboard by a large wave and carried out to sea along with the boat. The 10 on the starboard side clung to the boat but an hour later she began to break up and eight were washed overboard by another huge wave. By daylight only John Russel, of Key West, and a man named McBride of New York were left. They drifted out to sea on the cabin roof which was torn off in the storm. The *New York Times* reported Russel's tale:

> For five or six hours we floated on the raft. Then it turned turtle and broke up. When I saw McBride last he was fighting for his life in the water. I crawled up on a section of the capsized roof and drifted about on it for twenty-four hours. . . . Sharks gathered about the wreckage, but when they turned on their backs to attack me the heavy spikes in the timbers cut their snouts and they could not get at me. I prodded them with a piece of a boathook until I became too weak to drive them away.

Luckily, Capt. Knowles of the *El Paso* sighted Russel and sent a boat to rescue him. The only survivor of the ill-fated *Halpy*. As with many stories, another paper had a slightly different version.

It says there were 37 men on board the houseboat moored at Matecumbe. It also relates John Russel's story, which said he and eight others clung to piece of flooring after the boat broke up. At daybreak the flooring tipped over and he grabbed a piece of wreckage but was cut up by the protruding nails. Another man floated by on a door which had ropes attached but he drowned when it collided with other wreckage. Russel grabbed the rope and lashed together the door and some other pieces to make a raft. He floated another day and that night found himself surrounded by sharks. He ripped off a plank with nails on one end and beat off the sharks as best he could. By morning the sharks had all left. After 36 hours he was picked up by the steamer *El Paso*. Also reported the steamer *Alton* rescued 24 other survivors from one of the other houseboats and took them to Savannah. *Source:* 22; The Abbeville Press and Banner, 10/31/1906; Daily Press, 10/27/1906; NYT, 10/24/1906.

NO 26   QUARTER BOAT NO 5. F. E. C E. RAILWAY

Old postcard photo of an FEC quarterboat/houseboat. Courtesy of the Monroe County Library, Key West/Art and Historical Collection.

3) *PALM*—Gas tug, working for the FEC Railroad. Built 1904 at San Mateo, Florida, 38.9' x 10.2' x 3.1'. Capt. Charles Kelly and Engineer Martin were aboard when moored about ¼ mile from shore in the Florida Keys. A construction barge with bridge materials collided with her in the hurricane and sank the tug. The two men managed to jump onto the barge, but were soon washed overboard where they clung to some planks of wood and floated on these from 9 a.m. October 17 until 11 a.m. October 20 when they were spotted 60 miles from land and about 80 miles from Key West and picked up by the steamer *Montauk* (from Galveston bound for Liverpool) and were landed at Liverpool. *Source:* 10; The Sun, 11/20/1906.

1) Page 36. **Gus Shammel**—Built at Freeport, Florida, of Pensacola, 62' x 14.9' x 4'. *Source:* 10.

2) Page 36. **Carrie N. Chase**—Built in Boothbay, Maine, 69.5' x 20.1' x 8.1'. *Source:* 10.

3) Page 37. **Francis & Margery**—Of Pensacola, 74.2' x 19.7' x 7.4'. *Source:* 10.

4) Page 38. **Two Sisters**—built 1890 (correction). *Source:* 10.

5) Page 38. **Wm H. Warren**—Built at Harpswell, Maine, 56.9' x 18.2' x 6.3'. *Source:* 10.

6) Page 127. *St. Lucie*—She was anchored on the lee side of Elliot Key when a tidal wave engulfed the island killing about 250 on the island, along with 21 of the 97 on board. The steamer was sunk. She was from Miami for Knights Key with camp supplies. A *Barge* moored at Elliot Key was torn away from her moorings and later picked up off the Bahamas, and 50 of the 100 on board were reported as lost (probably another barge working on the FEC railroad). *Source:* 10; The Barre Daily Times, 10/20/1906.

1907

AVANTI—Norwegian three-masted iron hulled ship, from Pensacola bound for Uruguay, with lumber. Wrecked on Loggerhead Key, January 22, 1907. Crew and much of the cargo saved. Built 1875 in Glasgow, 261.4' x 39'.3' x 23.8', 1,818 gross tons. Now a popular dive and snorkel site known as the "Windjammer Wreck," lies in 18 to 21 feet of water with mooring buoys (see GPS coordinates at end of chapter). *Source:* 17; 33; 34; 35. *Note:* She was one of the many vessels that went aground in the 1906 hurricane at Pensacola and was saved.

Painting of the Norwegian ship *Avanti*, wrecked in 1907. Courtesy of Image: Aust-Agder Museum and Archive, Arendal, Norway.

2) *STERLING*—Norwegian bark, of Porsgrunn, built 1878 at Quebec, 1,296 tons, 202.6' x 37.6' x 23.1', from Pascagoula bound for Montevideo, with a cargo of pitch pine, wrecked on Molasses Reef, March 19, 1907. Originally

the full rigged ship *Polynesian*, but converted to a bark when sold to a new Norwegian owner in 1893. *Source:* 35; 39. (3)

3) *UNCLE SAM*—G/V, 14 tons, built 1903 at Holly Hill, Florida, of St. Augustine, burned on the Indian River, May 1, 1907, and all 78 on board saved. *Source:* 10. (7)

4) *RUBY*—Steamer, 17 tons, built 1880, of Georgia, 53' x 10.3' x 3.9', burned at Jacksonville, August 24, 1907. *Source:* 10. (7)

1) Page 38. *Florence Witherbee*—Of Pensacola, 95' x 17' x 6.5'. *Source:* 10.

2) Page 152. *Anna F*—Built at Mobile, 47.2' x 12.5' x 4.1'. *Source:* 10.

3) Page 226. *Rita*—Yacht, of New York, 56.4' x 18' x 4.4'. Possible Florida wreck. *Source:* 10.

1908

1) *TRINIDAD*—British barkentine, built 1891 at Kempt, Nova Scotia, by H. H. Greene, 690 tons, 158.2' x 36' x 16.1', sheathed with yellow (composite) metal. From Cuba bound for New York, with mahogany, wrecked during a storm off the Florida coast (believe near Jupiter). The crew were saved from the sinking ship after clinging to the rigging for five days and nearly starved. They were taken to Nassau. *Source:* The Morning Astorian, 4/12/1908. (Most likely British brig mentioned on page 371 of *Shipwrecks of Florida*, second edition.) (8)

2) *MAYFLOWER*—America's Cup Defender (won the race in 1886), 110 tons, 100' x 23.6' x 9.84', built in 1886 of oak and hard pine. Originally a sloop but re-rigged as a schooner in 1889. She was on her way to look for sunken treasure with a group of Harvard students. She was caught in a hurricane well off Florida's east coast and all on board saved by a fruit steamer. She was later seen drifting off the SE coast. Possible Florida wreck. *Source:* Evening Star, 10/7/1908; Virginia Citizen, 10/9/1908; Wikipedia. *Note:*

The ex-America's Cup winner *Mayflower*. Library of Congress Prints and Photographic Division/ Detroit Photographic Co.

The treasure company was called the Southern Research Co. Appears they were looking for the wreck of the *Concepcion* on the Silver Banks. Some newspapers reported some Jamaican divers had previously found it in 1902, and about 10,000 pieces of eight were retrieved and brought back to Jamaica. The *Mayflower* was going to pick up a Jamaican diver who said he knew where the wreck was after finding it while laying a submarine cable after the Spanish American War. The wreck was salvaged in 1687 by William Phipps and found again in 1978 by Burt Webber Jr., and much was salvaged. (8)

3) *MAGGIE*—Steamer, 19 tons, built 1893 at and from Mobile, 50' x 1' x 4.7', burned at Mulat, Florida, May 29, 1908. *Source:* 10. (7)

1) Page 153. *Melrose* (formerly the *W.H. Oler*)—Three-masted schooner, built 1880 at Bath, Maine, by D. Blaisdell, 693 tons, 150.9' x 35' x 17.4'. She had wrecked near Ocracoke Inlet, February 1908. Salvage was abandoned as she was full of water and her stern was coming apart. Don't know how some of the wreck managed to drift down to Hobe Sound (was some of this from when she wrecked in 1904?). Interesting note is she had previously wrecked off Florida in 1904 under Capt. Kelly. She was from Jacksonville bound for Nassau, with lumber, and capsized near Palm Beach (others say Lauderdale) just before sunset, October 15, 1904, by a large wave. She had a crew of eight and four passengers, two who were women. She righted, and the survivors, of which there were five, took to the rigging. Two were newlyweds, a Mr. and Mrs. Weller. One mast fell on Mrs. Weller and instantly killed her. Mr. Weller washed ashore near Palm Beach on a hatch cover. The captain, mate, and two crew also made shore. *Source:* 6; The Bennington Evening Banner, 10/20/1904; Daily Kennebeck Journal, 10/21/1904. *Note:* Lloyd's Register continues to list her in service until she wrecked again in 1908.

1909

1) *MARY SANFORD*—Schooner, Capt. Stone, of Wellfleet, Massachusetts, built 1881 at East Boston, 455 tons, 136 feet, left Morgan City bound for New York or Boston, January 6, 1909, and was abandoned off Florida's coast during a gale, January 31. One report says she struck some rocks and sprung a leak and then dismasted. Crew of nine abandoned her and took to their dory and were picked up a few days later by the British steamer *Mineola* and landed in France. Another says the steamer took off the crew from the wreck. *Source:* NYT, 2/16–27/1909; BP, 2/16/1909; Evening Star, 2/17/1908. (8)

2) *CLEOPATRA*—Schooner, Capt. Marton, left St. Andrews for Pensacola, January 23, 1909, with turpentine and rosin. Wrecked off the Panhandle during the January 1909 storm, and drifted for a couple of months until washing up on St. George Island around March 20. All on board had drowned and their bodies washed up on Hurricane Island weeks previous. A number of vessels had reported seeing the derelict vessel. *Source:* Indiana Evening Gazette, 3/20/1909; The Richmond Palladium and Sun-Telegram, 2/15/1909. (1)

3) *CELER*—Norwegian bark, built 1880 at Grimstad, Norway, Capt. Jensen, 650 tons, 154.3' x 32.4' x 18.9', from Pernambuco for Carrabelle, stranded and then broke in two, February 11, 1909, at SW Cape Shoal, about 12 miles east of Carrabelle. Sails, tackle, anchors, etc., were saved. *Source:* 35; The Pensacola Journal, 2/23, 3/21, 1909. (1)

4) *QUARTERBOAT #3*—Was lost at Cudjoe Key, when 700 pounds of dynamite exploded aboard her, killing three instantly, and severely wounding 12 others. Believe it was working on the FEC Railroad. *Source:* The Thibodaux Sentinel, 5/22/1909.

Photo of FEC *Quarterboat #3*, at Long Key Viaduct, 1906. Courtesy of the Monroe County Library, Key West/Art and Historical Collection.

5) *ZEEBURG*—Dutch steamship, of Amsterdam, 3,039 tons, built 1899 at Sunderland, by R. Thompson and Sons, 325' x 48.6' x 21.3'. Captain Von Rossen (or Rassen), from Hamburg bound for Jacksonville, with phosphate

fertilizer. She struck the south jetty at the entrance to the St. John's River five miles below Mayport, 25 miles from Jacksonville, which tore a hole in her side and filled the hold with six to 12 feet of water. Too rough for tugs to get to her and she eventually sank. The crew saved. *Source:* Daily Press, 9/28/1909; Washington Post, 9/27/1909; Atlantic Daily Telegraph, 9/22/1909. (6)

6) October 1909 hurricane at Key West.

There were about 100 vessels in the harbor when the hurricane struck. Only five remained after the storm, the rest either ashore or put to sea. Tugs *SYBIL* and the *SADIE* were both sunk at Bahia Honda. All 12 on board the *Sybil* were lost including Captain Parker except one deckhand who was found unconscious under a wheelbarrow. He relates that the other 11 grabbed the life preservers and jumped overboard feet first and that the preservers stayed around their feet and their heads went under water drowning them all, which doesn't make much sense. All were working on the FEC railroad. The crew of the *Sadie* survived. *Source:* NYT, 10/12/1909; Pomeroy Herald, 10/21/1909; Lincoln Nebraska State Journal, 10/14/1909. (3)

7) *FLORENCE R. HEWSON*—Schooner, of Annapolis Royal, Nova Scotia, 318 tons, built 1893 at Parrsboro, Nova Scotia, 133.9' x 31.3' x 12. Was abandoned during the hurricane. She first encountered the storm about 25 miles off Havana, eventually having to abandon her. The crew were picked up by the steamer *Pleroma* and taken to Key West. Possible Florida wreck. *Source:* NYT, 10/12/1909; LR, 1909. (8)

Key West Harbor after the 1909 hurricane. Courtesy of the Monroe County Library, Key West.

Fishing fleet docks after the 1909 hurricane at Key West. Courtesy of the Monroe County Library, Key West.

8) **Unk. VESSEL**—The steamer *Woton* reported a submerged wreck at Lat. 23°40' N, Long. 81° W. *Source:* Manchester Courier, 11/22/1909. (3)

1) Page 56. *Jimmie*—Built at Port Jefferson, New York, 43.9' x 16' x 4.2'. *Source:* 10.

The sidewheel steamer *Peerless*, pushing a barge. It was lost in the 1909 hurricane. Courtesy of the Monroe County Library, Key West/postcard #31, gift of Mr. J. Tedder.

2) Page 92. *Peerless*—Was working for the FEC Railroad as a fresh water supply boat.

3) Page 91. *Emma Eliza*—Built at and from Key West, 43.8' x 16.6' x 4.5'. *Source:* 10.

4) Page 371. *Coquimbo*—Built in Glasgow in 1876, 1,015 tons, 204.8' x 33.5' x 20.6'. Went aground January 31, 1909. *Source:* Norsk Maritime Museum.

Photo of one of the steel masts on the site of the Norwegian bark *Coquimbo*, wrecked in 1909 off Boynton Beach.

1910

1) *WILLENA*—A 60-foot yacht built in Oshkosh, of St. Louis bound for Havana, Capt. Halsey, was being towed by a tug, along with two barges, when she parted her cable during a storm, January 28, 1910, and smashed into one of the barges. The crew of six managed to grab some lines and get aboard the barge as the *Willena* was going to pieces. The barge soon parted from the tug and landed in St. Joseph's Bay. Pieces of the *Willena* washed up along the beaches. *Source:* NYT, 1/31/1910; Oshkosh Daily Northwestern, 1/31/1910, 2/9/1910. (1)

2) *LEBRA*—Yacht, Captain Charles M. S. Bennett (or Stuart Bennet, a writer of New York), left Marco, Florida, bound for Key West, and struck a rock jetty (another source says a piling for the FEC Railway) at the NW entrance to Key West Harbor, December 25, 1910, at full sail and both engines working and instantly went to pieces. The three on board managed to cling to the bottom of the overturned craft. Mr. Bennett, being badly injured, was swept off after a couple of hours. His wife grew hysterical and tried to jump in after him but was pulled to safety by Herman Parker, the friend of the Bennett's. He said she continually tried to join her husband, but he managed to hold her with one arm, and the other held onto the hull. By the next morning, she broke free and joined her husband. Parker was picked up by the pilot boat near the NW Lighthouse where the hull drifted ashore. Three others on board were also saved. *Source:* Norwich Bulletin, 12/28/1910; The Marion Daily Mirror, 12/28/1910; Washington Post, 12/28/1910. (3)

4) *YALE*—G/P, 14 tons, built 1903, of Jacksonville, 52' x 8' x 3.2', burned at Welaka, 8/3/1910. *Source:* 10. (7)

5) *HEARTSEASE*—Schooner, 16 tons, built 1882 at Roslyn, New York, of Key West, 52.3' x 14.8' x 3.9', foundered at Key West, October 17, 1910. *Source:* 10. (3)

6) *NABOB*—Sloop, broke from her moorings at the Marquesas and was swept to sea during a hurricane with the loss of all six on board. *Source:* The Times Dispatch, 10/21/1910. (3)

7) *VIVIAN*—Schooner, also swept to sea at the same time as the *Nabob* and lost, though nobody was on board at the time. Another schooner, the *Standard*, was also swept away at the Marquesas, but must have been recovered as it's listed in service for a few more years. *Source:* The Times Dispatch, 10/21/1910. (3)

1) Page 92. *Louisiane*—French transatlantic steamship. During a gale, she ran aground on Sombrero Reef with 547 passengers. All passengers were

safe and she was eventually refloated and went to New Orleans to be surveyed before sailing back to Havre. *Source:* London Standard, 2/3/1911. *Note:* See photo in chapter 4.

2) Page 93. *Edward T Stotesbury*—This source says stranded on Pigeon Key, a total loss. *Source:* Washington Post, 10/21/1910.

3) Page 127. *Alexander Jones*—She was a steam screw tug, 350 HP engine, of Wilmington. She had left Jacksonville October 12, bound for Knight's Key to try and salvage the *Edward T. Stotesbury*, which was stranded on the reef there, and tow her to Baltimore. By the next evening, they encountered the first of a hurricane, and the next morning while in the area of the Fowey Rock Light, the sides of the deck house were stove in and she was soon filling with water. Luckily, she was seen by a passing steamer, and Capt. W. A. Sanders, and the crew of seven were all saved by the steamer *Ennisbrook*, and none too soon, as the *Jones* sank right after they were gotten off at great peril to the *Ennisbrook*. According to the story reported in the *Biloxi Daily Herald*,

> The rescue was performed with the greatest difficulty and danger. Lines were thrown to the tug and she was hauled alongside. As the tug came in contact with the iron hull of the steamer the concussion caused her to fill—she was already more than half filled—and she immediately sank. The men all had hold of lines that had been thrown to them and had life preservers on. Two of the men lost their lines but others were thrown to them which they managed to grasp and fix around their bodies and they were hauled on board by the crew of the *Ennisbrook*.

The *Ennisbrook* fought the hurricane, which got even worse, for the next five days. The schooner the tug was sent to save was also lost during the hurricane. The *A. Jones* had been recently rebuilt and probably converted for use as a tug at that time. She was owned by the Wilmington Towing Company and was said she was one of the most powerful tugs working along the coast. *Source:* 10; Daily Press, 10/21/1910; Biloxi Daily Herald, 10/20/1910.

4) Page 183. *Magic City* (correct)—Barnette says she was removed in 1911 by the Army Corps of Engineers. *Source:* 7.

5) Page 183. *Wm. W. Converse*—Of Philadelphia for Cuba, with a cargo of coal, Capt. E. J. Miller, went to pieces during a hurricane on Tuesday afternoon, October 18, 1910. Captain and two of the crew were lost, one being killed by a piece of wreckage while in the surf having almost reached the shore. *Source:* The Times Dispatch, 10/21/1910.

6) Page 200. *Mawagra II*—G/Y, of Boston, 44.1' x 11.2' x 4.7'. *Source:* 10.

1911

1) *HANNAH M. BELL*—British steel screw schooner rigged steamship, built 1893 at Stockton by Ropner and Sons, of Stockton, 2,998 tons, 315' x 40.5' x 20.3', Captain Thomas, from Norfolk bound for Vera Cruz, with coal, ran aground on Elbow Reef, April 4, 1911, and soon broke up. Now a popular dive site which was known as "Mike's Wreck" for many years. See GPS coordinates at end of chapter. *Source:* LR, 1911; Marion Weekly Star, 5/6/1911; Sun Sentinel, 9/22/2012. *Note:* Some of the coal in the area is from the steamer *Quoque* (page 129) which grounded on top of the *Hannah* in 1920 and threw off much of her cargo of coal to lighten her. The *Quaque* floated off a few days later. (4)

2) *QUEEN*—Schooner, 40 tons, built 1892 at Eau Gallie, Florida, of Key West, 63' x 17.6' x 7', stranded at Phillips Inlet, May 9, 1911 (other reports say on beach at St. Andrews). She was an oil schooner owned by the Standard Oil Company. From Tampa bound for Panama City, loaded with oil in barrels. Believed all five of her crew were drowned. *Source:* 10; Lowell Sun, 5/12/1911. (1)

3) *WATER BOY*—G/T, 14 tons, built 1906 at New Orleans, of Pensacola, 52.9' x 13.4'x 3', exploded at East Pass, Florida, June 15, 1911. *Source:* 10. (1)

4) *WINFIELD S. SCHUSTER*—Schooner, built 1904 at Rockport, Maine, of Boston, 1,481 tons, 218' x 42.7' x 19.9', from Norfolk bound for Tampa, struck on Rebecca Shoal, October 27, 1911, and immediately sank. Her cargo of coal may have been saved. Crew saved. *Source:* 10; Galveston Daily News, 10/30/1911; Brownsville Herald, 10/31/1911. (3)

1) Page 39. *Belle*—from Boggy, Florida bound for Pensacola, went to pieces during a storm and sank in Choctawhatchee Bay. Captain Thomas's two children and two others drowned. *Source:* The Bennington Evening Banner, 4/28/1911.

2) Page 127. *Star of the Sea*—Of Boston, four-masted schooner, stranded on French Reef (another report says Molasses Reef). From Pensacola bound for San Juan, Puerto Rico, with 615,000 feet of lumber, most of which was saved. It was reported that she may be saved, but not listed in service after 1911 so most likely lost. *Source:* 10; BP, 12/7/1911.

3) Page 153. *Edithanna*—G/Y, built at Atlantic City, 54' x 15.4' x 4'. *Source:* 10.

4) Page 200. *Bertha Ritter*—Built at and of Jacksonville, 49.5' x 13' x 5'. *Source:* 10.

5) Page 200. *Hester*—Was 97.4' x 25.5' x 5', of Tampa. *Source:* 10.

1912

1) *DOVER*—Freight steamer (formerly the *Westover*), 617 tons, 165' x 28' x 12', built 1873 at Wilmington, of the Texas Steamship Co., went aground trying to enter the St. John's River at Mayport, October 5, 1912. She was abandoned after attempts to salvage her were unsuccessful. *Merchant Vessels of the U.S.* mistakenly listed her as wrecked in Louisiana. *Source:* 10; Kittanning Simpsons Daily Ledger, 10/7/1912; Galveston Daily News, 10/13/1912.

2) *MONARCH*—Tug, 143 tons, built 1882 at Charleston, of Pensacola, 105.9' x 22' x 11'. Well known off Florida, and was one of the filibusters bringing arms, ammo and men to Cuba during the insurrection there. She was on her way from Pensacola to Cuba with two barges in tow. They hoped to get coal at Sanibel Island first. Captains Mayo and Olaf Johanneson were in charge. Capt. Mayo said the accident was caused by the shifting sands and that the bar about four miles offshore had changed considerably. Capt. Mayo had ordered sounding to be taken and the depth was fine. When just about to throw the lead again, the bow drove into the sandbar off Boca Grande near the entrance to Charlotte Harbor. They tried to get her off, but the ocean soon became rough and battered the sternpost causing her to leak. Soon after she listed to port and her sides split, flooding her. They still tried in vain to get her off by throwing 190 tons of coal overboard to lighten her, but to no avail. They soon had to abandon her in the boat and rowed to the barges they had been towing where they waited until help arrived. The barges were saved. *Source:* 10; The Pensacola Journal, 11/21/1912, 12/15/1912. (2)

The schooner *Freddie Hencken*, wrecked on the Cape San Blas Shoals, in 1912. Courtesy of the State Archives of Florida.

1) Page 39. *Elzada*—Of Gulfport, 52.6' x 19.7' x 4.6', went ashore and soon broke up near Ft. Barrancas. Cargo of dross rosin. She was stripped of most everything and most cargo saved. *Source:* 10; The Pensacola Journal, 2/20/1912.

2) Page 39. *Freddie Hencken*. See photo.

3) Pages 183–84. *Emily B*—Lost 1/6/1912. *Source:* 10.

4) Page 200. *Cero*—G/Y, 51.2' x 17' x 5'. *Source:* 10.

5) Page 201. *W.W. Phipps*—Either a tug or gas cargo vessel, 37' x 10.8' x 3'. *Source:* 10.

6) Page 201. *Senrab*—Built at Camden, Maine, of Jacksonville, 52' x 12' x 7'. *Source:* 10.

1913

1) **UNK. WRECK**—Two steamers reported wreckage off the Keys. One reported logs floating at Lat. 24°51' N, 80°37' W. Another saw part of some wreckage of a sailing vessel about 20 feet long and 12 feet wide missing the bow and stern, at Lat. 25°21' N, 80°05' W. *Source:* The Philadelphia Inquirer, 5/20/1913. *Note:* Possibly part of the schooner *Venture* wrecked earlier? (4)

2) *MALWA*—Brigantine, of Quebec, 540 tons, 165.2' x 35' x 13.3', built 1901 at Black River, New Brunswick, from Trinidad for Gulfport, with asphalt, was abandoned in the Gulf of Mexico after being dismasted and in a sinking state, December 25, 1913. Crew were rescued. She was seen drifting December 26, 1913, at Lat. 25°42' N, Long. 85°57' W. Possible Florida wreck. *Source:* 20; Galveston Daily News, 12/27-31/1913. (8)

1) Page 57. *Vandalia*. See photo.

2) Page 93. *Clifford N. Carver*. See photo.

3) Page 128. *Lugano* (correct)—Iron steamer, 3,598 tons, 350.1' x 40.1' x 24', of Liverpool, built by the S.B. Co. Now a popular dive site in 25 to 30 feet of water on Long Reef, just south of the wreck of the *Mandalay* in the Biscayne National Park. You could easily dive both the same day. See GPS coordinates at end of chapter. *Source:* LR, 1913; National Park Service.

4) Page 128. *Venture*—Left Mobile, March 16, 1813, Captain D. H. Nisbet. *Waco Morning News*, March 23, 1913 reports: "The *Venture* sailed from Mobile last Sunday for Santo Domingo with a cargo of lumber and encountered a severe storm Tuesday. Most of the provisions were damaged in the

The schooner *Vadalia*, at the dock. Courtesy of the State Archives of Florida.

The schooner *Clifford N. Carver* aground on Tennessee Reef, 1913. U.S. Federal Document Collection, Special and Area Studies, George A. Smathers Libraries, University of Florida, Gainesville.

The steamer *Lugano* aground on Long Reef in 1913. Note the similarity to the *Alicia* (photo chapter 4). *Yachting Magazine* "Wreck Ashore," April 1942.

Another photo of the *Lugano* on the reef. Courtesy of the U.S. National Park Service, Biscayne National Park.

storm, and the crew was forced to take refuge on top of the cabin of the waterlogged schooner until rescued." Captain and crew of seven rescued by the British steamer *Reliance* and taken to Key West. A number of papers say they were found off Sand Key. *Source:* Evening Star, 3/23/1913. (3)

5) Page 129. **Samuel T. Beacham**—According to Capt. Fern of the British steamer, the *Beacham* attempted to cross her path and was cut almost in half, sinking within three minutes in the Florida Straight off Sandy Beach. They rescued the captain and one passenger from the schooner. *Source:* Harrisonburg Evening News, 4/4/1913.

6) Page 153. **Huntress**—Gas yacht, 78.9' x 22' x 5.7'. *Source:* 10.

1914

1) **COLUMBIA**—Passenger steamer (construction steamer for the Flagler system), 82 tons, built 1900 at Stillwater, Mississippi, of St. Augustine, 117.3' x 24' x 4', capsized and foundered near Conch Key, January 13, 1914. The second engineer, Charles Seymour, was lost. *Source:* 10; Atlanta Constitution, 1/14/1914. (4)

2) **F.J. LUCKENBACH**—Iron freight steamer, built 1886 at Sunderland, England, by R. Thompson and Son, 2,564 tons, 282.4' x 38.7' x 18.7', of New York. She was previously named the *Marie* and before that the *Euskaro*. Left Tampa, May 15, 1915, bound for Baltimore with a cargo of phosphate rock, and was never heard from again. Back in January, she had been in a collision in Tampa Bay with the steamer *Algiers*. May have been damaged more than the captain and owners thought. Captain A. K. Webb and 29 crew were lost. It's believed she sank somewhere off Florida's coast. Her lifeboat was found at Lat. 37°N, Long. 74.31°W, which could have drifted north in the Gulf Stream. Possible Florida wreck. *Source:* The Sun, 5/29/1914; Washington Times, 5/28/1914; The Evening Independent, 5/29/1914; LR, 1914. (8)

1) Page 57. **Mildred**—The Associated Press release says she sunk five miles southwest of the Tampa Bay entrance after the collision on November 19, 1914. Her topmast deck was just above water where she lay. The *Brazos*, of Tampa, which was being towed in that night by the tug *Coney*, parted her cable and washed up on the beach at Egmont Key. She was saved, but wrecked off Florida in 1917. *Source:* The Pensacola Journal, 11/20/1914; The Watchman and Southern, 11/25/1914.

2) Page 201. **Kennedy**—Built at Lyons, Iowa, 121.5' x 24.4' x 3.9'. *Source:* 10.

3) Page 201. *Melba*—Gas/fishing vessel, built at and from Jacksonville, 35.2' x 11.5' x 3.3'. *Source:* 10.

1915

1) *MATTIE WINSLOW*—Schooner, from Glasgow bound for Havana, was abandoned after striking a reef in a heavy sea off Florida, January 10, 1915. Crew picked up in their small boat the next day off Cape Florida by the steamer *Van*. *Source:* Atlanta Constitution, 1/12/1915. (5)

2) *BAY BELLE*—Yacht, struck a submerged wreck off the Fowey Rock Lighthouse, March 7, 1915, and sank in 18 feet of water. She was owned by millionaire E. O. Eshelby. All on board were saved by the lighthouse tender. *Source:* Alexandria Gazette, 3/8/1915. (4)

3) *MARY HOWARD*—Steamer (tow), 38 tons, built 1900 at Palatka, of Jacksonville, 54' x 18.6' x 5', burned at the mouth of Little Manatee River, 6/9/1915. *Source:* 10. (7)

4) *JOHN G. WHILDEN*, *GERTIE*, and **DIVE BOAT**—The *J. Whilden* was a fishing schooner of Mobile, built 1839 at Philadelphia, 51 tons, 78.3' x 18.8' x 6.9', wrecked during a hurricane near Tarpon Springs (another report says ashore at Port St. Joe), September 4, 1915, and eight of the nine on board were lost. It was also reported that a *dive boat* belonging to the sponge fishing vessel *Beatrice* was also missing with four men on board for the last week. Also feared all nine on board the schooner *GERTIE* may be lost as the schooner was seen the 3rd off Florida's gulf coast with masts gone and in a helpless condition. *Source:* Galveston Daily News, 9/9/1915; Washington Post, 9/6/1915. (2)

5) *DIAMONDFIELD*—Three-masted schooner (formerly the *Emma S. Lord*), 374 tons, built 1903 in Maine, 139.8' x 32.2' x 10.5', from Texas bound for Jamaica, with kerosene, gasoline, and motor parts. Foundered off Tillman, Florida (now Palm Bay, Brevard County). One report said found capsized and floating off Florida's coast. Most likely from the September 23 hurricane. Seven lives were lost. *Source:* 10. (5)

6) *NELLIE GRANT*—Schooner 19 tons, 43' x 15.3' x 7', built 1891 in Maine, of Tampa, and launch *SNAPPER*, owned by F. J. Stamm and W. A. Walshingham. Both lost off the beach at Boca Grande, December 1915. *Source:* 10; The Public Ledger, 12/17/1915. (2)

7) *MAY F*—Gas/cargo vessel, 19 tons, built 1913 at Middleboro, Florida, of Jacksonville, 50.6' x 14.7' x 5.9', burned at Black Creek, 12/22/1915. *Source:* 10; Kingston Daily Gleaner, 11/7/1917. (7)

1) Page 154. *Frances*—Gas yacht, built in Maryland, 60' x 17' x 4.5'. *Source:* 10.

2) Page 201. *Homer Hand*—Gas/passenger vessel, built at LaBelle, Florida, of Key West, 59.1' x 13.5' x 3.8'. *Source:* 10.

1916

1) *CARRIE STRONG*—Three-masted schooner, 473 tons, built 1882 at Thomasville, Maine, of Rockland, Maine, 151' x 35.3' x 12.2'. The captain was Oliver Slingsby, who usually was first mate, but took over as her regular captain stayed ashore for this voyage. She left Mobile for Matanzas June 29, with 373,000 feet of hard pine lumber. A hurricane swept this area July 5. The revenue cutter *Tallapoosa* went looking for vessels in distress after the storm and found the *Carrie Strong* on July 13, about 250 miles west of Key West, bottom up. As it was in a main shipping lane, they attempted to blow her up. They sent a yawl over to place dynamite, but hundreds of sharks attacked the yawl. Officers said they never saw anything like it before. They did find evidence after approaching the *Carrie Strong* that the entire crew had been devoured by the sharks. The attempt to sink her was not quite successful, so they towed her 180 miles to where they brought her inside the reef at the Dry Tortugas and beached her so she would not pose any hazards to navigation. *Source:* 10; The Washington Herald, 7/28/1916; Evening Star, 7/30/1916; BDG, 7/14/1916. (3)

SHARKS DEVOUR ENTIRE CREW OF WRECKED SHIP

(By the International News Service.)

Headline about the wreck of the *Carrie Strong*. *Washington Herald,* July 1916.

1917

1) *USS NEMES (S.P.424)*—Motorboat, built 1909 in Camden, New Jersey, 18 tons, 50.2' x 10.5' x 2.6', one 1-pounder and one machine gun, had pulled into Cottrell Bay, Key West, for cleaning, where she exploded and sank, August 21, 1917. *Source:* 14. (3)

Photo of the *USS Nemes* before the Navy bought her. Courtesy
of the Naval History & Heritage Command, catalog # NH 99983.

1) Page 94. *Santa Christina*—Newspapers reported that there was an explosion and she sunk about 50 miles off Havana and 29 crew and five passengers were picked up by the Cuban schooner *Teneriffe*. U.S. government
records say she was seen on fire 25 miles off Key West and that the Naval
vessels *SC-104* and *SC-320* rescued 34 passengers and crew. The *Alex Brown*
(SP-2725) then towed the hulk out of the shipping channel into Key West's
upper harbor. Now maybe some took to the boats and others remained on
the vessel and she drifted to where the she was seen off Key West? It was also
reported she was owned by both the W.R. Grace and Co. (probably previous
owner), and the New Orleans and South American Steamship Co. *Source:*
31; NYT, 7/10/1919; Pensacola Journal, 7/10/1919.

1918

1) *US Army Corps Hydraulic Dredge FLORIDA*—Built 1904 at Jacksonville,
371 tons, 152' x 29.9' x 7', foundered during a storm, July 3, 1918, off Crescent Beach. Three crew including Engineer J. W. Hackett (former Brigadier
General of the Florida National Guard) drowned. The 10 other crewmen
took to the lifeboat and landed on shore. Parts of the wreck were visible
from shore. *Source:* Thomasville Times Enterprise, 7/5/1918; 14. *Note:* The
wreck lies 1.2 miles off Crescent Beach and has been investigated by divers of the St. Augustine Lighthouse Archaeological Maritime Program and
information is on their website. *Source:* 10; 38. (6)

2) *HERALD*—Three-masted schooner, of New York, 499 tons, 144' x 33.9' x
10.2', built 1883 at Belfast, Maine, from Pensacola bound for Havana, with
lumber. Captain J. J. Peterson and crew of six were picked up by a steamer

and taken to Galveston after being damaged in a storm. She was seen abandoned and waterlogged at Lat. 23-44, Long. 85-56 (another report said she foundered at Lat. 25°28' N, Long. 86°14' W). Possible Florida wreck if drifted in Gulf Stream. *Source:* 10; BDG, 4/19/1918. (8)

1) Page 93. *F.A. Kilburn*—Listed at 997gt, 201' x 29.7' x 20', built at Fairhaven, California. *Source:* 10.

2) Page 94. *Lake City*—She was rammed amidships about 11:30 p.m., October 3, 1918, by the tanker *James McGee*, cutting her in two, about nine miles off Key West. She sank within three to five minutes. Most of the crew of 35 were asleep in their bunks and trapped. The radio operator, who was luckily on duty, said he only had time to sound the alarm and then jump overboard. The *McGee* lowered her boats immediately and picked up the five survivors. The accident was blamed on the fact that both vessels were running without any lights. *Source:* Evening Star, 10/6/1918; Sandusky Star Journal, 10/15/1918.

3) Page 184. *Ethel*—Freighter, built at and of Portland, Oregon, in 1918, was on her third voyage, 718 tons, 176.3' x 36.1' x 15.2', with a 400 HP engine, and may have been schooner rigged. From Santiago, Cuba, bound for Baltimore, with manganese ore, owned by the American Manganese Mfg. Co. Crew took to the boats and were picked up by the steamer *Langore* and landed in Cuba. *Merchant Vessels of the U.S.* says she was a gas-powered vessel and foundered off St. Augustine. Some newspapers say lost off Cuba. *Source:* 10: Racine Journal News, 11/2/1918; Daily Kennebunk Journal, 11/2/1918.

4) Page 228. *Lizzie E. Dennison*—Captain Burt Killand, of Mobile, was bound for Cuba, with lumber. She sprang a leak and foundered soon after, 25 miles off Titusville (on Hetzel Shoal). Captain and all eight of the crew landed at Titusville. *Source:* New Smyrna Daily News, 3/15/1918. (6)

1919

1) The following Navy patrol boats were wrecked or lost during the September 9, 1919, hurricane at Key West. Most were private vessels prior to being bought by the Navy during World War I.

a) *USS St. SEBASTIAN (S.P.470)*—Built in 1917 at Sebastian, Florida, wood motorboat, 50' x 12'4" x 3'5", and was anchored at North Beach Basin, Key West, and beat to pieces against the seawall there. Had one 1-pounder and one machine gun. *Source:* 14.

b) *USS COCO*—Served in a non-commissioned status. *Source:* 14.

The *USS Sebastian*. Courtesy of the Naval History and Heritage Command, catalog # NH 102172.

c) *USS HELENA (S.P. 24)*—Built in 1906 at Port Republic, New Jersey, 43' x 10' x 3', had one machine gun. She was wrecked at Key West on the 11th. *Source:* 14.

d) *USS KATHERINE K. (S.P. 220)*—A motorboat built in Baltimore in 1894, 55' x 12'4" x 4'2", 14 tons, had two 1-pounders, served as both a

The *USS Katherine K.* Courtesy of the Naval History and Heritage Command, catalog # NH 10955.

The *USS Sea Hawk*, at Key West. U.S. Navy photo in National Archives. In the Naval History and Heritage Command's web site, catalog # 80-G-1017188.

patrol boat and a tug. She had been sold by the Navy and was awaiting transfer when she was swept away in the hurricane. *Source:* 14.

e) *USS SEA HAWK (S.P. 2365)*—Wood hull boat built 1917 at Bristol, Rhode Island, 29 tons, 64'4" x 11'2", had one 1-pounder, was placed out of service at the end of the war and disappeared during the hurricane. *Source:* 14.

f) *USS PATROL #1 (S.P. 45)*—Motorboat built 1916 at Lynn, Massachusetts, five tons, 40' x 9' x 2'3", was beat to pieces in the North Beach Basin during the hurricane. *Source:* 14.

More September 1919 Hurricane losses. This was a very deadly hurricane for shipping, not only was the passenger ship *Valbanera* lost with all on board southwest of Key West, but the following vessels were also lost with a great loss of life.

a) Page 228. *Corydon*—Captain C. O. Christiansen, of the Ward Line, from Cuba bound for New York, with 23,850 bags of sugar. She encountered the hurricane on Sunday evening, and by Tuesday morning, it was apparent she was going to sink. No SOS was sent (was reported the captain refused to send one and also that the radio was out). Only one lifeboat managed to be launched, and of the 11 who jumped overboard, 10 managed to get

The *USS Patrol #1*. Courtesy of the Naval History & Heritage Command, catalog # NH 102114.

in the boat with the help of one seaman. It was said they saw the captain standing by the bridge, but he refused to jump and went down with the ship along with 27 others. The *Corydon* sank only moments later. The lifeboat capsized three times in the heavy seas, and only due to it being equipped with air tanks did it stay afloat, though it remained full of water. One seaman drank sea water and soon went mad, stabbing the mate. He was restrained but died later that day (first reported he went mad and jumped overboard). After 53 hours, they got the attention of the Fowey Rock Lighthouse keeper who radioed ashore. They drifted onto the beach and were taken in by a local family. The Miami Fish Co. schooner *Island Home* picked them up the next day. One of the survivors of the *Corydon*, recalled an omen he witnessed before she sank, which in his mind foretold of the doom awaiting this ship. A number of papers reported the tale of the wreck given by survivor F. Addison and others. He recalled that early Sunday morning, while still sailing in calm seas, he saw a black speck in the sky that became much larger as it approached the ship and circled round and round. It was a vulture, and it briefly landed on a spar, only to then continue to circle the ship. "I knew something was going to happen to the ship when I saw that bird," said Addison, "and when it kept following us mile after mile, I told the captain and the crew, but nobody would listen to me." *Source:* NYT, 9/12/1919; The Washington Herald, 10/16/1919; The Lakeland Evening Telegraph, 9/13/1919.

b) Page 228. *Larimer*—Another tanker lost in the hurricane, from Port Authur, Texas, bound for Philadelphia, with 31,000 barrels of oil, Capt.

Braun. Different reports had crew size from 33 to 42 men. *Source:* Evening Public Ledger, 9/22/1919.

c) Page 228. *Lake Conway*—This freighter was also lost during the hurricane. Had a cargo of coal, and another report says a crew of 31. *Source:* The Pensacola Journal, 9/22/1919.

d) Page 228. *Munisla*—This freighter carried flour, lumber, and other cargo. Other reports said she had a crew of 47. The captain of the steamer *Mielerio*, from Cuba for Mobile, reported seeing much wreckage, including the bridge of a lake type steamer, about 300 miles south of Mobile Bay, which he believed was that of the *Munisla*. *Source:* Evening Star, 9/23/1919; Ardmore Daily Ardmoreite, 9/26/1919.

A porthole and the letter "B" recovered from the wreck of the *Valbanera*. Now on display in The Archivo de Indianos Foundation-Museum of Emigration, Columbres, Spain. Courtesy of Fernando José Garcia Echegoyen.

e) Page 289. *Valbanera*—Resulted in the worst maritime loss of life off Florida in the 20th century, though what actually happened to her or any on board still remains a mystery.

The passenger steamer *Valbanera*. Was one of the worst maritime disasters off the coast of Florida. Courtesy of Fernando José Garcia Echegoyen.

End of September hurricane losses.

1) Page 57. *Millie R. Bohannan*—Capt. E. C. Bodden, from St. Andrews Bay for Puerto Rico, with 600,000 feet of lumber. She was abandoned during a gale and all the crew landed at Tampa. She was later set on fire 60 miles off Anclote Light as it posed a hazard to navigation. *Source:* Tulsa Daily World, 2/21/1919; The Millersburg Grit, 3/20, 1919.

2) Page 92. *Magnolia*—Correct date of loss is September 1919, not 1910.

3) Page 94. *Bayronto*—Steel schooner rigged steamer, 6,405 tons, built 1905 at Newcastle, by Armstrong, Whitworth and Co., 400' x 52' x 27', of London, loaded with wheat, from Galveston bound for Marseilles, was on its first trip since being torpedoed by a German sub in July 1918. All the crew saved. Eleven landed at Tampa and the others made it to Havana and Charleston. Eleven were picked up in an open boat September 17, 60 miles off Egmont Light. That vessel also had one survivor from an open boat from the *Lake Winona* (later found abandoned and saved) who had drifted for 10 days. The *Bayronto* drifted in the Gulf and finally sank 30 miles off Venice in about 100 feet of water. Now a popular dive site. *Source:* 29; LR, 1919; NYT, 9/22/1919. (2)

4) Pages 94–95. *Hugh De Payens*—Built at and of Rockland, Maine, 144' x 35.9' x 10.1', Capt. Atwood B. Norton, from Mobile for Ponce, Puerto Rico, with lumber, was abandoned in the September hurricane and the crew picked up by the steamer *Olinda*. The hulk drifted north until it washed ashore three miles south of Pablo Beach, 20 miles from Jacksonville. Masts were gone and she was in a damaged state. The fishing steamer *Cora P. White* tried to pull her off, but was unable to. *Source:* 10; Omaha Daily Bee, 9/18/1919; Richmond Times-Dispatch, 10/15/1919.

5) Page 155. *Sanibel*—Of Key West, 65.2' x 15.3' x 5.2'. *Source:* 10.

6) Page 184. *Daisy Farlin*—Crew saved by the tanker *Gulfmaid* off Brunswick, Georgia, November 21, 1919. Left Port Arthur, Texas, for Turin, October 28, 1919. *Source:* The Daily Ardmoriete, 11/22/1919.

7) Page 201. *Missinglink*—Steam/ferry, built at Mulat, Florida, of Pensacola, 64' x 22' x 3'. *Source:* 10.

1920

1) *ISIS*—U.S. Survey steamer, steel hulled, built 1902 at Newburgh, New York, 700 tons, twin screw, 180.4' x 24.8' x 11.6', G. T. Rude, Commander. Originally was a luxurious yacht built for A. G. Spalding and later sold to the U.S. government in 1915. Reported as aground with a hole in her hull and sunk five miles south of St. Augustine off Anastasia Island, January 15,

1920. An attempt to raise her in October 1920 failed and another attempt by the Salinger Ship Salvage Co. a few months later using lift bags (believe this was one of the first attempts to raise a vessel using these devices), also failed, though they did bring up brass fittings, two engines, a sand pump and a safe (still not opened when reported). The St. Augustine Lighthouse Archaeological Maritime Program says she wrecked when she ran onto the wreck of the *Florida* (1918), while looking to put a buoy on that wreck. *Source:* 4; 38; The News Scimitar, 11/15/1920; The Evening World, 5/2/1921.

2) *MIELERO*—Steam tanker, built in 1917 at Quincy, Mass, of New York, 5,853 tons, 389' x 54.7' x 29.3', from Matanzas bound for Philadelphia, with 1,600,000 gallons of molasses, broke in two and sank off the east Florida coast near the Georgia border, January 26, 1920. All onboard took to the two lifeboats which were separated after the second day in a storm. One was picked up five days later with 18 survivors, 125 miles off the Florida coast by the *Mielero's* sister ship *Sucrosa*. The other, with Capt. A. C. Simmons, his wife and two children, and eighteen crew members was yet to be heard from and feared lost. *Source:* 10; NYT, 1/31/1920, 2/4/1920; The Evening World, 1/30/1920; Dundee Courier, 1/31/1920. (6)

3) *JEANETTE* or *JEANNETTE*—Auxiliary three-masted schooner, 320 tons, Capt. Edgar Sammis, was reported to have sunk off the Florida coast, March 18, 1919. The crew arrived at Miami in the lifeboat on the 20th. She was from Havana bound for Philadelphia, with cement. Reported as American, but can't find her in the *Annual List of Merchant Vessels* (maybe Cuban). Possibly sank closer to the Bahamas. *Source:* BDG, 3/21/1919. (8)

4) *ALBERT SOPER* or *ALBERT*—British steamer, from Jacksonville bound for Havana, with lumber, is said to have sunk off Cape Canaveral, the night of September 24, 1920. Was under charter to the Bahamas-Cuban Co., Jacksonville. Was reported in a number of papers, but could find nothing else on a vessel of that name. One paper said steamer *Albert*, Capt. Soper. *Note:* There is a 600-ton German steamer *Albert Sauber*, listed in *Lloyd's Register* in 1921 as being built in 1920, but obviously wasn't lost in 1920. *Source:* Anaconda Standard, 9/26/1920; Bluefield Daily Telegraph, 9/26/1920; La Crosse Tribune and Leader-Press, 9/26/1920.

1) Page 129. *Quoque*—Shipping Board steamer, with cargo of coal, grounded on top of the wreck of the *Hanna M. Bell*, January 11, 1920, she threw much of her cargo of coal overboard to lighten her. Though earlier reports said she was going to pieces, was later reported she floated off at high tide on January 16, and proceeded to Key West for repairs. Checking *Merchant Vessels of the US*, the *Quoque* was removed from the 1920 *Merchant Vessel of the US* listings. I'm thinking she probably did reach Key West and was condemned,

as wreckage from her does not seem to be near the *Hannah Bell.* A 1922 newspaper reports the wreck as "gone from Elbow Reef" when investigated August 16, 1922, at Lat. 25°08'30" N, 80°15'30" W. Maybe it remained there for a while? *Source:* BDG, 1/16/1920; NYH, 8/28/1922.

2) Page 185. *Northwestern*—From Charleston bound for Havana, with coal. Capt. P. E. Jenassen. Foundered near Matanzas Inlet, with the loss of one life. *Source:* The Pensacola Journal, 3/24/1920.

3) Page 201. *Richmond*—Barge, built at Richmond, Maine, of Bath, Maine, 228' x 41.9' x 21.6'. Had 3,600 tons of coal on board. A report from Jacksonville dated May 24, 1920, says she was floated today at the South Jetty. She was never listed in service after 1920 though, so she may have sunk again, or was towed and condemned. *Source:* 9; Biddeford Daily Journal, 1/10/1920; The Sun and NY Herald, 5/28/1920.

4) Page 201. *Misery*—*Merchant Vessels of the US* lists her as a gas yacht, of New York, 55.7' x 15.8' x 7'. A newspaper report says an auxiliary schooner yacht, owned by naval architect Irwin Cox, of New York, which went ashore at the mouth of the St. John's River during a gale, March 16, 1920. Cox, his wife, and another couple clung to the rigging overnight and were rescued the next day by the pilot boat *Mota*, using lifelines. Vessel was a total loss. *Source:* Bridgeport Telegram, 3/18/1920.

1921

1) *SWORDFISH*—G/Y, 151 tons, built 1901 at and from New York, 116.8' x 17.7' x 4.9', burned near Amelia Island, 4/29/1921. *Source:* 10. (6)

2) *PAULINE G*—G/F, 13 tons, built 1911 in Pensacola, of Tampa, 58.1' x 9' x 5.5', burned at Key West, 7/14/1921. *Source:* 10. (3)

3) *VIOLA*—Smuggling two-masted schooner, Capt. Mentcal (alias-real name Hugo Wentzel), went aground 20 miles west of St. Andrews on West Bay on the outer beach, July 21, 1921, and was later burned to the water's edge. She was smuggling Chinese immigrants from Cuba into Florida who planned to go to Chicago. They were to meet a small boat about 20 miles off Pensacola, but when it never came, they cruised about for a couple of days but bad weather and lack of food forced them to look for a safe place to land and that's when they went aground. How many Chinese reported aboard varied, but was around 40. The Chinese got ashore and were abandoned, and the smugglers went to Pensacola and then split up. Twenty Chinese were soon found in the woods and most of the others soon after. Early reports said many died in the fire, but that was false. Authorities

soon arrested the mate Alfred Ullman who confessed the whole story. The captain and Chester Wing, who was in charge of the smuggling operation, were arrested a couple days later at DeFuniac Springs. The other two of the crew were eventually arrested and all were found guilty of smuggling. Wing got sentenced to 13 months, the captain to five, and two crew to four months. There was talk of arresting the owner of the *Viola* as they believe he burned it. *Source:* The Ocala Evening Star, 7/22/1921; Atlanta Constitution, 7/23/1921; The Pensacola Journal, 7/23–24/1921, 11/30/1921, 12/1/1921. (1)

4) *BON TEMPS*—G/Y, 17 tons, built 1905 in Boston, of Key West, 50.2' x 9' x 5', burned near Tampa, 10/2/1921. *Source:* 10. (2)

5) *MAPLEFIELD*—Three-masted schooner, Captain L. Saven, with lumber, ran into a gale about 60 miles off Pensacola, lost sails, and was filling with water. Unmanageable, she drifted toward the rocky shore when she was sighted by the steamer *Ulua*, Capt. Towell, a few miles off Pensacola. Seeing the distress signals and her crew waving for help, Captain Towell circled around to make a lee so they could lower the boat. The seas being too rough to do so, Towell then proceeded to lay down oil to calm the seas which enabled the *Maplefield*'s crew to lower the boat without capsizing it, and all made it safely onto the steamer. *Source:* NYT, 10/18/1921. (1)

6) October 25th Hurricane—Though the west coast of Florida around the Tampa area was hit hardest, the St. Augustine area up to Jacksonville also got hit. Most all the pleasure craft in Matanzas Bay were sunk, and the fishing smack *Dolphin* from there was feared lost. The steamer *Crescent* was high and dry at Tampa but unknown if saved as a number of vessels drove ashore were. The schooners *Aegina* and *Francis* were also lost (see chapter 9).

a) *SEHOME*—Schooner, 680 tons, 182' x 37.9' x 13.3', built 1899 in Washington, of Pensacola, from Mobile bound for Cuba, with 609,037 feet of pine lumber, was abandoned off the Florida coast in a waterlogged condition due to a hurricane, October 25, 1921, at Lat. 24°44'N, Long. 83°40'W, after drifting two days at sea, the lifeboats having been smashed. The crew lashed themselves to the remains of the ship. Crew were saved by the Italian vessel *Recca* and taken to Galveston. *Source:* San Antonio Light, 11/4/1921; Evening Star, 12/26/1921; Galveston Daily News, 10/30/1921; Richmond Times, 10/27/1921. (2)

b) *KONA*—Motor yacht, of Roslyn, New York, 60 feet, was found wrecked on the jetties at the mouth of the St. John's River, October 28, 1921. One of the crew washed up on the beach dead at Mayport and the rest have not been found. *Source:* The Evening World, 10/28/1921. (6)

c) *FAVORITE*—Steamer. A well-known Tampa steamer that sailed the area for years. She was torn from the Tampa Steam Way Co. dock on the Hillsborough River during the October hurricane and was wrecked ashore between the car barns and the Tampa Water Works Plant. It was a total loss, though some machinery was to be saved. *Source:* Sarasota County Times, 10/27/1921. (7)

The steamer *Favorite*, after the 1921 hurricane. U.S. Federal Document Collection, Special and Area Studies, George A. Smathers Libraries, University of Florida, Gainesville.

d) *GENEVIEVE*—Steamer, of the Home Line, was taking 25 passengers and some cargo across Tampa Bay when the beginning of the hurricane struck. She made it across, but was sunk 20 minutes after everyone disembarked after slamming into the docks, which smashed a hole in her side. Most cargo was saved afterward including a brand-new Harley Davidson motorcycle bought by the City of Tampa. *Source:* The Evening Independent, 10/27/1921. (2)

e) *HYPNOTIST*—Fishing smack, Capt. Ponia, of Tampa, sank after striking a submerged piling on the railroad bridge. Survivors made it to the beach at Coffee Pot. It had hundreds of pounds of fish and ice on board which were all lost. *Source:* St. Petersburg Times, 10/27/1921.

f) *AGNES BELLE*—Fishing schooner, of St. Petersburg, 29 tons, built 1877 at Milbridge, Maine, 58.4' x 18.3' x 6.6', Capt. Fred Ryan, was lost with all hands (seven men) during the hurricane off the Dry Tortugas. *Source:* 10; St. Petersburg Times, 11/8/1921. (3)

g) *SEVERITER, ESPANIA* (both sponge boats), *CONSTANTINOPLE, COR-NILLA* (both dive boats)—The battered hulks of the two sponge boats were found drifting about five miles west of Anclote Light with no trace of the crews, and the two dive boats were reported missing. *Source:* Ibid. (2)

1) Page 58. *Thomas B. Garland*—Was washed ashore at Tampa during the October hurricane, along with the former naval barge *Yenrut*, and former destroyer *Hopkins*. Unknown if other two salvaged. *Source:* Ibid.

The schooner *Thomas B. Garland* (in foreground), after the 1921 hurricane. U.S. Federal Document Collection, Special and Area Studies, George A. Smathers Libraries, University of Florida, Gainesville.

2) Page 155. *Thames*—Associated Press said it sank on October 25, 1921, about 14 miles north of Jupiter. Capt. E. J. Wuhl and all 15 of the crew made shore safely in the lifeboat at Gomez (Martin County). Also reported was a small wooden vessel ashore at the same place. *Source:* Ibid.

3) Page 203. *J.W. Sommerville*—I only mention her here as she was found in the Gulf dismasted and capsized 40 miles off the Dry Tortugas after the October 1921 hurricane. No trace of her crew was ever found. Not long after, she was picked up drifting bottom up off Tybee, Georgia (another source says the Coast Guard brought her to Key West). Though *Merchant Vessels* lists her as foundered in the Gulf in 1921, she was salvaged, became the *Nassauvian*, and later burned at Jacksonville in 1930. *Source:* 10.

End of 1921 Hurricane losses.

7) *GLENDOVER*—Yacht, of New Orleans, blew up off St. Andrews. One person was killed, one was missing, and two were badly burned, after one lit a match igniting gasoline fumes. *Source:* San Antonio Light, 12/5/1921; The Daily Times, 12/5/1921. (1)

1) Page 95. *Planter*—From Philadelphia bound for Mobile, with a cargo of coal, foundered in a storm about 30 miles off Key West. Capt. A. H. Owen and crew took to the boats, and all made it to Key West. *Source:* Atlanta Constitution, 8/19/1921.

2) Page 155. *Coniscliffe*—From Mobile bound for Arecibo, Puerto Rico. Vessel was sighted about 50 miles off the coast. Crew were rescued from their lifeboats by the British steamer *Parphenia*. *Source:* Bisbee Daily Review, 4/10/1921.

3) Page 155. *Osiris*—Dimensions are 109.5' x 19.7' x 7.1'. *Source:* 10.

1922

1) *COYLET*—Steamer, of Glasgow, 5,222 tons, built 1918 at Sunderland, 400' x 52.4' x 28.5', was recently converted from a cargo vessel to a tanker. From Avondale for New Orleans with gasoline, when she caught fire and was abandoned off Sand Key. Was last seen drifting and still burning 20 miles off Miami. *Source:* LR, 1922; Evening Star, 2/10/1922.

2) *COLT*—Fishing smack, left Pensacola in February 1922, and struck a reef and went to pieces. Capt. Wm. Smith and seven others were lost. One man, Edward Brooks, was the only survivor, being picked up off a makeshift raft 40 hours later. *Source:* Great Falls Tribune, 2/22/1922. (1)

3) *SARATOGA* (ex-Navy Subchaser)—Had been recently purchased from the Navy and was on a test run off Miami, April 30, 1922, with two men

on board named Truitt and Gardner. She started to leak badly which soon shut down the engine. With the launch half submerged, the two drifted on her for five days with no food or water, watching many vessels pass by. Almost giving up hope, she was accidentally run into by the schooner *Harry G. Deering*, who saved the two and brought them to Norfolk. *Source:* San Antonio Express, 5/9/1922; NYH, 5/9/1922. (8)

4) *PERCILER*—British schooner, from Nassau bound for Jacksonville for repairs, went ashore in a gale on the St. George Bar near the mouth of the St. John's River, May 1922. The crew made it to shore. *Source:* Norwich Bulletin, 5/30/1922; Jacksonville Daily Journal, 5/30/1922. (6)

5) *De Haviland 4* (Airplane)—Though not a shipwreck, this aircraft is worthy of noting. James "Jimmy" H. Doolittle, one of the greatest aviators of our time, attempted to set a record by flying across the country in under 24 hours starting from Jacksonville, refueling at Kelly Field, and finally landing at San Diego. In a specially constructed *De Haviland 4*, Doolittle took off at 9:35 p.m. from the gateway at Pablo Beach, Jacksonville, and was fine for the first 500 yards until he struck a sandbar and suddenly swerved toward the beach, went into a dive and went end over end tearing off one wing and a propeller, all while thousands on the beach watched. They soon found Doolittle standing knee deep in the surf unscathed. Not to be deterred, he attempted the same flight one month later from the same spot and succeeded in taking off and setting the record at 21 hours and 19 minutes. Some of this wreckage may still be buried in the surf, and if found, should end up at the Smithsonian Air and Space Museum. *Source:* NYT, 8/7/1922. (6)

6) *SHIRIN*—Converted yacht, exploded and sank three miles off Miami on its maiden voyage as a passenger and mail carrier bound for Nassau, September 11, 1922. There were over 20 passengers on board, plus the crew. An arrest warrant was issued for Capt. Sat Papas, who failed to show up for an inquiry regarding the tragedy. Six lives were lost. *Source:* Palatka Daily News, 8/13/1922. (5)

1) Page 42. *Colthraps*—One of the Hog Islander "Type A" built ships (89th launched from the Hog Island, Pennsylvania, yard), 390' x 54.2' x 27.1'. After catching fire, she was towed out into the bay where she settled in 18 feet of water. After the fire was put out, she was brought back into port for repairs, but sat idle for two years before she was sold for scrap and broken up. *Source:* 10; 18; The Pensacola Journal, 12/23/1922.

2) Page 96. *Caldwell H. Colt*—The nine on board clung to the wave swept deck for several days with no food or water, and one by one they were swept away until only three, including Captain L. A. Smith, were left. The steamer

El Orient saw the three and went to rescue them but before they could reach them, one man fell off the deck and drowned. The captain and the other were got on board but the seaman died from exhaustion and was buried at sea. Frank Brooks, who was swept off earlier, clung to a booby hatch and was picked up by a British tanker. *Source:* Sioux City Journal, 2/23/1922; Great Falls Tribune, 2/23/1922.

1923

1) *ROBERT B. BURNEY*—G/C, 38 tons, built 1906, of Tampa, 55.5' x 18.2' x 5.8', stranded at Boca Grande, 1/10/1926. *Source:* 10. (2)

2) *DRAGON*—G/Y, 19 tons, built 1907 at Tottenville, New York, 50.6' x 13.2' x 3.8', foundered at Miami, September 18, 1926. Possibly the same yacht *Dragon* that came in first in the New London to Bermuda yacht race in June 1926. *Source:* 10. (5)

3) *DOROTHY*—G/F, 14 tons, built 1908, of Charleston, 50' x 12' x 6.5', foundered by Mosquito Light Station, October 10, 1923. *Source:* 10. (6)

4) *CITY OF EVERETT*—Whaleback type tanker, 2,595 tons, built 1894 at Everett, Washington, 346' x 42.1' x 22.9'. An SOS was received from her on October 11, 1923, during a severe storm (may have been a hurricane), west of the Tortugas. Last call said she was going down stern first, and they were trying to lower the lifeboats. They gave the location as Lat. 24°30' N, Long. 86°00' W. She was never heard from again. Twenty-six men on board were lost. An extensive search was made, but no survivors or wreckage was found. *Associated Press* and most U.S. newspapers reported this. She may have been found 120 miles off the Florida coast a few years ago in 400 feet of water. *Source:* The Key West Citizen, 10/11/1923. (3)

1924

1) *RUSS*—Ex-60-foot subchaser, was used during prohibition to apprehend drug-runners off the coast of Florida, and was captained by Sheriff W. H. Dowling, who was the divisional prohibition chief for Florida and Puerto Rico. They were about 10 miles off Jacksonville when the *Russ* exploded. Dowling and the crew got safely into the vessel's dory, though three men had serious burns. The pilot boat *Meta* heard the explosion while out at sea, and rescued the men about two hours later and brought them to Jacksonville. *Source:* Evening Star, 3/28/1924.

2) **Unk. SCHOONER**—A major storm had hit the Fort Myers area, October 20. On the 25th, a three-masted schooner was found bottom up with both

bow and stern underwater off Marco Pass, about 75 miles south of Fort Myers, and her identity could not be determined though finders thought maybe a Spanish schooner. Another report a couple days later just says a two-masted schooner was seen abandoned and almost completely submerged between Cape Romano and Fort Myers. Reported it may be the missing *Adeliza*, from Nova Scotia, and said the wreckers may be able to salvage it. Both reports thought nobody had survived.

Now on November 4, it was reported that the aptly named steamer *Emergency Aid*, had rescued the crew of the Cuban schooner *Jubilee*, 80 miles north of the Tortugas, and had brought them to Key West. I thought this must be the schooner found abandoned. A couple days later it was reported that the "steel" schooner *Jubilee* was seen in the shipping lane at Lat. 25°30' N, 84°55' W, floating "high out of the water." On November 12, a number of papers then reported the American schooner *Jubilee* was found grounded on the Isle of Pines, Cuba, on the 11th. Now I found no "American" schooner by that name listed, so it was likely the Cuban schooner *Jubilee* that drifted south to Cuba and grounded. Could this be the schooner reported in October? That one was almost submerged and no name could be seen, but the *Jubilee* seen on the 7th was floating high out of the water. The *Jubilee* was said to be steel, but that was not mentioned about the schooner reported in October. Could a schooner bottom-up and almost submerged drift that far south? Possibly, but I'm inclined to think it was not the *Jubilee*, but another vessel altogether. *Source:* The Sunday Star, 10/26/1925; The Anniston Star, 10/30/1924; Atlanta Constitution, 11/5/1924; Galveston Daily News, 11/7/1924; Biloxi Daily Herald, 11/12/1924. (2)

3) *MARIE*—G/C, 13 tons, built 1911, of Tampa, 50.5' x 17' x 3.5', burned in Tampa Bay, 12/10/1924. *Source:* 10. (2)

1) Page 42. **Cornelius H. Callaghan** (Originally the *Percy R. Pyne 2nd*)— Built at Camden, Maine, 233' x 39.7' x 18.9'. The *Percy R. Pyne 2nd*, was originally listed as an Oil Vessel but in 1921 was listed as a schooner. One report says she went ashore and broke her back eight nautical miles from St. Andrew's Bay. *Source:* 10; The Times, London, 1/1924.

1925

1) *COTOPAXI*—Steamer, 2,351 tons, built 1918 by the Great Lakes Engineering Works, Ecorse, Michigan, of New York, 253.4' x 43.7' x 25.1', Capt. William Myers, from Charleston bound for Havana, with coal, was reported in late November as in distress off Jacksonville and never heard from again. All 32 of the crew were lost. *Note:* This ship has been associated with the Bermuda Triangle a number of times. It was in the director's cut of the

The steamer *Cotopaxi* in port. She went missing in 1925, which was a basis for many wild speculations. The Marine Historical Society of Detroit.

movie *Close Encounters of the Third Kind*, shown being found in the Gobi Desert, and in 2015, videos of it being found adrift off Cuba were circulated on YouTube and elsewhere, but was just a hoax. At the time the distress call was picked up at Jacksonville, there was a tropical storm sweeping the Florida coast, and the ship reported it was taking on water. Most papers reported it likely lost off the Florida coast. A week or so after the distress call, it was reported the crew was safe in both Havana and at Charleston, which both proved to be false. Lost due to the Bermuda Triangle, or sunk due to a storm? I'll say the later. *Source:* Gastonia Daily Press, 12/5/1925; LL, 1925. (8)

2) **Rum Runner SCHOONER**—From the Bahamas, with 2,000 cases of fine liquor, went aground and broke up during a storm, three miles south of Flagler Beach in the early morning of December 1, 1925. Six of the nine crewmen were drowned, the rest saved by Coast Guard. *Source:* Morning Herald, 12/2/1925. (6)

1) Page 58. *Gwalia*—Was a steam tug. Capt. R. D. Cogswell. It was towing the barge *Altamaha* loaded with gravel, from Mobile for Tampa, when it

parted her cable in a gale about 85 miles NW off Egmont. The tug was in a sinking condition and the crew took to the boat just as the tug sank. The boat had smashed into the sinking tug and stove a hole in the side. The 15 men in the boat had to both bail water and try and row to the drifting barge. It took them 13 hours to reach the barge, and any longer they may all have drowned. The six men on the barge got them all aboard. The barge was given some supplies by a passing vessel and days later was towed into Tampa by the Coast Guard cutter *Tallapoosa*. *Source:* Key West Citizen, 12/14/1925; Florence Morning News Review, 12/15/1925.

2) Page 156. **Wilbert S. Bartlett**—Had a full load of lumber, and all of the deck-load washed up onto the beach. Much was salvaged and used in the construction of local buildings. The wreck was off Hutchinson Island about halfway between Gilbert's Bar House of Refuge and the Inlet. *Source:* Elliot Museum, Stuart, Florida.

The schooner *Wilbert S. Bartlett*, wrecked off Hutchinson Island in 1925. Courtesy of the House of Refuge Museum, Stuart, Florida.

3)Page 186. **Comanche**—Of the Clyde Steamship Line, had a crew of 94 and 73 (or 167) passengers, was abandoned six miles off the St John's Bar. Reported that 10 passengers were missing, and many others injured, though later changed to one passenger lost and 13 injured. She was eventually

Image of the steamer *Comanche*, lost in 1925. Courtesy of the State Archives of Florida.

beached on the St. John's River, east of Jacksonville. The *S.S. Reaper* saved most all on board. The fire could be seen for miles. It was also later reported that some of the crew were drunk, and were throwing passengers out of the lifeboats, though one passenger says this was untrue, and that the crew did all they could to save passengers. There was an inquiry, though I don't know the outcome. *Source:* Mexia Daily News, 10/19/1925; Galveston Daily News, 10/18/1925; Athens Sunday Messenger, 10/18/1925; Evening Star, 10/20/1925.

Note: Right after this, the *Reaper* also saved the crew from the 185.5' long four-masted lumber schooner *Rosalie Hull*, from Savannah for Miami, with lumber, found wrecked "three miles south of Hetzel Light below St. Augustine," and reported to be breaking up. *Merchant Vessels* lists her as in-service until 1928 and as abandoned in 1929. *Source:* Key West Citizen, 10/22/1925.

4) Page 186. **Mohican**—Burned May 10, 1925, and later beached. All on board saved. *Source: 9.*

5) Page 202. **Bruce**—Passenger steamer, built at Freeport, Florida, of Pensacola, 82.4' x 22.6' x 4'. *Source: 10.*

6) Page 202. **Lavinia**—G/P built at Palatka, of Jacksonville, 58' x 13' x 3.6'. *Source: 10.*

7) Page 228. *Genessee*—Auxiliary schooner yacht originally built for William Vanderbilt in 1900, steel hulled, 120' long. She was a well-known vessel and was used by the Brown Exploring Company in 1920 to search for the lost treasure of Cocos Island. When wrecked it was owned by young millionaire Sylvanus Stokes Jr. of D.C., and bound for Miami. According to Mark Mondano's book, she went ashore three miles south of Sexton Plaza in Vero Beach, off Sand Point, November 3, 1925. All eleven on board were rescued. The vessel was a total loss. Local divers have found pieces of this wreck. *Source:* 23; San Antonio Light, 2/12/1928; NYT, 11/5/1925. (5)

8) Page 229. *William Russell*—Two-masted schooner, from Norfolk to Ft. Lauderdale, with building supplies, foundered off Olympia (now Hobe Sound). All nine on board saved. *Source:* The Key West Citizen, 11/30/1925. (5)

1926

1) *ALECIA*—G/P, 32 tons, built 1911 in New Jersey, of Miami, 56.7' x 13.5' x 5.7', burned at Turkey Point, May 25, 1926. *Source:* 10. (4)

2) *CALLIOPE*—Sloop rigged gas powered yacht, 55 feet, 20 tons, built 1925, owned by W. E. D. Stokes Jr. of New York, who was the son of a wealthy New York hotelier, wrecked off the beach on Merritt Island, March 15, 1926. The three on board got to shore safely. May be related to the millionaire by the same last name who wrecked his yacht *Genesee* the year before off Florida. *Source:* 10; NYT, 3/23/1926. (5)

3) *TWILIGHT*—G/Y, 65 tons, built 1915 on Long Island, New York, of Huntington, New York, 102' x 12.5' x 6.7', burned at West Palm Beach, April 28, 1926. *Source:* 10. (5)

4) *QUEEN OF NASSAU*—Formerly the Canadian gunboat *Canada*, built 1904 in England, 200' x 25', decommissioned in 1919, and later bought by developer Barron Collier (Collier County was named after him). From Miami bound for Tampa to transfer to the new owners from Mexico when the boilers failed and she took on water and sank off Alligator Reef, July 2, 1926. Captain Peter Songdahl got her to deeper water so as not to obstruct navigation. All the crew took to the boat and were saved. They watched her go down soon after leaving the ship. Now lies in 230 feet (see GPS coordinates at end of chapter). *Source:* 34; Monroe New Star, 7/3/1926. (4)

5) There were two hurricanes in 1926, one in July and the other in September. The July hurricane hit the Palm Beach and Jupiter area, and over **40 Yachts and Houseboats** were sunk in Lake Worth.

Wreck of the schooner *Robert L. Bean* off Santa Rosa Island in 1926. Courtesy of the State Archives of Florida.

The steamer *Thendara*, foundered in 1926. Courtesy of the Monroe County Library, Key West.

6) *V-1025*—F/V, sank off Florida. Captain and mate were picked up by an oil tanker about eight miles SW of Jupiter. *Source:* Key West Citizen, 8/7/1926. (5)

7) *CARSON OF NASSAU N.P.*—Schooner. The battered half of this schooner was found September 18, 1926, beached on Talbot Island, 2-1/2 miles off Mayport. No survivors were found. *Source:* Miami News Record, 9/19/1926.

8) *C.T. ROWLAND*—Barge, 282 tons, built 1893, 149.5' x 23.4' x 9.8', foundered off the Florida coast, 12/31/1926. *Source:* 10. (8)

1) Page 43. *Robert L. Bean.* See GPS coordinates at end of chapter.

2) Page 96. *John Henry Sherman*—G/F, built at and of Millville, Florida, 86.2' x 22.3' x 10.2'. *Source:* 10.

3) Page 96. *Thendara.* See photo.

4) Page 156. *Endurance*—Tug, 42 tons, 59.2' x 15.5' x 7.3', built 1925 at Norfolk, of the Oil Power Towing Co, New York. The barge she was towing also sank. *Source:* 10; NYT, 1/31/1926.

5) Page 156. *Lynn*—Was beat to pieces in the surf north of Palm Beach/Lake Worth Inlet. The *Lynn* and another barge were both lost by a tug trying to tow them in the inlet in rough seas. The other barge was saved. Three men and a woman abandoned her in the lifeboat and made shore safely. *Source:* Sarasota Herald, 2/18/1926.

6) Page 157. *Patricia*—O/V, 60 tons, 86.7' x 15' x 6.9', of New York. *Source:* 10.

7) Page 157. *Prins Valdemar*—After she was refloated, the hull was brought to shore at Bayfront Park and encased in concrete as a tourist attraction. Decay led to her being demolished in 1952, though her anchor is still on display at the Miami Yacht Club. *Source:* 7.

8) Page 158. *Richmond*—Was 135.3' x 26.5' x 9'. *Source:* 26.

1927

1) Page 97. *Rose Murphy*—Capt. J. G. Murphy was charged in a federal indictment three years later of conspiracy to purposely scuttle the vessel. The engineer was also indicted, but believe he committed suicide. Others of the crew were also to be arrested. *Source:* Anniston Star, 11/1/1930.

2) Page 186. *Piute*—O/C, 79 tons, built 1925, of Jacksonville, 64.4' x 21.2' x 4', stranded at Mosquito Inlet, 1/27/1927. *Source:* 10.

3) Page 202. **Swan**—Oil/passenger vessel, built at Biloxi, of Pensacola, 86.2' x 17.8' x 4.7'. *Source:* 10.

4) Page 229. **Maurice R. Thurlow**—Went ashore on Diamond Shoal, North Carolina, not off Florida. Crew abandoned her and she was later seen floating with no crew and was called a "phantom ship." *Source:* New Castle News, 10/21/1927.

5) Page 229. **Albert Meyer**—From Mobile for Jacksonville via Key West, with cedar logs for the box factory at Key West, Capt. O. Scott, went aground on the Marquesas in mud and could not be gotten off. The crew made Key West in the lifeboat. *Source:* Key West Citizen, 12/15/1927.

1928

1) **MOHAVE**—Oil/tender vessel (formerly U.S.Q.M.C. vessel), 25 tons, built 1907 in New Jersey, of Miami, 53.5' x 12.2' x 6.3', foundered at Palm Beach, 9/16/1928. *Source:* 10. (5)

2) **OKA SAN**—Gas/cargo vessel, 22 tons, built 1905, of Miami, 53' x 15.5' x 5', foundered at West Palm Beach, 9/16/1928. *Source:* 10. (5)

3) **CITY OF PUNTA BLANCA**—G/C, 19 tons, built 1911, of Everglades, Florida, 60' x 13.7' x 4.3', foundered at Punta Gorda, 9/17/1928. *Source:* 10. (2)

1) Page 59. **Wallace A. McDonald**—Crew swam to shore after she grounded. They saw her roll over and break up one mile off Piney Point. *Source:* 29.

2) Page 97. **Monroe County**—Ferry, built at Jacksonville, of Key West, 107.2' x 24' x 5.7'. *Source:* 10.

1929

1) **MARIA de LOS ANGELES**, and another Cuban *fishing Smack*—Both from Havana and both sunk off Long Boat Key, north of Sarasota Bay, during the September 1929 hurricane. Both crews landed safely on the beach in their lifeboats. *Source:* The Miami Herald, 9/30/1929. (2)

2) **JOAN MARIE**—A 60-foot British motorboat. Crew were rescued by the Coast Guard from the wreck after the September storm off Sand Key, about 10 miles from Cape Sable. *Source:* St. Petersburg Times, 10/1/1929. (3)

3) **ESMINE**—Was one of the Tarpon Springs sponge fleet. Reported missing after the September storm. Unknown if found. Coast Guard were looking for her. *Source:* Evening Independent, 10/1/1929. (2)

4) **Unk. FISHING SMACK**—A four-masted fishing smack believed to be Cuban, was found sunk in 11 fathoms of water, about 25 miles west of Anclote Light. Believed lost in the recent storm and fate of the crew was unknown. *Source:* Albert Lea Evening Tribune, 10/10/1929. (2)

1) Page 187. *Ada Tower*—Captain Hatfield (also the owner), wrecked off Atlantic Beach, Jacksonville. *Source:* Danville Bee, 10/10/1929.

2) Page 187. *Tamarco*—Built 1903 at Bath, Maine. Originally the *Hope Sherwood*. Wrecked off the beach 1/2 mile from the Bulow Coast Guard Station. One man was lost and five were saved. Newspapers and the Coast Guard all said she was a total loss. The *Hope Sherwood* was listed as abandoned in 1927, and was salvaged and became the *Tamarco* in 1928. *Merchant Vessels of the U.S.* then lists the *Tamarco* in service up until 1932, when it says she foundered off Flagler Beach, September 24, 1932. I think they made a mistake and meant September 1929 and should have taken her off the books at that time. *Source:* 10; Hammond Lake County Times, 10/5/1929; Thomasville Times Enterprise, 9/24/1929.

The wreck of the schooner *Tamarco*, 1929. Central Press Association photo, 1929.

1930

1) *MESSENGER*—Tug, was cast upon the beach near West Palm Beach, the night of November 9, 1930, and was pounded to pieces. She was on her way to Ft. Pierce to aid the grounded freighter *Lillian* there. Capt. Charles Russel and all six of the crew were rescued using lifelines provided by the Jupiter Lighthouse crew. *Source:* The Morning Herald, Uniontown, PA, 11/10/1930. (5)

1) Page 59. *Zalophus*—Should be mentioned this was owned by John Ringling, of circus fame, though he was not on board when she sank, though New York City Mayor Jimmy Walker was. All on board were rescued. *Source:* 29.

2) Page 130. *Northern Light*—Was being towed by the tug *Ontario* of Mobile, loaded with a cargo of phosphate, when she sank off Carysfort Reef at 2:20 a.m. during a storm. "Five sailors were tossed into the ocean and only one was saved by the *Ontario*." J. W. Heath was master of the barge. See GPS coordinates at end of chapter. *Source:* The Morning Herald, Uniontown, PA, 11/10/1930.

3) Page 130. *Eureka II*—Capt. Clarence Styles, was a 105-foot glass bottomed tourist boat. On December 14, 1930, she was on her way back from the area they called the "Marine Gardens" about 15 miles south of Miami Beach, with over 100 women, children, and men on board. Smoke was seen from the engine room and soon there were three explosions. All on board jumped overboard. One hundred twenty-five of the 135 on board were saved by two nearby yachts and a couple of fishing tugs. She burned and sank in ten feet of water. *Source:* Hagerstown Daily Mail, 12/15/1930.

1931

1) *POLLY B*—G/C, 30 tons, built 1909 at Titusville, of Tampa, 54.4' x 15.3' x 3.8', foundered at New Port Richey, August 25, 1931. *Source:* 10. (2)

2) *BURTON E. COE*—Steam/tow vessel, 42 tons, built 1897 at Tampa, of Apalachicola, 61.7' x 14.5' x 4.9', burned at Blountstown, Florida, September 28, 1931. *Source:* 10. (7)

1932

1) *EULALIA*—G/P, 17 tons, built 1915 in Virginia, of Miami, 53' x 12' x 4.8', burned at Key West, January 7, 1932. *Source:* 10. (3)

2) *DIXIELAND*—O/T, 14 tons, built 1906 at Jacksonville, of Miami, 57' x 20' x 3.6', stranded at Ft. Lauderdale, January 21, 1932. *Source:* 10. (5)

3) *SIXTY-FIVE* and the *SIXTY-SIX*—Barges, both 221 tons, built in 1910 in Minneapolis, of Tampa, both 139.5' x 30' x 6.7', both foundered at Phillips Inlet, 5/12/1932. *Source:* 10. (1)

1935

1) *BILLY JUNIOR*—G/Y, 31 tons, built 1925 at Bayonne, New Jersey, of Miami, 53' x 13' x 6.4', burned off Ft. Lauderdale, June 23, 1935. *Source:* 10. (5)

The schooner *Marie J. Thompson*, the largest sailing vessel ever built in the Bahamas. Courtesy of the Monroe County Library, Key West.

The wreck of the *Marie J. Thompson*. Courtesy of the Monroe County Library, Key West.

2) *HALLIE K*—G/F, 23 tons, built 1891 in MD, of Miami, 62.7' x 17.8 x 4.8', foundered 30 miles NE of Jupiter Light, December 13, 1935, crew saved. *Source:* 10. (5)

1) Page 97. *Marie J. Thompson*—Four-masted schooner, built at Harbour Island using some lumber from previously wrecked vessels, 695 tons, usually carried lumber. Sunk about one mile north of Key West in the flats and now a popular dive/snorkel site. She was the largest sailing vessel ever built in the Bahamas. See GPS coordinates at end of chapter. *Source:* Mel Fisher Maritime Heritage Society. See photo.

2) *Comet*—Page 162. G/Y, 65 tons, of Miami, 67.3' x 16.3' x 7.3'. *Source:* 10.

1936

1) *ADRENIA C*—G/Y, 19 tons, built 1916 in Michigan, of Detroit (fifth name she sailed under), 55.7' x 10' x 5', foundered in a storm off Florida in March 1936 with loss of two lives. *Source:* 10.

2) *NUNOCA*—British motor vessel (may also been schooner rigged), 190 tons, 110 feet, built in the Cayman Islands and was around four years old. She was a well-known mail and passenger vessel that regularly sailed between Tampa and the Caymans, sometimes stopping at the Isle of Pines in between. She left Georgetown, Grand Cayman, for Tampa, July 4 with 22 persons on board, including four women and two children. She was never heard from again. She had on deck 60 Texaco drums when she left. It was soon apparent that she was lost when many of the drums and wreckage began floating up along the Florida coast from the Tortugas up to Miami and many areas in between. A cargo hatch was also found 30 miles south of Tampa. Some of the Texaco drums were charred and other wreckage showed signs of an explosion (said there was both gasoline and diesel engines on board). A small life raft from the wreck was found off Key Largo. An extensive search was made but no bodies or survivors were ever found. Many of the passengers were from Florida. The Captain was Moses J. Kirkonnell, of Cayman Brac. He was from a seagoing family and became the fifth brother of the family to be lost at sea. *Source:* Kingston Gleaner, 7/22/1936, 8/11/1936; Biloxi Daily Herald, 7/22/1936; Zanesville Times Recorder, 7/22/1936. (8)

1) Page 162. *Elizabeth*—She was patched up and was towed off the reef and purposely sunk four miles off Miami in 720 feet of water, May 15, 1936. *Source:* Panama City Herald, 5/15/1936.

1937

1) *ALAMO*—O/C, 62 tons, built 1919 at St. Augustine, 57.4' x 15.7' x 4.9', burned at Dames Point on the St. John's River, July 27, 1937. *Source:* 10. (7)

1) Page 45. *Tarpon*—Foundered about 20 miles off East Pass. The body of Capt. W. G. Barrow was recovered near where she sank, along with the second mate. It was reported this was his 1,735th trip on the *Tarpon*. The Coast Guard began their search only after 23-year old Addley Baker swam to shore after 25 hours in the water and told of her sinking. There were 31 people on board. Nine more were rescued after clinging to some wreckage for 36 hours. Two others reached shore clinging to wreckage. The rest were feared lost. According to Baker, the *Tarpon* had run into stormy weather and was "shipping seas for hours before the pumps failed." He grabbed a life vest and made it to the deck just as she capsized. "The Tarpon turned over and we grabbed whatever we could. I held onto a plank for over an hour. Near me was Cecil Smith, another oiler (later rescued). I told him I saw land and was going to swim for it." If Baker hadn't made shore, many more may have been lost. *Source:* Biddeford Daily Journal, 9/3/1937; Biloxi Daily Herald, 9/3/1937. *Note:* Now a State Underwater Preserve and popular dive site. See GPS coordinates at end of chapter.

2) Page 130. *Hilton*—Cargo vessel, 68.6' x 14' x 6.4'. *Source:* 10.

1938

1) Page 97. *E.J. Bullock*—Standard Oil tanker, exploded 25 miles east of the Dry Tortugas, October 6, 1938. She had full tanks of gasoline and fuel oil and was from Lee's Bluff, Texas bound for Baltimore. Her radio went out, but luckily the tanker *O.M. Bernuth* saw smoke from about 10 miles away and picked up the crew from two lifeboats. Two crew were killed in the blast and one died later from his injuries. The cause of the explosion was not known, and the ship was on fire within minutes of the explosion. She sank one hour after the explosion. One lifeboat was found capsized near Jupiter Light nine days later. *Source:* Galveston Tribune, 10/7/1938; The Boone News-Republican, 10/17/1938; NYT, 10/7/1938; Sandusky Star Journal; 10/10/1938.

2) Page 162. *Eunice M*—G/C, built at and of New York, 75.2'x 14' x 6.1'. *Source:* 10.

3) Page 187. *Fortuna II*—O/F, 57.2' x 17.2' x 5.3'. *Source:* 10.

1939

1) *VENETIA*—G/Y, 81 tons, built 1920, of New York, 67.4' x 17' x 9.1', burned at Ft. Myers, February 24, 1939. *Source:* 10.

2) **Mystery VESSEL**—A report from Jupiter, Florida, on November 3, said that residents smelled a strong odor of fuel oil around 2 a.m. and a strong wind blew a film of the oil onshore covering buildings and trees. "Daybreak disclosed thick oil for hundreds of yards offshore and six miles up and down the coastline." A ship's door with brass fittings, a lifeboat, vibration proof light bulbs like those used in a ship's engine room, some shaving brushes "with a Swatstika for a trade mark," part of a radio room with small aluminum plates with German radio terms inscribed, and other ship's materials were strewn along the beach over the next few days. Oil barrels and a sea chest with a name of a sailor of New York were also washing up along the coast as far as Daytona Beach. Speculated it was a Nazi submarine tender or some other type German vessel. A lifeboat that washed up near Jupiter and had no ship's name but in German said "Sea Trade Union." A local seaman who saw the wreckage said it appeared the vessel either blew up of was torn apart in a storm (there had been a terrible storm a few weeks earlier). A caretaker in Hobe Sound said he saw a large piece of wreckage as big as a house floating northward. There was also speculation it could be from the 4,327-ton German tanker *Emmy Friedrich*, which was scuttled by her crew October 24 in the Caribbean Sea when confronted by a British warship. It had 39,000 barrels of oil on board loaded at Port Arthur just before the war in Europe started and then sailed to Mexico to avoid the blockade in the gulf. I could not find where it was scuttled, but it wasn't near Jupiter. Could any or all of it drifted north? A search was made offshore, but no sign of a wreck was found. I don't believe the mystery was ever solved. *Source:* Santa Fe New Mexican, 11/3/1939; Panama City News Herald, 11/8/1939; Biloxi Daily Herald, 11/4/1939; Evening Star, 10/22/1939; Sarasota Herald Tribune, 11/22/1939. (5)

1) Page 130. *Alyce B*—O/P, 53' x 15.9' x 4.8'. *Source:* 10.

1940

1) *REGINA*—Steel tanker barge, built 1904 at Belfast, 247' x 36' x 14', parted her cables while being towed during a storm and grounded off Bradenton Beach, March 8, 1940. Had 350,000 gallon of molasses on board. One life was lost. Now a State Underwater Preserve and popular dive site. See GPS coordinates at end of chapter (State preserves). *Source:* 36. (2)

2) *RHEIN HAMBURG*—German transport ship, built 1926 at Bremen, 543.8' x 58.2', had left Mexico and was being watched by allied ships. Hoping to escape into the Atlantic, she found herself pursued off the Tortugas and the German crew set fire to her in order to scuttle her on December 11, 1940. After a brief battle with the Dutch warship *Van Kinsbergen* and the British warship *Caradoc*, which fired 22 rounds into her, she sank, and the German crew were captured. She now lies in 240 feet of water and is a favorite dive site for tech divers. Capt. Billy Dean recovered her bell in 1991. See GPS coordinates at end of chapter. *Source:* 34; Florida Scuba News, 9/2000. (3)

3) *VIRGINIA B*—G/Y, 36 tons, built 1940 at and from Newark, 55.5' x 12.8' x 5.6', burned at Miami, 12/25/1940. *Source:* 10. (5)

1) Page 60. *Belmont*—Sank January 24, 1940, was found in 25 feet of water on the 26th with one lifeboat missing. News reports said it was 103 feet long. *Source:* Washington CH Herald, 1/27/1940.

1941

1) *SCURRY*—G/Y, 55 tons, built 1914 at Marco, of Miami, 70' x 16.6' x 3', burned at Coot Bay, Florida, 2/20/1941. *Source:* 10. (7)

2) *VENTURE*—O/Y, 48 tons, built 1907, of NY, 71.6' x 13.1' x 7', burned 3 miles off Miami Beach, 4/2/1941. *Source:* 10. (5)

WORLD WAR II

1942

1) *SEMINOLE*—Barge, 173 tons, built 1911, of Miami, 105' x 27.1' x 8', foundered at Lat. 25°52' N, Long. 79°20' W, October 4, 1942. *Source:* 10. (5)

1) Page 252. *Vamar*—Was once part of Admiral Byrd's Antarctic Expedition fleet and carried the plane that made the first ever flight over the south pole. Had left Port St. Joe for Cuba, when she sank under

The Dutch freighter *Laertes*, after being torpedoed by *U 109* (see page 261 *Shipwrecks of Florida*, 2nd edition). Courtesy of Henk Meurs and his web site: http://members.ziggo.nl/hmeurs/

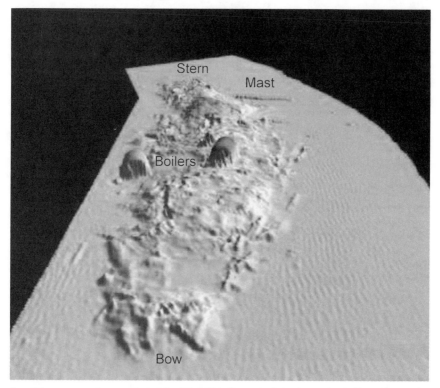

A multibeam sonar image of what the World War II wreck of the *Laertes* looks like today on the ocean floor. She had been demolished by the Navy after she sunk and now lies in 72 feet of water. Courtesy of Land and Sea Surveying Concepts, Inc., Merritt Island, Florida.

suspicious circumstances, some say to block the harbor entrance. Why she sank still remains a mystery. It's a popular dive site, less than four miles off Mexico Beach in 25 feet of water. See GPS coordinates at end chapter. *Source:* 36; www.mexicobeach.com.

2) Page 252. **Ontario**—From Puerto Cortes for Mobile with bananas. Owned by the United Fruit Co. All the crew made it safely in three lifeboats and were later picked up by the *USS Onyx*. When last seen she was burning and must have sunk soon after as attempts to find her failed. *Source:* 32.

3) Page 252. **San Pablo**—Was sunk on purpose by a secret military weapon, a radio-controlled boat with 3,000 pounds of explosives. That was high-tech back then, now a commonplace toy. Lies in 80 feet of water (see GPS coordinates at end of chapter). *Source:* 36.

4) Page 253. **Munger T. Ball** and the **Joseph M. Cudahy**—Both torpedoed the same day and in the same area. The *M.T. Ball*, Capt. Olsen, with 65,000

SS Munger T. Ball Sunk 4 May 1942

The tankers *Munger T. Ball* and the *Joseph M. Cudahy*. Both sunk the same day by U 507.
Note the similarity in appearance. www.armed-guard.com

SS Joseph M. Cudahy Sunk 4 May 1942

The *Joseph M. Cudahy*.

barrels of crude oil, was hit by two torpedoes and only four of the 34 on board survived as lifeboats could not be launched due to fire everywhere. It sank about 15 minutes later. The *J.M Cudahy*, Capt. Reed, with 77,444 barrels of crude and lube oil, saw the burning *Ball* and changed course for Tampa, but it too was torpedoed soon after and only 10 of the 37 on board survived. The hulk was found floating two days later by Navy patrol boat *USS Coral* (PY 15), and sunk by gunfire since it was a hazard to navigation. *Note:* In 2007, divers explored what was called the "Oil Wreck," 93 miles SW of Ft. Myers in 145 feet of water, but were not able to positively identify it, though believed likely one of these two wrecks. *Source:* uboat.net; wreck-diveguide.com (*Oil Wreck Expedition*, by David Miner, 4/23/2013).

5) Page 253. *Torny*—Built in Wilmington, Delaware, originally as the *War Crater*. From Cristobol for Panama City, with 3,650 tons of nitrate, Capt. Østerbø. Two crew (brothers Einar and William Ãnondsen) were killed in the fire room when the torpedo struck the starboard side, which also damaged the bridge. She sank in three minutes, barely enough time to launch the port lifeboats. As the midships slipped under water, the one lifeboat was in danger of being sucked into the still turning propellers. Eleven of the 15 on that boat jumped into the sea just as the *Torny* went down. All were pulled under with her, but all were able to swim back to the surface. The lifeboat missed the propellers by six inches! Those on the lifeboat and six in the motorboat with the captain soon found the other survivors who had been blown overboard by the explosion. There were 24 survivors. The U-boat soon came alongside and questioned them but soon left. They were spotted by an aircraft a couple of hours later which dropped a message to head east and also dropped two rubber rafts. Soon after, two Navy seaplanes landed near them and they were rescued and taken to the Pensacola Naval Air Station. *Source:* 40.

6) Page 254. *Faja de Oro*—One of six Italian tankers that were confiscated in Mexico at the start of the war. The *USCG Nemesis* rescued 28 survivors. *Source:* 31.

7) Page 254. *Gunvor*—From Mobile for Trinidad, Capt. Brynildsen, with a cargo of cars, tractors and mail. Though initially thought to have been

The Norwegian freighter *Gunvor* struck a mine and sunk in 1942. Courtesy of the Monroe County Library, Key West.

torpedoed, it appears she struck a friendly mine in a recently laid minefield by the U.S. Marines off the Keys to deter U-boats from sinking allied vessels. The 20 survivors got into the lifeboat and after searching for any other survivors, made it to Key West 14 hours later. See GPS coordinates at end of chapter. *Source:* 40.

8) Page 255. ***Bosiljka.*** See photo.

8) Page 255. ***Edward S. Luckenbach***—The Navy salvage vessel *Harjurand* (ARS-31), operated by the Merritt-Chapman and Scott Salvage Co., brought up 4,500 tons of ore and brought it to Tampa. The *Harjurand* also worked on the wreck of the *Gulfamerica* off Jacksonville. *Source:* 31.

9) Page 256. ***Port Antonio***—Built in Fevik, Norway, and was chartered by the United Fruit Co. She was from Puerto Barrios, Nicaragua, bound for Tampa, with coffee, and to await orders. The torpedo caused a massive explosion, and she sank within two minutes, taking Capt. Gundersen and 12 of the crew with her. She had broken in two, forming a V, before going under. Luckily, the starboard lifeboat became free and the survivors all eventually were pulled aboard it. After searching for and finding no more survivors, they made sail and rowed, landing at Santa Lucia, Cuba, 45 hours later. *Source:* 40.

The Yugoslavian freighter *Bosiljka*, sunk by a mine in 1942. Courtesy of the Monroe County Library, Key West.

The freighter *Edward S. Luckenbach*, sunk in 1942. Courtesy of the Monroe County Library, Key West.

10) Page 256. **Gulfstate**—Though never located, it's on NOAA's list of 87 ships deemed potential sources of pollution. It sank with 78,000 barrels of crude oil on board, destined for Portland, Maine. Though torpedoed,

Survivors of the *Gulfstate* being rescued by a Navy plane. Courtesy of the National Archives, College Park, Maryland.

SS Gulfstate Sunk 3 April 1943

The steam tanker *Gulfstate*, torpedoed by *U 155* in 1943. www.armed-guard.com

it supposedly did not break up, and I presume there must not have been much of an oil slick, indicating much may still remain on board. *Source:* Boat U.S. Magazine, October/November, 2013.

11) Page 258. *Benwood*—The Stavanger Maritime Museum in Norway was grateful enough to send me an extract from the log of the *Benwood* (the original is in the National Archives in Oslo) with the correct facts of her demise:

> Thursday 9th April 1942. Outside the Florida Coast on voyage from Port Tampa to United Kingdom with cargo of phosphate rock. . . .
> At 1.45 a vessel was observed coming towards us about 2-3 point on stg. Side with parallel course. The course was altered about 1 point to port, simultaneously giving two short blasts in the steam whistle. Some time afterwards the

The Norwegian freighter *Benwood* on the reef. Courtesy of the Monroe County Library, Key West.

meeting ship altered the course to stb. And gave one blast in the whistle. We replied with 2 blasts as there was no space to swing to stb. In order to go clear. As the collision could not be avoided, signaled full speed ahead and at the same time rang alarm to have the crew on deck. The collision occurred about 1.47. The colliding ship (*Robert C. Tuttle*) struck us in the bow. Stopped, and the damage examined and sounded all bilges and tanks. As the whole fo'c'sle head was smashed in and the water flowing into no.1 room and the forepart commenced to sink and at about 2.45 order was given to the crew to take to the boats. . . . The vessel grounded immediately after she was abandoned. The captain's and the 2nd Mate's lifeboats standing by the wreck the whole time. At dawn attempts were made to board the ship but the sea was too heavy. The midship and the after deck were partly above the water.

The captain hired a vessel and was able to get on board later that day, and the salvage vessel *Willet* arrived not long after. By the next day the *Willet* abandoned any hope of salvaging the vessel.

This was the first wreck I ever dove on in the Keys, and it is still one of the most popular dive sites in the upper Keys. The wreck lies in around 25–50 feet of water, and though much of the structure of the vessel was salvaged for the war effort, it's still a nice dive. *Note:* I've since read that Hurricane Irma recently uncovered more of this wreck previously buried under sand including an anchor. See GPS coordinates at end of chapter.

12) Page 259. **Potrero del Llano**—Attached photo of ship lists her at Lat. 25°48' N, Long. 79°58' W, when photo of her was taken. *Source:* NOAA.

The Mexican tanker *Potrero del Llano* on fire after being torpedoed by *U 564*. Courtesy of the National Archives, College Park, Maryland.

13) Page 261. *Cities Service Empire*—From Port Arthur for Philadelphia. The *Biddle* (DD-151) rescued 36 and brought them to Ft. Pierce. The *USCG Vigilant* saved two of three who were stuck on the burning hull fighting the fire, but the tanker blew up and sank when trying to reach the third. *Source:* 31.

14) Page 262. *Lubrafol*—She was from Aruba bound for New York, with 67,000 barrels of #2 heating oil. Had a total of 44 men on board (38 merchant men, and six Navy Armed Guards). Was torpedoed on the starboard side at number five tank about 3-1/2 mile off Hillsboro Inlet, and believe was also struck by a second torpedo. Soon she was on fire and the survivors abandoned her in three lifeboats, though one of these also caught fire. Two Coast Guard boats were soon on scene and landed the survivors at Boynton Beach. Thirteen men were lost and seven injured. *Source:* 32.

1943

1) *USN YP 438*—Destroyed by grounding at Port Everglades, Florida, March 20, 1943. *Source:* 19. (5)

2) *SUNSHINE*—Motor Yacht/Trawler, either 41 or 57 tons, foundered April 22 or 23, 1943, at approximate coordinates: Lat. 28.000273 N, Long. 84.999886 W. *Source:* 4; 10. (1)

1) Page 252. *Viking*—F/V, built at and from Pensacola, 71.4' x 20.4' x 9.4'. *Source:* 10.

2) Page 254. *Antonio Ensen*—Cuban freighter which collided with the Honduran schooner *Charta*. Captain Jose Prego. From Cuba bound for Tampa, with barrels of Cuban rum. One hundred fifty barrels were floating in the gulf after she sank. Both were running at night without lights as was required due to U-boat attacks. She sank within 10 minutes and all nine on board were rescued. Local diver John Marsden and his son identified the wreck which lay in 64 feet of water 12 miles off the Venice Jetties and recovered her anchor. Some machinery still remains. *Source:* Sarasota Herald Tribune, 11/1/1943; Information provided by John Marsden.

1944

1) *VITRIC*—Schooner barge, built 1911 at Noank, Connecticut, 165.6' x 36' x 15.5'. Was reportedly carrying 130,000 gallons of syrup and some Japanese motorcycles, when she sank off Key Largo. Supposedly identified due to the storage vats on the wreck. Some dive sites say she sank March 1944. I checked *US Merchant Vessel's* list, and she is listed up until 1945, and I could

not find her listed in the losses section after that, nor did I see any reports listed in the papers that I could access, so not verified. Now a popular tech dive site as it lays in 300 feet of water. *Source:* 34. (4)

2) *USS WARRINGTON* (DD-383)—Though she was many miles off Florida when she sank, it was reported lost off the Florida coast, her exact where-abouts unknown. A Navy destroyer, built 1937 at Kearny, New Jersey, 381' x 36'7" x 17'. When two days out of Norfolk in company with another naval ship headed to Trinidad, she encountered the beginnings of a hurricane, and by September 13, the storm was at its worse and she began to lose headway and water began to enter into the engine room. This caused an electrical outage, which caused her to lose steering and the engines. Winds were more than 150 mph, and the only pump that may have saved her was ripped from the deck and washed overboard. By noon, with the ship in a sinking state, the order to abandon ship was given, "By 1250, her crew had left the Warrington; and she went down almost immediately."

The horror didn't end there for the 43 men on one raft. By the next day only 26 remained on the raft, "The raft being flipped over by mountainous

The destroyer *USS Warrington*, sunk during a hurricane in 1944. Courtesy of the Naval History and Heritage Command, catalog # NH 62123.

waves. Next day only 15 remained and then a ship loomed out of the mist, and before they could move, struck the raft: squarely, smashing it aside." This caused three more men to lose their lives, but the ship heard the men's cries and stopped.

There were a number of tales of heroism, and a book about the disaster, the *Dragon's Breath, Hurricane at Sea*, by Commander Robert A. Dawes Jr., is definitely worth reading. One hero was the physician on board, Lt. Robert M. Kennedy, who refused to leave the ship as he had two badly injured patients.

This was printed in the *Jefferson Bee* newspaper after the disaster: "There will be no purple hearts for those who died. But men who know the sea and its power to destroy will remember the valiant crew of the *USS Warrington* as long as grey seas pile over the foc'sle of our fighting ships."

Of a total of 20 officers and 301 crewmen, only five officers and 68 crewmen were saved, making this one of the worst maritime disasters off the Florida coast in recent history. *Source:* 14; Jefferson Bee, 11/28/1944; Tipton Daily Tribune, 9/23/1944. (8)

3) *Army TUG*—Small tug known as an S.T. boat, from New Orleans with a stop in Panama City bound for Charleston, capsized during a tropical storm off Bradenton, October 18, 1944. The twelve civilian crew took to the dinghy but it capsized too, and eleven men drowned. Only the skipper survived. *Source:* NYT, 10/21/1944. (2)

1) Page 253. *Anona*—Originally a 117-foot steam yacht built in 1904 at Boston, steel-hulled. Eventually became a cargo vessel and recently found in 4,000 feet of water. Was carrying potatoes to the British West Indies when she sank. Crew were rescued by Navy PBY planes after two days in a raft. Credit: https://www.boem.gov/Environmental-Stewardship/Archaeology/Shipwrecks.aspx.

1945

1) *BAMBOO*—G/F, 21 tons, built 1930, of St. Augustine, 50.7' x 13.3' x 4.6', foundered between Ponce de Leon Inlet and Cape Canaveral, February 1, 1945. *Source:* 10. (6)

POST–WORLD WAR II

1945

1) *LIBERATOR*—O/F, 37 tons, built 1944 at St. Augustine, 50.2' x 16.6' x 6.2', lost off the St. Augustine Bar, 1/2 mile SE of the N. Jetties, December 13, 1945. *Source:* 10. (6)

1946

1) Page 252. *A.G.T.N. No.34*—Foundered November 22, 1946 (not 1942). *Source:* 10.

1947

1) *OCEAN QUEEN*—G/F, 23 tons, built 1911 at and from Biloxi, 52.2' x 18.2' x 3.7', burned at mouth of the Caloosahatchee River, November 30, 1947. *Source:* 10. (2)

2) *DELIVERANCE*—British motor schooner, of Bermuda, about 200 tons, went aground south of Ponte Vedra Beach, December 13, 1947. Crew were rescued and taken to the Coast Guard station at Mayport. Had 40 tons of scrap iron on board, and was sinking into the sand, her hold was full of water. Was on her way to Jacksonville for lumber. *Source:* 24; Daytona Beach Morning Journal, 12/15/1947. (6)

1) Page 60. *Okeechobee*—Built at lake Okeechobee, of Tampa, 78.9' x 26' x 4.8'. *Source:* 10.

2) Page 162. *Emma*—F/V, built at Brooklyn, of Miami, 58.1' x 16' x 7.5'. *Source:* 10.

3) Page 204. *Josephine H II*—Yacht, 51.3' x 13' x 6', built at Detroit, of Jacksonville. *Source:* 10.

1948

1) *BRUNHILDA*—G/Y, 34 tons, built 1929, of Buffalo, 52.9' x 13.6' x 5.3', burned at Lake Worth, 1/31/1948. *Source:* 10. (5)

2) *WESTERNER*—O/F, 46 tons, built 1947 at St. Augustine, of Fernandina, 54.7' x 16.6' x 6.9', burned 47 miles east of St. Augustine, March 15, 1948. *Source:* 10. (6)

3) *MAHANA*—G/F, 26 tons, built 1910 in Nyack, New York, of Key West, 55.4' x 13.4' x 5.6', foundered at Key West, September 21, 1948. *Source:* 10. (3)

4) *VAGABOND*—G/P, 12 tons, built 1908 at New York, of Key West, 56' x 8.6' x 4.5', foundered at Key West, September 21,1948. *Source:* 10. (3)

5) *RED SNAPPER*—O/F, 33 tons, built 1938 at Fernandina, 50.1' x 17.6' x 4', lost (cause unknown) 11 miles south of New Smyrna Light, December 25, 1948. *Source:* 10. (6)

1) Page 60. *Nandoma*—Yacht, built in Maine, of Chicago, 74.5' x 13.2' x 5.9'. *Source:* 10.

2) Page 162-3. *George C. Bell*—Freighter, 87.2' x 24.3' x 6.5'. *Source:* 10.

3) Page 163. *Vahadah*—G/Y of St. Augustine, 77.2' x 13' x 6.8'. *Source:* 10.

1949

1) *ICACOS*—G/Y, 39 tons, built 1927 at Bayonne, New Jersey, of Key West, 57.7' x 14' x 6.1', burned at Key West, January 13, 1949. *Source:* 10. (3)

2) *MISS CHARLESTON*—O/F, 40 tons, built 1946 at St. Augustine, of Charleston, 53.8' x 17.6' x 6.9', foundered at Lat. 29°35' N, Long. 81°03' W, January 15, 1949. *Source:* 10. (6)

3) *MISS ELLAZENA*—O/F, 19 tons, built 1921, of Jacksonville, 63' x 15' x 3.2', foundered at Lat. 30°23' N, Long. 81°26' W, July 1949. *Source:* 10. (6)

4) *TUNA*—G/Y, 30 tons, built 1917 at Boston, of Miami, 67.9' x 10.5' x 5.9', foundered off 33 St. on Lake Front at Lake Worth, 8/26/1949. *Source:* 10. (7)

5) *FALCON*—O/T, 20 tons, built 1936 in Biloxi, of Pensacola, 50.6' x 13.2' x 5.4', burned about 14 miles east of Pensacola, September 18, 1949. *Source:* 10. (1)

6) *LYNNHAVEN*—O/F, 65 tons, built 1917, of Fernandina, 74.5' x 19.4' x 6.1', burned in Fernandina Beach Harbor in 1949. *Source:* 10. (6)

1) Page 130. *Sunshine*—Yacht, built at Brooklyn, of Miami, 65.9' x 16.4' x 7.6'. *Source:* 10.

2) Page 204. *Norvell*—O/T, built at Chattahoochee, Florida, of Apalachicola, owned by Florida Gravel Co., 61' x 20' x 3.6'. *Source:* 10.

1950

1) *SULEW*—G/Y, 41 tons, built 1909 at Philadelphia, of Pensacola, 63' x 14.1' x 6.5', burned about 25 miles west of Aripeka, Florida, July 31, 1950. *Source:* 10. (2)

1) Page 60. *Seawave*—O/Y, of Miami, 61.5' x 14.3' x 5.9'. *Source:* 10.

1951

1) Page 60. *Desire*—F/V, built at Galveston, of Tampa, 84.4' x 16.1' x 8'. *Source:* 10.

2) Page 98. *Dayco*—O/F, 42 tons, built at Tarpon Springs, of Miami, 55' x 16.9' x 7'. *Source:* 10.

1952

1) Page 204. *Miss Jo*—O/F, built at St. Augustine, of Brunswick, GA, 48.6' x 16.8' x 6.5'. *Source:* 10.

1953

1) Page 60. *Petrel* (correct) and *USS PC 463*—The *Petrel* survived and did not sink, and the *USS PC 463* was damaged in the collision and survived, but was sunk for target practice using the new Mark 28 torpedo. *Source:* 29.

2) Page 99. *F.W. Sheper*—O/F, built at and from St. Augustine, 51.3' x 17.4' x 5.4'. *Source:* 10.

1954

1) *MISS BIRMINGHAM*—O/P, 13 tons, built 1939, of Tampa, 57.1' x 15' x 2.4', stranded at Blind Pass, Pinellas County, February 8, 1954. *Source:* 10. (2)

2) *R.E. HUFF*—O/V, 18 tons, built 1929, burned in the Florida Straight, February 17, 1954. *Source:* 10. (8)

3) *RONALD and DOROTHY*—O/F, 43 tons, built 1926 in Maine, 60.6' x 16.7' x 7.8', foundered 1/2 mile east, 17 miles from Dry Tortugas Light west, 3/4 north 44 miles from wreck buoy, May 6, 1954. *Source:* 10. (3)

4) *CLARA M*—O/F, 19 tons, built 1926, 52.2' x 15.1' x 4.6', foundered six miles off Miami Ship Channel to the north, June 10, 1954. *Source:* 10. (5)

5) *BERTHA R*—Tug, 275 tons, 117.5' x 28' x 13.5', built 1944 at City Island, New York, Capt. Thompson, owned by the Blue Stack Towing Co., Tampa. From New Orleans for Tampa with a crew of 11, and was towing a barge (*Blue Stack #93*), loaded with steel and Sulphur. On December 6, 1954, the barge came loose in heavy seas. After the line parted, they made two attempts to get a line attached, but on the second attempt, the barge smashed against the tug, causing her to leak badly. *Merchant Vessels* reported the collision at Lat. 28°9" N, Long. 86°7" W. Newspapers just said about 90 miles SW of Apalachicola. The captain had sent a distress call reporting having rudder problems and that they were taking on more water than the pumps could handle. After four hours they had to abandon ship in the two life rafts. After 16 hours afloat, seven survivors were rescued including the captain. A motorized lifeboat with a crew of 10 from the vessel *Helen Lykes* picked up four men from one lifeboat, but the seas being so rough and with high winds, were unable to return to the *Lykes*, but were later all rescued by the Coast Guard cutter *Cartigan*. The cutter soon picked up three more survivors, along with two bodies from the second life raft and found a third body nearby. Three men had died during the night. The first mate was still missing. *Source:* 10; Dixon Evening Telegraph, 12/7/1954; Monroe News Star, 12/8/1954; Sarasota Herald Tribune, 12/9/1954.

6) *DERELD*—O/F, 58 tons, built 1945 at and from St. Augustine, 57.2' x 18.8' x 7', burned about two miles NE of Tortugas Light, December 16, 1954. *Source:* 10. (3)

1) Page 61. *Blue Stack # 79*—Built at and from Tampa, 170' x 40' x 9.9'. *Source:* 10.

2) Page 99. *Elliot*—F/V, of New York, 72' x 14.2' x 8'. *Source:* 10.

3) Page 99. *Spot Pack*—F/V, built at Ipswich, Massachusetts, of Miami, 90.6' x 21.3' x 10.9', burned at Lat. 24°56'05" N, Long. 82°46'05" W. *Source:* 10.

1955

1) Page 99. *Blue Bonnet*—F/V, built at St. Augustine, of Tampa, 55.3' x 18.8' x 6.6'. *Source:* 10.

1956

1) *PHANTOM*—A 65-foot yacht, was hired by millionaire E. M. Loew (of Loew's Theaters and hotel fame), to take his employees to a floating restaurant off Key Biscayne to celebrate the construction of a new hotel in Miami. When about four miles off Miami, the two-decked yacht made a turn and flipped over on its side, throwing many of the passengers (either 53 or 56 on board) into the water. All were rescued and only a few had minor injuries. Unknown if yacht was salvaged. *Source:* Aberdeen Evening Express, 4/4/1956; Charleston Gazette, 4/4/1956. (5)

1) Page 45. *Jolly Roger*—F/V, built at Tarpon Springs, of Tampa, 49.6' x 16.5' x 6.7'. *Source:* 10.

1957

1) *MARY ANNE*—O/F, 21 tons, built 1946, of Tampa, 50.3' x 14.6' x 4.1', foundered about 40 miles west of Sanibel, 1/21/1957. *Source:* 10. (2)

1) Page 99. *Miss Columbia*—O/F, built at St. Augustine, of Tampa, 52.4' x 17.7' x 6.8'. *Source:* 10.

2) Page 99. *Santa Barbara*—O/F, built at 7 from St. Augustine, 51.1' x 17' x 6.5'. *Source:* 10.

3) Page 163. *Dragoon*—G/Y, built at and from New York., 74' x 15.1' x 7.5'. *Source:* 10.

4) Page 188. *Miss Ilse*—O/F, built at St. Augustine, of Charleston, 44.6' x 15.5' x 6'. *Source:* 10.

1958

1) *MISS CAMPECHE*—O/F, 56 tons, built 1951, of St. Augustine, 61.4' x 18.5' x 7.3', foundered about 60 miles NW of the Dry Tortugas, January 8, 1958. *Source:* 10. (3)

2) *WALLING III*—F/V, 66 tons, built 1953 at St. Augustine, of Tampa, 63.5' x 18.6' x 7.7', foundered about 70 miles SSW of Sanibel Light, at Lat. 25°37', Long. 83°43', December 15, 1958. *Source:* 10. (2)

3) *St. MARK*—O/F, 63 tons, built 1953 at St. Augustine, of Jacksonville, 58.7' x 18.5' x 8.2', collided with the *Amarante*, December 21, 1958, at Lat. 25°37' N; Long. 84°02' W. *Source:* 10. (2)

1) Page 46. *Supertest*—O/T, of Tampa, 58' x 18' x 6.6'. *Source:* 10.

2) Page 61. *Louanna*—F/V, of Fernandina, 67.2' x 20.3' x 7.7'. *Source:* 10.

3) Page 99. *Evening Star*—O/F, built at St. Augustine, of Tampa, 62.9' x 21.6' x 7.6'. *Source:* 10.

4) Page 189. *Elizabeth Perry*—O/F, of Jacksonville, 53.6' x 18.4' x 6.4'. *Source:* 10.

1959

1) *CAPTAIN TAP*—O/F, 41 tons, built 1959 in Georgia, 50' x 16.2' x 7.7', foundered off Cape Canaveral, March 7, 1959. *Source:* 10. (6)

2) *MARBAR-RON*—O/F, 35 tons, built 1955, of Charleston, 50.5' x 16.2' x 6.6', foundered at St. Augustine, November 9, 1959. *Source:* 10. (6)

1) Page 61. *Pamela Ann*—O/F, built at and from Miami, 58.5' x 17.6' x 7.4'. *Source:* 10.

2) Page 61. *Virginia Ann*—O/F, built St Augustine, of Tampa, 53.6' x 18.4' x 6.4'. *Source:* 10.

3) Page 61. *Louanna*—O/F, built at St. Augustine, of Fernandina, 67.2' x 20.3' x 7.7'. *Source:* 10.

4) Page 130. *Chimaera*—O/Y, built in Rhode Island, of Bar Harbor, 66.5' x 13.5' x 5.9'. *Source:* 10.

1960

1) *CAPTAIN RED*—O/F, 48 tons, built 1952 at St. Augustine, 53.6' x 18.4' x 6.4', burned off the Dry Tortugas, 1/1/1960. *Source:* 10. (3)

1) Page 46. *Cracker's Boys*—O/F, built at Fernandina, of Morgan City, 50.1' x 16.2' x 6.8'. *Source:* 10.

2) Page 100. *Emily A*—F/V, of Key West, 49' x 15.7' x 6.6'. *Source:* 10.

3) Page 100. *Cape Lookout*—O/F, of Corpus Christi, 49.6' x 16' x 5.8'. *Source:* 10.

4) Page 189. *Deepwater II*—O/F, built at St. Augustine, of Jacksonville, 52.5' x 17/1' x 7.3'. *Source:* 10.

5) Page 189. *Jackie B*—F/V, of Tampa, 52.6' x 16.8' x 6.4'. *Source:* 10.

6) Page 189. *D&D II*—Wood vessel, 55.3' x 17.3' x 7.9'. *Source:* 10.

7) Page 205. *Little David*—Built at San Francisco, of Miami, 59.3' x 22' x 4.8'. *Source:* 10.

1961

1) Page 61. *Mary E*—F/V, of Tampa, 48.5' x 11' x 8.1'. *Source:* 10.

2) Page 61. *Miss Margie*—F/V, of Jacksonville, 50.5' x 17.3' x 6.8'. *Source:* 10.

3) Page 62. *Santa Maria*—F/V, of Key West, 42' x 14.2' x 6.1'. *Source:* 10.

4) Page 62. *Rampant* (correct)—T/V of Tampa, 56' x 13.6' x 6'. Was originally a yacht, one of a few used by Thomas Edison for the Navy during World War I for research. *Source:* 10; 29.

5) Page 100 . *Buddy Lynn*—O/F, built at St. Augustine, 61.6' x 18.4' x 8.5'. *Source:* 10.

6) Page 163. *Arizona Sword*—Built in Portland, Oregon, of Tampa, 306.2' x 49.1' x 23.4'. Had 5,000 tons of sulfur on board. She broke up within minutes after her cable parted in 15-foot waves. Seven of the eight on board were lost. *Source:* 10; Joplin News Herald, 1/14/1961.

7) Page 163. *Antonia*—O/Y, of Cape Charles, Virginia, 73' x 15.8' x 7.2'. *Source:* 10.

8) Page 163. *Leonie*—G/Y, built in Camden, New Jersey, of New York, and owned by L. Guggenheim (of the Guggenheim Museum?), 100' x 20' x 9.8'. *Source:* 10.

1962

1) Page 100. *Joe Rizzo*—F/V, of Corpus Christi, 52.4' x 17.8' x 7'. *Source:* 10.

2) Page 100. *Grand Mar*—F/V, of Savannah, 48' x 15.5' x 6.9'. *Source:* 10.

3) Page 100. *Danny Boy*—F/V, of Key West, 48.1' x 16' x 5.9'. *Source:* 10.

4) Page 100. *Miss Sarah*—F/V, of Key West, 61.6' x 18.4' x 8.2'. *Source:* 10.

5) Page 100. *William R*—F/V, of Tampa, 59.5' x 17.9' x 7.7'. *Source:* 10.

6) Page 163. *Whereaway*—G/Y, built at Palm Beach, of Miami, 67' x 19.1' x 5.3'. Barnette says it may have been saved, though it is no longer listed in *Merchant Vessels* after 1962. Maybe renamed? *Source:* 7; 10.

7) Page 205. *Grace*—F/V, built and of St. Augustine, 41.3' x 14.8' x 6.8'. *Source:* 10.

8) Page 205. *Flying Cloud*—Yacht, of Miami, 50' x 14' x 9.6'. *Source:* 10.

1963

1) *EDDIE BOY*—O/F, 48 tons, built 1951 at St. Augustine, of Tampa, 53.6' x 18.4' x 6.4', burned November 20, 1963, at approx. Lat. 26°38' N, Long. 82°19' W. *Source:* 10. (2)

1) Page 100. *Comanche*—F/V, of Tampa, 58.7' x 18.5' x 8.2'. *Source:* 10.

1964

1) *ENCHANTRESS*—G/Y, 20 tons, built 1925 at Bath, Maine, 50.5' x 12' x 7.5', lost during a storm at Miami, January 13, 1964. *Source:* 10. (5)

2) *SEA STAR*—O/F, 65 tons, built 1953 at St. Augustine, 61.6' x 18.4' x 8.4', foundered about 90 miles SW of Tortugas Light, January 14, 1964. *Source:* 10. (3)

3) *MAYRA*—O/F, 24 tons, of Miami, 50.4' x 12.7' x 4.6', foundered 12 miles east of Ft. Lauderdale, March 3, 1964. *Source:* 10. (5)

4) *SOUTHERN DAWN*—O/F, 53 tons, built 1951 at Jacksonville, of Corpus Christie, 61.1' x 18.2' x 6.9', burned at approx. Lat. 27°, Long. 82°32', April 7, 1964. *Source:* 10. (2)

5) *MISS TUSCON*—O/F, 38 tons, built 1951 at St. Augustine, foundered at approximate Lat. 29°52', Long. 86°32', 10/16/1964. *Source:* 10. (1)

6) *SAND DOLLAR*—O/F, 52 tons, built 1956 at St. Augustine, 55' x 18.5' x 7.5', stranded about 15 miles south of Ponce De Leon Inlet, November 9, 1964. *Source:* 10. (6)

7) *PEGGY SUE*—O/F, 69 tons, built 1959 at Tarpon Springs, 61.3' x 19.3' x 8.5', foundered at approximate Lat. 24°19' N, Long. 82°56' W, December 12, 1964. *Source:* 10. (3)

1) Page 100. *Yellow Jacket*—F/V, of Key West, 43.3' x 16.3' x 6'. *Source:* 10.

1965

1) *SEABEE*—O/F, 44 tons, built 1947 at St. Augustine, 51.1' x 16.8' x 6.5', burned at Marathon, February 9, 1965. *Source:* 10. (4)

2) *WARRIOR*—Oil/cargo vessel, 26 tons, built 1941 at Fernandina, of Charleston, 51.4' x 15.6' x 4.3', foundered at Jacksonville, May 15, 1957. *Source:* 10. (6)

3) *ONAWA*—G/Y, 71 tons, built 1925 at Seattle, 76.4' x 15.6' x 9.7', foundered about 100 miles off Ft. Meyers, May 23, 1965. *Source:* 10. (2)

4) *PAPA JON*—O/Y, 74 tons, built 1952 in Sweden, 76' x 16' x 8', burned two miles south of the Sarasota Bridge, November 18, 1965. *Source:* 10. (2)

5) *MARANA*—O/Y, 93 tons, built 1922 in New Jersey, 70' x 17.9' x 9.2', foundered about 18 miles off Miami, December 28, 1965. *Source:* 10. (5)

1) Page 101. **Gulf Maid**—F/V, of Tampa, 48.6' x 16.8' x 6.7'. *Source:* 10.

2) Page 164. *Amaryllis*—Originally the *Cromwell Park*, built in Vancouver for the Canadian government for use in World War II, 7,147 tons, 441.6' x 57.2'. After she grounded on the beach on Singer Island during Hurricane Betsey, it became a tourist and surfer attraction, but soon after started leaking oil, caught on fire once, and became a safety hazard. The Army Corps pumped out the fuel, partially dismantled her, and towed her out to sea about 3/4 a mile offshore where she was sunk. Soon after, another vessel called the *Mizpah* was sunk as an artificial reef right next to her. Long before all the other artificial reefs were being sunk, this is where many other divers, including myself, would come to dive on a "wreck." The Gulf Stream comes closest to the Florida coast right in this area, and though the current wasn't always bad when diving here, I remember times when you had to fight the current getting down to these wrecks, having to hold my mask onto my face so it wouldn't be pulled off, and even having the purge valve on my regulator pushed in by the current. You definitely have to be aware of the current when diving these wrecks. The wreck lies in Lat. 26°47'17" N, Long. 80°00'58" W, in 100 feet of water. *Source:* Wikipedia.

1966

1) *FLIPPER TOO*—O/Y, 36 tons, built 1940, 51.5' x 13.2' x 6', burned between Egmont Key and Ft. Desoto, mouth of Tampa Bay, March 13, 1966. *Source:* 10. (2)

2) *GERTIE T*—G/F, 14 tons, built 1917, 51.5. x 14' x 2.6', lost during a hurricane at Key West, June 4, 1966. *Source:* 10. (3)

3) *RANGER III*—O/P, 27 tons, built 1950, 59.6' x 17.6' x 4', lost during a hurricane, July 1966, at Lat. 27°33' N, Long. 82°44' W. *Source:* 10. (2)

1967

1) *SINBAR II*—O/Y, 49 tons, built 1937 at Chicago, 64.7' x 14.8' x 5.1', foundered 15 miles NE of the Miami Sea-buoy, April 9, 1967. *Source:* 10. (5)

2) *CAPT. CHARLES*—O/F, 64 tons, built 1957 at St. Augustine, 61.6' x 18.4' x 8.5', burned at Lat. 25°50' N, Long. 82°16' W, 10/23/1967. *Source:* 10. (2)

3) *BAGS*—Trawler, 55' x 18' x 7', caught fire and sank in 1967 off the lower Keys. See GPS coordinates at end of chapter. *Source:* 4. (3)

4) **Unk. 70' F/V**—Was found in 1967 at approximate Lat. 24.49°N, Long. 81.677223°W. *Source:* 4. (3)

1968

1) *CAPT. JOE L*—O/F, 71 tons, built 1958 at Bayou La Batre, AL, 58.5' x 18.6' x 9.3', lost at Lat. 26°22' N, Long. 87°44' W, March 13, 1968. *Source:* 10. (2)

2) *SKYLARK II*—O/Y, 49 tons, built 1932 in New York, 62.4' x 14' x 7', burned about five miles off shore of Lake Worth, June 22, 1968. *Source:* 10. (5)

3) *KING FISH*—O/F, 47 tons, built 1949 at St. Augustine, 53.6' x 18.4' x 6.4', foundered WSW of the Tampa Bar, October 1, 1968. *Source:* 10. (2)

4) *SEA EAGLE*—O/F (wood), 65 tons, built 1953, stranded about 1/4 mile east of the N. Jetty, St. Augustine, November 11, 1968. *Source:* 10. (6)

1) Page 100. *Lainee K*—O/F, 35 tons, built 1945 at Miami, 56.2' x 16' x 7.3'. *Source:* 10.

2) Page 101. *Miss Lorraine*—O/F, 55.9' x 17' x 7.1'. *Source:* 10.

1969

1) *PIXIE*—O/F (wood), 64 tons, built 1954 at St. Augustine, 61.6' x 18.4' x 8.5', burned SW by S of Sanibel Light, Ft. Myers Beach, January 25, 1969. *Source:* 10. (2)

2) *MM 71*—Barge (steel), 91 tons, built 1944 at Houston, 186.7' x 33.7' x 10.7', foundered at Lat. 24°35', Long. 87°46', March 15, 1969. *Source:* 10. (3)

3) *SELMA*—O/Y (wood), 69 tons, built 1928 in Sweden, 77.4' x 16' x 6.9', burned about 1/2 mile east of the Fowey Rock Lighthouse, May 14, 1969. *Source:* 10. (4)

4) *FLYING CLOUD*—O/Y (composite), 28 tons, built 1911 in Rhode Island, 50' x 14' x 9.6', foundered in Lake Worth, July 1969. *Source:* 10. (5)

1970

1) *MARIE*—O/F (wood), 37 tons, built 1950 at St. Augustine, 51.3' x 16.4' x 7.1', foundered about 6.5 miles, NW of Boca Grande, January 31, 1970. *Source:* 10. (2)

2) *SEA KING*—O/F (wood), 63 tons, built 1952 at St. Augustine, 58.7' x 18.5' x 8.2', burned at Key West, February 17, 1970. *Source:* 10. (3)

3) *TIBOR*—O/V, 63 tons, built 1962, burned near West Palm Beach, March 30, 1970. *Source:* 10. (5)

4) *CONSOLIDATOR*—Panamanian freighter, 213-feet long, sank off Carysfort Reef around 3:30 a.m., May, 18, 1970. Seven of the crew were picked up about 20 miles south of Miami by the Coast Guard. *Source:* Biloxi Daily Herald, 5/18/1970. (4)

5) *AIPLE 100*—Barge (steel), 724 tons, built 1959, 256' x 50' x 22.1', foundered at Lat. 29°13' N, Long. 86°18' W, October 19, 1970. *Source:* 10. (1)

6) *MACHOTE*—Was an old 325-foot long freighter built in Norway in 1941. Moored in Tampa, she became a rusting hulk until finally forced to be towed to Europe to be scrapped along with another hulk. While in tow by an Italian tug, she encountered a number of problems, and finally sank about 23 miles east of Lake Worth Inlet in 1,200 feet of water, November 1, 1970. *Source:* 7; Naples Daily News, 11/2/1970. (5)

7) *SEA WITCH*—O/F (wood), 48 tons, built 1953 at key West, foundered at Lat. 24°48'30" N, Long. 83°06'30" W, November 8, 1970. *Source:* 10. (3)

8) *MR. MAX*—O/F (wood), 63 tons, built 1952 at St. Augustine, 58.7' x 18.5' x 8.2', foundered between Key West and Cuba, November 27, 1970. Possible Florida wreck. *Source:* 10. (8)

9) *CARA MIA*—G/Y (fiberglass), 31 tons, built 1961 in Michigan, 57' x 13' x 6.3', foundered 35 miles west of Cedar Key, December 29, 1970. *Source:* 10. (2)

1) Page 63. *118*—Steel/freight barge, 124.3' x 32' x 6.4'. *Source:* 10.

1972

1) *USS AMESBURY* (Alexander's Wreck)—This ex-naval vessel was bought with the intension of sinking her as an artificial reef in the gulf. While being towed, she ran aground in 1972, and before she could be refloated, a storm hit the area and she broke in two. She now lies in two parts in 30 feet. See GPS coordinates at end of chapter. *Source:* 32. (3)

The *USS Amesbury* at the Bethlehem Hingham Shipyard, Massachusetts, being outfitted, July 6, 1943. From the National Archives. Also on the Naval History and Heritage Command's web site, catalog # 19-N-85626.

1) Page 46. *Capt. Bill*—O/F (wood), built at St. Augustine, 69.2' x 20' x 7.9'. *Source:* 10.

2) Page 102. *USS Wilkes-Barre.* See GPS coordinates at end of chapter.

The *USS Wilkes-Barre* being sunk by the Navy off Key West. Courtesy of the Monroe County Library, Key West.

3) Page 190. *Joan & Ursala*—O/F (wood), built 1937 at Essex, Massachusetts, 69.5' x 18.1' x 8.9'. *Source:* 10.

1973

1) *ICE FOG*—O/T vessel (steel), 133 tons, built 1967 at New Orleans, 71.5' x 25' x 11.5', foundered in the Florida Straight, February 10, 1973. *Source:* 10. (8)

2) *DEBORAH ELLEN*—O/F (wood), 87 tons, built 1969 in North Carolina, 65.9' x 20.9' x 8.1', burned about 20 miles NW of the Smith Shoal Light, Lat. 24°43.2', Long. 81°55', April 15, 1973. *Source:* 10. (3)

3) *MISS FAY*—O/F (wood), 48 tons, built 1957, 51.1' x 17.4' x 7.6', collided with a submerged object, at Lat. 27°40', Long. 80°20', May 25, 1973. *Source:* 10. (5)

4) *FLYING EAGLE*—O/P (wood), 42 tons, built 1965 at Tarpon Springs, 51.4' x 17.2' x 4.3', collided with a submerged object, 50 miles NW of Ft. Meyers, September 7, 1973. *Source:* 10. (2)

5) *WILD HOG*—O/F (wood), 64 tons, built 1956 at St. Augustine, 61.6' x 18.4' x 8.5', was destroyed by high winds at Ponte Vedra Beach, October 18, 1973. *Source:* 10. (6)

1) Page 63. *YSD 71*—Steel, built in Charleston, 98.5' x 30' x 6.7'. *Source:* 10.

2) Page 102. *DC 715*—Steel barge, built at New Orleans, 260' x 60' x 22.6', owned by Dow Chemicals, Houston. *Source:* 10.

1974

1) *VAN MAR*—O/Y (wood), 31 tons, built 1969 at Homestead, 50' x 15' x 8.5', burned at Elliot Key, March 26, 1974. *Source:* 10. (4)

2) *BOWARD II*—Dredge (wood), 358 tons, built 1924 at Baltimore, 125' x 40' x 5.9', burned off Gadsen Point Cut C, Tampa Bay, July 26, 1974. *Source:* 10. (2)

3) *RMC 100*—Freight barge, 1,508 tons, built 1964 at Houston, 200' x 40' x 17.4', foundered at Lat. 27°28' N, Long. 79°08' W, October 6, 1974. *Source:* 10. (5)

4) *MARY ETTA*—O/V, 83 tons, built 1965, burned at Lat. 25°18', Long. 81°55', December 7, 1974. *Source:* 10. (3)

5) *MISS LETTIE*—O/V, 64 tons, built 1954, foundered at Miami, in 1974. *Source:* 10. (5)

1) Page 102. *Miss Five Eleven*—F/V, 61.6' x 18.4' x 8.5'. *Source:* 10.

1975

1) *TEGRA*—O/V, 69 tons, built 1929, foundered at WPB, January 1975. *Source:* 10. (5)

2) *TRADE WINDS*—O/P (wood), 14 tons, built 1942 in Michigan, 56.8' x 13.6' x 2.5', burned at New Smyrna Beach, February 1975. *Source:* 10. (6)

3) *MISS DEDE*—O/F (wood), 83 tons, built 1971 at St. Augustine, 66' x 19.1' x 9', collided with barge SBI 517, at Lat. 27°30' N, Long. 82°46' W, May 1975. *Source:* 10. (2)

4) *NORTHWIND*—Tug, 55 tons, built 1953. This was the vessel used by Mel Fisher and company while looking for the treasure galleon *Atocha*. She sprung a leak and capsized while the crew were asleep, with the tragic loss of Mel's son Dirk, daughter-in-law Angel, and diver Rick Gage, June 1975. She now lies in 40 feet of water, 3.5 miles SW of the Marquesas. *Source:* 10. (3)

5) *CAPT. GIBERSON*—O/P (wood), 41 tons, built 1961 in New Jersey, 59.7' x 19.1' x 3.6', foundered off Port Richey, November 20, 1975. *Source:* 10. (2)

6) *CORAL SEAS*—O/F (wood), 67 tons, built 1966, 62.2' x 18.3' x 8.4', burned 40 miles SSW of Ft. Myers, November 24, 1975. *Source:* 10. (2)

1976

1) **GULF BREEZE**—O/F (wood), 74 tons, built 1963 at St. Augustine, 65.9' x 18.2' x 8.3', stranded in St. Joseph Bay, Lat. 29°45.3' N, Long. 85°24.4' W, October 22, 1976. *Source:* 10. (1)

2) **MISS BESSIE M**—O/F (wood), 60 tons, built 1954, 61.6' x 18.4' x 8.5', foundered at Lat. 30°08' N, Long. 87°46' W, 12/9/1976. *Source:* 10. (1)

1977

1) **MISS IRMA**—O/F (wood), 99 tons, built 1968, 67' x 20.5' x 9.5', stranded with a submerged jetty near Key West, January 3, 1977. *Source:* 10. (3)

2) **MISS EILEEN**—O/F (wood), 64 tons, built 1958 at St. Augustine, 61.6' x 18.4' x 8.5', foundered off Cape Canaveral, February 10, 1977. *Source:* 10. (6)

3) **MISS ANN II**—O/F (wood), 46 tons, built 1950, 58.3' x 13.9' x 5.9', stranded at Lat. 24°20' N, Long. 82°24'30" W, May 1, 1977. *Source:* 10. (3)

4) **THE BACHELORS II**—O/V, 40 tons, built 1943, foundered 50 miles, 219 degrees from Destin, May 7, 1977. *Source:* 10. (1)

5) **GEMINI II**—O/F, 97 tons, built 1965, 67' x 20.3' x 9.6', burned at Lat. 24°43' N, Long. 82°12' W, May 16, 1977. *Source:* 10. (3)

6) **BELIEVER**—O/F (wood), 83 tons, built 1965 at St. Augustine, 66' x 19.1' x 9', collided with the Sunshine Skyway Bridge, May 19, 1977. *Source:* 10. (2)

7) **ERMA J II**—O/Y (fiberglass), 40 tons, built 1971, 53.5' x 16' x 7', collided with the wreck of the *USS Massachusetts*, at Pensacola, July 18, 1977. *Source:* 10. (1)

8) **BETSY**—O/F (wood), 63 tons, built 1953 at St. Augustine, 58.7' x 18.5' x 8.2', stranded about 50 yards west of Indian Rocks Beach, October 13, 1977. *Source:* 10. (2)

9) **DEMERARA**—O/F (wood), 74 tons, built 1962, 65.9' x 18.2' x 8.3', foundered off the Florida Coast, October 17, 1977. *Source:* 10. (8)

10) **GAIL EMMA**—O/F (wood), 64 tons, built 1958, 61.6' x 18.4' x 8.5', burned between Pulaski Light and East Key, Dry Tortugas, October 30, 1977. *Source:* 10. (3)

11) *PIRATE'S LADY*—A 75-foot Burger luxury yacht. See chapter 6. *Source:* Lavin, Andy. "The Yacht That Vanished." Power and Motoryacht Magazine, November 2008; The Panama City News Herald, 8/6 and 12/18/1983. (1)

1) Page 64. *Gunsmoke*—See chapter 6. *Source:* Ibid; 29.

1978

1) *SUSAN H*—O/F (wood), 99 tons, built 1966 at St. Augustine, 67' x 20.5' x 9.5', foundered off the jetties near Key West, January 4, 1978. *Source:* 10. (3)

2) *LITTLE ERNIE*—O/F (wood), 83 tons, built 1966, 66' x 19.1' x 9', foundered 1-1/4 mile, NNW from San Carlos Bay, Light No. 1, March 3, 1978. *Source:* 10. (2)

3) *CHARLES II*—O/T (steel), 47 tons, built 1960 in Wisconsin, 54.5' x 14' x 7', foundered at Lat. 28°56'12"N, Long. 83°02'12"W, March 17, 1978. *Source:* 10. (2)

4) *TOMADOR*—O/Y (wood), 78 tons, built 1969 at Annapolis, 71.3' x 17.2' x 7.9', burned off Ft. Lauderdale, May 1978. *Source:* 10. (5)

5) *GALE WINDS*—O/F (wood), 46 tons, built 1967, 51' x 17.3' x 6.9', foundered at Cape Canaveral, May 1978. *Source:* 10. (5)

6) *JODI ANN*—O/V, 48 tons, built 1945, burned off St. Joseph Pt, August 3, 1978. *Source:* 10. (1)

1979

1) *REX*—O/F (wood), 65 tons, built 1953 at St. Augustine, 61.6' x 18.4' x 8.4', foundered in a heavy sea about five miles from Tampa, January 21, 1979. *Source:* 10. (2)

2) *LARRY & MABEL II*—O/F (wood), 99 tons, built 1972 at St. Augustine, 67' x 20.5' x 9.5', collided with the *Cove Ranger*, March 16, 1979, at Lat. 24°32' N, Long. 83°29' W. *Source:* 10. (3)

3) *CAPTAIN H*—O/F (wood), 67 tons, built 1966, 62.2' x 18.3' x 8.4', foundered WNW of Key West, March 24, 1979. *Source:* 10. (3)

4) *LITTLE ALLEN*—O/F (wood), 44 tons, built 1958 in North Carolina, 54.7' x 17.8' x 6.9', foundered at Rebecca Shoals, April 1979. *Source:* 10. (3)

5) *GASPARILLA IV*—O/F (wood), 45 tons, built 1958, 50.5' x 18' x 7.8', burned about seven miles SE of Boca Grande Pass, June 5, 1979. *Source:* 10. (2)

6) *SEA ANGEL*—O/Y (wood), 14 tons, built 1953 at Tarpon Springs, 59.2' x 19.5' x 1.6', foundered about 30 miles off Palm Beach, June 9, 1979. *Source:* 10. (5)

7) *TOOTS*—O/F (fiberglass), 57 tons, built 1978 at Titusville, 64.1' x 18.5' x 7.5', burned at Lat. 25°33' N, Long. 83°45' W, June 24, 1979. *Source:* 10. (2)

8) *JESSIE A*—O/V, 52 tons, built 1957, foundered off Cortez, Florida, June 20, 1979. *Source:* 10. (2)

9) *THE SEA WITCH*—O/V, 46 tons, built 1959, foundered at approximate Lat. 25°N, Long. 81°55' W, September 2, 1979. *Source:* 10. (3)

10) *ALMA DEAN*—A 50' F/V, burned and sank in 1979 off Grassy Key. *Source:* 4. (4)

11) *ELMAR*—O/Y (wood), 99 tons, built 1943 in Massachusetts, 107.3' x 18' x 9.4', foundered 12.3 miles off the St. Johns River. No date, but reported in the 1980 *Annual List of Merchant Vessels*, and was in service in 1978 list, so likely lost in 1979. *Source:* 10. (6)

1980

1) *FLINTSTONE*—Shrimp boat, 76 tons, 57', sunk near the Dry Tortugas, February 8, 1980. See GPS coordinates at end of chapter. *Source:* 4; 10. (3)

1) Page 165. **North Easter**—Built at St. Augustine (wood), 61.6' x 18.4' x 8.5'. *Source:* 10.

1981–1982

1) *La NATIVITE* and the *ESPERANCIA*—These were two Haitian immigrant vessels that had a tragic ending and also hit close to home. It was late October and I had just arrived at daybreak for work at a construction site for some new townhomes on A1A in Hillsboro Beach. I soon saw police and ambulance vehicles everywhere. The 30 or so foot-long jerry-rigged Haitian boat *La Nativite* had capsized about a hundred yards off the beach and broke in two right in front of the multimillion-dollar homes along that stretch of coastline. Thirty-three Haitians drowned (19 men and 14 women). I could see people carrying bodies on stretchers and placing them in white vans. I tried to get to the beach to see what had happened, but the

police kept everyone off. That evening the news had the full story. It was reported later on that Captain Charles Joseph and his three mates made shore safely and escaped. One survivor, a Mr. Pierre, who was 23 years old and stayed to help pull survivors and bodies out of the water, was sent to a detention camp and was to be deported, along with most of the other survivors. His case went before a magistrate, but I don't know his final fate. What I saw that day has made me very grateful for having been born in this country.

Only five months later, in March 1982, another Haitian boat, the *Esperancia*, broke apart in the surf off Highland Beach, another town where homes of millionaires and now billionaires look over the Atlantic, and is only a few miles north of Hillsboro Beach. Twenty-one Haitians drowned there and nine survived.

1984

1) *PANKY*—Panamanian registered 285-feet freighter. She had sprung a leak which continued to get worse and which the pumps were no longer able to handle. On March 21, 1984, the 15 crewmembers took to the two lifeboats in 6 to 10-foot seas and 20 mph winds, and were spotted by a jet about 1/2 hour after she sank, about 100 miles west of Ft. Meyers. She was from Mobile for the Dominican Republic with 2,600 tons of lumber for the railroad. Two Coast Guard helicopters rescued all 15. *Source:* 4; Panama City News Herald, 3/22/1984.

1985

1) *ARBUTUS*—Ex-Coast Guard Tender, 997 tons, 174'7" x 33' x 12.3'. Was bought by Mel Fisher's salvage company and the engineless ship ended up anchored in the Quicksands, on the north end of the *Atocha* wreck site, where the hulk was used as a sentry vessel. Her hull eventually gave out, and her remains are still visible in 25 feet of water (some still protruding above the water). Previously, a Navy jet mistakenly strafed it when one person was aboard, thinking the rusty hulk was another vessel that the Navy used for target practice. Luckily it missed its target that day. (Don't know exact year it sank, but believe between around 1985.) Nice snorkeling site. *Source:* 10.

2) *CAP'N CRUNCH*—Was a 60-foot dive charter boat, had around 50 people on board when it sank and all were rescued. I remember hearing about it, as we were in the Keys at the time taking out a dive class off Islamorada. When we got back to the dock it was big news. I know everyone was rescued, but was told that some people were still underwater diving when it sank, and when they got back to where it was anchored, they saw her sitting

on the bottom. Never verified the story, but that would be a little discon-
certing if you were a diver, got back to where you hoped the anchor line
would be, only to find your charter boat sunk! Was a wood hulled vessel,
and the Coast Guard was soon was inspecting all the dive charter vessels in
the area after that debacle. Now a local dive site.

3) *TONGA*—Sailboat, supposedly owned by Hollywood actor Errol Flynn
at one time. Burned and sank off Snell Island in Tampa Bay in September
1985. *Source:* 4. (2)

1986

1) *JACQUELINE A*—Ex-minesweeper, built in 1927. From Port Canaveral
for Miami to convert for fishing. Wrecked on a reef north of Vero Beach,
August 10, 1986, and soon went to pieces. Her remains can still be seen at
low tide. *Source:* 23.

4) *CAPT. J*—Burned and sank in Tampa Bay in 1986. See GPS coordinates
at end of chapter. *Source:* 4.

1992

1) *ELIZABETH*—Tug, of Miami. Mysteriously sunk off Highland Beach in
August 1992. It was soon stripped of all materials. It made for a nice dive
in 35 feet of water. Haven't been there for a few years, but lies off the water
tower, and could be seen on a clear day as there's only sand around her. Last
time I was there, she had sunk fairly deep into the sand. May be covered
now.

1) Page 365. **Roatan Express**—Sank during a storm, October 1, 1992, and
had a cargo of containers, trucks, and cars—"has been listing heavily to
port, possibly because of a ruptured ballast tank, said one of the crew
members, Olden Ebanks." Captain Landon Gough had given his life jacket
to a passenger just before she sank. The captain went back to his cabin to
find another life jacket and a lady went back to get her purse and both
were presumed to have gone down with the ship. The 12 others on board
were rescued by the Coast Guard. *Source:* Northwest Florida Daily News,
10/2/1992. Now a popular tech dive and fishing location 84 miles off Ft.
Meyers in 187 feet of water.

The sunken tug *Elizabeth* off Highland Beach.

1993

1) *FANTASTICO*—Honduran freighter, 200-feet long, from Miami for Tampa, with phosphates (fertilizer), capsized in a severe storm about 70 miles SW of Ft. Myers, March 13 or 14, 1993. The Coast Guard heard her distress calls the night of the 13th during an extremely violent storm. They rescued three of the 10 on board, the other seven were lost. Lies on her side in 115 feet of water and a popular dive site now. See GPS Coord. *Source:* 29; Kingston Gleaner, 3/16/1993. (2)

1995

1) *CLUB ROYALE*—Casino ship, 234 feet long. I looked at her when she was docked at Port Everglades when I believe she was for sale. A captain friend asked me to check it out, and she looked like she definitely needed some work. She became a gambling ship after that. A bad decision to ride out Hurricane Erin and head out to sea from the Port of Palm Beach, ended in her sinking about 90 miles off Port Canaveral, August 2, 1995, and I remember hearing about her loss on the local news. A Coast Guard helicopter saved seven of the 10 on board despite strong winds and heavy seas,

though the captain, cook, and another went down with the ship. *Source:* Associated Press. (5)

1996

1) Page 372. **Mariner.** See photo.

The sailboat *Mariner* up against the rocks off Palm Beach.

1998

1) *JEAN CABOT*—The 80-foot vessel went ashore at Boca Raton, near the Deerfield Beach border, October 26, 1998. She had left Miami during a small craft advisory and was soon was taking on water. She drifted until coming ashore at Boca. The crew of three were found safe. Could not be salvaged and the wooden vessel was later broken up where she lay and scrapped. *Source:* Sun Sentinel, 10/28/1998. (5)

The *Jean Cabo*t on the beach at Boca Raton in 1998.

2000

1) *ANITA*—Freighter, of Port-au-Prince, 163-foot long, left Miami River docks, December 23, 2000, bound for Haiti. Some of the cargo consisted of 2,100 cases of plastic bags, and thousands of jugs and 150 drums of cooking oil, 13 cars, 700 tires, hundreds of cases of champagne and liquor, and other items. The brother of the chief mate of the ill-fated vessel thought it was overloaded and the cargo piled too high. This along with leaving Miami in 13 knot winds and 12-foot seas couldn't have helped, and he believed it capsized. Over the holiday weekend, the cargo from the vessel started to appear on beaches from Pompano Beach to Jupiter and even on Bonita Beach on the Gulf coast. Thousands of one-gallon jugs of Alberto cooking oil were washed up along Delray Beach, and thousands of plastic bags washed into Boynton Inlet and were caught in the mangroves. All 10 on board were feared lost, and a body discovered in the ocean about seven miles northeast of Ft. Pierce was believe to be one of the crew. *Source:* Sun-Sentinel, 12/28–29/2000. (8)

2002

1) *ROBERT JOYCE*—Schooner, 87 feet, sank in St. Andrew Bay, July 4, 2002, in 25 feet of water off Courtney Point. Been anchored there for about two years. Coast Guard managed to pump out around 3,000 gallons of diesel. Wreck is still reported there (see GPS coordinates at end of chapter). *Source:* 4; Panama City News Herald, 7/20/2002. (1)

2007

1) *CHRISTIE NICOLE*—Shrimper, 36 years old, had been followed by sharks which was nothing unusual for a fishing boat, but on January 29, 2007, the crew suddenly felt a big thud and thought they had hit something. Captain Roger Schmall said: "It bogged the engine down, and snapped the tail, and that's actually where we started with our problem." Turns out, a very large bull shark had rammed the vessel causing her to leak so badly, the pumps couldn't keep up with the incoming water. Being 100 miles off Ft. Meyers Beach didn't help any and I'm sure the crew was replaying scenes from the movie *Jaws* in their mind. They radioed a fellow shrimper, Henry Gore, who was fairly close by and who came to their rescue. The *Nicole* later sank after they were rescued. The story of "shark sinks boat" soon made the local news. *Source:* www.UnderwaterTimes.com, 2/5/2007. (2)

2008

1) *Freighter*—Name unknown, about 40–45 feet, was smuggling illegal immigrants into the country when it ran aground a few hundred yards offshore near Fisher Island (near Miami), October 31, 2008. At least five drowned. She had around 40 people on board, though a number jumped off the vessel when they saw the authorities approaching. She was of Dominican registry and most of the migrants were from there along with a few Brazilians. *Source:* Cedar Rapids Gazette, 11/1/2008. (5)

2015

1) *SERENA III*—The 106-foot mega-yacht, sank about 13 miles (either off Lauderdale-by-the-Sea, or Hillsboro Inlet) January 25, 2015. All 13 on board were rescued by the Coast Guard. She was from Brazil and just left Port Everglades bound for the Bahamas. She sank in less than two hours after the initial mayday call. Estimated to be worth around $13 million, and was only four years old. Why she sank remains a mystery. Crew said they thought they struck something coming out the Port, but there's a

well-marked channel out the inlet that hundreds of cruise and other ships use all the time. As she lies in about 1,200 feet of water, what happened may never be known. Video of her sinking can be seen on the internet. *Source:* Local News Channels. (5)

2016

1) *STEEL KELLY*—A 75-foot yacht, had tried to tow the 32-foot boat *John Deere Green*, which was in distress and taking on water, April 8, 2016. The *Green* had sent a mayday, and the Coast Guard went to the scene. Trying to help only ended up in disaster for the *Kelly*, as she sunk about 19 miles off Egmont Key. The two on board got on to the *Green* safely, and the Coast Guard was able to tow the *Green* into Bradenton. *Source:* News Channel 8. (2)

GPS COORDINATES

First listed are the 12 Florida State Preserve wreck sites. Then I list wrecks (both in this new book and in *Shipwrecks of Florida*) from Pensacola going east and down the western Florida coast to the Tortugas and around the Keys and up Florida's east coast to the Florida/Georgia border. I tried to list only wrecks with verified coordinates from largely government sources, but make no guarantees. Coordinates also vary from source to source. Storms also move wrecks, and bury wrecks under sand. Any dates listed after any shipwreck is the year it was lost. For anyone wanting to look on a map to see where a wreck lies using GPS coordinates or to convert coordinates to decimal/degrees, degrees/minutes/seconds, etc., I recommend the following website: http://boulter.com/gps/

State of Florida Underwater Preserve Shipwrecks: The state of Florida has 12 wreck sites that are now Underwater Preserves. I submitted the site of the *Lofthus*, which is now one of these preserves. I also positively identified the *SS Copenhagen* wreck when that site was first considered. Except for the *Tarpon*, most all of these are in shallow water and many have mooring buoys. All these sites are protected. For photos and more history on these, you can visit the state's website, www.museumsinthesea.com.

1) *USS Massachusetts* (1921)—N30°17.794', W87°18.727'. Off Pensacola.

2) *Tarpon* (1937)—N30°05.702', W85°56.555'. It's 7.8 miles off shore in 95 feet of water near Panama City.

3) *Vamar* (1942)—N29°53.941', W85°27.806'. Off Mexico Beach.

4) *City of Hawkinsville* (1922)—No GPS, it's in the Suwanee River, location in this edition, and on the state website.

5) *USS Narcissus* (1866)—N27°37.548', W82°47.991'. Off Egmont Key.

6) *Regina* (1940)—N27°28.135', W82°42.129'W. Just off Bradenton Beach.

7) *San Pedro*—See 1733 fleet wrecks.

8) *Half Moon* (1930)—N25°43.654', W80°08.069'. Just outside Bear Cut.

9) *SS Copenhagen* (1900)—N26°12.349', W80°05.108'. Off north end of Lauderdale-by-the-Sea.

The bow of the steamer *Copenhagen*. It lies about one-half mile from the main wreck site that is now a state underwater preserve.

The wreck of the *Copenhagen* looking north soon after she went aground on the reef. Courtesy of the State Archives of Florida.

10) *Lofthus* (1898)—N26°33.776', W80°02.309'. Just north of the Boynton Inlet.

11) *Georges Valentine* (1904)—N27°11.93', W80°09.787'. Lies 100 yards south of the Gilbert's Bar House of Refuge, in 22 feet of water

12) *Urca de Lima*—See 1715 fleet wrecks.

More Florida Shipwreck GPS Coordinates: Many of these GPS coordinates are from NOAA's Automated Wreck and Obstruction Information System (AWOIS), and though many more are listed in that system, I only used the ones that the coordinates were verified as good. Many others were only approximate locations, but anyone researching wrecks should check out their database. Here is the link to their chart site: https://wrecks.nautical-charts.noaa.gov/viewer/.

When I wrote the first two editions of *Shipwrecks of Florida*, I had to order the telephone book thick computer printout. It's also been updated since then. Many counties or municipalities also list the coordinates for wrecks, though most are of all the "artificial reefs" that have been sunk all along the Florida coasts over the years. I do not list these artificial reefs here. Only actual shipwrecks. I list unidentified wreck sites and a couple named wrecks that I could find no information on from NOAA's database that hopefully may be identified from information in this and my past books.

Another great source for the Florida Keys wrecks and reefs and which some of the coordinates were taken, is Cathy Sheehan's fantastic website whose link is: http://www.florida-keys-vacation.com/. It also gives additional history of the many Keys wrecks and includes some very nice photos of the many shipwrecks there.

For Martin and Brevard Counties, I suggest checking out Land and Sea Surveying's website: http://land-and-sea-surveying.com/. They offer two books, both online or hardcopy, listing offshore reefs and wrecks with additional history and photos of a number of World War II wrecks including multibeam sonar images.

There are numerous sources, but here are a few other websites with GPS coordinates for Florida reefs and wrecks:

a) State of Florida GPS coordinates for all artificial reefs and some actual wrecks: http://myfwc.com/media/131585/REEFS.pdf

b) Florida Keys: http://florida-keys-fishing.org/florida-keys-wrecks-gps.htm

c) Florida: https://www.floridagofishing.com/reefs/gps-coordinates-florida-fishing-boating-diving.html

d) (Example of a local county site) Destin area GPS coordinates: www.fishingdestinguide.com

Florida Wreck GPS Coordinates

1) **Unk Tug,** 70' x 25'—Located 1986 in 53 feet of water. N30°06.089', W87°23.503'.

2) **Old Hopper Barge**—120' x 40' x 15', in 51 feet of water. N30°13.133', W87°19.389'.

3) **Wood sailing vessel** aka *Catherine*—In 14 feet of water. N30°12.755', W87°15.993'.

4) *Sport*—Visible steel wreck, 100' long. N30°19.212', W87°14.465'.

5) *Rhoda* (1882)—N30°19.583', W87°14.988', in 21 feet of water.

6) *Cabradroca* (Early 20th century)—N30°21.839', W87°11.542'.

7) **Unk. Wreck**—In Pensacola Harbor. N30°25.770, W87°09.527'.

8) *San Pablo*—World War II freighter, now a popular dive site. N30°11.331', W87°13.041'.

9) **Old Steamer Wreck**—Some 30-gallon drums of rosin have been found on her. N30°26.583', W86°30.975'. In Choctawhatchee Bay.

10) **Wood Barge**—N30°26.504', W86°27.306'. In nine feet of water in Choctawhatchee Bay.

11) **Unk. Barge** (Boiler)—N30°25.407', W86°19.340'. In Choctawhatchee Bay.

12) **Unk. Wreck**—N30°27.605', W86°13.508'. In nine feet of water in Choctawhatchee Bay.

13) **Unk. Barge**—N30°25.427', W86°21.813'. In Choctawhatchee Bay.

14) *Robert L. Bean* (1926)—N30°23.262', W86°46.697' (approximate).

15) *Robert Joyce* (2002)—N30°08.350', W85°42.555'. In St. Andrew Bay.

16) *E.E. Simpson* (1930)—N30°03.215', W85°37.294'.

17) *Capt. J* (1986)—N27°47.008', W82°. In Tampa Bay.

18) *Dania* (Dredge-1958)—N27°45.293', W82°31.098' (in Tampa Bay).

19) **Unk. Barge**—N27°36.129', W82°49.536', in 24 feet of water and other wrecks nearby.

20) *Rhein Hamburg* (1940)—N24°56.116', W83°30.601'.

21) *U-2513* (1951)—N24°52.015, W83°18.594'.

22) *Capt. Craig*—N24°49.993, W82°02.948'.

23) *USS Sturtevant*—World War II wreck. N24°45.503', W82°01.301.

24) *Araby Maid* (1903)—N24°43.831', W83°28.955'.

25) *Bags* (1967)—Trawler—N24°42.225', W82°25.690'.

26) *Avanti*, aka "Windjammer Wreck" (1907)—N24°37.461', W82°56.564'.

27) *USS Amesbury* aka "Alexander's Wreck" (1972)—Bow is at: N24°37.366, W81°58.917.

28) *Flintstone* (1980)—N24°37.626, W80°42.590.

29) *Valbanera* (1919)—N24°33.480', W82°28.414'.

30) *HMS Looe* (1744)—N24°32.7000', W81°24.500'.

31) *USS Wilkes-Barre* (1972)—Bow is at N24°29.094', W81°33.202'.

32) *USS R-12*—World War II wreck. N24°25.210', W82°02.394'.

33) *USS S-16* (1945)—N24°25.207', W80°02.393'.

34) **Unk. Wreck**—Sunk 1985—N24°42.502', W81°57.407', in 11 feet of water.

35) **Unk. Wreck**—N24°41.004', W81°52.733'. In 24 feet of water.

36) **Unk. 60' F/V**—N24°39.400, W81°53.055'. In 24 feet of water.

37) **Unk. Barge**—Wrecked on rocks in 1976—N24°30.826', W81°55.359'.

38) *Marie J. Thompson* (1935)—N24°33.518', W81°48.534'.

39) **Unk. 110' wreck**—N24°27.507', W81°48.301'. Located in 2001.

40) **75' Shrimper**, aka "Joe's Tug"—N24°27.850', W81°44.270'. Popular dive site.

41) **Unk. 245' barge**—In shallow water. N24°32.589', W81°49.552'

42) *Gunvor*—World War II wreck. N24°56.925', W81°46.589'.

43) *Edward S. Luckenbach*—World War II wreck. N24°57.831', W81°53.269'.

44) *Bosiljka*—World War II wreck. N24°58.203', W81°52.804'.

45) **"Delta Shoal Barge"**—N24°37.78', W81°05.49'.

46) **"Ivory Wreck"**—A 17th or 18th century slaver found in the 1950s and many artifacts salvaged.—N24°37.780', W81°05.490'.

47) *North America* (1842)—N24°38.270', W81°05.605'. On Delta Shoal.

48) *Adelaide Baker* (1889)—In two areas, N24°42.14', W80°53.56'; and N24°42.175', W80°53.670'. In 20–25 feet of water.

49) **Unk. steamer wreck** aka "Duck Key Wreck"—N24°42.601', W80°52.659'. In 20–25 feet of water, two boilers and four stacks are still visible.

50) *Trespasser*—A 60-foot vessel. N25°50.7055', W80°25.8942'.

51) **19th century schooner** aka "Brick Wreck"—N24°44.311', W80°57.659'. In 12 feet of water.

52) *Queen of Nassau* (1926)—N24°47.165', W80°39.546'.

53) **75-foot Trawler** aka "Cannabis Cruiser"—Found by divers in 110 feet in the late 1970s full of marijuana. N24°49.584', W80°38.590'.

54) *USS Alligator* (1822)—N24°51.079', W80°37.102'. A recent survey of the wreck has led some to believe this is not the *Alligator*, but an entirely different vessel.

55) *Slabdova* (1887)—N25°01.00', W80°22.53'.

56) *Benwood* (World War II)—N25°03.160', W80°20.020'.

57) *Northern Light* (1930)—N25°05.040', W80°21.643'.

58) *Hannah M Bell* (1911)—N25°08.673', W80°15.393'.

59) *City of Washington* (1917)—N25°08.788', W80°15.355'.

60) *Tonawanda* (1866)—N25°08.850', W80°15.462'.

61) *HMS Winchester* (1695)—N25°12.179', W80°13.517'.

62) *Thiorva* (1894)—N25°16.927', W80°12.425'.

63) **Unk. 35' wreck**—N25°31.123', W80°18.387'.

64) *Alicia* (1905)—Steamer, 1905. N25°24.705', W80°07.660'.

65) *Lugano* (1913)—N25°26.639', W80°07.717'.

66) **Unk. 60' Barge**—N25°31.552', W80°17.950'.

67) **Unk. 40' wood wreck** (believe an old sponge fishing vessel)—N25°31.813', W80°15.588'. In Biscayne Bay.

68) **Unk. Wreck**—N25°34.798', W80°13.755'.

69) **Visible steel hull**—25°35.404', 80°09.733'. In two feet of water.

70) **Barge**—N25°38.841', W80°09.772'.

71) **Two barges**—N25°41.151', W80°10.814'.

72) **Unk 40' wreck**—25°43.060', W80°11.963'. In nine feet of water.

73) *Adamelia*—Sunk in 1960? in 23 feet and demolished. N25°40.523', W80°06.486'.

74) *Half Moon* (1930)—N25°43.627', W80°08.071'. In two to three feet of water.

75) **Unk. 61' Wreck**—N26°46.953', W80°00.648'. In 78 feet of water.

76) *Hydro Atlantic* (1987)—N26°19.5000', W80°03.043'. In 184 feet of water.

77) *Inchulva* (1903)—N26°27.267', W80°03.549'.

78) **Unk. Wreck**—N28°18.482', W80°27.420'. In 52 feet of water.

79) **Unk. Wreck**—N28°03.944', W80°52.654'. In 48 feet of water.

80) *Mohican* (1925)—In 32 feet of water. N28°23.837', W80°32.107'.

81) *Laertes*—World War II wreck. N28°28'41.9189", W80°22'00.3703". In 72 feet of water.

82) *Leslie*—World War II wreck. N28°36'13.5463", W80°16'21.4955". In 80 feet of water.

83) *Ocean Venus*—World War II wreck. N28°23'22.5183", W80°17'43.1253". In 80 feet of water.

84) *Cities Service Empire*—World War II wreck. N28°23.785614', W80°02.799442'. In 240 feet of water.

85) *Pan Massachusetts*—World War II wreck. N28°19.965205', W80°00.014154'. In 300 feet of water.

86) **110' Barge**—N30°16.554', W80°19.264'. In 57 feet of water.

87) *Casablanca*—Steel hull 200'+ long, N30°17.522', W80°49.278'. In 83 feet of water.

88) *Barge*—N30°20.828', W81°12.973'. In 59 feet of water.

89) *Roslyn B.* Hudgins—N30°22.361', W80°53.988'.

90) *Unk.* Wreck—N30°22.361', W80°53.988'.

91) *Unk.* Wreck—N30°23.260' , W81°10.513'. In 53 feet of water.

92) *Unk.* Wreck—N30°23.301', W81°10.215'. In 64 feet of water.

93) *Unk.* Wreck—N30°23.335', W81°10.616'. In 61 feet of water.

94) *Unk.* **Wreck**—N30°23.670', W81°10.306'. In 62 feet of water.

95) *Unk.* **Wreck**—N30°23.355', W81°20.838'. In 43 feet of water.

96) *Unk.* **Wreck**—N30°24.779', W81°15.683'. In 46 feet of water.

97) *175' Steel Barge*—N30°25.283', W81°12.453'. In 47 feet of water.

98) *55' Tug*—N30°25.359', W81°13.489'. In 57 feet of water.

99) *Barge*—N30°25.657', W81°14.429'. In 45 feet of water.

100) *110' Barge*—N30°25.812', W81°13.736'. In 63 feet of water.

101) *World War II period wreck*—N30°27.162', W81°19.321'. In 54 feet of water.

102) *Unk.* **Wreck**. Has mast and propeller. N30°30.928', W81°12.498'. In 43 feet of water.

103) *Barge*—N30°32.999', W81°07.382'. In 56 feet of water.

104) *Barge*—N30°38.736', W81°12.870'. In 53 feet of water.

105) *Atlantic Sun*—N30°42.433', W81°24.298'. In 11 feet of water near Jetty.

9

Post-1900 Wrecks under 50 Feet

In the first and second editions, I didn't list many vessels under 50 feet, but have been asked by folks that do ocean surveys, and by divers, snorkelers, and fishermen, if I could include these smaller vessels to help them identify the many targets they've found while conducting magnetometer, side scan, or sub bottom surveys, or just while fishing, diving or snorkeling. A wreck 35 feet long is still substantial, and some of these also have a tale to tell. Unless otherwise noted, all information on these was gathered from the annual *List of Merchant Vessels of the United States*.

Here are the abbreviations for this section: Sch (Schooner); Schy (schooner yacht); Slp (sloop); Brg (barge); G/V (gas vessel); G/P (gas passenger vessel); G/C (gas cargo vessel); G/F (gas fishing vessel); G/T (gas tow vessel); G/Y (gas yacht); P/G (pilot boat gas); P/O (pilot boat oil); O/V (oil vessel); O/P (oil passenger vessel); O/T (oil tow vessel); O/C (oil cargo vessel); O/F (oil fishing vessel); O/Y (oil yacht); Cat (catboat).

A vessel's tons listed are gross tons, unless otherwise noted. All vessels listed are commercial vessels, unless listed as a yacht or otherwise. Latitudes are all north, and longitudes are all west.

1902

1) *J.N. Coombs*—Sch, 17 tons, built 1897 at Carrabelle, of Cedar Keys, 38.3 x 14 x 4.5, foundered at Big Pass, Florida, 7/8/1902, crew saved.

1904

1) *Kitty Hor*—Cat, 17 tons, 41.5 x 13.7 x 4.8, of Key West, stranded near Marco, Florida, 11/15/1904.

1905

1) *Annie*—Sch, 5 tons, built 1871 at Cedar Keys, of Tampa, 27.6' x 10' x 3', stranded in Coots River, 1/5/1905.

2) *Engle*—Slp, 6 tons, built 1900, foundered near Sarasota, 3/29/1905.

3) *Volunteer*—Sch, 26 tons, built 1888 at Key West and from there, 49.2 x 17.4 x 5.5, foundered at Sand Key, 1/16/1905.

1906

1) *D.W.*—Slp, 5 tons, built 1904, of Pensacola, 29' x 11.7' x 2.5', stranded in Pensacola Bay,

9/27/1906.

2) *Gracie S*—Sch, 9 tons, 36 x 13.1 x 3.9, built 1897, of Pensacola. Stranded in Pensacola Bay, 9/27/1906.

3) *Irma*—Sch, 6 tons, built 1888 in Massachusetts, 39.2 x 12.2 x 3.5, of Pensacola, stranded at Pensacola, 9/27/1906.

4) *Jas. P. Collins*—Sch, 13 tons, built 1895, 38.8 x 14.8 x 4.5, of Pensacola, stranded at Pensacola, 9/27/1906.

5) *Marietta*—G/V, 9 tons, built 1905 at and of Apalachicola, 34.6' x 11.9' x 5.1', foundered at West Pass, Apalachicola Bay, 12/12/1906.

6) *Moccasin*—Sch, 15 tons, built 1888 at Key West and from there, 39 x 17 x 4.4, foundered at Knights Key, Florida, 10/15/1906.

7) *Palm*—G/T, 12 tons, built 1904 at San Mateo, Florida, of St. Augustine, 38.9' x 10.2' x 3.1', stranded at Long Key in the hurricane, 10/18/1906 (see story in main wreck section regarding the hurricane).

8) *Pelican*—Sch, 13 tons, 42 x 13.7 x 3.8, of Tampa, stranded at Pass Grille, Florida, 10/2/1906.

9) *Pinta*—Yawl, 9 tons, built 1896 at Cocoa, of St. Augustine, 35.7 x 12 x 2.6, burned at Cocoa, 5/21/1906.

10) *Sarah*—Slp, 11 tons, built 1877, of Pensacola, 37.7 x 13.5 x 3.6, stranded at Pensacola, 9/27/1906.

11) *Sidney*—Sch, 7 tons, built 1874 in and from Key West, 32.8 x 12.5 x 3.8, foundered off Matecumbe, 10/18/1906.

12) *Silver Heel*—Sch, 10 tons, built 1898 at Bamboo Key, Florida, of Key West, 34 x 1.2 x 4.3, stranded off Miami, 10/18/1906.

13) *Sparta*—Sch, 6 tons, built 1891 in Rhode Island, of St. Augustine, 34.4 x 12.3 x 3.8, foundered by Pappy's Bayou, Florida, 10/10/1906.

14) *Sunbeam*—Sch, 7 tons, built 1885 in New York, of Key West, 37.8 x 10.2 x 3. Foundered off Cutler, Florida, 10/18/1906.

15) *Thistle*—G/V, 10 tons, built 1897 at Ormond, Florida, of Key West, 42.2' x 10.6' x 6.4', stranded at Key Largo, 10/18/1906.

16) *Two Brothers*—Sch, 12 tons, built and from Key West, 36 x 14.8 x 4.1, stranded at Elliot Key, 10/18/1906.

1907

1) *Dash*—Sch, 17 tons, built 1897 at Miami, of Key West, 43.6' x 14.3' x 3.3', stranded off Woman's Key, 1/11/1907.

2) *Elsia Marie*—Slp, 16 tons, built 1901, 30' x 14.8' x 4.5', of Cedar Keys, foundered between Anclote and Egmont Keys, 3/22/1907.

3) *Fawn*—Sch, 11 tons, built 1889 in Mississippi, of Mobile, 44' x 14' x 3.8', stranded off Santa Rosa Island, 12/13/1907.

4) *Osinnipiac*—G/T, 14 tons, built 1870 in New Haven, of Key West, 48' x 11.3' x 3.4', foundered between Key West and Miami, June 1907.

1908

1) *Annie C*—G/P, 9 tons, built 1907 in Kissimmee, of Tampa, 30.4' x 8.2' x 3.2', stranded at Kissimmee, 9/15/1908.

2) *Flora*—Sch, 5 tons, built 1882 at Key West and from there, 31.5' x 10.4' x 3.1'. Foundered off Key Largo, 4/27/1908.

3) *Ida*—Sch, 11 tons, built 1886, of Pensacola, 43' x 15.2' x 3.5', burned in Santa Rosa Sound, 10/9/1908.

4) *Helene*—G/Y, 19 tons, built 1907, burned at New Berlin, Florida, 2/15/1908. *Note:* Same source (Merchant Vessels of the U.S.) also says she was lost November 1907.

5) *Noal*—Sch, 14 tons, 43' x 14.3' x 3.5', built 1892 at Brunswick, Georgia, of Key West. The Life Saving Svc. Reports say she sunk in 1908 with the loss of two lives in the Shark River. Still listed in service in 1909 but not after that.

6) *Xibalda*—Sch, 13 tons, built 1892 at Boggy Bayou, of Pensacola, 34.8″ x 13.9' x 3.1', stranded in Choctawhatchee Bay, 4/23/1908.

1909

1) *Cleopatra*—G/V, 13 tons, built 1878 at Freeport, FlrL, of Pensacola, 41.7'x 16.5' x 3.8', stranded at St. George's Island, 3/25/1909.

1910

1) *A.A. Fletcher*—G/Sch, 15 tons, built 1910, foundered at East Pass, Santa Rosa Island, 11/28/1910. Owned by the Bay Fisheries, Co, St. Andrews. Went to the assistance of a man in a small sailboat who capsized and was drifting out to sea. It was caught in the breakers and the men on board narrowly escaped death themselves. The stranger was presumed drowned. *Source:* The Pensacola Journal, 12/1/1910.

2) *Ada B*—Sch, 9 tons, built 1887 at Apalachicola, of Key West, 36.5' x 11.4' x 3.9', stranded at North Cape, Florida, 10/17/1910.

3) *E.W. Smith*—Sch, 9 tons, built 1901 at Punta Gorda, of Key West, 46' x 12.6' x 3', foundered at San Carlos Pass, Florida, 10/17/1910.

4) *Florida*—Sch, 8 tons, built 1881 at Key Largo, of Key West, 34.2' x 11.4' x 2.9', foundered at the Tortugas, 11/29/1910.

5) *Gracie J*—G/P, 12 tons, built 1908, of Jacksonville, 45.6' x 9.7' x 3.8', burned on the St. John's River, 12/28/1910.

6) *May Flower*—Sch, 12 tons, built 1886 at Biloxi, of Key West, 38.2' x 15.2' x 3.4', stranded at Plover Key, Florida, 10/17/1910.

7) *Rosa Albury*—Sch, 16 tons, built 1878 at Biloxi, of Key West, 37.5' x 14.6' x 4.6', foundered off Bay Keys, Florida, 10/17/1910.

8) *Saturn*—G/V, 14 tons, built 1891 at Marco, FL, of Key West, 32.5' x 12' x 3.4', stranded on Marco Bar, 10/17/1910.

1911

1) *E. Hempstead*—Sch, 19 tons, built 1886 at East Pass, of Pensacola, 46' x 16.2' x 4.7', foundered off East Pass, 10/13/1911.

2) *Lady Clara*—G/P, 13 tons, built 1907 at and from Jacksonville, 44.5' x 9.7' x 3.8', burned at Grassy Point, Florida, 6/24/1911.

3) *Marie*—G/C, 13 tons, built 1899 at Indianola, Florida, of St. Augustine, 49.8' x 15' x 2.6', burned in Indian River, 4/27/1911.

4) *Mary Eliza*—Sch, 13 tons, of Key West, 42.5' x 13.2' x 4.8', stranded off Garden Key, Tortugas, 12/5/1911.

5) *Seminole*—G/V, 6 tons, built 1908 at Apalachicola and from there, 35.7' x 8.9' x 4.2', burned at Franklin, Florida, 3/4/1911.

6) *Tyre*—G/V, 13 tons, built 1901, burned at Jacksonville, 7/28/1911.

7) *Vixen*—G/V, 14 tons, built 1888 at and from Jacksonville, burned at Silver Springs, 8/26/1911.

1912

1) *C.A. Pierce*—G/P, 13 tons, built 1885 at and from Key West, 36' x 12" x 3.6', stranded 1912, at Marco, Florida.

2) *Emerald*—Sch, 17 tons, built 1878 at and from Key West, 42' x 15.5' x 5', foundered off Bay Keys, 2/15/1912.

3) *Jolly Tramp*—Slp, 7 tons, built 1892 in Tampa, of Pensacola, 25.4' x 11.5' x 1.8', stranded at Cape Sable, Florida, 9/6/1912.

4) *Lottie*—Sch, 19 tons, built 1894 at Mary Esther, Florida, of Pensacola, 47' x 20.3' x 4', burned in Choctawhatchee Bay, 5/5/1912.

5) *Ruby W*—G/T, 16 tons, built 1911 at Green Cove Springs, of Jacksonville, 45.2' x 11.6' x 5.6', burned at Orangedale, Florida, 8/4/1912.

6) *Selma S*—G/C, 17 tons, built 1911 at Green Cove Springs, of Jacksonville, 44.4' x 14.3' x 5', burned at Sanford, 11/21/1912.

7) *W.W. Phipps*—G/C, 13 tons, built 1906 at Gulf City, Florida, of Tampa, burned in Tampa Bay, 11/4/1912.

1913

1) *Awixa*—G/T, 11 tons, built 1886 at Islip, New York, of Jacksonville, 30' x 12' x 4', collided with the steamer *Crescent* at Palatka, 11/26/1913.

2) *Hattie Mae*—G/C, 10 tons, built 1906 at and from Tampa, 37' x 10.6' x 3', burned in Tampa Bay, 1/16/1913.

3) *Marie*—G/Y, 11 tons, built 1910 in and from New Jersey, 41.2' x 9.5' x 3.2', burned on Matanzas River, Florida, 4/22/1913.

4) *Mary C*—G/P, 14 tons, built 1910 at and from Jacksonville, 35.2' x 11.6' x 4.3' burned at Mayport, 4/11/1913.

1914

1) *Alma S*—G/P, 19 tons, built 1911 at Dames Point, Florida, of Jacksonville, 47.2' x 12.3' x 3.5', burned at Jacksonville, 12/14/1914.

2) *Annie B*—G/C, 12 tons, built 1900 at and from Jacksonville, 41.1' x 9.7' x 3.8', burned at the mouth of Thomas Creek, Florida, 11/28/1914.

3) *Callie B*—G/P, 14 tons, built 1909 at Middleburg, Florida, of Jacksonville, 49.3' x 14.2' x 4.5', burned on the St. John's River, 4/14/1914.

4) *Fannie S*—G/P, 7 tons, built 1908 at and from St. Augustine, 27' x 9.8' x 2.6', burned on the St. Sebastian River, 10/30/1914.

5) *Irene Albury*—G/C, 14 tons, built 1888 at Scranton, MS, of Key West, 48.4' x 17.6' x 3.1', foundered off Long Key, 1/22/1914.

6) *Markab*—Sch, 16 tons, built 1888 at New York, of Key West, 44.4' x 12.2' x 4.2', struck the pier at Pigeon Key and sunk, 8/14/1914.

7) *Mary Celina*—G/C, 14 tons, built 1902 in Biloxi, of Mobile, 49' x 16.9' x 2.4', stranded at Cape Canaveral, 5/18/1914.

8) *Mizpah*—G/P, 14 tons, built 1914 at Riverview, Florida, of Jacksonville, 41.7 x 11.8 x 4.4, burned at Black Creek, Florida, 4/14/1914, and all 30 on board saved.

1915

1) *Curlew*—G/V, 11 tons, built 1909, burned at Donaldson's Landing, Florida, 11/15/1915.

2) *Gertrude*—G/P, 12 tons, built 1905 at New York, of Jacksonville, 43' x 11' x 3.1', burned on Nassau River, 2/11/1914.

3) *Gretchen*—G/T, 17 tons, built 1911 in Florida, of Jacksonville, 39.7' x 11.9' x 3.9', burned at Pablo Creek, Florida, 8/25/1915.

4) *Onawanda*—G/P, 11 tons, built 1906 at St. Andrew, Florida, of Tampa, 46.5' x 11.4' x 5.3', burned on Manatee River, 4/9/1915, all 19 on board saved.

1916

1) *Foam of the Sea*—G/V, 18 tons, built 1866, foundered at New River Inlet, 2/22/1916.

2) *Water Gypsy*—G/V, 14 tons, built 1890, of Chicago, 46.5' x 11.4' x 5.3', burned at Gulf City, Florida, 5/19/1916.

1917

1) *Pilgrim*—G/C, 18 tons, built 1904 at West Palm Beach, of Jacksonville, 48.5' x 12.4' x 3.9', burned at Miami in 1917.

2) *Virginia*—Slp, 8 tons, built 1909 in and from Georgia, 33.8' x 13' x 3', stranded at Lake George, Florida, 8/16/1917.

1918

1) *Alert*—G/P, 13 tons, built 1910, of Jacksonville, 45' x 10.2' x 3.5', foundered at Black Creek, Florida, 2/22/1918.

2) *Brilliant*—G/F, 12 tons, built 1900 in Florida, of Pensacola, 37.7' x 14' x 4.1', stranded at Santa Rosa Island, 1/3/1918.

3) *Olympia*—G/Y, 8 tons, built 1899, burned on St. Lucie River, 3/24/1918.

4) *Ruth*—G/C, 13 tons, built 1901 at Punta Gorda, of Miami, 40' x 12.4' x 2.9', burned in 1918 in Lake Okeechobee.

5) *Unk. 40' bootlegger*—This 40-foot boat foundered just off the beach at St Augustine, October 1918, while smuggling liquor. The two on board swam to shore and escaped. *Source:* Palatka Daily News, 10/31/1918.

6) *Willie*—G/V, 11 tons, built 1908, 40.2' x 10.1' x 2.9', burned at Six Mile Creek, Florida, 8/8/1918.

1919

1) *Cleo*—Slp (freight), 6 tons, built 1894, of Key West, 32.4' x 12.2' x 3.2', foundered at Key West in 1919.

2) *Hiawatha*—G/P, 13 tons, built 1903 at Courtney, Florida, of St. Augustine, 41.6' x 13.2' x 2', burned at Courtney, Florida, 7/13/1919.

3) *Trojan*—G/T, 17 tons, built 1902, 41' x 13.5' x 3.6', foundered at Key West, 9/17/1921.

4) *White Squadron*—Sch Barge, 10 tons, built 1897 at Key Largo, of Key West, 41.2' x 8.6' x 3', foundered in Key West Harbor in 1919.

1920

1) *Saverio Marca Stella*—Sch, 9 tons, built 1910, stranded at Anna Maria Key, 12/8/1920.

1921

1) *Aegina*—Fishing schooner, 18 tons, built 1909 at Tarpon Springs, 47' x 15.9' x 5.9', of Tampa, lost during the October hurricane. *Source:* St. Petersburg Times, 11/8/1921.

2) *Big Bazoo*—G/C, 12 tons, built 1881 at Pensacola, of Apalachicola, 40.7' x 14.6' x 3.9', foundered NW of Egmont Lighthouse, 10/25/1921.

3) *Bobble*—G/V, 10 tons, built 1920, burned at Key West, 1/4/1921.

4) *E.C. Knight*—G/F, 13 tons, built 1902 at Punta Gorda, of Key West, 44.2' x 13' x 3', burned near Punta Gorda, 2/28/1921.

5) *Francis*—Sch, 14 tons, built 1910 at Tarpon Springs, of Tampa, 43' x 13.7' x 4.4', foundered SW of Egmont Key, 10/25/1921, during the hurricane. Six crew saved by another schooner.

6) *Osceola*—G/V, 9 tons, built 1911, burned at Miami, 3/17/1921.

7) *Pilot*—P/G, 11 tons, built 1916 in Massachusetts, of Key West, 38.5' x 8.6' x 4', burned at Sand Key, 12/21/1921.

1922

1) *Dohema*—G/V, 16 tons, built 1911 of Morehead City, 39.9' x 10.8' x 3.9', foundered south of the St. Augustine Light, 10/15/1922.

2) *White Seal*—G/P, 14 tons, built 1905, 44' x 9.3' x 3', stranded at Lake Worth Inlet, 12/24/1922.

1923

1) *Emwal*—G/V, 26 tons, built 1913, burned at Dearing Channel, Florida, 2/11/1923.

2) *Hyrandale*—G/V, 15 tons, built 1913, stranded at Mosquito Inlet, 5/11/1923.

3) *Lady Bird*—G/T, 12 tons, built 1907 at Key West, 33.8' x 12' x 2.4', of Tampa, burned at Steinhatchee, 9/7/1923.

4) *Margaret*—G/V, 16 tons, built 1902, burned at Palatka, 3/29/23.

5) *Nerald*—G/V, 17 tons, built 1922, abandoned off Palm Beach, 4/1/1923.

6) *Orion*—G/P, 13 tons, built 1910 at Chicago, of St. Augustine, 36.8' x 10.4' x 3.2', burned in St. Andrews Bay, 6/1923.

1924

1) *Lilla*—G/Y, 8 tons, built 1916, foundered at Key West, 10/20/1924.

2) *Nereides*—G/Y, 16 tons, built 1916 on Long Island, New York, of Tampa, 43.2' x 11.2' x 5.1', burned 6/20/1924 at Palma Sola, Florida, 6/20/1924.

3) *Ripple*—G/P, 15 tons, built 1920 at New Smyrna, of St. Augustine 38' x 14' x 7.6', burned in Halifax River, Florida, 8/7/1924.

4) *Russ*—G/V, 18 tons, built 1916, burned on the St. John's Bar, 3/27/1924.

5) *Shadow II*—G/P, 14 tons, built 1916 at Miami, of Charleston, 49.2' x 9' x 4.6', exploded at Fernandina, 11/17/1924.

6) *Willy Jane*—G/P, 7 tons, built 1920 at New Smyrna, of St. Augustine, 30' x 11.5' x 3.5', stranded at Mosquito Inlet, 10/29/1924.

1925

1) *Clara A*—A 40-foot charter pleasure craft, had a large party of people from Kansas on board. Captain Arnold attempted to go out Sebastian Inlet 10/11/1925, but decided it was too rough and turned around capsizing while doing so, drowning 14 on board including two children. Some of the party did survive. *Source:* Gastonia Daily Gazette, 10/12/1925.

2) *Eola*—P/G, 10 tons, built 1921 at Salem, OR, of Key West, 40.9' x 9.1' x 4.6', stranded at Key West, 5/9/1925.

3) *William Curry*—G/P, 17 tons, built 1881 at Key West, of Miami, 42.1' x 14.5' x 4.2', burned at Black Water Bay, 4/29/1925.

1926

1) *Annie J*—G/Y, 9 tons, built 1915, foundered at Cape Canaveral, 5/18/1926.

2) *Eola*—G/C, 9 tons, built 1910 at Key West, of Miami, 34.5' x 10' x 2.6', foundered off the Florida coast, September 1926.

3) *Hawaiian*—O/V, 6 tons, built 1917 in New Jersey, of Miami, 33.8' x 9.8' x 3.7', stranded at Miami, 9/18/1926.

4) *Hypnotist*—G/C, 19 tons, built 1903 in Mississippi, of Tampa, 43.2' x 16.7' x 5.7', stranded at Mullet Key, 9/16/1926.

5) *Ida*—Sch, 10 tons, built 1914 at tarpon Springs, of Tampa, 36.5' x 13' x 4.1', stranded at Boca Grande, 2/18/1926.

6) *Liberty*—G/C, 20 tons, built 1870 at and from Key West, 42.5' x 17.3' x 4', stranded at Key West, 10/20/1926.

7) *M.B.*—G/T, 15 tons, built 1913 at Jacksonville, of Miami, 37.5' x 9.5' x 4.8', foundered at Miami, 9/18/1926.

8) *Mayflower*—G/P, 15 tons, built 1914 in and from Virginia, 45.3' x 11.6' x 4', stranded at Ojus, Florida, 9/1926.

9) *Queen Henrietta*—G/Y, 23 tons, built 1919, of Clearwater, 47.3' x 11.2' x 5.9', burned at Cowpen Island, Florida, 3/12/1926.

10) *Snug*—G/Y, 27 tons, built 1920 in Maryland, of Miami, 42' x 14.5' x 4.5', burned at Angel Fish Creek, 1/9/1926.

11) *Virginia Lee II*—G/Y, 17 tons, built 1925 in Bremen, Germany, of Cortez, Florida, 47.2' x 9.9' x 5.3', foundered at Miami Beach, 8/18/1926.

12) *W.D. Cash*—Sch (freight), 10 tons, built 1876 at Marco, Florida, of Tampa, stranded at Mullet Key, 8/24/1926.

13) *William G. Vance*—Sch, 17 tons, built 1971 at and from Key West, 38.8' x 15.3' x 4.4', foundered in Key West Harbor, 10/20/1926.

1927

1) *Dorryn*—G/P, 11 tons, built 1901 at New York, of Tampa, 39.4' x 9.5' x 4', burned at Tampa, 7/11/1927.

2) *May E*—G/P, 24 tons, built 1920 at Jacksonville, of Miami, 47' x 16' x 2.8', burned at South Bay, Florida, May 1927.

3) *Nimrod*—G/F, 19 tons, built 1900, of Tampa, 42.4' x 16.2' x 5', stranded at Bradenton, 5/12/1927.

1928

1) *Asa M. Lowe*—G/T, 14 tons, built 1880 at Manatee, Florida, of Tampa, 39.6' x 15' x 4.4', burned at Chattahoochee, Florida, 12/27/1928.

2) *Dorothy L*—G/Y, 18 tons, built 1912 in Mich., of Daytona Beach, 47.2' x 10.4' x 4.9', foundered at Cape Canaveral, 3/28/1928.

3) *Flapper*—O/F, 11 tons, built 1923 in Georgia, of Brunswick, 32.9' x 11.8' x 4.4', foundered at Panama City, 3/23/1928.

4) *Lydia C*—G/Y, 15 tons, built 1908, burned at Lake Worth Harbor, 3/3/1928.

5) *Orca*—G/Y, 15 tons, built 1917, burned at Eau Gallie, 12/6/1928.

6) *Stone II*—G/T, 15 tons, built 1908 at New York, of Tampa, 44.4' x 14' x 5', burned at Gulf City, Florida, 3/22/1928.

7) *Surprise*—G/F, 8 tons, built 1915, of Georgia, 29.4' x 11.3' x 3.6', foundered at Panama City, 12/31/1928.

8) *Three Brothers*—G/F, 15 tons, built 1914 at San Blas, of Tampa, 36.4' x 12.5' x 3.6', burned at Lagrange Bayou, Florida, in 1928.

9) *W.F. Favorite*—G/P, 14 tons, built 1912 at New York, of Atlantic City, foundered off Miami 9/18/1928.

1929

1) *Alma*—G/C, 9 tons, built 1922, of Jacksonville, 34.4' x 11.1' x 3', burned at Georgetown, Florida, 1/29/1929.

2) *Petrel*—G/C, 14 tons, built 1901 in New Jersey, of Miami, 39.5' x 14' x 3.5', burned in the Palm Beach Canal, July 1929.

1930

1) *Australia*—O/P, 14 tons, built 1886 at Los Angeles, of Tampa, 43.2' x 12.6' x 3.6', burned in Tampa Bay, 10/4/1930.

2) *Lagoon*—G/P, 8 tons, built 1904 at Titusville, of St. Augustine, 34.5' x 10.9' x 1.8', foundered off Cape Canaveral Light, 4/13/1930.

3) *Juanita*—G/C, 7 tons, built 1907 at and from Apalachicola, 41.5' x 9.6' x 3.9', burned at Chattahoochee River Landing, 10/25/1930.

1931

1) *Eclipse*—G/F, 8 tons, built 1930 at and from Michigan, 30.7' x 9.3' x 4.4', burned at Daytona Beach, 7/5/1931.

2) *Josie B*—G/F, 12 tons, built 1928 at Fernandina, of St. Augustine, 40.2' x 12.2' x 4.3', burned at St. Augustine, 4/13/1931.

3) *Rosa*—G/F, 11 tons, built 1918, of Brunswick, Georgia, 33' x 11/6' x 4', stranded at Cape Canaveral, 2/16/1931.

1932

1) *Chum*—G/Y, 17 tons, built 1925 in New Jersey, of Miami, 42' x 11.5' x 5.1', burned at Key Largo, 10/25/1932.

2) *Edward Westerbeke*—G/F, 10 tons, built 1896 at New York, of St. Augustine, 35.5' x 14.1' x 3.6', stranded at Cape Canaveral, 3/5/1932.

3) *General Hancock*—G/F, 17 tons, built 1880 at Key West, of Tarpon Springs, 44.7' x 15.6' x 5.5', stranded in Tampa Bay, 7/14/1932.

4) *KCAM*—G/T, 12 tons, of Jacksonville, 41.5' x 11' x 4', burned at Sisters Creek, Florida, 9/9/1932.

1933

1) *Imperial*—O/V, 17 tons, built 1926, burned at Mayport, 12/25/1933.

2) *Sunshine*—O/V, 15 tons, built 1929, burned at Fernandina, 11/27/1933.

1934

1) *Gladys*—G/F, 16 tons, built 1932 at and from St. Augustine, 39.8' x 12.4' x 4.6', collided with the Bethel Shoal Buoy, 4/11/1934.

2) *Miss America*—G/F, 17 tons, built 1922 at St. Mary's, Georgia, of St. Augustine, 41' x 11' x 6', stranded at St. Augustine, 2/9/1934.

3) *Pieces of Eight*—G/Y, 18 tons, built 1924 in Nova Scotia, of Philadelphia, 47.7' x 13' x 6.1', stranded at Bahia Honda, 2/11/1934.

4) *Porpoise*—G/P, 14 tons, built 1911 in Michigan, of Tampa, burned in Tampa Bay, 5/13/1934.

5) *President*—O/V, 13 tons, built 1928, burned at Mayport, 1/17/1934.

1935

1) *Agnes A*—O/F, 10 tons, from Fernandina, 35.4' x 10.6' x 4.5', stranded at New Smyrna Inlet, 4/29/1935.

2) *Florence D*—O/Y, 29 tons, built 1931, burned at Miami Beach, 6/8/1935.

3) *Lorraine*—G/V, 8 tons, built 1925, lost off Miami in a hurricane, 11/4/1935.

4) *Mystic*—G/V, 27 tons, built 1928, burned at Ft. Lauderdale, crew saved, 6/24/1935.

5) *Roma*—G/V, 10 tons, burned at mouth of the Weeki Wachee River, 12/12/1935.

6) *Sea Beam*—O/F, 18 tons, built 1929 at and from Fernandina, 39.4' x 13.4' x 4.5', stranded at Matanzas, 4/8/1935.

7) *Trio*—G/P, 16 tons, built 1913 at Oyster Bay, of Miami, 35.7' x 12.6' x 3.8', foundered 10 miles north of Cape Sable, Florida, in a hurricane, 9/3/1935.

1936

1) *Costa Diva*—G/F, 13 tons, built 1860 in New York, of Tampa, 40.9' x 12.7' x 4.6', burned 10 miles north of Ft. Piece on the Indian River, 2/4/1936.

2) *Olga*—O/F, 13 tons, built 1928 at Fernandina, of St. Augustine, 41' x 12.4' x 4', stranded 1.5 miles south of Chester Shoal Coast Guard Station at Cape Canaveral, 1/5/1936.

3) *Wayland Jr.*—O/T, 13 tons, built 1924, of Jacksonville, 42.9' x 12.4' x 3.8', collided and sunk at Mayport, 3/2/1936.

1937

1) *Echo*—O/T, 15 tons, built 1904 at Fogartyville, Florida, of Pensacola, 47.5' x 10.9' x 3.6', burned off Apalachicola, 4/3/1937.

2) *Estrella*—G/P, 9 tons, built 1934 at Bay Harbor, of Pensacola, 31.2' x 9.7' x 5', stranded at Hurricane Island, St. Andrews Bay, 1/5/1937.

3) *Miss St. Augustine*—O/F, 17 tons, built 1928 at St. Augustine, 40' x 13.3' x 6.7', stranded at Ponce de Leon Light, 11/23/1937.

4) *Sadell*—G/V, 10 tons, built 1903 at Key West, 31' x 12.7' x 3.7', foundered between Egmont Key and Tampa Bay, 11/20/1937.

5) *Sea Ranger*—G/F, 15 tons, built 1920 at Fernandina, 39.5' x 12.4' x 4.6', foundered at Fernandina, 9/30/1937.

6) *Sioux*—G/T, 8 tons, built 1913 at Dames Point, Florida, 35' x 10.3' x 3.6', burned at Flagler Beach, 11/20/1937.

7) *Triumphant*—O/F, 13 tons, built 1928 at Fernandina, of St. Augustine, 37.8' x 12.8' x 4.5', stranded two miles south of St. Augustine Inlet, 1/27/1937.

1938

1) *Dione*—G/Y, 18 tons, built 1900 at Baltimore, 42.5' x 14.2' x 5.6', stranded at St. Pete, 9/21/1938.

2) *Mist*—G/V, 19 tons, built 1933, burned 9/15/1938, at mouth of the Chattahoochee River.

3) *Whistler*—G/F, 18 tons, built 1913 at Norwalk, 44.2' x 12.5' x 7', burned two miles NE of Ft. Pierce Light, 12/13/1938.

1939

1) *Atlantic*—G/P, 11 tons, built 1913 at Melbourne, of St. Augustine, 35.3' x 12.6' x 2.9', foundered in Lake Apopka, 3/1/1939.

2) *Providence II*—O/F, 18 tons, built 1926 at Fernandina, 42' x 12.6' x 4.8', stranded three miles south of Mosquito Lagoon, 11/19/1939.

1941

1) *Doris Oliver*—O/F, 13 tons, built 1927 at St. Augustine, of New Orleans, 38' x 12.6' x 4.4', burned at St. Augustine, 11/3/1941.

2) *J.C. Byers*—G/F, 9 tons, built 1911 in Michigan, of St. Augustine, 42.8' x 11.7' x 3.2', foundered 1 1/4 mile south of St. Augustine, 2/27/1941.

3) *James B*—O/P, 10 tons, built in Bayonne, New Jersey, of Miami, 37' x 10.1' x 4.8', burned in Pensacola Bay, 9/4/1941.

4) *Souwester*—O/F, 19 tons, built 1936 at and from Fernandina, 40' x 14' x 4.8', foundered off Cape Canaveral, 10/13/1941.

1942

1) *Margaret A*—G/F, 23 tons, built 1925 in North Carolina, of St. Augustine, 48.4' x 14.8' x 4.5', burned in Sheepshead Cut, New Smyrna, 4/30/1942.

2) *Miss Brunswick*—O/F, 15 tons, built 1927 at Fernandina, of Jacksonville, 39.5' x 12.4' x 4', foundered off New Smyrna, 11/8/1942.

1943

1) *Edalia*—O/F, 15 tons, built 1927 at Fernandina, of St. Augustine, 41.3' x 12.6' x 4', stranded near New Smyrna, 3/25/1943.

2) *Osceola II*—G/P, 19 tons, built 1905 at and from New York, 48.3' x 12.9' x 4.9', stranded at New Smyrna Beach, 10/2/1943.

1944

1) *Kathryn Jean*—O/F, 16 tons, built 1928 at St. Augustine, of Fernandina, 40.9' x 13' x 4.8' foundered by the North Shoal Buoy, Cape Canaveral, February 1944.

2) *Lapwing*—G/F, built 1932 at Fernandina, of St. Augustine, 35' x 10' x 4.4', burned at Ponce de Leon Inlet, 7/7/1944.

1945

1) *Creel Brothers*—G/C, 12 tons, built 1906 at and from Apalachicola, 39.4' x 13' x 3.3', foundered at East Point, Florida (date unknown—reported in Merchant Vessels annual report in 1945).

2) *Egret*—G/P, 9 tons, built 1942 at Merritt Island, of Miami, 29.5' x 12.2' x 4.3', foundered at Canaveral Beach, October 1945.

3) *Hobo*—O/T, 14 tons, built 1919 at St. Andrews, of Tampa, 48.9' x 12.4' x 4', foundered on the Hillsborough River, 7/9/1945.

1946

1) *Adena II*—G/V, 21 tons, built 1930 in New York, of Tampa, 46' x 11.2' x 5.1', burned near Snacks Bayou on the west shore, Old Tampa Bay, 5/30/1946.

2) *Arrow*—G/F, 12 tons, of Miami, 42.8' x 10' x 4.7', burned at Marathon, 3/18/1946.

3) *Mickey & Donna*—O/V, 24 tons, built 1942, foundered at Ponce de Leon Inlet, 12/30/1946.

4) *Piggy*—G/F, 12 tons, built 1925 in North Carolina, of Jacksonville, 41.2' x 10.8' x 3.1', foundered in Sisters Creek, November 1946.

5) *Pinta*—O/F, 23 tons, built 1929 in and from St. Augustine, 42.3' x 14.2' x 5.5', foundered at St. Augustine Inlet, January 1946.

6) *Sunshine*—G/V, 19 tons, built 1899, exploded 40 miles SW of Egmont Key, 9/1/1946.

1947

1) *Alexander C*—G/F, 11 tons, built 1925 at St. Augustine, of Jacksonville, 36.6' x 11.6' x 4.2', foundered at Lat. 30-30; Long. 81-29', July 1947.

2) *Beede*—G/F, 10 tons, built 1900, 39.1' x 13.3' x 4', foundered half mile off U.S. Maritime Station, Tampa Bay, 9/22/1947.

3) *Elsie Lee*—G/F, 11 tons, built 1927, of Tampa, 32.3' x 10.2' x 4.4', foundered in Lake Worth, September 1947.

4) *Gary Owen*—G/F, 13 tons, 39' x 12.9' x 5.7', foundered five miles NE of Fowey Rock Light, 5/15/1947.

5) *Jumbo*—G/V, 14 tons, built 1883 in New York, of Bridgeport, 40.6' x 10.8' x 6.1', burned off Key Largo, 12/16/1947.

6) *Loice L*—O/F, 12 tons, built 1923 in Louisiana., of New Orleans, 35.3' x 10.8' x 4.2' foundered at sea off Key West, February 1947.

7) *Portarista*—O/F, 12 tons, built 1924 at Tarpon Springs, of Tampa, 39' x 13.4' x 4.8', stranded on Pass a Grille Beach, 12/28/1947.

1948

1) *Barbara*—G/F, 13 tons, built 1930 at and from Key West, 42.2' x 14.3' x 3.3', lost at Key West in a hurricane, 9/21/1948.

2) *Boy Mac*—G/P, 10 tons, built 1925 at New York, of Key West, 32.7' x 10.4' x 4.2', foundered at Key West, 9/21/1948.

3) *Evelyn*—G/V, 9 tons, foundered at Key West, 9/21/1948.

4) *Greyhound*—G/P, 13 tons, built 1927 at St. Pete, of Key West, 44.5' x 10.3' x 3.2', foundered at Key West, 9/21/1948.

5) *Helen*—G/P, 15 tons, built 1938 at Miami, of Key West, 39.4' x 11' x 5.1', foundered at Key West, 9/21/1948.

6) *Puerta*—G/F, 9 tons, built 1928 at and from Key West, 30' x 11.2' x 4', foundered at Key West Bight, 9/21/1948.

7) *Rosalie I*—O/F, 23 tons, built 1922 in Virginia, of Savannah, 48' x 13' x 5', burned at Matanzas Inlet, 1/24/1948.

8) *Southern Queen*—O/F, 24 tons, built 1943 at St. Augustine, of Savannah, 42.8' x 10.5' x 5.9', stranded at New Smyrna Beach Inlet, 12/26/1948.

9) *Tartar*—G/Y, 15 tons, built 1927 at Fernandina, of Jacksonville, 41.7 x 12.8' x 4', foundered at Lat. 27°30' N, 80°15' W, 3/6/1948.

10) *W.F. Ferguson*—G/F, 8 tons, built 1922 at Tarpon Springs, of Tampa, 37.5' x 13' x 4.7', burned off Sea Horse Reef (near Cedar Keys), 7/12/1948.

1) Page 188. *Sea Breeze*—O/F, built at and from St. Augustine, 46.7' x 17.1' x 5.6'.

2) Page 188. *Uncle Sam*—O/F, 26 tons, built 1940 at St. Augustine, of Brunswick, GA, 44.8' x 16.3' x 5.8', stranded one mile south of Ponce de Leon Inlet, 2/27/1948.

1949

1) *Avis G. Abel*—G/F, 30 tons, built 1917 at Norfolk, of Key West, 49' x 13' x 5.1', burned at Key West, 1/17/1949.

2) *Carmen Louise*—O/F, 18 tons, built 1939 at Tarpon Springs, of Tampa, 42.2' x 14.5' x 5.7', burned 40 miles west of Anclote Light, 9/23/1949.

3) *J.E. Grady*—Sch (passenger), 12 tons, built 1896 at Apalachicola, of Pensacola, 37.5' x 10.7' x 5.4', foundered on St. Joe Bar, Pensacola, 9/4/1949.

4) *Maria*—O/F, 23 tons, built 1948 at St. Augustine, of Charleston, 41.5' x 15.9' x 6.6', burned at Lat. 30°50' N; 81°15' W, 12/12/1949.

5) *Osprey*—G/F, 14 tons, built 1928 at Osprey, Florida, of Miami, 39.7' x 10.6' x 4', burned at Ft. Myers Beach, 3/5/1949.

6) *Sonny Boy*—O/F, 28 tons, built 1931 at and of St. Augustine, 40.5' x 15.5' x 5.6', foundered forty miles off Cape Canaveral, 11/22/1949.

7) *Spray*—G/P, 12 tons, 33.6' x 10.3' x 5.3', burned about 30 miles east of Miami, 8/5/1949.

1950

1) *Democratia*—O/F, 13 tons, built 1924 at Tarpon Springs, of Tampa, 38.5' x 15.7' x 5.1', foundered at Cedar Keys in a hurricane, 9/5/1950.

2) *Sea Wolf*—G/P, 9 tons, of Jacksonville, 28' x 12.4' x 4.4', burned at Lat. 30°19'40"N; Long. 81°36'40"W, 6/18/1950.

3) *Wild Wind*—G/P, 7 tons, built 1930, of Tampa, 29.1' x 9.1' x 3.8', foundered off Clearwater Beach, 9/6/1950.

4) *Wood Duck II*—G/P, 14 tons, built 1944 at and from Miami, 36.7' x 12.3' x 4.5', burned about one mile off Key Largo, 1/9/1950.

1951

1) *Amelia*—O/C, 27 tons, built 1945 at and from Jacksonville, 42.2' x 12.4' x 6.8', burned at Lat. 30°33'48" N, Long.80°23'17" W, 9/7/1951.

2) *Beatrice*—O/F, 10 tons, built 1932 at St. Augustine, of Charleston, 34' x 12' x 3.9', foundered off Cape Canaveral, 1/16/1951.

3) *Dorsyl*—G/T, 13 tons, built 1932 in Connecticut, of Miami, 35.2' x 10.5' x 3.8', foundered halfway between Tarpon Springs and Cedar Key, 2/5/1951.

4) *Gen. Papagos*—O/F, 15 tons, built 1934 at Tarpon Springs, of Tampa, 38.9' x 14.1' x 4.8', burned 30 miles off Cedar Keys, WNW of Horse Light, 1/6/1951.

5) *Ida III*—G/P, 10 tons, of Miami, 32.4' x 9' x 4.6', burned in the channel between Marco and Naples, 6/15/1951.

6) *Neptune*—G/F, 12 tons, built 1938 at Miami, of Jacksonville, 36.8' x 11' x 4.8', burned at Lat. 29°01' N, Long.80°50' W, 4.15.1951.

1) Page 98. *Joan C*—O/F, built in St. Augustine, of Charleston, 40.5' x 16.2' x 5.2'.

2) Page 188. *Marion*—O/F, built at and from St. Augustine, 46.3' x 16.2' x 6.2'.

1952

1) *Jenkins McCoy*—G/V, 9 tons, built 1947 at and from Miami, 33.2' x 10.5' x 3.1', foundered in Tavernier Creek, 8/15/1952.

1953

1) *Irene II*—G/F, 10 tons, built 1949 in Connecticut, of St. Augustine, 32.8' x 12.4' x 4.6', burned in Gasparilla Sound, north of Boca Grande Island, 8/17/1953.

2) *Mary Jane*—O/F, 11 tons, built 1943 at New Orleans, of St. Augustine, 33.8' x 10.3' x 4.7', foundered one mile off Crescent Beach, 7/31/1953.

3) *Miss Priscilla*—G/F, 10 tons, built 1946 in North Carolina, of Miami, 38.4' x 11.2' x 3.4', Collided with the M/V *Big Lady* off the Dry Tortugas, 5/4/1953.

1954

1) *Alice*—G/F, 13 tons, built 1942 in Miami, of Miami, 49.6' x 12.7' x 4/1', stranded off Vero Beach, 11/6/1954.

2) *C.D. Ergas*—O/F, 10 tons, of Tarpon Springs, 36' x 12.3' x 5.1', burned 40 miles west of Cedar Key, 9/10/1954.

3) *Doc M*—G/V, 10 tons, built 1949, 28.6' x 12.4' x 4.9', foundered about 35 miles off New Smyrna, 11/5/1954.

4) *Penquin*—G/F, 14 tons, built 1936, 34.1' x 10.4' x 3.4', foundered at Baker's Haulover Inlet, Miami, 12/7/1954.

5) *Quo Vodis*—G/P, 8 tons, built 1929, 27.3' x 10.6' x 4', burned at Mangrove Inlet, three miles SSW of Boca Grande, 4/17/1954.

6) *R.E. Huff*—O/V, burned in the Florida Straight, 2/17/1954.

1955

1) *Capt. Phil*—O/F (wood), 22 tons, built 1937 at Fernandina, 40.9' x 14.3' x 5.2', foundered in the Gulf of Mexico off Key West, April 1955.

2) *Cookie*—G/P, 9 tons, built 1954, of Perth Amboy, 31.8' x 11.1' x 4.5', collided with the *Cavallier De La Salle*, 7/9/1955, 35 miles due west of Key West.

3) *Ginger*—O/V, 22 tons, built 1955, foundered 40 miles off Daytona Beach, 11/20/1055.

4) *Greece*—G/F, 12 tons, built 1928 at Tarpon Springs, of Tampa, 39' x 13.2' x 5.1', stranded one mile, SE of the Egmont Bar, Tampa Bay, 7/30/1955.

5) *Jean*—G/P, 14 tons, built 1945, of Tampa, 37.6' x 14.2' x 3.9', foundered 25 miles west of John's Pass, 11/15/1955.

6) *Jean Frances*—O/F, 16 tons, built 1947 at and from Apalachicola, foundered off Cape San Blas, 11/26/1955.

7) *Martha*—O/P, 13 tons, built 1938, of Tampa, 40.7' x 11.8' x 5.2', burned at Channel Stake 80, ICW, south of Sarasota, 5/23/1955.

8) *Rowena*—O/F, 11 tons, built 1919, of St. Augustine, 46.5' x 12.9' x 4.1', foundered off Mayport, 1955.

1956

1) *Admiral*—G/P, 14 tons, built 1912 in New York, of Miami, 41.3' x 16' x 4.1', foundered 18 miles NE of Port Everglades, 3/9/1956.

2) *Golden K*—G/P, 14 tons, built 1927 at Key West, of Miami, 37' x 11/6' x 5.2', burned about 18 miles east of Key West, 6/10/1956.

3) *Neptune*—O/F, 19 tons, built 1947, 45.7' x 13.7' x 5.1', stranded at Ponte Vedra Beach, 8/1/1956.

4) *Sea Spray*—G/P, 10 tons, built 1939, of West Palm Beach, 31.7' x 10.7' x 4.3', burned about three miles NW of Conch Key, Lat. 24°50' N, Long. 80°55' W, 6/21/1956.

5) *St. Nicholas*—O/F, 11 tons, built 1925 at Tarpon Springs, of Miami, 38.8' x 13.7' x 4.7', foundered about one mile west of Key Biscayne, 5/12/1956.

6) *The Birmingham Queen*—O/V, 11 tons, built 1954, foundered off Panama City, 7/22/1956.

1957

1) *Aqueos Speridon*—O/F, 14 tons, built 1927 at Tarpon Springs, of Tampa, 35.3' x 13.8' x 5.2', foundered about three miles off Tarpon Springs, 7/23/1957.

2) *Artmar*—G/P, 7 tons, built 1942, 30.8' x 10.2' x 3.6', foundered at Key West, 12/17/1957.

3) *Cactus*—G/F, 13 tons, built 1938 at and of Key West, 35.2' x 11.6' x 5.1', stranded in NW Channel off Key West, 2/23/1957.

4) *Judy K*—G/V, 13 tons, built 1931, 46' x 11.2' x 4.9', stranded on a sandbar off St. John's Pass, 11/28/1957.

5) *Mollie and Me*—O/F, 14 tons, built 1931, 40.5' x 12.1' x 4.7', burned off Cape Canaveral in 1957.

6) *Smiles*—O/F, 13 tons, of Apalachicola, 40.5' x 12.6' x 3.5', burned in St. Vincent Sound, Apalachicola, 5/1/1957.

7) *Peace II*—O/F, 20 tons, built 1943 at St. Augustine, of Key West, 39.6' x 15.3' x 5.2', foundered about 8 miles west of Key West, 12/15/1957.

8) *Star Dust*—G/F, 11 tons, built 1952, of Tampa, 29.8' x 10.6' x 5.3', foundered about 20 miles off Honeymoon Isle, 9/13/1957.

1958

1) *Americana*—O/C, 14 tons, built 1940, of Miami, 40' x 13.5' x 4.5', burned about two miles north of Key Largo, 7/27/1958.

2) *Argosy*—G/Y, 25 tons, built 1947 in New Jersey, of New York, 43.7' x 12.2' x 5.9', burned about seven or eight miles off Miami, 5/27/1958.

3) *Bounty*—G/P, 11 tons, built 1936 at Jacksonville, of Tampa, 35.6' x 11' x 5.6', was lost somewhere between Miami and Bimini, January 1958.

4) *Mary L*—O/F, 14 tons, built 1929, 44.5' x 12.2' x 4.3', stranded off Daytona Beach, 1/3/1958.

5) *Revonoc*—A new two-mated racing yawl with a 37 hp Mercedes Benz auxiliary diesel engine, 13 tons, built 1957 in New York, 42' x 11' x 6', from Key West for Miami, was lost during a storm. Most believe somewhere in the Florida Keys, probably on 1/3/1958, when a major winter storm hit the area. It was owned by wealthy New York publisher and sportsman, Harvey Conover. Conover was a well-known yachtsman who had sailed with many

including Dick Bertram. *Yachting* magazine was just one of the many his company published. Was believed wreckage found 75 yards off East Washerwoman Shoal was the *Renovoc*, due to the red, white, and blue paint on the wreckage which was the same color as the *Revonoc*. It was never reported that this wreckage was verified as the *Revonoc*, even though the builder was sent down to view the site, so likely was another vessel (*Merchant Vessels* does list it as lost off Marathon). An extensive search was made, divers checked the Marathon area wreckage, and it was reported in papers all over the United States. Was feared he along with his wife, son, daughter-in-law, and another were lost. Her dingy, the *Revonoc Jr.*, was found floating off Jupiter. Another theory is she sank off Key Largo due to a lead keel and a section of a spar found in Hawk's Channel in 1964, but also never verified. Where she actually wrecked remains a mystery, though most say it must have wrecked on a reef in the Keys. The storm was quite intense and it was also reported that two 55-foot fishing vessels from St. Augustine for Key West were missing, the 29-foot sponge boat *Little Nickie* off Tarpon Springs, and the 32-foot fishing vessel *Times* off Naples. Finding that Mercedes diesel motor would likely solve this mystery. *Source:* 10; Farmington Daily Times, 1/7/1958; Redlands Daily Facts, 1/9–18/1958; Scott, Thomas A. *Histories and Mysteries: The Shipwrecks of Key Largo*, 1994; Pacific Stars and Stripes, 1/12/1958.

6) *Sailfisher*—G/F, 12 tons, built 1949, of Miami, 33.3' x 11.2' x 5', burned at Lat. 26°55'15" N, Long. 80°01'15" W, 8/26/1958.

7) *Elizabeth*—O/F, 9 tons, built 1918 at tarpon Springs, of Apalachicola, 35.9' x 11.6' x 4.6', burned in the gulf off St. Vincent's Island, 6/11/1958.

8) *Sun Quest*—O/P, 14 tons, built 1946 at Baltimore, of Tampa, 40.5' x 12.7' x 5.6', stranded off San Marco Island, 3/14/1958.

1959

1) *Bahamian*—G/P, 22 tons, built 1938 at and from Miami, 42.9' x 11.9' x 5.4', burned about 1.5 miles east of Ragged Key, 5/10/1959.

2) *Byrn Mawr*—G/P, 9 tons, built 1914 at Anclote Pass, of Tampa, 35.5' x 9' x 4.4', foundered in ten fathoms, west by south of Tarpon Light, 1/16/1959.

3) *David Harris*—O/F, 33 tons, built 1954 at St. Augustine, of Jacksonville, 46.3' x 16.8' x 6.1', stranded at Ponte Vedra, 7/19/1959.

4) *Emma Louise*—O/F, 9 tons, built 1931, of Charleston, 37' x 10' x 3.2', foundered at Carrabelle, 5/12/1959.

5) *Judy II*—G/P, 12 tons, built 1936, of Miami, 35.6' x 10.1' x 4.6', foundered at the entrance to Port Inglis, Florida, 4/21/1959.

6) *Marieta K II*—G/V, 13 tons, built 1935, burned about three miles west of Clearwater Beach, 4/18/1959.

7) *Miss Fleta*—O/F, 30 tons, built 1951, 42.1' x 16.1' x 7.1', collided with vessel *Big Mike*, about 40 miles west of Key West, 3/24/1959.

8) *Miss Lou*—G/V, 12 tons, built 1955, burned about 35 miles off Naples, 5/12/1959.

9) *Paul Taylor*—O/V, 15 tons, lost in a storm about 40 miles west of Boca Grande, 6/16/1959.

10) *Sailgr*—O/V, 28 tons, built 1952, foundered at Lat. 29°12'; Long. 83°36', 10/11/1959.

11) *Sharron*—O/F, 12 tons, built 1945, of Miami, 39.9' x 10.8' x 4.1', foundered about three miles west of Marathon, 2/27/1959.

12) *The Pixie P*—O/Y, 16 tons, built 1955, of West Palm Beach, 36.2' x 12.1' x 6.5', foundered at approx. Lat. 26-13'-01" N, Long. 80-10'-09" W, 10/11/1959.

13) *Wil-Don-Jon*—Fishing vessel, seven tons, built 1948, of Charleston, 33.7' x 10.9' x 2.8', collided with a submerged object, three miles south of St. Augustine, 7/15/1959.

1960

1) *Angler*—G/F, 11 tons, built 1938, of Miami, burned off Cape Florida, 11/3/1960.

2) *Blue Nose*—G/F, 18 tons, built 1922, of New York, 45.6' x 11.5' x 5', foundered off Port Everglades, 8/6/1960.

3) *Georgia Queen*—O/P, 10 tons, built 1948, of Apalachicola, 36.8' x 10.7' x 4.1', foundered about 10 miles SW of Dog Island, 9/3/1960.

4) *Manatee*—G/F, 11 tons, built 1911, of Tampa, 46' x 13.1' x 3.9', stranded at mouth of St. Lucie Inlet, 5/8/1960.

5) *Salty Dog II*—G/Y, 10 tons, built 1954, 30.6' x 10.1' x 4.5', lost during a hurricane at Marathon Shores, 9/15/1960. *Source:* 14. (4)

6) *Sea Gull*—G/F, 12 tons, built 1934, of Miami 38.4' x 11.1' x 4.6', burned about 20 miles SW of Cape Romano, 7/20/1960.

7) *Sheri Ina*—14 tons, built 1940, burned at Pelican Harbor, 4/8/1960.

1961

1) *Eleanor*—G/P, eight tons, built 1933 at and from Miami, 33.3' x 9.9' x 5.5', foundered at Sand Key, 11/15/1961.

2) *Ginger*—O/F, eight tons, built 1947, of St. Augustine, 45.3' x 17.2' x 8.1', foundered in Nassau Sound, about five miles from Jacksonville, 10/27/1961.

3) *Gladys*—G/P, 12 tons, built 1947 in North Carolina, 37.5'x 11.6' x 3.2', burned between Naples and Big Marco, 7/26/1961.

4) *Goblin*—G/Y, 25 tons, built 1930, 46.2' x 13.6' x 7.3', foundered at sea shortly after being stolen at Ft. Lauderdale, 2/2/1961.

5) *Hi Hey*—O/V, 14 tons, built 1960, burned about 12 miles due west of Pass-a-Grille, Florida, 4/14/1961. At Lat. 27°08'N, Long. 83°02'W.

6) *Lucy*—G/V, 7tons, built 1956, 33.1' x 8.8' x 3.3', burned in the Suwanee River by Suwanee, 7/23/61.

7) *Marjie B*—G/P, 10 tons, built 1937, of Tampa, 34.6' x 11.6' x 6.2', foundered off Dog Island near Carrabelle, 5/1/1961.

8) *St. Christopher*—G/Y, 11 tons, built 1953, lost about two miles off Hillsboro Inlet, 12/19/1961.

9) *Two Sisters*—O/F, 24 tons, of Pensacola, 39.1' x 12.8' x 7.3'. Foundered about 30 miles SW of Panama City, 11/14/1961.

1962

1) *Frances*—O/F, 13 tons, built 1948, of Charleston, 35.9' x 12.4' x 4.1', foundered near St. Augustine, 7/8/1962.

2) *Julia*—O/P, 10 tons. Built 1918 in New Hampshire, of Tampa, 37.7' x 9.1' x 4.4', foundered about 12 miles west of Homosassa, 5/1/1962.

3) *Joanie B*—G/V, 8 tons, built 1959, burned at Man of War Key, off Everglades National Park, 8/5/1962.

4) *Jockiel V*—O/V, 20 tons, built 1960, burned at Ocean Reef, Key Largo, 10/17/1962.

5) *Margin*—O/F, 14 tons, built 1929 in Maine, of Tampa, 41' x 11.2' x 4.5', stranded at St. John's Pass, Madeira Beach, 11/4/1962.

6) *Seabiscuit*—G/P, 13 tons, built 1948, of Miami, 38.6' x 11.4' x 4.8', burned about 1/4 mile off Crandon Park Marina, 2/4/1962.

7) *Symi*—O/F, 13 tons, built 1922 at Tarpon Springs, of Apalachicola, 39.9' x 13.5' x 5.1', lost off Pass-a-Grille Beach, 3/7/1962.

1963

1) *Caroline Kid*—O/F, 30 tons, built 1949 at St. Augustine, of Key West, 44.7' x 15.9' x 6.6', foundered NW of Smith Shoal Light, 12/5/1963.

2) *Elma M*—G/F, 6 tons, built 1947, 30.0' x 9.2' x 2.1', burned in front of Pirate's Cove, Manatee Point, Ports Salerno, 12/3/1963.

3) *Jacko*—O/F, 11 tons, built 1942, of Key West, 37.2' x 10.7' x 4.4', foundered about 12 miles south of Big Marco Pass, south of Naples, 9/25/1963.

4) *John E. Betis*—O/V (dredge), 10 tons, built 1950, of Miami, 28.4' x 12' x 4.5', stranded 1.5 miles south of Jacksonville Beach, 6/24/1963.

5) *Kendall D. Wade*—O/F, 18 tons, built 1945, of Apalachicola, 43.1' x 14.5' x 4.7', burned in Apalachicola Bay, 9/9/1963.

6) *Lucky*—O/P, 13 tons, built 1940, of West Palm Beach, 39.6' x 10.9' x 4.2', burned about two miles west of Clearwater, 7/8/1963.

7) *Lucky Penny*—G/P, 10 tons, built 1947, of West Palm Beach, collided with a submerged anchor 40 feet SE of the SE corner of the north jetty at Boynton Inlet, 1/5/1963.

8) *Mako*—O/V, 12 tons, built 1944, of Key West, 33.8' x 10.2' x 4.3', foundered off Anna Maria Island near Bradenton, 7/19/1963.

9) *Snapper II*—G/Y, 22 tons, built 1937 in Ohio, 45.5' x 11' x 5.5', burned in Indian Creek, Miami Beach, 8/19/1963.

10) *Sunshine*—O/C, 12 tons, built 1928 at Miami, of Tampa, 47.8' x 11.5' x 3.3', burned off the south tip of Longboat Key in New Pass, Sarasota, 4/7/1963.

11) *Trump*—O/F, 6 tons, built 1943 at Tarpon Springs, of Tampa, 27.8' x 9.4' x 3.7', collided with a submerged rock at Hell's Hole, Homosassa River, 10/21/1963.

1964

1) *Adak*—O/V, 17 tons, built 1940, wrecked during a storm at Lat. 27°09', Long. 83°33', 10/15/1964.

2) *Bobby Lee*—O/F, 15 tons, built 1947, 40' x 12.4' x 4', foundered at Ft. George, Florida, 9/9/1964.

3) *Dolores II*—G/Y, 13 tons, built 1960 in New Jersey, 34.5' x 11.1' x 4.8', lost in a hurricane, 8/27/1964 at Miami Beach.

4) *Don Pancho*—G/Y, 15 tons, built 1935 at Conch Key, 43.3' x 12.1' x 4.4', burned at Marathon, 4/20/1964.

5) *Gypsy Queen*—G/F, 14 tons, built 1936, of Miami, 37.9' x 11.5' x 5.6', burned about five miles east of Baker's Haulover, Miami, 11/19/1964.

6) *Mariposa*—O/Y, 22 tons, built 1929 in Maine, 47.5' x 14.7' x 7.5', lost during a storm near St. Petersburg Beach, 7/25/1964.

7) *Polaris*—G/Y, 12 tons, built 1948 in Nova Scotia, 35.4' x 11.2' x 5.7', foundered off Juno Beach, 3/29/1964.

8) *Rebecca*—O/F, 11 tons, built 1957 at and from Key West, 35.6' x 11/6' x 4.7', was lost in a storm near Marquesas Key, 10/14/1964.

9) *Sea Ward*—G/V, 24 tons, built 1928, lost during a hurricane at Miami, 8/27/1964.

10) *Sweet Angeline*—O/P, 14 tons, built 1937, 47.2' x 11.4' x 4.3', foundered at Marathon, 4/7/1964.

1965

1) *Alice*—G/V, 17 tons, built 1910, foundered near Ft. Lauderdale, 2/22/1965.

2) *Goblin II*—G/F, 10 tons, built 1941, 30.2' x 10.2' x 4.8', lost in the Florida Straight, 11/9/1965.

3) *King Fish*—G/F, 10 tons, built 1938, 33.2' x 10' x 4.6', foundered in Sarasota Harbor, 12/15/1965.

4) *Leslie Ann*—O/F, 38 tons, built 1959 at Tarpon Springs, 49.7' x 16.5' x 7.9', foundered off St. Pete, 10/14/1965.

5) *Libby Ann*—G/V, 13 tons, built 1932, foundered about 10 miles SW of the Whistle Buoy off Egmont Key, 2/25/1965.

6) *Little Bill*—O/F, 36 tons, built 1960 at St. Augustine, 46' x 15.7' x 6.8', lost during a hurricane at Key West, 9/8/1965.

7) *Little Husky*—G/F, 11 tons, built 1935, 31.8' x 9.9' x 4.3', lost during a hurricane at South Creek, Key Largo, 9/8/1965.

8) *Luck Star*—G/P, 13 tons, built 1928 at Tampa, 30.6' x 10.4' x 4.9', foundered about 10 miles from Key West, 11/7/1965.

9) *Margarete A III*—G/P, 18 tons, built 1938 in New Jersey, 37.5' x 11.6' x 4.9', lost in a storm off West Palm Beach, 9/6/1965.

10) *Miss Manning*—G/F, 9 tons, built 1945 in FL, 31.5' x 10' x 4', foundered in lower Biscayne Bay, 6/27/1965.

11) *Moana*—G/F, eight tons, built 1958 at Salerno, Florida, 32.6'x 12' x 6', burned at Eau Galle, 7/20/1965.

12) *Peg*—G/Y, 10 tons, built 1940 at Baltimore, 28.7' x 10' x 4.2', foundered about 100 yards south of Clearwater, 4/22/1965.

13) *Picarona*—G/Y, 18 tons, built 1938, 37' x 13.4' x 5.3', stranded on Spoil Island, about ½ mile off Port Everglades, 2/9/1965.

14) *South Wind*—G/P, 12 tons, built 1930, 37' x 10.5' x 4.9', stranded 1/2/ mile south of Lake Worth Pier, 6/6/1965.

15) *Trouvaille*—G/Y, 17 tons, built 1918 in New Jersey, 40.8' x 14.3' x 4.1', lost during a hurricane at Melbourne, 10/12/1965.

16) **Walden**—G/Y, 13 tons, built 1964 at Miami, 31' x 17.3' x 6', collided with a sunken object, 3/17/1965, three miles off Govt. Cut, Miami.

1966

1) *Betty Ruth*—O/V, 38 tons, built 1953, foundered at approximate Lat. 24°42'N, Long. 82°44' W, 2/3/1966.

2) *Captain Harry*—O/F, 10 tons, built 1949, 44.6' x 15.5' x 31, burned about eight miles NW of Smith Shoal Light, Key West, 7/2/1966.

3) *JJ Hanson*—O/F, 27 tons, built 1937 at St. Augustine, 44.2' x 15.6' x 5.6', burned about two miles off Port Canaveral, Lat. 28°22' N, Long. 80°34' W, 3/15/1966.

4) *Lucky R*—G/F, 6 tons, built 1936, 30.6' x 10' x 4.4', stranded in the surf off the Seminole Golf Course, Juno Beach, 2/8/1966.

5) *Miss Juanita*—O/P, 11 tons, built 1940 in Virginia, 38.2' x 10.5' x 4.6', foundered in Ponce De Leon Inlet, 12/8/1966.

6) *Miss Stella*—G/V, 10 tons, built 1957, burned about two miles west of Clearwater Beach, 7/22/1966.

7) *Princess*—O/P, 14 tons, built 1943, 40.4' x 11.3' x 5.1', foundered at Lat. 28°34', 83°20', 10/13/1966.

8) *Ranger II*—G/F, 17 tons, built 1933 in New York, 48.4' x 14' x 4.7', foundered at Lat. 26°11' N, Long. 82°11' W, SW of Ft. Myers, 3/9/1966.

9) *Sea Star*—O/F, 13 tons, built 1932 at Brooklyn, 36' x 10.3' x 4.7', foundered at approximate Lat. 28°N, Long. 82°W.

10) *Silver Star*—O/F, 20 tons, built 1951 in North Carolina, 42.5' x 13.9' x 4.7', foundered 30 miles, NW of Rebecca Shoals, Dry Tortugas, 5/4/1966.

11) *Sunrise Tomorrow*—G/V, 21 tons, built 1964, burned at Sanford, 11/6/1966.

12) *VaVaVoom III*—G/V, 17 tons, built 1959, burned in Biscayne Bay, 12/22/1966.

1967

1) *Alice M*—O/F, 30 tons, built 1958 in North Carolina, 45.4' x 15.4' x 6.3', burned nine miles off Ft. Myers Beach, 11/4/1967.

2) *Captain Ike Lewis*—O/F, 44 tons, built 1950 at St. Augustine, 48.6' x 16.8' x 6.5', collided with the jetty in the St. Johns River at Mayport, 4/5/1967.

3) *Fern G*—G/F, 6 tons, 26.5' x 9' x 4.4', foundered about 50 yards off Marathon, 6/1/1967.

4) *Izaak Walton*—O/F, 20 tons, built 1926 at Cape May, New Jersey, 44.5' x 13.1' x 4.8', foundered at Lat. 27°35' N, Long. 82°48' W, 5/23/1967.

5) *Miss Gigi*—G/V, 10 tons, built 1965, burned at Yankeetown, Florida, 6/8/1967.

6) *Pappy*—G/P, 10 tons, built 1953 in CA, 36.6' x 11.2' x 3.8', stranded at Lat. 28°13' N, Long. 80°36' W, 4/7/1967.

7) *Reef Corsair*—O/P, 14 tons, built 1955 in North Carolina, 38.1' x 12.7' x 4.6', foundered one mile south of Elbow Light, 5/20/1967.

1968

1) *Connie Sue*—O/V, 26 tons, built 1965, burned about 1,500 yards NW of Clearwater Marine Ways, Clearwater, 1/25/1968.

2) *Cracker Jack*—O/V, 13 tons, built 1966, burned 200 yards west of the Anclote Light, Tarpon Springs, 6/15/1968.

3) *Firebird*—G/Y, eight tons, built 1954 in Maine, 32.3 x 10.4 x 6.3, foundered about eight miles east of Fowey Rock Lighthouse, 5/20/1968.

4) *Gulf Pride*—O/P, 11 tons, built 1955 at Ozona, Florida, 38' x 11.4' x 4.4', foundered about 45 miles west of Anclote Light off Tarpon Springs, 7/24/1968.

5) *Kingfisher*—Oil-Pilot boat, 10 tons, built 1932 at WPB, 33.9' x 9.8' x 4.4', foundered at Lat. 30°24' N, Long. 81°18' W, 5/11/1968.

6) *Lady Lou*—G/P, 12 tons, built 1958 in Maine, 35.2' x 11.7' x 4.7', burned about 1/2 mile off Pt. Charles, Florida, 9/9/1968.

7) *Maria*—O/Y (wood), 42 tons, built 1964 in New Jersey, 49.1' x 14.7' x 7.7', burned 17 miles ENE of Port Everglades, 3/11/1968.

8) *Mystery II*—O/F (wood), 14 tons, built 1936 in New Jersey, 42.2' x 12.9' x 4.1', collided with a Japanese ship about 40 miles west of Egmont Key, Tampa, 11/12/1968.

9) *Patty Jo*—O/V, 11 tons, built 1923, foundered off the South Jetties, 500' south of No. 5 marker, Mayport, September, 1968.

10) *Rodonsetta*—O/F, 32 tons, built 1946 at St. Augustine, 41.5' x 11.2' x 6', foundered off Ft. Myers, 5/2/1968.

11) *Sinbad*—G/V, 8 tons, built 1966, burned about three miles off Hallandale Beach, 9/14/1968.

12) *Striper*—G/F (wood), 13 tons, built 1939 at New Bedford, lost in a storm, 6 miles west of Venice, Florida, 11/10/1968.

13) *Wanderlust*—G/V, 24 tons, built 1956, burned at mile marker 17 in the ICW, between Clearwater and Dunedin, 2/4/1968.

1969

1) *Blue Marlin*—G/P (wood), 12 tons, built 1951 at Miami, 35.7' x 11.5' x 5.2', foundered at Stuart, January 1969.

2) *Camille*—O/F, 8 tons, built 1911 at Key West, 29.9' x 9.3' x 4.3', foundered at Buoy #7, SE Channel, Key West, 10/24/1969.

3) *Ella*—O/F (wood), 10 tons, built 1936 at Biloxi, 38' x11.3' x 3.6', foundered at Lat. 29°48' N, Long. 87°57' W, 3/16/1969.

4) *J.H. Pierpoint*—O/F (wood), 31 tons, built 1972 in Virginia, 49.7' x 12.9' x 6.7', lost during a storm at Pensacola, 12/29/1969.

5) *Jeannie*—G/F, 14 tons, built 1948 in Michigan, 32.1' x 10.3' x 4.9', burned in Santa Rosa Sound, at approximate Lat. 30°25' N, Long. 87°11' W, 3/14/1969.

6) *Janet*—G/P (wood), 12 tons, Lost during a storm in St. Johns River near Bayard Point, and south of Green Cove Springs, 3/1/1969.

7) *Jeannie*—G/F (wood), 14 tons, built 1948 in Michigan, 32.1' x 10.3' x 4.9', burned in Santa Rosa Sound, at approximate Lat. 30°20' N, Long. 87°11' W, 3/14/1969.

8) *Lady Luck*—G/P (wood), 13 tons, built 1940 in Maine, 35.8' x 11.4' x 3.1', foundered in the Otela River, N. Miami Beach, May 1969.

9) *SDC 2*—Freight barge (steel), 23 tons, built 1955 at Miami, 34.9' x 20' x 3.6', lost in a storm approximately 20–30 miles off Key West, 11/10/1969.

10) *Sampan*—O/Y, 13 tons, built 1946 in VA, 39.6' x 10' x 3.9', foundered at Wabasso, believe around 1969.

11) *Scotchie*—35 tons, built 1949 at St. Augustine, foundered off Ft. Lauderdale, May 1969.

12) *Seco No. 2*—O/T (steel), 8 tons, built 1955, 26' x 11' x 5.9', foundered about 20–30 miles north of Key West, 11/10/1969.

13) *Voyager II*—G/V, 12 tons, built 1951, burned near Key Largo, 3/23/1969.

1970

1) *3C*—O/V, 15 tons, built 1945, foundered near southern tip of Mullet Key, near entrance to Tampa Bay, 11/28/1970.

2) *Flying Dutchman*—G/F (wood), nine tons, built 1960 at Pensacola, 33' x 10.1' x 4.3', burned in Bayou Chica, Pensacola, 7/3/1970.

3) *Mare Amo*—O/Y (fiberglass), 14 tons, built 1968 at Tarpon Springs, 41' x 23.5' x 5', foundered 50 miles east of Daytona, 12/31/1970.

4) *Mary*—O/V, 29 tons, damaged due to an explosion in 1970 on the Miami River. She was then towed to sea off Miami and sunk.

5) *Sea Fever*—G/Y (fiberglass), 26 tons, built 1960 in North Carolina, 40.4' x 13' x 6.3', burned near the 79th St. Causeway, Biscayne Bay, 1/31/1970.

6) *Sea Gull*—O/P (wood), 44 tons, built 1965 in New Jersey, 49.1' x 15.7' x 7.6', burned about 12 miles off Port Everglades, 12/13/1970.

7) *Sherry Diane*—O/T (steel), 29 tons, built 1965 in TX, 41.8' x 15' x 6.1', foundered 15 miles WNW of Key West, 1/17/1970.

8) *Shirley M*—F/V (wood), 18 tons, built 1936, 40.3' x 13.2' x 3.8', collided with an unknown object near Rebecca Shoals, 8/20/1970.

9) *Tarpon Lady*—O/P (wood), 13 tons, built 1956 at Pinellas Park, 48.9' x 19' x 3.3', foundered about 25 miles west of Tarpon Springs, 10/6/1970.

10) *The Night Cap II*—G/Y (steel), 12 tons, built 1964 in Minnesota, 33.1' x 9.7' x 2', burned near Long Boat Pass Bridge, Sarasota, 6/11/1970.

11) *Trienin IV*—G/Y (wood), 15 tons, built 1950 in New York, 32.3' x 10.6' x 5', foundered about one mile east of Marathon, 2/4/1970.

12) *Uncle Sam*—O/V, believe 37.5', foundered in Choctawhatchee Bay at Ben's Lake, 4/6/1970.

13) *Wing Ding*—O/Y (wood), 28 tons, built 1962, 42.1' x 12.8' x 7.4', burned five miles off NW Cape, Florida, in Gulf, 5/4/1970.

1) Page 190. *Lady M. Johnson*—Built 1947 at New Berlin, Florida, 41.4' x 17.5' x 8.'

1971

1) *Daisy Mae*—O/P (wood), 25 tons, built 1963 in North Carolina, 43' x 15.5' x 6.9', foundered at Lat. 27°40' N, Long. 84°07' W, 5/15/1971.

2) *Drift Two*—G/P (wood), 10 tons, built 1959 at Pompano Beach, 31.4' x 12/2' x 5.4', burned four miles west of Sarasota, 9/6/1971.

3) *Enchantress III*—O/Y (wood), 26 tons, built 1951 in New York, 43.6' x 12.8' x 7', stranded on Carysfort Reef, 1/23/1971.

4) *Gindy III*—O/Y (fiberglass), 24 tons, built 1969 in North Carolina, 40.7' x 14' x 6.3', burned off Palm Beach Inlet, 4/8/1971.

5) *Greyhound*—O/P (wood), 11 tons, built 1923, 38.4' x 9.9' x 4', foundered about 200 yards north of the John Gorrie Bridge, Apalachicola, 3/28/1971.

6) *Hercel Ann*—G/P (wood), 13 tons, built 1940 at Everglades, 34.6' x 10.9' x 4.2', foundered in Chokoloskee Bay, 12/27/1971.

7) *La Dolce Vita*—G/Y (wood), 28 tons, built 1965 in New Jersey, 43.1' x 14.1' x 6.2', stranded on a reef in the Keys, March 1971.

8) *Lorraine*—O/F (wood), 13 tons, built 1948 at Tarpon Springs, 39.4' x 13.1' x 5.1', stranded off St. George Island, November 1971.

9) *Miss Manatee*—O/F (wood), 36 tons, built 1968 at Tarpon Springs, 46.8' x 17.6' x 6.1', stranded in lower Tampa Bay off Passage Key, 4/7/1971.

10) *Pengor II*—O/Y (wood), 29 tons, built 1948 at Jacksonville, 49.3' x 14.1' x 7.3', burned off Florida, July 1972.

11) *Syndag*—O/F (wood), 10 tons, built 1936 in Virginia, 36' x 11.2' x 4.2', burned about 1/2 mile SE of Horseshoe Beach, 9/27/1971.

12) *Ta Maru Too*—O/P (wood), 12 tons, built 1932 in New Jersey, 41.6' x 12' x 4.8', foundered about 1/2 mile off Haulover Beach, Dade County, 1/5/1971.

13) *U N Me II*—G/F (wood), 10 tons, built 1942 at Baltimore, 29.3' x 10.2' x 5', foundered off 35th St., Marathon, June, 1971.

1972

1) *Barabara K*—O/V, 16 tons, built 1958, foundered 35 miles west of John's Pass, 4/26/1972.

2) *Condor*—G/Y (wood), 12 tons, built 1948 in New Jersey, 33' x 9.9' x 6', foundered 100 yards off Govt. Cut, Miami, 7/4/1972.

3) *Georgia Mae*—O/F (wood), 10 tons, built 1944 in South Carolina, 35.9' x 10.6' x 3.5', foundered by SW corner of Egmont Key, 12/17/1972.

4) *Lady Gay*—O/P (wood), 12 tons, 34.1' x 11/6' x 4.5', foundered 70 miles west of Ft. Myers, 2/19/1972.

5) *Mima Fay*—O/V, 47 tons, built 1942, lost in a storm off St. Augustine Beach, 12/16/1972.

6) *Ruth Lee*—G/F, (wood), 13 tons, built 1952 in N.C., 38.5' x 12.3' x 4.1', sunk off St. Augustine, July 1972.

7) *Six CS*—O/Y (wood), 36 tons, built 1952, 47.3' x 14.3' x 7.4', foundered about 20 miles east of Ft. Lauderdale, 10/7/1972.

8) *Starr L*—O/P (wood), 17 tons, built 1949 at Fernandina, 37.3' x 12.8' x 5.2', foundered five miles west of New Pass, Sarasota, 2/19/1972.

9) *The Flying Dutchman*—O/Y (wood), 40 tons, built 1953 in Michigan, 48.6' x 14' x 7.2', stranded in Ponce Inlet, off Smyrna Beach, 4/21/1972.

10) *Timucuan*—O/T (steel), nine tons, built 1956 at Miami, 27' x 11.6' x 3.8', foundered at St. Pete Beach, 4/11/1972.

11) *Tuna*—G/F (wood), six tons, built 1921 at Sarasota, 27.1' x 8.4' x 4.3', foundered near New Pass, Sarasota, 2/13/1972.

12) *Turnabout*—O/F (wood), 40 tons, built 1950 at St. Augustine, 46' x 16.8' x 6.8', stranded at the entrance of the NW Channel, Key West, 4/10/1972.

13) *Wahoo*—O/F (wood), 11 tons, built 1953 in Michigan, 32.6' x 10.9' x 4.9', lost near Ft. Walton Beach, 3/1/1972.

1) Page 190. *Miss Libby*—Built in North Carolina (wood), 45.4' x 15.4' x 6.3'.

1973

1) *Ingomar*—O/V, 21 tons, built 1967, burned off Haulover Beach, 5/31/1973.

2) *Flo Jo II*—G/P (wood), 11 tons, built 1953 in New Jersey, 32.6' x 10.6' x 11.9', foundered five miles west of the north end of Clearwater Beach, 5/27/1973.

3) *Jocko II*—G/V, 10 tons, built 1950, foundered 650 yards off 87th St., Miami, 4/10/1973.

4) *Maribo*—O/F (wood), 17 tons, built 1958 at Jacksonville, 34.6' x 12.9' x 5', lost in a storm at the S. Jetty at the mouth of the St. Johns River, 2/9/1973.

5) *Melody*—G/Y (wood), eight tons, built 1964 in New Jersey, 30' x 10.8' x 4.1', foundered off Hollywood, 2/28/1973.

6) *Misty*—G/P (wood), 9 tons, built 1968 in Pennsylvania, 28' x 10.8' x 4.7', burned in St. Andrews Bay, August 1973.

7) *Night Hawk*—O/V, 23 tons, built 1970, burned sometime in 1973 at Lat. 28°27.3' N, Long. 80°28' W.

8) *Shirley Ann*—O/F (wood), 15 tons, built 1946 at Pt. St. Joe, 39.5' x 13.3' x 3.5', collided with a motorboat off Redfish Pt., St. Andrews Bay, 6/2/1974.

9) *Sue*—G/F (wood), 9 tons, built 1964 at Pensacola, 32.1' x 9.8' x 4', stranded about one mile west of Perdido Pass, 5/29/1974.

10) *Venture*—O/V, 33 tons, built 1949, foundered at the mouth of the St. Johns River, Mayport, 11/6/1973.

1974

1) *Anna Marie*—O/F (wood), 21 tons, built 1937 at Tarpon Springs, 45.5' x 15.8' x 5.4', foundered off Ft. Myers Beach, 8/2/1974.

2) *Mary Ann*—G/V, 7 tons, built 1935, foundered at Islamorada, November 1974.

3) *Miss Lula*—O/F (wood), 30 tons, built 1954, 45.6' x 15.4' x 6.5', stranded off Ponte Vedra at Lat. 30°14' N, 81°22' 28" W.

1975

1) *Blue Skies*—O/Y, 22 tons, built 1967 in New Jersey, 39' x 13.5' x 6.4', burned about 2.5 to 3 miles SE of Lake Worth Inlet, 9/22/1975.

2) *El Pescador*—O/V, 19 tons, built 1957, foundered 100 yards east of Pacific Reef Light, 3/28/1975.

3) *Ginger Ann*—G/P (wood), seven tons, built 1939 at Palma Sola, Florida, 30.7' x 9.8' x 3.6', foundered at Bonita Springs, 6/10/1975.

4) *Granada*—O/Y (wood), 20 tons, built 1929 at Bayonne, New Jersey, 40.2' x 11.5' x 5.7', foundered 12 miles south of Alligator Reef Light, 3/30/1975.

5) *Jackie K*—G/F (wood), 7 tons, built 1947 at Ft. Pierce, 30' x 9.8' x 4.4', foundered at Riviera Beach, 4/10/1975.

6) *Liddle Darlin*—O/V, 18 tons, built 1963, foundered on Bethel Shoals, 2/25/1975.

7) *Partner*—O/F (wood), 36 tons, built 1960 at St. Augustine, 44.9' x 16.4' x 7.4', burned at Pensacola, 5/3/1975.

8) *Ponce*—O/F (wood), eight tons, 33.5' x 8.8' x 4.2', foundered in Sparkman Channel, Tampa, 12/12/1975.

9) *Sawsea*—G/Y (fiberglass), 35 tons, built 1971 in Maryland, 46' x 15' x 4.1', burned at west coast of Florida, by Lake Okeechobee, 12/18/1975.

10) *Scylla*—O/P (wood), 21 tons, built 1939 in Massachusetts, 38.3' x 11/3' x 5.6', burned in Choctawhatchee Bay, 10/19/1975.

11) *Tamarack*—G/Y (wood), 21 tons, built 1970 in New Jersey, 37' x 12.5' x 7', foundered in Lake Worth Inlet, 1/14/1975.

12) *The Hobo*—O/P (wood), 11 tons, built 1958 at Titusville, 33.5' x 11' x 5.1', lost in a hurricane at Grand Lagoon, Panama City, 9/23/1975.

13) *The Sandpiper*—G/Y (wood), 17 tons, 44.9' x 13.1' x 5.5', foundered in Lake Cusic, Jacksonville Beach, 1975.

14) *White Marlin*—O/P (wood), 14 tons, built 1937 in New Jersey, 37.8' x 11' x 5.7', foundered four miles west of Destin Florida Pass, 6/22/1975.

1976

1) *Dori Malyn*—O/F (wood), 16 tons, built 1943 at Tarpon Springs, 40.8' x 13.9' x 6.1', stranded at Lat. 27°58' N, Long. 82°50' W, 5/18/1976.

2) *Edna Oliver*—O/F (wood), 18 tons, built 1930 at Fernandina, 40.9' x 14' x 4.9', foundered in Tampa Bay, 11/23/1976.

3) *Evy Gee II*—O/V, 19 tons, built 1966, collided with an unknown object at the St. Lucie Inlet, 12/6/1976.

4) *Janthina*—O/P (wood), 14 tons, built 1952 in Virginia, 39.7' x 12.2' x 4.8', burned at Lake Worth, 10/16/1976.

5) *Rig*—G/P (wood), 13 tons, built 1937 in Ohio, 37.3' x 10.7' x 5.2', burned at Marathon, 3/26/1976.

6) *Robert L*—O/F (wood), 14 tons, built 1938 in New York, 40' x 12.8' x 5', foundered about 40 miles west of John's Pass, in the gulf, 8/15/1976.

7) *Sport Fisherman*—O/P (fiberglass), nine tons, built 1974 at Destin, 28.4' x 11.8' x 4.8', burned in St. Andrews Bay, 7/8/1976.

8) *Therese Michelle*—O/V, 13 tons, built 1949, burned at Key West, 5/1/1976.

9) *Tiki*—O/F (wood), seven tons, built 1965 at Chokoloskee, 26.6' x 10.4' x 3.8', foundered seven miles off Marco Island, 10/12/1976.

1977

1) *Albacore*—O/F (wood), 43 tons, built 1971 at Tarpon Springs, 45.7' x 16.1' x 10.5', stranded in Boca Grande Channel, 3/22/1977.

2) *Bettie D*—O/Y (fiberglass), 23 tons, built 1969 in Wisconsin, foundered at Lat. 25°05' N, Long. 82°10' W, 10/2/1976.

3) *Big Gizmo*—O/F (wood), 14 tons, built 1963 at Key West, 34.5' x 12.7' x 5', foundered off Orange Point, Florida, 11/17/1977.

4) *Lucky Star*—O/F (wood), 25 tons, built 1946 in North Carolina, 39.7' x 13.4' x 6', foundered off Truman Square Annex, near Key West, 8/15/1977.

5) *Mar Mac*—O/P (wood), seven tons, built 1936 in Michigan, 29.8' x 9.2' x 4.7', stranded at New Pass off Ft. Meyers, 1/11/1977.

6) *Miss Kristie*—O/V, seven tons, built 1963, burned in the Barron River, Everglades City, 8/17/1977.

7) *Perseverance*—O/P (wood), eight tons, built 1949, 33.4' x 11' x 3.2', foundered in Egmont Channel, 5/21/1977.

7) *Sandy D III*—O/Y (fiberglass), 38 tons, built 1971 in New Jersey, 48' x 14.5' x 8.4', foundered off WPB, 1/29/1977.

8) *Sunshine Lady*—O/V, 15 tons, built 1977, burned at Titusville, 6/16/1977.

9) *Trade Winds*—O/F (wood), 14 tons, built 1941 at Brooklyn, 36.6' x 11.9' x 6', collided with the Courtney Campbell Bridge, Old Tampa Bay, 4/4/1977.

1978

1) *Christine*—O/V, 21 tons, built 1968, burned in the ICW near Hobe Sound, 4/7/1978.

2) *Echo*—G/F (wood), 22 tons, built 1958 at Tarpon Springs, 48' x 14.3' x 3.9', foundered at approximate Lat. 26°48' N, Long. 83°40' W, 1/14/1978.

3) *Evening Star*—O/F (wood), 14 tons, built 1965 at Panama City, 35' x 14.7' x 3.4', burned about one mile off White City, Florida, 5/13/1978.

4) *Joppa*—O/V, 17 tons, built 1976, burned five miles north of Smith Shoals Light, 2/17/1978.

5) *Maximus*—O/V, 35 tons, built 1958, stranded 25 miles east of Miami, 3/20/1978.

6) *Pisces*—O/V, 15 tons, built 1972, foundered at Lat. 24°34.6', Long. 81°06.3', 5/2/1978.

7) *Silver Queen*—O/P (wood), 14 tons, built 1960 at Tarpon Springs, 33.7' x 13.2' x 5.3', foundered about 22 miles west of Egmont Key, 6/17/1978.

8) *Stowaway V*—O/Y (fiberglass), 29 tons, built 1972 in North Carolina, 48.7' x 14.6' x 6.2', burned off Chuck (likely meant Duck) Key, Florida, 7/1/1978.

9) *Tail Chaser*—O/V, 13 tons, built 1970, stranded at Stuart, 8/16/1978.

10) *Three Bros*—O/F (wood), 19 tons, built 1963 at Panacea, 42.4' x 12.2' x 5', stranded in Shark Bayou, Destin, 4/27/1978.

11) *Wisdom*—O/V, 14 tons, built 1973, burned off the coast of Vero Beach, 9/3/1978.

1979

1) *Capt. Dave*—O/P (wood), 13 tons, built 1959 in Maine, 35.6' x 13' x 5.9', foundered in 23 fathoms in the south area of the Florida Middle Ground, August 1979.

2) *Dori Lew IV*—O/Y (fiberglass), 11 tons, built 1974 in New Jersey, 33.6 x 12.5 x 4', destroyed by a hurricane at WPB, 9/6/1979.

3) *Flying Star II*—O/P (wood), 12 tons, built 1953 in Virginia, 37.4' x 11.7' x 4.8', foundered about 40 miles west of Weeki Wachee, 6/9/1979.

4) *Jo Le*—O/F (fiberglass), 17 tons, built 1973 at Ft. Lauderdale, 34' x 12.8' x 6.1', burned in Spanish Channel at No Name Key off Big Pine Key, 7/20/1979.

5) *M Friz*—O/V, 45 tons, built 1970, burned at Ft. Myers, 10/19/1979.

6) *Michele Jenene*—O/F (fiberglass), 17 tons, built 1976 at Miami, 36.7' x 11.5' x 6.5', foundered about 50 miles WNW of St. Pete, 1/20/1979.

7) *Miss Cachita*—O/V, nine tons, built 1977, foundered off Key Largo, 6/8/1979.

8) *Miss Darlene*—O/F (wood), 13 tons, built 1974 in VA, 42.4' x 12.5' x 3.5', burned 10 miles, 150° from the Sombrero Light, off Marathon, 8/26/1979.

9) *Patricia Anne*—O/F (fiberglass), nine tons, built 1978 at Key West, 30.6' x 11.3' x 3.7', burned off Big Pine Key, 7/20/1979.

10) *Rita M*—O/F (wood), 13 tons, built 1948 at New Orleans, 31' x 12.1' x 5.3', burned at approximate Lat. 28°13' N, Long. 83°58' W, 9/21/1979.

11) *Teddybear*—O/Y (wood), 33 tons, built 1948 in Virginia, 48.7' x 14.6' x 5.1', foundered 17.5 miles off Jacksonville, July 1979.

12) *Tiger*—O/F (wood), 7 tons, built 1952 in Maryland, 29.5' x 9.6' x 3.9', burned 35 miles south of Daytona Beach, June 1979.

1980

1) *Aeolus*—O/V, 12 tons, built 1980, burned 14 miles south of Panama City at Lat. 29°54.3' N, Long. 85°52' W, 12/4/1980.

2) *Anita*—O/P (fiberglass), 21 tons, built 1973 at Key West, 37.9' x 13.2' x 5.3', burned at Alligator Point, Lat. 30°08.2' N, Long. 85°43.5' W, 6/18/1980.

3) *Capt. Ben Michell*—G/P (wood), 10 tons, 36.4' x 12.5' x 3.4', foundered at Lat. 30°01'N, Long. 85°W, 10/30/1980.

4) *Joynt Effort II*—O/V, 28 tons, built 1968, foundered about 70 miles SW of Naples, 5/3/1980.

5) *Mele Kai*—G/P (wood), 15 tons, built 1958 at Miami, 38.1' x 12.7' x 5.2', foundered about six miles SE of Lake Worth Inlet, 1/2/1980.

6) *Patricia Anne*—O/V, nine tons, built 1978, burned off Big Pine Key, near Spanish Channel, 8/8/1980.

7) *Sandpiper II*—O/V, 18 tons, built 1980, foundered 85 miles NW of Clearwater, 11/5/1980.

1998

1) *A 30' pleasure boat*—Smuggling Cubans to Florida, capsized near Elliot Key, 12/18/1998. Had 36 people on board, nine were rescued, eight were found dead, and others were missing. *Source:* NYT, 12/16/1998.

2002

1) *Panther*—A 31-foot tour boat built in 1968 sank in eight feet of water with 29 tourists on board on the fringe of the Everglades National Park. All on board safe. Unknown if saved (was moved but still in water). *Source:* Sun Sentinel, 1/1/2003.

2003

1) *Third Wish*—A 32-foot sailboat was abandoned after the three on board were rescued by Florida Fish and Wildlife Conservation Commission

officers in rough seas in the Gulf, November 9, 2003. The sailboat was found two weeks later between two sandbars off the Topsail Hill State Preserve, Walton County, Florida. *Source:* Sun Sentinel, 11/25/2003.

2007

1) *Madame Glenda*—A 42-foot fishing boat, of St. Petersburg, struck a submerged object and sank about 53 miles northwest of Key West, 10/27/2007. The four fishermen on board were saved by the Coast Guard. *Source:* Sun Sentinel, 10/28/2007.

2008

1) *Seas A Lady*—Sport fisherman, fiberglass hull, about 47 feet, broke from her Port Everglades sea buoy anchor, 9/28/2008, and washed up on shore along Galt Ocean Mile, Ft. Lauderdale. Parts of her hull and fuel tank, but no engines, were washed up on the beach.

Wreckage from the *Seas A Lady*, washed up on Ft. Lauderdale Beach, 2008.

Large capstan from an unknown wreck off Palm Beach County.

The late Carl Ward on his dive boat. Navy veteran, police detective, and avid wreck diver, he was a pleasure to dive with.

Dive partner Don Kree, looking through the glass bottom portal on Carl Ward's dive boat.

Old Hugh C. Leighton, Co. postcard of the "Old Wreck." It's the *James Judge*, pages 151 and 152 in *Shipwrecks of Florida*, 2nd edition. From author's collection.

Some cannons (likely from the 1733 Spanish fleet) in front of the old McKee Treasure Museum in Islamorada, shortly after it closed.

Diver using a suction dredge on a Florida ship-wreck site.

Some treasure is edible. Author with his "trea-sure" on the 1715 "Nieves" site.

Author's daughter Monica, ready to dive on a shipwreck.

Author with the late Dan Wagner, who filmed many documentaries on Florida shipwrecks including "What Dreams are Made Of." He was one of the first YMCA dive instructors and ran the live-aboard dive vessel *Impossible Dream*.

Many vessels are simply abandoned, like this old hulk in the Florida Keys.

Bibliography

The Internet offers a wealth of sources for anyone doing research and more is added every day. Many U.S. government records are now available online going back to the 18th century.

I researched hundreds of newspapers and periodicals (many online now), and I simply listed those sources by name and date after each wreck where applicable, except in chapter 9, which almost all are from one source described at the beginning of that chapter.

The most commonly used newspapers I've abbreviated as per the list, and that abbreviation with the date will appear after each applicable wreck. *Lloyd's List* and *Lloyd's Register* are also abbreviated with year or date referenced. Any further sources will have the corresponding numbers listed after each wreck.

a) Adams Sentinel (Gettysburg): AS

b) Bells Weekly Messenger (London): BWM

c) Boston Daily Globe: BDG

d) Boston Post: BP

e) Boston Morning Post: BMP

f) Edinburgh Advertiser: EA

g) Gazette of the United States and Daily Advertiser (Philadelphia): GUS

h) Georgian: G

i) Lloyd's List: LL

j) Lloyd's Register: LR

k) London Daily Advertiser: LDA

l) London Evening Post: LEP

m) London St. James Crescent: LSJC

n) New Orleans Daily Crescent: NODC

o) New York Herald: NYH

p) New York Times: NYT

q) New York Tribune: NYTR

r) Republican and Savannah Evening Ledger: RSEL

s) Savannah Republican: SR

t) Savannah Daily Republican; SDR

u) Savannah Morning News: SMN

v) Savannah Daily Morning News: SDMN

w) Savannah Daily Georgian; SDG

x) Savannah Georgian; SG

y) Shipping and Mercantile Gazette (London): SMG

Other Sources

Books, government records, etc. *Note:* Please see the bibliography in *Shipwrecks of Florida*, where all the information on the previous listed shipwrecks was obtained.

1) *1733 Spanish Galleon Trail*. Tallahassee: Florida Dept. of State. (Pamphlet-no date).

2) Adams, William Henry Davenport. *Great Shipwrecks, A Record of Perils and Disasters at Sea—1544 to 1877*. London: Thomas Nelson and Sons, 1880.

3) Albion, Robert G. *Square Riggers on Schedule*. Princeton, NJ: Princeton University Press, 1938.

4) *Automated Wreck and Obstruction Information System (AWOIS)*. U.S. Department of Commerce, National Oceanic and Atmospheric Administration (NOAA). Rockville, MD, 2018. Now online: https://www.nautical-charts.noaa.gov/data/wrecks-and-obstructions.html/

5) Baker, George E. *Swamp Sailors, Riverine Warfare in the Everglades 1835–1842*. Gainesville: University Press of Florida, 1975.

6) Baker, William Avery. *A Maritime History of Bath, Maine, and the Kennebeck River Region, Vol. I and II*. Bath: Marine Research Society of Bath, 1873.

7) Barnette, Michael C. *Encyclopedia of Florida Shipwrecks, Vol.1*. Association of Underwater Explorers, 2010.

8) Bass, George F. *History of Seafaring*. New York: Walker and Co., 1972.

9) Bonifacio, Claudio. *Galleons and Sunken Treasure*. Merritt Island, FL: Signum Ops, 2010.

10) Congressional Information Service (CIS). *United States Serial Set Index, Part 1–11*, and *Records of the National Archives*. The U.S. government sources used are from *List of Merchant Vessels of the U.S.* (which the earliest I found was 1868 and published annually-provided most information), *Annual Reports of the U.S. Life-Saving Service, 1876–1914*, and The Congressional Hearing Records from 1846. Many of the annual List of *Merchant Vessel of the U.S.*, and the annual *Life-Saving* records, can be found online. The CIS records on microfilm are still available in many large libraries.

11) Colledge, J. J. *Ships of the Royal Navy*. Annapolis, MD: Naval Institute Press, 1987.

12) Cutler, Carl C. *Queens of the Westers Ocean*. Annapolis, MD: United States Naval Institute,

1967.

13) Chaunu, Huguette et Pierre. *Seville et L'Atlantique (1505–1650)*. Paris: S.E.V.P.E.N., 1955.

14) *Dictionary of American Naval Fighting Ships, Vols. 1–8*. Washington: Navy Department, Office of the Chief of Naval Operations, Naval History Division, 1963 and 1977. (Available online through the Naval History and Heritage Command website): https://www.history.navy.mil/research/histories/ship-histories/danfs.html/.

15) Earle, Peter. *The Treasure of the Concepcion*. New York: Viking Press, 1979.

16) Fismer, Carl, and Sam Milner. *Uncharted Waters*. Melbourne, FL: Sea Dunes Publishing, 2015.

17) Friar, Linda. "The Windjammer Wreck-A Diver's Haven." S. Dade News Leader, 6/8/2014.

18) Goldberg, Mark H. *The "Hog Islanders."* Kings Point, NY: American Merchant Marine Museum, 1991.

19) Kafka, Roger, and Roy L. Pepperburg. *Warships of the World*. New York: Cornell Maritime Press, 1946.

20) *List of Vessels on the Registry Books of the Dominion of Canada.* Ottawa: Department of Marine and Fisheries. (Annual list).

21) Lytle, William M., and Forrest R. Holdcamper. *Merchant Steam Vessels of the Unites States 1790–1868, "The Lytle-Holdcamper List."* New York: The Steamship Historical Society of America, 1952 and 1975.

22) Mc Carthy, Kevin. *Thirty Florida Shipwrecks.* Sarasota, FL: Pineapple Press, 1992.

23) Mondano, Mark R. *Divers Guide to Shipwrecks-Cape Canaveral to Jupiter Light.* Roseland, FL: Sandman Productions, 1991.

24) Quinn, William P. *Shipwrecks Along the Atlantic Coast.* Orleans, MA: Parnassus Imprints, 1988.

25) Romans, Capt. Bernard. *A Concise Natural History of East and West Florida.* New York: 1775.

26) Snediker, Quentin, and Ann Jensen. *Chesapeake Bay Schooners.* Centreville, MD: Tidewater Publishers.

27) Survey of Federal Archives. *Ship Registers.* Though I could include these under #10 (National Archive Records), these were published by individual states/custom districts around the U.S. between 1938 and 1942. The Federal Archives, along with many states, through both a community and women's project program, compiled a list of shipping records from old custom houses, etc., before they were possibly lost forever. Included records from districts like New Bedford, New Orleans, Philadelphia, Boston, Providence, Plymouth, Newport, Machias, Saco, Barnstable, etc. Each district produced and printed their own records. These are available in the National Archives though some are also available online.

28) Viele, John. *The Florida Keys, Volume 2, True Stories of the Perilous Straights.* Sarasota, FL: Pineapple Press, 1999.

29) Watts, Leon. *Shipwrecks of Florida's West Coast.* Self-published, 1999.

30) Weatherill, Richard. *The Ancient Port of Whitby and Its Shipping.* Whitby: Horne and Son, 1908.

31) Williams, Greg H. *Civil and Merchant Vessel Encounters with United States Navy Ships, 1800–2000.* Jefferson, NC: McFarland and Company Publishers, 2002.

Websites

32) http://armed-guard.com/ships.html/. Merchant Marine database, especially for World War II.

33) https://digitalmuseum.no/search/. Stavanger Maritime Museum.

34) http://www.florida-keys-vacation.com/. Florida Keys wreck sites, history, and photos.

35) http://kulturnav.org/. Database for Norwegian ships.

36) http://museumsinthesea.com/ and http://floridapanhandledivetrail .com/. State of Florida's Underwater Preserves and Panhandle wrecks.

37) https://research.mysticseaport.org/. Mystic Seaport Museum's online digital records including: a) *American Lloyd's Registry of American and Foreign Shipping* (Annual list starting in 1857). The Society of American Lloyd's. b) *Record of American and Foreign Shipping* (Annual list starting in 1867). New York: American Shipmaster's Association.

38) http://staugustinelighthouse.org/. Lighthouse Archaeology Maritime Program (LAMP).

39) http://skipshistorie.net/. Norwegian ships database.

40) http://www.warsailors.com/. (Norwegian merchant fleet 1939–1945).

41) Late addition. Gaines, W. Craig. *Encyclopedia of Civil War Shipwrecks*. Baton Rouge: Louisiana State University Press, 2008.

Suggested Reading and Further Material Sources

Also see those listed in *Shipwrecks of Florida*.

1715 Fleet

1) Armstrong, T. L., and Gore, Tommy. *The Rainbow Chasers Tricentennial Yearbook*. Merritt Island, FL: Signum Ops, 2015.

2) Marx, Robert F. *The Quest for the Queen's Jewels*. Merritt Island, FL: Signum Ops, 2015.

3) Westrick, Robert F. *Finding the Fleet*. Self-published, 2015.

1733 Fleet

1) Ward, Carl. *Shipwreck in the Florida Keys 1733*. Self-published, 2013.

2) Weller, Robert. *Galleon Alley*. Lake Worth, FL: Crossed Anchors Salvage, 2001.

Other

Shipwrecks, Maritime history, Maritime Archaeology, etc.

1) *A History of Shipwrecks, and Disasters at Sea*, Vols. 1–4. London: Whittaker and Co, Ave-Maria Lane, Gilbert and Rivington, Printers, 1835.

2) Carlile, Capt. Tim. Land and Sea Surveying. *Offshore Martin County; Offshore Brevard County*. Merritt Island, FL. 2014.

3) Crile, Barney and Jane. *Treasure Diving Holidays*. New York: Viking Press, 1954.

4) Crooks, David S. *Sunken Treasure Books*. Self-published, 2002.

5) Dean, James, and Steven Singer. *Shipwrecks of Broward County*. Self-published, 1985.

6) Ellms, Charles (compiled by). *Shipwrecks and Disasters at Sea*. New York: Richard Marsh, 138 William-St., 1836.

7) Fine, John Christopher. *Treasures of the Spanish Main*. Guilford, CT: Lyons Press, 2006. Great photos including a two-page photo of a 1715 fleet gold coin which I found.

8) Fowler, William M. Jr. *Rebels Under Sail. The American Navy during the Revolution*. New York: Charles Scribner's Sons, 1976.

9) Grocott, Terence. *Shipwrecks of the Revolutionary and Napoleonic Eras*. Great Britain: Caxton Publishing Group, 2002.

10) Harbron, John D. *Trafalgar and the Spanish Navy*. Oxford: University Printing House, 1988.

11) José Garcia Echegoyen, Fernando. *El Misterio del Valbanera*. Aqualargo Editores SL, 2001.

12) Layson, J. F. *Memorable Shipwrecks and Seafaring Adventures*. London: Walter Scott, 1907.

13) Link, Marion Clayton. *Sea Diver*. New York: Rinehart and Co., 1959.

14) Marx, Robert, and Jenifer Marx. *New World Shipwrecks 1492–1825*. Dallas: Ram Publishing, 1994.

15) Marx, Robert F., with Jenifer Marx. *The Search for Sunken Treasure*. Toronto: Key Porter Books Limited, 1993. Just some of the many books by Robert Marx regarding shipwrecks.

16) *Notable Shipwrecks, Being Tales of Disaster and Heroism at Sea.* London: Cassell and Company, 1898.

17) Oppel, Frank, and Meisel, Tony (edited by). *Tales of Old Florida.* Secaucus, NJ: Castle, 1987.

18) *Perils and Adventures on The Deep.* London: Thomas Nelson, 1844.

19) Shippen, Edward. *Naval Battles of the World and Our New Navy.* James C. McCurdy, 1894.

20) *Shipwrecks and Tales of the Sea.* London: W. and R. Chambers, 1887.

21) Smith, C. Fox, ed. *Adventures and Perils.* London: Michael Joseph, 1936.

22) *The Book of the Ocean, and Life on the Sea.* Auburn: John E. Beardsley, 1850.

23) *The Fisherman's Own Book.* Gloucester: Proctor Brothers, Publishers, 1882.

24) *The New Register of Shipping.* London: Society of Merchants, Ship-Owners, and Under-Writers. (Annual list similar to *Lloyd's Register* starting in 1798.)

25) *Thrilling Narratives of Mutiny, Murder and Piracy, a Weird Series of Tales of Shipwreck and Disaster, from the Earliest Part of the Century to the Present Time, with Accounts of Providential Escapes and Heart-Rending Fatalities.* New York: Hurst and Co., Publishers, no-date (likely late 1800s).

26) Weller, Bob. *True Stories of Sunken Treasure.* Lake Worth, FL: Crossed Anchors Salvage, 2005.

27) Weller, Bob. *Salvaging Spanish Sunken Treasure.* Lake Worth, FL: Crossed Anchors Salvage, 1999.

Piracy/Privateering

1) Bager, Ferdinand (translated from Spanish by). *Dying Declaration of Nicholas Fernandez, Who with Nine others were Executed in Front of Cadiz Harbor, December 29, 1829. For Piracy and Murder on the High Seas.* 1830. Available in the Law Library of Congress.

2) Benjamin, S. W. S. *Sea-Spray or Fact and Fancies of a Yachtsman.* New York: Benjamin and Bell, 1887.

3) Bradlee, F. B. C. *Piracy in the West Indies and Its Suppression.* Salem, MA: Essex Institute, 1923. Reprinted by Macdonald and Jane's, London, 1970–1974.

4) Daly, Charles P., First Judge of the Court of Common Pleas of the City of New York. *Are the Southern Privateersmen Pirates? Letter to the Hon. Ira Harris, U.S. Senator.* New York: December 21, 1861. (Available in the Law Library of Congress and a great reference.)

5) Gibbs, Charles (his confession retold). *Confessions and Execution of the Pirates, Gibbs and Wansley.* New York: Christian Brown, No. 211 Water St., New York, 1831. Another book is *The Confession of Chas. Gibbs alias James Jeffreys.* Boston: 1831 (available in the Law Library of Congress).

6) Gibbs, Joseph. *Dead Men Tell No Tales: The Lives and Legends of the Pirate Charles Gibbs.* South Carolina: University of South Carolina Press, 2007.

7) Cordingly, David. *Under the Black Flag.* New York: Random House, 1995.

8) French, Joseph Lewis, ed. *Great Pirate Stories.* New York: Brentano's, 1925.

9) Kaserman, James, and Kaserman, Susan. *Florida Pirates.* Charleston, SC: History Press, 2011.

10) McCarthy, Kevin. *Twenty Florida Pirates.* Sarasota, FL: Pineapple Press, 1993.

11) *Piracy and Murder. Particulars of the Horrid and Atrocious Murders, Committed by Four Spaniards of the Captain, Passengers, and Crew of the Brig Crawford.* New York: E.M. Murden and A. Ming, Jr., 1827 (Available in the Law Library of Congress—story from court records).

12) Saxon, Lyle. *Lafitte the Pirate.* Gretna, LA, 1989.

13) Wansley, Thomas J. (his confession retold). *Trial and Sentence of Thomas J. Wansley and Charles Gibbs, for Murder and Piracy, On board the Brig Vineyard.* New York: Christian Brown, 211 Water St, 1831.

14) Whitehead, David W. *CryptoQuest Field Guide to Florida Pirates and Their Buried Treasure.* Self-Published, 2008.

Anchors

1) Curryer, Betty Nelson. *Anchors, An Illustrated History.* Annapolis: Naval Institute Press, 1999.

Florida Keys Wreckers

1) Viele, John. *The Florida Keys, Volume 2, The Wreckers.* Sarasota: Pineapple Press, 2001.

Websites

Besides the sites listed at the end of chapter 8 in the GPS coordinate section and a few others in that chapter, plus those in the bibliography, here are just a few more. The internet offers a wealth of other sites, and one only has to search.

1) Maritime Museum of Denmark. Link to shipwrecks post 1893: http://mfs .dk/velkommen-ms-videnscenter/arkiv/registre/dansk-soeulykke-statistik/

2) Naval History and Heritage Command: https://www.history.navy.mil/

Online *Dictionary of American Naval Fighting Ships*:

https://www.history.navy.mil/research/histories/ship-histories/danfs.html

3) National Park Service (Florida Wrecks).

https://www.nps.gov/subjects/travelfloridashipwrecks/index.htm

4) Reefs and wrecks around Florida: https://florida.greatestdivesites.com

5) Shipwreck coin and artifact reference book: https://enrada.com/

6) Great videos of many Keys wrecks and reefs with GPS coordinates are Don Ferguson's Keys Dive Guide video: https://www.facebook.com/ KeysDiveGuide/

Glossary

Here are a few terms used in describing cargoes, measurements, and nautical terms found in this book. Most ship types are noted in *Shipwrecks of Florida*.

1) Ballast—A heavy material (could be rocks/stones/ore/lead or iron bars (pigs), etc., used in the bottom of a vessel for stability and a desired draft. Later vessels used water tanks or lead keels.

2) Bilged—Refers to the damaging of the lower hull of a vessel, causing water to enter the ship.

3) Beam-ends—As in "a ship thrown on its beam-ends," a vessel healed over so far on one side as its deck is nearly vertical.

4) Barrel or "bbl"—A cask usually about 31.5 gallons.

5) Cochineal—A red dye derived from a dried-out insect found in Mexico and Central America, and also from a certain berry.

6) Coppered—Refers to copper sheathing on the bottom of a wood vessel to protect it from the Teredo worm and from growth of barnacles and sea grass. Other materials were also used on the bottom of ships such as lead, zinc, and composite metals.

7) Deal—Board or plank, usually of fir or pine.

8) Divi-divi—Small shrub or tree from tropical America whose pods are used for tanning and dyeing.

9) Dory—Originally the name for the native dugouts along the Mosquito Coast of Central America, but later the name for a boat with a narrow, flat bottom, flaring sides and a high bow.

529

10) Dyewood—Any type wood used in the dyeing process.

11) Fathom—Unit of measure equal to six feet.

12) Flotsam—Any part of wreckage of a vessel found floating in the ocean or lake.

13) Foundered—To fill with water and sink.

14) Frigatilla—Smaller type frigate, or "fragata," with a shallower draft.

145 Fustic—The wood/dyewood from a tropical tree used to make a light yellow dye.

16) Gig—A narrow and light ship's boat.

17) Guano—Bat dung.

18) Hogshead or "hhd"—A large cask usually measuring 63 gallons, though can vary from 63–140 gallons.

19) Indigo—A blue dye obtained from a number of different plants.

20) Jalap—A dried tuberous plant root, in which a light yellow powder is derived from, used in medicine.

21) Jetsam—Any materials or cargo from a vessel intentionally thrown overboard to lighten a ship, usually in some sort of peril.

22) Jolly-boat—Small boat driven with oars.

23) League—A unit of measure which varied over time and is used as a nautical or land measurement. For the purposes of this book, it is usually meant to be three nautical miles.

24) Leeward—Direction in which the wind blows. Opposite of windward.

25) Lighter—Usually a type of barge or vessel used to transport goods from ship to shore.

26) Logwood—A heavy, brownish-red heartwood from the West Indies and Central America used for making dye.

27) Lugger—Usually a two-masted vessel, with a lugsail (four-sided sail). A nimble craft used in the coastal trade, but also used by pirates, privateers, smugglers, and fishermen.

28) Manila—A fibrous plant material used in making, rope, fabric, etc.

29) Melada—A thick and valuable type of molasses.

30) Nautical Mile—Rounded off to 6,080 feet, it differs from the standard mile used on land.

31) Packet-boat—Vessel that usually sailed between two ports carrying mail, but also goods and passengers.

32) Piastre—A Spanish "piece of eight," though also a monetary unit of other nations.

33) Pig—Usually a bar of soft iron used for ballast.

34) Pipe—A large cask for wine, rum, oil, etc. Equal to around four barrels or two hogsheads.

35) Pitchpine—Any of the pine wood that turpentine is derived from.

36) Polacca—A sailing vessel formerly used in the Mediterranean, having a combination of square and lateen (a triangular sail) sails on two or three masts.

37) Puncheon—A large cask of varying capacity, though usually of 80 gallons.

38) Rosin—This is the amber or yellowish residue left over from distilling turpentine, and was used in making varnish, printing ink, etc.

39) Seron—A parcel or bale, wrapped in animal hide.

40) Sheathing—As with word "coppered," a vessel "sheathed" had her hull area under water protected using a number of different materials including copper, lead, zinc, composite or "yellow" metals, or other materials.

41) Shook—Set of staves, enough to make a barrel or hogshead.

42) Snow—Large two-masted type brig.

43) Specie—Money in coin form.

44) Staves—Thin wood pieces used to make barrels, casks, etc.

45) Sundries—Refers to small cargo items of minor value.

46) Tallow—Fatty tissue from animals used in the making of candles, soap, etc.

47) Tierces—Can be a cask or vessel with a capacity of 42 gallons. Also used as a unit of measurement equal to 42 gallons.

48) Xebec—Small three-mated vessel which was popular in the Mediterranean. Nimble and fast, but difficult to manage.

49) 16th to mid-19th century New World Spanish coinage terms—The following can have other definitions, although for the purpose of this book, they mean the following: a) Escudo—refers to a gold Spanish coin. b) Doubloon— Initially a "two" escudo coin; eventually came to mean any

Spanish gold coins. c) Piece-of-eight—A silver eight-real Spanish dollar or peso. d) Real or reales (plural)—Spanish silver coin was used until replaced in 1868 by the peseta; they were the most common currency used through-out the world for many years. e) Cob—These were crudely made coins that were cut from a bar of silver or gold and hand stamped with a hammer and die. Shapes can vary greatly. The Mexico mint started making these in 1536 and the last ones at the Potosi mint in 1773, when the "milled" coins took over. f) Royal—Unlike a cob coin, these were a very limited produced 8 escudo (or 8 real) presentation piece (nicely struck and round) from some New World mints meant for royalty. Note: Spanish coins in this time period came in ½, 1, 2, 4, and 8 denominations. See *Shipwrecks of Florida* for photos.

The Harbor Bar
By Charles Burr Todd

A ship has crossed the harbor bar,
It darts on the ship far out at sea,
The sunlight glinting on sail and spar:
It tears and rends her with savage glee,
Whither she goes, who knows? Who knows?
And, lo! A wreck drifts wild and free.
She carries pearl of lustrous hue,
Costly fabrics from far Hindoo,
The sea has crossed the harbor bar,
A tender maid to her lover true.
It hears a potent voice from afar:
Whither it goes, who knows? who knows?
The wind has crossed the harbor bar,
Rising upon a land of palms,
All armed and panoplied for war:
It throws a wreck to sea-walled farms,
Whither it goes, who knows? who knows?
And a lifeless maid to her lover's arms.

The Fisherman's Own Book, 1882.